American Urban Politics in a Global Age

The Reader

SIXTH EDITION

EDITED BY

Paul Kantor
Fordham University

Dennis R. Judd
University of Illinois at Chicago

Longman
New York San Francisco Boston
London Toronto Sydney Tokyo Singapore Madrid
Mexico City Munich Paris Cape Town Hong Kong Montreal

Editor-in-Chief: Eric Stano
Marketing Manager: Lindsey Prudhomme
Production Coordinator: Scarlett Lindsay
Project Coordination, Text Design, and Electronic Page Makeup:
    S4Carlisle Publishing Services
Senior Cover Designer/Manager: Nancy Danahy
Cover Photo: City reflected in Cloud Gate sculpture in Millennium Park, at dusk;
    Kim Karpeles, photograher; © Axiom Photographic Agency/Getty Images, Inc.
Senior Manufacturing Buyer: Alfred C. Dorsey
Printer and Binder: RR Donnelley & Sons Company/Harrisonburg
Cover Printer: RR Donnelley & Sons Company/Harrisonburg

Library of Congress Cataloging-in-Publication Data

American urban politics in a global age : the reader/edited by Paul P. Kantor,
Dennis R. Judd.—6th ed.
    p. cm.
Includes bibliographical references.
ISBN 978-0-205-74545-6
1.   Urban policy—United States. 2.   Municipal government—United States.
3.   Metropolitan government—United States.   I. Kantor, Paul, 1942–
II. Judd, Dennis R.
    HT123A6664 2010
    320.8'50973—dc22   2009017279

Longman
is an imprint of

1 2 3 4 5 6 7 8 9 10—DOH—12 11 10 09

www.pearsonhighered.com

ISBN-13: 978-0-205-74545-6
ISBN-10:   0-205-74545-8

To my grandchildren, Dylan, Miranda, Jake, Weston, Wyatt, Eliza, and Katie: you make the world go round!

Dennis R. Judd

To my wonderful daughter, Elizabeth, and her global generation.

Paul Kantor

CONTENTS

PREFACE

The globalization of America's cities, suburbs, and urban regions has unleashed so many dramatic changes in local politics that political scientists have had to rethink their approaches to the study of the city. Social and political developments in the first decade of the twenty-first century are so far-reaching and profound in social meaning that they are altering our assumptions about the nature of urban politics. For this reason, we have assembled readings for this sixth edition that highlight: the intense competition among cities in the international marketplace; the new attention given to urban culture in promoting cities; the fears and rivalries among groups over efforts to privatize public spaces; the political competition over new issues of race, ethnicity, and inequality, and the emergence of a multiethnic metropolis; the novel efforts to address the costs of urban sprawl; and the intergovernmental politics that helps determine how well cities cope with terrorism and natural disasters that overwhelm local resources. These developments are so transformative that we have been forced to substantially re-conceive our task, with the result that *American Urban Politics in a Global Age* is quite different from earlier editions in much of its content.

However, it is important to acknowledge the degree to which many of the "new" urban issues are actually rooted in the past. In our introductory essay we place the global age in historical context and highlight the continuities that have defined American urban politics since the nation's founding. In the first century, when cities spread across the frontier, they engaged in a frenetic competition for primacy and power and coped with the political effects of massive immigration—just as they do today. In the late nineteenth and twentieth centuries, cities emerged as industrial centers, but then slid into decline as a result of suburbanization and, finally, the end of federal urban programs. In the global era, as we have noted, intense inter-urban competition and ethnic and racial rivalries drive local politics. The issues of federalism have also become important because of the limited capacity of cities to respond to all of the problems that confront them.

In all three periods, urban leaders have tried to promote local economic prosperity, but they have had to do so within the constraints of democratic processes. Dynamic tension between these two imperatives has shaped city politics in the past, and it continues to do so in the global age. This is because the American political order constitutes a merger of capitalism and democracy, or to put it differently, it joins a process in which popular elections and give-and-take among groups co-exists with private institutions and markets that supply necessary resources in exchange for profit. Local governments and cities are part of this political order.

The selections making up Part One of the book shed light on the economic imperatives that are reshaping urban America. They examine how contemporary urban politics is shaped by economic competition and the choices that cities make in mapping out their future well-being. The selections in Part Two comment on the complex and sometimes contested governance of the multiethnic metropolis. The chapters examine how governance takes placed not only within the public realm of cities and suburbs, but also within privatized urban enclaves. In all of these spaces, groups jostle for influence and control.

Part Three is concerned with the politics and governance of our socially fractured metropolitan areas. Some of the selections deal with sprawl and the attempts to respond to its problems. Other selections examine federal-local governmental relations and comment upon how effective decentralized political system copes with major problems that overwhelm the resources of local political systems.

Although the Internet and electronic libraries provide ready access to information about urban politics, students often find these sources overwhelming. Worse, they are lacking in selectivity and context. This volume overcomes these deficiencies. It brings together a selection of readings that represent some of the most important trends and topics in urban scholarship today. These are placed in context by means of editors' essays at the beginning of each chapter. These essays explain how each reading fits into the thematic context and highlight particularly important insights, from these readings. This book is a suitable companion for any good urban politics text, but its organization and themes fit particularly well with Dennis R. Judd and Todd Swanstrom's *City Politics*, a textbook also published by Longman Publishers.

Although not every area of importance for the study of urban politics could be included, we believe these reading selections provide depth and scope for students trying to understand politics in urban America through the work of some of our nation's leading scholars. This Sixth Edition of *American Urban Politics in a Global Age: The Reader* captures many of the new and old dynamics that shape the politics of America's cities. We wish to thank Eric Stano, our Longman political science editor, for championing this book. His interest, ideas, and encouragement were essential to this enterprise. We also wish to thank the professional reviewers for their helpful comments and suggestions: John Bretting, University of Texas—El Paso; Michael Coulter, Grove City College; Aubrey Jewett, University of Central Florida; Kenneth Fernandez, University of Nevada—Las Vegas; Tim Mead, University of North Carolina—Charlotte, Platon Rigos, University of South Florida—Tampa; Linda Shafer, Allegheny College; Allan Wallis, Colorado University—Denver; Frank Popper, Rutgers University—New Brunswick; and Mark Chubb, Portland State University.

PAUL KANTOR
DENNIS R. JUDD

GOVERNING THE METROPOLIS IN THE GLOBAL ERA

Globalization has intensified competition among cities, quickened the pace of immigration, and changed spatial relationships within metropolitan areas. Cities have been thrown into intense interurban competition because investors send their money to wherever it yields the highest profits. People from low-wage parts of the world are moving in large numbers to places that afford opportunity; frequently, this means they move to urban areas. So many travelers and tourists move about each year that they have become a permanent fixture of the local landscape and the economies of all larger cities. Cities and urban regions are at the center of these globalization processes and are deeply affected by them. If "all politics is local," as a congressman famously observed decades ago, the phrase can now be interpreted to mean that the processes of globalization can be understood best by the imprint they leave on local communities.

Cities of all sizes, including those in the suburbs, compete in the global economy; as in the past, they can ill afford to leave their fortunes to chance. Intense interurban competition is not new; in the nineteenth century, for example, cities fought hard for railroad connections that would tie them into the emerging industrial economy. More recently, the global economy has favored investments in postindustrial business sectors such as finance, real estate, insurance, and a variety of service activities. In global cities all over the world highly educated white-collar professionals—for example, corporate managers, management consultants, legal experts, accountants, computer specialists, financial analysts, media and public relations specialists—work in clusters of downtown skyscrapers.[1] Likewise, cities further down the urban hierarchy try to define a niche that will secure their futures. Suburbs have gotten into the act, too; in effect, urban areas are free-trade zones where cities offer various subsidies to attract malls, big-box stores, and affluent residents.

Economic competition among jurisdictions will remain a basic fact of the global era into the foreseeable future. By the early twentieth century, cities occupied well-defined places in the industrial urban hierarchy. Globalization has torn that system apart. In the global era, cities are dependent on the decisions made by highly mobile, transnational corporations. New technologies in computers, communications, materials, production, and business organization have enabled businesses to disperse many of their activities to far-flung locations in suburbia, the Sunbelt, and foreign production sites. Many traditional industrial activities that once were undertaken in cities, such as steelmaking and garment and appliance manufacturing, have migrated to lower-cost locations in foreign countries in the Asian Rim, the Caribbean, Mexico, and South and Central America. The so-called global office has become commonplace: large corporations have concentrated their administrative activities in major cities while decentralizing all other business operations to a multitude of sites.

The competitive struggle for economic prosperity has enormous implications for local politics and public policy. Globalization keeps local officials fixated on economic matters for the simple reason that the rules of the game are constantly changing. Yesterday it was manufacturing; today it is a complex mix of services and the economic benefits flowing from tourism and culture. All cities try to get their share, but the options available to them are limited, and especially so for poorer and smaller places. This economic imperative can be read by observing the transformation of city skylines. In recent decades, restored waterfronts and historic buildings, gleaming office towers, luxury hotels, convention centers, sports stadiums—and the list goes on—have sprung up in central cities everywhere. Cities commonly try to attract investment by offering such lures as historic tax credits, tax subsidies, and public improvements. Surrounding suburbs try to outdo one another to influence the location of development projects such as retail clusters and office parks. To attract the most affluent workers in the globalized service economy, all cities must offer a high level of urban amenities.[2]

The public subsidies required to build new infrastructure and amenities draw critical comments in the letters sections of local newspapers because it often appears that local governments do little else but support development and respond to the needs of business. In most cities, however, public officials try to achieve—or appear to achieve—some kind of balance. At least to some degree, the ballot box acts as a counterweight. All but the most homogeneous and prosperous local communities must manage a complex politics marked by interest-group competition and racial, ethnic, and class differences. An increasing volume of capital flows may be a defining feature of globalization, but so also is the movement of people across borders and from place to place. The logic of the marketplace treats cities purely as locations for private economic activity, but the political logic of democratic processes motivates public officials to build political support for what they seek to accomplish.[3]

In the United States, local governments are especially dependent upon the marketplace because they receive so little aid from upper-level governments. In most other Western nations, much of the basic infrastructure and many of the services provided to citizens originate from central governments. Most West European city governments do not have to rely on private lenders to raise money for capital projects; those are generally financed by national governments. The relative absence of intergovernmental aid forces U.S. cities to support their activities through local revenues, and these quickly dry up unless adequate tax sources can be found. This is a major reason why the economic and political imperatives are often so difficult to negotiate.

To trace the contours of today's urban politics, we have organized *American Urban Politics in a Global Age* into three parts. Part One contains selections highlighting the thesis that the economic imperative powerfully shapes contemporary urban politics. Part Two is made up of selections dealing with the governance imperative: How are competing political demands of citizens reconciled with the economic pressures? In the global era, as in the past, local governments are forced to respond to issues connected to race, space, and ethnicity.

The selections in Part Three comment on the fragmentation of power and authority in America's governmental system. America's metropolitan regions are fractured into multitudes of governments, which makes it difficult to respond to important problems connected to sprawl. The way governments are organized matters, both at the metropolitan level and beyond. The haphazard response to the catastrophic damage inflicted on New Orleans by Hurricane Katrina in August 2005 called into question whether the intergovernmental system of the United States can effectively respond not only to natural disasters, but also to less-publicized problems, such as poverty and inadequate schooling and housing. In the remainder of this essay, we summarize the themes that the selections are meant to address.

Part One: Globalization and the Economic Imperative

If we place today's urban politics in historical context, the differences as well as the continuities come into focus. In the United States, fierce interurban competition has always worked as a mainspring animating urban politics. In the nineteenth century, local elites were active promoters of local growth because they instinctively understood that some cities—but not all—would prosper in the international urban system that was emerging in the industrial age. Before industrialization, the major obstacles to local economic growth were physical barriers that impeded the exchange of goods between a rural hinterland and the city, and between the city and other commercial centers. With the coming of railroads in mid-century, competition among cities became truly national in scope. Cities everywhere, big or small, new or old, could use railroad lines to penetrate their hinterland in the expectation that they could gather up the trade of the backcountry and channel it through to their own commercial streets. Individual cities, as public corporations, provided massive assistance to railroad companies that agreed to build connecting lines. The federal and state governments offered assistance to the railroads as well, but the cities provided the most of all.

The selections in Part One make it clear that there is a close parallel with the politics of growth in today's cities. As in an earlier era, today's civic boosters are fired with the conviction that the fate of their cities cannot be left to chance. In the postwar era, when suburbanization and deindustrialization threatened to plunge the cities into permanent decline, downtown business interests mobilized to preserve their investments. In city after city, coalitions led by aggressive mayors and corporate CEOs led campaigns to revitalize the downtowns. For nearly half a century, the politics of cities revolved around these coalitions and their preferences. They spearheaded the efforts to build convention centers, renew business districts, improve streets and streetscapes, build sports facilities, and improve parks and green spaces.

An emerging literature in urban politics shows that globalization has dispersed power more widely and reduced the influence of the CEO-led organizations. Corporate buyouts, mergers, and the internationalization of corporate structures have reduced the ranks of business leaders interested in local politics. In their stead, a new leadership has emerged that reflects the shape of the new economy: developers, the leaders of nonprofit organizations, and professionals working in cultural institutions have filled the gap left by the lagging interest of corporate CEOs. Since the 1990s, tourism and culture have led the revitalization of many central cities. The new political leadership translates culture into policies that often seem heavily weighted in favor of tourists and affluent downtown residents. High-end residential and tourist enclaves exist in virtually all cities whatever their racial and ethnic makeup, and policies to promote such developments are nearly universal. This has created competition and often confrontation among groups over neighborhood changes and city policies. As in the past, city politics often pivots around the economic imperative, even though the specific political actors have changed.

Part Two: Governing the Multiethnic Metropolis

As important as the economic imperative may be, a political logic also acts as a dynamic feature of urban politics. This dynamic is not new to the global era. In the nineteenth century, a rapidly expanding urban electorate became an enduring fixture in the politics of cities. This development radically changed the complexion of local politics. By the 1840s, property qualifications to vote were abolished almost everywhere, a reform that enhanced the influence of immigrant voters. After the Civil War, city populations exploded when waves of immigrants from abroad and migrants from rural areas came in search of jobs in the factories. Wide-open political struggles began to replace oligarchic control by business elites. A new generation of politicians organized party machines as a way of mobilizing the urban electorate by buying loyalty and favors with cash, jobs, contracts, and other material inducements. Whatever their merits or shortcomings, the machines gave the immigrants a voice in local politics. This new-found influence became the lightning rod for many of the political conflicts of the late-nineteenth and early-twentieth centuries.

The parallels with urban politics today are plain to see. An immigrant floodtide has made cities and urban regions more racially and ethnically diverse than ever before. More immigrants came to the United States in the 1990s than in any previous decade in the nation's history, and the flow is certain to continue well into the twenty-first century. The social and political effects of large-scale population movements are dramatically evident in big global cities such as Miami, New York, Chicago, and San Francisco. In these cities—and even in some smaller places—the new immigration has changed the complexion of local politics.

The diverse ethnic makeup of the globalized metropolis constitutes a sharp break from the previous urban pattern. In the years after World War II, white flight to the suburbs combined with the mass migration of blacks to the central cities created a metropolis characterized by high levels of racial segregation and sometimes violent racial confrontation. The movements into and out of the cities created a nearly unbridgeable social chasm that threatened to rend the fabric of American society. As blacks moved into central-city neighborhoods, whites resisted, often violently. These tensions began to ease by the 1970s when blacks became incorporated into local politics systems. A black political leadership first emerged in the central cities, and over time blacks have been elected to political office throughout the federal system.

Immigration has unleashed far-reaching changes. Immigrants from Asia, Latin America, the Caribbean, and Eastern and Central Europe now constitute a substantial and growing proportion of the residents of America's cities and of its suburbs. As the ethnic complexion of cities has become more diverse, urban politics has increasingly become defined by a process of interethnic bargaining. A power struggle is taking place between newly arrived immigrants, African Americans, and middle- and upper-class residents. It has become clear that there is no singular "minority" interest; instead, the new immigrants often compete with blacks in the electoral arena and beyond. Coalitions, sometimes quite temporary and fragile, have replaced the clear racial divisions of the past. Sometimes the tensions are difficult to manage. At the same time, it must be recognized that the presence of minorities in positions of political leadership has reduced the mutual suspicions and hostilities that characterized interracial and interethnic relations just a few decades ago.

Not long ago these observations would have applied mainly to the central cities. But unlike the past, immigrants of all ethnic backgrounds are now settling in the suburbs as much as in the central cities. The old urban pattern, with a troubled central city surrounded by rank on rank of suburbs, is breaking down. The new urban pattern is extremely complex. In central cities, rising levels of social inequality characteristic of U.S. society are written on the urban landscape. Affluent downtown and gentrified neighborhoods are sharply separated from the neighborhoods inhabited by the urban poor. High-rise condominium and townhouse developments sometimes sit only a block or two from neighborhoods with extreme levels of poverty. Affluent empty-nesters and young professionals are moving back downtown. Central cities are once again becoming hotspots for culture, nightlife, and fun, but a few blocks away the scene may be very different. In cities facing the social problems that arise from immigration and social polarization, it should occasion no surprise that the debate over policies that seem weighted heavily in favor of affluent downtown residents should become highly contentious.

In the suburbs, a parallel process has been unfolding. In the 1990s, when Asians and Latinos settled in the suburbs in large numbers, a large proportion of both groups ended up in ethnic enclaves that were sharply separated from whites,[4] although these groups were less segregated in the suburbs than in the central cities.[5] Many suburbs are becoming multiethnic. In some of these suburbs a politics of interethnic bargaining has evolved that looks very much like the political process that has evolved in the central cities over a long period, in which minorities have become, or are in the process of becoming, incorporated into electoral politics and institutions. In other suburbs, a politics of marginalization, distrust, and hostility carries the day. Metropolitan areas are typically fragmented into a multitude of separate jurisdictions. Often, immigrants are sharply separated from the neighborhoods inhabited by affluent residents. For example, during the 1990s two streams moved to Orange County, California, just outside Los Angeles: highly educated professionals and foreign-born immigrants. The two streams could hardly have been more different: high-income families making more than $150,000 per year jumped by 184 percent in the county, but at the same time the number of foreign-born immigrants increased by 48 percent.[6] Commenting on these trends, a noted demographer said the county could go in two directions: either a "mostly gated-community-type mentality" or "Immigrants start integrating into middle-class areas, so you have a blended suburbia."[7]

A multiethnic metropolis has emerged that requires a high degree of political dexterity to manage the demands made by various groups. Some urban residents seem to be opting out of the demands of governance altogether by retreating from the public realm into protected, privatized enclaves. Enclaves have proliferated in suburbs just as they have in central cities. A large proportion of urban residents commute from subdivisions, gated communities, townhouse developments, and condominium complexes to high-rise downtown office buildings or suburban office parks, drive to enclosed malls and mall complexes for shopping, and commute to entertainment and tourist bubbles to enjoy themselves.[8] Escape from the public realm fragments the metropolis not only into separate suburban jurisdictions, but also into privatized enclaves that separate affluent from poorer residents more purely than before.

In addition to immigration, other global pressures are relentlessly changing the responsibilities of local governments. International terrorism is bringing the dark side of globalization into the largest cities, particularly since 9/11. The terrorist threat has precipitated a political scramble to seek defensive measures and redefine how important public spaces, such as airports, tall buildings, subways, and crowded commercial centers, should be watched and made safe. Local governments, as first responders, are frontline participants in the struggle for homeland security.

Part Three: Sprawl, Federalism, and the Divided Metropolis

In recent years, urban sprawl has blossomed as an important public policy issue. The sprawled metropolis has spawned a set of highly publicized issues such as traffic congestion and gridlock, uncontrolled development, and air pollution, but governance must be added to the list as one of the most intractable problems. For decades, movements sprang forth seeking the regional consolidation of governments, but attempts to achieve this goal failed decade after decade. Although comprehensive reform proved to be elusive, other, more modest steps have been taken to reduce the quality of governance and to reduce inequality among jurisdictions. For example, in Minnesota, the state legislature approved a modest tax-sharing plan, wherein wealthier jurisdictions would share some of the tax revenues created by attracting development with less wealthy suburbs.

The debates about the consequences of sprawl have run the gamut; some have said it is simply an outcome of prosperity, which gives Americans the opportunity to constantly improve their circumstances; others have decried the proliferation of suburban malls, the spiderweb of superhighways that crisscrosses the landscape, and the spread of housing tracts that seem to go on forever. For the New Urbanists, much of the solution for tract housing developments, big-box retailing, and expressways is more compact planned developments that mix uses and design traffic grids, streets, and neighborhoods to human scale.

Debates about the appropriate scale and governance of our metropolitan areas have been given new urgency by international pressures resulting in rising energy prices. As suburban and city residents confront the reality of dramatically more expensive costs of gasoline, fuel oil, natural gas, and electricity, recalculating the desirability of sprawled living styles is unavoidable. Distances to work and home acquire a new meaning. Regional policy is becoming a pocketbook issue.

The slow and disorganized response to the devastation wrought on New Orleans by Hurricane Katrina in August 2005 raised important questions about the complicated governmental system of the United States. The terrorist attacks of September 11, 2001, also raised the alarm. It is not only regions that are fragmented; the governmental structure of the nation is as well, and as the disaster revealed, it was difficult for national, state, and local authorities to work together. What is the proper relationship between the federal government and the cities? Do cities possess the capacity to respond to all problems that may face them? Since the withdrawal of federal urban programs in the 1980s, cities have been on their own. At the same time, there are signs of creeping federal regulation and mandates, but often without adequate funding to assist local governments in meeting their obligations. For the most part, local governments have stepped up to the daunting challenge posed by revitalizing local economies at a time of limited federal assistance. But large-scale disasters pose a different kind of problem that may require a closer relationship between cities and federal government. The nation's federal system is in flux, and its future evolution will dramatically shape the capacity of cities to govern.

CHAPTER 1

THE POLITICAL ECONOMY OF URBAN GOVERNANCE

ENTREPRENEURIAL CITIES

City politics can be understood as a bargaining process over the policy priorities and public expenditures of local governments. These negotiations, whether they are conducted as open battles fought out between electoral candidates or in other arenas, become highly contentious because, as public corporations, cities are invested with significant public powers that can be used for a variety of purposes. As Paul E. Peterson points out in Selection 1, there are constant debates about the "public interest" that cities ought to pursue. Some people might demand that cities spend their public resources on "redistributive" policies designed to help those most in need. Others might promote the view that city governments should do little more than provide the services necessary to make the city a healthy and functional environment. Peterson's view is that cities must at all costs avoid policies that redistribute resources from businesses and affluent residents to those with fewer resources. Instead, he argues, cities have no choice but to support policies that will stimulate economic growth. Such policies, he says, respond to a "unitary interest" that all urban residents hold in local economic vitality: "It is in the city's interest . . . to help sustain a high-quality local infrastructure generally attractive to all commerce and industry." This logic dictates that even the social health of a city depends upon its economic prosperity: "When a city is able to export its products, service industries prosper, labor is in greater demand . . . tax revenues increase, city services can be improved, donations to charitable organizations become more generous, and the social and cultural life of the city is enhanced."

In Peterson's analysis, the leaders of cities cannot leave economic growth to chance because cities compete with one another. City governments are unable to control the movement of capital and labor across borders. In contrast to the national government, they lack the authority to regulate immigration, currency, prices, and wages, or the import or export of goods and services. City governments, therefore, are constrained to compete for capital investment or suffer decline in the economic well-being of the community. Cities occupy a particular space, but businesses can move; therefore, if the local business environment is not pleasing to them, investors and businesses will go elsewhere. This logic drives cities to minimize taxes, avoid expensive regulations, and offer a variety of subsidies to business. If they heed Peterson's injunction, politicians will resist the clamor of all political interests that might compromise the preferences of business in any way.

The book from which the Peterson selection is taken ignited a controversy among urban scholars—a controversy that has not died down completely even after more than two decades. (Peterson's book was published in 1981.) Many scholars took Peterson to task for his apparent assertion that growth benefits everyone. Others accused him of ignoring the complexities of local politics by pointing out that the mix of local policies differs substantially from city to city depending on population demographics, the political influence and the degree of political participation of various groups, and governmental powers and structures. The importance of local prosperity is likely to always be high on the agenda, but politicians must also mobilize sufficient political support to remain in office; in other words, they must win elections. Mayors must often perform a delicate balancing act that requires them to protect and enhance the economic base of a city while at the same time mobilizing sufficient political support to remain in office and implement their policies.

Partially in response to Peterson's book, a literature on "urban regimes" emerged that provided detailed descriptions of the process by which local policy priorities were decided. The leading book, *Regime Politics* (1989), by now a classic in the field of urban politics, was based on a detailed case study of postwar politics in Atlanta. As described by Clarence N. Stone in Selection 2, the two most powerful partners of what he called the "urban regime" in Atlanta included the mayor and the city's downtown business elite. In his study, Stone pointed out that governmental officials were motivated to join the coalition because they lacked the resources to do much about Atlanta's economic problems on their own. Likewise, the business community required a local government capable of coordinating the massive resources necessary for saving the downtown from decline. By working together, all the participants could accomplish goals that none of them could achieve on their own. Stone noted, "What makes governance in Atlanta effective is not the formal machinery of government, but rather the informal partnership between city hall and the downtown business elite. This informal partnership and the way it operates constitute the city's regime; it is the same means through which major policy decisions are made." For Stone, governance in Atlanta was achieved by *partnership* rather than by control exercised by a few powerful individuals.

Globalization has changed the internal politics of cities in fundamental ways. Following Stone's book, the literature in urban politics documented the overwhelming influence of business elites in promoting economic growth and downtown revitalization. Elizabeth Strom points out in Selection 3 that the alliances forged between powerful mayors and downtown business elites are being replaced by looser coalitions dominated by real estate developers, nonprofit institutions, and public-sector agencies. Downtown is no longer "the seat of corporate power;" instead, American downtowns have become transformed into entertainment spaces and locations for upscale residences. The owners and managers of condominium towers, cultural facilities, convention centers, sports venues, and entertainment complexes, working closely with public development agencies, cooperate, as needed, to promote an environment that will be mutually beneficial. In Strom's view, the result is that the ambitious civic agenda once promoted by business elites has given way to a politics driven by a narrower set of issues. Downtown interests remain influential, but they do not necessarily dominate the local political landscape.

1

Paul E. Peterson

THE INTERESTS OF THE LIMITED CITY

Like all social structures, cities have interests. Just as we can speak of union interests, judicial interests, and the interests of politicians, so we can speak of the interests of that structured system of social interactions we call a city. Citizens, politicians, and academics are all quite correct in speaking freely of the interests of cities.[1]

Defining the City Interest

By a city's interest, I do not mean the sum total of the interests of those individuals living in the city. For one thing, these are seldom, if ever, known. The wants, needs, and preferences of residents continually change, and few surveys of public opinion in particular cities have ever been taken. Moreover, the residents of a city often have discordant interests. Some want more parkland and better schools; others want better police protection and lower taxes. Some want an elaborated highway system; others wish to keep cars out of their neighborhood. Some want more inexpensive, publicly subsidized housing; others wish to remove the public housing that exists. Some citizens want improved welfare assistance for the unemployed and dependent; others wish to cut drastically all such programs of public aid. Some citizens want rough-tongued ethnic politicians in public office; others wish that municipal administration were a gentleman's calling. Especially in large cities, the cacophony of competing claims by diverse class, race, ethnic, and occupational groups makes impossible the determination of any overall city interest—any public interest, if you like—by compiling all the demands and desires of individual city residents.

Some political scientists have attempted to discover the overall urban public interest by summing up the wide variety of individual interests. The earlier work of Edward Banfield, still worth examination, is perhaps the most persuasive effort of this kind.[2] He argued that urban political processes—or at least those in Chicago—allowed for the expression of nearly all the particular interests within the city. Every significant interest was represented by some economic firm or voluntary association, which had a stake in trying to influence those public policies that touched its vested interests. After these various groups and firms had debated and contended, the political leader searched for a compromise that took into account the vital interests of each, and worked out a solution all could accept with some satisfaction. The leader's own interest in sustaining his political power dictated such a strategy.

Banfield's argument is intriguing, but few people would identify public policies as being in the interest of the city simply because they have been formulated according to certain procedures. The political leader might err in his judgment; the interests of important but politically impotent groups might never get expressed; or the consequences of a policy might in the long run be disastrous for the city. Moreover, most urban policies are not hammered out after great controversy, but are the quiet product of routine decision making. How does one evaluate which of these are in the public interest? Above all, this mechanism for determining the city's interest provides no standpoint for evaluating the substantive worth of urban policies. Within Banfield's framework, whatever urban governments do is said to be in the interest of their communities. But the concept of city interest is used most persuasively when there are calls for reform or innovation. It is a term used to evaluate existing programs and to discriminate between promising and undesirable new ones. To equate the interests of cities with what cities are doing is to so impoverish the term as to make it quite worthless.

The economist Charles Tiebout employs a second approach to the identification of city interests.[3] Unlike Banfield, he does not see the city's interests as a mere summation of individual interests but as something which can be ascribed to the entity, taken as a whole. As an economist, Tiebout is hardly embarrassed by such an enterprise, because in ascribing interests to cities his work parallels both those orthodox economists who state that firms have an interest in maximizing profits and those welfare economists who claim that politicians have an interest in maximizing votes. Of course, they state only that their model will assume that firms and politicians behave in such a way, but insofar as they believe their model has empirical validity, they in fact assert that those constrained by the businessman's or politician's role must pursue certain interests. And so does Tiebout when he says that communities seek to attain the optimum size for the efficient delivery of the bundle of services the local government produces. In his words, "Communities below the optimum size seek to attract new residents to lower average costs. Those above optimum size do just the opposite. Those at an optimum try to keep their populations constant."[4]

Tiebout's approach is in many ways very attractive. By asserting a strategic objective that the city is trying to maximize—optimum size—Tiebout identifies an overriding interest which can account for specific policies the city adopts. He provides a simple analytical tool that will account for the choices cities make, without requiring complex investigations into citizen preferences and political mechanisms for identifying and amalgamating the same. Moreover, he provides a criterion for determining whether a specific policy is in the interest of the city—does it help achieve optimum size? Will it help the too small city grow? Will it help the too big city contract? Will it keep the optimally sized city in equilibrium? Even though the exact determination of the optimum size cannot presently be scientifically determined in all cases, the criterion does provide a useful guide for prudential decision making.

The difficulty with Tiebout's assumption is that he does not give very good reasons for its having any plausibility. When most economists posit a certain form of maximizing behavior, there is usually a good commonsense reason for believing the person in that role will have an interest in pursuing this strategic objective. When orthodox economists say that businessmen maximize profits, it squares with our understanding in everyday life that people engage in commercial enterprises for monetary gain. The more they make, the better they like it. The same can be said of those welfare economists who say politicians maximize votes. The assumption, though cynical, is in accord with popular belief—and therefore once again has a certain plausibility.

By contrast, Tiebout's optimum size thesis diverges from what most people think cities are trying to do. Of course, smaller communities are often seeking to expand—boosterism may be the quintessential characteristic of small-town America. Yet Tiebout takes optimum size, not growth or maximum size, as the strategic objective. And when Tiebout discusses the big city that wishes to shrink to optimum size, his cryptic language is quite unconvincing. "The case of the city that is too large and tries to get rid of residents is more difficult to imagine," he confesses. Even more, he concedes that "no alderman in his right political mind would ever admit that the city is too big." "Nevertheless," he continues, "economic forces are at work to push people out of it. Every resident who moves to the suburbs to find better schools, more parks, and so forth, is reacting, in part, against the pattern the city has to offer."[5] In this crucial passage Tiebout speaks neither of local officials nor of local public policies. Instead, he refers to "economic forces" that may be beyond the control of the city and of "every resident," each of whom may be pursuing his own interests, not that of the community at large.

The one reason Tiebout gives for expecting cities to pursue optimum size is to lower the average cost of public goods. If public goods can be delivered most efficiently at some optimum size, then migration of residents will occur until that size has been reached. In one respect Tiebout is quite correct: local governments must concern themselves with operating local services as efficiently as possible in order to protect the city's economic interests. But there is little evidence that there is an optimum size at which services can be delivered with greatest efficiency. And even if such an optimum did exist, it could be realized only if migration occurred among residents who paid equal amounts in local taxes. In the more likely situation, residents pay variable prices for public services (for example, the amount paid in local property taxes varies by the value of the property). Under these circumstances, increasing size to the optimum does not reduce costs to residents unless newcomers pay at least as much in taxes as the marginal increase in costs their arrival imposes on city government.[6] Conversely, if a city needs to lose population to reach the optimum, costs to residents will not decline unless the exiting population paid less in taxes than was the marginal cost of providing them government services. In most big cities losing population, exactly the opposite is occurring. Those who pay more in taxes than they receive in services are the emigrants. Tiebout's identification of city interests with optimum size, while suggestive, fails to take into account the quality as well as the quantity of the local population.

The interests of cities are neither a summation of individual interests nor the pursuit of optimum size. Instead, policies and programs can be said to be in the interest of cities whenever the policies maintain or enhance the economic position, social prestige, or political power of the city, taken as a whole.[7]

Cities have these interests because cities consist of a set of social interactions structured by their location in a particular territorial space. Any time that social interactions come to be structured into recurring patterns, the structure thus formed develops an interest in its own maintenance and enhancement. It is in that sense that we speak of the interests of an organization, the interests of the system, and the like. To be sure, within cities, as within any other structure, one can find diverse social roles, each with its own set of interests. But these varying role interests, as divergent and competing as they may be, do not distract us from speaking of the overall interests of the larger structural entity.[8]

The point can be made less abstractly. A school system is a structured form of social action, and therefore it has an interest in maintaining and improving its material resources, its prestige, and its political power. Those policies or events which have such positive effects are said to be in the interest of the school system. An increase in state financial aid or the winning of the basketball tournament are events that, respectively, enhance the material well-being and the prestige of a school system and are therefore in its interest. In ordinary speech this is taken for granted, even when we also recognize that teachers, pupils, principals, and board members may have contrasting interests as members of differing role-groups within the school.

Although social roles performed within cities are numerous and conflicting, all are structured by the fact that they take place in a specific spatial location that falls within the jurisdiction of some local government. All members of the city thus come to share an interest in policies that affect the well-being of that territory. Policies which enhance the desirability or attractiveness of the territory are in the city's interest, because they benefit all residents—in their role as residents of the community. Of course, in any of their other social roles, residents of the city may be adversely affected by the policy. The Los Angeles dope peddler—in his role as peddler—hardly benefits from a successful drive to remove hard drugs from the city. On the other hand, as a resident of the city, he benefits from a policy that enhances the attractiveness of the city as a locale in which to live and work. In determining whether a policy is in the interest of a city, therefore, one does not consider whether it has a positive or negative effect on the total range of social interactions of each and every individual. That is an impossible task. To know whether a policy is in a city's interest, one has to consider only the impact on social relationships insofar as they are structured by their taking place within the city's boundaries.

An illustration from recent policy debates over the future of our cities reveals that it is exactly with this meaning that the notion of a city's interest is typically used. The tax deduction that homeowners take on their mortgage interest payments should be eliminated, some urbanists have argued. The deduction has not served the interests of central cities, because it has provided a public subsidy for families who purchase suburban homes. Quite clearly, elimination of this tax deduction is not in the interest of those central city residents who wish to purchase a home in the suburbs. It is not in the interest of those central city homeowners (which in some cities may even form a majority of the voting population), who would then be called upon to pay higher federal taxes. But the policy might very well improve the rental market in the central city, thereby stimulating its economy—and it is for this reason that the proposal has been defended as being in the interest of central cities.

To say that people understand what, generally, is in the interest of cities does not eliminate debate over policy alternatives in specific instances. The notion of city interest can be extremely useful, even though its precise application in specific contexts may be quite problematic. In any policy context one cannot easily assert that one "knows" what is in the interest of cities, whether or not the residents of the city agree. But city residents do know the kind of evidence that must be advanced and the kinds of reasons that must be adduced in order to build a persuasive case that a policy is in the interest of cities. And so do community leaders, mayors, and administrative elites.

Economic Interests

Cities, like all structured social systems, seek to improve their position in all three of the systems of stratification—economic, social, and political—characteristic of industrial societies. In most cases, improved standing in any one of these systems helps enhance a city's position in the other two. In the short run, to be sure, cities may have to choose among economic gains, social prestige, and political weight. And because different cities may choose alternative objectives, one cannot state any one overarching objective—such as improved property values—that is always the paramount interest of the city. But in as much as improved economic or market standing seems to be an objective of great importance to most cities, I shall concentrate on this interest and only discuss in passing the significance of social status and political power.

Cities constantly seek to upgrade their economic standing. Following Weber, I mean by this that cities seek to improve their market position, their attractiveness as a locale for economic activity. In the market economy that characterizes Western society, an advantageous economic position means a competitive edge in the production and distribution of desired commodities relative to other localities. When this is present, cities can export goods and/or services to those outside the boundaries of the community.

Some regional economists have gone so far as to suggest that the welfare of a city is identical to the welfare of its export industry.[9] As exporters expand, the city grows. As they contract, the city declines and decays. The economic reasoning supporting such a conclusion is quite straightforward. When cities produce a good that can be sold in an external market, labor and capital flow into the city to help increase the production of that good. They continue to do so until the external market is saturated—that is, until the marginal cost of production within the city exceeds the marginal value of the good external to the city. Those engaged in the production of the exported good will themselves consume a variety of other goods and services, which other businesses will provide. In addition, subsidiary industries locate in the city either because they help supply the exporting industry, because they can utilize some of its by-products, or because they benefit by some economies of scale provided by its presence. Already, the familiar multiplier is at work. With every increase in the sale of exported commodities, there may be as much as a four- or fivefold increase in local economic activity.

The impact of Boeing Aircraft's market prospects on the economy of the Seattle metropolitan area illustrates the importance of export to regional economies. In the late sixties defense and commercial aircraft contracts declined. Boeing laid off thousands of workmen, the economy of the Pacific Northwest slumped, the unemployed moved elsewhere, and Seattle land values dropped sharply. More recently, Boeing has more than recovered its former position. With rapidly expanding production at Boeing, the metropolitan area is enjoying low unemployment, rapid growth, and dramatically increasing land values.

The same multiplier effect is not at work in the case of goods and services produced for domestic consumption within the territory. What is gained by a producer within the community is expended by other community residents. Residents, in effect, are simply taking in one another's laundry. Unless productivity increases, there is no capacity for expansion.

If this economic analysis is correct, it is only a modest oversimplification to equate the interests of cities with the interests of their export industries. Whatever helps them prosper redounds to the benefit of the community as a whole—perhaps four and five times over. And it is just such an economic analysis that has influenced many local government policies. Especially the smaller towns and cities may provide free land, tax concessions, and favorable utility rates to incoming industries.

The smaller the territory and the more primitive its level of economic development, the more persuasive is this simple export thesis. But other economists have elaborated an alternative growth thesis that is in many ways more persuasive, especially as it relates to larger urban areas. In their view a sophisticated local network of public and private services is the key to long-range economic growth. Since the world economy is constantly changing, the economic viability of any particular export industry is highly variable. As a result, a community dependent on any particular set of export industries will have only an episodic economic future. But with a well-developed infrastructure of services, the city becomes an attractive locale for a wide variety of export industries. As older exporters fade, new exporters take their place and the community continues to prosper. It is in the city's interest, therefore, to help sustain a high-quality local infrastructure generally attractive to all commerce and industry.

I have no way of evaluating the merits of these contrasting economic arguments. What is important in this context is that both see exports as being of great importance to the well-being of a city. One view suggests a need for direct support of the export industry; the other suggests a need only for maintaining a service infrastructure, allowing the market to determine which particular export industry locates in the community. Either one could be the more correct diagnosis for a particular community, at least in the short run. Yet both recognize that the future of the city depends upon exporting local products. When a city is able to export its products, service industries prosper, labor is in greater demand, wages increase, promotional opportunities widen, land values rise, tax revenues increase, city services can be improved, donations to charitable organizations become more generous, and the social and cultural life of the city is enhanced.

To export successfully, cities must make efficient use of the three main factors of production: land, labor, and capital.[10]

Land

Land is the factor of production that cities control. Yet land is the factor to which cities are bound. It is the fact that cities are spatially defined units whose boundaries seldom change that gives permanence to their interests. City residents come and go, are born and die, and change their tastes and preferences. But the city remains wedded to the land area with which it is blessed (or cursed). And unless it can alter that land area, through annexation or consolidation, it is the long-range value of that land which the city must secure—and which gives a good approximation of how well it is achieving its interests.

Land is an economic resource. Production cannot occur except within some spatial location. And because land varies in its economic potential, so do the economic futures of cities. Historically, the most important variable affecting urban growth has been an area's relationship to land and water routes.

On the eastern coast of the United States, all the great cities had natural harbors that facilitated commercial relations with Europe and other coastal communities. Inland, the great industrial cities all were located on either the Great Lakes or the Ohio River–Mississippi River system. The cities of the West, as Elazar has shown, prospered according to their proximity to East-West trade flows.[11] Denver became the predominant city of the mountain states because it sat at the crossroads of land routes through the Rocky Mountains. Duluth, Minnesota, had only limited potential, even with its Great Lakes location, because it lay north of all major routes to the West.

Access to waterways and other trade routes is not the only way a city's life is structured by its location. Its climate determines the cost and desirability of habitation; its soil affects food production in the surrounding area; its terrain affects drainage, rates of air pollution, and scenic beauty. Of course, the qualities of landscape do not permanently fix a city's fate—it is the intersection of that land and location with the larger national and world economy that is critical. For example, cities controlling access to waterways by straddling natural harbors at one time monopolized the most valuable land in the region, and from that position they dominated their hinterland. But since land and air transport have begun to supplant, not just supplement, water transport, the dominance of these once favored cities has rapidly diminished.

Although the economic future of a city is very much influenced by external forces affecting the value of its land, the fact that a city has control over the use of its land gives it some capacity for influencing that future. Although there are constitutional limits to its authority, the discretion available to a local government in determining land use remains the greatest arena for the exercise of local autonomy. Cities can plan the use of local space; cities have the power of eminent domain; through zoning laws cities can restrict all sorts of land uses; and cities can regulate the size, content, and purpose of buildings constructed within their boundaries. Moreover, cities can provide public services in such a way as to encourage certain kinds of land use. Sewers, gas lines, roads, bridges, tunnels, playgrounds, schools, and parks all impinge on the use of land in the surrounding area. Urban politics is above all the politics of land use, and it is easy to see why. Land is the factor of production over which cities exercise the greatest control.

Labor

To its land area the city must attract not only capital but productive labor. Yet local governments in the United States are very limited in their capacities to control the flow of these factors. Lacking the more direct controls of nation-states, they are all the more constrained to pursue their economic interests in those areas where they do exercise authority.

Labor is an obvious case in point. Since nation-states control migration across their boundaries, the industrially more advanced have formally legislated that only limited numbers of outsiders—for example, relatives of citizens or those with skills needed by the host country—can enter. In a world where it is economically feasible for great masses of the population to migrate long distances, this kind of restrictive legislation seems essential for keeping the nation's social and economic integrity intact. Certainly, the wage levels and welfare assistance programs characteristic of advanced industrial societies could not be sustained were transnational migration unencumbered.

Unlike nation-states, cities cannot control movement across their boundaries. They no longer have walls, guarded and defended by their inhabitants. And as Weber correctly noted, without walls cities no longer have the independence to make significant choices in the way medieval cities once did.[12] It is true that local governments often try to keep vagrants, bums, paupers, and racial minorities out of their territory. They are harassed, arrested, thrown out of town, and generally discriminated against. But in most of these cases local governments act unconstitutionally, and even this illegal use of the police power does not control migration very efficiently.

Although limited in its powers, the city seeks to obtain an appropriately skilled labor force at wages lower than its competitors so that it can profitably export commodities. In larger cities a diverse work force is desirable. The service industry, which provides the infrastructure for exporters, recruits large numbers of unskilled workers, and many manufacturing industries need only semiskilled workers. When shortages in these skill levels appear, cities may assist industry in advertising the work and living opportunities of the region. In the nineteenth century when unskilled labor was in short supply, frontier cities made extravagant claims to gain a competitive edge in the supply of ordinary labor.

Certain sparsely populated areas, such as Alaska, occasionally advertise for unskilled labor even today. However, competition among most cities is now for highly skilled workers and especially for professional and managerial talent. In a less than full-employment economy, most communities have a surplus of semiskilled and unskilled labor. Increases in the supply of unskilled workers increase the cost of the community's social services. Since national wage laws preclude a decline in wages below a certain minimum, the increases in the cost of social services are seldom offset by lower wages for unskilled labor in those areas where the unemployed concentrate. But even with high levels of unemployment, there remains a shortage of highly skilled technicians and various types of white collar workers. Where shortages develop, the prices these workers can command in the labor market may climb to a level where local exports are no longer competitive with goods produced elsewhere. The economic health of a community is therefore importantly affected by the availability of professional and managerial talent and of highly skilled technicians.

When successfully pursuing their economic interests, cities develop a set of policies that will attract the more skilled and white collar workers without at the same time attracting unemployables. Of course, there are limits on the number of things cities can do. In contrast to nation-states, they cannot simply forbid entry to all but the highly talented whose skills they desire. But through zoning laws, they can ensure that adequate land is available for middle-class residences. They can provide parks, recreation areas, and good-quality schools in areas where the economically most productive live. They can keep the cost of social services, little utilized by the middle class, to a minimum, thereby keeping local taxes relatively low. In general, they can try to ensure that the benefits of public service outweigh their costs to those highly skilled workers, managers, and professionals who are vital for sustaining the community's economic growth.

Capital

Capital is the second factor of production that must be attracted to an economically productive territory. Accordingly, nation-states place powerful controls on the flow of capital across their boundaries. Many nations strictly regulate the amount of national currency that can be taken out of the country. They place quotas and tariffs on imported goods. They regulate the rate at which national currency can be exchanged with foreign currency. They regulate the money supply, increasing interest rates when growth is too rapid, lowering interest rates when growth slows down. Debt financing also allows a nation-state to undertake capital expenditures and to encourage growth in the private market.

At present the powers of nation-states to control capital flow are being used more sparingly and new supranational institutions are developing in their place. Market forces now seem more powerful than official policies in establishing rates of currency exchange among major industrial societies. Tariffs and other restrictions on trade are subject to retaliation by other countries, and so they must be used sparingly. The economies of industrialized nations are becoming so interdependent that significant changes in the international political economy seem imminent, signaled by numerous international conferences to determine worldwide growth rates, rates of inflation, and levels of unemployment. If these trends continue, nation-states may come to look increasingly like local governments.

But these developments at the national level have only begun to emerge. At the local level in the United States, cities are much less able to control capital flows. In the first place, the Constitution has been interpreted to mean that states cannot hinder the free flow of goods and monies across their boundaries. And what is true of states is true of their subsidiary jurisdictions as well. In the second place, states and localities cannot regulate the money supply. If unemployment is low, they cannot stimulate the economy by increasing the monetary flow. If inflationary pressures adversely affect their competitive edge in the export market, localities can neither restrict the money supply nor directly control prices and wages. All of these powers are reserved for national governments. In the third place, local governments cannot spend more than they receive in tax revenues without damaging their credit or even running the risk of bankruptcy. Pump priming, sometimes a national disease, is certainly a national prerogative.

Local governments are left with a number of devices for enticing capital into the area. They can minimize their tax on capital and on profits from capital investment. They can reduce the costs of capital investment by providing low-cost public utilities, such as roads, sewers, lights, and police and fire protection. They can even offer public land free of charge or at greatly reduced prices to those investors they are particularly anxious to attract. They can provide a context for business operations free of undue harassment or regulation. For example, they can ignore various external costs of production, such as air pollution, water pollution, and the despoliation of trees, grass, and other features of the landscape. Finally, they can discourage labor from unionizing so as to keep industrial labor costs competitive.

This does not mean it behooves cities to allow any and all profit-maximizing action on the part of an industrial plant. Insofar as the city desires diversified economic growth, no single company can be allowed to pursue policies that seriously detract from the area's overall attractiveness to capital or productive labor. Taxes cannot be so low that government fails to supply residents with as attractive a package of services as can be found in competitive jurisdictions. Regulation of any particular industry cannot fall so far below nationwide standards that other industries must bear external costs not encountered in other places. The city's interest in attracting capital does not mean utter subservience to any particular corporation, but a sensitivity to the need for establishing an overall favorable climate.

In sum, cities, like private firms, compete with one another so as to maximize their economic position. To achieve this objective, the city must use the resources its land area provides by attracting as much capital and as high a quality labor force as is possible. Like a private firm, the city must entice labor and capital resources by offering appropriate inducements. Unlike the nation-state, the American city does not have regulatory powers to control labor and capital flows. The lack thereof sharply limits what cities can do to control their economic development, but at the same time the attempt by cities to maximize their interests within these limits shapes policy choice.

Local Government and the Interests of Cities

Local government leaders are likely to be sensitive to the economic interests of their communities. First, economic prosperity is necessary for protecting the fiscal base of a local government. In the United States, taxes on local sources and charges for local services remain important components of local government revenues. Although transfers of revenue to local units from the federal and state governments increased throughout the postwar period, as late as 1975–76 local governments still were raising almost 59 percent of their own revenue.[13] Raising revenue from one's own economic resources requires continuing local economic prosperity. Second, good government is good politics. By pursuing policies which contribute to the economic prosperity of the local community, the local politician selects policies that redound to his own political advantage. Local politicians, eager for relief from the cross-pressures of local politics, assiduously promote goals that have widespread benefits. And few policies are more popular than economic growth and prosperity. Third, and most important, local officials usually have a sense of community responsibility. They know that, unless the economic well-being of the community can be maintained, local business will suffer, workers will lose employment opportunities, cultural life will decline, and city land values will fall. To avoid such a dismal future, public officials try to develop policies that assist the prosperity of their community—or, at the very least, that do not seriously detract from it. Quite apart from any effects of economic prosperity on government revenues or local voting behavior, it is quite reasonable to posit that local governments are primarily interested in maintaining the economic vitality of the area for which they are responsible.

Accordingly, governments can be expected to attempt to maximize this particular goal—within the numerous environmental constraints with which they must contend. As policy alternatives are proposed, each is evaluated according to how well it will help to achieve this objective. Although information is imperfect and local governments cannot be expected to select the one best alternative on every occasion, policy choices over time will be limited to those few which can plausibly be shown to be conducive to the community's economic prosperity. Internal disputes and disagreements may affect policy on the margins, but the major contours of local revenue policy will be determined by this strategic objective.

2

Clarence N. Stone

URBAN REGIMES

What makes governance in Atlanta effective is not the formal machinery of government, but rather the informal partnership between city hall and the downtown business elite. This informal partnership and the way it operates constitute the city's regime; it is the means through which major policy decisions are made.

The word "regime" connotes different things to different people, but in this [selection] regime is specifically about the *informal arrangements* that surround and complement the formal workings of governmental authority. All governmental authority in the United States is greatly limited—limited by the Constitution, limited perhaps even more by the nation's political tradition, and limited structurally by the autonomy of privately owned business enterprise. The exercise of public authority is thus never a simple matter; it is almost always enhanced by extraformal considerations. Because local governmental authority is by law and tradition even more limited than authority at the state and national level, informal arrangements assume special importance in urban politics. But we should begin our understanding of regimes by realizing that informal arrangements are by no means peculiar to cities or, for that matter, to government.

Even narrowly bounded organizations, those with highly specific functional responsibilities, develop informal governing coalitions.[1] As Chester Barnard argued many years ago, formal goals and formal lines of authority are insufficient by themselves to bring about coordinated action with sufficient energy to accomplish organizational purposes,[2] commitment and cooperation do not just spring up from the lines of an organization chart. Because every formal organization gives rise to an informal one, Barnard concluded, successful executives must master the skill of shaping and using informal organization for their purposes.

Attention to informal arrangements takes various forms. In the analysis of business firms, the school of thought labeled "transaction cost economics" has given systematic attention to how things actually get done in a world full of social friction—basically the same question that Chester Barnard considered. A leading proponent of this approach, Oliver Williamson,[3] finds that what he terms "private orderings" (as opposed to formal and legal agreements) are enormously important in the running of business affairs. For many transactions, mutual and tacit understanding is a more efficient way of conducting relations than are legal agreements and formal contracts. Williamson quotes a business executive as saying, "You can settle any dispute if you keep the lawyers and accountants out of it. They just do not understand the give-and-take needed in business."[4] Because informal understandings and arrangements provide needed flexibility to cope with nonroutine matters, they facilitate cooperation to a degree that formally defined relationships do not. People who know one another, who have worked together in the past, who have shared in the achievement of a task, and who perhaps have experienced the same crisis are especially likely to develop tacit understandings. If they interact on a continuing basis, they can learn to trust one another and to expect dependability from one another. It can be argued, then, that transactions flow more smoothly and business is conducted more efficiently when a core of insiders form and develop an ongoing relationship.

A regime thus involves not just any informal group that comes together to make a decision but an informal yet relatively stable group *with access to institutional resources* that enable it to have a sustained role in making governing decisions. What makes the group informal is not a lack of institutional connections, but the fact that the group, *as a group*, brings together institutional connections by an informal mode of cooperation. There is no all-encompassing structure of command that guides and synchronizes everyone's behavior. There is a purposive coordination of efforts, but it comes about informally, in ways that often depend heavily on tacit understandings.

From Clarence N. Stone, "Urban Regimes: A Research Perspective" and excerpt from "Conclusion" from *Regime Politics: Governing Atlanta*, 1946–1988, pp. 3–12, 238–245. © 1989 by the University Press of Kansas. Reprinted by permission of the University Press of Kansas.

If there is no overarching command structure, what gives a regime coherence? What makes it more than an "ecology of games"?[5] The answer is that the regime is purposive, created and maintained as a way of facilitating action. In a very important sense, *a regime is empowering.* Its supporters see it as a means for achieving coordinated efforts that might not otherwise be realized. A regime, however, is not created or redirected at will. Organizational analysis teaches us that cognition is limited, existing arrangements have staying power, and implementation is profoundly shaped by procedures in place.[6] Shrewd and determined leaders can effect purposive change, but only by being attentive to the ways in which existing forms of coordination can be altered or amplified.[7]

We can think of cities as organizations that lack a conjoining structure of command. There are institutional sectors within which the power of command may be much in evidence, but the sectors are independent of one another.[8] Because localities have only weak formal means through which coordination can be achieved, informal arrangements to promote cooperation are especially useful. *These informal modes of coordinating efforts across institutional boundaries are what I call "civic cooperation."* In a system of weak formal authority, it holds special importance. Integrated with the formal structure of authority into a suprainstitutional capacity to take action, any informal basis of cooperation is empowering. It enables community actors to achieve cooperation beyond what could be formally commanded.

Consider the case of local political machines. When ward politicians learned to coordinate informally what otherwise was mired in institutional fragmentation and personal opportunism, the urban political machine was created and proved to have enormous staying power.[9] "Loyalty" is the shorthand that machine politicians used to describe the code that bound them into a cohesive group.[10] The political machine is in many ways the exemplar of governance in which informal arrangements are vital complements to the formal organization of government. The classic urban machines brought together various elements of the community in an informal scheme of exchange and cooperation that was the real governing system of the community.

The urban machine, of course, represents only one form of regime. In considering Atlanta, I am examining the governing coalition in a nonmachine city. The term "governing coalition" is a way of making the notion of regime concrete. It makes us face the fact that informal arrangements are held together by a core group—typically a body of insiders—who come together repeatedly in making important decisions. Thus, when I refer to the governing coalition in Atlanta, I mean the core group at the center of the workings of the regime.

To talk about a core group is not to suggest that they are of one mind or that they all represent identical interests—far from it. "Coalition" is the word I use to emphasize that a regime involves bringing together various elements of the community and the different institutional capacities they control. "Governing," as used in "governing coalition," I must stress, does not mean rule in command-and-control fashion. Governance through informal arrangements is about how some forms of coordination of effort prevail over others. It is about mobilizing efforts to cope and to adapt; it is not about absolute control. Informal arrangements are a way of bolstering (and guiding) the formal capacity to act, but even this enhanced capacity remains quite limited.

Having argued that informal arrangements are important in a range of circumstances, not just in cities, let me return to the specifics of the city setting. After all, the important point is not simply that there are informal arrangements; it is the particular features of urban regimes that provide the lenses through which we see the Atlanta experience. For cities, two questions face us: (1) Who makes up the governing coalition—who has to come together to make governance possible? (2) How is the coming together accomplished? These two questions imply a third: What are the consequences of the *who* and *how?* Urban regimes are not neutral mechanisms through which policy is made; they shape policy. To be sure, they do not do so on terms solely of the governing coalition's own choosing. But regimes are the mediating agents between the ill-defined pressures of an urban environment and the making of community policy. The *who* and *how* of urban regimes matter, thus giving rise to the further question of *with what consequences.* These three questions will guide my analysis of Atlanta.

Urban Regimes

As indicated above, an urban regime refers to the set of arrangements by which a community is actually governed. Even though the institutions of local government bear most of the formal responsibility for governing, they lack the resources and the scope of authority to govern without the active support and cooperation of significant private interests. An urban regime may thus be defined as the *informal arrangements by which public bodies and private interests function together in order to be able to make and carry out governing decisions.* These governing decisions, I want to emphasize, are not a matter of running or controlling everything. They have to do with *managing conflict* and *making adaptive responses* to social change. The informal arrangements through which governing decisions are made differ from community to community, but everywhere they are driven by two needs: (1) institutional scope (that is, the need to encompass a wide enough scope of institutions to mobilize the resources required to make and implement governing decisions) and (2) cooperation (that is, the need to promote enough cooperation and coordination for the diverse participants to reach decisions and sustain action in support of those decisions).

The mix of participants varies by community, but that mix is itself constrained by the accommodation of two basic institutional principles of the American political economy: (1) popular control of the formal machinery of government and (2) private ownership of business enterprise.[11] Neither of these principles is pristine. Popular control is modified and compromised in various ways, but nevertheless remains as the basic principle of government. Private ownership is less than universal, as governments do own and operate various auxiliary enterprises from mass transit to convention centers. Even so, governmental conduct is constrained by the need to promote investment activity in an economic arena dominated by private ownership. This political-economy insight is the foundation for a theory of urban regimes.[12]

In defining an urban regime as the informal arrangements through which public bodies and private interests function together to make and carry out governing decisions, bear in mind that I did not specify that the private interests are business interests. Indeed, in practice, private interests are not confined to business figures. Labor-union officials, party functionaries, officers in nonprofit organizations or foundations, and church leaders may also be involved.[13]

Why, then, pay particular attention to business interests? One reason is the now well-understood need to encourage business investment in order to have an economically thriving community. A second reason is the sometimes overlooked factor that businesses control politically important resources and are rarely absent totally from the scene. They may work through intermediaries, or some businesses may even be passive because others represent their interests as property holders, but a business presence is always part of the urban political scene. Although the nature of business involvement extends from the direct and extensive to the indirect and limited, the economic role of businesses *and the resources they control* are too important for these enterprises to be left out completely.

With revived interest in political economy, the regime's need for an adequate institutional scope (including typically some degree of business involvement) has received significant attention. However, less has been said about the regime's need for cooperation—and the various ways to meet it.[14] Perhaps some take for granted that, when cooperation is called for, it will be forthcoming. But careful reflection reminds us that cooperation does not occur simply because it is useful.

Robert Wiebe analyzed machine politics in a way that illustrates an important point: "The ward politician . . . required wider connections in order to manage many of his clients' problems. . . . Therefore clusters of these men allied to increase their bargaining power in city affairs. But if logic led to an integrated city-wide organization, the instinct of self-preservation did not. The more elaborate the structure, the more independence the ward bosses and area chieftains lost."[15] Cooperation can thus never be taken as a given; it must be achieved and at significant costs. Some of the costs are visible resources expended in promoting cooperation—favors and benefits distributed to curry reciprocity, the effort required to establish and maintain channels of communication, and responsibilities borne to knit activities together are a few examples. But, as Wiebe's observation reminds us, there are less visible costs. Achieving cooperation entails commitment to a set of relationships, and these relationships limit independence of action. If relationships are to be ongoing, they cannot be neglected; they may even call for sacrifices to prevent alienating allies. Forming wider connections is thus not a cost-free step, and it is not a step that community actors are always eager to take.

Because centrifugal tendencies are always strong, achieving cooperation is a major accomplishment and requires constant effort. Cooperation can be brought about in various ways. It can be induced if there is an actor powerful enough to coerce others into it, but that is a rare occurrence, because power is not usually so concentrated. More often, cooperation is achieved by some degree of reciprocity.

The literature on collective action focuses on the problem of cooperation in the absence of a system of command. For example, the "prisoner's dilemma" game instructs us that noncooperation may be invited by a number of situations.[16] In the same vein, Mancur Olson's classic analysis highlights the free-rider problem and the importance of selective incentives in inducing cooperation.[17] Alternatively, repeated interactions permit people to see the shortcomings of mutual noncooperation and to learn norms of cooperation.[18] Moreover, although Robert Axelrod's experiments with TIT FOR TAT computer programs indicate that cooperation can be instrumentally rational under some conditions, the process is not purely mechanical.[19] Students of culture point to the importance of common identity and language in facilitating interaction and promoting trust.[20] Size of group is also a consideration, affecting the ease of communication and bargaining among members; Michael Taylor, for example, emphasizes the increased difficulty of conditional cooperation in larger groups.[21]

What we can surmise about the urban community is thus twofold: (1) cooperation across institutional lines is valuable but far from automatic; and (2) cooperation is more likely to grow under some circumstances than others. This conclusion has wide implications for the study of urban politics. For example, much of the literature on community power has centered on the question of control, its possibilities and limitations: to what extent is domination by a command center possible and how is the cost of social control worked out. The long-standing elitist-pluralist debate centers on such questions. However, my line of argument here points to another way of viewing urban communities; it points to the need to think about cooperation, its possibilities and limitations— not just any cooperation, but cooperation of the kind that can bring together people based in different sectors of a community's institutional life and that enables a coalition of actors to make and support a set of governing decisions.

If the conventional model of urban politics is one of social control (with both elitist and pluralist variants), then the one proposed here might be called "the social-production model." It is based on the question of how, in a world of limited and dispersed authority, actors work together across institutional lines to produce a capacity to govern and to bring about publicly significant results.

To be sure, the development of a system of cooperation for governing is something that arises, not from an unformed mass, but rather within a structured set of relationships. Following Stephen Elkin, I described above the basic configuration in political-economy terms: popular control of governmental authority and private ownership of business activity. However, both of these elements are subject to variation. Populations vary in characteristics and in type of political organization; hence, popular control comes in many forms. The economic sector itself varies by the types of businesses that compose it and by the way in which it is organized formally and informally. Hence there is no one formula for bringing institutional sectors into an arrangement for cooperation, and the whole process is imbued with uncertainty. Cooperation is always somewhat tenuous, and it is made more so as conditions change and new actors enter the scene.

The study of urban regimes is thus a study of who cooperates and how their cooperation is achieved across institutional sectors of community life. Further, it is an examination of how that cooperation is maintained when confronted with an ongoing process of social change, a continuing influx of new actors, and potential break-downs through conflict or indifference.

Regimes are dynamic, not static, and regime dynamics concern the ways in which forces for change and forces for continuity play against one another. For example, Atlanta's governing coalition has displayed remarkable continuity in the post-World War II period, and it has done so despite deep-seated forces of social change. Understanding Atlanta's urban regime involves understanding how cooperation can be maintained and continuity can prevail in the face of so many possibilities for conflict.

Structure, Action, and Structuring

Because of the interplay of change and continuity, urban regimes are perhaps best studied over time. Let us, then, take a closer look at historical analysis. Scholars make sense out of the particulars of political and social life by thinking mainly in terms of abstract structures such as democracy and capitalism. Although these are useful as shorthand, the danger in abstractions is that they never capture the full complexity and contingency of the world. Furthermore, "structure" suggests something solid and unchanging, yet political and social life is riddled with contradictions and uncertainties that give rise to an ongoing process of change and adjustment. Much of the change that occurs is at the margins of basic and enduring relationships, making it easy to think in terms of order and stability. Incrementalists remind us that the present is the best predictor of the near future. But students of history, especially those accustomed to looking at longer periods of time, offer a different perspective. They see a world undergoing change, in which various actors struggle over what the terms of that change will be. It is a world shaped and reshaped by human efforts, a world that never quite forms a unified whole.

In historical light, social structures are less solid and less fixed than social scientists have sometimes assumed. Charles Tilly has argued that there is no single social structure. Instead, he urges us to think in terms of multiple structures, which "consist of shifting, constructed social relations among limited numbers of actors."[22] Philip Abrams also sees structures as relationships, relationships that are socially fabricated and subject to purposive modification.[23]

Structures are real but not fixed. Action does not simply occur within the bounds set by structures but is sometimes aimed at the structures themselves, so that a process of reshaping is taking place at all times. Abrams thus argues that events have a two-sided character, involving both structure and action in such a way that action shapes structures and structures shape actions. Abrams calls for the study of a process he labels as "structuring," by which he means that events occur in a structured context and that events help reshape structure.[24]

Abrams therefore offers a perspective on the interplay of change and continuity. This continuity is not so much a matter of resisting change as coping with it. Because the potential for change is ever present, regime continuity is a remarkable outcome. Any event contains regime-altering potential—perhaps not in sudden realignment, but in opening up a new path along which subsequent events can cumulatively bring about fundamental change.[25] The absence of regime alteration is thus an outcome to be explained, and it must be explained in terms of a capacity to adapt and reinforce existing structures. Events are the arena in which the struggle between change and continuity is played out, but they are neither self-defining nor free-formed phenomena. They become events in our minds because they have some bearing on structures that help shape future occurrences. It is the interplay of event and structure that is especially worthy of study. To identify events, one therefore needs to have some conception of structure. In this way, the researcher can focus attention, relieved of the impossible task of studying everything.

There is no escaping the necessity of the scholar's imposing some form of analysis on research. The past becomes known through the concepts we apply. Abrams sees this as the heart of historical sociology: "The reality of the past is just not 'there' waiting to be observed by the resurrectionist historian. It is to be known if at all through strenuous theoretical alienation."[26] He also reminds us that many aspects of an event cannot be observed in a direct sense; too much is implicit at any given moment.[27] That is why the process, or the flow of events over time, is so important to examine. That is also why events are not necessarily most significant for their immediate impact; they may be more significant for their bearing on subsequent events, thus giving rise to modifications in structure.

Prologue to the Atlanta Narrative

Structuring in Atlanta is a story in which race is central. If regimes are about who co-operates, how, and with what consequences, one of the remarkable features of Atlanta's urban regime is its biracial character. How has cooperation been achieved across racial lines, particularly since race is often a chasm rather than a bridge? Atlanta has been governed by a biracial coalition for so long that it is tempting to believe that nothing else was possible. Yet other cities followed a different pattern. At a time when Atlanta prided itself on being "the city too busy to hate," Little Rock, Birmingham, and New Orleans pursued die-hard segregation and were caught up in racial violence and turmoil. The experience of these cities reminds us that Atlanta's regime is not simply an informal arrangement through which popular elections and private ownership are reconciled, but is deeply intertwined with race relations, with some actors on the Atlanta scene able to overcome the divisive character of race sufficiently to achieve cooperation.

Atlanta's earlier history is itself a mixed experience, offering no clear indication that biracial cooperation would emerge and prevail in the years after World War II. In 1906, the city was the site of a violent race riot apparently precipitated by inflammatory antiblack newspaper rhetoric.[28] The incident hastened the city's move toward the economic exclusion and residential segregation of blacks, their disenfranchisement, and enforcement of social subordination; and the years after 1906 saw the Jim Crow system fastened into place. Still, the riot was followed by modest efforts to promote biracial understanding, culminating in the formation in 1919 of the Commission on Interracial Cooperation.

Atlanta, however, also became the headquarters city for a revived Ku Klux Klan. During the 1920s, the Klan enjoyed wide support and was a significant influence in city elections. At this time, it gained a strong foothold in city government and a lasting one in the police department.[29] In 1930, faced with rising unemployment, some white Atlantans also founded the Order of Black Shirts for the express purpose of driving blacks out of even menial jobs and replacing them with whites. Black Shirt protests had an impact, and opportunities for blacks once again were constricted. At the end of World War II, with Atlanta's black population expanding beyond a number that could be contained in the city's traditionally defined black neighborhoods, another klanlike organization, the Columbians, sought to use terror tactics to prevent black expansion into previously all-white areas. All of this occurred against a background of state and regional politics devoted to the subordination of blacks to whites—a setting that did not change much until the 1960s.

Nevertheless, other patterns surfaced briefly from time to time. In 1932, Angelo Herndon, a black Communist organizer, led a mass demonstration of white and black unemployed protesting a cutoff of work relief. Herndon was arrested, and the biracial following he led proved short-lived. Still, the event had occurred, and Atlanta's city council did in fact accede to the demand for continued relief.[30] In the immediate postwar period, a progressive biracial coalition formed around the successful candidacy of Helen Douglas Mankin for a congressional seat representing Georgia's fifth district. That, too, was short-lived, as ultra-conservative Talmadge forces maneuvered to reinstitute Georgia's county-unit system for the fifth district and defeat Mankin with a minority of the popular vote.[31]

It is tempting to see the flow of history as flux, and one could easily dwell on the mutable character of political alignments. The Atlanta experience suggests that coalitions often give expression to instability. Centrifugal forces are strong, and in some ways dis-order is a natural state. What conflict does not tear asunder, indifference is fully capable of wearing away.

The political incorporation of blacks into Atlanta's urban regime in tight coalition with the city's white business elite is thus not a story of how popular control and private capital came inevitably to live together in peace and harmony. It is an account of struggle and conflict—bringing together a biracial governing coalition at the outset, and then allowing each of the coalition partners to secure for itself an advantageous position within the coalition. In the first instance, struggle involved efforts to see that the coalition between white business interests and the black middle class prevailed over other possible alignments. In the second instance, there was struggle over the terms of coalition between the partners; thus political conflict is not confined to "ins" versus "outs." Those on the inside engage in significant struggle with one another over the terms on which cooperation will be maintained, which is one reason governing arrangements should never be taken for granted.

Atlanta's urban regime therefore appears to be the creature of purposive struggle, and both its establishment and its maintenance call for a political explanation. The shape of the regime was far from inevitable, but rather came about through the actions of human agents making political choices. Without extraeconomic efforts by the city's business leadership, Atlanta would have been governed in a much different manner, and Atlanta's urban regime and the policies furthered by that regime might well have diverged from the path taken. History, perhaps, is as much about alternatives not pursued as about those that were. . . .

The Political Ramifications of Unequal Resources

From Aristotle to Tocqueville to the present, keen political observers have understood that politics evolves from and reflects the associational life of a community. How people are grouped is important—so much so that, as the authors of the *Federalist* essays understood, the formation and reformation of coalitions [are] at the heart of political activity. Democracy should be viewed within that context; i.e., realizing that people do not act together simply because they share preferences on some particular issue.

Overlooking that long-standing lesson, many public-choice economists regard democracy with suspicion. They fear that popular majorities will insist on an egalitarian redistribution of benefits and thereby interfere with economic productivity. As worded by one economist, "The majority (the poor) will always vote for taxing the minority (the rich), at least until the opportunities for benefiting from redistribution run out."[32] In other words, majority rule will overturn an unequal distribution of goods and resources. This reasoning, however, involves the simple-minded premise that formal governmental authority confers a capacity to redistribute at the will of those who hold office by virtue of popular election. The social-production model of politics employed here offers a contrasting view. Starting from an assumption about the costliness of civic cooperation, the social production model suggests that an unequal distribution of goods and resources substantially modifies majority rule.

In operation, democracy is a great deal more complicated than counting votes and sorting through the wants of rational egoists. In response to those who regard democracy as a process of aggregating preferences within a system characterized by formal equality, a good antidote is Stein Rokkan's aphorism, "Votes count but resources decide."[33] Voting power is certainly not insignificant, but policies are decided mainly by those who control important concentrations of resources. Hence, governing is never simply a matter of aggregating numbers, whether for redistribution or other purposes. . . .

Of course, the election of key public officials provides a channel of popular expression. Since democracy rests on the principle of equal voting power, it would seem that all groups do share in the capacity to become part of the governing regime. Certainly the vote played a major role in the turnaround of the position of blacks in Atlanta. Popular control, however, is not a simple and straightforward process. Much depends on how the populace is organized to participate in a community's civic life. Machine politics, for example, promotes a search for personal favors. With electoral mobilization dependent upon an organizational network oriented toward patronage and related considerations, other kinds of popular concerns may have difficulty gaining expression.[34] The political machine thus enjoys a type of preemptive power, though the party organization is only one aspect of the overall governing regime.

On the surface, Atlanta represents a situation quite different from machine politics. Nonpartisan elections and an absence of mass patronage have characterized the city throughout the post-World War II era. Yet it would hardly be accurate to describe civic life in Atlanta as open and fluid. Nonpartisanship has heightened the role of organizations connected to business, and the newspapers have held an important position in policy debate. At the same time, working-class organizations and nonprofit groups unsupported by business are not major players in city politics.

Within Atlanta's civic sector, activities serve to piece together concerns across the institutional lines of the community, connecting government with business and each with a variety of nonprofit entities. The downtown elite has been especially adept at building alliances in that sector and, in doing so, has extended its resource advantage well beyond the control of strictly economic functions. Responding to its own weakness in numbers, the business elite has crafted a network through which cooperation can be advanced and potential cleavages between haves and have-nots redirected.

Consider what Atlanta's postwar regime represents. In 1946, the central element in the governing coalition was a downtown business elite organized for and committed to an active program of redevelopment that would transform the character of the business district and, in the process, displace a largely black population to the south and east of the district. At the same time, with the end of the white primary that same year, a middle-class black population, long excluded from power, mobilized its electoral strength to begin an assault on a firmly entrenched Jim Crow system. Knowing only those facts, one might well have predicted in 1946 that these two groups would be political antagonists. They were not. Both committed to an agenda of change, they worked out an accommodation and became the city's governing coalition. The alliance has had its tensions and even temporary ruptures, but it has held and demonstrated remarkable strength in making and carrying out policy decisions.

To understand the process, the Atlanta experience indicates that one must appreciate institutional capacities and the resources that various groups control. That is why simple preference aggregation is no guide to how coalitions are built. The downtown elite and the black middle class had complementary needs that could be met by forming an alliance, and the business elite in particular had the kind and amount of resources to knit the alliance together.

Politics in Atlanta, then, is not organized around an overriding division between haves and have-nots. Instead, unequally distributed resources serve to destabilize opposition and encourage alliances around small opportunities. Without command of a capacity to govern, elected leaders have difficulty building support around popular discontent. That is why Rokkan's phrase, "Votes count but resources decide," is so apt.

Unequal Resources and Urban Regimes

Regimes, I have suggested, are to be understood in terms of (1) who makes up the governing coalition and (2) how the coalition achieves cooperation. Both points illustrate how the unequal distribution of resources affects politics and what differences the formation of a regime makes. That the downtown elite is a central partner in the Atlanta regime shapes the priorities set and the trade-offs made. Hence, investor prerogative is protected practice in Atlanta, under the substantial influence of the business elite *within* the governing coalition. At the same time, the fact that the downtown elite is part of a governing coalition prevents business isolation from community affairs. Yet, although "corporate responsibility" promotes business involvement, it does so in a way that enhances business as patron and promoter of small opportunities.

Similarly, the incorporation of the black middle class into the mainstream civic and economic life of Atlanta is testimony to its ability to use electoral leverage to help set community priorities. The importance of the mode of cooperation is also evident. Although much of what the regime has done has generated popular resistance, the black middle class has been persuaded to go along by a combination of selective incentives and small opportunities. Alliance with the business elite enabled the black middle class to achieve particular objectives not readily available by other means. This kind of enabling capacity is what gives concentrated resources its gravitational force.

The pattern thus represents something more than individual cooptation. The black middle class as a group benefited from new housing areas in the early postwar years and from employment and business opportunities in recent years. Some of the beneficiaries have been institutional—colleges in the Atlanta University system and a financially troubled bank, for example. Because the term "selective incentives" implies individual benefits (and these have been important), the more inclusive term "small opportunities" provides a useful complement. In both cases, the business elite is a primary source; they can make things happen, provide needed assistance, and open up opportunities. At the same time, since the downtown elite needs the cooperation of local government and various community groups, the elite itself is drawn toward a broad community-leadership role. Although its bottom-line economic interests are narrow, its community role can involve it in wider concerns. Selective incentives, however, enable the elite to muffle some of the pressure that might otherwise come from the larger community.

Once we focus on the regime and the importance of informally achieved cooperation, we can appreciate better the complex way in which local politics actually functions.

Public-choice economists, fearful that democracy will lead to redistribution, misunderstand the process and treat politics as a causal force operating in isolation from resources other than the vote. That clearly is unwarranted. Atlanta's business elite possesses substantial slack resources that can be and are devoted to policy. Some devotion of resources to political purposes is direct, in the form of campaign funds, but much is indirect; it takes on the character of facilitating civic cooperation of those efforts deemed worthy.

The business elite is small and homogeneous enough to use the norms of class unity and corporate responsibility to maintain its cohesion internally. In interacting with allies, the prevailing mode of operation is reciprocity, reinforced in many cases by years of trust built from past exchanges. The biracial insiders have also been at their tasks long enough to experience a sense of pride in the community role they play. Even so, the coalition is centered around a combination of explicit and tacit deals. Reciprocity is thus the hallmark of Atlanta's regime, and reciprocity hinges on what one actor can do for another. Instead of promoting redistribution toward equality, such a system perpetuates inequality.

Reciprocity, of course, occurs in a context, and in Atlanta, it is interwoven with a complex set of conditions. The slack resources controlled by business corporations give them an extraordinary opportunity to promote civic cooperation. Where there is a compelling mutual interest, as within Atlanta's downtown elite, businesses have the means to solve their own collective-action problem and unite behind a program of action. Their resources also enable them to create a network of cooperation that extends across lines of institutional division, which makes them attractive to public officials and other results-oriented community groups. In becoming an integral part of a system of civic cooperation, Atlanta's business elite has used its resource advantage to shape community policy and protect a privileged position. Because the elite is useful to others, it attracts and holds a variety of allies in its web of reciprocity. The concentration of resources it has gathered thus enables the elite to counter demands for greater equality.

Social Learning versus Privilege

Instead of understanding democratic politics as an instance of the equality (redistribution)/efficiency (productivity) trade-off, I suggest an alternative. Policy actions (and inactions) have extensive repercussions and involve significant issues that do not fit neatly into an equality-versus-efficiency mold. There is a need, then, for members of the governing coalition to be widely informed about a community's problems, and not to be indifferent about the information. That is what representative democracy is about.

For their part, in order to be productive, business enterprises need a degree of autonomy and a supply of slack resources. It is also appropriate that they participate in politics. However, there are dangers involved in the ability of high-resource groups, like Atlanta's business elite, to secure for themselves a place in the governing coalition and then use that inside position along with their own ample resources to shape the regime on their terms. Elsewhere I have called this "preemptive power,"[35] and have suggested that it enables a group to protect a privileged position. The ability to parcel out selective incentives and other small opportunities permits Atlanta's business elite to enforce discipline on behalf of civic cooperation by vesting others with lesser privileges—privileges perhaps contingently held in return for "going along."

The flip side of discipline through selective incentives is a set of contingent privileges that restrict the questions asked and curtail social learning. Thus, one of the trade-offs in local politics can be phrased as social learning versus privilege. Some degree of privilege for business may be necessary to encourage investment, but the greater the privilege being protected, the less the incentive to understand and act on behalf of the community in its entirety.

The political challenge illustrated by the Atlanta case is how to reconstitute the regime so that both social learning and civic cooperation occur. The risk in the present situation is that those who govern have only a limited comprehension of the consequences of their actions. Steps taken to correct one problem may create or aggravate another while leaving still others unaddressed. Those who govern can discover that only, it seems, through wide representation of the affected groups. Otherwise, choices are limited by an inability to understand the city's full situation.

No governing coalition has an inclination to expand the difficulties of making and carrying out decisions. Still, coalitions can be induced to attempt the difficult. For example, Atlanta's regime has been centrally involved in race relations, perhaps the community's most difficult and volatile issue. Relationships within the governing coalition have been fraught with tension; friction was unavoidable. Yet the coalition achieved a cooperative working relationship between the black middle class and the white business elite. In a rare but telling incident, black leaders insisted successfully that a 1971 pledge to build a MARTA spur to a black public-housing area not be repudiated. The newspaper opined that trust within the coalition was too important to be sacrificed on the altar of economizing. Thus the task of the governing regime was expanded beyond the narrow issue of serving downtown in the least expensive manner possible; concerns *can* be broadened.

Although no regime is likely to be totally inclusive, most regimes can be made more inclusive. Just as Atlanta's regime was drawn into dealing with race relations, others can become sensitive to the situations of a larger set of groups. Greater inclusiveness will not come automatically nor from the vote alone. Pressures to narrow the governing coalition are strong and recurring. Yet, if civic cooperation is the key to the terms on which economic and electoral power are accommodated, then more inclusive urban regimes can be encouraged through an associational life at the community level that reflects a broad range of perspectives. The problem is not an absence of associational life at that level but how to lessen its dependence on business sponsorship, how to free participation in civic activity from an overriding concern with protecting insider privileges, and how to enrich associational life so that nonprofit and other groups can function together as they express encompassing community concerns.

This step is one in which federal policy could make a fundamental difference. In the past, starting with the urban-redevelopment provision in the 1949 housing act and continuing through the Carter administration's UDAG program, cities have been strongly encouraged to devise partnerships with private, for-profit developers, thus intensifying already strong leanings in that direction. Since these were matters of legislative choice, it seems fully possible for the federal government to move in another direction and encourage nonprofit organizations. The federal government could, for example, establish a program of large-scale assistance to community development corporations and other nonprofit groups. Some foundations now support such programs, but their modest efforts could be augmented. Programs of community service required by high schools and colleges or spawned by a national-level service requirement could increase voluntary participation and alter the character of civic life in local communities. It is noteworthy that neighborhood mobilization in Atlanta was partly initiated by VISTA (Volunteers in Service to America) workers in the 1960s and continued by those who stayed in the city after completing service with VISTA. This, however, is not the place to prescribe a full set of remedies; my aim is only to indicate that change is possible but will probably require a stimulus external to the local community.

Summing Up

If the slack resources of business help to set the terms on which urban governance occurs, then we need to be aware of what this imbalance means. The Atlanta case suggests that the more uneven the distribution of resources, the greater the tendency of the regime to become concerned with protecting privilege. Concurrently, there is a narrowing of the regime's willingness to engage in "information seeking" (or social learning). Imbalances in the civic sector thus lead to biases in policy, biases that electoral politics alone is unable to correct.

A genuinely effective regime is not only adept at promoting cooperation in the execution of complex and nonroutine projects, but is also able to comprehend the consequences of its actions and inactions for a diverse citizenry. The promotion of this broad comprehension is, after all, a major aim of democracy. Even if democratic politics were removed from the complexities of coordination for social production, it still could not be reduced to a set of decision rules. Arrow's theorem shows that majority choices cannot be neutrally aggregated when preference structures are complex,[36] as indeed they are bound to be in modern societies.

Democracy, then, is not simply a decision rule for registering choices; it has to operate with a commitment to inclusiveness. Permanent or excluded minorities are inconsistent with the basic idea of equality that underpins democracy. That is why some notion of social learning is an essential part of the democratic process; all are entitled to have their situations understood. Thus, to the extent that urban regimes safeguard special privileges at the expense of social learning, democracy is weakened.

Those fearful that too much community participation will lead to unproductive policies should widen their own understanding and consider other dangers on the political landscape. Particularly under conditions of an imbalance in civically useful resources, the political challenge is one of preventing government from being harnessed to the protection of special privilege. The social-production model reminds us that only a segment of society's institutions are under the sway of majority rule; hence, actual governance is never simply a matter of registering the preferences of citizens as individuals.

The character of local politics depends greatly on the nature of a community's associational life, which in turn depends greatly on the distribution of resources other than the vote. Of course, the vote is significant, but equality in the right to vote is an inadequate guarantee against the diversion of politics into the protection of privilege. If broad social learning is to occur, then other considerations must enter the picture. "One person, one vote" is not enough.

3

Elizabeth Strom

University of South Florida

RETHINKING THE POLITICS OF DOWNTOWN DEVELOPMENT

Those interested in both the physical and political changes reshaping the downtowns of large American cities can find themselves engaged in two parallel conversations. In the first, found among urbanists from many fields as well as in the popular press, we learn that much of the new (e.g., post-1980) development in American city centers has been focused on activities we might characterize as "consumption"—professional sports, cultural institutions, themed shopping districts, and housing are now taking over areas once dominated by banks, corporate headquarters, and department stores. Downtowns, we learn, are now developed and marketed as mixed districts in which retail, housing, and entertainment may even come to overshadow traditional central business district (CBD) functions.

The second is a conversation mostly among political scientists and political sociologists, who have been interested in the various stakeholders (elected officials and bureaucrats; corporate leaders and peak business associations; neighborhood organizations) who have sought to shape downtown. In this narrative, business elites with a financial and symbolic stake in the economic health of the central business district began mobilizing in many cities during the 1940s and 1950s to protect their investments, which were in many cases thought to be "sunk" and immobile—Richard King Mellon, the Pittsburgh financier who mobilized resources behind the redevelopment of downtown Pittsburgh in the 1940s, explained his commitment to his city as an outgrowth of his business interests: "We have a lot of property here. We can't very well move out the banks" (Fitzpatrick, 2000). Business leaders worked with entrepreneurial mayors and development officials, leveraging federal urban renewal funds to shore up downtowns. Although in some cities these downtown-focused coalitions were eventually challenged by neighborhood-based groups seeking a more equitable share of public investment dollars, the basic political science narrative—that downtown development is the project of the city and region's most powerful economic elites—has not been revised.

But if downtown is now less a seat of corporate power and more a "place to play" (Fainstein & Judd, 1999), do these assumptions still hold? If indeed the value and use of downtown land has changed over the past four decades, would not that suggest that the nature and relative strength of downtown development interests would have

From Elizabeth Strom, "Rethinking the Politics of Downtown Development," *Journal of Urban Affairs*, Vol. 30, No. 1 (2008), pp. 37–50, 58–61. Copyright © 2008 Urban Affairs Association. Reprinted by permission of Wiley-Blackwell.

shifted as well? This article posits that in many U.S. cities, downtowns are no longer the region's economic heart, and they are therefore unlikely to generate the sort of political power assumed in earlier political science studies. I study the players in peak, downtown-focused business organizations as a way to understand who in the business community is most engaged in downtown development issues, and to generate hypotheses about how further research could shed light on the relationship between the geography and the politics of the American downtown.

Narrative One: The New Downtown Is Fun!

Whether for a leisurely walk next to the Reedy River Falls or a night of music and fast-paced entertainment, Downtown Greenville is the place to go for fun just about any day of the week.

From the Greenville, South Carolina, website[1]

Downtown is a great place to attend family friendly events, dine at one of the 170 plus restaurants, visit over 30 attractions and over 200 retail and service establishments. With over 17 new restaurants and 22 new retail stores that have opened since 2003, you owe it to yourself to come see what all the "fun" is about. Have fun in downtown St. Louis.

From the Downtown St. Louis Partnership website[2]

Over the past two decades, much of the new development in American downtowns has been the construction of cultural facilities, convention centers, and sports venues. Often these projects have been undertaken with the goal of encouraging tourism, seen by many economic development officials as an important new growth industry (Judd et al., 2003). In addition, city officials and business leaders have better recognized the competitive advantages of central cities for functions like culture and nighttime entertainment, as downtowns can offer amenities (access to mass transit, a dense and historically interesting built environment) with which sprawling suburbs cannot easily compete. Downtowns are now marketed as exciting areas in which to be enriched (by museums and concert halls) and entertained (by professional sporting events and themed restaurants). Downtown, we learn from promotion groups, is now officially "fun."

In many downtowns, moreover, market-rate housing has become a major part of the built environment.[3] The growing popularity of market-rate downtown housing is by now even reflected in census data, which show an increase in downtown populations, with more downtown residents who are college educated and who own their homes (Birch, 2005; Perlman, 1998).[4] The trend toward renovating industrial lofts into living space has been underway, at least in some cities, for several decades (Zukin, 1982). Now even office buildings have been repackaged for residential use, as apartments are seen as ways to rescue obsolete, class B office stock in cities like Denver, Tampa, St. Louis (Sharoff, 2001), and Los Angeles (Bergsman, 2004), where a recent study found continued increases in residential population, alongside decline in downtown employment (DiMassa, 2007).

New entertainment spaces and residential districts are often heralded (by city officials and by the local press, if not always by academics—see Fainstein & Judd, 1999; Hannigan,

1998) as signs of a downtown "revival" or "comeback." This narrative of revival, however, overshadows (and indeed, is often intended to overshadow) the key underlying trend found in many American metropolitan areas: downtown is no longer the center of the region's economic life. The traditional CBDs are no longer necessarily their region's largest office markets or their largest employment nodes. In most metropolitan areas, a majority of jobs are found well outside the traditional CBD (Glaeser & Kahn, 2001). And only a few downtowns continue to dominate their metro area office markets. In the cities studied by Lang (2003), traditional downtowns contained about one-third of the area's office space. He and other sources (see, for example, Center City District, 2006) note wide variation between more centralized MSAs (New York, Boston, San Francisco, Pittsburgh, and Chicago are examples) and the most decentralized areas (Las Vegas, Phoenix, Miami, and Houston) where CBDs may contain less than 20% of the region's office space (Center City District, 2006). Both Lang and the Center City District find that the downtown share of the office market is decreasing over time. For example, Philadelphia contained just 27% of its region's office space in 2005, which was down from 41% in 1993—a reflection of the much faster pace of growth in its suburbs (Center City District, 2006).

CBD office space had also, traditionally, been the most expensive in the region (indeed, urban economic theory's "bid-rent curve" assumes that the highest land values will always be at the center (Alonso, 1960)). That has also changed. Quite often, newer, peripheral office developments are pricier than the average center city building. The most expensive offices in Atlanta are found in the Buckhead neighborhood (within the city limits, but miles from the downtown); the Philadelphia region's costliest offices are on the suburban Main Line (Center City District, 2006).

And that's why we find office buildings converted into condominiums, banks renovated into theaters, and 50-acre football stadium/parking complexes usurping commercial districts: too few companies are compelled to be downtown, leaving space for more land-intensive and less profitable uses (Ford, 2003). The trend toward big-footprint projects like stadiums and convention centers in downtowns, or of converting office buildings into loft apartments, may be framed by city boosters as signs of an urban resurgence, but in some fundamental way they indicate that a city's downtown has lost its function as the key economic hub and real estate powerhouse of the region.

Narrative Two: Downtown as the Center of Power

These changes in land use and economic geography would seem to presage fundamental changes in the urban political economy, but students of urban politics have not yet begun to grapple with their implications. Although there are political scientists who find new ways to write about downtown development (Fainstein, 1994; McGovern, 1998; Turner, 2002), the basic political science downtown development paradigm first developed decades earlier has not been questioned: the redevelopment of the city's center is seen as the project of the most essential regional economic stakeholders who will reap immediate material and longer-term symbolic advantages from a robust urban core. They work in coalition with elected officials and appointed redevelopment directors who gain clear political advantage from their association with the city's

dominant economic interests. Much of the urban political science literature on downtown development has been an exploration of these stakeholders and their mutual interests in the physical redevelopment of the city's center (Dahl, 1961; Mollenkopf, 1983;
Salisbury, 1964; Stone, 1989; Wolfinger, 1974).

The Peak Business Association: Downtown Development Catalyst

The peak downtown business association has been at the center of downtown development since emerging in the 1940s (Fogelson, 2001), and it has been the focus of much
urban development literature. The best known and most successful of these organizations played a dominant role in shaping policies to redevelop their downtowns. Some
(e.g., Central Atlanta Progress) did so with an explicitly downtown focus; others
(Greater Philadelphia Movement, Allegheny Conference on Community Development)
were regional organizations that gave priority to a downtown redevelopment agenda.
To ensure their effectiveness, many of these organizations restricted membership to the
most prominent businesses (in contrast to Chambers of Commerce that represent all
businesses) and required the participation of a company's CEO.

In cities like Boston (Mollenkopf, 1983), San Francisco (McGovern, 1998; Mollenkopf,
1983); Atlanta (Stone, 1989), and Cleveland (Swanstrom, 1985) these groups shaped
urban renewal policies and influenced local electoral politics, using these organizations
as vehicles with which to "look more broadly, both in time and area," than other local
interests were able to do (Stone, 1989, p. 21). The Bay Area Committee, formed in
San Francisco in 1946, included the Chief Executives of 23 of the 27 regional Fortune
500 companies, as well as the heads of the four major banks and two newspapers
(McGovern, 1998; Mollenkopf, 1983). In Pittsburgh, extensive infrastructure improvement and downtown redevelopment came about when a politically connected mayor,
David Lawrence, joined forces with local business leadership, led by financier Richard
King Mellon (Ferman, 1996; Sbragia, 1989). Redevelopment in downtown Milwaukee
was spearheaded by the Greater Milwaukee Committee, whose membership, according
to its 1955 annual report, "owned or managed businesses representing one-fourth of the
city's total assessed value of business property" (Norman, 1989, p. 184). Either these
business leaders literally invested in downtown, by dint of their ownership of its real
estate, or they depended on getting customers/clients to come to downtown locations,
or they would derive symbolic benefit from a robust downtown. In all the scholarly
work on this topic, there is a stated or implied link between a business firm's concerns
with profitability, its presence in or near a city's central business district, and its
progrowth activism.

These peak organizations have been identified in the political science literature as
central to the project of downtown development, both because they symbolized the
collective interests of the most powerful economic actors, and because, by mobilizing
this power into an organizational vehicle, they could have real impact on a city's electoral politics and on its redevelopment policies. They would seem, therefore, to be useful institutions to study if one wishes to see whether the private interests guiding
downtown development have changed over the years. Are these economic interests
still mobilized into peak organizations engaged in downtown development? If not,
what do changes in private sector downtown leadership tell us about larger changes
in the urban political economy?

Tracking Downtown Changes through Peak Organization Leadership

To understand how urban business leadership has changed, and to suggest the implications of these changes for downtown politics, I have examined the leadership of three such peak organizations in earlier decades. These are the Greater Philadelphia Movement (GPM, formed in 1948), the Greater Baltimore Committee (GBC, formed in 1956), and Central Atlanta Progress (CAP, formed in 1941, when it was called Central Atlanta Improvement Association). I have sought to identify the companies represented on these boards (which I have labeled "leadership companies"), ascertain the sectors in which these companies operated, and discover whether those companies are still in operation (and still in operation in those cities). Although these companies hardly represent any kind of random sample of locally based companies, it is fair to say that these organizations generally have represented the largest, most politically active companies in the area (the Greater Baltimore Committee, for example, specifically sought to engage the heads of the region's largest one hundred businesses). I have used the board of directors or members lists for the years available: 1960 and 1965 for GPM, 1962 for GBC, and 1970 for CAP.

As Table 1 indicates, 26% of these "leadership companies" from the 1960–1970 period were still present in their region or city in 2006; 35% have either gone out of business, been bought out by another corporation headquartered elsewhere, or moved out of the region. It is quite likely that all or most of the 42 (29%) firms for which I could find no information are also defunct, so the percentage of firms represented on these boards that are no longer in the region is likely to be well over 50%. Atlanta has had the highest retention rate, which may reflect the fact that the board list is more recent, but could also speak to the greater economic success of Atlanta, which today has twice as many Fortune 500 headquarters as either Philadelphia or Baltimore, even though it has a smaller population than either of those cities.

The "leadership companies" have been broken down by sector in Table 2. "Other professional service" firms include advertising, accounting, and architecture/engineering. Finance and insurance includes all manner of banks, investment firms, and insurance agencies. The admittedly clumsy "miscellaneous corporate" category includes all those companies not described in any other category (these run the gamut from manufacturers to energy producers to communications and transportation firms to retail establishments).

In Table 3, we see that some sectors have had a more stable presence than others. Law firms seem to be the most likely to have remained intact in their cities, especially

Table 1 Percentage of GPM (1960, 1965), GBC (1962), and CAP (1970) Members Still Active in Region in 2006

Peak Org.	No. of Firms in City	No. of Firms in Suburbs	No. of Firms Gone	No. of Whereabouts Unknown
GPM	11 (31%)	4 (11%)	13 (37%)	7 (19%)
GBC	13 (15%)	11 (13%)	28 (31%)	35 (41%)
CAP	14 (56%)	0	11 (44%)	0

Note. Totals for all three groups: 38 (26%); 15 (10%); 52 (35%); 42 (29%).

Table 2 Downtown Leadership, 1960–1970

	Atlanta, Baltimore, and Philadelphia		
	Central Atlanta Progress, 1970 $n = 25$	Greater Baltimore Committee, 1962 $n = 87$	Greater Philadelphia Movement, 1960 and 1965 $n = 36$
Real estate	0	6 (7%)	0
Law	1 (4%)	2 (2%)	8 (22%)
Other professional services	1 (4%)	9 (10%)	2 (6%)
Finance and insurance	10 (40%)	31 (36%)	7 (20%)
Miscellaneous corporate	13 (50%)	37 (43%)	15 (42%)
Nonprofit and education	0	0	2
Public	0	0	0
Other/cannot determine	0	2 (2%)	2 (6%)

Table 3 Stability of 1960–1970 Leadership Firms by Sector (of Firms Whose Sector Could be Determined), GPM, GBC, and CAP Combined

	In Region (City or Suburb), 2006	Not in Region (Moved, Merged or Went Out of Business)	Fate Cannot Be Determined
Real estate ($n = 6$)	2	1	3
Law ($n = 12$)	12	0	0
Other prof. services ($n = 11$)	3	2	6
Finance and insurance ($n = 47$)	14	17	16
Misc corporate ($n = 22$)	10	9	3
Manufacturing ($n = 28$)	9	11	8
Retail ($n = 13$)	1	11	1

in Philadelphia, where eight of the eleven companies from the GPM lists that are still active in Philadelphia are law firms.

In all three cities, the boards of the 1960s and 1970s were dominated by the insurance, banking, financial, and "miscellaneous corporate" sectors (Table 4 gives further breakdown of the dominant corporate sectors found in this category in each city).

On the other hand, the "miscellaneous corporate" category has shown larger decline. First, industrial producers and energy firms had been part of the downtown leadership in earlier decades—both Philadelphia and Baltimore groups had included representatives from major regional subsidiaries of companies like Bethlehem Steel and General Electric, and local companies like Sun Oil. Although a few industrial producers remain in these regions (examples include Black and Decker in Baltimore), the decline in industrial employment since 1970, both nationally and in urban areas, has been documented (Harrison & Bluestone, 1982).

**Table 4 Most Frequently Represented Sectors in the "Miscellaneous Corporate Category,"
CAP, GBC, and GPM Boards, 1960–1970**

	Atlanta	Baltimore	Philadelphia
Retail (department stores)	4	7	2
Energy/Utilities/Communication (local phone companies)	6	4	2
Manufacturing	3	23	10

But some of the other companies in the "miscellaneous corporate" category represent sectors that, to both scholars and practitioners of an earlier era, seemed particularly place-bound. Local utilities and newspapers had played an important role in downtown growth coalitions (Logan & Molotch, 1987), their deep interest in promoting the local economic base clearly linked to the nature of their business. But even these companies have become less tied to central cities. First, both industries have been able to adjust to the realities of a more dispersed metropolitan region, and have developed their suburban client bases, becoming less dependent on downtown business. Moreover, deregulation, mergers, and acquisitions have changed the nature of both industries. Today, many utilities are part of regional conglomerates with less focus on particular central cities. Newspapers, similarly, are likely to be controlled by one of several national chains such as the McClatchy Company (which owns newspapers in 30 markets) or Gannett. Thus, the conditions in downtown Atlanta, or Philadelphia, or Chicago are simply not as significant a business factor for them as they had once been. Others in this category include transportation and communication companies, which have been affected by industry-wide sea changes since 1970. Local Bell Telephone companies have disappeared, as have regional rail lines such as Philadelphia's Reading or Baltimore's Western Maryland Rail.

The most strikingly transformed sector in this "miscellaneous corporate category" is retail, and specifically the once iconic downtown flagship department store. The presidents of these stores were often extremely active in shaping downtown development coalitions (Cohen, 2007), and heavily engaged in civic affairs, sponsoring parades in cities like New York and Detroit, and underwriting the costs of a museum in Newark. Their often large, elaborate downtown buildings were seen as emblematic of the identity of a city's center (Isenberg, 2004). Today, the list of remaining downtown flagship department stores is short indeed. Where a downtown houses a department store it is most likely part of a national chain such as Cincinnati-based Federated Department Stores, which over the years has bought up such downtown fixtures as Macy's, Bloomingdale's, and A&S (New York City); Rich's (Atlanta), Filene's (Boston), Marshall Field (Chicago), Goldsmith's (Memphis), Burdine's (Miami), and Strawbridge's (Philadelphia). As a result of this industry reshuffling, only one of the retailers whose heads had sat on these leadership boards is still in operation (Haverty's Furniture in Atlanta). The decline of the downtown department store is felt in the city's economy, in its downtown power structure, and in its built environment—in some cases flagship stores have simply been demolished (as was Hudson's in downtown Detroit, to the consternation of preservationists—see McGraw, 2002) or reused, as is the case of Muse's seven-story downtown Atlanta store, now loft apartments.

"Leadership companies" in the area of banking and insurance have been similarly depleted in our case study cities. The heads of local banks had been among the most eager participants of urban-renewal era downtown coalitions. These institutions surely seemed to be exceptionally place-bound. Federal regulations made it difficult for banks to operate beyond their local areas, so their fate seemed to be intertwined with the local economy and the value of local real estate. But deregulation has led to a consolidation in the banking industry, as those banks that managed to remain solvent have frequently been bought up by one of five or six national banking giants (Dymski, 1999). Whereas in the 1960s cities like Philadelphia and Baltimore would have been home to some eight or ten substantial, locally controlled banks, today such cities may have no locally controlled banks at all. Richard King Mellon's claim that he cannot "just move our banks," it turns out, was not completely accurate.

The local implications of these industry-wide changes can be found when we look at the fate of leadership companies in this sector. Of the financial institutions represented on the 1960–1970 boards, just 14 of the 47 are still active in their regions. These include a few insurance companies (although some are now part of larger "groups" based in New York or Europe) and a few financial service firms that have remained active. T. Rowe Price and Legg Mason, for example, are two large financial service groups that have remained headquartered in Baltimore. The banks represented on leadership boards, however, have been far less stable. The Greater Philadelphia Movement had six bank presidents on its board in 1960, representing the major local banks of that decade. By 2000 not one of those banks existed. In Baltimore, two of the banks whose presidents served on the Greater Baltimore Committee board in 1962 are still headquartered in Baltimore. The remaining six that could be traced have been bought up by banks in Atlanta, Buffalo, and Charlotte. Atlanta has been the beneficiary of some of this merger activity, as the Atlanta-based Suntrust has emerged as a national leader. Nonetheless, five other local banks have since been absorbed into either Bank of America or Wachovia, and another has been closed. In some cases, too, bank buildings are now put to uses that suggest the new function of the central city built environment: architecturally significant bank buildings in Philadelphia now house the Ritz-Carlton and Loews hotels; San Diego's First National Bank building has been converted to condominiums, and the former Western National and Eutaw Savings Banks in Baltimore now house the France-Merrick Performing Arts Center.

In sum, we see that the most economically dominant companies that had once spearheaded downtown redevelopment in Atlanta, Baltimore, and Philadelphia in the 1960s are largely gone (Hodos, 2002; Holloway & Wheeler, 1991). Apparently, the "place-based" economic interests whose downtown "sunk costs" made them appear as permanent fixtures of the downtown landscape a few decades ago were not as permanent as they had seemed. The literature focused on the urban renewal era could not have anticipated just how many core members of the downtown-based business groups would flee.

Of course, the loss of these particular firms in these particular industries need not suggest the economic decline of the central city—after all, these firms could well have been replaced by other firms in newly dominant industries, in which case the political base of downtown could, despite these changes, remain intact. But there are several reasons to suggest that this has not been the case.

Downtown Leadership Today

If so many of the firms that had been engaged in downtown development and advocacy have disappeared, is there still a "downtown business interest" articulated in city politics? There is, but I would argue it represents different segments of the business community, and, perhaps related to these sectoral shifts, it organizes itself differently. Today's downtown coalitions are geographically narrower, represented by groups focused only on the downtown (although in some cases their board membership may overlap with the boards of regional groups). At the same time, they have extended their constituency to include nonprofit executives and public officials, very few of which could be found on the boards of 1960–1970.

These contrasts can best be seen by comparing downtown leadership boards of the earlier era with those active today. Ideally, I would have liked to accomplish this by comparing the board figures for GPM, GBC, and CAP from the 1960s–1970s, to those of 2006. I have indeed done this in the case of Atlanta. But in the cases of Philadelphia and Baltimore, a methodological problem emerged, one that is in itself very revealing of the political shifts in downtown leadership. Many of the peak business organizations identified with downtown advocacy in the 1950s and 1960s have either disappeared, or have shifted their focus to broader, regional issues like economic competitiveness, transportation, and education. Meanwhile, downtown-specific organizations have been created in many cities, and these have taken up the downtown-focused agenda first advocated by these earlier business groups. So, for example, the Greater Philadelphia Movement merged, transformed, emerged as Greater Philadelphia First in the 1980s, which in 2003 merged into the regional Chamber of Commerce (ironically, perhaps, as the group had originally formed with the goal of distinguishing the downtown-based corporate and banking concerns from those of regional industrialists—see Adams et al., 1991). By then, it had become largely focused on regional issues, such as encouraging foreign investment and regional cooperation (Hodos, 2002), with no focus on downtown development. But GPM had, in the late 1950s, spun off the Old Philadelphia Development Corporation, intended to help implement the ambitious Society Hill urban renewal plan. The OPDC had ultimately extended its reach to the traditional CBD, renaming itself the Central Philadelphia Development Corporation. The CPDC is thus the real successor to the downtown mission of the Greater Philadelphia Movement.

The Greater Baltimore Committee has remained active, but has dropped its downtown agenda, and today has a purely regional focus. The organization's website notes its historical role in spurring downtown development, but today: "The GBC's mission is to improve the business climate of the Baltimore region by organizing its corporate and civic leadership to develop solutions to the problems that affect the region's competitiveness and viability." Its current priorities are development of biotechnology industries; support for regional transportation; and support for minority business development.[5] Meanwhile, downtown businesses have created the Downtown Partnership of Baltimore to attend to their specific concerns. Although this organization has no "genetic" ties to the Greater Baltimore Committee, it would be the logical place to look for a picture of business leadership in the downtown. In other cities as well, older organizations that had included downtown development as part of a broader agenda have seemed to move in a regional direction while dedicated downtown groups have taken up the central city revitalization banner.[6]

Business leadership concerned with the downtown has thus, at least in some cities, shifted its organizational vehicle from corporate-based, peak business organizations that included citywide and regional interests to organizations more narrowly engaged in the development and maintenance of the CBD. Upon closer observation, it is clear that the business sectors represented by these organizations, and their organizational goals, have changed as well. Table 5 shows the sectoral breakdown of downtown group

Table 5 Downtown Leadership, 2006

	Atlanta, Baltimore, Philadelphia		
	Central Atlanta Progress/Atlanta Downtown Improvement District *n* = 72	Downtown Partnership of Baltimore/Downtown Management District *n* = 64	Center City District/Central Philadelphia Development Corporation *n* = 56
Real estate	18 (25%)	16 (25%)	15 (27%)
Law	8 (11%)	12 (19%)	9 (16%)
Other professional services	7 (10%)	4 (6%)	9 (16%)
Finance and insurance	4 (6%)	11 (17%)	8 (16%)
Miscellaneous corporate	28 (39%)	4 (6%)	5 (9%)
Nonprofit and education	10 (14%)	9 (14%)	3 (5%)
Public	6 (8%)	8 (13%)	1 (2%)
Other/cannot determine	2 (3%)	0	2 (4%)

board members in 2006. Whereas the older organizations were dominated by corporations (including manufacturers and retailers), banks and insurance companies (see Table 2), board membership for the contemporary groups includes scant corporate representation. Atlanta is the exception to this trend; CAP's board still includes such local institutions as Coca-Cola, Delta Airlines, Turner Broadcasting, and BellSouth. Nonetheless, even in Atlanta many of these corporations seem to have lost some of their downtown Atlanta focus, sending vice presidents rather than CEOs to represent them. The local press has frequently commented on the diminished clout of CAP, noting its failure to see its favored projects through, and bemoaning the decline of civic leadership in the downtown (Salter & Scott, 1991; Saporta, 2000; Saporta, 2003). This is consistent with other literature, which suggests that as corporations stretch their geographic presence, they may become less engaged, economically or politically, in their headquarters city. As Kanter notes, "large businesses supplying global customers have weaker ties to specific regions" (2000, p. 166), and most certainly have a reduced interest in the fate of the region's downtown.

In place of banks, corporations, and department stores, we see greater representation of the public and nonprofit sectors. The older boards had no public participation, and the only nonprofit representation was in Philadelphia, where both a construction union and the University of Pennsylvania were part of the leadership coalition. Today, in contrast, most downtown groups include several public representatives *ex officio*, suggesting a more formalized cooperation between private and public interests in downtown development and management.

We also see an increase in nonprofit representation, which includes universities, nonprofit hospitals, and cultural institutions. This suggests the greater importance of large nonprofits as economic actors: Universities and their medical centers are the largest private employers in Philadelphia, New Haven, and the San Francisco Bay Area (Strom, 2005; Wallack, 2005)—and unlike those Mellon-owned banks, they really *cannot* move. Major cultural institutions are increasingly embraced by downtown business leaders as key actors in economic development efforts, and there is now enormous ideological and organizational overlap between downtown booster groups, tourism promoters, and cultural advocates (Strom, 2003).

The dominant business sector on downtown boards today is the real estate industry. On all of today's boards, real estate interests (which include developers and leasing agents) represent approximately a quarter of all representatives. This percentage actually undervalues the importance of real estate to these organizations, however, as many of the law firms and "other professional service" firms (which include a number of architectural firms) are very closely tied to the real estate industry. The combined representation of real estate, nonprofit, and public sectors—three sectors virtually absent from the earlier boards—now comprises about half of the board in Atlanta (47%) and Baltimore (52%), and over a third in Philadelphia (35%). The constituency working for CBD development, at least as represented on peak business association boards, has clearly changed in ways that reflect the changing value and function of the downtown as productive economic space.

Today's downtown groups also rely on organizational and financial structures that were not found among urban renewal-era groups: the self-financed Business Improvement Districts (BIDs), which are state-enabled special assessment districts in which property owners pay toward the provision of enhanced public services in their district.[7] Today, nearly every downtown development group manages or has a dotted-line relationship to a BID; many downtown BIDS were formed at the urging of downtown organizations and their constituent businesses, no doubt, in some cases as a way to ensure a sufficient income stream to support the organization (Briffault, 1999). These groups, then, function largely as service organizations, collecting fees from local property owners in exchange for providing services, the most common of which include maintenance, façade and street improvements, and marketing (Mitchell, 2001).[8] BIDs and their services have become a key part of the mobilization of downtown interests, because these organizations can then keep a constituency together around the appeal of a service organization; with the special assessment powers they experience limited "free rider" problems (Briffault, 1999; Mitchell, 2001).

One does find variation among downtown groups and BIDs, with better-established organizations led by strong boards and/or experienced and knowledgeable directors playing roles beyond simple service provision.[9] The Center City group in Philadelphia does a great deal of research and planning (see their website, http://www.centercityphila.org/ for examples of their reports); the Downtown Seattle Association has been active in addressing the problems of affordable housing and homelessness in that city's downtown (Harrell, 2004; Slobodzian, 2005). In Charlotte the Center City Partners board, which unlike many downtown boards still includes many top corporate leaders, functions almost as the downtown planning and marketing arm of both the city and the corporate sectors; plans commissioned by the organization have in several instances been adopted as the official plan of the city. But most downtown groups today are no longer the vehicles of the region's top employers, so they have come to rely more on the skills of their staff (the directors of the downtown groups in both Philadelphia and Seattle have been with their organizations many years, and are well-known and respected figures in political, business, and academic circles), and more generally the professionalization of downtown promotion and management.[10]

The Political Implications of the New Downtown

How and Why the New Downtown Coalition Is Different

It is clear that the economic base of the downtown leadership has changed, and it is safe to say that downtown is no longer a primary focus of the largest regional economic interests. What is less clear is whether that has an impact on the ability of downtown interests to shape the city's development agenda. Does it matter that the remaining downtown growth interests are developers, brokers, university presidents, and city officials rather than bankers and manufacturers? I would hypothesize that it does, but I admit this hypothesis requires considerably more testing. In theory at least, the significant presence of nonprofit and public officials surely gives these groups a different agenda than their all-private sector predecessors would have had. Although it would be naïve to claim that public officials and nonprofit leaders always engage in urban redevelopment with democratic and eleemosynary goals, it is clear that such leaders are responsible to different constituencies than are their private sector counterparts (Strom, 2005). For public and nonprofit officials, maximizing economic returns is only one of many goals. Nonprofit organizations are responsible to boards of trustees who may place a higher priority on issues like organizational prestige. Public officials need to garner votes from a broad, geographically dispersed constituency, but also care about the reputation of their cities among investors and other political leaders. Certainly, many public officials support the efforts of BIDs to provide enhanced services without dipping into public coffers, although some government leaders may share the concerns of critics who wonder whether this form of privatization has negative consequences for democratic governance (Briffault, 1999). At any rate, the inclusion of public officials on these leadership boards represents a number of trends in the maturation of various "public-private partnership models" (Friedan & Sagalyn, 1989) but it can surely suggest at least some loss of preeminence on the part of the private sector downtown leadership, which can no longer depend on an active cadre of CEOs, and must invite public officials to be part of their decision-making processes in order to gain attention and support.

I would further argue that the replacement of corporate and banking CEOs with real estate developers and managers has altered the position of these downtown associations as well. First, the real estate industry is less central to a region's economic base and its promoters are therefore in a weaker institutional position to operate as insiders in a progrowth regime. Does this mean that real estate developers and owners have no economic significance or political clout? Of course not. Real estate interests can, and in some cities do play a prominent role as campaign funders, and their political largesse can give individual real estate developers excellent access to decision makers. Studies of downtown development have highlighted the centrality of the property development process, which can shape many aspects of a city's center (Fainstein, 1994). At the very least, real estate development has a huge symbolic resonance, for it is the reshaping of the physical built environment—the ribbon cutting ceremonies, the "cranes on the skyline" (Healey & Barrett, 1990) that give political leaders the opportunity to claim credit for positive change. David Harvey notes the importance of the continued construction and destruction of the built environment as part of capitalist reproduction, and points to what he calls the "speculator-developer" as playing a key "coordinating and stabilizing function" in this process (Harvey, 1985, p. 68).

But real estate remains, in Harvey's analysis, a secondary circuit of capital, auxiliary to primary production. Real estate is reactive—its value reflects the eagerness of other sorts of economic actors to locate in a particular place. If city boosters can persuade major corporations to locate in their center, *some* developer will be happy to take advantage of this opportunity.[11] In more concrete terms, real estate is not an export industry;[12] it does not have a large employment base (construction of course is an important part of the job market but construction jobs are largely sub, or sub-sub-contracted, so there is no direct line between a developer and this workforce). Individual developers may use tools such as campaign contributions to open access channels to public decision makers, but cities are not generally in competition for the favors of specific developers the way they are for car makers, pharmaceutical firms, or even football franchises. Indeed, Friedland and Palmer's analysis might suggest that the high level of engagement of real estate interests in activities such as campaign fund-raising indicates their lack of structural power—the most central economic actors, those with the power of exit, need not exert time and energy in these efforts to influence decision makers (Friedland & Palmer, 1984). That real estate now appears to be such a dominant industry in some cities may say more about the dearth of other productive activities than it does about the potential of real estate alone to generate significant economic activity.

My claim here is not that real estate developers—or for that matter, the directors of nonprofit hospitals and universities—wield no influence in the politics of downtown development. Rather, I would maintain that they have influence over a narrower set of issues, with power that is more tactical (e.g., they can draw on it to fight particular, site-specific battles) than structural (e.g., capable of setting a political agenda). Real estate dominated groups, for better or worse, may also have a less ambitious civic agenda. Real estate owners and developers are probably not going to make significant material and symbolic investments of the kind made by companies like GM (in Detroit) or Prudential (in Newark)—it is not in their self-interest or part of their corporate culture to do so. But they also are less likely to play a prominent role trying to shape significant civic or political debates—when real estate is one's primary business, the key question is whether resources will be devoted to block X or block Y, and there may be less of an identification with and commitment to a larger civic agenda.

I further hypothesize that the proliferation of the "business improvement district" model as a way of mobilizing resources around downtown development suggests that this new coalition has different kinds of collective active issues than did earlier groups, which were more reliant on voluntary activities (donations of money and the involvement of corporate CEOs) than on mandated contributions such as those underwriting BID budgets. The creation of BIDs that focus on services and festivals recognizes the survival needs of organizations that cannot count on a base of major employers to sustain them; rather, they rely on material incentives and seek alliances with public and nonprofit officials.

These hypotheses, however, require further testing, as there is surprisingly little research on the local organization of downtown real estate interests.[13] There is also little scholarly research about peak business associations in the post-urban renewal period; a better understanding of the factors behind the shifting missions and leaderships of groups like the Greater Baltimore Committee or the Allegheny Conference for Community Development would provide additional insight into the changing balance of power in downtown governance. Using organizational and newspaper archives and interviews, for example, a researcher could learn when and why such organizations abandoned downtown issues. These methods could also reveal any clear relationships between the sectoral representation on organizational boards and the agendas pursued by these organizations. Additional research could be done on various companies represented on downtown association boards to learn from them first-hand how they view the political roles of their organizations.

Is "Downtown versus the Neighborhoods" Still a Key Political Cleavage?

Urban political scientists, on the one hand, have long been interested in powerful downtown elites; on the other hand, they have shown a great deal of interest in the challenges to these groups, often represented by neighborhood associations adept at utilizing both the electoral arena and other means of protest (DeLeon, 1992; Ferman, 1996; Mollenkopf, 1983). In some cities, would-be mayors successfully attacked downtown development policies, and indeed made their pledges to redirect resources from the central business district to struggling neighborhoods central to their election campaigns. Pete Flaherty, for example, was elected mayor of Pittsburgh in 1969 with the backing of a newly mobilized neighborhood movement (Ferman, 1996); San Francisco voters used the ballot box to challenge downtown interests both by electing sympathetic mayors and councils, and by passing voter initiatives that limited downtown development (DeLeon, 1992; McGovern, 1998). In 1983, Boston voters eliminated mayoral candidates known for their support of downtown development and sent two neighborhood activists, Mel King and Ray Flynn, to compete in a run-off. Flynn, who went on to be elected mayor, reflected, "In 1983, there was a feeling that the downtown interests didn't respect the neighborhoods of Boston. . . . That's how Mel King and I got nominated in 1983. We represented fighters. People knew we were two tough neighborhood guys who were going to stand up to the powerful interests of the city and fight for the neighborhoods" (Nolan, 1993). Some of the political conflicts between populist Dennis Kucinich's supporters and Cleveland's business community reflected this dynamic as well (Swanstrom, 1985).

Is "downtown vs. the neighborhoods" still a key cleavage in U.S. urban politics? I hypothesize that opposition to downtown development is less likely to be the point around which today's urban populist groups mobilize than would have been the case a few decades earlier. To support this hypothesis I have only anecdotal (and admittedly slim anecdotal) evidence. Former Boston Mayor Flynn noted that it was no longer a feature of electoral politics in his city (Nolan, 1993), and interviews with elected officials in Seattle suggested a similar dampening of tensions. In recent elections in Newark, Cleveland, and New York, just to name a few cities, the lines of cleavage did not seem to run between defenders and detractors of downtown development. Of course, there will always be political conflict over the spatial distribution of public resources, but I would argue that in most cities "downtown" is no longer seen as the enemy of those who advocate investment in their own residential neighborhoods.

If indeed this claim is true, there could be many explanations, including the successes of some earlier challengers to downtown who succeeded in implementing growth caps and linkage policies. But I would also argue that downtown simply is not the sort of target it once was. As at least in some cities, downtown has lost corporate headquarters, office space, and symbolic clout, perhaps it has seemed less threatening to neighborhood advocates as well. Moreover, today's downtown groups are busy with activities it is hard to dislike—who is against clean streets, better lighting, and farmers' markets? Indeed, in interviews, some downtown organization leaders explicitly talked about the importance of their food fairs and art walks as effective ways to broaden political support for downtown investment (see endnote 10). New downtown developments are in many cases, as well, championed by a new set of supporters—cultural leaders, university administrators—and are marketed not as buttoned-down business centers but as hip, edgy spaces. Downtown groups are intent on reshaping and marketing downtown as a place to see a ball game, grab a beer, or live in trendy, artist-inspired lofts. As central city areas gain residential population, they themselves become "neighborhoods."

This is an admittedly hard hypothesis to test rigorously. One could choose cities that had manifested downtown versus neighborhood cleavages and study selected elections over time to see if these issues remained salient. Finer-grained case studies of those cities in which electoral politics had once pitted the interests of downtown business against the interests of neighborhood residents could reveal some shifts in electoral rhetoric around development issues, and that such research could help further the goal of better understanding the politics of the new downtown.

In conclusion, American central business districts have undergone dramatic changes in function over the past four decades, and it should be expected that these functional changes would be accompanied by changes in political organization and influence. In an earlier era, the downtown was usually the region's largest employment node and home to its key retailing and financial activities. Regional business leaders saw a healthy downtown as crucial to the success of their enterprises, and they worked, often through peak business organizations, to push for downtown revitalization alongside other business concerns. Today, many of the key business institutions, once at the heart of the downtown coalition, are gone. Downtowns are now less dominant as either economic centers or as the basis of political power. While corporate interests in many cities still work toward downtown improvements, this cause is less central to their mission, and less connected to a broader regional business agenda. Those most concerned with downtown are now real estate interests, who seek allies among nonprofit organizations and forge connections to cultural institutions.

CHAPTER 2

CITIES IN A GLOBAL WORLD

THE NEW URBAN ECONOMY AND LOCAL POLITICS

Three changes in global capitalism have transformed urban economies: the replacement of industrial with service-sector jobs, the deconcentration of business activities and urban residents, and the emergence of an international competition among cities. In Selection 4, H. V. Savitch and Paul Kantor trace these developments. They argue that the radical deconcentration of businesses and population began around the middle of the twentieth century as changes in communication, technology, transportation, and production processes enabled more and more businesses to leave central cities in favor of lower-cost locations in suburbia and the Sunbelt. Where jobs went, people followed. By the end of the century, these movements had transformed the United States into a predominantly suburban nation.

Savitch and Kantor also show that the deindustrialization of urban economies changed how Americans make a living. The United States has become less dependent on industry and hard goods production because business activity has shifted decidedly into services. Where cities once pursued smokestack industries, they now are converting old warehouse, seaport, and industrial districts to tourist destinations, downtown malls, and office centers. In places where armies of blue-collar workers in factories fueled city growth, today it is more likely to be driven by white-collar managers and technicians meeting face-to-face in downtown offices, business parks, and upscale restaurants. Finally, the authors describe how globalization has made cities, suburbs, and even whole regions part of an international marketplace. The latter is characterized by rapid communication, transnational business activities, and a complex linkage among workers, managers, and cultures all over the world.

Savitch and Kantor argue that this "great transformation" is a source of new political challenges for cities of all kinds. Older as well as newer urban centers must compete on a wider playing field as places to work and live. Those who lose in this game of competition struggle to find ways of coping with their diminished fate. Yet the authors do not conclude that local governments are prisoners of the forces of internationalization. Rather, they argue, "there is a variation in the response to globalization." This is not only because cities vary in their resources or capacity. Local responses also reflect the "distribution of power within a city." Globalization has changed the nature of urban politics: the makeup of political coalitions, the relative influence of various interests, and the ability of new groups to mobilize. Cities are not blank slates to be written upon. They are dynamic places, capable of choosing how to respond to the challenges that face them.

In Selection 5, Royce Hanson, Harold Wolman, David Connolly, Katherine Pearson, and Robert McManmon describe the way that globalization has changed the internal political dynamics of cities. As in the past, corporate CEOs continue to play a pivotal role in local politics, but power is more widely shared. In most cities in the postwar era, they joined in forming powerful organizations made up almost exclusively of corporate leaders. Hometown bankers and corporate elites were extremely important in providing capital for redevelopment efforts. Mergers, buyouts, and the internationalization of finance and corporate management have made the participation of the earlier generation of civic elites "shallower, more transient, and less influential." They still play important roles, but tend to participate in broad-based coalitions that represent a wide variety of interests. At the same time, the urban agenda has become regional, and the influence of mayors has weakened. According to Hanson et al., local business organizations are as apt to work with state and federal officials as with local officials in pursuing urban development projects. These arrangements have made mayors less important; in the past they might have led a powerful downtown coalition, but today they play an important role only when they have something to bring to the table.

It is important to re-emphasize that the politics of cities varies substantially. Their choices depend on a combination of the options available to them and the contours of the local political landscape. If local politics is not sufficiently open and inclusive, citizens may come up empty-handed when public officials give away too much in the deal-making that goes on between business and government. Selection 6, by Richard Foglesong, illustrates this point. In his brief story of the coming of Disney World to Winter Park, Florida, Foglesong describes how the transformation of that community by America's entertainment giant was dominated by private purposes and unexpected public consequences. Although Disney promised to build a model city for people to live in, what eventually materialized was a megacomplex entertainment center that is run purely as a business. This was possible in part because the Disney Corporation managed to win the legal right to incorporate itself as a virtual city-state controlled by the company while enjoying regulatory powers and privileges normally reserved by law to popularly elected local governments. Without a resident citizen population, the government of Epcot became—to use Foglesong's phrase—"a Vatican with mouse ears." As such, company executives could make key decisions without having to answer to any local residents other than a handful of their own employees.

In Selection 7, Paul Kantor and H.V. Savitch argue that local officials can sometimes gain considerable influence in guiding their own development even though the pressures to compete are intense. Scholars have sometimes depicted cities as junior partners to business in the global development game. In theory, business investors have many cities and regions to choose from; cities are often desperate to attract their money and employees. In their comparative analysis of cities in the United States and Western Europe, Kantor and Savitch show that the real world is not always so one-sided. The authors describe how city bargaining advantages relative to business are not uniform; sometimes business actually is the junior partner. The explanation is that the bargaining advantages of cities can be enhanced by market conditions, local political systems, and national urban policies. For example, some city governments have the advantage of a very favorable market environment for attracting or keeping business; not all are desperate to chase every dollar investors offer. Sometimes this is because there are businesses—entertainment parks, for example—with such large sunk costs that they cannot easily move elsewhere.

Alternatively, some global cities, such as London, Tokyo, and New York, serve as global anchors for industries like financial services; this limits the economic competition they face from smaller cities. Still others may have such highly diversified economies that jobs that are lost are easily replaced. In all these circumstances, economic advantages can favor cities, not investors. This, in turn, makes it possible for these city governments to act with greater independence and promote development policies that generate more community benefits than others can.

As the authors note, bargaining advantages are not always economic in nature. Cities that have highly democratic political systems are better able to resist business demands. Cities with access to assistance from national governments that take an active role in urban affairs also are better able to extract concessions from the private sector and limit business power. Savitch and Kantor's comparative research suggests that the role of national governments in supporting their cities may be pivotal. U.S. cities tend to have fewer bargaining advantages than their counterparts in Western Europe—largely because of the limited role of the federal government in regulating local economic development activity.

4

H. V. Savitch and Paul Kantor

CITIES IN THE INTERNATIONAL MARKETPLACE

An enormous transformation engulfs the industrial world. The rapidity and consequences are unparalleled. The change is breathtaking. The ancient world lasted for three thousand years, the medieval age for less than a millennium, and the industrial era for about a century. Our postindustrial society has been brought about in roughly three decades, and its pace is quickening. This new revolution has already remade the economic fabric of society, radically altered the behavior of capital, broken down national boundaries, and is remodeling government.

This transformation is particularly profound within liberal democratic states in North America and Western Europe. Since 1970, these states have shed their older industrial capacity and have become societies dominated by the tertiary sector—business, professions, services, high technology, and government. Within these societies capital has changed its configuration. It is more nimble and more multinational.[1] "Flexible production" and "just-in-time inventory" are not only techniques for quick action but they have also changed the operations of capitalism. Corporate ownership is not confined solely to a single nation but can span the globe, putting management in the hands of unlikely collaborators. Archrivals continue their rivalries but also find themselves in partnership with one other; fiercely competing one day and collaborating the next. The giant plane-manufacturer Airbus is a case in point. Its operations are a product of a European high-tech faceoff with America. At the same time, it buys products from its American nemesis, Boeing, and 40 percent of Airbus components are made in the United States.

Migration is another part of the story. Counting refugees alone, one finds that within the last decade 4.3 million have flocked into Germany, France, Italy, and the United Kingdom. Over one million have turned to the United States and Canada.[2] Recent immigrants now make up roughly 10 percent of these last two societies. While North America is regarded as the traditional immigrant haven, the numbers in Western Europe have exploded. During the past decade European officials expected that more than 25 million legal or illegal immigrants would settle on that continent.[3] Meanwhile birth rates of nationals within most Western countries have flattened or declined. The birth rate crisis is most acute in France and Italy, where the newborn cannot keep pace with the rate of mortality. As those birthrates continue to plummet, Europeans will have to rely on even more immigrants to support high living standards and generous pensions.

On the political front transnational pacts have nurtured the transformation by facilitating the movement of goods, people, and common policies across boundaries. The most prominent of these pacts are in the West and include the European Union (EU), which comprises fifteen nations, and the North American Free Trade Association (NAFTA), composed of the United States, Canada, and Mexico.[i] The EU already has a supranational government and bureaucracy that imposes policy on member nations. NAFTA is not that far advanced, but it has begun to affect political life in North America by forcing choices over freer trade, currency supports, and labor policy.

Technology plays a central role in this transformation. Just as previous periods may have been driven by steam locomotion (1780–1840), rail transportation (1840–90), electric power (1890–1930), or petroleum energy (1930–70), so the current era is propelled by the transmission of information. The last quarter of the twentieth century was appropriately called "the information age," and it portended revolutionary technological achievements into this millennium.

By now it may be a commonplace observation that warrants repeating. Ordinary people are communicating faster, they are more directly in touch with events, and they often exchange information person to person. The new world of cyberspace is just one technology that allows this. At the dawn of the postindustrial age, during the mid-1970s, just 50,000 computers existed in the world. That number has now rocketed to 556 million, giving common individuals access to each other across the globe. More than half of Americans and more than a quarter of Western Europeans own computers. In North America and Western Europe, big and small cities are hard-wired for instant communication. Carriers, like BBC or CNN, have established global news networks, allowing the world to witness the same events at the same time. Impressions are created instantly, and reactions occur swiftly. The decreasing cost of telephone service and the spread of fiber optic cables (simultaneously transmitting 1.5 million conversations within the diameter of a human hair) catapulted personal information to new levels. By the year 2000 international telephone calls reached an all-time high of 100 billion minutes.[4] None of these developments can create democracy, but collectively they assure wider dissemination of information, they facilitate freer exchange among people, and they hold potential for greater accountability between rulers and the ruled. Under these conditions, it becomes increasingly difficult to monopolize information, control public opinion, or ignore citizen demands.

The combination of economic, demographic, technological, and political change is cumulative, and will continue to impact the social order. No society encapsulates this transformation more than urban society. Cities are the crucibles through which radical experiments become convention. They are concentrated environments in which people adapt and their resilience is tested. They are the world's incubators of innovation— made possible by critical mass, diversity, and rich interaction. And cities have steadily grown over the centuries to fulfill that role. In the tenth century one of the world's largest cities, Cordoba, held just 300,000 people. Later Constantinople became the leading metropolis and held half a million people. By the eighteenth century London had surpassed every other Western city with one million inhabitants. In the twentieth century New York rose to ascendancy with several million people. Now in the twenty-first century Tokyo, São Paulo, and Mexico City have climbed above ten million inhabitants.

What is more, cities have complemented their role as global innovators with geo-physical centrality. Despite enormous changes in technology, cities remain at the juncture of world transportation, as transit points for business, science, and travel of every stripe. This puts cities at the very pivot of transformation. Few statistics demonstrate this better than air traffic. . . .

In just nine short years average passenger traffic jumped by 51 percent while cargo increased by 131 percent. Already a global transit point, Paris more than doubled both its air passengers and cargo, Seoul showed a similar doubling in passengers and cargo, while Amsterdam and London also showed impressive gains. All told, every one of these cities registered gains, and we note that these advance have been made on very substantial bases. Cities are continuing to grow in this global transformation, and indeed are at its very heart. Despite the dip in passenger air traffic after September 11, that transformation is likely to continue and cities will resume their station at the junctures of air travel.

This tells us something not only about the future, but also about the recent past. Cities have been the terrain on which technological, social, and global transformation has taken place. Cities hold the machinery that furnishes each era with a distinct product; they are the progenitors of national culture; and, they are the great mixing cauldrons that supply a unique human hybrid. In providing all of these functions, cities continually remake themselves, reconstruct their productive base, and adapt their physical environment to the necessities of the time.

We examine this transformation . . . along three distinct trajectories: 1) the deindustrialization of urban economies, 2) the deconcentration of older cities, and 3) the globalization process. As we shall see, cities are not necessarily the passive recipients of this change, but have the capacity to guide it and shape its impact. . . .

Deindustrialization: For What?

Just thirty years ago, cities in North America and Europe were bustling with factories, workshops, warehouses, and open air markets. While the great primate cities of New York, London, and Paris had always held financial houses and corporate headquarters, they also were balanced by textile manufacture, light industry, chemical production, and warehousing.[ii]

At the same time, secondary cities took on the heavy lifting. Cleveland, Pittsburgh, Birmingham, Newcastle, Essen, Lille, and Turin were centers for tool and dye making,

automobile manufacture, and steel production. These industrial towns were complemented by cities of passage. New Orleans, Liverpool, Marseilles, Hamburg, and Naples
were glorious ports, which boasted the world's finest bistros and bawdiest night life.

Secondary cities were the workshops of the industrial world. They also housed
large numbers of blue-collar families in a rich social milieu. From London's East End to
New Orleans's Garden District, neighborhoods anchored the social life of the city. To be
sure, the housing was often substandard and the neighborhoods overcrowded, but they
spawned a host of vibrant institutions. Labor unions, shops, schools, churches, and
social clubs bound communities together, allowed citizens to connect to public institutions, and gave the city meaning.

The bulk of those factories are now gone and many of the ports are closed. Some
workers hold on to remnants of the old economy, some have joined the ranks of the
unemployed, and others have found jobs elsewhere. While some working-class neighborhoods are intact, others have been gentrified and enriched with boutiques and
expensive specialty shops. Still other inner-city neighborhoods now accommodate
immigrants who bring with them a new culture, different foodstuffs, and an altogether distinct way of life (from tea salons to mosques). A substantial number of old
neighborhoods, mostly in America and Great Britain, have not been recycled for the
gentry or for immigrants. Instead they have fallen into disuse: the houses are abandoned, stores are boarded up, sidewalks are littered, and streets are dangerous. Many
social institutions are gone—either they have disappeared or taken new form in the
suburbs. . . .

Deindustrialization is generating uneven development and social imbalance. . . .
Some cities remain in decay while others have succeeded in remaking themselves.
Chicago, Cleveland, Madrid, and Rotterdam saw the collapse of blue-collar employment. Some of these same cities (Madrid and Rotterdam) made up their losses in manufacture through white-collar employment. Other cities like Cleveland, Philadelphia,
and St. Louis have not yet recovered from this trauma. The crises of transformation are
more widespread in Anglo-American cities than on the European continent. American
cities were particularly hard hit, and account for the bulk of those that have yet to
recover. In part, this is due to the nineteenth- and early-twentieth-century genesis of
American central cities as locations for heavy industry. This is also true for some British
cities (Newcastle, Liverpool, Glasgow). Continental cities mostly developed in the trad-
ing eras of the seventeenth and eighteenth centuries, and wealth was largely vested in
the urban core. Thus, the ecological structure of European cities permitted them to shift
more easily to tertiary economies.[iii]

By and large, primate cities did well. London emerged as the banking center where
capital could be concentrated, New York as a producer of financial instruments where
loans and mergers could be consummated, and Paris as a seat for corporate headquarters and professional services where deals could be struck. Each of these cities
carved out niches for themselves as command posts in a larger world economy.[5] In large
measure London, New York, and Paris became the forerunners of postindustrialism and
established the pace for others.[6] To be sure, these cities already had thriving nests of
banks and corporate headquarters, and they were able to build upon economies of
agglomeration. Yet primate cities are complex, and during the 1950s high finance made
up just a fraction of their economies. Manufacture, ports, and warehousing held the bulk
of employment, and losses in these sectors were enormous. After deindustrialization

struck, London, New York, and Paris had to refill huge holes in their economies just to stay even.

Secondary cities show greater variation in outcome. Cleveland experienced fiscal collapse in 1978, and nearly 40 percent of its residents are now below the poverty line.[7] Detroit and countless other rustbelt cities in America suffered a similar fate.[8] By contrast, Pittsburgh guided its shrinkage, revived its economy through research and technology, and kept its downtown healthy. In France, grimy, industrial Lille was rebuilt as the crossroads for Northern Europe. Industrial Glasgow has acquired a new downtown, but the rest of the city remains mired in decline.

Port cities have also turned out differently from one another. New Orleans and Liverpool fell into deep decline and have yet to recover. For a while, Hamburg reeled under successive economic blows, but recovered by modernizing its port and diversifying its industry. Today it is one of Europe's success stories and exults in the fact that it has more millionaires per capita than any other city on the continent.[9] Rotterdam, too, managed a partially successful transition by retaining its role as Europe's leading port and by building commercial linkages with Amsterdam and Utrecht.

Deindustrialization has also paved the way for new types of cities. So-called new-age boomtowns or sunbelt cities owe their urban form to late-twentieth-century technology.[10] Their economies usually are based on computers, software, electronics, space technology, or other emerging economic sectors. Their social structure is founded on middle-class outlooks, small families, and private housing. Especially in North America, new-age boomtowns enjoy an abundance of space, and their development spreads out along the corridors of modern freeways.

The United States has a concentration of these cities in its southwest and counts among them Phoenix, Houston, Albuquerque, and San Diego. Canada's boomtowns are found in its westerly open spaces and include Calgary and Vancouver. Boomtowns are not as common in Europe, which is already highly urbanized and lacks much vacant land. Nevertheless, European versions of these cities can be found in Southeast London (Croydon) and Oxford, in Grenoble and Montpellier, in Bavaria (Munich), and in the smaller towns of Italy's Northeast.

In America these boomtowns grew rapidly during the late 1960s and through the 1970s. Upheavals in petroleum and real estate sometimes threw cities like Houston into shock. But Houston recovered and continues to grow. In Canada, Vancouver is fueled by investments from Hong Kong, and it continues to lead that nation. The picture in Europe is hazy, though cities like Oxford and Grenoble have embraced high technology and believe that they are Europe's answer to the Silicon Valley.

In a nutshell, cities in North America and Europe changed substantially during the previous three decades. While the most successful became postindustrial, that status represented a dominant layer of activity, superimposed upon a diminished base of manufacture, shipping, and skilled trades. Less successful cities underwent shrinkage, though many of these managed to secure some postindustrial activity (small downtowns, tourism, stadiums, and exhibition centers). New-age boomtowns thrived on a combination of office employment, services, electronics, and light industry—set in the midst of universities, research centers, and low density development.

This reshuffling of the urban hierarchy has brought old and new cities into a competitive scramble to secure their economic well-being. As old industries decline and new investment patterns emerge, citizens and politicians are drawn into finding a niche for their communities in the new economic order. In the process, cities may be gripped by a certain angst—internal conflicts over means and ends, a belief that if a community does not grow it will surely die, and a rush to move faster.

Deconcentration: The Spreading Urban Landscape

The great transformation has also influenced human settlement and mobility. Overall, central cities have lost population. This deconcentration of population encompasses a range of different demographic processes, some healthy for cities, others not. Deconcentration entails movement away from places. This includes a movement out of healthy central cities, which allows remaining residents more space and gives departing residents more economical accommodations. We call this *dedensification*. Of course, dedensification also involves movement toward other places. This includes a burgeoning of low-density, metropolitan peripheries, brought about by rising living standards and a desire for single-family housing in the suburbs. It can also mean an entry into newer boomtowns and a search for fresh opportunities and economic betterment (new migration). This kind of movement can facilitate prosperity. On the other hand, deconcentration can also entail an exodus from urban cores because of decaying conditions, leaving these cities as segregated reservations for the poor. We refer to this as *decline*. In this case, population loss usually leaves cities in deeper distress.

Just as population loss does not necessarily mean decline, population growth does not always mean prosperity. Impoverished growth can occur when people move off rural land in search of opportunities elsewhere and fail to find them. We label this *impaction*. Migration into or around cities can also be accompanied by poorer living conditions and unemployment. The upshot has been massive growth without commensurate development. While this experience is uncommon among more mobile North Americans, it does occur in Africa and Latin America. A few European cities have grown while living conditions deteriorated. Whether accompanied by affluence or poverty, new migration and impaction create sprawling urban regions or megalopoli.[11]

In the United States, deconcentration often meant urban decline. As cities lost employment and neighborhoods decayed, some people escaped to the suburbs, while others remained behind in segregated ghettos. Even major cities that managed to remake themselves incurred the ravages of decline because whole neighborhoods fell apart. New York and Chicago did manage population gains during the past decade, but white residents continued to flee and the gains were due to immigration from Latin America or Asia. Population decline was rampant in secondary cities, where immigration was marginal and could not offset losses. Detroit, Cleveland, and St. Louis, once cities with close to or above a million residents, shrunk to less than half that size. Even after devastating losses of the 1970s and 1980s, the past decade was scarcely better, with those cities losing between 5 and 10 percent of their population.[12]

At the same time, urban deconcentration brought enormous prosperity to sunbelt boomtowns and swelled their suburbs. Boomtowns are the paragons of what we think of as urban *growth*. These areas experienced dramatic increases in residential populations, which gave rise to new shopping malls, office complexes, and single-family houses. The transformative years saw a virtual upheaval of inner-city populations, a massive shift of the white middle class into new settlements, and the trek of blacks and Hispanics into what remained of the urban cores.[13]

Some cities in Europe also suffered urban decline and now resemble their American counterparts. For the most part, however, European deconcentration was more genteel, taking the form of urban dedensification. Having begun in the Middle Ages and matured in the industrial era, Europe's cities were already overcrowded. Families often lived in small apartments within congested communities where shopping, recreation, schools, and factories were tightly clustered. Some urban theorists hailed this as the realization of community, but the relatives were less quaint.[14] Space was scarce, private bathrooms often absent, and sanitary conditions dubious. By the 1970s, if people could afford to live in the city, they bought extra space and renovated. If not, they moved out.

A push-pull operated in European cities to shift populations around. The rich, the upwardly mobile, and the single people stayed. Modest income families left because of financial pressures, but were also attracted by the ease of living outside the central city. In contrast to the United States, suburbs were built for those who could not afford to live closer to the center. The best of these were in outlying villages, in "new towns," or further away in new-age boomtowns; and they accommodated middle-class citizens. They were clean, spacious, and featured supermarkets, playgrounds, and schools woven into the residential fabric. The worst, were, low-income projects built in segregated edges or as extensions to impacted cities. They were massive, dingy concrete blocks that accommodated immigrants.

In sum the great transformation produced massive population shifts with different kinds of consequences. . . . Despite differences in geography, size, and population, major cities across the industrial West have undergone economic restructuring, brought on by similar forces. On both continents, populations spread throughout metropolitan areas. Suburbs and boomtowns radically expanded and urbanization proceeded apace. Rural areas shrank and fewer people earned their living through agriculture. Distant towns and rural villages lost population and, in some instances, fell into near vacancy. All told, we see substantial variation among these cities. The ramifications are deeply political. Citizens face a new set of urban challenges, driven by deindustrialization, migration, and a need to adapt.

Global Sweep, Local Brooms

Globalism is an encompassing concept; it covers a broad range of activities, and it has brought both positive and negative results. Foremost among its characteristics is free trade. Open markets rest on a theory of competitive advantage, whereby each locale finds it beneficial to produce goods or services it can most efficiently turn out and to use international markets to acquire products that are best made elsewhere. This has sharpened and refined the division of labor among nation-states. The upshot is an explosive process, in which productivity, consumption, and participation rise at exponential rates. As we have seen and will continue to explore, urban growth has been nothing short of colossal, but it has also been accompanied by deep inequalities and paradoxes.[15]

Fundamentally, globalism and its attendant free trade are derived from a technological revolution that has shrunk time and distance. We have already mentioned the revolutionary effects of instant communication, and here we amplify how that technology allows nations to achieve deeper levels of economic integration within competitive markets. By now, advanced technology moves $1.5 trillion around the world each day. In the United States international flows of bonds and equities are fifty-four times higher today than in 1970. The comparable figures for Germany and Japan are sixty and fifty times higher. Other research has shown that international trade sustains the global patterning and has brought about changes in economic relationships, social structure, and the significance of geographical place.[16]

A corollary characteristic is standardization. Once goods and information are alike, they become recognizable and interchangeable. Common standards of measurement, universal criteria, interchangeable parts, and identical symbols are essential for globalization. Just as the grid system of streets helped land-development, so too does standardization facilitate globalization. This includes a common currency, established procedures for registering and enforcing patents, and compatible mechanical or electronic equipment. Licenses and professional certification have also become standardized in order to allow human resources to flow across boundaries. Even sports has become standardized. The Olympic Games and Olympic committees legitimate certain sports and sanction rules through which athletic contests are held. Traditionally, American baseball has been capped by the misnomer of a "World Series." Up until recently this was entirely an American affair, but increasingly players and even some teams have been drawn from other nations. The progressive universality of sports today is incontrovertible.

Another wave of global change is heavily political. Globalization has magnified the intercourse between states, localities, and social movements across the world.[17] Signs of this are visible in the rise of multilateral organizations, regional pacts, and talk of a borderless world. States, localities, nongovernmental organizations, and labor increasingly ignore old boundaries and are driven more than before by the seemingly contradictory stimuli of cooperation and competition. For some this has opened new worlds of opportunity, where masses of people can be mobilized for democratic ends. This interaction, both on site and across cyberspace, makes government more accountable and also more replaceable. For others, globalism signifies a concentration of wealth and power, and a threat of lower living standards. This has led to a perilous instability and a thunderous reaction from both left- and right-wing protestors.[iv]

An additional wave of globalization is sociocultural. This involves diffusion of a more open, multipolar, and multicultural society in which migration is a major by-product.[18] What distinguishes current migration from preceding movements is its truncated and temporary patterns of settlement. Commonly, single men live abroad for lengthy periods, while sending remittances to the homeland. When whole families do migrate, they often are treated as long-term aliens, rarely assimilating, and even children born in the host country may not acquire citizenship. Indeed, the telecommunications revolution has given permanency to this temporary status. Cheap, efficient technology compresses space and time, enabling groups to retain homeland ties and preserve indigenous culture. Overseas, ethnic culture is now said to thrive in "transnational space" in which language, habit, and tradition continue regardless of geography.[19]

These aspects of globalization also foster a greater sense of mutual vulnerability. Free trade and competitive advantage have made societies more efficient, but they have also made societies more fragile and susceptible to crisis. In a matter of minutes, turmoil in a single great bank can upset finance at the other end of the world. Currency fluctuations can overturn decades of progress, hitting those at the bottom of the economic scale hardest. As economies become more integrated, localities share more closely both the good and bad times of globalization. Through the 1990s Taipei, Tel Aviv, and Santiago experienced an unprecedented boom. After 2000 the global economy was hit by recession and those cities went bust. The more integrated and the more synchronized the locality with globalization, the greater the upturn and the steeper the downturn.

Vulnerability has many dimensions. Disease travels as swiftly as airline flights and has acquired an international character. The recent exuberance and then depression of stock markets as well as the AIDS epidemic are unfortunate examples of this exposure. Still another dark side of globalism is the spread of terrorism.[20] The ease of travel, instantaneous communication, and quick transfer of money make it possible for terrorists to do their work and attack fragile international linkages.[v] International terror most vividly illustrates the underside of global interdependence. The multinational character of its actors and the slippery content of its operations are especially well suited for porous boundaries. . . . It was at the seams of globalization where international cities and international terror were tragically joined on September 11.

How do cities fit into this overall picture? One might suppose that globalization makes cities less important, as they are swept into a common world of economic competition and social interchange. Presumably, people could be located anywhere, and conduct business via the Internet from a mountaintop retreat.[21] In fact, the opposite is true—at least for some cities. A knowledge-based economy has accelerated face-to-face and informal contact. It has increased an appetite for conferences, seminars, and annual meetings. Additionally, business searches for that extra edge that comes from personal contact.

Globalization also has generated a need for central direction in which financial, legal, and professional services are concentrated within a common locale. Cities have made free trade much easier to accomplish, they have facilitated a new international division of labor, and they have absorbed waves of migration.[22] While not all cities have been blessed with these advantages, many are still efficient and enormously productive work stations for the postindustrial era. Whether one selects a handful of global cities, a larger number of primate cities, or a sampling of regional ones, urban centers lead national productivity, and their total output in goods and services has quickened during the last few decades.[23]

Rising urbanization has occurred concomitantly with globalization and is associated with rising GDP. Metropolitan areas of Europe and North America grew rich during the transformation, though clearly as the process matures the rate of urbanization flattens. . . .

Globalization has not made all urban places alike. Where you live and work matters more than ever in accessing jobs, income, public amenities, schools, and green space. These things are contingent upon "place." Location does make a huge difference. Neat suburban residential enclaves, edge cities, busy commercial downtowns, urban ghettos, vacated industrial areas, and campus-like office parks are all part of a complex urban fabric that differentiates opportunities. Some cities have taken advantage of those opportunities and the enormous wealth that springs from global trade. By the end of the millennium, Foreign Direct Investment (FDI) had reached an all-time high of $865 billion. While it is not possible to trace that investment to every locality, an overwhelming proportion of it went to advanced industrial nations, mostly located in the West. Banks held that money and facilitated investments, and almost all of these institutions were located in major cities. Moreover, along with investment flows, banking assets have gushed over the last few decades. . . .

Even during this short period, most banks substantially increased their holdings. In some cases the aggregation of capital crested by over 300 percent. Place often shapes perspective, and location cannot help influencing decisions. More than ever, cities serve as the command and control centers of those decisions. They have benefited not just from saturated white-collar employment and offshoot industries, but also from their strategic placement in international capital markets. Not all of this has produced salutary results. There are always paradoxes and contradictions connected to change, and the impact of globalization on cities is no exception.

One paradox is that while most metropolitan areas have become wealthier, they also contain rising numbers of the poor. In Western Europe 10 percent of city residents are classified as poor, while the percentage rises in suburbs to roughly 20 percent. The United States reverses these proportions, so that central cities and suburbs respectively hold 21 percent and 9 percent of residents who fall below the poverty line.[24] Quite expectedly, migrants searching for opportunities in cities account for a substantial portion of the poor. More than 50 percent of the populations in New York and Toronto are classified as either ethnic minorities or foreign born. In Paris, the percentage is above 15 percent.

Another paradox is that urban transformation has both expanded the sphere of central cities and shrunk it. In some ways deconcentration has extended central cities by making suburbanites dependent upon them for income, investment, jobs, and culture. One can see this in the huge numbers of commuters pouring into urban cores each day as well as in the many monetary transactions (mortgages, business loans, venture capital) that occur between city financial institutions and the hinterlands. In other ways, deconcentration has also meant an escape from the central city and has created an altogether new urban form. Green cities have sprung up in the more distant countryside and eliminated distinctions between urban and rural life. A newer urban life is built around asphalt, glass, trees, and grass, and it functions apart from traditional central cities.

Still another oddity is that while transformation has made cities into hard-working centers of productivity, it has also made them into sites of gluttonous leisurely consumption. Scholars often write about the dichotomy between investment and consumption whereby different locales tend toward one or the other.[25] Postindustrial cities have united these dichotomies. Complementing an enormous white-collar apparatus of producer services is a burgeoning industry in leisure and consumption. The rise of the office-complex city has been accompanied by the rise of the tourist city. Cities are today in the midst of what Judd and Fainstein describe as a "tourist bubble," whose growth is among the fastest in the world.[26]

Put in historical perspective, these paradoxes are not unusual. Cities have always grown or shrunk alongside technological advance. The introduction of elevators and steel framing allowed for skyscrapers but broke up traditional neighborhoods. Metro lines were a boon for central business districts, but a bust for out-of-the-way small towns. Invention is often a conveyance for what Schumpeter called "creative destruction"[27] and brought about very different results. . . .

"Glocal" Choices

Deindustrialization, deconcentration, and globalization have put cities on trajectories of change. It is this unusual blend of global challenge and local response that confronts us, and this combination is sometimes denoted by the inelegant terms "glocal" or "glocalization."[28] Like the industrial revolution before it, this revolution can be decisively influenced by government as well as other social institutions.[29] Governments have responded to these challenges in diverse ways. First, leaders and citizens have made strategic decisions about *what kind of community* they want. Some political leaders look to the marketplace for strategic direction, placing a high priority on gaining a competitive advantage for their communities. They ask, how can we find our niche in the regional, national, or world market? What can we do best? Where can we garner capital investment? How can we grow by helping business operate more efficiently? For cities that choose competition, answers to these questions have produced a variety of strategic responses. We see cities remaking waterfronts into tourist attractions, refurbishing downtowns with office towers and convention halls, and trying to attract big bang events such as the World Cup, Expo, or Olympic games, as well as revenue sources such as sports teams, theme parks, or gaming casinos.

Cities then do not just react to the movement of capital but act upon these forces. Although local governments have only limited control over the marketplace, they use public power to engage it. They do so whenever land is recycled, development rights are granted, housing is built, taxes are collected, or capital is borrowed. Moreover cities can profoundly affect factors of production. They can lower overhead costs by building bridges, ports, and airfields. They can tighten up or loosen controls over air pollution. Cities can even affect labor costs by making it easier or more difficult for individuals to access welfare benefits.[30] In making decisions over these issues, cities struggle to resolve an array of problems and influence their own restructuring.

Some leaders try to induce capital investment by reducing risks for business. They may put up bonds that guarantee the building of stadiums or convention halls, they may underwrite loans to potential investors, and they may find themselves forming public private-partnerships in order to assure private investors of unified backing.[31] Cities also aggressively solicit business by lobbying for private capital, bidding for company headquarters, or establishing international offices to stimulate trade.

Cities seeking competitive advantages may also tolerate increased migration, allow informal economies to flourish, and facilitate the supply of cheap goods and services. They may countenance permissive building codes, lax licensing, and an abundance of substandard housing. These newfound resources explain the partial resurgence of textile manufacture in some cities, where old-fashioned sweatshops arise and where illegal immigrants are exploited as low-cost labor. The upscale life-style of postindustrial cities generates a demand for low-paying service jobs. A virtual night shift of unskilled workers commutes into downtowns to clean the office towers, staff the restaurants, and drive the taxicabs. The "reverse commute" of marginal workers into affluent suburbs also helps to maintain an attractive low cost of living.

Alternatively, cities sometimes defy the swells of the marketplace. Local leaders can remain politically sensitive and rely on a logic of populist, anti-growth policies.[32] This logic may well clash with the rationality of the marketplace. Cities may resist the lure of growth and opt for preservationist or caretaker strategies.[33] They may want to protect historic neighborhoods, guard surrounding farmland, or prohibit large discount outlets and suburban malls. Some fear higher taxes and increased congestion. They may want to remain as quiet residential communities.

Large and small cities have resisted economic growth by invoking moratoria on the construction of office towers, using zoning exactions to force concessions from developers, adopting strict architectural codes, requiring underground facilities for automobile parking, and setting aside large tracts for open space.[34] In Western Europe the upsurge of "green parties" has affected urban policies. Green legislators have placed controls on housing costs, limited the price of apartment rentals, and closed off streets to automobiles. Reciprocally, they have used public funds to renovate housing, protected rights of squatters, and reserved sections of the streetscape for bicycles. Populist movements have sometimes arisen to challenge the power of corporate decision makers in places such as Cleveland, Ohio, the Mon Valley in Pennsylvania, and Liverpool, England.

There is variation in the response to globalization. In important ways, world competition has sparked a quest for capital investment and growth. In other ways, the free exchange of ideas and possibilities for collaboration has enabled groups to mobilize. Some scholars have found evidence of a new urban politics based on social issues, increased diversity, and a concern for the environment.[35] They also envision globalized cities as hothouses for the spread of postmaterialist values with its emphasis on citizen activism.[36] The concerns of migrant workers coupled to environmental and populist sentiment could generate counterpressures. Whatever the outcomes, globalization is not a leveling process, and it has created new alternatives.

Who makes decisions over *what* is another question of choice. This ultimately depends upon the existence of assets and the distribution of power within a city. Some scholars argue that urban decision-making is shaped by economics, and they stress growth and competition as the predominant force. From this perspective, cities must give priority to economic growth because they are disciplined by a market that punishes them with loss of jobs and tax revenue.[37] Other scholars argue that political preferences matter more than economic pressures. They see powerful leaders, coalitions, regimes, and growth machines operating to shape economic preferences.[38] There is something to both interpretations. Cities are certainly limited by the assets at their disposal, and they cannot deal with global change unless they have the wherewithal to do so. By the same token, dealing with change requires initiative, and coalitions must be built by political entrepreneurs who mobilize groups and classes.

The important questions deal not only with differences of alternatives taken, but also with the reasons why some cities might be able to choose particular alternatives. Are there structural characteristics that are common to cities choosing similar strategic alternatives? If so, can they be identified and how do they interact? Likewise, do cities that share similar strategic responses to globalism also share similar cultural or political characteristics? If so, what are these and how do they operate? Can we make sense of these varying influences on choice and put them into some logical schema? Finally, what are the lessons learned from this inquiry? Does the international marketplace have a tendency to homogenize cities so that they become alike, or are cities becoming more dissimilar? Given the tension between the global and the local, can one decide which side, if any, prevails? . . .

The classic development conflict occurs between "anti-growth" and "pro-growth" coalitions, and includes such debates as whether to adopt building moratoria and preserve historic districts or aggressively recruit private investors and turn downtowns into rows of towering office complexes. This conflict often encompasses a political component where the sides are poised for battle—neighborhood groups, preservationists, and environmentalists on one side versus developers, chambers of commerce, and media boosters on the other. Pro-growth impulses are often driven by a desire to standardize development (trade centers, office towers, tourist attractions) and expand the contributions of multinational firms in the local economy. Anti-growth impulses frequently stem from a desire for citizen participation and local autonomy.[39] These tensions reflect the degree to which local development agendas are influenced by the international market.

Looking at the situation more broadly, we can appreciate that issues of international import are fought on local battlegrounds, and that ultimately these conflicts change the character of cities. Many local challenges and responses have global proportions; decisions flow to and from an international marketplace. This marketplace can either saturate cities with massive investment and political pressure or marginalize them. Either way, cities must respond by accommodating, managing, or resisting these forces.

5

Royce Hanson, Harold Wolman, David Connolly, Katherine Pearson, and Robert McManmon

GLOBALIZATION AND LEADERSHIP IN AMERICAN CITIES

Corporate civic elites have played a major role in the building, rebuilding, governance, and functioning of major American cities. In fact, some of the most important policy innovations and development projects in American cities during the 20th Century were initiated, supported, or brought to fruition by key business leaders and peak organizations of local chief executive officers (CEOs). Recent urban literature has suggested, however, that there may be increasing disengagement of corporate elites from civic efforts, largely as a result of pervasive economic trends affecting locally owned and based businesses. Ironically, such disengagement comes during a time when federal aid

From Royce Hanson, Harold Wolman, David Connolly, Katherine Pearson, and Robert McManmon, *Corporate Citizenship and Urban Problem Solving: The Changing Civic Role of Business Leaders in American Cities.* A Report to the Brookings Institution Urban and Metropolitan Policy Program. Washington, DC: George Washington Institute of Public Policy, June 2006, pp. 1, 10–18, 25–27, 29, 34. Reprinted by permission of the Brookings Institution. www.brookings.edu/metro

to cities has been curtailed and greater reliance has been placed on the private sector to solve urban problems, leaving many cities with increasing limited means to undertake major initiatives.

Since the End of World War II, CEO-led organizations such as the Allegheny Conference, the Twin Cities Citizen's League, the Greater Baltimore Committee, the Dallas Citizen's Council, and analogous organizations in Atlanta, Cleveland, Detroit, Kansas City, St. Louis, San Francisco, and Milwaukee occupy legendary status as power brokers and agenda setters in their communities. Often founded by executives of local corporations that grew to national or international scale, these organizations were able to mobilize their corporate members' personal devotion to community, their deal-making talent, and their ability to commit corporate financial resources to address redevelopment, environmental quality, transportation, health care, and education issues in their respective cities. In some cases, their initiatives transformed whole sections of cities, both physically and economically. In others, they managed sensitive local issues such as the desegregation of public schools and the integration of restaurants, hotels, theaters, and other places of public accommodation.

The power and influence of these organizations began to wane after the mid-1970s, however, as economic restructuring-deregulation, reorganization and suburbanization of major industries took hold, and demographic changes produced shifts in political leadership. By this time, professional and business service firms and nonprofit organizations had begun to displace manufacturers as the principal employers of many regions. Successive waves of mergers and acquisitions started to transform many local banks and other businesses from corporate headquarters to branches of larger corporations headquartered in other cities, or even other countries. And new executives, often with tenuous career ties to the locality, gradually began to replace the generation of home-town entrepreneurs and business titans that built their corporations and established CEO-led civic organizations in places where they had deep roots.

Corporate engagement in urban problem solving depends heavily on the heads of major firms located in an area being actively involved in the civic life of their communities—in other words, the extent to which they are willing and able to lend their personal leadership skills, time, ideas, and the slack resources of their firms (executive and professional talent and money) to the arts, education, hospitals, workforce development programs, sports and cultural facilities, and, especially, major economic development projects. The changes in economic structure discussed above have altered the level and nature of this engagement over the past several decades, however.

Substantial changes in an area's manufacturing, services, and FIRE [Finance, Insurance, Real Estate] sectors, and in the number and strength of its largest firms, have had numerous implications for the engagement of corporate CEOs in urban issues. In the case of the FIRE sector, the gain or loss of major banks and other financial institutions has had an effect on both financial contributions to civic causes and, perhaps even more important, the leadership of the corporate community. Declining employment in the traditional manufacturing sector has been accompanied by the demise or relocation of major firms, and with them the loss of prominent CEOs to the region's leadership ranks. And business demands on executives of newer, fast-growing manufacturing firms appear to leave them little time for civic activities.

The universal increase in the services sector presents a more complex situation for civic engagement. It appears to be accompanied almost everywhere by the growth of nonprofit organizations in education and health care, as well as expansion of business services in some areas. In other areas, growth in services may be more oriented to small firms and consumer services. Nonprofit firms tend to have fewer slack resources than large corporations, and their executives may see themselves more as potential beneficiaries of civic engagement by private CEOs than as leaders in the mobilization of private sector economic and civic power. But as they often have a larger stake in the well being of their city and region, they can be important additions to corporate civic organizations. At the same time, executives of business service firms—such as law, accounting, consulting, and public relations—may replace manufacturers and bankers in the leadership echelons of business, but the organizational culture of the partnerships from which they come may be fundamentally different from those of the corporations they serve.

The presence of Fortune 500 companies provides at least the opportunity to engage those firms and their CEOs in civic life. But with the move of major corporate headquarters to the suburbs, it's not surprising that many executives have shifted their interests away from the city toward more regional issues. And as local Fortune 500 companies are acquired and become branches or divisions of larger corporations with home offices removed to distant places, the managers of those residual branches often have less latitude in their activities and ability to commit financial and other resources to civic projects.

Finally, the culture of business engagement in a metropolitan area and the character of its civic institutions are important factors in determining how corporate executives address urban issues. Some cities have strong traditions of business statesmanship where corporate executives are expected by their peers to take on important civic leadership responsibilities and their firms are expected to make generous contributions to charities and public causes. Where business leaders have created organizations and networks that can mobilize economic resources and talent to influence public policy or economic activity they are more likely to find satisfaction in civic engagement, reinforcing their commitments.

All told, it's clear that economic restructuring has affected CEO engagement in cities and metropolitan areas in myriad and profound ways.

New Patterns of Civic Engagement by Corporate CEOs

Associations composed solely of CEOs were created to bring together in a small, exclusive forum an area's largest employers—those local companies who could make "on the spot" commitments of their firm's resources to support a development project, a change in public policy, a mayoral campaign, a bond referendum, or other major civic initiative. R. L. "Uncle Bob" Thornton, the founder of the Dallas Citizens Council in the late 1930s, famously called its members his city's "Yes and No men." In some cases—as was the case with creation of Cleveland Tomorrow in 1982—the leading business titans of the city regarded the chamber of commerce as slow-moving, ineffective, and primarily designed to provide member services rather than solve big problems. Moreover, they found chamber deliberations tedious and time-consuming. They preferred gatherings among peers in a boardroom, receiving a quick briefing by a colleague or a senior staff officer, and reaching a quick consensus on what to do, how to allocate its costs and responsibilities among the group, and how best to use their influence and money to make it happen.

These organizations typically allowed only CEOs of the largest corporate employers to be members. The banks, utilities, newspaper, department stores, and manufacturers were the mainstays. Professional partnerships and real estate developers often were excluded, and CEOs of nonprofit institutions—universities, hospitals, and foundations— were rarely invited to join. They might have been among a region's largest employers, but their executives rarely had authority to commit unbudgeted resources and they were more likely to be beneficiaries of a civic initiative than instigators of one.

Total membership in some cities was 50 or fewer; in larger urban areas it might include two hundred or more. A small executive committee or board of directors made decisions, usually out of public view. Typically, only CEOs could participate in deliberations or decisions—no substitutes were allowed. In early years, there may have been no staff. Later an executive director or president may have been selected to carry out the decisions of the board and help its officers set the agenda. Additional staffs tended to be small.

Influence flowed from the economic power of the members, the long identification of their firms with the city, and their own deep affection for it. They often regarded their success and that of their companies as bound to the success of the city. Once a course of action had been agreed upon, they used their power to rebuild sections of town, influence the location of public facilities and development projects, make and break mayors, and allocate the resources of foundations they controlled to projects and programs they deemed worthy of support. In Pittsburgh, Atlanta, Cleveland, Baltimore, St. Louis, and Dallas they formed governing coalitions with mayors and managers to undertake major civic improvements. Even in cities where such governing regimes were transitory or unstable they were a force with which public officials had to reckon.

Changes in the role and influence of corporate leadership organizations were beginning to be apparent by the mid-1970s in most metropolitan areas. Many experienced large turnover in membership in the ensuing two decades as waves of mergers and acquisitions transformed local corporate headquarters, converting icons of local industry into mere branches of distant firms. Executive suites were populated with a new generation of managers, many of whom had no local roots and were on career trajectories that involved frequent transfers to branches in other cities. All these institutional changes were accompanied by relocation of many headquarters offices to the suburbs. The combination of these forces led to changes in the nature of civic engagement by business leaders, their commitment to city and region, and the membership and structure of many of their organizations.

The Loss of the Hometown Bankers

Of all the economic sectors, the deregulation and reorganization of banking have had the most pervasive effect on business organizations engaged in urban and regional problem solving. Prior to 1980 most major U.S. cities contained headquarters of one or more major regional banks. National and international banking headquarters were located in only a few of the largest cities. But in the massive reorganization of banking that followed deregulation and the collapse of the real estate and savings and loan industries in the late 1980s, many of the nation's great regional banks were acquired by national and international financial systems headquartered in other cities and were transformed into regional subsidiaries. Bank CEOs with deep roots in and allegiance to their region, some of them reaching back several generations of banking families, were often replaced by managers for whom success was measured by promotion to run a bank in a more important market, and eventually to the bank's central headquarters.

The executive officers of business-civic organizations were virtually unanimous in stressing the importance of bankers to the leadership of their organizations and the financial support of major civic projects. The older generation of hometown bankers had been almost universally engaged in civic affairs, leading peak business organizations and chambers of commerce, and serving as the catalysts in raising funds from their peer executives for civic projects. Many were leaders in the creation of CEO-only organizations in cities such as Pittsburgh, Dallas, Baltimore, Cleveland, and Houston. But while bank executives remain mainstays of corporate civic leadership, in cities where the central headquarters of a bank has been lost through consolidations or mergers, CEO-led civic association executives generally reported a negative effect on civic leadership in general and on their organizations in particular. As one association put it: "Banks used to be the leading civic contributor. Not anymore unless a bank headquarters is in your city." Another said that 20 years ago, "if one wanted to launch a major civic project, you'd go to the CEO of the local bank. You can't do that anymore; the banker doesn't have as much clout, but is probably working harder and devoting more time to the community."

In many cities, CEOs of national or international banking systems continue to play important leadership roles in their headquarters cities. After Wells Fargo Bank moved its headquarters to San Francisco, for example, its executives assumed major leadership positions in area affairs. Its corporate CEO chairs the California Business Roundtable and the COO is treasurer of the Bay Area Council. In Cleveland, National City Corp. and KeyBank CEOs were leaders of Cleveland Tomorrow and played key roles in its merger with the Cleveland Growth Association to form the Greater Cleveland Partnership. Minneapolis-St. Paul remains the headquarters city for three banking systems, and they are among the strongest supporters of the Citizens League. Their executives see a clear business self-interest in helping solve the region's problems. In Pittsburgh, CEOs of PNC Financial Services Group and Mellon Bank are active board members of the Allegheny Conference.

In other areas, the CEOs of major banks headquartered in a city have passed responsibility for representing the bank in urban and regional affairs to a second-in-command, or the head of the regional division. In part this is a function of the demands on the system CEO's time from far-flung branches, investors, and regulators. Although SunTrust's headquarters remains in Atlanta, for example, it is the regional executive who serves on the board of Central Atlanta Progress.

In cities that have lost bank headquarters, the key to engagement of the new generation of bankers appears to be the autonomy of the regional CEO within the overall system, the corporate culture of the parent corporation, and the length of an executive's tenure in the city. In some cities, the loss of hometown bankers may result in reductions in charitable contributions. In others, it may be that a regional bank CEO lacks authority to commit resources without home office approval. And yet, elsewhere, the regional bank CEO may have had both autonomy and interest in participating in civic life, but is promoted or transferred just as he or she is beginning to know the area well and is ready to take on a major leadership role. In one city, the president of the CEO-based civic association observed that the three major banks changed their role in the community when their leadership changed even though these "local presidents" generally could make commitments to the community without going back to home office.

For example, when Bank of America moved its headquarters from San Francisco to Charlotte, its representation on the Bay Area Council was shifted from the system CEO to the head of the California office, and the strong leadership the bank had provided in the business community was effectively lost. In Milwaukee, the head of the USBank was active in the Greater Milwaukee Committee, but after two years was moved to another city. By contrast, in Houston, where locally-owned banks were acquired by out-of-state systems, the regional executives remain mainstays of the Greater Houston Partnership. Regional executives of J. P. MorganChase, Bank One, Wells Fargo, and Bank of America are typically responsible for branches in a number of states and all play a fairly substantial role in Houston's civic life. For the most part, these banks have been in Texas for some time and they bring in executives that know the market and the city.

General Consequences of Economic Restructuring for CEO Civic Engagement

While the reorganization of banking often produced the most dramatic changes in CEO engagement in urban problem solving, the broader shifts in the economic landscape of urban areas have exacerbated those effects. In addition to banking headquarters, most cities lost locally owned utilities, newspapers, centrally located department stores, and manufacturing companies. Seven of the urban areas in this study lost Fortune 500 companies over the past 20 years, 12 gained them, and in only one—Phoenix—the number stayed constant. But whether they gained or lost big companies, many regions simply now have fewer top executives among whom to spread civic work, and those executives often lack either the interest or experience in civic affairs.

In response, many CEO organizations have expanded their membership to include a broader range of executive talent such as heads of higher education institutions, medical centers, foundations, and business service partnerships in law, accounting, and consulting firms. Several organizations have merged with the regional chambers of commerce and other business-oriented organizations in order to save staffing, time, and financial resources, and to achieve greater solidarity among all sizes and types of business so they can be more effective in achieving common economic and policy goals. Whether retaining a CEO-only membership or becoming part of a merged business partnership, the paid professional executives and staffs of peak business organizations have continued to play a larger and more visible role in civic leadership. And, finally, almost all of the organizations have de-emphasized their engagement in central city affairs and increased their involvement in regional economic development policy.

The Pool of CEO Civic Leaders Is Shallower, More Transient, and Less Influential The pool of executives from which civic leadership can be drawn has become different in its makeup than in prior generations, and it is shallower. Regardless of whether an urban area had an increase or decrease in the number of major corporations, almost all experienced a substantial change in the composition and level of civic leadership by CEOs.

In some urban areas, there are simply fewer corporate headquarters from which talent can be drawn. One CEO, who is a leader in his city's civic life, lamented: "If one turned back 20 years, there were maybe 50 active executives . . . there are now 17. About half of the ones that had been active are gone, there were others that didn't care or were not engaged . . . There are fewer corporate leaders engaged than in the past."

Another pointed out that today's world for CEOs is very different from that of a generation ago. Then, he said, a dozen CEOs knew each other and were always in town. A phone call from their most respected colleague could bring them together within a day, and they could each pledge a million dollars to support a project. "CEOs, whether they want to or not, cannot be gathered effectively anymore," he said. "My travel time has gone up to 50 percent. . . . And, everything is public. I can't invest $2 million dollars of shareholders' money [on a project] that probably won't work, like they did back then. Everything is public now, and you just don't do it."

These comments were mirrored in those of the president of one of the older CEO civic associations: "There is much higher turnover in executive ranks than in past years, as a result of mergers and acquisitions. Globalization has resulted in an incredible increase in the amount of travel for CEOs. The recession only increased their travel requirements. I can no longer have regular meeting schedules for committees, but must poll members to find a 'best' time for meetings. It's tough to get participation. Some are willing to get involved in short term projects." Another said he had such difficulty in scheduling meetings that he now often goes to member firms to make presentations and seek support for projects.

Although the power, cohesion, and engagement of past CEOs are probably exaggerated and even mythic in some cities, there were substantial agreement among the association executives that even where the number of corporate central headquarters has increased, some of the new CEOs are only lightly engaged, if at all, in the civic life of the community or the organization of their peers. In the case of many fast growing firms, such as those in information technology and biomedicine, this may be due to the fact that they have not yet reached plateaus that give their leaders time to devote to civic causes. These executives have not had the opportunity to be mentored for leadership by an older generation of CEOs, and many of their companies have not yet developed an internal culture of civic engagement. For other executives, there may simply be a reluctance to get involved in local civic affairs. Many heads of regional offices of corporations, for example, tend to be more attached to the corporation and their careers than to the cities in which they currently find themselves. Because their assignments tend to be short-term, these CEOs may be especially reluctant to take on projects that require several years to complete or that present hazards to their reputation for effectiveness.

Certainly some new CEOs are deeply engaged in civic life, serving on multiple boards and in a variety of leadership and philanthropic endeavors. But particularly in the case of regional executives, their frequent rotation complicates civic leadership. A number of the association executives tell of grooming an energetic executive for leadership positions, only to have him transferred to another city just as he reaches a key position of influence. This transience deprives an area of a cadre of senior business statesmen, whose long experience in a community can provide valuable counsel and institutional memory for the civic system. And because newly arriving CEOs lack long association with and knowledge of the communities in which they find themselves, they are generally more dependent on their own community affairs staffs and the professional staffs of their civic associations. Their effectiveness in problem solving thus rests on the quality of their briefings, pre-meeting negotiations, and post-event follow through by staff. Their roles, therefore, have shifted from substantive to symbolic engagement, and from fashioning policies and solutions to bestowing legitimacy on or championing decisions formulated by professional staff.

Further exacerbating these issues is the fact that CEOs of regional offices or divisions of corporations headquartered elsewhere, like their counterparts in banking, tend to have less autonomy than the generation of homegrown owner-CEOs that preceded them. Twelve of the 19 organizations for which information was obtained for this study reported a decline in the decision-making autonomy of some of their members whose firms had become regional offices of corporations headquartered elsewhere. Even when a local executive's proposal is approved, the need for central headquarters approval of major commitments of resources can slow launching of projects and can also make executives cautious about tendering support that goes beyond their signature authority.

The Role of Nonprofit Employers and Foundations Has Grown As the extent and nature of CEO engagement in civic organizations has changed, so too has the composition of their memberships. The nonprofit sector—particularly universities, medical centers, and foundations—has provided a substantial component of the growth in the service employment in most regions, and its engagement in civic affairs has become increasingly important to CEO organizations and the communities they serve.

Universities and medical centers are now the largest employers in many metropolitan areas. They are often incubators of new businesses and supply much of the creative, technical, professional, and management talent that both old and new industries require for success. The chief executives of these institutions have become important members of the peak business organizations in their regions. Community college presidents have increasingly been added, as their institutions are deeply engaged in workforce development, business incubation, and development of minority workers and managers.

Presidents of universities and medical centers tend to have less autonomy to allocate resources and less control of their boards and organizations than top business CEOs. Still, even though they may be supplicants and beneficiaries of the slack resources of corporate donors more often than grantors of resources to others, there are important advantages to including them in the civic organizations of the economic elite. First, most of them cannot move to other locations, and thus tend to have a strong and continuing interest in the quality of life of their areas. Universities are not subject to acquisitions and mergers, although private and some nonprofit medical centers are targets of consolidators. Second, they produce entrepreneurial, professional, and technical talent, and marketable patents to fuel the area's economy. Finally, university and medical center campuses serve as anchors and magnets for growing economic sectors such as information technology, arts, and biomedicine. All the CEO-led civic associations we studied have added higher education and medical institutions to their membership.

A growing number of civic organizations also include local private foundations, although a few exclude foundations as a matter of policy, either feeling that they do not want their agendas to be influenced by foundation priorities, or that their connections with the foundations are sufficiently strong through the overlapping board memberships of CEOs. Private foundation assets have ballooned in many cities, making them important players in establishing the civic agenda, particularly in areas that have lost locally owned banks. A foundation executive pointed out that they differ from the CEOs in that civic issues are the "day job" of the foundation presidents and their staffs.

One of the by-products of industrial reorganizations has been the creation of new private foundations or substantial increases in funding for existing foundations with a substantial focus on local giving. But the foundations are less interested in economic development initiatives—the primary priority for CEO organizations—and instead tend to focus their grants and programs on social, education, health care, and community issues. Although one or more local foundations in most urban areas can be counted on to support projects initiated by the leading business organization, most make relatively few grants for economic development, as such.

A significant exception to foundation reticence in entering the economic development arena has occurred in the Cleveland area. Led by the Cleveland and Gund foundations based in Cleveland, and Akron's GAR Foundation, 70 foundations in northeastern Ohio pooled resources in 2004 to create a three-year $30 million Fund for Our Economic Future. The Fund's objective is to frame a regional economic development agenda designed to produce a long-term economic transformation of the region, track economic progress, and invest in promising initiatives. Initial grants have supported projects and institutions created by the civic organizations of the business elite, but the foundations appear to be staking out new ground, which, while complementary to the business agenda, aims to engage a broader set of stakeholders and issues.

The key to this more aggressive role for foundations in territory once largely occupied by the corporate leadership appears to be a combination of the size of the resources leading foundations can bring to bear on problems and the changing role of foundation executives. Several urban areas have foundations that can easily match levels of corporate largess. Atlanta, Milwaukee, Kansas City, Pittsburgh, Central Indiana, and Philadelphia are home to major foundations with as much flexibility and potential leverage as Cleveland's, should they choose to use it to influence the regional agenda. This can be especially important at a time when corporate leaders tend to have less autonomy in making civic investments, and are less personally attached to the region where they are currently located. Like the universities and medical centers, the foundations are not moving. And although their executives may be mobile, they are increasingly expected by their boards to make strategic investments that can produce improvements in urban conditions, rather than repeatedly fund traditional clients.

Organizational Agendas Have Shifted to the Region The shift toward a regional agenda has been pervasive among CEO-led civic associations, whether they have merged with other groups or have steadfastly retained their independence of the larger and more inclusive chambers of commerce. The number that have added "Greater," "Regional," "Metro," or "Area" to their names is indicative of the regional emphasis and reflects dispersion into the suburbs of members' corporate headquarters and other major facilities, as well as the growth of metropolitan areas.[1]

With agendas that typically include transportation systems, economic growth, regional workforce development, and business taxes, the leadership and professional staff of these organizations increasingly deal with state officials instead of mayors. Most retain a central city portfolio in large-scale development projects or K-12 education—which also involves a major state policy component—and maintenance of close relationships with mayors and other local elected officials remains important to their effectiveness. Even among these, however, the uneven experience of business leaders in building and maintaining governing coalitions with mayors has led them to work in what are often more hospitable regional arenas.

At the same time, based on their business experience, their members recognize that the economy functions on a regional scale, and therefore have concluded they can be effective in matters of economic development only if they work on a regional, statewide, or multi-state scale. It is also probable that the lack of CEOs with long and deep attachments to the central city, in contrast with the generation that founded many of the organizations, makes the region a more comfortable environment for more transient executives. Regional issues are more common across the country and more transferable to new venues than central city issues, making them more attractive to executives that rotate through several places in the new corporate environment.

A few organizations, such as the Bay Area Council (BAC) and the Central Indiana Corporate Partnership (CICP), have never considered themselves to be anything but regional organizations and they have no "city" agenda. Both organizations work largely with state and federal officials, and only incidentally with local officials, leaving individual city and county issues to the local chambers of commerce. The Bay Area Council holds a monthly meeting of the major chambers, some of which are members of BAC. The Central Indiana Corporate Partnership has even less connection to individual cities or counties. CICP focuses on macroeconomic strategies to address issues confronting Central Indiana and usually does not pursue a "business" agenda, as such. The MetroHartford Alliance chose the region as the only scale at which they could mount an effective strategy for economic competitiveness in an area that contains a proliferation of small local governments.

Only a few peak business organizations continue to define their mission primarily in central city and "downtown" terms. These include Central Atlanta Progress, the Federal City Council (in Washington, DC), and Detroit Renaissance. Each may be involved in some regional activities, but these are generally supportive of their central city mission. The Federal City Council, for example, is strongly focused on improving schools and libraries in the central city and on major urban development projects such as the Anacostia waterfront and a new baseball facility. Detroit Renaissance and Central Atlanta Progress have focused on CBD and major in-town redevelopment projects.

Governing Alliances with Mayors Have Weakened Regionalism is both a cause and effect of weakened alliances between some business-based civic organizations and central city mayors. These informal alliances in cities such as Pittsburgh, Atlanta, Dallas, Cleveland, and Baltimore produced historic achievements in urban development and public policy. They often endured over many years and different mayoral administrations and were based on the recognition that, as one mayor put it, "I could get elected without the business leaders, but I could not govern without them." On the other hand, only city government could provide much of what business leaders needed—whether it was land, zoning, infrastructure, tax changes, or investments in safety, education, and other services. Mayors realized they needed business support to leverage public investments and to provide legitimacy for important policy initiatives and projects. Their support was also critical in extracting help from state and federal governments.

We found no city where such an alliance was once a defining feature of its governance that currently claimed it had been sustained to the present day. In some places, there does remain a good, even warm relationship between mayors and business leaders and their civic organizations. But even in these cities, it appears to depend heavily on the approach of the incumbent mayor toward business leadership. And because, over time, mayors have varied substantially in their ability to relate to CEOs, whether due to their own political agendas and base, or to lack of understanding of what business leaders can do and how to approach them, there has been growing disenchantment with the mayoralty, despite occasionally rekindled romances with specific mayors. Whether they offered and initiatives were rebuffed, ignored, or scorned, mayoral influence on the agenda of a city's major business organization has declined.

In no city was the relationship with the mayor described as a central feature of the organization, although a number of organizations report that they regularly work in alliance with mayors on major projects. Most acknowledge, however, that the relationship can vary widely from incumbent to incumbent and few seem to have strongly institutionalized relationships—even in cities where public-private regimes once characterized their governance. An association executive summarized his long experience that spanned two cities:

> The relationship differs based on the official. There are two categories of officials: those who are for things and those who are against things. I like working with those who are for things. Some make a career of being opposed to bad things, rather than those who work for the good things. I like those who accept an idea and work for it. The mayor of [the executive's current city] is for things and is enjoyable to work with. In [the executive's former city], the mayor was against new ideas. In cities, it's increasingly important to have a good relationship with the mayor [and the] governor, and . . . it's important to have a relationship with Congress to get your share of federal earmarks. Most cities don't know how to do this, but we have a good delegation and [our organization] works well with them. One of the trends of the future will to go after more federal help than ever before.

Another opined that:

> There is an interdependent relationship of the highest order with political leaders. They can't do much without us. The [CEOs] can support or oppose tax issues effectively. There are also many things the [organization] wants—e.g., downtown redevelopment, better state funding of education—that have to have support of political leaders. At times the relationships are difficult. The [organization] will sometimes support things about which it is not enthusiastic to avoid the risk of damage to more important things that are high on its agenda. The quality of the relationship varies with the officeholder. The previous mayor had not been supported by most of the . . . members, but after his election he came to the [organization] and said we needed to work together. A close working relationship was established. He took advice and consulted . . . before undertaking major projects. The current mayor had lots of support from business leaders, but tends to take them for granted. [This mayor] has a very different style and does not have a big circle of advisers. The big change has been that there is no longer an accepted power structure in the city.

These comments were typical of opinions expressed by most other association executives, even those with strong central city and downtown agendas. The change in relationship with mayors appears to be idiosyncratic rather than follow any historical trend. Describing his organization's relationship with four successive mayors, one association executive said it was "poisonous" with one, who feared that asking business for help would be perceived as weakness; "good" with another, "OK" with a third, and "wonderful" with the current incumbent, "who has been able to exist comfortably in both the political and business communities, has brought business into the fold, and [has] taken advantage of services donated to the city."

The reduction in the autonomy of many of a region's CEOs, and in their familiarity with its political system, combined with executive suite turnover and demands on their time produce impediments to swift, bold, and sustained civic action. Dispersion of headquarters across the region, the consolidation of banking, and the loss of dominant home-grown CEOs means that if a city once had a self conscious and cohesive economic "establishment," it probably no longer has one. There simply are fewer "go to" corporate leaders who can mobilize their peers in support of major projects. These conditions induce caution toward taking on "wicked" central city issues, where attempt to ameliorate them can beget new problems that escalate the stakes and widen the conflict. While it may be in their firms' interests to solve such problems, engaging them can be a major drain on time and do little to enhance the career of a branch executive. Buying the naming rights to a sports facility, leading the United Way campaign, or becoming a patron of a museum, university, hospital, or zoo is less hazardous to the reputation of both the firm and its local CEO.

6

Richard Foglesong

WHEN DISNEY COMES TO TOWN

"It was as though they'd put a gun to our head," said the director of tri-county planning. "They were offering to invest $600 million. And there was the glamour of Disney. You could hardly say no to that. We were all just spellbound."

They had come from around the state to hear, finally, what Disney's new East Coast theme park would look like. The new Republican governor and most of his cabinet were there. So was half the legislature. Bankers, developers and a planeload of reporters filled out the audience. Everyone was clamoring to hear Disney's proposal, but the politicians, in particular, were anxious to know what the giant entertainment company would demand of the state legislature.

The project was Walt Disney World; the year was 1967; the place was Winter Park, Fla., outside Orlando, where the pooh-bahs had gathered to hear Disney's plans for a regional theme park. There are significant differences between 1960s Florida and 1990s Virginia, of course—Floridians were relatively untutored in the consequences of urban growth, while Virginians today are not so naive—yet the odd familiarity of the Winter Park scene highlights some of the more striking parallels between Disney's Orlando project and its present-day plans for a park in Haymarket. Then, as now, Disney's proposal was accompanied by hardball lobbying from the company, hoopla from business

From "When Disney Comes to Town," by Richard Foglesong, as appeared in *The Washington Post Magazine*, May 15, 1994. Richard Foglesong is Professor of Politics at Rollins College in Florida. Reprinted by permission of the author.

interests, enthusiastic support from a Republican governor and a struggle over the financing of roads. Then—as now—the Walt Disney Co. proved more powerful than local critics or media skeptics, hiring the right lobbyists and nurturing the right legislators. Then—as now—Disney got what it wanted from the state.

Given these similarities, it's instructive to consider the disparity between the plan that Disney laid out on that heady day in Winter Park and what actually transpired in Central Florida. Simply put, the California company proposed one kind of development, which it used to gain special governmental powers, and then built something else. And yet Floridians, blinded by the pixie dust, hardly noticed. Then—as now?—people were mesmerized by the Disney mystique.

The big news about the Florida project, initially, was its much-vaunted plan for a model city where ordinary people would make their homes and go about their lives in an idealized setting. This was a concept that had been brewing for some time: Two years before the Winter Park presentation, Walt Disney, speaking at a Florida press conference, rhapsodized about building a "City of Tomorrow." In the following months, the City of Tomorrow became an obsession with Walt, according to Disney biographer Bob Thomas. The company already knew how to build an amusement park, Walt insisted; so he focused his attention on what he was soon calling "an experimental prototype community of tomorrow"—or Epcot.

But the company's commitment to Epcot depended on the creative leadership of one man—Walt himself. In the fall of 1966, Orlando banker and power broker Billy Dial flew to California to meet with the 64-year-old Disney. Worried about the showman's health, he asked over lunch: "Mr. Disney, if you walked out of this restaurant and were hit by a truck, what would happen to the Orlando project?" Walt responded: "Absolutely nothing. My brother runs this company, I just piddle around."

Dial was unpersuaded, and with good reason: Three weeks later, he was in New York at the Bankers Trust Co. when he received a hurried phone call from Disney executive Donn Tatum, who said simply, "Walt is dead." It was December 15, 1966, and Walt Disney had died from lung cancer before almost anyone realized he was ill. His death left the company directionless—creatively at least—and Epcot, which had existed mostly in his head, in a state of flux. Roy Disney, the company's financial mastermind and Walt's older brother, was 73 and had already announced his plans to retire.

Roy agreed to stay on and, after polling senior executives, gave the East Coast project his blessing and directed that it be called *Walt* Disney World as a tribute to his brother. Disney execs knew little of Walt's Epcot plans, however, so they focused instead on building a Disneyland-type amusement park; as Disney Vice President Card Walker would later observe, "It was the thing we knew best."

Indeed, Walt's comments on a May 23, 1966, memo suggest that he himself had privately backed away from the model city vision before he died. In the memo, which was found in Walt's desk and is now kept at the Disney Archives in Burbank, Calif., Florida attorney Paul Helliwell sketched out the problem of allowing permanent residents at Epcot. If people lived there, they would vote there, diluting the company's political control of the property. It seems that Walt's thoughts were headed in a similar direction: On the memo, every time Helliwell referred to "permanent residents," Walt crossed it out and substituted "temporary residents/tourists."

Yet the company persisted in hyping Epcot as the centerpiece of Walt Disney World. When, shortly after Walt's death, Roy addressed that SRO crowd in Winter Park, he touted Epcot. The highlight of the press conference was a 25-minute color film, Walt's last screen appearance, in which he described Epcot as the "heart" of the Florida project, a vibrant community where people would "live and work and play." In the film and in the accompanying press release, the company said Epcot would "serve a new population of 20,000."

Following the Winter Park press conference, Roy and Republican Gov. Claude Kirk flew to Jacksonville, where they filmed a joint presentation that was shown along with the Epcot film on statewide television. Floridians thus saw Walt, in a posthumous appearance, describing Epcot as a working community that would always be on the cutting edge of technology and urban design. The film was unequivocal in this depiction; yet, a decade later, a Disney spokesman would state that the model city concept was "only one visual presentation of one way to go." The film was likewise shown to the Florida legislature as it began work on the Disney legislation.

If, after Walt's death, the company was uncommitted to building a true residential community, why did company officials present this as the crux of their proposal? In part it was because the Epcot film was so visually compelling—with Walt alive on screen, offering his futuristic vision of Epcot and appealing for lawmakers' support. But it was also for legal reasons best explained in the Helliwell memo.

In that memo, Helliwell expressed concern about state and local laws that might limit the company's "freedom of action" in developing its 43-square-mile property. He proposed a Disney-controlled government with regulatory powers "superseding to the fullest extent possible under law state and county regulatory authorities." There was just one hitch: Under Florida law, as Helliwell explained, planning and zoning authority could only be exercised by a popularly elected government. To escape external land-use controls, the company had to submit to control by voters. Disney attorneys, however, found a clever way to avoid this fate.

Their proposed legislation called for a two-tier system of government. The top tier, embracing an area twice the size of Manhattan, was the Reedy Creek Improvement District. It would be controlled by the landowner, its board of supervisors elected on the principle of one acre equals one vote. Since Disney owned the land, Disney would elect the board. The bottom tier consisted of two municipalities, Bay Lake and Lake Buena Vista, each having a handful of residents who would be trusted Disney employees living in company housing. Officially, planning and zoning authority was vested in these two municipalities. Their residents would elect a government and then—ingeniously—transfer administrative responsibility for planning and zoning to the Reedy Creek District.

By this legal magic, the company was able to comply with the law and still enjoy regulatory immunity. The charter made it possible for the Reedy Creek government to regulate land use, provide police and fire services, license the manufacture and sale of alcoholic beverages, build roads, lay sewer lines, construct waste-treatment plants, carry out flood projects—even build an airport or nuclear plant, all without local or state approval. The company was creating a sort of Vatican with Mouse ears: a city-state within the larger state of Florida, controlled by the company yet enjoying regulatory powers reserved by law for popularly elected governments.

To acquire such powers, the company had to convince the Florida legislature that Epcot would be a bona fide community. Paul Helliwell, acting as lobbyist, frequently used the term "resident" in describing the company's plans. Disney lobbyists also told lawmakers that Disney would include "public school sites and other public needs in their two cities," according to an April 22, 1967, article in the Orlando Sentinel-Star. And Helliwell told legislators, few of whom had read the thick Reedy Creek charter, that the company was not asking for anything "that had not been done before." At best the statement was half-true: The charter combined the powers available in three kinds of special districts. But Florida had not combined those powers in one district before.

In persuading the legislature to adopt this legislation, the California company ably plied the old-boy system. A good example is a meeting between J. J. Griffin, a former state representative who became a Disney lobbyist, and the powerful president of the Senate, Verle Pope. Griffin had started a long-winded explanation of the weighty Reedy Creek charter when Pope stopped him. "J. J.," he said, "I just have one question. Is this good for Florida?" Griffin answered, "Yes, sir, I believe it is." Whereupon Pope said, "Well, that's good enough for me." (The anecdote is recounted by Griffin in the film "Florida's Disney Decade," produced by Disney.)

With Pope's blessing, the legislation sailed through the Senate, passing unanimously and without debate. In the House there was one dissenting vote, from Miami. Less than an hour after the vote, the State Road Board approved emergency funding for Disney's road requests. And finally, the Florida Supreme Court ruled in 1968 that the Reedy Creek District was legally entitled to issue tax-free municipal bonds. The bonding power would "greatly aid Disney interests" but would nevertheless benefit the "numerous inhabitants of the district," the court ruled.

What about those "numerous inhabitants" today? How fares the city where 20,000 would "live and work and play"? Sure enough, in 1982, 11 years after the turnstiles began spinning at Disney World, the company opened something called Epcot. Yet today, there are more hotels than homes on Disney property. Between the two cities of Bay Lake and Lake Buena Vista, there are 43 residents living in 17 mobile homes—all nonunion Disney supervisors and their families, who safeguard the company's political control of its property.

Disney is also designing a huge mixed-use development called "Celebration," billed as a further realization of Walt's urban vision. While some permanent housing is scheduled for Celebration, it will be de-annexed from the Reedy Creek District—making it impossible for homeowners to vote in Disney elections. Celebration will also have time-share units, whose temporary occupants will not have voting rights. The model city described by Walt, promoted by Roy and dangled before Florida lawmakers by Disney lobbyists has never come about; the promises of 1967 are the stuff of history.

7

Paul Kantor and H. V. Savitch

CAN POLITICIANS BARGAIN WITH BUSINESS?

In the summer of 1989, United Air Lines announced it was planning a new maintenance hub that would bring nearly a billion dollars in investment and generate over 7,000 jobs for the region lucky enough to attract it. Within a few short months, officials in over

90 localities were competing for the bonanza and were tripping over one another in an effort to lure United. Denver offered $115 million in incentives and cash, Oklahoma City sought to raise $120 million, and localities in Virginia offered a similar amount. The competition for United was so keen that cities began to bid against one another and asked that their bids be kept secret.

United was so delighted at the level of bidding that it repeatedly delayed its decision in anticipation the offers would get even better. Nearly two years later, city officials in nine finalists were enhancing their incentives, courting United executives, and holding their breaths. Reflecting on the competition, Louisville Mayor Jerry Abramson quipped, "We haven't begun to offer up our firstborn yet, but we're getting close. Right now we are into siblings."[1]

Except for the extremity of the case, there is nothing new about cities questing for private capital. Cities compete with one another for tourism, foreign trade, baseball franchises, and federal grants. Yet, there is another side to this behavior. Although 93 cities competed for the United hub, many others did not, and some cities would have resisted the corporate intrusion (Etzkowitz and Mack 1976; Savitch 1988). When United stalled and raised the ante, Kentucky's governor angrily withdrew, complaining that he would "not continue this auction, this bidding war. There is a point at which you draw the line" ("Governor turns down UAL," *Courier-Journal*, 18 October 1991). In Denver, the legislature's majority leader protested, saying, "United has a ring and is pulling Colorado by the nose." With those remarks and heightening resentment, public opinion began to pull the state away from the lure of United ("UAL bidding goes on," *Courier-Journal*, 22 October 1991).

Such cases do not seem uncommon. Although many cities are willing to build sports stadia, others have turned down the opportunity. For instance, when Fort Wayne, Indiana, declined to go beyond its offer of a short-term low-interest loan to obtain a minor-league baseball team, the franchise was taken elsewhere (Rosentraub and Swindell 1990). Although officials in some cities trip over one another in efforts to attract business by lowering taxes, officials in others raise them. Over the last three years, Los Angeles, New York, and Denver have increased business taxes. Notwithstanding high taxes and locational costs, business continues to seek out such cities as San Francisco, Tokyo, London, Toronto, and Frankfurt.

Nevertheless, the literature on urban politics has not systematically examined such "nondecisional" cases (Bachrach and Baratz 1962) to probe the precise circumstances under which local governments can influence the capital investment process. . . .

. . . We propose that questions of how, when, and why local government can influence economic development are best answered by treating political control as something that springs from bargaining advantages that the state has in political and economic exchange relationships with business. Variations in local-government influence are strongly tied to the ways in which the larger political economy distributes particular bargaining resources between the public and private sectors.

From Paul Kantor and H. V. Savitch, "Can Politicians Bargain with Business? A Theoretical and Comparative Perspective on Urban Development," *Urban Affairs Quarterly*, Vol. 29, No. 2, pp. 230–255. Copyright © 1993 by SAGE Publications, Inc. Journals. Reproduced with permission of SAGE Publications, Inc. Journals in the format Textbook via Copyright Clearance Center.

Following Lindblom (1977), we find that it is useful to regard this context as a liberal-democratic system in which there is a division of labor between business and government (Kantor 1988; Elkin 1987). The private sector is responsible for the production of wealth in a market system in which choices over production and exchange are determined by price mechanisms. For its part, the public sector is organized along polyarchal lines (Dahl 1971; Dahl and Lindblom 1965) in which public decisions are subject to popular control. Public officials may be viewed as primarily responsible for the management of political support for governmental undertakings; business leaders can be considered essentially managers of market enterprises.

This perspective suggests that even though public and private control systems are theoretically separate, in reality they are highly interdependent. So far as government is concerned, the private sector produces economic resources that are necessary for the well-being of the political community—including jobs, revenues for public programs, and political support that is likely to flow to public authorities from popular satisfaction with economic prosperity and security. For business, the public sector is important because it provides forms of intervention into the market that are necessary for the promotion of economic enterprise but that the private sector cannot provide on its own. Such interventions include inducements that enable private investors to take risks (tax abatements and tax credits), the resolution of private conflicts that threaten social or economic stability (courts, mediation services), and the creation of an infrastructure or other forms of support (highways, workforce training).

Conceptualized in this manner, business and government must engage in exchange relationships (bargaining) to realize common goals. This is done by using bargaining advantages that derive from three dimensions or spheres of interdependence: market conditions, popular-control systems, and public-intervention mechanisms. . . .

Our analysis suggests that there is substantial variation among local governments in their ability to bargain. We also suggest that bargaining advantages tend to be cumulative—that is, the more advantages a city holds, the greater its ability to bargain. Finally, we suggest that because bargaining is a product of political and economic circumstance, so is urban development. Although it may not be possible for a city to manipulate all the variables affecting its bargaining position, most cities can manipulate some and thereby shape its own future. . . .

Markets and Public Control of Urban Development

There is little doubt that a businesses' greatest bargaining resource in urban development is its control over private wealth in the capital investment process. It is this dimension of business-government relations that Peterson's (1981) market-centered model of local politics describes. The logic of this model is that cities compete for capital investment by seeking to attract mobile capital to the community; failure to meet the conditions demanded by business for investment leads to the "automatic punishing recoil" (Lindblom 1982) of the marketplace as business disinvests. This notion has been variously interpreted to suggest that business inherently holds a dominant position (Fainstein et al. 1986; Mollenkopf 1983; Logan and Molotch 1987; Jones and Bachelor 1986; Kantor 1988).

Although the market-centered model is a powerful tool for analyzing development politics, it does not fully capture the bargaining relationships that logically derive from it. Specifically, the market perspective tends to highlight only those advantages that accrue to business. Yet, the marketplace works in two directions, not one. If we look at specific market conditions and bargaining demands, it becomes apparent that government also can use the market to obtain leverage over business. Thus we will present a number of common market-centered arguments and show their other side.

The Cities-Lose-If-Business-Wins Argument

In the market model, public and private actors represent institutions that compete to achieve rival goals. Business pursues public objectives only insofar as they serve private needs; if important business needs are not met, local government experiences the discipline of the marketplace as capital and labor seek alternative locations.

Yet, in this description of market dynamics, cases in which local government and business may also share the same goals (as distinct from the same interests) are ignored; in such instances the market model no longer indicates business advantage in the development process. Thus a local government may have an interest in raising public revenue by increasing retail sales while shopkeepers and investors have an interest in maximizing profits. Though their interests are different, they may share the common goal of bringing about higher sales through expanded development. When this happens, bargaining between government and business shifts from rivalry over competing goals to settling differences over how to facilitate what already has been agreed on. This kind of scenario enhances the value of bargaining resources that are mostly owned by the public sector. Development politics focuses on such things as the ability to amass land, grant legal privileges and rights, control zoning, provide appropriate infrastructure, and—not least—enlist public support. Because alternative means of promoting growth are important choices (Logan and Swanstrom 1990), substantial bargaining leverage over development outcomes is placed in the hands of those who manage the governmental process, a point that Mollenkopf (1983) underscored in his study of urban renewal politics.

Yet, this partial escape from the market often is not recognized. Peterson (1981) considered the sharing of interests and goals to be one and the same. Other scholars have often assumed that there is an inherent conflict between private and public goals (Stone and Sanders 1987; Logan and Swanstrom 1990; Swanstrom 1986). However, a strong case can be made that business and government often share common goals. Although they cannot logically share interests, public officials, motivated by different stakes, frequently choose to pursue economic objectives that are also favored by business (Cummings 1988). Although some critics reject progrowth values, these values tend to be supported broadly by local electorates (Logan and Molotch 1987, 50–98; Vaughn 1979; Crenson 1971).

To take a different tack on former head of General Motors Charles Wilson's aphorism, scholars may be too anxious to suggest that if it is good for General Motors, it must be bad for Detroit. Yet, local officials and their publics do not always share this logic. When government and business perceive common goals, such perceptions can have a powerful effect on opportunities for political control over the urban economy. Under these conditions, the ability of political authorities to create political support for specific programs and their willingness to use public authority to assist business can become important bargaining resources for achieving their own interests. At the very least, the extent to which agreement between business and local government is a byproduct of political choice rather than of economic constraint should be a premise for empirical investigation instead of an a priori conclusion.

The Capital Mobility Argument

This argument encompasses an assumption that bargaining advantages accrue to business as it becomes more mobile. Historically, private capital was more dependent on the local state than it is today (Kantor 1988). Technological advances in production, communications, and transportation have enhanced the ability of business to move more easily and rapidly. Changes in the organization of capital, especially the rise of multilocational corporations, have increased business mobility and made urban locations interchangeable. Automation, robotics, and the postindustrial revolution are supposed to enhance capital mobility. Fixed capital has been nudged aside by a new postindustrial technology of flexible capital (Hill 1989; Parkinson, Foley, and Judd 1989).

It would seem to follow that increasing capital mobility must favor business interests. Yet, this conclusion does not always follow, if one considers specific cities and businesses that are caught up in this process of economic globalization. Capital is, in fact, not always very portable. Although cities are frequently viewed as interchangeable by some corporations, many cities retain inherent advantages of location (e.g., Brussels), of agglomeration (e.g., New York), of technological prowess (e.g., Grenoble), or of political access (e.g., Washington, D.C.). The dispersion of capital has triggered a countermovement to create centers that specialize in the communication, coordination, and support of far-flung corporate units. Larger global cities have captured these roles. Much of postindustrial capital has put enormous sunk costs into major cities. One of the more conspicuous examples is the Canadian development firm of Olympia and York, which has invested billions of dollars in New York, London, Ontario, and a host of other cities. As Olympia and York teeters on the edge of collapse, banks, realty interests, and mortgage brokers are also threatened. It is not easy for any of these interests to pull up stakes.

There has been a fairly stable tendency for corporate headquarters operations, together with the ancillary services on which headquarters depend, to gravitate to large cities that have acquired the status of world business centers (Sassen 1988; Noyelle and Stanback 1984). New York's downtown and midtown, London's financial district and its docklands, Paris's La Defense, and Tokyo's Shinjuku are some outstanding examples of postindustrialism that [have] generated billions in fixed investments. Movement by individual enterprises away from such established corporate business centers is unlikely for various reasons, including that this kind of change imposes costs on those owning fixed assets in these locations and disrupts established business networks.

Cities that have experienced ascendant market positions have not been reluctant to cash in on this. When property values and development pressures rose in downtowns, local politicians used the advantage to impose new planning requirements and demand development fees. In San Francisco, a moratorium on high-rise construction regulates the amount and pace of investment (Muzzio and Bailey 1986). In Boston and several other large cities, linkage policies have exacted fees on office development to support moderate-income housing (Dreier 1989). In Paris, differential taxes have been placed on high-rise development and the proceeds used to support city services (Savitch 1988). One should also recognize that market conditions are not immutable.

Local governments may be subject to the blandishments of business at an early stage of development, when there is great eagerness for development and capital has wide investment choices. However, once business has made the investment, it may be bound for the long term. Thus bargaining does not stop after the first deal is struck, and the advantages may shift.

This occurred in Orlando, Florida, where Disney World exacted early concessions from the local governments, only to be faced with new sets of public demands afterward (Foglesong 1989). Prior to building what is now a vast entertainment complex near Orlando, Disney planners capitalized on their impending investment and won huge concessions from government (including political autonomy, tax advantages, and free infrastructure). However, as Disney transformed the region into a sprawling tourist center, local government demanded that the corporation relinquish autonomy and pressured it to pay for physical improvements. Disney struggled to defeat these demands but eventually conceded. With huge sunk investments, Disney executives had little choice but to accommodate the public sector.

So although some industries have grown more mobile, others have not. The issue turns on the relative costs incurred by business and by government when facilities, jobs, and people are moved. How relative costs are assessed and the likelihood that businesses will absorb them influence the respective bargaining postures of business and government.

The City-Cannot-Choose Argument

In the market model, business makes investment choices among stationary cities; because cities cannot move, powerful bargaining advantages accrue to business in the urban development process and supposedly this enables them to exact what they want from local governments. Although this is sometimes the case, it is also true that local communities may have investment choices as well. Some local governments can make choices among alternative types of business investment. In particular, economic diversification enables local political authorities to market the community in a particular economic sector (e.g., as a tourist city, as a research or technical center, or as a sound place in which to retire). Furthur, economic diversification enhances a locality's ability to withstand economic pressure from any particular segment of the business community. This has occurred in cities as far ranging as Seattle, Singapore, and Rome, enabling them to maintain powerful market positions for years, despite profound changes in the world and national economies.

Experience teaches city officials to sense their vulnerabilities and develop defenses against dominance by a single industry. Through diversification, these cities can gain a good deal of strength, not only in weathering economic fluctuations but in dealing with prospective investors. Houston's experience after oil prices crashed moved city leaders to develop high-technology and service industries (Feagin 1988). Pittsburgh's successful effort to clean its air gave that city a new economic complexion. Louisville's deindustrial crisis was followed by a succession of new investments in health services, a revival in the transportation industry, and a booming business in the arts (Vogel 1990).

Diversification, which was so instrumental in strengthening the public hand, was actually made possible by government coalitions with business.

The advantages of diversification are most apparent when these cities are compared to localities that are prisoners of relatively monopolistic bargaining relations with business. Officials in single-industry towns are strongly inclined to accommodate business demands on matters of development because they lack alternative sources of capital investment. Crenson (1971) found this pattern in Gary, Indiana, where local officials resisted proposals for pollution control because they feared that U.S. Steel would lay off workers. Similarly, Jones and Bachelor (1986) described how Detroit leaders weakened their market position when they sought to preserve the city's positions as a site for automobile manufacturing. When worldwide changes in the auto industry eroded Detroit's traditional competitive advantages, political leaders fought to subsidize new plants and to demolish an otherwise viable residential neighborhood.

Neither Gary's steel-centered strategy nor Detroit's auto-centered strategy has stemmed their economic decline. The lesson for urban politicians is clear: Instead of vainly hanging on to old industry, go for new, preferably clean business. More than most politicians, big-city mayors have learned well and are fast becoming major economic promoters (Savitch and Thomas 1991).

The City-Maximizes-Growth Argument

Although the market model is built on the supposition that it is in the interest of cities to promote economic growth, not all localities seek to compete in capital markets. To the extent that communities ignore participation in this market, they do not have to bargain with business over demands that they might choose to bring to the bargaining table. Santa Barbara, Vancouver, and Stockholm are cities that have consisted growth and instituted extensive land-use controls. These cities are in enviable positions as they deal with business and developers.

Aside from major cities, there are smaller communities that do not seek to compete for capital investment such as suburban areas and middle-size cities that after years of expansion, now face environmental degradation. Even if these localities have a stake in maintaining competitive advantages as bedroom communities or steady-state mixed commercial/residential locales, their bargaining relationship with business is more independent than in relatively growth-hungry urban communities (Danielson 1976). University towns, in which a self-sustaining and alert population values its traditions, have managed to resist the intrusions of unwanted industry. Coastal cities, which seek to preserve open space, have successfully acquired land or used zoning to curtail development.

Moreover, there are cities in which governmental structures reduce financial pressure and are able to resist indiscriminate development. Regionalism and annexation have enabled cities to widen their tax nets, so that business cannot easily play one municipality off against another. Minneapolis-St. Paul, Miami-Dade, and metro Toronto furnish examples of localities banding together to strengthen their fiscal positions and turn down unwanted growth. In Western European and other non-American nations, cities are heavily financed by central government, thereby reducing and sometimes eliminating the pressure to attract development. For these cities, growth only engenders liabilities.

Popular-Control Systems and Urban Development

Democratic political institutions not only provide means of disciplining public officials, but they constrain all political actors who seek governmental cooperation or public legitimation in the pursuit of their interests. The reality of this is suggested by the fact that business development projects frequently get stopped when they lack a compelling public rationale and generate significant community opposition. This has occurred under varying conditions and in different types of cities. In Paris, neighborhood mobilization successfully averted developers (Body-Gendrot 1987); in London, communities were able to totally redo urban renewal plans (Christensen 1979); in Amsterdam and Berlin, local squatters defied property owners by taking over abandoned buildings; after the recent earthquake in San Francisco, public opinion prevailed against the business community in preventing the reconstruction of a major highway. The existence of open, competitive systems of elections and other polyarchal institutions affords a means by which nonbusiness interests are able to influence, however imperfectly, an urban development process in which business power otherwise looms large.

But do institutions of popular control afford political authorities with a valuable bargaining resource in dealing with business? Are democratic institutions loose cannons that are irrelevant to political bargaining over economic development? From our bargaining perspective, it would appear that these institutions can provide a resource upon which political leaders can draw to impose their own policy preferences when the three conditions described in the following paragraphs are satisfied.

First, public approval of bargaining outcomes between government and business must be connected to the capital-investment process. This is often not the case because most private-sector investment decisions are virtually outside the influence of local government. Even when the characteristics of private projects require substantial public-sector cooperation, many decisions are only indirectly dependent on processes of political approval. Economic-development decisions have increasingly become insulated from the mainstream political processes of city governments as a result of the proliferation of public-benefit corporations (Walsh 1978; Kantor 1993). As power to finance and regulate business development has been ceded to public-benefit corporations, the ability of elected political leaders to build popular coalitions around development issues has shrunk because it makes little sense to appeal to voters on matters that they cannot influence.

On the other hand, the importance of this bargaining resource increases as issues spill over their ordinary institutional boundaries and into public or neighborhood arenas. When this occurs, elected political authorities gain bargaining advantages by putting together coalitions that can play a vital role in the urban development game. Consequently, even the most powerful public and private developers can be checked by politicians representing hostile voter coalitions.

In New York, Robert Mose's slide from power was made possible by mounting public discontent with his later projects and by the intervention of a popular governor who capitalized on this to undercut Moses's position (Caro 1974); Donald Trump's plans for the Upper West Side of Manhattan incurred defeats by a coalition of irate residents, local legislators, and a hostile mayor (Savitch 1988); a major highway (Westway) proposal, sponsored by developers, bankers, and other business interests, was defeated by community activists who skillfully used the courts to question the project's environmental impact.

Second, public authorities must have the managerial capability to organize and deliver political support for programs sought by business. Credible bargaining requires organizing a stable constituency whose consent can be offered to business in a quid pro quo process. However, political authorities clearly differ enormously in their capacity to draw on this resource. In the United States, the decline of machine politics, the weakening of party loyalties and organizations, and the dispersal of political power to interest groups have weakened the capacity of elected political authorities. To some extent, this has been counterbalanced by grassroots and other populist-style movements that have provided a broad base for mayors and other political leaders (Swanstrom 1986; Dreier and Keating 1990; Savitch and Thomas 1991; Capek and Gilderbloom 1992).

In contrast, in Western European cities, the stability and cohesion displayed by urban party systems more frequently strengthen political control of development. In Paris, extensive political control over major development projects is related to stable and well-organized political support enjoyed by officials who dominated the central and local governments (Savitch 1988). In London, ideological divisions between Conservative and Labour parties at the local and national levels limit the ability of business interests to win a powerful role, even in cases involving massive redevelopment such as Covent Garden, the construction of motorways, and the docklands renewal adjacent to the financial city. For example, changes in planning the docklands project were tied to shifts in party control at both the national and local levels. Given the political significance of development issues to both major British parties, it was difficult for nonparty interests to offer inducements that were capable of splitting politicians away from their partisan agendas (Savitch 1988).

Similarly, even highly fragmented but highly ideological political party systems seem capable of providing a powerful bargaining resource to elected governmental authorities. In Italy, many small parties compete for power at the national and local levels. Although this is sometimes a source of political instability, the relatively stable ideological character of party loyalties means that elected politicians are assured of constituency support. Consequently, this base of political power offers substantial bargaining advantages in dealing with business. According to Molotch and Vicari (1988), this enables elected political authorities to undertake major projects relatively free from business pressure. In Milan, officials planned and built a subway line through the downtown commercial district of the city with minimal involvement of local business.

Third, popular-control mechanisms are a valuable bargaining resource when they bind elected leaders to programmatic objectives. If political authorities are not easily disciplined for failure to promote programmatic objectives in development bargaining, business may promote their claims by providing selective incentives (side payments), such as jobs, campaign donations, and other petty favors, to public officials in exchange for their cooperation. When this happens, the bargaining position of city governments is undermined by splitting off public officials from their representational roles—and the process of popular control becomes more of a business resource.

In America, where partisan attachments are weak and where ethnic, neighborhood, and other particularistic loyalties are strong, political leaders are inclined to put a high value on seeking selective benefits to the neglect of programmatic objectives. Although populist mayors have sometimes succeeded in overcoming these obstacles (Swanstrom 1986; Dreier and Keating 1990), the need to maintain unstable political coalitions that are easily undermined by racial and ethnic rivalries limits programmatic political competition. For example, in Detroit and Atlanta, black mayors have relied heavily on economic development to generate side payments that are used to minimize political opposition; this is facilitated by the symbolic importance that these black mayors enjoy among the heavily black electorates in the two cities. Consequently, they have been able to hold on to power without challenging many business demands (Stone 1989; Hill 1986). In contrast, in Western Europe, where political party systems more frequently discipline public officials to compete on programmatic grounds, bargaining with business is less likely to focus on side payments. As suggested earlier, in France, Italy, and Britain, votes are more often secured by partisan and ideological loyalties and reinforced by progammatic competition than by generating selective incentives for followers.

In sum, city governments vary enormously in their capacity to draw on the popular-control process in bargaining over development. The proximity of electoral competition to development, the capability of officials to organize voter support, and the extent of competition over programmatic objectives are crucial factors that weaken or enhance the resources of city governments.

State Intervention
and Urban Development

. . . Ironically, integrated national governmental systems appear to enhance local governmental control of urban development, and political structures that decentralize the regulation of market failures afford less local governmental influence. Political systems that accord a powerful urban regulatory role for the national government limit local political authority in urban planning, of course. Yet, these more centralized systems can often work to enhance local governmental bargaining power with the private sector; they do this by making it easier for governments to contain capital movement (overriding private decision making), as well as by permitting localities to draw on the resources, regulatory apparatus, and political support of higher levels of government.

Contrasts between American and some Western European cities illustrate the different bargaining implications of each system. The United States is unique in the degree to which urban public capital investment is highly decentralized. Although the national government provides grants to support highway and other capital projects, this aid is spotty and unconnected to any system of national urban planning. Most important, responsibility for financing most local infrastructure is highly decentralized. Consequently, local and state governments have little choice but to find an administrative means of extracting revenues from the private sector that gives priority to satisfying investor confidence. To market long-term debt, public corporations must contend with investor fears that borrowed funds might be diverted to satisfy political pressures, rather than used for debt repayment. Consequently, major urban infrastructure development is in the hands of public corporations that are only indirectly accountable to urban electorates. These corporations are well known for courting private investors and treating them as constituents rather than as bargaining rivals (Caro 1974; Walsh 1978).

The European experience is quite different. There, most capital expenditures are supported by the central government. In France, upwards of 75% of local budgets are financed by central government; in Holland, the figure is 92%. This relieves some of the pressure on local authorities to compete with one another for capital investment to finance basic services. Local governments in Europe are capable of dealing with business from a position of greater strength. Beyond this, national government is not as dependent on private capital as local government is and can turn to vast financial and regulatory powers to reinforce public bargaining on the part of national and local governmental authorities.

The case of La Defense, just outside of Paris, is instructive of how state-business relations have been managed in Western Europe. During the 1960s, the national government planned to build another central business district for Paris on the vacant fields of La Defense. Despite skepticism by private investors, funds were allocated by the national government. Just as the project was launched, it was confronted by a fiscal crisis. French business looked on as La Defense reeled from one difficulty to another, and the enterprise was mocked as a "white elephant." The national government responded quickly, infusing the project with funds from the treasury, from nationalized banks, and from pensions. To buttress these efforts, the government clamped down on new office construction within Paris and used other carrots and sticks to persuade corporations that La Defense was the wave of the future. The effort worked, and La Defense became a premier site as an international business headquarters.

La Defense was not built in unique circumstances. To the contrary, it demonstrates the cumulative effect of centralized policy intervention on urban development. It is not unusual for governments throughout Western Europe to pour infrastructure into a particular development area, to freeze the price of surrounding land to prevent speculation, to construct buildings in the same area by relying on public corporations, and to design all the structures in the development site. The last public act is usually to invite private investors to compete for the privilege of obtaining space. Only then does bargaining begin. . . .

Comparison of . . . two antipodal cities [—Amsterdam and Detroit—] permits us to illustrate the cumulative consequences of differences in bargaining resources for political control of business development. To begin with market conditions, Amsterdam has a highly favorable market position because it is at the center of Holland's economic engine—a horseshoe shaped region called the Randstad. The cities of the Randstad (Amsterdam, Utrecht, Rotterdam, and the Hague) form a powerful and diversified conurbation that drives Holland's economy, its politics, and its sociocultural life. Amsterdam itself is the nation's political and financial capital. It also holds light industry, is a tourist and historic center, and is one of northern Europe's transportation hubs. Although Amsterdam has gone through significant deindustrialization (Jobse and Needham 1987) and has lost 21% of its population since 1960, it has transformed its economy to residential and postindustrial uses and is attractively positioned as one of the keystones of a united Europe.

Detroit's market conditions are dramatically less favorable. It is situated in what was once America's industrial heartland and what is now balefully called the Rustbelt. Known as America's Motor City, its economy revolved around automobile manufacture. Deindustrialization and foreign competition have taken a devastating toll. In just three decades, Detroit lost more than half its manufacturing jobs and 38% of its population (Darden et al. 1987). Nearly half the population lives below the poverty line, and one quarter is unemployed (Nethercutt 1987). Detroit has tried to come back to its former prominence by rebuilding its downtown and diversifying its economy for tourism and banking. But those efforts have not changed the city's market posture. Jobs and the middle class continue to move to surrounding suburbs, and any possible conversion of the Rustbelt economy appears slim when viewed against more attractive opportunities elsewhere.

The differences in popular control of these two cities are equally stark. Amsterdam is governed by a 45-member council that is elected by proportional representation (the council also elects a smaller body of aldermen) and is well organized and easily disciplined by the voters. Political parties have cohesive programs geared to conservative, social democratic, centrist, and leftwing orientations. Political accountability is reinforced by a system of elected district councils that represent different neighborhoods of the city. These councils participate in a host of decentralized services including land use, housing, and development.

In contrast, Detroit's government is poorly organized in respect to promoting popular control of economic development. A nine-member city council is elected at large and in nonpartisan balloting. Detroit's mayor [in 1993], Coleman Young, has held power for 16 years and has based his administration on distributing selective benefits, especially city jobs and contracts, while focusing on downtown project development (Hill 1986; Rich 1991). The system affords scant opportunity for neighborhood expression, and the city's singular ethnic composition (Detroit is 75% black) is coupled to a politics of black symbolism that impedes programmatic accountability and pluralist opposition. Indeed, one scholar has described Detroit as ruled by a tight-knit elite (Ewen 1978); two other researchers believed that the city's power was exercised at the peaks of major sectors within the city (Jones and Bachelor 1986).

The two cities also differ dramatically in respect to modes of policy intervention. Like many European cities, Amsterdam is governed within an integrated national planning scheme. The Dutch rely on three-tier government, at the national, regional, and municipal levels. Goals are set at the uppermost levels, master plans are developed at the regional level, and allocation plans are implemented at the grass roots. A municipalities fund allocates financial support based on population, and over 90% of Amsterdam's budget is carried by the national treasury.

By contrast, Detroit stands very much alone. While "golden corridors" (drawn from Detroit's former wealth) have sprung up in affluent outskirts, the suburbs now resist the central city. Attempts at creating metropolitan mechanisms to share tax bases or to undertake planning have failed (Darden et al. 1987). Over the years, federal aid has shrunk and now accounts for less than 6% of the city's budget (Savitch and Thomas 1991). State aid has compensated for some of Detroit's shortfalls, but like most states, Michigan is at a loss to do anything about the internecine struggles for jobs and investment.

Given the cumulative differences along all three dimensions, the bargaining outcomes for each city are dramatically opposite. Under the planning and support of national and regional authorities, Amsterdam has managed its deindustrialization—first by moving heavy industry to specific subregions (called *concentrated deconcentration*) and later by locating housing and light commerce in abandoned wharves and depleted neighborhoods. The Dutch have accomplished this through a combination of infrastructure investment, direct subsidies, and the power to finance and build housing (Levine and Van Weesop 1988; Van Weesop and Wiegersma 1991). Amsterdam's capacity to construct housing is a particularly potent policy instrument and constitutes a countervailing alternative to private development. Between 50% and 80% of housing in Amsterdam is subsidized or publicly built. This puts a considerable squeeze on private developers, who face limitations and availability as well as zoning, density, and architectural controls. As a condition of development, it is not uncommon for commercial investors to agree to devote a portion of their projects toward residential use (Van Weesop and Wiegersma 1991).

Indeed, the bargaining game in Holland is titled toward the public sector in ways that seem unimaginable in the United States. Freestyle commercial development in Amsterdam has been restricted, so that most neighborhoods remain residential. Because of massive housing subsidies, neighborhoods have lacked the extremes of wealth or poverty. Even squatting has been declared legal. Abandoned buildings have been taken over by groups of young, marginal, and working-class populations—thus leading to lower-class gentrification (Mamadouh 1990).

All this compares very differently to the thrust of development outcomes in Detroit. The case of Poletown provides a stark profile of Detroit's response to bargaining with the private sector (Fasenfest 1986). When General Motors announced that it was looking for a new plant site, the city invoked the state's "quick take" law, allowing municipalities to acquire property before actually reaching agreement with individual owners. To attract the plant and an anticipated 6,000 jobs, the city moved more than 3,000 residents and 143 institutions (hospitals, churches, schools, and businesses) and demolished more than 1,000 buildings. To strike this bargain, Detroit committed to at least $200 million in direct expenditures and a dozen years of tax abatements. In the end, the bargaining exchange resulted in one lost neighborhood and a gain of an automobile plant—all under what one judge labeled as the "guiding and sustaining, indeed controlling hand of the General Motors Corporation" (Jones and Bachelor 1986).

In many respects, Poletown reflects a larger pattern of bargaining. The city is now trying to expand its airport. At stake are 3,600 homes, more than 12,000 residents, and scores of businesses. The city and a local bank also have their sights set on a venerable auditorium called Ford Hall. The arrangement calls for razing Ford Hall and granting the developers an $18 million no-interest loan, payable in 28 years. When citizen protests stalled the project, developers threatened to move elsewhere. Since then, Detroit's city council approved the project (Rich 1991).

The polar cases of Amsterdam and Detroit reveal something about the vastly different development prizes and sacrifices that particular cities experience as a result of their accumulated bargaining advantages. Amsterdam is able to use public investment to extract concessions from investors and enforce development standards in a process conducted under public scrutiny. Detroit offers land, money, and tax relief to attract development in a process managed by a tight circle of political and economic elites.

Political Control of Urban Development

By examining urban development from a state-bargaining perspective, we are able to identify some critical forces that influence local governmental control over this area of policy. From this vantage point, public influence over urban development appears to be tied to differences in market conditions, popular control mechanisms, and public policy systems because these interdependent spheres powerfully affect the ability of politicians to bargain with business. . . .

By using our bargaining perspective, future researchers may be able to overcome the limitations of extant theory and better understand the actual political choices of local communities in economic development.

CHAPTER 3

DEVELOPMENT POLITICS
AND URBAN CULTURE

CULTURAL STRATEGIES OF URBAN DEVELOPMENT

Tourism/entertainment, culture, and urban amenities have been extremely important for the revitalization of downtowns and urban economies. Old cities have an advantage in developing these sectors. Jobs are connected to amenities; the affluent residents who live downtown want to commute less but also prefer to live in an environment with exciting street life, nightlife, culture, and entertainment. With their historic architecture, public monuments, redeveloped waterfronts, and older neighborhoods, cities are uniquely positioned to provide an exciting urban culture. Partly for this reason, for the first time in a half century, cities seem to be indispensable to their metropolitan regions.

A leading urban scholar, Richard Florida, has identified the rise of "the creative class" to explain the recent emphasis on tourism, culture, and entertainment. In Selection 8, Florida argues that the creative class, which is composed of highly educated professionals with rarified intellectual, analytic, artistic, and creative skills, frequently regard lifestyle as more important than a particular job in choosing a place to live. The members of this class demand social interaction, culture, nightlife, diversity, and authenticity, which have become identified with historic architecture, renovated buildings, old neighborhoods, special features such as trendy bars and music, and a certain measure of urban grit. Florida indicates that the creative class tends to reject the "canned experiences" associated with tourist enclaves. Instead, the creative class has become the basis for a political movement that demands a high level of urban amenities, both public and private, in the downtowns and neighborhoods they frequent. The result is a revival of the downtown and of inner-city neighborhoods after decades of decline.

In Selection 9, Elizabeth Strom points out that as the traditional economic base of cities has weakened, culture and the arts have become increasingly important for urban revitalization. Whatever other problems they may face, older cities hold a distinct advantage over suburbs in building a new economy based on culture and arts because of the presence of renovated waterfronts, historic districts, museums, concert halls, opera galleries, and "high culture" assets. Strom describes how a close collaboration between the private and public sectors has emerged to enhance the presence of culture downtown. Promoters of culture and arts seek public funding for their efforts. At the other end of the bargain, city officials perceive cultural and art institutions as industries that can help drive urban revitalization. Strom believes that this close collaboration raises questions: Does the commercialization of culture exclude artistic endeavors that do not draw big crowds or long lines? Does it bias public support for the arts in favor of events that have quick audience potential, but diminish sustained support for museums and concert halls after they are built? Ultimately, is the quality of life in cities improved or degraded by the new culture-development alliance?

In Selection 10, Kevin Fox Gotham describes the campaigns to brand New Orleans as an entertainment destination from the 1990s to the present, and to re-brand in the aftermath of the havoc caused by Hurricane Katrina. He points out that cities everywhere have attempted to project a distinctive image designed to attract visitors and investment. What is often overlooked is that branding is a political project that benefits some interests more than others; typically, for example, historic downtowns and cultural attractions are promoted while neighborhoods are ignored. For decades, New Orleans was branded as the birthplace and home of Mardi Gras, jazz music, and a distinctive culture and cuisine. This long-nurtured image was put in mortal danger by the disaster wrought by Hurricane Katrina. Gotham's account reveals that the efforts to recover the city's image has had political consequences. Branded and standardized entertainment venues have been favored because these can be sharply separated from neighborhoods devastated by the flood. Though the entertainment venues are branded as the "authentic" New Orleans, it is easy for visitors to spend time in the city without seeing any evidence of problems that continue to plague most New Orleans neighborhoods; truly, "the French Quarter's a world to itself." Ironically, "disaster tourism" also has been promoted as an alternative; visitors are provided standardized, carefully managed tours of flooded neighborhoods. The policies employed to nurture New Orleans' revival revolve around subsidies designed to favor investors who are willing to bring in capital for hotels and other tourist venues.

The New Orleans experience is important for what it reveals about "quality of life" and tourism politics in many cities. The revitalization of cities has been beneficial, but not for everyone equally. For tourism promoters, poor people, the homeless, and in New Orleans' case, the displaced, are unpleasant realities that visitors usually are not invited to see.

8

Richard Florida

THE POWER OF PLACE
The Creative Class

As I walked across the campus of Carnegie Mellon University on a delightful spring day, I came upon a table filled with young people chatting and enjoying the spectacular weather. Several had on identical blue t-shirts with "Trilogy@CMU" written across them—Trilogy being an Austin-based software company that often recruited our top students. I walked over to the table. "Are you guys here to recruit?" I asked. "No, absolutely not," they answered, seeming taken aback by the very question. "We're not recruiters. We're just hangin' out, playing a little Frisbee with our friends." How interesting, I thought. They've come to campus on a workday, all the way from Austin to Pittsburgh, just to hang out with some new friends.

I noticed one member of the group sitting slouched over on the grass, dressed in a tank top. This young man had spiked multicolored hair, full-body tattoos and multiple piercings in his ears—an obvious slacker. "So what's your story?" I asked. "Hey man, I just signed on with these guys." As I would later learn, he was a gifted student who had just inked the highest-paying deal of any graduating student in the history of his department, right at that table on the grass, with the recruiters who do not "recruit," because of course that would be pushy and not cool.

What a change from my own college days, when students would put on their dressiest clothes and carefully hide any counterculture symptoms, in order to show recruiters that they could fit in. Here the company was trying to fit in with the student. Trilogy had wined and dined this young man over margaritas in Pittsburgh and flown him to Austin for private parties in hip nightspots and aboard company boats. When I called the recruiters to ask why, they answered, "That's easy. We wanted him because he's a rock star." Moreover, "when big East Coast companies trek down here to see who is working on *their* project, we'll wheel him out"—blowing the customers' minds with his skill and coolness.

But something bigger struck me: Here was another talented young person leaving Pittsburgh. That was exactly the problem that had started me on this line of research in the first place. My adopted hometown has a huge number of assets. Carnegie Mellon is one of the world's leading centers for research in information technology. The University of Pittsburgh, right down the street, has a world-class medical center. Pittsburgh attracts hundreds of millions of dollars per year in university research funding and is the sixth largest center for college and university students, on a per capita basis, in the country. It is hardly a cultural backwater. The city is home to three major sports franchises, renowned museums and cultural venues, a spectacular network of urban parks, remarkable industrial-age architecture, and truly great urban neighborhoods with an abundance of charming yet affordable housing. It is a friendly city, defined by strong communities and a strong sense of pride. In the 1985 Rand McNally survey, Pittsburgh was ranked "America's Most Livable City," and it has continued to score high on such lists ever since.

Yet the economy putters along in a middling flat-line pattern. Both the core city and the surrounding metropolitan area lost population in the 2000 census. And those bright young university people keep leaving. Most of Carnegie Mellon's prominent alumni of recent decades—like Vinod Khosla, among the best known of Silicon Valley's venture capitalists, and former faculty member Rick Rashid, now head of R&D at Microsoft—went elsewhere to make their marks. Pitt's vaunted medical center, the place where Jonas Salk created his polio vaccine and the site of the world's premier organ-transplant program, has inspired only a handful of entrepreneurs to build biotech companies in Pittsburgh.

Over the years I have seen the community try just about everything possible to remake itself, and I was personally involved in many of these efforts. The region has launched a multitude of programs to diversify its economy away from heavy industry into high technology. It rebuilt its downtown virtually from scratch, invested in a new airport and developed a massive new sports complex for the baseball Pirates and the football Steelers. It devotes considerable effort to attracting and retaining talented young people. But nothing, it seems, can reverse the tide of people and companies leaving.

I vividly recall the day one of our university's most famous spin-off companies, Lycos, left town. I was on leave at Harvard's Kennedy School and opened the morning paper only to find a story reporting the company's relocation to Boston. Carnegie Mellon researchers had developed the Lycos catalog-and-search technology in the earliest days of the commercial Internet. The technology had then been licensed to the Boston-based venture capital firm CMGI, which built a company around it. At first, Lycos headquarters were in Boston but the engineering offices and the technical operations, a considerable enterprise, were kept in Pittsburgh. But now that was moving as well. According to a number of my colleagues who were close to the situation, the main reason was that Boston offered lifestyle options that made it much easier to attract top managerial and technical talent.

With all of this whirring in the back of my brain, I asked the young man with the spiked hair why he was going to a smaller city in the middle of Texas, a place with a small airport and no professional sports teams, without museums and high-art cultural amenities comparable to Pittsburgh's. The company is excellent, he told me. It has terrific people and the work is challenging. But the clincher was: "It's in *Austin!*" "Why is that good?" I asked. There are lots of young people, he explained, and a tremendous amount to do, a thriving music scene, ethnic and cultural diversity, fabulous outdoor recreation, and great nightlife. That's what mattered—not the symphony or the opera, which he enjoyed but would not feel comfortable attending. What's more, Austin is affordable, unlike Silicon Valley, another place that offered the kinds of work he desired. He was right: Austin ranked as the fourth most affordable place for information-technology workers like him, with a pay differential of more than $18,000 over the San Francisco Bay area, when cost-of-living differences are taken into account.[1]

"I can have a life in Austin," he concluded, not merely a job. When I asked him about Pittsburgh, where he had chosen to go to college, he replied that he had lived in the city for four years and knew it well. Though he had several good offers from Pittsburgh high-tech firms, he felt the city lacked the lifestyle options, cultural diversity and tolerant attitude that would make it attractive to him. As he summed it up, "How would I fit in here?"

Thus a question that lies at the heart of our age, and that would drive much of the research for this book:

> How do we decide where to live and work? What really matters to us in making this kind of life decision? How has this changed—and why?

The usual answer is "jobs." That certainly is what most economists would say. People go to places in pursuit of the most attractive positions and the greatest financial rewards. But jobs are not the whole story. People balance a host of considerations in making decisions on where to work and live. What they want today is different from what our parents wanted, and even from what many of us once thought we wanted. And while the young man with spiked hair and impressive tattoos is not representative of everyone in the Creative Class, my research shows that the same basic kinds of things he liked about Austin are representative of the traits many look for in choosing a place to live. A number of consistent themes emerge from my research:

- The Creative Class is moving away from traditional corporate communities, Working Class centers and even many Sunbelt regions to a set of places I call Creative Centers.

- The Creative Centers tend to be the economic winners of our age. Not only do they have high concentrations of Creative Class people, they have high concentrations of creative economic outcomes, in the form of innovations and high-tech industry growth. They also show strong signs of overall regional vitality, such as increases in regional employment and population.
- The Creative Centers are not thriving for such traditional economic reasons as access to natural resources or transportation routes. Nor are they thriving because their local governments have given away the store through tax breaks and other incentives to lure business. They are succeeding largely because creative people want to live there. The companies then follow the people—or, in many cases, are started by them. Creative centers provide the integrated eco-system or habitat where all forms of creativity—artistic and cultural, technological and economic—can take root and flourish.
- Creative people are not moving to these places for traditional reasons. The physical attractions that most cities focus on building—sports stadiums, freeways, urban malls and tourism-and-entertainment districts that resemble theme parks—are irrelevant, insufficient or actually unattractive to many Creative Class people. What they look for in communities are abundant high-quality amenities and experiences, an openness to diversity of all kinds, and above all else the opportunity to validate their identities as creative people.

Limits of the Conventional View

Several perspectives dominate the debate over the role of place in our economy and society. While not opposed to each other in every respect, they are seldom in agreement. Perhaps the greatest of all the New Economy myths is that "geography is dead." With the Internet and modern telecommunication and transportation systems, the thinking goes, it is no longer necessary for people who work together to *be* together, so they won't be. This end-of-geography theme has been with us since experts predicted that technologies from the telegraph and the telephone to the automobile and the airplane would essentially kill off the cities. In his widely read 1998 book *New Rules for the New Economy*, Kevin Kelly wrote, "The New Economy operates in a 'space' rather than a place, and over time more and more economic transactions will migrate to this new space."[2] Kelly then qualifies this to some degree: "Geography and real estate, however, will remain, well . . . real. Cities will flourish, and the value of a distinctive place, such as a wilderness area, or a charming hill village, will only increase." Still he reiterates that "People will inhabit places, but increasingly the economy inhabits a space."

Never has a myth been easier to deflate. Not only do people remain highly concentrated, but the economy itself—the high-tech, knowledge-based and creative-content industries that drive so much of economic growth—continues to concentrate in specific places from Austin and Silicon Valley to New York City and Hollywood, just as the automobile industry once concentrated in Detroit. Students of urban and regional growth from Robert Park and Jane Jacobs to Wilbur Thompson have long pointed to the role of places as incubators of creativity, innovation and new industries.[3] Moreover, the death-of-place prognostications simply do not square with the countless people I have interviewed, the focus groups I've observed, and the statistical research I've done. Place and community are more critical factors than ever before. And a good deal of the reason for this is that rather than inhabiting an abstract "space" as Kelly suggests, the economy itself increasingly takes form around real concentrations of people in real places. There are several theories that seek to account for the continued importance of place in economic and social life. Let's take a look.

One view suggests that place remains important as a locus of economic activity because of the tendency of firms to cluster together. This view builds on the seminal insights of the economic Alfred Marshall, who argued that firms cluster in "agglomerations" to gain productive efficiencies. The contemporary variant of this view, advanced by Harvard Business School professor Michael Porter, has many proponents in academia and in the practice of economic development.[4] It is clear that similar firms tend to cluster. Examples of this sort of agglomeration include not only Detroit and Silicon Valley, but the *maquiladora* electronics- and auto-parts districts in Mexico, the clustering of makers of disk drives in Singapore and of flat-panel displays in Japan, and the garment district and Broadway theater district in New York City.

The question is not whether firms cluster but why. Several answers have been offered. Some experts believe that clustering captures efficiencies generated from tight linkages between firms. Others say it has to do with the positive benefits of co-location, or what they call "spillovers." Still others claim it is because certain kinds of activity require face-to-face contact.[5] But these are only partial answers. As I have already noted and will show in greater detail, the real force behind this clustering is people. Companies cluster in order to draw from concentrations of talented people who power innovation and economic growth. The ability to rapidly mobilize talent from such concentrations is a tremendous source of competitive advantage for companies in the time-driven Creative Economy.

An alternative view is based on Robert Putnam's social capital theory. It basically says that regional economic growth is associated with tight-knit communities where people and firms form and share strong ties.[6] Putnam and others have tried to use social capital theory to account for the performance of high-tech industrial clusters like Silicon Valley, arguing that the networks of people and firms in these places constitute a form of social capital. But these high-tech centers do not approximate the classic social capital model. Rather they are centers of loose ties, of economic and social diversity. The Creative Class people I have interviewed in these places do not desire the strong ties and long-term commitments associated with traditional social capital. Rather they prefer a more flexible, quasi-anonymous community—where they can quickly plug in, pursue opportunities and build a wide range of relationships.

Human Capital and Economic Growth

Over the past decade or so, a potentially more powerful theory for city and regional growth has emerged. The basic idea behind this theory is that people are the motor force behind regional growth. Its proponents thus refer to it as the "human capital" theory of regional development.

Economists and geographers have always accepted that economic growth is regional—that it is driven by and spreads from specific regions, cities or even neighborhoods. The traditional view, however, is that places grow either because they are located on transportation routes or because they have endowments of natural resources that encourage firms to locate there. According to this conventional view, the economic importance of a place is tied to the efficiency with which it can make things and do business. Governments employ this theory when they use tax breaks and highway construction to attract business. But these cost-related factors are no longer the key to success.

The proponents of the human capital theory argue that the key to regional growth lies not in reducing the costs of doing business, but in endowments of highly educated and productive people. This clustering of human capital is even more important to economic growth than the clustering of companies, because as Ross DeVol of the Milken Institute points out, "You attract these people and you attract the industries that employ them and the investors who put money into the companies." Joel Kotkin captures the essence of the human capital view when he writes that:

> Traditionally, human intelligence tends to cluster in places where industry and commerce draw them. This has been true from the time of ancient Mesopotamia and Rome through early modern Amsterdam and New York. Yet at the same time, brainpower could be highly concentrated in certain places—like New England or the Minneapolis region, other regions with more relative brawn—such as industrial Detroit or Buffalo, would still lead economic growth, luring highly skilled workers when needed. . . . This "brawn to brain" shift profoundly alters the importance of "place." Under the new regime of geography, wherever intelligence clusters evolve, in the small town or the big city, so too will wealth accumulate. Moreover, these clusters are far less constrained by traditional determinants such as strategic water-way location, the abundance of raw materials or the proximity to dense concentrations of populations.[7]

The human capital theory—like many theories of cities and urban areas—owes a debt to Jane Jacobs. For a long time academic economists ignored her ideas, but in the past decade or two, some very prestigious ones have taken them up in earnest and tried to develop empirical proof of their validity. Decades ago, Jacobs noted the ability of cities to attract creative people and thus spur economic growth.[8] The Nobel Prize-winning economist Robert Lucas sees the productivity effects that come from the clustering of human capital as the critical factor in regional economic growth, referring to this as a "Jane Jacobs externality." In a widely circulated e-mail he went so far as to suggest that she should be considered for a Nobel in economics herself. Building on Jacobs's seminal insight, Lucas contends that cities would be economically infeasible if not for the productivity effects associated with endowments of human capital:

> If we postulate only the usual list of economic forces, cities should fly apart. The theory of production contains nothing to hold a city together. A city is simply a collection of factors of production—capital, people and land—and land is always far cheaper outside cities than inside. . . . It seems to me that the "force" we need to postulate to account for the central role of cities in economic life is of exactly the same character as the "external human capital.". . . What can people be paying Manhattan or downtown Chicago rents for, if not for being near other people?[9]

Studies of national growth find a clear connection between the economic success of nations and their human capital, as measured by the level of education. This connection has also been found in regional studies of the United States. In a series of studies, Harvard University economist Edward Glaeser and his collaborators found considerable empirical evidence that human capital is the central factor in regional growth.[10] According to Glaeser, such clustering of human capital is the ultimate cause of regional agglomerations of firms: Firms concentrate to reap the advantages that stem from common labor pools—not merely, according to Glaeser, to tap the advantages from linked networks of customers and suppliers as is more typically argued. Research by one of Glaeser's Harvard graduate students, Spencer Glendon, shows that a good deal of city growth over the twentieth century can be traced to those cities' levels of human capital at the beginning of the century.[11] Places with greater numbers of highly educated people grew faster and were better able to attract more talent. Research by Patricia Beeson, an urban economist at the University of Pittsburgh, supports this view. Her ongoing work explores how investments in various sorts of infrastructure have affected city and regional growth since the mid-nineteenth century. She finds that investments in higher education infrastructure predict subsequent growth far better than investments in physical infrastructure like canals, railroads or highways.[12]

Creativity and Place

The human capital theory says that economic growth will occur in places that have highly educated people. This begs the question: Why do creative people cluster in certain places? In a world where people are highly mobile, why do they choose to live in and concentrate in some cities over others and for what reasons?

While economists and social scientists have paid a lot of attention to how companies decide where to locate, they have virtually ignored how people do so. This is the fundamental question I sought to answer. With little in the way of academic studies or literature to guide me, I began simply by asking people how they make their decisions about where to live and work. I started with my students and colleagues at Carnegie Mellon and then turned to friends and associates in other cities. Eventually I began to ask virtually everyone I met about this. The same answer kept coming back. People said that economic and lifestyle considerations both matter, and so does the mix. In reality, people were not making the career decisions or geographic moves that the standard theories said they should: They were not slavishly following jobs to places.

Gradually I came to see my perspective as distinct from the human capital theory. A colleague of mine even gave it a name, the "creative capital theory." Essentially my theory says that regional economic growth is driven by the location choices of creative people—the holders of creative capital—who prefer places that are diverse, tolerant and open to new ideas. It thus differs from the human capital theory in two respects: (1) It identifies a type of human capital, creative people, as being key to economic growth; and (2) it identifies the underlying factors that shape the location decisions of these people, instead of merely saying that regions are blessed with certain endowments of them. . . . [L]et me share the findings from my interviews and focus groups that provide invaluable insights on what creative people actually value in locations.

Thick Labor Markets

When asked about the importance of employment, the people in my interviews and focus groups repeatedly say they are not looking just for a single job but for many employment opportunities. The reason, they tell me, is simple. They do not expect to stay with the same company for very long. Companies are disloyal and careers are increasingly horizontal. To be attractive, places need to offer a job market that is conducive to a horizontal career path. In other words, places have to offer a *thick labor market*.

In this way, place solves a basic puzzle of our economic order: It facilitates the matching of creative people to economic opportunities. Place thus provides a labor pool for companies who need people and a thick labor market for people who need jobs. The gathering of people, companies and resources into particular places with particular specialties and capabilities generates efficiencies that power economic growth. It is for this reason that I say place is becoming the central organizing unit of our economy and society, taking on a role that used to be played by the large corporation.

Lifestyle

The people in my focus groups tell me that lifestyle frequently trumps employment when they're choosing where to live. Many said they had turned down jobs, or decided not to look for them, in places that did not afford the variety of "scenes" they desired— music scene, art scene, technology scene, outdoor sports scene and so on. Some recounted how they or their friends had taken jobs for economic reasons, only to move elsewhere for lifestyle reasons. In the course of my research, I have come across many people who moved somewhere for the lifestyle and only *then* set out to look for employment there.

People today expect more from the places they live. In the past, many were content to work in one place and vacation somewhere else, while frequently getting away for weekends to ski, enjoy a day in the country or sample nightlife and culture in another city. The idea seemed to be that some places are for making money and others are for fun. This is no longer sufficient. The sociologists Richard Lloyd and Terry Nichols Clark of the University of Chicago note that "workers in the elite sectors of the postindustrial city make 'quality of life' demands, and . . . increasingly act like tourists in their own city."[13] One reason is the nature of modern creative work. Of course people still go away at times, but given their flexible and unpredictable work schedules, they want ready access to recreation on a "just-in-time" basis. When putting in a long day, for instance, they may need an extended break in the middle to recharge their batteries. Many who do this tell me a bike ride or run is a staple of their day-to-day productivity. And for this, a beach house or country getaway spot doesn't do them much good. They require trails or parks close at hand.

Nightlife is an important part of the mix. The people I talked to desired nightlife with a wide mix of options. The most highly valued options were experiential ones— interesting music venues, neighborhood art galleries, performance spaces and theaters. A vibrant, varied nightlife was viewed by many as another signal that a city "gets it," even by those who infrequently partake in nightlife. Interestingly, one of the biggest complaints of my focus groups had to do with cities where the nightlife closes down too early. The reason is not that most of these people are all-night partyers, but with long work hours and late nights, they need to have options around the clock. . . . As one person in a focus group summed it up: "I want the option available, when I want to do it."

A survey by one of my students, Erica Coslor, found that nightlife is indeed an important component of a city's lifestyle and amenity mix. Defining nightlife as "all entertainment activities that happen after dark," Coslor examined what younger Creative Class people (her respondents ranged in age from early twenties into their thirties) desire in urban nightlife. The highest-rated nightlife options were cultural attractions (from the symphony and theater to music venues) and late-night dining, followed by small jazz and music clubs and coffee shops. Bars, large dance clubs and after-hours clubs ranked much farther down the list. Most of her respondents desired a mix of entertainment options and safe and reliable "after-hours transportation." She also identified a strong preference for "on-demand entertainment." A third of Coslor's survey respondents said that "nightlife" plays a role in where they choose to live and work. She found that it takes a variety of activities coming together to create that *gestalt* that is nightlife.[14] Time and again, the people I speak with say these things are signals that a place "gets it"—that it embraces the culture of the Creative Age; that it is a place where they can fit in.

Social Interaction

People have always, of course, found social interaction in their communities. But a community's ability to facilitate this interaction appears to be more important in a highly mobile, quasi-anonymous society. In his book *A Great Good Place,* Ray Oldenburg notes the importance of what he calls "third places" in modern society. Third places are neither home nor work—the "first two" places—but venues like coffee shops, bookstores and cafés in which we find less formal acquaintances. According to Oldenburg, these third places comprise "the heart of a community's social vitality" where people "hang out simply for the pleasures of good company and lively conversation."[15]

Creative Class people in my focus groups and interviews report that such third places play key roles in making a community attractive. This is because the two other sources of interaction and stability, the family and workplace, have become less secure and stable. People are more likely to live alone, and more likely to change jobs frequently. Third places fill a void by providing a ready venue for acquaintance and human interaction.

The importance of third places also arises from the changing nature of work. More of us do not work on fixed schedules and many of us work in relative isolation—for instance, in front of a keyboard at home, as I often do. Reliable human contact is thus hard to come by, and e-mail or phone interruptions provide only a limited form. So I frequently take a break and head to the coffee shop down the street just to see people on the street; or I take a bike ride to recharge, then head to the cafe to see my associates there. Many people I interview say they do much the same thing.

Diversity

My focus group and interview participants consistently listed diversity as among the most important factors in their choice of locations. People were drawn to places known for diversity of thought and open-mindedness. They actively seek out places for diversity and look for signs of it when evaluating communities. These signs include people of different ethnic groups and races, different ages, different sexual orientations and alternative appearances such as significant body piercings or tattoos.

Small wonder that when a group of students visited my house recently, and I asked them where they wanted to live after graduation, highly diverse Washington, D.C., was the favorite. A Korean student liked it "because there's a big Korean community," meaning Korean religious institutions, Korean grocery stores and Korean children for his children to play with. Likewise an Indian student favored it for its large Indian population, an African-American for its large black professional class, and a gay student for the community around DuPont Circle.

But there's more at work here than expatriates who only want to be around people like themselves. It's the differences, not just the sameness, that are the benefit. A young female premedical student of Persian descent summarized the many criteria for diversity:

> I was driving across the country with my sister and some friends. We were commenting on what makes a place the kind of place we want to go, or the kind of place we would live. And we tried to list [the factors]. . . . We said: It has to be open. It has to be diverse. . . . It has to have a visible gay community; it has to have lots of different races and ethnic groups. It has to have people of all ages and be open to young people. It has to have people who *look* different.[16]

Like the diverse workplace, a diverse community is a sign of a place open to outsiders. And just as domestic partner benefits convey that a potential employer is open and tolerant, places with a visible gay presence convey the same kind of signal. Some said they oriented their location search to such places, even though they are not gay themselves. Others actively sought out gay neighborhoods for their amenities, energy, safety and sense of community. Younger women in particular said they liked to live in gay neighborhoods because they are "safe." As with employers, visible diversity serves as a signal that a community embraces the open meritocratic values of the Creative Age.

Diversity also means "excitement" and "energy." Creative-minded people enjoy a mix of influences. They want to hear different kinds of music and try different kinds of food. They want to meet and socialize with people unlike themselves, to trade views and spar over issues. A person's circle of closest friends may not resemble the Rainbow Coalition—in fact it usually does not—but he or she wants the rainbow to be available.

An attractive place doesn't have to be a big city, but it has to be cosmopolitan—a place where anyone can find a peer group to be comfortable with, and also find other groups to be stimulated by; a place seething with the interplay of cultures and ideas; a place where outsiders can quickly become insiders. In her book *Cosmopolitan City*, Bonnie Menes Kahn puts it very simply.[17] She says a great city has two hallmarks: tolerance for strangers and intolerance for mediocrity. These are precisely the qualities that appeal to members of the Creative Class—and they also happen to be qualities conducive to innovation, risk-taking and the formation of new businesses.

Authenticity

Places are also valued for authenticity and uniqueness, as I have heard many times in my studies. Authenticity comes from several aspects of a community—historic buildings, established neighborhoods, a unique music scene or specific cultural attributes. It comes from the mix—from urban grit alongside renovated buildings, from the commingling of young and old, long-time neighborhood characters and yuppies, fashion models and "bag ladies."

People in my interviews and focus groups often define "authenticity" as the opposite of generic. They equate authentic with being "real," as in a place that has real buildings, real people, real history. An authentic place also offers unique and original experiences. Thus a place full of chain stores, chain restaurants and nightclubs is not authentic: Not only do these venues look pretty much the same everywhere, they offer the same experience you could have anywhere. One of my Creative Class subjects, emphasizing the way people are attracted to the authenticity and uniqueness of a city, used the two terms together as a combined phrase.

> I'm thinking in particular of the Detroit Electronic Music Festival. Here was a free concert that drew a million people the first year . . . and featured a stellar lineup of Detroit and some national performers and DJs, a great boon to the city and its image. This year, they . . . start to drop Detroit artists in favor of more well-known national acts. So more people come, but the event is losing much of the uniqueness/authenticity that makes people want to come to this event from around the world.[18]

Music is a key part of what makes a place authentic, in effect providing a sound or "audio identity."[19] Audio identity refers to the identifiable musical genre or sound associated with local bands, clubs and so on that make up a city's music scene: blues in Chicago, Motown in Detroit, grunge in Seattle, Austin's Sixth Street. This is what many people know about these cities and the terms in which they think of them; it is also the way these cities promote themselves.

Music in fact plays a central role in the creation of identity and the formation of real communities. Sounds, songs and musical memories are some of the strongest and most easily evoked. You can often remember events in your life by what songs were playing at the time. Simon Frith writes that music "provides us with an intensely subjective sense of being sociable. It both articulates and offers the immediate *experience* of collective identity. Music regularly soundtracks our search for ourselves and for spaces in which we can feel at home."[20]

In fact, it is hard to think of a major high-tech region that doesn't have a distinct audio identity. In addition to Seattle and Austin, consider the San Francisco Bay Area. It was home to perhaps the most creative music scene of the 1960s with the Grateful Dead, Jefferson Airplane, Mamas and the Papas, Haight-Ashbury and the seminal Monterey Pop Festival. Chapel Hill, North Carolina, at the heart of the Research Triangle, was recently named as having one of the best local music scenes in the country. Technology and the music scene go together because together they reflect a place that is open to new ideas, new people and creativity. And it is for this reason that frequently I like to tell city leaders that finding ways to help support a local music scene can be just as important as investing in high-tech business and far more effective than building a downtown mall.

Other kinds of "soundtracks" are important besides music. As Creative Class people like to say, an authentic place has a distinct "buzz." The sociologists Lloyd and Clark write of a sculptor who told them, "I came to Chicago because that was where the conversation was." This kind of soundtrack cannot be dubbed into a place. It is played and sustained by the creative people who live there—who *choose* to live there.

Identity

Place provides an increasingly important dimension of our identity. Fewer people today find lifelong identity in the company for which they work. We live in a world where many traditional institutions have ceased to provide meaning, stability and support.

In the old corporate-driven economy, many people took their cues from the corporation and found their identity there. Others lived in the towns where they grew up and could draw on the strong ties of family and long-term friends. As the Berkeley sociologist Manuel Castells has noted, "the power of identity" has become a defining feature of the insecure, constantly changing postmodern world.[21]

The combination of where we live and what we do has come to replace who we work for as a main element of identity. Forty years ago, some would likely identify themselves by saying "I work for General Motors" or "I'm with IBM." Today our tattooed friend is more likely to identify himself by saying "I'm a software developer and I live in Austin" rather than "I work for Trilogy." I travel by plane a lot and have noticed that the standard conversation-starter has changed. Ten years ago, people were likely to ask, "Where do you work?" Today it's "Where do you live?"

With the demise of the company-dominated life, a new kind of pecking order has developed around places. Place is becoming an important source of status. To some extent, this has always been true. Places like Paris, London and New York City have always been high on the status order. Elsewhere, people were content to substitute the economic status that came from a good job with a prestigious company for the status of place. But now the people in my focus groups and interviews tell me they are likely to move to places that convey high status.

Many Creative Class people I've studied also express a desire to be involved in their communities. This is not so much the result of a "do-good" mentality, but reflects their desire to both actively establish their own identity in places, and also to contribute to actively building places that reflect and validate that identity. In Pittsburgh, for instance, a group of young people in creative fields, ranging from architecture and urban design to graphics and high-tech, has formed a loose association that they dubbed "Ground Zero" (the group was formed and took its name before the World Trade Center tragedy). The group emerged on its own out of a series of brainstorming sessions that I organized in early 2000 to gain insight into the lifestyle and other concerns of young Creative Class people. While the initial impetus for the group was to combat a redevelopment plan that would have replaced an authentic downtown shopping district with a generic urban mall, they quickly began to focus their efforts on shaping the creative climate and identity of the city. Their initial "manifesto" speaks so directly to the nexus of creativity, place and identity that it is worth reproducing here in full.

Creative Friends,

Now is the time for us to come together to Speak Up and Act Up.

We the people who make things, who make the culture of this city, need to connect and engage. We want you to come and join us.

We all hear about how to make Pittsburgh a better place to be a consumer or a sports fan or an entrepreneur. We hear about strategies to suck in the young suburban consumers so they can park their cars, shop and leave.

This isn't us. We are already here. We are actively creating, whether it be food, stories, photographs, music, video games, paintings, buildings, performance or communities. We are making the culture of this city. We already know what makes Pittsburgh unique, interesting and attractive to people of all ages. We want to work to preserve its authenticity as a place; to make it more authentic.

We want to capitalize on what is already here, not destroy, demolish or suppress it. We want City policy that encourages culture to grow from within instead of promoting removal and replacement. We will then work proactively through ALL forms of media to make our voice heard. To make our city better.

    We want to provoke awareness, discussion, argument, debate, and maybe even local pride (?) through what we will accomplish. And we want the voice of young creators to be heard loud and clear by those who make public policy.

The Ground Zero people have launched a variety of efforts to realize their vision, from organizing edgy community arts events to working to organize a shuttle-bus system, the "Ultra-Violet Loop," to establish "connectivity" between the various neighborhoods that make up Pittsburgh's street-level cultural mix. In doing so, they have sought to implant their creative identity into the urban fabric of the city.

The role of place in our identity is also evident in the growing struggles over who controls places. Some of the great conflicts of our age are the displacement of existing residents from their communities—their identities. I got a first-hand taste of this on a warm night in Seattle's up-and-coming Belltown neighborhood in May 2000. Walking down newly fashionable First Avenue with its mix of high-tech companies, high-end residences and nice restaurants, our group came upon a rag-tag band banging on drums and bellowing: "Say no to the construction noise." Jolted by the commotion, well-dressed yuppies emerged onto the street to see what it was about. A boisterous debate broke out between them and the protesters over who were the neighborhood's "true" residents.

Quality of Place

All of the factors that go into Creative Class location decisions are, together, so powerful that I have coined a term to sum them up: *quality of place*. I use the term in contrast to the more traditional concept of quality of life. It refers to the unique set of characteristics that define a place and make it attractive. Generally, one can think of quality of place as having three dimensions:

- *What's there*: the combination of the built environment and the natural environment; a proper setting for pursuit of creative lives.
- *Who's there*: the diverse kinds of people, interacting and providing cues that anyone can plug into and make a life in that community.
- *What's going on*: the vibrancy of street life, café culture, arts, music and people engaging in outdoor activities—altogether a lot of active, exciting, creative endeavors.

The quality of place a city offers can be summed up as an interrelated set of experiences. Many of them, like the street-level scene, are dynamic and participatory. You can do more than be a spectator; you can be part of the scene. And the city allows you to modulate the experience: to choose the mix, to turn the intensity level up or down as desired, and to have a hand in creating the experience rather than merely consuming it. The street buzz is right nearby if you want it, but you can also retreat to your home or other quiet place, or go into an urban park, or even set out for the country. This is one reason canned experiences are not so popular. A chain theme restaurant, a multimedia-circus sports stadium or a prepackaged entertainment-and-tourism district is like a packaged tour: You do not get to help create your experience or modulate the intensity; it is thrust upon you.

Many members of the Creative Class also want to have a hand in actively shaping the quality of place of their communities. When I addressed a high-level downtown revitalization group in Providence, Rhode Island, in the fall of 2001, a thirty-something professional captured the essence of this when he said: "My friends and I came to Providence because it already has the authenticity that we like—its established neighborhoods, historic architecture and ethnic mix." He then implored the city leaders to make these qualities the basis of their revitalization efforts and to do so in ways that actively harness the energy of him and his peers. He said that Creative Class people like him seek places that are themselves a challenge and where they can help craft the future. Or as he aptly put it: "We want a place that's not done."

Quality of place does not occur automatically; rather it is an ongoing dynamic process involving the coming together of several different aspects of a community. The sociologist Richard Lloyd of the University of Chicago provides a vivid description of how this occurred in Chicago's Wicker Park neighborhood.

> Wicker Park was a relatively obscure, low-income neighborhood in the 1980s populated largely by Puerto Rican and Mexican immigrants who struggled against receding opportunities in the postindustrial landscape. With its relatively high crime rates and its abundance of derelict buildings leftover from a bygone era, the neighborhood would have seemed a poor candidate for the current proliferation of high-tech enterprises. However in the 1990s it underwent a striking transition. In 1989, the Northwest Tower lent its nickname to an annual "Around the Coyote" festival, designed to advertise the growing numbers of young artists who lived and worked in the neighborhood. The local rock-and-roll scene gained national recognition in the early part of the decade, leading *Billboard* magazine to anoint Wicker Park "cutting edge's new capital." The concentration of young artists, along with the establishment of associated amenities including boutiques, performance venues, coffee shops and galleries transformed the image of the neighborhood from a space of postindustrial decay to a privileged site of urban culture. This in turn has abetted the development of new profit-generating practices.[22]

It has also given rise to gentrification and displacement of long-term residents as Lloyd notes. . . .

Some of my critics like to argue that many people who work in high-tech industries tend to be blandly conservative and prefer homogeneous communities and traditional lifestyles of the sort found in middle-class suburbs. They find evidence in the fact that so many high-tech people live in suburban enclaves like northern Virginia, the heart of Silicon Valley or the Seattle suburbs. My response is simple. These places are all located within major metropolitan areas that are among the most diverse in the country and offer a wide array of lifestyle amenities. In fact, these places are themselves a product of the openness and diversity of the broader areas. Had the Silicon Valley–San Francisco area not been receptive years ago to offbeat people like the young Steven Jobs, it could not have become what it is.

What people want is not an either/or proposition. Successful places do not provide just one thing; rather they provide a range of quality of place options for different kinds of people at different stages in the life course. Great cities are not monoliths; as Jane Jacobs said long ago, they are federations of neighborhoods. Think about New York City and its environs. Young people, when they first move to New York, live in places like the East Village, Park Slope, Williamsburg or Hoboken, where rents are more affordable and there are lots of other young people. When they get a little older and earn a little more, they move to the Upper West Side or maybe to SoHo; earn a little more and they can go to the West Village or the Upper East Side. Once marriage and children come along, some stay in the city while others relocate to bedroom communities in places like Westchester County, Connecticut, or the New Jersey suburbs. Later when the kids are gone, some of these people then move back to the city and buy a co-op overlooking the park or a duplex on the Upper East Side.

Members of the Creative Class come in all shapes, sizes, colors and lifestyles; and to be truly successful, cities and regions have to offer something for them all.

9

Elizabeth Strom

CULTURE, ART, AND DOWNTOWN DEVELOPMENT

American cities have rediscovered their cultural resources. During the past two decades, city officials have learned to value the historic communities that their predecessors have been eager to raze; have dubbed desolate, derelict warehouses "arts districts"; and have committed local tax dollars to their museums and performing arts complexes, many newly built or recently expanded. A survey of 65 U.S. cities (those with populations of 250,000 and above) finds that 71 major performing arts centers and museums have been either built or substantially expanded since 1985.[1] From Charlotte's Blumenthal Hall, to Los Angeles' Getty Museum, to Seattle's Benaroya Hall, a cultural building boom is clearly under way.

Of course, cultural facilities have always concentrated in urban areas. What is new and interesting, first, is that so many new facilities have been built in a relatively short time span, and so many have been built outside traditional cultural centers such as New York, Boston, Chicago, and San Francisco.[2] Second, whereas once the arts were considered a luxury, supported by philanthropy and enjoyed by an elite group of connoisseurs, today's cultural institutions are constructed as an explicit part of a city's economic revitalization program. This shift reflects changes both in the political economy of cities and in the organization and mission of highbrow cultural institutions. This article examines these changes and shows how they have led to an increasingly close and mutually beneficial relationship between urban political, economic, and cultural entrepreneurs.

The urban cultural building boom, this article maintains, represents a confluence of three related trends. First, cities seeking to attract businesses with quality-of-life amenities are eager to support the development of cultural institutions, especially in their once moribund centers. They believe that these institutions will increase the city's symbolic capital and catalyze other, unsubsidized commercial activities. Second, cultural institutions are

From Elizabeth Strom, "Converting Pork into Porcelain: Cultural Institutions and Downtown Development," *Urban Affairs Review,* Vol. 38, No. 1, pp. 3–21, copyright © 2002 by SAGE Publications, Inc. Reprinted by permission of SAGE Publications, Inc.

drawn by their own economic needs and by the imperatives of their funding sources to seek broader audiences and exploit more commercial, income-generating strategies. They are able to achieve these goals without completely sacrificing their aesthetic legitimacy because, third, the boundaries between high culture—once their dominant domain—and popular culture have blurred. Cultural institutions today are thus better positioned than those of 100 years ago to become active stakeholders in urban growth politics.

Culture in the Growth Coalition: Why Business and Political Leaders Need the Arts

Business elites have long recognized that the prestige of high arts institutions could bring economic benefit to their hometowns, but policies explicitly drawing on the arts to achieve economic development goals have only recently become common. The urban renewal projects of the 1950s and 1960s occasionally included cultural institutions—landmarks such as New York's Lincoln Center and Washington's Arena Stage were built on sites cleared of tenement housing with the support of city development officials, business elites, and the cultural institutions that would inhabit them (Toffler 1964, 1973). However, during this period, most city planners and business-people still saw investments in culture as incidental to the main city development goals of industrial retention and office and housing development.

By the 1980s, the dominant urban development policy paradigm had shifted away from "smokestack chasing" in which cities competed for investment by offering lower costs (Bailey 1989). Competing for corporate headquarters and producer service firms, economic development practitioners realized, required more than just abating taxes and improving infrastructure. Clark (2000) maintains that today's educated workers are more likely to choose appealing locations, most notably those with attractive natural and cultural resources, and then consider their employment options. In this model, firms that rely on highly skilled labor have greater incentive than ever to either choose amenity-rich locations or to strive to improve the quality of life in their headquarters city. As cities compete for mobile, skilled workers and the firms that employ them, low taxes may be less important than riverfront parks, sports arenas, and historic districts. Moreover, city officials have become ever more aware of the economic importance of tourism and have put a great deal of energy into building and enlarging convention centers (Sanders 1998), subsidizing new hotels, and attracting major retailers (Friedan and Sagalyn 1989; Hannigan 1998; Judd 1999).

Cultural institutions represent an important element of the recreational infrastructure thought to make a city more appealing to tourists and investors (Eisinger 2000; Hannigan 1998). Corporations have come to see the presence of local arts institutions as a business asset, and their support for such organizations represents good business sense as much as philanthropy. Ford Motor's marketing director, who was asked why his company has nearly single-handedly kept Detroit's opera company solvent, noted that the presence of such an institution made it easier to recruit white-collar employees (Bradsher 1999). Donors to the New Jersey Performing Arts Center made this point as well (Strom 1999).

City governments and place-based business elites have become more intent on marketing their cities. Local boosterism, of course, is hardly new, but today professionals with large budgets have replaced the well-intentioned amateurs of an earlier era (Ward 1998; Holcomb 1993). Moreover, as is true throughout the business world, city promoters have moved from a model of *selling*, where one tries to persuade the buyer to purchase what one has, to *marketing*, where one tries to have what the buyer wants (Holcomb 1993). Marketers do not merely come up with a catchy jingle; they seek to remake the city, or at least the most visible part of the city, to conform to the expectations of the affluent consumers they want to attract. Cultural institutions, associated with beauty, good taste, and higher purpose, become singularly important symbolic assets for image-conscious marketers.

At the same time, development practitioners and scholars began to appreciate that the arts comprise a wealth-generating economic sector, one in which urban areas retain a competitive advantage. Since the 1980s, the economic impact of the arts has received considerable attention. In major cultural capitals like New York, the "culture industry," as the production and consumption of the arts is called, comprises an important economic sector (National Endowment for the Arts 1981; The Port Authority of New York and New Jersey 1993). Even in less obvious places, the culture industry plays a measurable economic role (Perryman 2000).

Cultural projects are valued for more than their direct economic impact. They are built in locations well situated to transform waning downtowns, obsolete factory districts, and disregarded waterfronts. New museums and performing arts centers now feature architectural designs that embrace and enhance their surroundings, rather than isolate their audiences from the city around them, as had been the case in an earlier generation (Russell 1999). And the new projects have been seen as a means of bringing life—and economic impulse—to central cities that are too often deserted after business hours. Philadelphia's Kimmel Center for the Performing Arts, it is hoped, will anchor new economic activity in Center City, where until recently check-cashing businesses and nude dance halls were as common as restaurants and theaters. During the past decade, Seattle has built two major arts facilities downtown: a new home for the Seattle Art Museum, opened in 1991, and Benaroya Hall, a performing arts complex built primarily for the Seattle Symphony, which opened in 1998. Seattle business leaders credit these cultural institutions with a downtown revival that includes the development of several major retail complexes and a 40% increase in the number of people living downtown since 1990 (Byrd 1997).

The arts can also lend greater legitimacy to other urban development efforts. One hundred years ago, urban arts patrons were quite clear about their hope that cultural institutions would serve to placate a growing immigrant working class (Horowitz 1976). As Boston entrepreneur Henry Lee Higginson wrote in 1886, "Educate and save ourselves and our families and our money from mobs!" (Quoted in Levine 1988, 205). The social control function of urban arts institutions today is far subtler. To David Harvey (1989), the contemporary urban spectacle—which includes ephemera like street fairs and festivals, as well as more institutionalized cultural facilities and entertainment districts—has become a way of co-opting the oppositional politics of the 1960s. To others, the presence of culture, especially serious, nonprofit culture, can serve to legitimize urban redevelopment among those who would not normally see themselves as its beneficiaries. Large-scale urban renewal projects can be made more palatable to voters and opinion shapers (if not always to those displaced in their wake) when they are packaged as new cultural centers or filled with public art (Miles 1998). In the words of a National Endowment for the Arts official,

> The arts . . . are like Mom and apple pie; they're consensus-makers, common ground. People can easily focus on the arts activities in a new project, instead of dwelling on the complicated costs and benefits public support for private development activity usually entails. (Quoted in Clack 1983, 13)

Arts organizations therefore represent a significant and unique component of the amalgam of downtown consumption palaces Judd (1999) has labeled the "tourist bubble." Urban scholars have analyzed the actors in the urban tourism and entertainment infrastructure, including retail mall developers, convention center operators, and major-league sports franchises, to understand why they are drawn to participate in downtown real estate projects (Friedan and Sagalyn 1989; Rosentraub 1997; Danielson 1997; Sanders 1998). Cultural institutions, however, have not received similar attention from urban political economists, even though their incorporation into urban growth politics begs explanation. Urban scholars have not asked why an elite cultural institution, whose legitimacy has long been based on its ability to showcase the most serious, academically sanctioned art, might join with those seeking to develop and market the city to the widest possible audience. Today's cultural institutions, however, have been affected by some of the same pressures as city governments. Living in a more competitive environment in which entrepreneurship and marketing are held to be the key to their survival, arts organizations have themselves been transformed.

Culture, Consumption, and Revitalization: Why Arts Institutions Need Urban Development

Cultural institutions are not just the objects of urban development schemes: They have themselves become active promoters of revitalization and place marketing activities, and they have done so to realize their own institutional goals. Cultural facilities, especially art museums, must expand to remain "competitive" in the art world, and their expansion needs often place them at the center of local development plans. They have at least five important reasons for wanting to be part of the area's revitalization.

First, some of their concerns about the city's economic health may derive from the interests of their trustees (Logan and Molotch 1987). In nearly every city, there is considerable overlap between those who are prominent in the city's highest business circles and those who are active on cultural boards. One study found that 70% of the members of Louisville's most prestigious development organizations also served on the boards of cultural organizations. (In contrast, those active in peak economic development groups were far less likely to be found on human service agency boards, suggesting the unique importance of arts organizations to those most concerned with the city's development) (Whitt and Lammers 1991). It would be a mistake, however, to assume that major cultural organizations are mere extensions of profit-seeking trustees. Cultural board members usually grant the arts professionals a great deal of autonomy in running the institution's operations. Nominations to the most prestigious nonprofit institution boards are coveted; those invited to join are unlikely to jeopardize the hard-earned esteem of their peers by asserting a self-serving agenda (Ostrower 1998).[3] The business interests of board members provide a context for institutional decision making, but they are unlikely to be the primary imperative pushing cultural organizations toward a development agenda.

Second, cultural institutions need to bring their customers—the cultural audiences—to them. People are unlikely to visit a place if the surrounding community is thought to be dangerous. Many cultural consumers are not arts aficionados willing to go anywhere to see, say, a particular Rembrandt, but rather those for whom arts events are part of an entertainment experience. Not only will high crime and extensive physical deterioration put a cultural institution at a disadvantage, but so also will a dearth of amenities like good restaurants.

Third, numerous studies indicate the extent to which cultural institutions depend on tourist visits (the Port Authority of New York and New Jersey 1993; McDowell 1997). New York's Museum of Modern Art estimates that two-thirds of its visits are from out-of-towners, and half of those come from overseas.[4] Of those who visited the Los Angeles County Museum of Art Van Gogh exhibition in 1999, 56% came from outside Los Angeles (Morey and Associates 1999). Cultural institutions therefore have a strong interest in the city's overall appeal to tourists.

Fourth, cultural institutions are heavily dependent on the availability of local volunteers (there are 2.5 volunteers for every paid museum staff member, according to the American Association of Museums). Location in an impoverished city or in a declining neighborhood may make it more difficult to recruit volunteers. Fifth, wealthy individuals and corporations, which provide the program funds for many cultural organizations, usually focus their giving in their hometowns. When a corporation fails or relocates, local arts organizations lose an important source of support.

In sum, arts organizations in thriving areas will have more visitors, more volunteers, and greater fund-raising success than those in depressed areas.

It is clear that arts organizations benefit when their cities are economically healthy. Moreover, cultural groups are learning that they can benefit when they are perceived as one of the sources of that economic health. Today, preparing a study of one's economic impact seems to be a staple of large arts organizations and local arts councils. Such studies are of questionable economic merit (Cwi and Lyall 1977)—as Eisinger (2000, 327) notes, "Consultants hired by project proponents often seem to pull their multipliers out of thin air." But their purpose is not rigorous cost-benefit analysis; rather, they are tools used by arts groups in their efforts to gain funding and political support. The claim that flourishing arts institutions are important to the urban economy has given arts advocates a rationale to appeal for government support even when tight budgets and political controversies might make public arts funding difficult to obtain (Wyszomirski 1995).

By emphasizing their importance to local revitalization, arts administrators have also been able to gain access to new funding sources. The construction of the New Jersey Performing Arts Center (NJPAC) was supported by $106 million in state contributions, mostly from funds earmarked for economic development activities. Such a large sum would not have been made available for a cultural project had it not been able to claim an important regional economic impact—New Jersey's entire annual cultural budget has never been higher than $20 million (Strom 1999). Arts projects in Louisville, Seattle, and Philadelphia all received generous capital grants from state governments, grants that were clearly tied to the economic mission of these institutions. Similarly, major arts institutions are receiving support from private sources that are more interested in urban revitalization than in art. New Jersey financier Ray Chambers, a man who had never shown much interest in cultural activities but who was deeply committed to the future of Newark, spearheaded the development of NJPAC. Clothing manufacturer Sidney Kimmel made clear in remarks broadcast on local radio that his $15 million donation to Philadelphia's new performing arts center was in support of the center's urban revitalization promises. Arts institutions can show funders that their contributions are not mere charity but rather serve as investments in the city's economic future.

New Audiences, New Patrons: Why Today's Cultural Institutions Are Well Positioned to Participate in Urban Development

Funding and Organizing High Culture

Cultural institutions may have long had a clear interest in the city's economic health, but only recently have they emerged as ideal partners for the sorts of growth-oriented coalitions described in Mollenkopf (1983), Logan and Molotch (1987), and Stone (1989). The participation of cultural institutions in urban development coalitions has been facilitated by far-reaching changes in arts patronage and arts management ongoing at least since the 1960s. If nineteenth-century institutions looked to wealthy families for financial support, since that time the private collector/patron has been largely eclipsed by more institutionalized forms of funding.[5] Many wealthy families now route their donations through foundations, the largest of which have professional staffs. Since the mid-1960s, the single most important patron of high culture has been the government. The National Endowment of the Arts will have a budget of about $115 million in 2001–2002, and the 50 state governments have allocated $447.5 million for arts and cultural programs in fiscal year 2001 (National Association of State Arts Agencies 2001). During the 1970s, corporate funding became an increasingly significant source of support. According to the Business Committee for the Arts, corporate support for culture increased from $22 million in 1967 to $1.16 billion in 1997,[6] and corporate arts funding tripled during the 1975–1985 period (DiMaggio 1986).

Changes in arts funding affect arts programming in ways that have implications for economic development policies. More so than private patrons, government agencies and corporate donors seek programs with broad audience appeal (Zolberg 1983; Alexander 1996). The National Endowment for the Arts (NEA) and the state arts councils are eager to associate with programs whose popularity can translate into political support for their efforts. For businesses, cultural donations are a "highbrow form of advertising" (Alexander 1996, 2), as corporations seek to attach their names to programs that are highly visible and prestigious. A well-placed, $200,000 cultural donation, according to one corporate foundation official, can have the same impact as $50 million in paid advertising.[7] Government and corporate funding influence the form of cultural offerings as well as the content. Few corporations want to fund a museum's operations; they prefer to attach their name to special, traveling exhibitions that attract large crowds in a number of cities. Alexander (1996) correlates the growth of government and corporate funding with the increasing number of special, "blockbuster" exhibits mounted by museums (and there may well be similar parallels in other kinds of arts institutions). Museum managers see such events as opportunities to attract large, paying audiences (many museums charge for such special exhibits) and generate new members who will continue to support the museum once the special exhibit has moved on.[8]

If such big-ticket events bring benefits for museum managers, they also fit well into the marketing strategies of urban development and tourism officials. Indeed, arts advocates, economic development officials, and the tourism industry have, since the mid-1990s, consciously sought to promote "cultural tourism." An estimated 50 cultural tourism programs have been founded in state, county, and local convention and visitors bureaus, and two national networks, Partners in Tourism (which is sponsored by American Express) and the Cultural Tourism Alliance, hold conferences and publish newsletters on cultural tourism. The Los Angeles County Museum of Art Van Gogh exhibition that drew so many out-of-town visitors had been promoted heavily by the Los Angeles Convention and Visitors Bureau, which advertised "Van Gogh weekend packages" in such upscale publications as *The New Yorker*. The convergence of interests is clear: City marketing officials, arts funders, and ultimately publicity-conscious cultural administrators all find benefit in mounting large, well-publicized exhibits or performances that attract big audiences.[9]

The Shifting Brows

Highbrow arts institutions would have limited value as economic development catalysts, however, if they were catering to a narrow stratum of social elites and art connoisseurs. But a dramatic shift in the way culture is framed and classified has made an expansion of art audiences possible. Boundaries between serious and popular art, and between the audiences who enjoy them, have become increasingly blurred. Of course, even the high-low distinctions that seemed so secure at midcentury were hardly inevitable; rather, scholars have shown them to be largely a product of the mid- to late-nineteenth century (DiMaggio 1982; Levine 1988). In the earlier part of the nineteenth century, concerts might include pieces by Bach or Haydn as well as popular fare; an evening of Shakespeare might be interspersed with acrobatic performances; and fledgling museums displayed works of established, serious artists next to curios (DiMaggio 1982). Even in the late nineteenth century, museums such as Philadelphia's Pennsylvania Museum unapologetically celebrated industrial design alongside European painting (Conn 1998). Such catholic sensibilities soon vanished in favor of more rigid classification schemes that made some cultural artifacts the exclusive terrain of those with education and money. Cultural objects that had once been universally enjoyed, including Shakespearean plays and Italian operas, were reinterpreted so that their more accessible elements were abandoned, and they became the property of the possessors of cultural capital (Levine 1988). That this reclassification took place in the decades surrounding the turn of the century was not accidental: It represented a response on the part of the upper classes to the growing presence and political strength of an increasingly vocal and politically mobilized working class. Defining an elite culture created a safe haven for the upper classes, who could rely on their association with high cultural goods to legitimize their class position (Horowitz 1976; Bourdieu 1984).

High art and popular culture also became institutionally segregated. Earlier in the nineteenth century, high culture had been marketed through the same commercial mechanisms as popular fare. The Swedish opera singer Jenny Lind made a wildly popular American tour in the 1850s under the sponsorship of P. T. Barnum, and European ballerina Fanny Ellsler, who toured the United States from 1840 to 1842, managed to become the darling of economic and cultural elites while still acquiring a mass following and making good profits selling Fanny Ellsler brand garters, stockings, corsets, and shaving soap (Levine 1988).

By the late nineteenth century, however, high and low art forms each had their own institutional home. Profit-driven entrepreneurs disseminated popular culture. The newly created nonprofit corporation, on the other hand, become the vehicle for disseminating high culture. Museums and orchestras so organized had a mix of public and private purposes that suited their patrons. As private corporations, they remained under the control of their appointed trustees. Because they relied on charitable donations, and not on popular political support, they could maintain high standards of elite culture. And because they were nonprofit, they could make claims to have a broader public purpose than a fully private, profit-seeking operation, thus justifying appeals for public support (DiMaggio 1982). Disseminated through the nonprofit corporation, the artifacts of serious culture could maintain their distance from the marketplace.

Today, however, the distinctions so carefully honed in the nineteenth century have become blurred. Rigid classifications fell under attack from several fronts. Gans (1974, 1999) notes a convergence of tastes dating back to the 1920s. The emergence of the middlebrow provided middle classes with more accessible versions of elite art, and today you do not need highbrow credentials to visit a blockbuster event at an art museum or enjoy a foreign film. At the same time, there was a "gentrification" of lowbrow arts, as elite artists and musicians explored jazz and folk art (Peterson 1997). Today, more modern and accessible art forms like jazz, modern dance, film, and photography can be created and consumed in many different venues and at many different levels, challenging the sorts of hierarchies described by Bourdieu (1984). Moreover, theoretical and empirical evidence suggests that the typical upper-class cultural consumer is no longer the snob, whose consumption of elite culture was linked to his or her rejection of other cultural forms, but the "omnivore," who consumes traditional high culture but also partakes of a variety of popular genres (Peterson and Kern 1996). The possibilities for mixing audiences of different classes and art of different genres are far greater today than they were at the turn of the nineteenth century.

The boundaries separating the organization of elite and popular culture have shifted as well. High culture remains the domain of elite, nonprofit institutions, but it is increasingly marketed with reference to the symbols and presentations of popular culture and supported by commercial market mechanisms. Museum shops no longer merely sell postcards and art books. They now feature a whole range of merchandise, some replicas of objects in their collections, some using motifs from objects in their collection (e.g., famous paintings printed on scarves and umbrellas), and some having little to do with their collections but presumably gaining value just by their association with great art. Museums and performing arts centers boast full-scale, four-star restaurants that become part of a city's lure to tourists, and their staffs include people with the business skills needed to help such enterprises run profitably (Alexander 1996).

The obscuring of cultural boundaries has important implications for the value of culture as an element of urban revitalization. Not only can cultural institutions take advantage of the market for arts-associated products. They can also broaden their programmatic offerings without losing their core constituencies. Today's arts organization trustees, apparently mindful of the need to appeal to broader audiences, are able to accept the use of popularizing techniques and commercial marketing without feeling that their elite status is compromised (Ostrower 1998). The Metropolitan Museum features Hollywood costumes; the Guggenheim showcases motorcycles and the work of fashion designer Armani. They do this while displaying their collections of European paintings and Greek sculpture, retaining their base of upscale donors and remaining highly desirable conveyers of status for those fortunate enough to be named to their boards.

Performing arts institutions have exhibited an even greater eclecticism than museums. Because performances are very time limited, a theater's programming can simultaneously appeal to diverse audiences. Indeed, many of today's performing arts centers, built with the goal of having maximum economic impact, contain multiple performance spaces, so that radically different types of performances can take place on the same evening (Rothstein 1998). One need only peruse the calendars of America's leading performing arts centers to find intriguing juxtapositions, as Broadway shows share the theater complex with symphony orchestras, country fiddlers, and travel lectures. In November 2000, just to offer one example, the Tulsa Performing Arts Center's calendar included the Broadway musical Showboat, Brahms Oratorio music, the Moscow String Quartet, the U.S. Marine Band, and a pops concert of Frank Sinatra hits. On one very busy Saturday in February 1998, West Palm Beach's Kravis Center for the Performing Arts hosted singers Steve Lawrence and Eydie Gorme, the Gospel Gala, and the Emerson String Quartet. This is exactly the mix we might expect given the new relationship between the brows. On one hand, distinctions are maintained—these performances all took place in different halls, most likely attracting different audiences who probably conducted themselves according to different codes of behavior. On the other hand, these audiences apparently did not feel that their enjoyment of their brand of art was compromised by their proximity to others enjoying a different kind of performance. A few may have even come back another night to attend one of the other shows.

As long as cultural institutions could not easily cut across genres, their usefulness as vehicles of economic development was limited. They could function as elite establishments, bringing prestige to their city and perhaps attracting a few well-heeled tourists and an occasional amenity-oriented business. However, they would seldom draw large enough crowds or identify with broad enough consumption opportunities to be considered commercial catalysts. On the other hand, organizations offering popular fare might bring in the crowds but would be less likely to earn the support of political and social elites or serve to improve a city's symbolic capital. But this has changed, as we can see when we observe those performing arts center calendars. The Broadway musicals pay the bills. The ethnically diverse programming assures broader political legitimacy. The European art, the symphonic music, the elegant galas affirm an institution's highbrow bona fides to social and economic elites. Institutions of high culture fulfill their unique role within today's urban growth coalitions precisely because they can catalyze profit-generating activities, while bringing their nonprofit, noncommercial credentials with them.

DiMaggio and Powell have theorized that organizations working together in the same "organizational field" come to share structural characteristics to facilitate their relations in a process that is shaped by resource dependencies as well as shared professional norms (DiMaggio and Powell 1983). Peterson has applied this theory to the study of cultural institutions and arts patrons, noting that arts organizations have become more professionalized (there are now 40 graduate programs in arts administration) and specialized as arts funding has shifted from private patronage to bureaucratic support (Peterson 1986). The organizational field of cultural production and consumption can perhaps today be expanded to include not just arts organizations and their funders but also the local officials who are involved in developing and marketing the city's cultural offerings. The marriage of culture and development is thus facilitated by the shared goals and norms of their advocates, and increasingly it is institutionalized through cultural tourism offices, arts district promotional agencies, or national collaboratives like the Institute for Community Development and the Arts, a project uniting the advocacy group Americans for the Arts with the United States Conference of Mayors. All are involved in selling an image of an urbane place of cultural sophistication, in which the museum or performance hall lends its panache to the city around it, which reciprocates by creating an atmosphere that promotes the consumption of culture.

Art and the Economy: A Changing Relationship

The cultural life of American cities has always had a complex relationship to the local political economy. Local cultural landscapes were shaped by social rivalries and boosterist regional competition. Such revered institutions as New York's Metropolitan Opera, for example, were created to display the wealth of newly rich industrialists (Burrows and Wallace 1999); the patrons of Chicago's now renowned art museum and symphony sought to assert their cultural parity with Boston and New York (Horowitz 1976). If late-nineteenth and early-twentieth-century patrons could appreciate the potential benefits that accrued to those who built cultural centers, however, for those founding nineteenth-century museums and concert halls—in contrast to today's cultural entrepreneurs—economic gain remained subtext. Cultural institutions of their era were built to show off wealth, not to generate it. Reporting on the opening of the (at that time very modestly housed) Newark Museum in 1909, the local press proclaimed, "The city is rich! A part of the wealth of its citizens should be invested in paintings, sculpture and other art objects" (Newark Museum 1959, 7). Businessman and arts patron Joseph Choate, speaking at the Metropolitan Museum's opening, stressed the museum's function as an uplifting source of beauty and urged men of wealth to "convert pork into porcelain, grain and produce into priceless pottery, the rude ores of commerce into sculpted marble, and railroad shares and mining stocks . . . into the glorified canvas of the world's masters" (Tomkins 1970, 23). Today, the relationship between the city's economy and its cultural institutions is understood very differently. Kicking off a fund-raising drive for the expansion of the Newark Museum—the same museum celebrated as a symbol of local prosperity in 1909—New Jersey Governor Tom Kean touted the museum and other urban cultural assets as "catalysts of rebirth," "creating the kind of public image needed for growth and new jobs" (Courtney 1984). Countless public officials and donors have similarly proclaimed their support for culture as a means of spurring an economic revival (Byrd 1997; Davies 1998).

The association of economic development and culture has by now become commonplace, and commentary on this new relationship is largely laudatory. There have been a few cautionary voices: Some urban scholars have expressed concern that an urban development strategy whose primary goal is to attract outsiders to privatized entertainment spaces can be undemocratic and exclusionary (Eisinger 2000; Judd 1999), diverting public funds from projects of more direct benefit to most urban residents (Strom 1999). Even those cultural facilities deemed successful will never generate the tax revenue and employment to make them appear to be good investments in a cost-benefit analysis (National Endowment for the Arts 1981),[10] giving rise to the same critiques that have been leveled against subsidized sports and convention venues (Sanders 1998; Rosentraub 1997). Of course, unlike convention center and sport stadium proponents, cultural advocates have never argued that they could justify public subsidy purely through their production of direct economic benefits. Rather, the arts are said to increase the value of other products and deliver noneconomic benefits as well. Many museums and performing arts centers have effective outreach and education programs that make them genuinely accessible. Surely no other "tourist bubble" institution can make such a claim.

Cultural institutions themselves may face conflicts when they adapt their mission to that of the city's economic development strategists. Hoping for the biggest possible impact on their central city areas, economic development proponents are eager to build new museums and concert halls, and less concerned with sustaining these institutions once they are built. Individual and corporate donors also like to contribute to capital campaigns, where their largesse can be rewarded with wall plaques and naming opportunities. As a result, bricks and mortar investments may be favored over support for cultural programs; smaller arts organizations may be overlooked in favor of the larger groups better able to document their economic clout.

The need to prove their economic mettle to political allies and funders becomes yet one more pressure on cultural institutions already hard-pressed to disseminate great art while paying their bills. The fine arts can certainly be "popular," drawing large audiences. There is also art that is unlikely to play to full houses or attract long lines because it is difficult or challenging or cutting-edge. If arts institutions are primarily seen as mechanisms for urban revitalization and are valued for their ability to draw large numbers of people to city hotels and restaurants, they may be less willing or able to realize the scholarly or educational aspects of their work. To be sure, urban development stakeholders are hardly the only ones pushing arts institutions toward a more commercial, less scholarly mission. And museum curators have often been clever at mounting the kinds of shows that will draw the crowds and pay the bills to gain resources to support more esoteric or challenging programs (Alexander 1996). However, too much focus on the arts institutions' economic role may obscure the fact that making money for the city can never be their primary purpose.

10

Kevin Fox Gotham

Tulane University

(RE)BRANDING THE BIG EASY
Tourism Rebuilding in Post-Katrina New Orleans

Urban Branding and the Promotion of Place

Urban branding stands at the nexus of global forces of transnational flows and networks of activity, and local forces of territorial embeddedness and place particularity. Unlike other brands that people buy and sell in markets, a branded place is spatially fixed, non-transportable, and consumed by people at the point of production. On one hand, branding is a global process of homogenization and standardization with numerous powerful corporate brands circulating in the international market place. Economically, branded goods are extra-local, generic, and not constrained by local habits or idiosyncrasies. Corporate brands like Coca-Cola, Nike, and McDonalds are centrally conceived and lack locally based networks and communal ties. On the other hand, urban branding is a process of differentiation and diversification whereby local tourism organizations, arts and cultural facilities, museums, and historic preservation groups harness and construct place images and help produce tourist sites to attract consumers and investment to a particular locale. According to Destination Marketing Association International, an international network of more than six hundred convention and visitor bureaus in more than twenty-five countries,

> A brand is more than a name, logo, or slogan and it is not built only through advertising. Genuine brands are the result of a comprehensive strategy that encompasses the entire destination *experience* from the visitor and prospective visitor point of view. . . . Brand names are well known but similar, like supermarkets, car dealerships, and fast-food restaurants. The distinguishing factor that sets a "real" brand apart from others is its set of distinctive characteristics and its experience. . . . You get to be a real brand *only* when your customers (visitors) say you are distinctive. (Brand Strategy Inc. 2004)

Around the world, convention and visitor bureaus have embraced and implemented branding strategies to clearly define their local attractions, differentiate them from competitors in the minds of visitors, and create a "promise" that frames the destination experience for visitors. Slogans like "Live Large, Think Big" (Dallas), "City of

---

Angels" (Los Angeles), and "Country Music Capital of the World" (Nashville) are part of the repertoire of local urban branding and represent strategic efforts to identify a city's image and establish a singular personality (International Association of Convention and Visitor Bureaus [IACVB] 2005; Stafford 2005; Miroff 2006). In contrast with the homogeneity and standardized nature of corporate brands, branded spaces and cities valorize cultural diversity and project images that attempt to convince people that they are relatively unique, distinctive, and original.

The main goals of urban branding are to reimagine a city, forge place-based identities, and control consumer impressions and understandings of a particular locale (Evans 2003). Yet branding is more than a strategic and rationalized form of place promotion and marketing. According to Greenberg (2000, 228), urban branding is about constructing and shaping an "urban imaginary" understood as a "coherent, historically based ensemble of representations drawn from the architecture and street plans of the city, the art produced by its residents, and the images of and discourse of the city as seen, heard, or read in the movies, on television, in magazines, and other forms of mass media." Urban imaginaries are not uniform or coherent but are plural, conflicting, contested, and power-laden. For this reason, urban branding aims to create a clear, singular, and consumer-oriented version of the urban imaginary capable of "attracting desirable consumers, repelling undesirable ones, and maximizing consumer spending" (Chatterton and Hollands 2003, 26). Seen in this way, urban branding is a form of place-based "impression management" (Goffman 1957) that relies on evocative storytelling to manage and control the interpretations people have about a city, and socialize visitors and residents to view the city in a particular way. Unlike conventional place promotion that is concerned with selling place images to get the consumer or investor to travel to or invest in the city, urban branding is geared to adapting, reshaping, and manipulating (i.e., simulating) images of the place to be desirable to the targeted consumer. Moreover, the significance of branding as opposed to advertising is that the former seeks to obliterate distinctions between commodities and their representations to the extent that the image becomes the reality (Gibson 2006; Moor 2003, 7). Insofar as possible, tourism boosters employ branding to generate an infinite set of referentials in which one product and activity refers to another through a set of intense associations and pleasurable experiences across time and space.

Another major component of urban branding involves the use of sophisticated niche marketing techniques. As reflected in the work of Lily Hoffman (2003), David Harvey (2001), J. Allen Scott (2004, 2000), and other urban scholars, niche marketing refers to the development of new forms of cultural fragmentation, differentiation, and specialization that split consumers and markets into ever smaller segments or niches, resulting in heterogeneity rather than homogeneity. Unlike mass marketing which advertises products for mass audiences, the goal of niche marketing is to produce images and other referents that appeal to the tastes and expectations of particular niche groups or market segments (Cohen 2003; Slater 2002). According to Novelli (2005, 5):

> The clear premise is that the market should not be seen as some simplistic homogeneous whole with general needs, but rather as sets of individuals with specific needs relating to the qualities and features of particular products. Thus we can speak of a "niche market" as a more narrowly defined group whereby the individuals in the group are identifiable by

the same specialized needs or interests and are defined as having a strong desire for the products on offer.

Niche markets do not exist a priori but are created by erasing the diversity of social groups and defining and thus homogenizing families, baby boomers, senior citizens, gays and lesbians, and African- and Hispanic-Americans as consumers. In tourism marketing, all groups and subcultures—except non-consumers—are scrutinized as possible niche markets. Branding aids in the production and reproduction of niche markets by constructing and disseminating images of local culture and cultural products that reflect travel trends and niche tourists' ways of viewing the world. That is, the different representations of local culture including what is distinctive and unique about different places are chosen among a variety of vocabularies, symbols, and codes to convince specific niche groups to travel to particular locales to consume the markers of local culture. Indeed, profit making and organizational survival dictate that tourism agencies create more and more niches because each new niche group amounts to a new market to tap into to create consumer demand to travel and spend money. The rise of ethnic heritage tourism, cultural tourism, ecotourism, geo-tourism, gastronomic tourism, and adventure tourism, among many others, reflects the growth of niche marketing in tourism promotion (Lin 1998; Urry 2002; Sheller and Urry 2004; Yuen 2006).

A further element of branding is the attempt to blur the boundaries between tourist and nontourist practices and make different and disparate social activities indistinguishable from tourism.[1] Early urban work by Michael Sorkin (1992) and colleagues expressed concern that the growth of tourism and related spread of theme-park characteristics to cities was eroding past distinctions between tourism and other aspects of urban culture. More recent urban research by Clark (2004), Gottdiener (2001), and Lloyd (2005), among others, draws attention to broad sociocultural transformations that have spearheaded the development of new highly themed and regulated entertainment spaces characterized by liminality, staging, and fantasy—all commonly identified with tourist sites. In these and other accounts, tourism amalgamates with consumption practices and urban entertainment activities to become part of the broader urban culture with no clear boundaries. Over the last decade, tourism organizations around the world have launched strategic branding campaigns to elide the distinction between residents and tourists, to urge residents to acquire the consumption practices and visual orientation characteristic of tourists. Local advertisements in New Orleans and elsewhere encourage residents to be tourists in their own hometown. Yet, unlike tourists, residents are locked into everyday local struggles and conflicts, shared experiences of the mundane and commonplace, and collective practices to create stable rules and traditions to give meaning to their lives as members of a community. Such actions are the antithesis of touristic experiences that are explicitly designed to be worry-free, spectacular, extraordinary, and short-term. These inherent problems complicate the branding process and make it difficult to evaluate whether branding is "successful," produces intended outcomes, or generates unforeseen and negative consequences. As I show, the implementation of urban branding in New Orleans has faced an array of conflicting prerogatives and expectations because the object of branding consists of many stakeholders with diverse and divergent interests and concerns. Like all places, New Orleans cannot be represented as a consistent brand because perceptions, interpretations, and understandings of the city vary among residents and local organizations.

Branding New Orleans: Tourism Development before Hurricane Katrina

Tourism in the New Orleans metropolitan area has grown tremendously in the postwar era. In 1960, local leaders formed the Greater New Orleans Tourist and Convention Commission (GNOTCC), a forerunner to the current New Orleans Metropolitan Convention and Visitors Bureau (NOMCVB), to promote New Orleans on an international scale and plan for long-range tourism development. During the 1970s and 1980s, political and economic elites joined forces to build the Louisiana Superdome, the Riverfront Mall, the Ernst Morial Convention Center, the Aquarium of the Americas, and a variety of other tourist attractions. Since the 1980s, the city has hosted many mega-events, including the 1984 World's Fair, periodic Super Bowls and (Nokia) Sugar Bowls, the NCAA basketball tournaments, the Jazz and Heritage Festival, and the Essence Festival (Lauria, Whelan, and Young 1995). The hotel industry has grown considerably over the last few decades as indicated by the skyrocketing number of hotel rooms in the metropolitan area. The number of hotel rooms increased from 4,750 in 1960; to 10,686 in 1975; and 19,500 in 1985. In 1990, the metropolitan area had approximately 25,500 hotel/motel rooms. This figure increased to 28,000 in 1999 and more than 33,000 by 2004. As of December 2006, approximately 180 metropolitan area hotels and motels were operating with 28,500 rooms in inventory. Prior to Hurricane Katrina, 265 hotels had an inventory of 38,338 rooms (New Orleans Tourism Marketing Corporation [NOTMC] 2006). Much of the increase in hotels and hotel rooms has been fueled by the growth in the convention market and industry. New Orleans hosted 172 conventions in 1960; 1,000 conventions in 1975; 1,453 conventions in 1990; 2,485 conventions in 1995; and 3,556 conventions in 2000. In recent years, lackluster economic growth and the lingering effects of the September 11, 2001, disaster have depressed the convention industry. Nevertheless, overall convention attendance increased more than twenty times from 1960 to 2001, a development that reflects the growth of a vast tourism infrastructure of restaurants, festival promotions, professional sports, hotel and motel accommodations, university programs in tourism management and service, and so on.[2]

The development of a tourism infrastructure in New Orleans can be situated with reference to wider economic and sociocultural changes that affected the city and the state of Louisiana in the postwar decades. Economically, New Orleans's status as a military shipbuilding port and center of chemical and petroleum processing underwent a major decline in the 1950s and later (Lewis 2005). During the 1970s, a statewide coalition of business leaders formed the Council for a Better Louisiana (CABL) to remedy the state's lagging economic growth and attract new sources of capital investment. "In the economic outlook for Louisiana, a hard fact is that the production of oil and gas which has supported much business activity is on the downturn," lamented the CABL in 1977. "Reserves are being depleted, and the state needs to promote other bases for economic growth such as tourism" (Craig 1977). Demographically, massive losses in urban population in the decades after 1960 coincided with beginnings of a long-term erosion of the tax base of the city. Various studies and newspaper reports from the mid-1960s forward document the city's revenue problems.[3] In the two decades after 1964, the percent distribution of property taxes for New Orleans dropped from 33.3% of total revenue to 9.8%. During the same time, the city became more reliant on sales tax revenue with the percent distribution of sales tax increasing from 33.5% of total revenue in 1964 to 57.3% in 1984.[4] The loss of revenue from property taxes and increased dependence on sales taxes reflect the passage of several statutes by the state of Louisiana during the 1970s that significantly reduced the ability of local governments to raise revenue.[5] Fiscal constraints imposed by the state government combined with the suburbanization of people and businesses weakened the ability of New Orleans to fund government operations and provide public services. As a result, by the late 1970s, the city was facing a fiscal crisis, financially pressured to develop new policies and strategies to leverage consumption-based investment focusing on tourism and entertainment.

Since the 1970s, New Orleans has engaged in various forms of place promotion and marketing to enhance local distinctiveness and project a favorable image to a global audience to attract visitors and tourism investment. What is different in the 1990s and later, however, is the creation of specialized tourism organizations and the strategic use of branding to fragment and diversify tourists and insinuate tourism practices more deeply into the everyday life of New Orleans. In the late 1990s, political and economic elites created the New Orleans Tourism Marketing Corporation (NOTMC), the New Orleans Multicultural Tourism Network (NOMTN), and the Mayor's Office of Tourism and Arts to represent local tourism businesses, create new business opportunities, and capitalize on the burgeoning niche market industry. The opening of NOMCVB offices in several foreign countries, the legalization of gambling in Louisiana in the 1990s, and the building of a Harrah's casino also reflect concerted efforts to expand tourism and promote the city on a global scale. In 2001, the NOTMC launched a major marketing campaign to brand New Orleans as a place of "authentic fun." The NOTMC's Annual Report of 2002 noted:

> The new comprehensive branding campaign focused on the food, music, ambience, and good times New Orleans offers any time of the year. It marks a shift from the purely direct-response approach of prior years by adding a strong image component. In our creative testing in 2001, the concept of "authentic fun" and the message "happenin' every day" got very positive responses. In 2002, it delivered as tested. Our Summer Campaign pushed traditional inquiries 10% beyond the previous year's campaign.

During this time, the NOTMC and the NOMCVB established a synergistic "marketing partnership" that included public relations, e-mail campaigns, and direct marketing to generate awareness of New Orleans as a holiday destination, and as a place of year-round and all-day and night entertainment. In 2003, the NOMCVB began "disseminating a strategically crafted set of core messages that 'brand' the city as a premier destination." According to the NOMCVB's 2003 Annual Report, "The NOMCVB is branding New Orleans . . . as an energetic and vibrant city not only to visit but also in which to live, work, and do business. The CVB's communication emphasizes New Orleans's unique blend of European, African, and Caribbean culture and its preeminence as a center for art, music, and food." At the same time, the NOMCVB is "branding itself as the national leader in best practices and customer service."

Many urban researchers view urban branding as a process of simplifying and reducing the complexity of urban reality to a few transparent and easily understood themes, symbols, and slogans. Yet it is important to note that distinguishing a place is only one component in the larger process of branding local attributes, activities, and products. In the 1990s, major companies began branding themselves and their products as expressions of New Orleans culture. Hotel Monteleone, the city's oldest hotel, has attempted to brand itself as a New Orleans literary landmark (Hotel Monteleone 2006). Advertisements from the Brennan family restaurants proclaim that they are "responsible for fostering a culinary tradition that many regard as the epitome of New Orleans fine dining . . . and Brennan-branded restaurants are now in business in Houston, Las Vegas and Anaheim, California" (McNulty 2005). In addition, Southern Comfort has launched a major branding campaign to brand itself as an "authentic" New Orleans tradition by emphasizing that the Southern Comfort secret formula was developed on Bourbon Street. In these and other cases, companies seek to merge their commercialized images with New Orleans imagery to forge emotional connections between the city and visitors. The goal of these corporate promotions is to convince consumers that by buying their products they are, in fact, receiving the New Orleans experience and with that an impression of value.

One of the so-called "benefits" of effective urban branding, according to the World Tourism Organization (WTO 2006), is that a branded place can "serve as a base for the promotion of other products" including film brands, music brands, and other cultural product brands. We can see this brand extension and brand amplification process in the attempt by city officials and tourism boosters to brand jazz music as authentically New Orleans to generate inward investment and stimulate the growth of a local music industry. In 2002, local leaders established the New Orleans Jazz Orchestra as a nonprofit jazz education and performance organization that had as its purpose "the celebration, proliferation, and structured branding of New Orleans jazz" and the development of a "New Orleans based jazz tourism programming." Central to this initiative has been the emphasis on "building national awareness about the role New Orleans has played and continues to play in American culture." Advertisements proclaim "New Orleans jazz is a way of life for New Orleanians" and New Orleans's "spirit created America's only indigenous music" (New Orleans Jazz Orchestra 2005). These strategic efforts supplement a major branding campaign launched by the mayor's Office of Economic Development in August 2004 to "facilitate future collaboration among the businesses and entities that promote Jazz." As New Orleans Mayor C. Ray Nagin puts it, "New Orleans is the birthplace of Jazz and Jazz is the foundation for all music in America. We need to capitalize on this and begin branding the world-wide appeal of Jazz as a uniquely New Orleans experience" (City of New Orleans 2004).

The attempt to brand New Orleans as the birthplace and home of jazz music intersects with other organized efforts to brand food and history as signs of local authenticity. In my interviews, tourism professionals proclaim that food, music, and history constitute the "holy trinity" of New Orleans tourism that unites the diverse cultural attributes of the city into a set of easily recognized and evocative themes. Urban branding is about identifying the most relevant associations between these three elements and strengthening their links to the New Orleans brand. The triad's lack of specificity leaves it open to diverse interpretations while creating a chain of signifiers to interconnect diverse leisure activities. Branding New Orleans as a site of delicious food, quality music, and rich history fulfills several strategic tourism objectives including attracting diverse kinds of niche tourists and generating business opportunities within the local tourism industry. Another objective is to minimize the uncertainty of urban reality by presenting a transparent and understandable image of New Orleans and its cultural products. Overall, branding seeks to enhance the calculability, predictability, and efficiency of consuming places. Producing and circulating brand values—food, music, and history—is tantamount to rearranging commodity-images into chains of meaning and cultural signification to make New Orleans attractive and accessible to the imagination. Yet as Hollands and Chatterton (2003, 367) note, the branding of products and services on the basis of their physical attributes have increasingly given way to distinguishing them through their expressive or "'product surrounding' qualities—aesthetic and emotional elements." In short, a distinctive feature of urban branding is the production of interconnected signs, images, and evocative themes that has the capacity to provide memorable and entertaining experiences. This in turn relates to a point made by Judd (2003) that urban branding and related urban place building campaigns are a process of symbolic differentiation and specialization to "coach" tourists on what to do, where to go, and how to feel.

Rebranding New Orleans: Tourism Rebuilding in the Aftermath of Hurricane Katrina

In the aftermath of the Katrina disaster, the NOMCVB, NOTMC, and other tourism organizations have elaborated on their past branding campaigns and/or created new campaigns to alter people's perceptions and images of New Orleans using brand elements such as new slogans and logos. Novel slogans and themes seek to counter negative imagery and publicity, and reconstitute and amplify New Orleans's brand identity. In April 2006, the Louisiana Recovery Authority earmarked $30 million for tourism and convention marketing. The NOMCVB is using a portion of this money to "reimage and rebrand" the Ernest N. Morial Convention Center, the site of an internationally televised humanitarian crisis in the days after Hurricane Katrina (Mowbray 2006). The NOTMC, whose hotel tax-dependent budget was negatively affected by the Katrina disaster, has joined forces with the Louisiana Office of Tourism to launch a new branding campaign with "Fall in Love with Louisiana All Over Again" as the main slogan. The NOTMC is continuing its "New Orleans: Happenin' Every Day" slogan while establishing new institutional collaborations to leverage funds and seek new sources of financing. The New Orleans Multicultural Tourism Network (NOMTN) has adopted the slogan "Do You Know What It Means to Miss New Orleans? We Know You Do" to rebrand New Orleans as a multicultural destination. These slogans project a conflict-free and nostalgic image of New Orleans, divert attention from the reality of human suffering and physical destruction, and construct a narrative of past grandeur to stimulate consumer desires to travel to the city. To paraphrase Greenberg (2000), recent post-Katrina urban branding campaigns function not only as "texts-on-cities" but power-laden "texts-as-cities" that position tourism professionals and organizations as important voices in the articulation of the city's collective identity and thus ultimately the urban brand.

Before Katrina, local tourism organizations and city leaders focused on attracting international hotel chains and entertainment corporations such as Harrah's casino, Planet Hollywood, and House of Blues, among others, as expedients to branding New Orleans as a music and entertainment city. These branding efforts have accelerated in the aftermath of Katrina as city and state leaders announced in May 2006 their desire to create a twenty-acre performance arts park to be anchored by a new National Jazz

Center in downtown New Orleans (New Orleans Jazz Orchestra 2006; Mowbray, Krupa, and Thomas 2006). In addition, preeminent developers such as Donald Trump have planned major condominium developments while Harrah's casino has launched a major expansion of its 450-room hotel. In particular, Harrah's has joined with the NOMCVB and city leaders to redevelop the area from the French Quarter to the Morial Convention Center into an urban entertainment destination anchored by new restaurants, a themed jazz club, upscale bars, and global retail firms. In 2005, the city of New Orleans hired a marketing firm to seek corporate sponsors for future Mardi Gras celebrations and contract with television networks to broadcast carnival parades nationwide. In September 2006, The U.S. Department of Housing and Urban Development (HUD) approved $28.5 million to distribute to seventeen tourism offices and organizations in Louisiana to promote their venues. State and local leaders and tourism officials have earmarked this money to finance a national tourism campaign similar to one used by New York City after the September 11, 2001, disaster (Scott 2006). These developments complement the $185 million spent to repair and improve the Superdome stadium, which reopened in September 2006.

Much of the impetus for the development of tourism in post-Katrina New Orleans involves planning for branded and standardized entertainment experiences, commodified and privatized spaces to maximize consumption, and a strong desire to increase the value of corporate brands. Three recent developments reveal the way in which new types of tourism planning and rebuilding are altering the New Orleans landscape. First, tourism professionals are implementing new urban rebranding campaigns to present an image of "authentic" New Orleans as clearly demarcated, disconnected, and segregated from flooded neighborhoods. Indeed, promotional efforts depict the French Quarter and other tourist spaces as hermetically sealed enclaves that are safe and crime-free. Tourism boosters are seeking to attract new visitors, especially those like Dorothy Washington from Philadelphia who told a wire-service reporter in July 2006, "Really, I haven't seen any sign of the hurricane or crime. The French Quarter's a whole world to itself" (Foster 2006). Second, Katrina has inspired a new industry of "disaster tourism" that involves the circulation of people to flooded neighborhoods in the safety and security of a guided tour bus. Beginning in January 2006, Gray Line New Orleans Bus Tours began offering its "Hurricane Katrina: America's Worst Catastrophe!" tour through devastated neighborhoods. The bus tour presents flooded neighborhoods as spectacular and entertaining sites to visit. Like other tours and place marketing efforts, Gray Line invests ordinary places with the status of tourist attractions that have historical and cultural significance thereby mobilizing travelers to visit them. New Orleans neighborhoods affected by Katrina are remade into abstract representations, with viewers constituted as consumers and disaster constructed as a consumable spectacle. What is important is that the constitution of flooded neighborhoods as tourist sites reflects conscious and strategic efforts to capitalize on the tourist's desire for the dramatic, spectacular, and unusual. Disaster tourism depends on the commodification of leisure and the transformation of tragic events into entertaining attractions that can deliver extraordinary experiences. Katrina bus tours compose New Orleans's urban landscape into a collage of fixed and static images that are marketed and interpreted for tourists.

Third, political and economic elites have pushed for the development of lucrative tax subsidies to attract corporate brands to invest in New Orleans and help finance the rebuilding effort. Indeed, urban branding is corporate-driven to the extent that international firms possess the institutional capacity to leverage huge amounts of capital to invest in some places rather than others. State and local officials and elites are looking to the passage of tax credits by the state of Louisiana in 2005 and 2006 to spur the development of a music and film industry. In addition, tourism professionals are seeking to leverage incentives provided through the federally created Gulf Opportunity Zone (GO Zone) to subsidize the planning and building of new entertainment spaces and attractions along Canal Street and near the French Quarter.[6] According to Stephen Perry, president of the NOMCVB,

> New Orleans has, over the last 10 years, made food its dominant brand. If we were able to rebrand the city, not only nationally but internationally, and put the food brand on one pillar and create one of the most dynamic live music centers of all sorts—with theater, cabaret, live local and national jazz—combined with the GO Zone, which goes towards infrastructure, plus the historic tax credits, that's the future. . . . What draws customers now in America is entertainment product. We can combine that with our natural authenticity. We can reach a level that we've never been to before. . . . We know it works in San Diego, Memphis, Austin, Nashville, and we know it changed the face of Las Vegas. This for us should not be a dream. This is something we can't live without. . . . [We] will not only restore confidence of locals but we'll realize dreams of what we always thought it could be. And we can do it in 36 to 48 months. (Coviello 2006)

Perry and other tourism professionals are looking to the example of Branson, Missouri, on how to brand New Orleans as an entertainment destination. With little prior existence as a tourism or entertainment center, Branson has become a major magnet for visitors with musicals, comedy, and variety shows. "I believe people yearn for culture. I believe that it's a matter of 'if you build it, they will come,'" according to entrepreneur Roger Wilson who is working with the NOMCVB to revitalize downtown New Orleans (Coviello 2006). These remarks suggest that branding is not only designed to attract affluent and upscale consumers and visitors to spend money in the city, but is driven by the need to increase the value of corporate brands and to legitimate urban branding as necessary and imperative to rebuilding New Orleans.

CHAPTER 4

THE CITIES: THE POLITICS OF INTERETHNIC BARGAINING

THE NEW GROUP POLITICS

Competition, conflict, and accommodation along racial and ethnic lines is a key element in the process of globalization, as is the dispersal of all groups to the suburbs. This development has profound consequences for city politics. New and older groups compete for living space and access to jobs, sharpening rivalries among people of different racial, ethnic, and social class backgrounds. In order to govern, political leaders must struggle to mobilize new voter coalitions and attempt to satisfy the political claims of voters who have different priorities and life experiences. Thus, city politics is often characterized by political confrontation and accommodation as diverse populations assert their presence and identity in local political systems.

Rising racial tensions over neighborhood space became a dominant feature of city politics decades ago. This set the stage for interracial political conflicts that sometimes reached crisis proportions. In Selection 11, Thomas J. Sugrue examines the seeds of racial confrontation in Detroit. Abundant jobs in the industrial cities during World War II drew black workers to northern cities, and once the war was over the migration picked up even more steam. In 1940, blacks made up just 9.3 percent of Detroit's population; by 1970, the proportion had increased to 63 percent. In Sugrue's account, whites attempted to keep blacks from moving into white neighborhoods by organizing homeowners' associations and citizen's groups and by resorting to intimidation and violence. White homeowners felt economically vulnerable to economic downturns and changes in the workplace, and they projected onto blacks their insecurities. The overcrowded slums that blacks were forced to live in projected a real-life image of the problems that whites feared. The resistance to black movement into white neighborhoods assumed some of the aspects of war. Racial change in the neighborhoods occurred in block-by-block skirmishes, with whites making a, slow retreat.

Although the city/suburban racial divide inherited from the past still persists in America's metropolitan areas, things are changing. Newer immigrants are establishing an uneven but growing political presence in urban politics. Early in the last century, some immigrants—in particular, the Irish—were able to find a voice in the party machines. That avenue is no longer available, but the ballot box still gives them powerful leverage. In Selection 12, Reuel Rogers focuses on coalition building in cities where new and old minority immigrant groups compete for power. He wonders whether the newcomers will forge coalitions with their native-born counterparts, particularly African-Americans. In the past, many believed that race-based alliances between nonwhite immigrants and African-Americans were likely since both experienced racial discrimination and frequently share other group characteristics that give them common cause.

Using the case of Caribbean and American-born blacks in New York City, Rogers notes the absence of alliances between these groups over many years. Common racial interests have not been sufficient to overcome a pattern of interminority tensions and political competition. Rogers explains that race alone is not a satisfactory foundation for coalition building between these two groups. He finds that competition for political turf frequently divides Caribbean and African-American blacks. Entrenched African-American elites have an interest in resisting the mobilization and inclusion of newer Caribbean blacks in order to preserve their hold on jobs and power. For their part, Caribbean minorities seek political recognition and their leaders give priority to constituency building within their own enclave. Rogers also believes that governmental institutions play a part in dividing these two groups. In particular, he says that New York City's decentralized electoral system rewards mobilization of ethnic groups and targeted appeals that become divisive. In addition, the city's one-party politics and lack of rich networks of community-based organizations encourages political faction. The author concludes that race is unlikely to form a stable foundation for governance in big cities like New York for some time, if ever.

The election of racial minorities is of great importance in a nation divided by race. Cities and local governments led the way in offering opportunities for racial and ethnic minorities to win public offices since the 1970s. African-American and Latino candidates have become increasingly successful in winning mayoral and local council elections in cities all over the United States even though their success in gaining national offices lagged. When Barack Obama won the presidential election in 2008, it represented a turning point in race relations. Yet the election of black candidates is an uncertain step with unknown consequences. Does it herald the beginning of a new politics with diminished racial tensions? Or does it trigger greater racial antagonism as white voters resist black political gains? Do black political leaders manage to pull voters together as they govern or does experience with minority government lead to fears of racial favoritism among citizens?

In Selection 13, Zoltan Hajnal surveys mayoral elections during the 20th century. He reports that white voters generally became more accepting of African mayoral candidates. Equally important, Hajnal's analysis suggests that black leadership plays an important role in changing the voting behavior of whites and the way white Americans think about black candidates. He proposes an informational model of voting behavior to understand this. The model assumes that when black challengers run for mayoral office, many white residents are uncertain about the consequences of black leadership and fear electing such candidates. But after electing blacks to office, white voters find that their fears are not born out. Most whites realize the world under black leadership is not all that much different than under white leadership. This encourages more deracialized electoral politics as whites become willing to consider voting for black candidates. Hajnal believes this model of voting explains white voting behavior in mayoral elections involving black candidates better than electoral theories that predict unchanging racial prejudice or backlash among white voters.

Hajnal's upbeat findings about the declining role of racial prejudice in urban politics have far-reaching implications for our entire political system. Perhaps most important, they suggest that opportunities for black leaders in local politics may be a source of profound change in racial attitudes beyond city halls. Whether the positive role of black leadership in changing white attitudes will continue or spread to other governmental levels remains an open question, however. Political competition based on class, racial, and ethnic differences is likely to remain an enduring feature of city politics as long as other sources of social division remain less important. As populations change and age, new urban political coalitions will be forged.

11

Thomas J. Sugrue

RACIAL CONFRONTATION IN POSTWAR DETROIT

The Rise of the Homeowners' Movement

Between 1943 and 1965, Detroit whites founded at least 192 neighborhood organizations throughout the city, variously called "civic associations," "protective associations," "improvement associations," and "homeowners' associations."[1] Few scholars have fully appreciated the enormous contribution of this kind of grassroots organization to the racial and political climate of twentieth-century American cities.[2] Their titles revealed their place in the ideology of white Detroiters. As civic associations, they saw their purpose as upholding the values of self-government and participatory democracy. They offered members a unified voice in city politics. As protective associations, they fiercely guarded the investments their members had made in their homes. They also paternalistically defended neighborhood, home, family, women, and children against the forces of social disorder that they saw arrayed against them in the city. As improvement associations, they emphasized the ideology of self-help and individual achievement that lay at the very heart of the American notion of homeownership. Above all, as home and property owners' associations, these groups represented the interests of those who perceived themselves as independent and rooted rather than dependent and transient.

The surviving records of homeowners associations do not, unfortunately, permit a close analysis of their membership. From the hundreds of letters that groups sent to city officials and civil rights groups, from neighborhood newsletters, and from improvement association letterheads, it is clear that no single ethnic group dominated most neighborhood associations. Names as diverse as Fadanelli, Csanyi, Berge, and Watson appeared on the same petitions. Officers of the Greater Detroit Homeowners' Association, Unit No. 2, in a blue-collar northwest Detroit neighborhood, included a veritable United Nations of ethnic names, among them Benzing, Bonaventura, Francisco, Kopicko, Sloan, Clanahan, Klebba, Beardsley, Twomey, and Barr. Groups met in public-school buildings, Catholic and Protestant churches, union halls, Veterans of Foreign Wars clubhouses, and parks. Letters, even from residents with discernibly "ethnic" names, seldom referred to national heritage or religious background. Organizational newsletters and neighborhood newspapers never used ethnic modifiers or monikers to describe neighborhood association members—they reserved ethnic nomenclature for "the colored" and Asians (and occasionally Jews). The diversity of ethnic membership in neighborhood groups is not surprising, given that Detroit had few ethnically homogeneous neighborhoods by midcentury. But the heterogeneity of Detroit's neighborhoods only partially explains the absence of ethnic affiliation in remaining records. Homeowners and neighborhood groups shared a common bond of whiteness and Americanness—a bond that they asserted forcefully at public meetings and in correspondence with public officials. They referred to the "white race," and spoke of "we the white people." Some called for the creation of a "National Association for the Advancement of White People," and others drew from the "unqualified support of every white family, loyal to white ideas."[3]

Detroit was a magnet for southern white migrants, but there is no evidence of a distinctive southern white presence in neighborhood organizations. "Hillbillies," as they were labeled, were frequently blamed for racial tension in the city, but their role was greatly exaggerated. Most of them dispersed throughout the metropolitan area, and quickly disappeared into the larger white population. There were a few concentrations of poor white southerners in the city, like the Briggs neighborhood near Tiger Stadium. Even in these neighborhoods, however, they tended not to form civic or political organizations. Scattered evidence from voter surveys suggests that they tended to vote solidly Democratic; indeed, in 1949 and 1951 they were more likely to support liberal candidates than were Italians and Poles. In addition, as historical anthropologist John Hartigan has shown, southern whites often lived in close proximity to blacks with little long-term resistance. Most importantly, a 1951 public opinion survey found that "Southerners who now live in Detroit express no more negative attitudes about Negroes and are no more in favor of segregation than are people from other parts of the country." The racial politics of Detroit's neighborhood associations were thoroughly homegrown.[4]

Racial exclusion had not always been the primary purpose of neighborhood associations. Real estate developers had originally created them to enforce building restrictions, restrictive covenants and, later, zoning laws. Their members served as watchdogs, gathering complaints from neighbors and informing the City Plan Commission of zoning violations. Frequently, they lobbied city officials for the provision of better public services such as street lighting, stop signs, traffic lights, and garbage pickup. Improvement associations were also social clubs that welcomed new neighbors and brought together residents of adjacent streets for events such as block parties, dinner dances, and excursions to local amusement parks or baseball games. They sponsored community cleanup and home improvement competitions. Their newsletters included admonitions to association members to drive safely, announcements of local dinner dances, neighborhood gossip, and home improvement and homemaking tips.[5]

During and after World War II, these organizations grew rapidly in number and influence, as hundreds of thousands of working-class whites became homeowners for the first time. Detroit's industrial workers had used their relatively high wages, along with federal mortgage subsidies, to purchase or build modest single-family houses on the sprawling Northeast and Northwest sides. The proportion of owner-occupied homes in the city rose from 39.2 percent in 1940 to 54.1 percent in 1960.[6] Yet the working-class hold on affluence was tenuous. Many city residents had spent a large part of their life savings to buy a home, and they usually had little else to show for their work. Most

Detroiters viewed homeownership as a precarious state, always under siege by external forces beyond their control. Even those who held steady employment found that
mortgage or land contract payments stretched family budgets to the breaking point. In
a comprehensive survey of Detroit residents conducted in 1951, Wayne University sociologist Arthur Kornhauser found that white Detroiters ranked housing needs as the
most pressing problem in the city. Homeownership required a significant financial sacrifice for Detroit residents: the most frequent complaint (voiced by 32 percent of respondents) was that the cost of housing was too high.[7] To a generation that had
struggled through the Great Depression, the specter of foreclosure and eviction was
very real. For working Detroiters, the vagaries of layoffs, plant closings, and automation jeopardized their most significant asset, usually their only substantial investment—
their homes.

Homeownership was as much an identity as a financial investment. Many of
Detroit's homeowners were descendants of immigrants from eastern and southern
Europe, for whom a house and property provided the very definition of a family. They
placed enormous value on the household as the repository of family values and the
center of community life. In addition, for many immigrants and their children, homeownership was proof of success, evidence that they had truly become Americans.
A well-kept property became tangible evidence of hard work, savings, and prudent
investment, the sign of upward mobility and middle-class status.[8]

To white ethnics, homeownership was more than the product of individual enterprise. Detroiters, by and large, lived in intensely communal neighborhoods. In Detroit's
working-class districts, houses were close together on small lots. Day-to-day life was
structured by countless small interactions among neighbors; little was private. Property
maintenance, behavior, and attitudes seldom escaped the close scrutiny of neighbors.
Reinforcing the ties of proximity were the common bonds of religion. In the mid-1950s,
about 65 percent of Detroit's population was Roman Catholic; the white population was
probably closer to 75 or 80 percent Catholic. Catholic familial and institutional bonds
ordered urban life in ways that cannot be underestimated. Paul Wrobel, a third-generation
Polish American, recalled that life in the heavily Catholic East Side neighborhood of
his youth "centered around three separate but related spheres: Family, Parish, and
Neighborhood." In largely Catholic neighborhoods, improvement associations grew
out of parish social organizations, frequently held meetings in church halls, and often got
material and spiritual support from pastors. Improvement associations in largely Polish
neighborhoods on Detroit's East Side, reported the Mayor's Interracial Committee
(MIC), "conform to the bounds of Catholic Church parish lines rather than subdivisions."
Although many Catholic clergy supported civil rights, priests at some Detroit-area
churches encouraged their parishioners to support homeowners' associations, for fear
that black "invasions" would hurt parish life. Parishioners at Saint Andrew and Saint
Benedict, a large Catholic church in a racially changing southwest Detroit neighborhood, were active in the Southwest Civic Improvement League. MIC officials reported a "prevailing sentiment of antagonism and fear" and a "feeling that this
investment [in a new parish school building] and the social life of the church will be
affected by the movement out . . . of large numbers of church members."[9] Catholic
parishes were not the only bases for homeowners' groups, however. White civic associations also found religious and political support among evangelical Protestants. Many
white fundamentalist churches, such as the Temple Baptist Church and the Metropolitan

Tabernacle, fostered racial prejudices and often sponsored neighborhood association meetings.[10]

The homeowners' movement, then, emerged as the public voice of proud home-owners who defined themselves in terms of their tightly knit, exclusive communities. But the simultaneous occurrence of economic dislocation and black migration in postwar Detroit created a sense of crisis among homeowners. Both their economic interests and their communal identities were threatened. They turned to civic associations to defend a world that they feared was slipping away. Increasingly, they blamed blacks for their in-security. In the era of open housing, responding to the threat of black movement into their neighborhoods became the raison d'être of white community groups. One new group, the Northwest Civic Association, called its founding meeting "So YOU will have first hand information on the colored situation in this area," and invited "ALL interested in main-taining Property Values in the NORTHWEST section of Detroit." The Courville District association gathered together residents of a northeast Detroit neighborhood to combat the "influx of colored people" to the area, and rallied supporters with its provocatively enti-tled newsletter, *Action!* When a black family moved onto Cherrylawn Street on the city's West Side, between six hundred and a thousand white neighbors attended an emergency meeting to form a neighborhood association. The founders of the Connor-East Home-owners' Association promised to "protect the Area from undesirable elements." Members of the San Benardo Improvement Association pledged to keep their neighborhood free of "undesirables"—or "Niggers"—as several who eschewed euphemism shouted at the group's first meeting. Existing organizations took on a new emphasis with the threat of black "invasion." In 1950, Orville Tenaglia, president of the Southwest Detroit Improve-ment League, recounted his group's history: "Originally we organized in 1941 to promote better civic affairs, but now we are banded together just to protect our homes." The league was engaged in a "war of nerves" over the movement of blacks into the community.[11]

The issues of race and housing were inseparable in the minds of many white Detroiters. Economically vulnerable homeowners feared, above all, that an influx of blacks would imperil their precarious investments. "Stop selling houses to the colored," advocated one white Detroiter. "Where would we move? No place—poor people have no place to move," he added. "What is the poor people to do?" Speaking for homeowners who felt threatened by the black migration, a self-described "average American housewife" wrote: "What about us, who cannot afford to move to a better location and are surrounded by colored? . . . Most of us invested our life's savings in property and now we are in constant fear that the neighbor will sell its property to people of different race."[12] Kornhauser found that race relations followed a close second to housing in Detroiters' ranking of the city's most pressing problems. Only 18 percent of white respondents from all over the city expressed "favorable" views toward the "full acceptance of Negroes" and 54 percent expressed "unfavorable" attitudes toward inte-gration. When asked to discuss ways in which race relations "were not as good as they should be," 27 percent of white respondents mentioned "Negroes moving into white neighborhoods." 22 percent answered that the "Negro has too many rights and privileges; too much power; too much intermingling." Another 14 percent mentioned "Negroes' undesirable characteristics." Only 14 percent mentioned the existence of discrimination as a problem in race relations.[13]

Whites in Detroit regularly spoke of the "colored problem" or the "Negro problem."[14] In their responses to open-ended questions, Kornhauser's informants made clear what they meant by the "colored problem." Of blacks: "Eighty percent of them are animals," stated one white respondent. "If they keep them all in the right place there wouldn't be any trouble," responded another. "Colored treat the whites in an insolent way," added a third white, "They think they own the city." A majority of whites looked to increased segregation as the solution to Detroit's "colored problem."[15] When asked, "What do you feel ought to be done about relations between Negroes and whites in Detroit?" a remarkable 68 percent of white respondents called for some form of racial segregation— 56 percent of whites surveyed advocated residential segregation. Many cited the Jim Crow South as a model for successful race relations.[16]

Class, union membership, and religion all affected whites' attitudes toward blacks. Working-class and poor whites expressed negative views toward blacks more frequently than other respondents to Kornhauser's survey. 85 percent of poor and working-class whites supported racial segregation, in contrast to 56 percent of middle-income and 42 percent of upper-income whites. Union members were slightly "less favorable than others towards accepting Negroes." CIO members were even more likely than other white Detroiters to express negative views of African Americans—65 percent— although more CIO members were also likely to support full racial equality (18 percent) than ordinary white Detroiters. And finally, Catholics were significantly more likely than Protestants to express unfavorable feelings toward blacks.[17]

Neighborhood groups responded to the threat of "invasion" with such urgency because of the extraordinary speed of racial change. Most blocks in changing neighborhoods went from being all-white to predominantly black in a period of three or four years. They also reacted viscerally against the tactics of blockbusting real estate brokers, whose activities fueled their sense of desperation. Whites living just beyond "racially transitional" areas witnessed the rapid black movement into those areas. They feared that without concerted action, their neighborhoods would turn over just as quickly.

White Detroiters also looked beyond transitional neighborhoods to the "slum," a place that confirmed all of their greatest fears. Whites saw in the neighborhoods to which blacks had been confined in the center city area, such as Paradise Valley, a grim prophecy of their own neighborhoods' futures. The rundown, shabby appearance of inner-city housing, the piles of uncollected garbage, and the streets crowded with children and families escaping tightly packed apartments seemed confirmation of whites' worst fears of social disorder. To them, the ghetto was the antithesis of their tightly-knit, orderly communities. They also noticed the striking class difference between blacks and whites. The median family income of blacks in Detroit was at best two-thirds of that of whites between the 1940s and the 1960s. Although the poorest blacks were seldom the first to move into formerly white neighborhoods (in fact black "pioneers" were often better off than many of their white neighbors), whites feared the incursion of a "lowerclass element" into their neighborhoods.[18]

To white Detroiters, the wretched conditions in Paradise Valley and other poor African American neighborhoods were the fault of irresponsible blacks, not greedy landlords or neglectful city officials. Because housing was such a powerful symbol of "making it" for immigrant and working-class families, many Detroit whites interpreted poor housing conditions as a sign of personal failure and family breakdown. Wherever blacks lived, whites believed, neighborhoods inevitably deteriorated. "Let us keep out the slums," admonished one East Side homeowners' group. If blacks moved into white neighborhoods, they would bring with them "noisy roomers, loud parties, auto horns, and in general riotous living," thus depreciating real estate values and destroying the moral fiber of the community. A middle-aged Catholic woman living in a racially changing Detroit neighborhood offered a similar view. Blacks "just destroy the whole neighborhood," she told an interviewer. "They neglect everything. Their way of life is so different from ours."[19] A Northwest Side neighborhood association poster played on the fears of white residents afraid of the crime that they believed would accompany racial change: "Home Owners Can You Afford to . . . Have your children exposed to gangster operated skid row saloons? Phornographic [sic] pictures and literature? Gamblers and prostitution? You Face These Issues Now!"[20]

As black joblessness rates rose in the 1950s, such fears were not totally without basis. As more and more young African American men faced underemployment or unemployment, many spent time hanging out on streetcorners, a scene that whites found threatening. And as the city's economy began its downward spiral in the mid-1950s, rates of burglary, robbery, and murder began to rise. In the city's poorest black neighborhoods, an alternative economy of gambling, drugs, and prostitution flourished. Even though whites were seldom the victims of black-initiated crimes, Detroit's white-owned daily newspapers paid special attention to black-on-white crimes, giving prominent billing to murders and rapes. Often sensationalistic accounts mentioned the race of a black perpetrator, but seldom, if ever, mentioned that of whites.[21]

Whites also commonly expressed fears of racial intermingling. Black "penetration" of white neighborhoods posed a fundamental challenge to white racial identity. Again and again, neighborhood groups and letter writers referred to the perils of rapacious black sexuality and race mixing. The politics of family, home, and neighborhood were inseparable from the containment of uncontrolled sexuality and the imminent danger of interracial liaisons. Neighborhood newsletters ominously warned of the threat of miscegenation. One Northwest Side newspaper praised a Common Council candidate with a banner headline: "Kronk Bucks Mixing Races." Members of the Courville District association discussed "interracial housing," "interracial marriage," and "interracial dancing in our schools and elsewhere." Proximity to blacks risked intimacy. "Do you want your children to marry colored?" asked one woman at an improvement association rally in 1957. At a meeting at Saint Scholastica Catholic Church in northwest Detroit nine years later, fears of racial intermarriage remained the most pressing concern. Parishioners expressed concerns about the supposed sexual potency of black men.[22]

The undistilled sentiments of youth offer a revealing glimpse into the racial attitudes that undergirded Detroit's battles over housing. In the mid-1940s, a teacher at the all-white Van Dyke School in northeast Detroit asked students in a sixth-grade class to write essays on "Why I like or don't like Negroes." The students frequently mentioned cleanliness, violence, and housing conditions as grounds for disliking blacks, and often offered pejorative comments about blacks' living habits. Several students expressed concerns about black neighbors. "They are durty fighters and they do not keep their yardes clean," wrote one sixth-grader. In the words of another student, "they try to mix in with white people when they don't want them." A classmate stated that "they wanted to live out on Van Dyke and we didn't want them to." Another argued (in words that must have come right from his parents) that "if you give them a inch they take a mile and they are sneaky." Mary Conk drew up a list which encapsulated most of her classmates' sentiments:

1. Because they are mean
2. And they are not very clean
3. Some of them don't like white people
4. They leave garbage in the yard and it smells
5. And in the dark the skare you
6. And they pick you up in a car and kill you at nite
7. And they start riots

Most of the students at the Van Dyke School had never lived near a black person. Few spoke from experience. But the children, fearful of the prospect of blacks as neighbors, expressed attitudes that they had heard again and again from their parents and friends. As white Detroiters continued to fight against black movement throughout the city, they ensured that subsequent generations of children and adults would share Mary Conk's fears about blacks.[23]

Life was good for Easby Wilson in the spring of 1955. The city was in a recession, but Wilson was still steadily employed on the day shift at the Dodge Main plant. At a time when many of his fellow black workers were being laid off, Wilson was lucky. He had saved enough money so that he, his wife, and their five-year-old son could move from the crowded and run-down Paradise Valley area to the quiet, leafy neighborhood around the Courville School on Detroit's Northeast Side. The Courville area was popular with Dodge Main workers because it was affordable, attractive, and only three miles from the plant. Wilson could drive from his house to the factory gate in about ten minutes, or take a fifteen-minute bus ride down Dequindre Avenue.[24]

After looking at a few houses in March 1955, the Wilsons chose a modest frame house on Riopelle Street. They knew that the neighborhood was predominantly white and had heard rumors of racially motivated violence in changing Detroit neighborhoods. But their real estate agent reassured him that "the situation" (a euphemism for race relations) "was fine." What the broker failed to tell them was that they were breaching an invisible racial boundary by buying a house west of Dequindre Avenue. The neighborhood to the east of Dequindre had a rapidly growing black population, but only one other black family lived on the blocks to the west. The Wilsons also did not know that over the preceding decade, white residents of the surrounding neighborhood had formed a powerful homeowners' association to resist the black "invasion" of their area, had harassed whites who offered their houses to blacks, and had driven out several black newcomers. Less than two years before the Wilsons bought their house, neighbors in the same block had threatened a white family who put their house on the market with a black broker.[25]

Shortly after the Wilsons closed on the real estate deal, their new house became a racial battleground. Indignant white neighbors launched a five-month siege on 18199 Riopelle. In late April, just before the Wilsons moved in, someone broke into the house, turned on all the faucets, blocked the kitchen sink, flooded the basement, and spattered black paint on the walls and floors. Later that day, after the Wilsons cleaned up the mess and left, vandals broke all the front windows in the house. Despite the noise, no neighbors reported the attack to the police. On Tuesday, April 26, the Wilsons moved in. The onslaught escalated. White members of the Cadillac Improvement Association approached the Wilsons and demanded that they sell the house. That evening, someone threw a stone through the bathroom window. For two straight nights, the phone rang with angry, anonymous calls.

On Friday, after dinner, a small crowd gathered on Riopelle Street in front of the Wilsons' house. They were soon joined by more than four hundred picketing and chanting whites, summoned by young boys who rode their bikes up and down the street, blowing whistles. The crowd drew together a crosssection of neighborhood residents: as Mrs. Wilson reported, "it was children; it was old people; it was teen-agers; in fact all ages were there." Demonstrators screamed epithets. "You'd better go back where you belong!" shouted an angry neighbor. A rock shattered the dining room window. Trapped inside, Easby Wilson could barely contain his rage. "He lost his head" before he was calmed by his wife and a police officer. The following evening, more protesters filled the street in front of the Wilson house; despite police surveillance, someone threw a large rock toward the house so hard that it stuck in the asbestos siding.

In the aftermath of the demonstrations, some of Wilson's friends from UAW Local 3 stood guard occasionally on the Wilsons' porch. The police stationed a patrol car near the house twenty-four hours a day. Gradually the pickets subsided, but over the next two months, hit-and-run vandals launched eggs, rocks, and bricks at the Wilsons' windows, splashed red, black, and yellow paint on the facade of the house, and put several snakes in the basement. An older white woman who lived next door threatened the family and was caught one evening pouring salt on the Wilsons' lawn. "At night," reported Mrs. Wilson, "when the lights are out, you can expect anything." Despite the police protection, the attacks went unabated; in fact many of the attacks occurred while police officers sat in their car nearby. At the end of the second month of the siege, Mrs. Wilson was exasperated. "I don't know whether it's worthwhile. I believe in Democracy; I believe in what my husband fought for [in World War II]. . . . They fought for the peace and I wonder if it's worthwhile. I have a question in my mind: where is the peace they fought for—where is it?"

The beleaguered Wilsons reported a "terrific strain" because of the incidents. Easby Wilson suffered from a mild heart condition that was aggravated by the stress of constant harassment. Their son Raymond, a five-year-old, began having "nervous attacks," waking up in the middle of the night complaining that he felt like "something was crawling over him, maybe ants." Raymond's affliction proved to be the last indignity the Wilsons would suffer. They moved out of their Riopelle Street house when a psychologist warned the Wilsons that Raymond risked "becoming afflicted with a permanent mental injury" because of the relentless attacks. The siege on the Wilsons, and other attacks on black newcomers to the area, served as an effective deterrent to black movement onto the streets west of Dequindre Avenue, between McNichols and Seven Mile Roads. In 1960, almost five years after the Wilsons were driven out, only 2.9 percent of the area's residents were black.[26]

Violent incidents like the attacks on the Wilsons' home were commonplace in Detroit between the Second World War and the 1960s. The postwar era, as a city race relations official recalled, was marked by many "small disturbances, near-riots, and riots." The city "did a lot of firefighting in those days." White Detroiters instigated over two hundred incidents against blacks moving into formerly all-white neighborhoods, including harassment, mass demonstrations, picketing, effigy burning, window breaking, arson, vandalism, and physical attacks. Most incidents followed improvement association meetings. The number of attacks peaked between 1954 and 1957, when the city's economy was buffeted by plant closings, recession, and unemployment, limiting the housing options of many white, working-class Detroiters. Incidents accelerated again in the early 1960s, reaching a violent crescendo in 1963, when the Commission on Community Relations reported sixty-five incidents. A potent mixture of fear, anger, and desperation animated whites who violently defended their neighborhoods. All but the most liberal whites who lived along the city's racial frontier believed that they had only two options. They could flee, as vast numbers of white urbanites did, or they could hold their ground and fight.[27]

The violence that whites unleashed against blacks was not simply a manifestation of lawlessness and disorder. It was not random, nor was it irrational. In the arena of housing, violence in Detroit was organized and widespread, the outgrowth of one of the largest grassroots movements in the city's history. It involved thousands of whites, directly affected hundreds of blacks, mainly those who were among the first families to break the residential barriers of race, and indirectly constrained the housing choices of tens of thousands of blacks fearful of harassment and physical injury if they broke through Detroit's residential color line. The violent clashes between whites and blacks that marred the city were political acts, the consequence of perceptions of homeownership, community, gender, and race deeply held by white Detroiters. The result of profound economic insecurities among working- and middle-class whites, they were, above all, desperate acts of neighborhood self-determination, by well-organized community groups, in response to an array of social and economic changes over which they had little control.

Racial incidents encoded possession and difference in urban space. Residents of postwar Detroit carried with them a cognitive map that helped them negotiate the complex urban landscape. In a large, amorphous twentieth-century city like Detroit, there were few visible landmarks to distinguish one neighborhood from another. But residents imposed onto the city's featureless topography all sorts of invisible boundaries— boundaries shaped by intimate association, by institutions (like public-school catchment areas or Catholic parish boundaries), by class, and, most importantly, by race. As the city's racial demography changed in the postwar years and as blacks began to move out of the center city, white neighborhood organizations acted to define and defend the invisible boundaries that divided the city. Their actions were, in large part, an attempt to mark their territory symbolically and visibly, to stake out turf and remind outsiders that to violate those borders was to risk grave danger.[28]

The sustained violence in Detroit's neighborhoods was the consummate act in a process of identity formation. White Detroiters invented communities of race in the city that they defined spatially. Race in the postwar city was not just a cultural construction. Instead, whiteness, and by implication blackness, assumed a material dimension, imposed onto the geography of the city. Through the drawing of racial boundaries and through the use of systematic violence to maintain those boundaries, whites reinforced their own fragile racial identity. Ultimately, they were unsuccessful in preventing the movement of blacks into many Detroit neighborhoods, but their defensive measures succeeded in deepening the divide between two Detroits, one black and one white. On one side of the ever-shifting, contested color line were insecure white workers who expressed their racial sentiments politically and depended on the most extreme among them to patrol racial borders. On the other side of the line were blacks, initially optimistic about the prospects of residential integration, but increasingly unwilling to venture into territory they justifiably considered hostile.

Territoriality

For those white Detroiters unwilling or unable to flee, black movement into their neighborhoods was the moral equivalent of war. As the racial demography of Detroit changed, neighborhood groups demarcated racial boundaries with great precision, and, abetted by federal agencies and private real estate agents, divided cities into strictly enforced racial territories. In the postwar years, white urban dwellers fiercely defended their turf. They referred to the black migration in military terms: they spoke of "invasions" and "penetration," and plotted strategies of "resistance." White neighborhoods became "battlegrounds" where residents struggled to preserve segregated housing. Homeowners' associations helped whites to "defend" their homes and "protect" their property.[29]

In defended neighborhoods, white organizations served as gatekeepers by diplomacy and by force. Their goal was nothing short of the containment of Detroit's black population, a domestic Cold War to keep the forces of social disorder, represented by blacks, at bay.[30] White community organizations served the double function of social club and neighborhood militia. On the Lower West Side, homeowners formed the "Property Owners Association" in 1945 to combat the expansion of the black West Side into their neighborhood with "every means at our command."[31] "United Communities are Impregnable," noted founders of the National Association of Community Councils, a grandiosely named "protective, vigilant, American organization" on the West Side.[32]

Most neighborhood improvement associations that battled black newcomers assumed a paramilitary model of organization. The Courville District Association divided the neighborhood into "danger spots," that were "in the process of disintegration by an influx of colored families in the past year." Each section had "captains" and "supervisors" who would lead residents to "retard and diminish this influx, and prevent our white families from exodus."[33] Residents of the De Witt–Clinton area adapted the civil defense system from World War II to their new racial battleground. They formed as "Unit Number 2" of the Greater Detroit Neighbors Association (later renamed the De Witt–Clinton Civic Association) in 1949, a full seven years before the first black family attempted to move into the area. "Block wardens" were responsible for the defense of every street in the area. Residents of other Wyoming Corridor neighborhoods invited De Witt–Clinton officials to help them organize in 1955, 1956, and 1957. They formed a tightly knit network of neighborhood groups that covered every subdivision along the West Side's racial frontier and that shared leadership and passed on information about black movements in the area.[34]

One of the most important roles of improvement associations was to mark the city's racial borders. Frequently, groups used signs to make visible the invisible boundaries of race. In November 1945, for example, white residents of a neighborhood that was beginning to attract blacks to its low-rent apartments posted a sign on a building: "Negroes moving here will be burned, Signed Neighbors."[35] Residents of a West Side street posted "Whites Only" and "KKK" on a house sold to a black family.[36] Blacks seeking homes on American Street in Saint Luke's parish could not miss two large signs at each end of the block that boldly proclaimed "ALL WHITE."[37] Protesters in front of a new house built for an African American in the "white section" of the Seven Mile–Fenelon area carried signs reading, "If you're black, you'd better go back to Africa where you belong."[38] Signs often greeted the first black families who crossed invisible racial lines, warning them of their proper place in the city. The first black family to cross into the Northeast Side neighborhood surrounding Saint Bartholomew's parish in 1963, for example, was greeted with a sign that read "Get back on the other side of 7 Mile."[39] And countless variations on the theme "No Niggers Wanted" (posted on a West Side house in 1957) appeared throughout the city. Signs sometimes conveyed a more subtle message. Some whites in neighborhoods threatened by racial change attempted to stake their turf and deter "blockbusting" real estate agents by posting signs declaring "This House is Not for Sale."[40]

Often protesters chose boundaries as the site of demonstrations. In the Seven Mile–Fenelon area, in November 1948, two men burned an effigy at the corner of Nevada and Conley, only a block from the Sojourner Truth site, on the edge of their threatened white neighborhood. Their ominously simple symbolic act made clear to blacks the risks of crossing racial barriers. When private developers announced plans to construct homes in a formerly all-white section of the area to be sold "on a non-restricted basis," Seven Mile–Fenelon residents tore down signs advertising the new homes and vandalized the houses that breached the racial divide.[41] In the Courville area, residents of Nevada and Marx Streets joined a "car parade," for the purpose of "keeping undesirables out." Led by a sound truck, the paraders ritualistically marked the line that they did not want breached.[42]

In the crucible of racial change, white protesters targeted and stigmatized outsiders whom they believed threatened their communities. The consummate outsiders were blockbusting real estate agents, who violated community boundaries and acted as the catalyst of racial "invasions." In 1948, a coalition of homeowners' organizations published a list of brokers who sold homes to blacks and encouraged members to "Get busy on the phone." Even though the pamphlet asked members to "Never threaten or argue," whites in defended neighborhoods regularly called and harassed offending brokers. Especially galling to white groups was the prominence of blacks and Jews in real estate firms conducting business in changing neighborhoods. Both suffered relentless abuse from members of community groups. When Nathan Slobin, a Jewish real estate agent working in the Lower West Side, sold a home on Poplar Street to a black family, un-named women barraged him with over a hundred phone calls, many with "obscene and menacing language." Area residents carrying antiSemitic signs picketed his office and his home. Members of the Seven Mile–Fenelon Association threatened Charles Taylor, a black real estate broker who worked with contractors in the area, and warned him that any new homes for blacks constructed north of Stockton Street "will be burned down as fast as you can build them."[43] In the Courville area, white residents made death threats to a real estate agent who sold a house to a black family. On Woodingham, a crowd catcalled James Morris, a black real estate agent showing a house to a black family. In another incident on Woodingham, the police demonstrated their solidarity with protesting whites when they arrested Morris, after he had requested police intervention to quell the hostile mob that had gathered. On nearby Tuller and Cherrylawn Streets, gangs of youths harassed black real estate agents and their clients.[44]

Equally galling to residents of defended communities were white neighbors who listed their homes with known blockbusting real estate agents. Protesters reserved special venom for white "race traitors" who sold their homes to African Americans. Frequently, threats were ominous. Whites hid behind the cloak of anonymity "to intimidate and terrify white people who might sell to Negroes." In one case, Mrs. Florence Gifford, a Lower West Side white woman who offered her house with a black real estate agent, received a hundred phone calls over a ten-day period in early 1948. All the calls came from women, but only three were willing to identify themselves, all members of the neighborhood improvement association. Callers threatened property damage and offered more vague warnings like "It will be too bad if you sell to Negroes." Protesters also followed blockbusting white sellers to their new neighborhoods and tried to poison their relations with their new neighbors. Lower West Side picketers tracked Edward Brock to his new house on Detroit's far West Side, and circulated copies of his business card to his new neighbors along with a handbill that read: "WATCH ED BROCK . . . IS ATTEMPTING TO PUT COLORED IN OUR *WHITE* NEIGHBORHOOD 3420 HARRISON. HE WOULD DO THE SAME TO YOU!!" In 1956, white residents of Ruritan Park followed Mr. and Mrs. Peter Hays to their new suburban Livonia home after they sold their Detroit house to a family suspected to be black. They warned the Hays' Livonia neighbors that the couple was "just the type who would sell a home to Negroes."[45]

Occasionally, community groups sought reprisals in the workplace. In 1955, the president of one neighborhood association gleefully reported that his group "had taken care of the white seller on his job." The owner of the chain store where the seller worked "asked us not to boycott [his] business because of this man." In 1957, protesters on Cherrylawn Street tried a similar tactic, threatening officials at Federals Department Store with a boycott if they did not fire Stella Nowak, a white woman who had sold her house to an African American family. Such threats deterred many whites from being the first on a block to sell to blacks.[46]

Threats were most effective when combined with diplomacy. In well-organized neighborhoods, delegations from improvement associations approached parties involved in the sale of a house to offer them alternatives. Often, community groups offered to purchase the house, usually for a sum greater than the asking price. If they lacked the financial resources, delegations often simply approached buyers and sellers and warned them of the dire consequences of breaching the residential color line. By approaching the offending seller or customer, whites presented a united community front, making clear their determination to preserve the neighborhood's racial homogeneity.[47]

Black resisters were the exception rather than the norm. White-initiated violence or the threat of it was a powerful deterrent to black pioneers. The effect of white resistance was to create a sieve through which a relatively small number of black Detroiters passed. The Seven Mile–Fenelon Association's activity did not fully preserve the racial status quo in the area, but it severely limited the residential options open to black home buyers, and slowed black residential movement. 26 percent of the population in the area was black in 1940, and only 35 percent was black in 1950. Considering that 250 black families had moved into the Sojourner Truth project, black movement to other parts of the neighborhood was at best incremental. 1960 census data make more clear the dynamics of racial transition in the area. Blacks were confined to the section of the neighborhood sandwiched between Conant Gardens and Sojourner Truth and to certain blocks immediately to the east.[48] Whites maintained the invisible boundary of race along Dequindre Avenue and slowed black movement further west. In 1960, the section of Courville west of Dequindre was only 2.7 percent black.[49] The De Witt–Clinton area also preserved its racial homogeneity for nearly fifteen years. Although the neighborhoods to the east steadily gained black population, from 1949, when they formed an association, to 1963, not a single black family successfully moved into the neighborhood.[50]

The one exception to the norm was the Lower West Side. The number of blacks living in the area increased between 1940 and 1950, but relatively slowly. Of the entire area, only 11.2 percent of the population was black in 1950; and over one-third of the black population was concentrated in the one census tract closest to the Tireman–Grand Boulevard area. By 1960, however, all but one of the tracts in the former turf covered by the Property Owners Association had a black population of at least 30 percent, but the western part of the district attracted more blacks and fewer whites.[51]

By preoccupying blacks in block-by-block skirmishes, and hastily retreating when blacks finally "broke a block," residents of defended neighborhoods offered a small safety valve to residents of the overcrowded inner city. The rearguard actions of the defended neighborhoods essentially preserved— indeed strengthened—the principle of racial segregation in housing. They protected the homogeneity of all-white neighborhoods beyond the contested blocks. Over the long run, most of the defended neighborhoods became majority black communities. Whites, as one observer noted, "hold 'til the dam bursts, then run like hell." Those whites who remained were, with a few exceptions, older people who could not afford to move.[52]

Detroit was not alone in its pattern of racial violence. Urban whites responded to the influx of millions of black migrants to their cities in the 1940s, 1950s, and 1960s by redefining urban geography and urban politics in starkly racial terms. In Chicago and Cicero, Illinois, working-class whites rioted in the 1940s and 1950s to oppose the construction of public housing in their neighborhoods. White Chicagoans fashioned a brand of Democratic party politics, especially under mayors Martin Kennelly and Richard Daley, that had a sharp racial edge. In Newark, New Jersey, in the 1950s, blue-collar Italian and Polish Americans harassed African American newcomers to their neighborhoods. And in the postwar period, white Philadelphians and Cincinnatians attacked blacks who moved into previously all-white enclaves, and resisted efforts to integrate the housing market.[53] Countless whites retreated to suburbs or neighborhoods on the periphery of cities where they prevented black movement into their communities with federally sanctioned redlining practices, real estate steering, and restrictive zoning laws.[54]

Racial violence had far-reaching effects in the city. It hardened definitions of white and black identities, objectifying them by plotting them on the map of the city. The combination of neighborhood violence, real estate practices, covenants, and the operations of the housing market sharply circumscribed the housing opportunities available to Detroit's African American population. Persistent housing segregation stigmatized blacks, reinforced unequal race relations, and perpetuated racial divisions.

A visitor walking or driving through Detroit in the 1960s—like his or her counterpart in the 1940s—would have passed through two Detroits, one black and one white. Writing in 1963, sociologists Albert J. Mayer and Thomas Hoult noted that blacks in Detroit "live in essentially the same places that their predecessors lived during the 1930s—the only difference is that due to increasing numbers, they occupy more space centered around their traditional quarters."[55] Segregation in housing constrained black housing choices enormously. Whole sections of the city and the vast majority of the suburbs were entirely off limits to blacks. Racial discrimination and the housing market confined blacks to some of Detroit's oldest and worst housing stock, mainly that of the center-city area, and several enclaves on the periphery of the city.[56] Through sustained violence, Detroit whites engaged in battle over turf, a battle that had economic and social as well as political and ideological consequences.

But more than that, it added to Detroit blacks' already deep distrust of whites and white institutions. Speaking to an open housing conference in 1963, the Reverend Charles W. Butler, a prominent African American minister and civil rights advocate, reminded his audience of the anger that seethed among Detroit's blacks. "The desire and ability to move without the right to move," he argued, "is refined slavery." Butler summed up his remarks with a warning that racial segregation "spawned and cultivated the spirit of rebellion. . . . This rebellion is evident in many forms, from nonviolent resistance to vandalism. This rebellion is proof positive that the Negro has grown weary of being the eternal afterthought of America." Racial violence left blacks in neighborhoods increasingly bereft of capital, distant from workplaces, and marginalized politically. In a city deeply divided by racial violence, it was only a matter of time before blacks retaliated. The results of housing segregation, in combination with persistent workplace discrimination and deindustrialization, were explosive.[57]

12

Reuel R. Rogers

MINORITY GROUPS AND COALITIONAL POLITICS

The current wave of non-White immigrants to American cities has prompted a range of important empirical and normative questions for political scientists to ponder. One of the most widely considered is how these newcomers will alter coalition dynamics in demographically diverse cities such as New York and Los Angeles, where alliances are a do-or-die fact of political life. Some researchers have speculated that the non-White racial status of the immigrants and their vulnerability to discrimination will lead them to forge coalitions with native-born minorities, specifically African-Americans (Jennings 1997; Marable 1994; Henry and Munoz 1991). Combating racial discrimination has long been a central political preoccupation for American-born Blacks. Scholars who subscribe to the "minority group" view believe that it will also be a chief concern for the new, non-White immigrants. Their conclusion is that this shared interest will become a powerful basis for interminority alliances, unifying African-Americans and their foreign-born counterparts. In short, this perspective anticipates a grand rainbow coalition among native-born Blacks and recent non-White immigrants from Latin America, Asia, and the Caribbean.[1]

But in cities with significant numbers of African-Americans and non-White newcomers, race-based alliances among these groups generally have proven to be an elusive political goal. Stable coalitions between native-born Blacks and their foreign-born

From Reuel R. Rogers, "Race-Based Coalitions among Minority Groups: Afro-Caribbean Immigrants and African-Americans in New York City," *Urban Affairs Review*, Vol. 39, No. 3, pp. 283–317, copyright © 2004 by SAGE Publications, Inc. Reprinted by permission of SAGE Publications, Inc.

counterparts have not been much in evidence in cities around the country. In New York, for instance, political figures as varied as Al Sharpton and Fernando Ferrer have tried to foster an alliance between African-Americans and Latinos with only the most limited results (Falcon 1988; Mollenkopf 2003). At the other end of the Atlantic seaboard in Miami, African-Americans and Cubans have been at odds for decades (Warren and Moreno 2003). Tensions also have simmered between African-Americans and Asians in Los Angeles (Sonenshein 2003b). In short, political relations between Blacks and recent non-White immigrants have been marked more often by conflict than by cooperation. Although race-based coalitions among native-born Blacks and foreign-born minority groups are widely expected, it turns out that they are actually quite rare.

The rarity of such alliances has led some researchers to speculate that African-Americans are more likely to find themselves in grim political isolation than in any grand rainbow coalition with non-White immigrants (Mollenkopf 2003). A few observers even dismiss the idea of race-based alliances altogether as a misguided and losing electoral strategy in increasingly diverse, multiracial cities, where immigration has scrambled the old Black-White, biracial political calculus (Sleeper 1993). Whatever their future prospects, race-based coalitions between African-Americans and non-White immigrants have not had much success to date.

Why have such race-based alliances been difficult to foster? A number of studies have noted the political conflicts between Blacks and non-White immigrants, to be sure. But very few have provided detailed analyses of why the racial commonalities they share have not been enough to override differences and produce stable alliances between them. . . .

The Case Study

This article takes up that question with a case study analysis of political relations between African-Americans and Afro-Caribbean immigrants in New York City.[2] These two groups of Black New Yorkers—one native and the other foreign born—together furnish a highly instructive case for exploring why the race-based alliances anticipated by the minority group view have not come to fruition. By the logic of the minority group perspective, rainbow alliances among non-Whites should be most likely when the racial commonalities between them are strong and the racial divisions separating them from Whites are pronounced and politically salient. The strategy for this analysis, then, was to identify a case that fully meets those conditions to give the minority group hypothesis a favorable test.

African-Americans and Afro-Caribbean immigrants living in New York City do just that. As Blacks, the two groups share the same ascriptive racial category, encounter similar forms of discrimination and disadvantage, and have a number of political and economic interests in common. True enough, they also have a history of occasional intergroup tensions, which could undermine any potential for a race-based political alliance between them. Yet the minority group perspective would maintain that racial commonalities, shared interests, and the potential benefits of a race-based coalition should override the intermittent interethnic conflicts.

The analysis reveals, however, that Afro-Caribbeans and African-Americans in New York—like non-White groups elsewhere—have not had much success at fostering a sturdy race-based coalition. I find that relations between Afro-Caribbean and African-American leaders typically have deteriorated in the face of interest conflicts over descriptive representation. The critical role that interest convergence plays in coalition building has been well established by scholars (Sonenshein 2003a). When interests are at odds, alliances crumble, or fail to develop for that matter. But rather than leaving the analysis at that conventional wisdom, the article explores why the racial commonalities the two groups share have not compelled them to settle these differences, as the minority group perspective would predict. It would be simplistic not to expect divisions of some kind among non-White groups. The challenge of any coalition is to overcome the inevitable intergroup differences and emphasize commonalities and compromises. Scholars who subscribe to the minority group view believe that race provides much of the incentive to do so.

I offer evidence from a series of interviews with Afro-Caribbean political leaders, however, that race is not always the unifying category that minority group scholars expect it to be. My analysis of the interview data shows that race, despite its potential as a rallying point, has serious limits as a linchpin for coalitions among non-Whites. In fact, it actually may heighten divisions among racial minority groups by emphasizing some interests over others. The analysis specifies and traces the conditions under which such differences tend to manifest, even in the face of strong racial affinities such as the ones shared by Afro-Caribbean and African-American New Yorkers.

I then turn from the internal dynamics between these two groups to consider whether any external factors may also help to explain why they have been unable to capitalize on their commonalities to forge a stable alliance. I argue that two key New York City political institutions—its parties and elections—have tended to undermine the intraracial commonalities between these two constituencies; these institutions, in fact, often have exacerbated the interethnic conflicts over descriptive representation between them. I also speculate that the lack of an institutional vehicle to bring African-American and Afro-Caribbean elites together to emphasize shared racial interests, address disagreements, and find compromises has also made it difficult for them to sustain a coalition. In sum, the article draws two major conclusions from the case study. First, race has serious limits as a site for coalition building among non-White groups. Second, whatever potential it does hold may be undermined by a city's political institutions. More generally, the article suggests that the literature on coalition building among non-White minorities in cities should be more attentive to how the complexities of race play out in intergroup relations and how institutions shape these dynamics.

The Minority Group Theoretical Perspective

With so few cases of successful race-based alliances between non-White immigrants and African-Americans in the literature, the question is why they are expected to develop at all. Why would scholars who advance the minority group perspective predict such a coalition in light of such limited empirical evidence? First, their expectations rest on the bedrock of dominant historical patterns in American politics. Race has been a long-standing and stubborn dividing line in local, state, and national politics in the United States. "Indeed, throughout American politics, the racial barrier redefined opinions, attitudes, and alignments" (Sonenshein 2003b, 334). In urban politics, race has been a key axis for the ideological divisions and interest conflicts that dominate campaigns, make and break political alliances, and shape voting preferences. For much of that history, Blacks and Whites have been on opposite sides of the dividing line. But even when groups of Blacks and Whites have managed to forge alliances, racial issues often have been the touchstone for interest and ideological convergence between the two (Browning et al. 2003).

Although some observers believe that the new non-White immigrants will blur and diminish the significance of the racial divide in urban politics, minority group scholars predict that it will hold. Only instead of pitting Whites against Blacks, it will divide Whites and non-Whites. Even with limited empirical evidence to date of race-based coalitions between Blacks and the new immigrants, minority group scholars infer from the long history of racial division in this country that such alliances are still likely to develop. They reason that as non-White newcomers meet racial barriers such as the ones African-Americans have encountered, the probability of their making political common cause with their native-born Black counterparts will increase.

Beyond the dominant patterns of racial division in this country, minority group scholars also take their analytic cues from theories of African-American politics. More specifically, the minority group view draws much of its inspiration from the literature on "linked racial fate" in African-American politics (Dawson 1994a; Tate 1993). Scholars have found that African-Americans remain a unified voting bloc in many cities, despite growing class divisions within the population (Stone and Pieranunzi 1997; Reed 1988). Dawson and others contend that the persistence of the racial divide and anti-Black discrimination in American life are what keep middle- and low-income African-Americans in relatively close political step. African-Americans, the argument goes, share a "linked fate" insofar as they all inevitably confront racial disadvantages. Race is, in short, a powerful political common denominator among African-Americans, trumping the divisions between the middle class and the poor. It is essentially the linchpin unifying middle- and low-income Blacks in an intraracial coalition. Similarly, minority group scholars predict that race will override the differences between African-Americans and the new immigrants and encourage them to forge political alliances.

The Prima Facie Case for an Afro-Caribbean and African-American Alliance

There are good reasons to expect this prediction to hold for non-White groups in New York City, particularly African-Americans and Afro-Caribbean immigrants. First, racial division and inequality have long been salient features of life in the city. Immigration has increased New York's demographic diversity in recent decades, to be sure: Foreign-born minority groups from Latin America, Asia, and the Caribbean have proliferated, while the numbers of native-born Whites and Blacks have declined. But even in the face of these new patterns of population diversity, familiar racial divisions remain. The city's political and economic sectors are marked by a pronounced racial divide, with well-off Whites often on one side and relatively disadvantaged non-White minorities on the other.

New York's Racial Divisions

New York's racial minorities have made significant advances in the past few decades, to be sure. Blacks, Latinos, and Asians have gone from having virtually no presence on the city council in the 1970s to a level of representation now almost proportionate to their numbers in the population. Racial minorities likewise have elected their own representatives to the state legislature and Congress, as well as to three of the city's five boroughs presidencies (Mollenkopf 2003). There are also signs of minority progress in the economy. Among the more notable trends from the past decade are the increases in Black incomes, Asian educational progress, and Latino business growth (Lewis Mumford Center for Comparative Urban and Regional Research 2002).

But the picture is not altogether sanguine. Even with these advances by racial minorities, Whites continue to enjoy a disproportionate share of the power, influence, and rewards in both the economic and political spheres of New York life. Table 1 indicates that significant disparities remain between the city's White and minority populations on key indicators of economic well-being. White New Yorkers outpace their minority counterparts by a substantial margin in median income. One recent study also uncovered a wide racial gap in neighborhood quality among New York residents (Lewis Mumford Center for Comparative Urban and Regional Research 2002). Whites tend to live in areas of the city with higher incomes, more homeowners, greater numbers of degree holders, and lower poverty rates than their minority counterparts.

Similarly, although New York's minorities have enjoyed considerable political gains in the past two decades, they nonetheless have much less substantive policy influence than Whites do. That is, they have less access to the political levers that actually control policy outcomes. Mollenkopf (2003) noted,

> With the exception of Congressman Charles Rangel . . . none of the city's minority legislators . . . wields great influence within their legislative bodies. . . . The city's minority legislators can and do extract rewards from the White leaders of their bodies, but they do not exert a strong and independent influence on the overall allocation of public benefits. (pp. 121–22)

At the mayoral level, minorities largely have been at the margins or outside of the electoral and governing coalitions assembled by New York's chief executive. Several of the elections for the top office have been racially divisive. What is more, the mayoralty has been occupied by a succession of White politicians. Aside from the short-lived

Table 1 Median Income by Groups in New York City

Year	All Groups	Non-Hispanic Blacks	Non-Hispanic Whites	Hispanics	Asians
2000	38,293	50,920	35,629	27,881	41,338
1990	38,706	47,325	31,955	20,402	41,350

Source: Data are from Lewis Mumford Center for Comparative Urban and Regional Research (2002).
Note: Median income for both years adjusted for 2000 dollars.

administration headed by African-American David Dinkins, minorities have not played a leading role in the city's mayoral regimes. Although several have relied on a modicum of minority support, they have been dominated largely by Whites. Blacks, Latinos, and Asians mostly have occupied subordinate positions, if any at all.

Racial Commonalities between Afro-Caribbeans and African-Americans

Although the divisions separating Whites and non-Whites in New York are pronounced and politically salient, there is no reason to believe that they alone would compel a race-based alliance among the city's minority constituencies. The minority group view holds that such divisions are necessary but not sufficient to produce the predicted coalition. According to this perspective, alliances among non-Whites are probable, not only when there is a sharp racial divide in the political system but also when there are strong commonalities among the minority groups. By that logic, minority group scholars perhaps would not be surprised to find that African-Americans have not been able to forge a sustained alliance with the city's Latino or Asian constituencies (Falcon 1988; Mollenkopf 2003).[3]

After all, there are notable cultural, ideological, economic, and even racial differences between native-born Blacks and these immigrant groups. Many Latinos, for instance, do not identify as non-Whites or racial minorities, unlike African-Americans who largely do. In short, the racial commonalities between African-American New Yorkers and their Asian and Latino counterparts are limited; the differences among these groups arguably match or outweigh the similarities.

For African-Americans and Afro-Caribbean immigrants, however, there is a much stronger argument to be made for racial commonalities. The two groups of Black New Yorkers appear to have considerable mutual interests and incentives for forging a race-based alliance. Consider the prima facie case. First, Afro-Caribbeans and African-Americans obviously share the commonality of Black skin color in a country where discrimination against Blacks has a long history. . . .

The two groups experience higher levels of residential segregation than any other population in New York (Lewis Mumford Center for Comparative Urban and Regional Research 2003). Put another way, both Afro-Caribbeans and African-Americans are confined to overwhelmingly Black sections of the city.[4] The neighborhoods where the two groups live tend to be more economically distressed than majority-White areas. Afro-Caribbeans and African-Americans are exposed to the same neighborhood problems, whether they be failing schools, concentrated poverty, or crime. These two groups thus often have overlapping interests in contests over the distribution of public services and resources to city neighborhoods.

Both Afro-Caribbeans and African-Americans also have had their share of neighborhood-level tensions with Whites. Quite a few of New York's most serious cases of interracial conflict from the past two decades have involved either Afro-Caribbeans or African-Americans and White residents. In the late 1980s and early 1990s, the city was convulsed by a series of violent attacks against Blacks by groups of Whites. All but one of these incidents involved an Afro-Caribbean victim (Waters 1996). The two groups also have had turbulent relations with the city's mostly White police force. There is no need to rehearse individual instances of conflict here. But suffice it to say that there have been complaints about police brutality and misconduct from both the African-American and Afro-Caribbean communities.

Finally, Afro-Caribbean immigrants and African-Americans have similar partisan attachments. The two groups are more heavily Democratic than any other constituency—White or non-White—in the New York City electorate. Although first-generation Afro-Caribbean immigrants do not have the same long-standing, historical ties to the party as their native-born counterparts, they nonetheless have favored the Democratic line almost as much as African-Americans in their voting and registration patterns.

This shared party allegiance does not necessarily mean that Afro-Caribbeans and African-Americans have identical ideological outlooks. Indeed, Afro-Caribbean election districts are consistently several points less Democratic than African-American districts. Although both groups tend to be fairly liberal in their political outlooks, there are shades of difference between them on particular policy questions. Afro-Caribbeans, for instance, are supportive of liberal immigration policies, whereas African-Americans are more ambivalent (Fuchs 1990; Rogers 2000). A few case studies also have suggested that Afro-Caribbeans may be a little less supportive than their native-born counterparts of government solutions to social problems (Rogers 2000; Waters 1999). Still, there is no evidence of deep ideological divisions between these two overwhelmingly Democratic constituencies.

Support for the party has led to gains for African-Americans and Afro-Caribbean immigrants at the elite level. African-Americans have secured leadership positions in the Democratic county organizations. The party also has incorporated a handful of Afro-Caribbean elites in recent years. Even with these gains, both groups have less power within the party than Whites do. In Queens and the Bronx, Whites continue to control a disproportionate share of the leadership positions and influence within the Democratic Party; only in Manhattan, and in Brooklyn to a lesser extent, have African-Americans been able to wield a decisive share of power in the party organization. After many decades of unwavering allegiance to the Democratic Party, then, native-born Blacks still do not match their White counterparts in their level of influence over the organization. Afro-Caribbeans, on the other hand, are marginal players, as the party continues to ignore the vast majority of these immigrants.

All in all, the racial commonalities between African-Americans and Afro-Caribbean immigrants are more than skin deep. The two groups have a number of experiences, interests, and partisan viewpoints in common. They also boast a solid cadre of leaders who regularly interact within New York's Democratic Party. All these factors—common interests, shared ideology, and familiar leadership, coupled with the pronounced racial divide in New York City politics—would appear to pave the way for a race-based alliance between Afro-Caribbean immigrants and African-Americans. This is not to say that there are no potential divisions between the two groups. Yet the minority group view would argue that their commonalities and the strategic appeal of a race-based coalition should override such divisions. This perspective recognizes a clear imperative for these two groups of Blacks to "close racial ranks" and forge a stable political alliance (Kasinitz 1992; Carmichael and Hamilton 1967).

Race-based mobilization represents an alternative route into politics for the thousands of Afro-Caribbean immigrants who have been neglected by the Democratic Party. Outnumbered by African-Americans, these newcomers might find it hard to resist the strategic benefits of combining with their native-born counterparts to build a larger

Black constituency and thereby achieve incorporation. Likewise, such mobilization could also serve as a potent source of political leverage for African-Americans seeking to enlarge their share of government resources and influence on the direction of public policy. With their combined numbers, the two groups could comprise a powerful minority bloc of voters with the potential to decide election outcomes.

The Empirical Case: A Coalition That Never Came

Yet Afro-Caribbean and African-American New Yorkers thus far have been unable to establish a stable coalition. For all their prima facie commonalities, the two groups have been no more successful at fostering a race-based alliance than their non-White counterparts in other cities. There have been instances of political cooperation and common cause between them, to be sure. In 1989, for example, Afro-Caribbean and African-American voters lined up solidly behind Dinkins in his successful first bid for the mayoralty. Together, the two groups were the single largest bloc of voters to support Dinkins in the election (Arian et al. 1991). Since then, these two groups of Black ethnics have also joined together at the voting booth to support high-profile Democratic candidates for state- and citywide office, such as Senator Hillary Clinton and unsuccessful mayoral candidate Mark Green.

Similarly, the episodes of police brutality in Black neighborhoods in the late 1990s galvanized hundreds of Afro-Caribbeans and African-Americans to take to the streets and demand greater police accountability. Both the Dinkins election and the protests against police brutality appealed to the sense of racial solidarity among African-Americans and Afro-Caribbeans. The two instances might well have been viewed as promising precursors to the race-based coalition anticipated by minority group scholars. But these cases of mutual support were episodic and short lived.

Patterns of Conflict

Relations between Afro-Caribbean immigrants and African-Americans over the past two decades more often have been marked by a stubborn undercurrent of tension. My interviews with Afro-Caribbean elites reveal a pattern of friction in the political relationship between the two groups. The conflicts have not extended to rank-and-file Afro-Caribbean and African-American constituents. Nor have they revolved around anything such as competing economic interests, substantive policy differences, or ideological disagreements. Rather, the conflicts typically have been confined to the elite level and have centered mostly on matters of political turf. More specifically, African-American and Afro-Caribbean leaders have clashed over attempts by the latter group to secure descriptive representation and carve out political influence for a distinct Caribbean constituency. African-American leaders have resisted these efforts, whereas their Afro-Caribbean counterparts have complained about the opposition from their fellow Black leaders.

My interview respondents noted that African-American politicians have long been resistant or lukewarm to the prospect of Afro-Caribbean mobilization. One interviewee

(November 22, 1996) conjectured that African-American opposition to Caribbean participation was one impediment to greater electoral representation for the immigrant group. As he explained, Afro-Caribbeans have yet to achieve a level of representation proportionate to their numbers, "partially because there has been opposition from African-American leaders." Caribbean Action Lobby (CAL) member and former state senator Waldaba Stewart (interview, May 2, 1997) recalled that many African-American politicians were either slow or unwilling to acknowledge the emergence of an Afro-Caribbean ethnic constituency in the 1980s.

> Ten, fifteen years ago, African-Americans—many of them—took the position that the only relevant issues were African-American issues, and in many respects ignored the growing Caribbean bloc. . . . In the 1980s, they didn't even want us to run for political office.

Indeed, as Kasinitz (1992) has recounted in his study, African-American politicians consistently opposed or refused to support Afro-Caribbean candidates for elective office in the 1980s.

The pattern continued into the 1990s. Consider former city councilwoman Una Clarke's account of her 1991 bid for a legislative seat. Clarke was seeking to represent a heavily Caribbean district in Brooklyn; her victory made her the first Caribbean-born member of the city council. Her account of the campaign underscores her perception that African-American leaders have often resisted Afro-Caribbean mobilization. The Jamaican-born politician (interview, December 13, 20, 1996) recalled,

> I helped to elect almost every African-American in central Brooklyn, and when my time came to run they were far and few in between that supported me. . . . There was not a single African-American that considered themselves "progressive" that did not come to me and did not ask for my support, and for whom I gave it. So when my time came, I thought that everybody was gonna rally around me, that there would not even be a campaign. . . . "Look your time has come." . . . Nothing of the sort happened.

In a 1999 interview, the former city councilwoman lamented, "I never saw bias until I ran in 1991. When I entered office the street talk was 'Why do these West Indians feel they have to be in politics?' " (Dao 1999). To be fair, Clarke did have the support of African-American Congressman Major Owens, who perhaps recognized that backing her would carry important symbolic value in his own increasingly Caribbean district. But staunch opposition to Clarke's campaign came from African-American Clarence Norman, Brooklyn's Democratic county leader. Norman ran his own candidate, fellow African-American Carl Andrews, for the council seat and led an ultimately aborted legal challenge to Clarke's victory in the aftermath of the election. Clarke and Norman have managed to build a cordial, if somewhat delicate, relationship since then (*New York Carib News* 1996a).

The former city councilwoman and other elite respondents also noted that African-American leaders generally have been slow to court Afro-Caribbeans as a distinct constituency. When asked whether African-American politicians reach out to Caribbean-American voters, one campaign organizer (interview, November 24, 1996) replied tersely, "Not enough. And when they do, they reach out half-heartedly." Another respondent (interview, July 5, 1997) offered,

> [Clarence] Norman has enormous political clout because he is the head of the Democratic Party in Brooklyn. From time to time, I've heard Caribbean leaders, including Una Clarke,

that he would support other people than them. I'm not sure if that's the case. But I would like to see him in more [Caribbean] events. I would like to see him reach out more to the community.

Clarke rated White politicians slightly higher than African-Americans on outreach to the Caribbean population. She (interview, December 13, 20, 1996) elaborated, "I think White politicians [unlike their Black counterparts] feel compelled to do that kind of outreach. Yes. Marty Markowitz is a well-known example. And I can give other examples too."

More recently, some African-American leaders—Dinkins, Owens, Sharpton, and Rangel—have begun to make their own appeals to the immigrant community. Owens and Sharpton have been particularly vocal about incidents of police brutality involving immigrants from the Caribbean, Latin America, and Africa. Their efforts are clearly intended to acknowledge the growing numbers of foreign-born newcomers to the city and perhaps to prevent conservative interests from pursuing divide-and-conquer tactics among New York's minority constituencies. But some of my respondents still characterize these efforts by African-American leaders as begrudging or lukewarm. One (interview, November 22, 1996) recalled Dinkins's early outreach to Caribbean-Americans. "Oh, we had a rough time getting Dinkins out into the Caribbean community. . . . They say that there were some people in Dinkins's camp who were very anti-Caribbean—African-American people." In sum, many Afro-Caribbean elites remain convinced that some African-American politicians still regard the prospect of Caribbean mobilization with ambivalence or resistance.

Key historical episodes in the relations between Afro-Caribbean and African-American political elites tend to support the views of these respondents. One of the most well known instances of conflict between the two groups came during former mayor Ed Koch's 1985 bid for reelection. A group of approximately 150 politically active Afro-Caribbeans established "Caribbeans for Koch" to back the incumbent mayor's campaign. Support for Koch in the Afro-Caribbean immigrant community was hardly widespread or deep. But the group's aim was largely symbolic. That is, to secure greater access to the mayor and City Hall for Afro-Caribbean immigrants—especially since Koch would likely be reelected. Caribbeans for Koch was thus an early attempt by Afro-Caribbean elites to signal the emergence of their immigrant community as a distinctive ethnic constituency with its own aspirations to political power (Kasinitz 1992, 253).

Whatever the motivation, Caribbeans for Koch was met with a torrent of angry criticism from African-American political leaders. Their outrage was fueled by two major concerns. First, anti-Koch sentiment was pervasive in the African-American community. African-American leaders accused the mayor of fomenting anti-Black racism and exacerbating the city's racial problems with his incendiary rhetoric. In their view, then, Caribbeans for Koch showed complete disregard for the mayor's troubling record on race relations; that insensitivity was perhaps all the more incensing to African-American leaders because it came from a group of Black immigrants, who were expected to be equally as outraged by the mayor's record on race as their native-born counterparts.

Second, Caribbeans for Koch was established at the same time that African-American leaders were attempting to "close ranks" and mount an independent political initiative to replace Koch with a Black mayor. The Coalition for a Just New York brought together scores of Black politicians and activists to identify a candidate and support his campaign. The expectation by organizers was that the group would mobilize Blacks and other minority New Yorkers to help ensure electoral victory. The coalition was riven by internal division, though; their African-American candidate ran a poor campaign and lost. Yet many African-Americans strongly criticized Caribbeans for Koch for working at cross-purposes with the coalition, flouting the goals of African-American political leadership, and undermining the larger struggle for Black empowerment. As one of my elite respondents recalled, the African-American leader of the Coalition for a Just New York, Al Vann, publicly reproached Afro-Caribbean leaders for pursuing divisive strategies. "They were not happy with us [Caribbean American leaders]. Al Vann called our attempts to organize on our own tribalism" (interview, November 22, 1996). The supporters of the Coalition for a Just New York essentially saw this attempt at independent Caribbean mobilization as a strain against the tether of racial solidarity.

There have been more recent political conflicts between the two groups involving issues of racial unity and representation. In fact, the tensions have become more palpable as growing numbers of Caribbean politicians run for elective office in the name of a distinct Afro-Caribbean ethnic constituency. As the numbers of Afro-Caribbean New Yorkers have increased steadily over the past two decades, so too has the political viability and likelihood of such ethnically targeted campaigns by Caribbean politicians. These attempts by Afro-Caribbean political entrepreneurs to organize their fellow immigrants into a distinct voting bloc still engender occasional criticism and resistance from some African-American leaders.

A number of Afro-Caribbean candidates joined the fray in the last round of New York City elections by making direct appeals to their coethnics. The most notable instance was the 2000 race for Brooklyn's Eleventh Congressional District seat between nine-term incumbent Owens and former city councilwoman Clarke. Blacks comprise 55% of the district population; more than two-thirds of them trace their roots to the Caribbean. The large numbers of Afro-Caribbeans in the district is a striking example of how immigration has transformed this stretch of central Brooklyn over the past few decades. Despite these demographic shifts, African-American Congressman Owens had held on to his seat since 1982 without a serious electoral challenge. That is, until he faced a fierce test from Clarke in the 2001 Democratic primary. Although Owens won the primary and went on to retain the seat in a lopsided general election victory, the race was one of the most bitter of the campaign season.

Practically none of the rancor between the two candidates was driven by actual issue disagreements. Rather, it was fueled by two very emotionally charged factors. First, there was the underlying tableau of political betrayal. The two were long-time political allies before Clarke announced her candidacy. Owens described himself as a former mentor to the councilwoman (Hicks 2000b). He thus saw her bid to replace him as an act of political betrayal. Clarke, on the other hand, dismissed the talk of betrayal as a distraction from her true motivation for mounting her campaign: that is, to serve the district's constituents. As she put it, "Too much has been made of friendship. It's about leadership and effectiveness. I don't think he's kept up with the needs of the changing community" (Hicks 2000a). Note that Clarke's mention of the "changing community" might be taken as a thinly veiled reference to the increasing numbers of Caribbean immigrants in the district. Her allusion hints at the other factor that fueled the rancor of the contest between these two candidates.

Even more significant than this personal tableau was the pall of interethnic conflict that hung over the race. Clarke made a point of trumpeting her Caribbean roots, appealing directly to her coethnics, and painting her opponent as anti-immigrant. Her goal clearly was to announce the presence of a distinct Caribbean constituency within the majority Black Eleventh District. Even more critically, she sought to emphasize her affinity with these immigrant voters while at the same time raising doubts about the incumbent's sensitivity to their concerns. Owens, in turn, condemned Clarke for couching her campaign in what he described as a divisive ethnic chauvinism (Hicks 2000a). His complaint was echoed by a number of African-American leaders who sent Clarke a letter urging her to abandon her candidacy. The congressman lamented that Clarke's tactics would split Brooklyn's Black community and undermine the larger cause of Black empowerment. His complaints practically echoed those directed against Caribbeans for Koch by African-American leaders more than 15 years earlier.

Case Study Analysis

The conflicts over descriptive representation between Afro-Caribbean and African-American leaders are striking for how often the question of racial unity is invoked. The fact that racial solidarity has not provided the incentive for the two groups to overcome these differences belies the predictions of the minority group view. The steady recurrence of such conflicts suggests that even racial commonality has its limits as a potential coalition linchpin.

The Limits of Racial Solidarity

The interviews and historical evidence indicate that African-American politicians have had one prevailing criticism against their Afro-Caribbean counterparts in the conflicts over descriptive representation. They complain that the immigrants' efforts to appeal to a separate Afro-Caribbean constituency are divisive and antithetical to the cause of racial solidarity and greater Black empowerment.[5] This lament typically greets electoral campaigns by Caribbean politicians seeking to rally, mobilize, or acknowledge their coethnics as a distinct constituency. The logic behind this line of criticism is straightforward. Appealing separately to Afro-Caribbean immigrants, the complaint goes, is tantamount to splitting apart Black New Yorkers, which in turn undermines Black political power. African-American political leaders have grown increasingly concerned about these potential divisions over the past decade, as the numbers of non-White immigrants in the city have expanded. Their worry is that conservative political interests will look to exploit or even sow divisions between African-Americans and these new immigrant constituencies, thereby dousing any potential for a liberal rainbow coalition led by Blacks. It is the classic divide-and-conquer strategy. Divisions between native- and Caribbean-born Black New Yorkers, they contend, might be put to those very political designs. In short, some African-Americans argue that the mobilization of Afro-Caribbeans as a distinct constituency is ultimately a threat to Black racial solidarity and empowerment.

Afro-Caribbeans, on the other hand, insist that the opposition from African-American leaders is unfair and that appeals to racial unity are beside the point. More precisely,

Afro-Caribbean politicians note that the immigrant community is large enough to warrant its own representatives and has distinctive concerns that cannot be taken for granted or glossed over with appeals to Black racial solidarity. My elite respondents were emphatic on this point. One (interview, December 14, 1996) offered,

> I think because we [Caribbean-Americans] have some separate interests, we have a responsibility to be a distinct bloc, be it around immigration and immigration reform, be it around trade with the Caribbean. I think that we can play a pivotal role. . . . We have that obligation. And I think it's a mistake to use skin color to be the only criterion. To use skin color as the only criterion stifles both African-Americans and Caribbean-Americans.

Another respondent gave a more concise reply to the same question. He (interview, November 23, 1996) explained, "Caribbean-Americans are a distinct bloc. Of course, we share many of the same concerns of African-Americans. But we have our own needs and concerns that you just can't dismiss or take it for granted that they [African-Americans] will understand." A community activist answered the charge that Afro-Caribbean mobilization promotes divisiveness within New York's Black population this way.

> Our comment is that you have different Caucasian or White groups, you have the Irish, the Italian, the this and that. What's wrong with us? Why can't we have that too? Just because we're originally, say from Africa, does that mean we have to think and act the same way? Don't we [Caribbean-Americans] have our own needs and issues? (interview, May 2, 1997)

Furthermore, many resent what they perceive to be African-American leaders' implicit assumption that Afro-Caribbeans will be relegated to junior status in any alliance between the two groups. In a 1996 interview, for example, Clarke bristled when she was asked about African-American county leader Norman's aim to consolidate Black political power in the heavily Caribbean 43rd AD. "There are over 300,000 Caribbean Americans in Central Brooklyn. What consolidation are we talking about here? Nobody will relegate us to second class status" (*New York Carib News* 1996b). It is clear that Clarke's objection is not necessarily to the prospect of a unified Black political bloc; in fact, she and many of the Caribbean-American leaders I interviewed were supportive of the notion of a coalition between the two groups. But her worry is that the political goals and interests of Afro-Caribbean immigrants will be subordinated in any such alliance.

Clarke's concern illuminates an important analytic point about alliances built around the idea of racial solidarity. The former city councilwoman noted that African-American leaders insist on serving as racial agents on behalf of Afro-Caribbean immigrants by appealing to the notion of group unity,[6] but in doing so, they often diminish or ignore the distinctive ethnic interests of their foreign-born counterparts. Appeals to racial group unity or collective racial interests—such as the ones made by Vann, Norman, and Owens more recently—are almost always articulated in an effort to advance very specific agendas, which ultimately favor some interests over others. Vann's Coalition for a Just New York, for instance, invoked the goal of racial group unity to criticize and discourage independent mobilization by Afro-Caribbean politicians. The coalition's expectation was that all Black New Yorkers, native- and foreign-born alike, should fall in line with their hand-picked candidates and issue positions. Their notion of group unity, then, was one in which their agenda took precedence over other interests within New York's Black community, such as Afro-Caribbeans' desire for their own share of political influence.

Of course, racial solidarity in politics does not necessarily prescribe or authorize a particular agenda, set of positions, or slate of candidates. Indeed, calls to racial unity might well be seen as an invitation to discuss and reach negotiated stances on such issues. Yet appeals to racial solidarity often implicitly privilege one set of interests over others without any open debate. Even worse, the resulting bias takes cover beneath the rhetorical gloss of "natural" or "collective" racial interests that benefit the population as a whole. Consequently, interests that ought to be debated or evaluated for how they affect different constituents are instead deemed to be settled and beyond question. The case of African-Americans and Afro-Caribbeans in New York demonstrates that the group that happens to have more influence—whether by virtue of numbers, longer political history, or whatever—has the advantage of framing the agenda in this way. African-American elites in New York thus have often taken the lead in prescribing what is required for a race-based alliance or minority empowerment, even if that agenda is not necessarily conducive to the interests of Afro-Caribbeans or other non-White groups.

Furthermore, the case demonstrates that the notion of racial group unity not only favors specific interests and agendas but also can be used to impose discipline and gatekeeping. Appeals to racial group solidarity are often made in the service of mobilization efforts. But the tensions between African-American and Afro-Caribbean politicians show that racial group unity is a two-edged sword that can also be used to discourage mobilization by particular interests within the Black population, or any minority constituency for that matter. To discipline specific constituencies within the population, dominant elites often stake out certain positions and label them as the ones most in keeping with the aims of racial empowerment and the political preferences of Blacks as a whole.[7] Any interests that appear to deviate from those positions are then conveniently challenged for threatening group unity, the "true" preferences of Blacks, or the cause of empowerment. The criticisms lodged against Caribbeans for Koch by the leaders of the Coalition for a Just New York are an obvious example of this tactic.

Owens employed a similar strategy against Clarke in their 2000 primary battle. The congressman tried to portray the city councilwoman as a supporter of Mayor Rudolph Giuliani, who was notoriously unpopular among Blacks during his tenure in office. He also charged that Clarke had been silent on the issue of police brutality, about which the vast majority of Black New Yorkers were acutely concerned. In contrast, he noted that he had engaged in demonstrations to protest incidents of brutality and had even been arrested (Hicks 2000a). Owens essentially waved his civil rights credentials in support of Blacks, while implying that Clarke had none to show. The strategy served to brand the Caribbean-born candidate as a kind of race traitor, a politician out of step with Black interests and the goal of Black empowerment. Tactics such as these are likely to play a role in the conflicts between Afro-Caribbean and African-American leaders, precisely because questions of racial unity so often come into play.[8]

Why Interest Conflicts Over Descriptive Representation

The analysis demonstrates why race is not the ultimate unifying category that minority group scholars expect it to be, even for two groups of Blacks. Yet the question that remains is why the interest conflicts between Afro-Caribbean and African-American elites have focused on descriptive representation. African-Americans have achieved higher levels of influence in New York City politics than have Afro-Caribbeans and other non-White groups.

As the dominant minority group in the Democratic Party, in fact, African-Americans have been able to control a significant share of the material rewards. Mobilization by Afro-Caribbean newcomers, or any other minority group for that matter, could potentially threaten their hold on these political prizes. Entrenched African-American elites thus have a rational interest in maintaining the status quo and resisting Afro-Caribbean mobilization.

Afro-Caribbeans and African-Americans are concentrated in many of the same election districts. The ascension of an Afro-Caribbean to political office could mean the displacement of an African-American incumbent. Several respondents explained this competitive intergroup dynamic.

> There definitely is competition and conflict between the two groups sometimes, especially in politics. Part of the problem is, if you want to call it, we are fighting for the same political offices in the same election districts. We're fighting for the same piece of the pie. And African-Americans probably think if Caribbean people get elected they will lose out on their share. (interview, November 28, 1996)

The result is often African-American resistance to Caribbean political initiative and organization. As Clarke (interview, December 13, 20, 1996) put it, "The [African-American] attitude is 'don't try passing me. I've been here.'"

Battles over political turf and representation between the two groups thus devolve into zero-sum struggles. The conflicts are not simply over political office but also access to the government jobs and other prizes that come with it. For some African-American politicians, then, the interest in political self-preservation trumps any vision for race-based mobilization and coalition building between them and their Caribbean-born counterparts. Afro-Caribbean elites, on the other hand, worry that their interest in greater descriptive representation and policy influence will be trumped by African-American political prerogatives.

The competition between African-Americans and Afro-Caribbeans is arguably reminiscent of earlier historical conflicts among White ethnic groups. There were, for example, fierce battles over patronage and positions within the Democratic Party between Jewish and Italian New Yorkers. But there is an important distinction between those earlier interethnic conflicts and the current tensions between African-American and Afro-Caribbeans. The earlier competition for patronage and public jobs among Irish, Italian, and Jewish ethnics was diminished, or at least moderated, as one or the other group moved into private-sector employment and up the socioeconomic ladder. Italian politicians, for instance, had less of a stake in holding on to government jobs when their coethnics began to find success in private-sector professions. They were thus gradually inclined to relinquish patronage positions in government to their Jewish rivals.

Today's African-American political elites, however, are much more reluctant to concede public-sector jobs and positions to their Caribbean-born counterparts. Their determination to hold on to these forms of public patronage is not surprising. Discrimination historically has made it difficult for African-Americans to find jobs and move up the career ladder in the private sector. Government, in contrast, has long furnished them with fair and ample employment opportunities. Indeed, public-sector jobs have helped foster the expansion of a stable African-American middle class in New York and other cities. The incentive to hold on to these public-sector jobs is thus much greater for African-Americans than it was for White ethnics in the past century. To put it more bluntly, the stakes are higher.

African-Americans thus arguably have legitimate reason to worry about Afro-Caribbean political mobilization. Their concern is likely compounded by the widespread perception that Whites often view these foreign-born Blacks more favorably than African-Americans (Waters 1999).[9] Any potential advancement by Afro-Caribbeans essentially raises the specter not only of political displacement but also economic backsliding for African-Americans. By this light, Afro-Caribbeans look less like a racial in-group and potential coalition partner for native-born Blacks and more like a competing out-group that could threaten African-Americans' share of political power and public-sector resources. That threat of competition and displacement calls into question a key assumption of the minority group perspective: that is, that non-White groups are likely to find common cause and grounds for coalition building in their shared racial experiences. For all the galvanizing power that race carries, this has not been the case with African-American and Afro-Caribbean New Yorkers. Clearly, even presumed common racial interests have their limits.

Electoral Institutions

Another weakness of the minority perspective is a failure to consider how institutional factors might influence the way groups perceive and frame their interests. Racial inequalities and divisions in the political system provide considerable impetus for African-Americans, Afro-Caribbeans, and other non-Whites to forge a race-based alliance, to be sure. But whether groups opt to coalesce and capitalize on common interests—racial or otherwise—or go it alone depends to some degree to the incentive structure of the political system. The prospects hinge on how political institutions frame group perceptions about interests, competition, rewards, and so on. In the case of Afro-Caribbeans, the interviews make it clear that the immigrants are inclined to elect their own coethnics to political office rather than having African-Americans serve as their racial agents. The question is how the immigrants came to value ethnic over racial representation.

It turns out that New York's elective institutions may very well dispose them to do so. The city's electoral structure encourages groups to organize and think of themselves primarily as ethnic cohorts, rather than as racial constituents. Electoral jurisdictions in New York City closely follow the outlines of ethnic neighborhoods. The scores of community board, city council, and state assembly seats in New York are based on districts that often track the boundaries of residential enclaves bearing the unmistakable stamp of particular ethnic groups. It is not too much of an exaggeration, then, to conclude that the basic political jurisdiction in the minds of New York politicians and perhaps its voters is the ethnic neighborhood. It is the fundamental unit of the city's political cartography. New York's "city trenches," to borrow Katznelson's (1981) famous phrase, are its ethnic neighborhoods.

Consider the 40th city council district seat, formerly held by Caribbean-born Una Clarke and now occupied by her daughter. The city created this district in 1991 specifically to accommodate the proliferation of Caribbean immigrant enclaves in central Brooklyn. Most of the pressure to establish the seat came from Afro-Caribbean politicians. The new district essentially gave the ethnic group an opportunity to garner its own share of political representation. As Stewart of CAL (interview, May 2, 1997) put it, "We [Caribbean politicians] noticed that other groups had districts to represent their people, we felt we should have some too." His remark suggests that the decision to push for a heavily Caribbean city council district was not merely the result of constituent pressure or elite initiative. Rather, it was encouraged by politicians' perceptions of the institutional logic of the city's electoral districts. Once institutional arrangements are in place, they tend to influence how elites understand their interests, their ties to constituents, and their relations with other groups. Sure enough, the 40th city council seat has come to be held perpetually and predictably by a Caribbean politician, fulfilling the logic of the district's original design.

More generally, the city's electoral battles are waged from these ethnic neighborhood trenches. The most obvious way for an aspiring politician to build a constituent base in New York is to rally and mobilize voters in ethnic neighborhoods. If a politician can put together a sizable, cohesive bloc of ethnic votes at the neighborhood level, he or she essentially can become a serious player in New York's political game. Politicians are thus often encouraged to make ethnic group appeals. Ethnic politics has long been a staple of political life in American cities, to be sure. The ethnic and immigrant enclaves across New York City are a hard-to-miss source of votes. But the close continuity between the design of the city's electoral institutions and the pattern of its ethnic neighborhoods reinforces this ethnically conscious form of political organization and mobilization. Ethnic appeals are practically dictated by the logic of the city's political jurisdictions.

Some researchers have argued convincingly that this neighborhood-based system of representation serves to regulate and perhaps mute interethnic tensions (Skerry 1993; Mollenkopf 1999). On this view, the system channels interethnic conflicts that might otherwise spill over into the streets and translates them to the bargaining table of the political process where they can be managed or resolved. That may explain why cities like New York and San Antonio, which both boast this kind of neighborhood-based system, have been less susceptible to volatile intergroup clashes than Los Angeles, where no such system exists. Nevertheless, this electoral institutional design simply transfers the potential for interethnic tension from the neighborhood to the elite level, where leaders are often encouraged to position themselves and relate to each other as representatives of particular ethnic groups. The interethnic conflicts thus move from the neighborhood level to the party system, the campaign trail, and the legislature.

It is no wonder, then, that relations between Afro-Caribbean and African-American political elites have been plagued by interethnic tensions over descriptive representation. The potential for interethnic conflict between these two groups of Black leaders is fairly telegraphed in the pattern of Black neighborhood settlement across New York City. Recall that African-Americans and Afro-Caribbean immigrants often live in adjoining neighborhoods or even share the same ones. When these areas are carved up into electoral jurisdictions, they easily become arenas for ethnically tinged, intraBlack bickering over descriptive representation. When a district that was predominantly African-American is somehow redrawn to give growing numbers of Afro-Caribbean immigrants a numerical advantage, the strategic incentive for Caribbean political entrepreneurs to make targeted ethnic appeals is hard to resist.

There are a few who avoid playing the ethnic card in campaigns. State Senator John Sampson is a good example. This second-generation Afro-Caribbean New Yorker has largely refrained from making exclusive appeals to his coethnics.[10] He instead campaigns to Blacks generally and scrupulously avoids the interethnic schisms that have erupted among the city's Black leaders. But most other Afro-Caribbean politicians have followed the ethnic strategy. The price of giving into the temptation is the danger of engendering interethnic conflict with African-American political elites faced with the specter of electoral displacement. The primary battle between Clarke and Owens is just one of the more well-known recent examples. But several cases fit this predicted pattern.

A simple historical comparison helps to demonstrate how the institutional design of New York's electoral districts shapes intergroup dynamics. It is no coincidence that the tensions over descriptive representation between Afro-Caribbean and African-American political elites have emerged only in the past two decades. Prior to 1989, the city council was not composed of the 51 neighborhood-based seats it boasts today. Rather, it consisted of 10 at-large districts, with 2 designated for each of the five boroughs (Macchiarola and Diaz 1993). Council members were elected on a borough-wide basis. Unlike the current neighborhood-based system, the at-large configuration compelled officeholders and candidates to make broad appeals beyond the boundaries of the city's ethnic enclaves.

An Afro-Caribbean politician with aspirations to the city council, for instance, could hardly afford to target only Caribbean voters in select neighborhoods. Minority candidates could win only by making wide cross-ethnic and sometimes cross-racial appeals. Earlier generations of Afro-Caribbean politicians thus refrained from marketing themselves as ethnic representatives of a distinct Caribbean constituency or appealing exclusively to their coethnics. Rather, they attempted to speak for Blacks at large and did not draw a distinction between themselves and their African-American counterparts (Kasinitz 1992; Watkins-Owens 1996). Consequently, there were almost no interethnic tensions over descriptive political representation between the two groups in that earlier era. This is not to say that there were no conflicts at all between Afro-Caribbeans and African-Americans. There were the inevitable cultural clashes and occasional conflicts over jobs when the immigrants first began migrating to New York (Vickerman 1999; Watkins-Owens 1996; Foner 1985; Hellwig 1978; Reid 1939).

Yet the friction between the two groups did not have much of a political dimension.[11] Ethnicity was simply not a major source of division or conflict among Blacks in the electoral sphere. With the shift to neighborhood-based city council seats, however, there is greater electoral incentive for Afro-Caribbean politicians to engage in the kind of ethnically targeted appeals that lead to tensions with African-American leaders. The past two decades have thus seen a marked increase in political conflicts between the two groups. Although this historical shift is not conclusive evidence, it does suggest indirectly that institutional configurations have some casual impact on intergroup racial and ethnic dynamics.

A brief comparison across cities also makes the point. The city of Hartford, like New York, is home to a sizable minority population of American- and Caribbean-born Blacks. Both groups, in fact, comprise roughly similar proportions of the minority population in both cities, although New York fairly dwarfs Hartford in absolute numbers. African-Americans in Hartford, like their counterparts in New York, also have enjoyed greater levels of electoral representation and influence than the city's other minority constituencies. But in the past decade, the other groups have started to make their own serious bids for political power. Afro-Caribbean leaders in Hartford have begun to organize their coethnics to participate in politics, much like their fellow Black immigrants in New York have been doing for the past two to three decades.

Yet these efforts by Hartford's Caribbean-born residents have generated considerably less friction and resistance from African-American leaders there than have the attempts by their counterparts in New York. A number of factors may explain this difference in intergroup dynamics, to be sure. But one important variable may be the design of Hartford's electoral institutions. Unlike New York's neighborhood-based city council districts, Hartford's legislature is composed of at-large seats. By the logic of the at-large electoral design, ethnically targeted campaigning must be balanced by broader appeals to other constituencies, which ultimately may serve to moderate or minimize interethnic conflict. It bears noting that the Hartford comparison is also not conclusive support for the casual impact of electoral institutions on intergroup dynamics, but it is certainly suggestive.

In the New York case, it should be emphasized that the interethnic tensions between these two groups of Black leaders took shape as Afro-Caribbean ethnic enclaves have developed and expanded to proportions large enough to leave an imprint or have an impact on the pattern of neighborhood-based electoral districts in boroughs such as Brooklyn and Queens. Prior to the 1980s, Caribbean settlements in these areas were too small to have much of an influence on the design of the city's system of elective representation or stand alone as a politically viable ethnic constituency. What is more, African-American and Afro-Caribbean political leaders could talk of representing the city's Blacks without drawing any further ethnic distinctions. Representing Blacks essentially meant African-Americans by and large. With the dramatic growth of the Caribbean immigrant population over the past few decades, however, intra-Black ethnic distinctions have taken on political salience. The potential for intergroup conflict is now reinforced by the city's electoral institutions.

The Absence of an Institutional Mechanism

Still, a final question remains: Why have the two groups been unable to resolve these interethnic differences over descriptive representation to build a coalition around their intraracial common interests and shared policy concerns? If New York's electoral institutions have encouraged or exacerbated the interethnic conflicts between Afro-Caribbean and African-American political leaders, the absence of certain other kinds of institutions have made those differences difficult to bridge. Sonenshein (2003b) was correct that shared interests, ideological compatibility, personal ties, and strong leadership are all essential for forging sturdy intergroup alliances. But his formulation overlooks one other important building block. Institutions are equally as important as interests, ideology, personal relations, and leadership for cultivating and sustaining coalitions. Viable institutions provide a framework for groups to engage in social learning, that is, articulate shared interests, acknowledge distinct ones, reinforce ideological commitments, solidify personal ties, and identify promising leaders.[12]

Race-based alliances among non-White groups do not simply spring from some essential racial viewpoint or presumptive group interest. Rather, such coalitions require an institutional mechanism for expressing and mobilizing substantive, shared racial interests—a point that proponents of the minority group view sometimes miss or overlook. Blacks in Chicago, for instance, developed a network of community organizations in the early 1980s that proved crucial to the election of the city's first Black mayor in 1983 (Grimshaw 1992). This institutional framework allowed Black Chicagoans to negotiate internal divisions, identify a strong mayoral candidate in Harold Washington, and muster the voter mobilization necessary to win the election.

Similarly, institutional networks have been critical to successful intergroup coalition building in cities such as Atlanta (Stone 1989). The absence of such an institutional vehicle for New York's Afro-Caribbean and African-American political leaders largely explains their failure to override interethnic tensions and build an enduring race-based alliance.

The Democratic Party may appear, at first blush, to be a potentially viable institutional site for Afro-Caribbean and African-American elites to organize a race-based movement. By virtue of their combined numbers inside the party, the two groups have the makings of a powerful caucus capable of a reform. The overwhelming attachment of African-American and Afro-Caribbean voters to the Democratic Party also gives these leaders the electoral clout necessary for mounting such a challenge. In fact, a Black reform impulse surfaced in the party's Brooklyn organization in the mid-1970s. But it faded as infighting erupted and many of the erstwhile insurgents made peace with the regular Democratic machine. Since then, there has been no major, viable movement for insurgency by Blacks in Brooklyn or the other borough party organizations.

The failure of African-Americans and Afro-Caribbeans to mount an insurgent movement from within the Democratic Party confirms the long-standing common sense of V.O. Key's (1949) 50-year-old observation about one-party systems. Key argued that one-party systems tend to be breeding grounds for factionalism. Factions, he noted, give rise to personality-driven politics that focus on invidious status or group distinctions and drown out substantive policy issues. Hence, one-party systems, such as New York's Democratic organization, are notoriously unsuitable institutions for launching and sustaining reform movements. It is no wonder then that African-American and Afro-Caribbean leaders have been unable to put together an insurgent coalition from within New York's dominant Democratic party. Their relations within the party show all the symptoms of Key's diagnosis: squabbles over turf between individual politicians and disagreements over descriptive representation that deteriorate into interethnic schisms. Congruent with Key's predictions, tensions between Afro-Caribbean and African-American political leaders in the party tend to obscure the substantive issues in which they may share a common racial interest or mutual understanding.

Despite the dominance of the Democratic Party in New York City politics, there is a modest Republican organization that conceivably could serve as a site for establishing a reformist coalition. Mollenkopf (1992, 89) reminds us that the Republican Party played this role in New York politics for many decades, uniting "discontented elements of the city electorate into potent, if short-lived, fusion movements." But it no longer does so today. The Republican Party has lost much of its organizational muscle and has transformed into a more conservative institution. As Mollenkopf (1997, 105) noted, "The Republican party has forsaken its traditional role as the organizational kernel of reform." Even more significantly, the party has made virtually no effort to court African-American and Afro-Caribbean voters. There is thus little chance that African-Americans and Afro-Caribbeans will mount a race-based movement for reform from either the Republican or Democratic Party.

Parties, however, hardly exhaust the list of potential institutional sites from which Afro-Caribbean and African-American New Yorkers could cultivate and sustain a reformist alliance. In fact, minority group scholars note that insurgent movements for greater racial inclusion typically begin from bases outside the conventional party system. Movements for African-American political empowerment and racial reform, for example, historically have begun in churches, civic groups, and neighborhood-based service organizations. These institutions provide a critical site for African-Americans to delineate their interests, clarify ideology, groom leaders, and strike alliances with other groups (Dawson 1994a).[13] In cities such as Chicago and Atlanta, African-Americans used these sites to forge reformist alliances with liberal Whites (Grimshaw 1992; Kleppner 1985; Stone 1989).

In New York, African-Americans attempted to sustain reform movements from a network of community-based organizations in the 1970s and early 1980s. The short-lived insurgent movement led by Al Vann in the 1970s took root in this network (Green and Wilson 1989). Vann's race-based alliance, the Coalition for Community Empowerment (CCE), brought together African-American politicians with ties to Brooklyn's Black churches and the community action programs spawned by President Johnson's War on Poverty and Mayor John Lindsay's liberal neighborhood government policies. The alliance included figures such as Congressman Owens and Assemblyman Norman, who traced their political beginnings to this network of community-based institutions. A handful of Afro-Caribbeans were also involved in the coalition, although none in leadership positions. Most of them had ties to community-based institutions, particularly school and community boards.

In the context of this institutional network, alliance members united around a shared vision for greater Black political empowerment, community control, and racial reform. As members were elected to the state and city legislatures, the alliance became a virtual party within Brooklyn's Democratic Party. The movement collapsed in the early 1980s, however, as its institutional base began to decay. The network of community-based agencies that had furnished an organizational framework for the movement was absorbed by the local city government and lost much of its political independence. Many of these agencies fell into disarray in the face of fiscal retrenchment and federal funding cutbacks. The African-American churches that had also supplied leaders for the movement remained an important part of some Brooklyn neighborhoods, but they struggled to attract younger parishioners. Consequently, they were no longer a leading source of leadership for Black politics in Brooklyn. Bereft of its independent institutional base, the CCE began to lose its way. Internal divisions surfaced, former insurgents were absorbed into the regular party organizations, and the push for reform ebbed.

Just as the movement was deteriorating in the 1980s, the CCE came into conflict with Afro-Caribbean elites who were seeking to win seats on the state assembly. Most of these Afro-Caribbean candidates had no ties to the institutional network that had spawned the African-American-led CCE movement. They were largely entrepreneurial lone wolves, such as Trinidadian-born Anthony Agard, or endorsees of immigrant organizations, such as Panamanian-born Stewart of the CAL. In short, they had no institutional ties to the African-American politicians involved in the CCE. The organization fiercely opposed the Afro-Caribbean candidates in their races for the state legislature. Without a shared institutional framework to build trust and dialogue, African-American politicians in the CCE and Afro-Caribbean elites were unable to resolve their differences in the interest of their shared racial goals.

The Future of Race-Based Coalitions

Not much has changed since then. The absence of an institutional mechanism for uniting and building trust between Afro-Caribbean and African-American elites diminishes the prospects of race-based mobilization. Of course, there have been small pockets of mutual cooperation and attempts at shared institution building in parts of Brooklyn and Queens—in political clubs and elsewhere. Recently, for example, native and foreign-born Black New Yorkers established a citywide organization to ensure that their numbers in the population are accurately reflected in the decennial census (John Flateau, personal communication, June 16, 2000). It is too early, however, to tell if the organization will last, especially since it has yet to face the difficult challenges posed by the city's electoral politics; reapportionment, for instance, could easily trigger the usual conflicts over descriptive representation. All in all, then, none of these recent organizational efforts have quite taken firm root; most have been ad hoc and short lived.

One potential institutional network that already has the benefit of longevity is New York's constellation of public unions. Emerging research on labor union activity in cities such as New York and Los Angeles over the past decade suggests that these institutions are beginning to serve a key role in the political adjustment of new immigrants to the United States (Wong 2000). This marks a radical break with a long, notorious history of anti-immigrant activity among American labor unions. Scholars speculate that changing demographic and economic realities have precipitated this shift. The growing numbers of non-White immigrants in American manufacturing and service-sector jobs, coupled with the overall decline in union membership, has compelled labor leaders to recruit these newcomers (Greenhouse 2000).

What is more, the new generation of labor union leaders are drawn largely from the ranks of native-born racial minority groups. African-Americans, for example, are at the helm of several active unions in New York. These native-born Blacks and their Caribbean-born counterparts, in fact, comprise a significant share of the membership in two of the city's most powerful public employee unions, Local 1199 of hospital workers and District Council 37 of city workers. By sharing these institutional vehicles, the two groups can engage in the kind of social learning and mutual search for shared interests that make coalition building easier. It may turn out that these unions prove to be the most promising institutional site for identifying leaders skilled in bridging the intergroup divisions among Afro-Caribbeans, African-Americans, and other racial minority populations. Still, there is an important caution to bear in mind. Much like local party machines, unions historically have been prone to internal wars of ethnic and racial succession (Mink 1986). Whether these union organizations can navigate those potential pitfalls well enough to become a stable site for a race-based alliance remains to be seen.

Some observers speculate that the ideological fervor for race-based mobilization has diminished, with the successes of the civil rights movement and the measurable minority group progress of the past few decades (Sleeper 1993). Simply put, the claim is that race-based movements are politically passé. Post-civil rights concerns, the argument goes, do not generate the same sense of urgency and consensus among minorities that fueled the civil rights movement. The conclusion is that race-based mobilization will be unlikely or difficult to foster in the current ideological climate. Yet Afro-Caribbean and African-American outrage over issues such as police brutality suggests that there are still grounds for race-based mobilization.

This study, however, shows that racial commonalities are not enough to generate an alliance of minority groups; indeed, appeals to racial unity actually may privilege some interests over others and thus heighten divisions among non-White groups. What is more, the institutional design of a city's electoral system may exacerbate these differences. To avoid these perverse effects, political leaders looking to foster race-based alliances must turn to neighborhood and community institutions. Without an institutional framework to identify shared issue concerns, acknowledge distinct interests, and generate dialogue, stable coalitions between African-Americans and Afro-Caribbeans or other racial minority newcomers will be difficult to generate.

13

Zoltan L. Hajnal

BLACK INCUMBENTS AND A DECLINING RACIAL DIVIDE

In a nation that has long been divided by race, the election of black leaders is of great historic importance. But it is in many ways an uncertain step with unknown consequences. Black leadership raises both meaningful possibilities and real risks, especially when African Americans are elected in racially mixed areas. After winning elections, black officials must lead communities that are racially diverse and often bitterly divided. How does white America respond to African American leadership? We have anecdotal evidence from various cases, but we know very little about the general pattern and ultimate consequences of black leadership: We don't know whether minority political leadership tends to exacerbate or reduce racial tension, whether black incumbents are more or less successful than their white counterparts in subsequent elections, or under what political, economic, and racial conditions white support can be maintained or increased over time.

The Information Model

The information model suggests that black leadership should significantly change the voting behavior of whites and the way white Americans think about black candidates because the candidates' terms impart critical information that greatly reduces uncertainty and dispels white fears about blacks and black leadership. The logic is fairly straightforward. When black challengers run for office, many white residents are uncertain about the consequences of black leadership and fear that black leaders will favor the black community over the white community, thereby reversing the racial status quo. To prevent this from happening, large segments of the white community are

From Zoltan L. Hajnal, *Changing White Attitudes Toward Black Political Leadership*, pp. 14, 15, 41–54, 60–66, 72. © Zoltan L. Hajnal 2007. Reprinted with the permission of Cambridge University Press.

apt to mobilize to prevent a black electoral victory. But if a black challenger is able to overcome white opposition and win office, most white fears are not borne out. Black leadership may lead to marginal changes to a few aspects of black well-being, but for the vast majority of the white community, the world under black leaders is strikingly similar to the world under white leaders. Once black officeholders have the opportunity to prove that black leadership generally does not harm white interests, uncertainty should fade, whites' views of blacks and black leadership should improve, and more whites should be willing to consider voting for black candidates. Black leadership therefore serves an important although difficult to observe informational role.

The critical question is not whether whites will vote for blacks but *under what circumstances* they will vote for blacks. And, more specifically, what difference does black incumbency make? Does experience under black incumbents change the way whites think about black candidates, make them more willing to support black incumbents, and reduce the role of race in biracial electoral contests?

Does Incumbency Matter?

To begin to answer these questions, I collected data on white voting patterns in a representative sample of mayoral elections involving black candidates. I collected these data with two goals in mind. My first goal was to provide as direct an assessment as possible of the impact of incumbency on the white vote. To do so, I amassed data on white voting patterns in sets of two mayoral elections in cities that have experienced a transition to black leadership. For each case, I contrast the white vote in the first election, in which a black challenger ran successfully against a white incumbent to become the first black mayor of the city, with the white vote in the election immediately following, in which the black mayor ran for reelection against a white opponent.[1] By comparing sets of two elections that involve the same black candidates, I am able to assess the effects of incumbency on the white vote directly. I confine my analysis to general or run-off elections rather than primaries to avoid complications introduced by multiple candidacies and voter disinterest. To analyze other aspects of the electoral outcome, I also collected data on overall turnout and the margin of victory in each election.

My second goal was to be as comprehensive as possible in order to ensure that the results of the data analysis are representative. Since all previous studies had considered only a small number of cases, I decided to create a complete data set that included all relevant cases across the country. To do this, I compiled a set of the entire universe of cases for cities with populations of over 100,000 that fit the criteria just outlined. In total, there were fifty-two elections in twenty-six cities. While this is admittedly a small number, it represents two-thirds of the cases of white-black transition in large American cities. What is happening in this set of cases, then, should be more or less what happens generally when a white mayor is replaced by a black mayor in a large American city.

It is also important to note that my selection criteria do not appear to have created a set of cities with exceptionally liberal or especially racially tolerant white populations. Although some of the cities, such as San Francisco, Minneapolis, and Seattle, are generally seen as liberal, others, including Memphis, Birmingham, and Houston, would be much more likely to be labeled conservative, and still others, Durham and Hartford, for example, fall somewhere in the middle. As we will see, most whites in these cities were not ready for black leadership and not particularly racially tolerant when black candidates were trying to win the mayoralty for the first time. On the contrary, black challengers in many of these cities faced nearly unanimous opposition. And, in many cases, whites turned out in record numbers to try to prevent a black victory. In fact, a comparison of the racial attitudes of white residents in these cities prior to the election of a black mayor with the racial attitudes of white residents in other cities using the survey data from the ANES found no consistent or substantial differences in white views. For these cities, the key to black victory was the black vote, not white support. This comports with existing research that suggests that the size of the black community and the resources of the black community are much more important in determining the success of black candidates than the nature of the white community (Karnig and Welch 1980).

To illustrate how white voters respond to black mayoral leadership, Table 2 presents a comparison of black challenger and black incumbent elections. The numbers tell a fairly clear story: when the same black candidate runs for reelection for the first time as an incumbent, the proportion of white voters who support that candidate grows by an average of 6 percentage points, from 30 to 36 percent of all white voters. A six-point shift in the vote is certainly not unheard of in American elections, and one could argue that this change represents relatively little movement on the part of white voters. Yet this relatively small change is clearly important, for if whites were reacting to incumbent black mayors as they have responded to other forms of black empowerment in the past, we would have seen the opposite: a white backlash characterized by heightened mobilization and resistance. Similarly, if prejudice were the main factor behind white opposition to black candidates, we would most likely see no change at all. The fact that white support grew, even if by a small amount, is very informative.

The growth in white support is more impressive when one considers that whites in these cities had only two or four years (depending on the length of a mayoral term) to experience black leadership. In cities like Los Angeles and Newark, where the same black mayor ran repeatedly for reelection, white support grew with each election. According to Sonenshein (1993), Tom Bradley's white support in Los Angeles grew in each of his first four elections. All told, his white support almost doubled from 32 percent in 1969 to 62 percent in 1985. Thus, the six-point shift may represent only the first step in growing white acceptance of black leadership. In addition, this analysis in some ways understates the exceptional nature of the white support that these black incumbents won. I do not compare the average challenger to the average incumbent but instead focus only on the most successful black challengers. Most black challengers lose their electoral bids. Thus, if I had included a cross-section of all black challengers, the contrast

Table 2 Voting Patterns in Black Challenger and Black Incumbent Elections

	Black Challenger	Black Incumbent
White voters for black candidate (%)	30	36
Margin of victory (%)	12	21
Turnout of registered voters (%)	59	52

between support for challengers and support for incumbents would be much greater. The limited data that are available attest to this point. In an analysis of a series of city council and mayoral elections in Atlanta, Bullock (1984) found that incumbency more than doubled white crossover voting. His findings were echoed in an analysis of the vote in mayoral and council elections in New Orleans (Vanderleeuw 1991).

It is worth noting that the black candidates in the sample gained substantial white support as incumbents *despite the fact* that they did not get the boost in electoral resources that most incumbents receive. For most white candidates, incumbency has enormous benefits: it usually means more endorsements, more money, and weaker opponents. This is much less true for the black candidates in my sample. Largely because they needed tremendous resources to be elected in the first place, the majority of these twenty-six black candidates garnered few new electoral resources as incumbents. In 81 percent of the cases, they received no new Democratic Party endorsement when they ran as incumbents. In 62 percent of the cases, they gained no new endorsements from local newspapers. These black incumbents also tended to face strong white challengers. Specifically, 62 percent of the incumbents faced opponents who had the same or a higher level of experience than their opponents in the challenger election. The candidates were able to muster only marginally greater financial resources as incumbents, and one-third actually raised less money than they had as challengers. It would make little sense, then, to attribute the growing white support for these candidates to the conventional resources of incumbency.

The six-point increase in the percentage of white residents who voted black was not the only significant change from the challenger to the incumbent elections. There was an even sharper decline in the absolute number of white voters who opposed the black candidates. Across all twenty-six cities, the number of white votes for the white candidate declined by 19 percent on average between the challenger and the incumbent elections. This result suggests that as many as one-fifth of all white voters who opposed black leadership may have changed their minds sufficiently either to support the black candidate or to choose not to vote at all. As a consequence of both the drop in voter turnout and the higher level of support for the black incumbents, the incumbents' average margin of victory jumped from 12 percent in the challenger elections to 21 percent in the incumbent elections, leading to victory for the black incumbents in all but three cities.

The final factor to consider is voter turnout. Table 2 reveals that turnout decreased substantially in the black incumbent elections. In a little over half of the challenger elections, turnout had reached or exceeded record levels. On average, it exceeded the national average by over 10 percentage points. But this mobilization quickly faded away when blacks ran as incumbents: across the twenty-six cities, turnout dropped from almost 59 percent in challenger elections to 52 percent in incumbent elections, falling in many cases to average or below average levels. In Charlotte, for example, where Harvey Gantt faced well-known white Republican city council members in both of his elections, voter turnout fell by over 15 percentage points from 50 percent in Gantt's challenger run to 34 percent, near the historic norm, in his reelection bid. From this data, it seems that black incumbency at the mayoral level transforms extraordinary black challenger elections into more ordinary contests for reelection.

The opposition that the black challengers faced was by no means totally erased when they ran as incumbents, of course. The data in Table 2 indicate that large numbers of white voters continued to oppose the black incumbents. But in the average case, after a few years of black incumbency, white Americans became more accepting of black leadership. Again, the most remarkable aspect of this shift was not its size but the fact that there was any positive change at all. Peter Eisinger noted, in his study of Atlanta and Detroit, how sharply the elections of black representatives in those cities contrasted with expectations: "What has occurred is particularly noteworthy when it is set against the history of race relations in those two cities themselves, against the habits of racial oppression in American society in general, and indeed against a virtually worldwide tendency to deal with ethno-racial political competition by violent means" (Eisinger 1980: xxi). In many cities, even city residents themselves seemed surprised at their mayoral election's outcome. As one reporter in Birmingham put it, "This city, once branded by the Rev. Martin Luther King Jr. as 'the most thoroughly segregated in America,' accomplished something Tuesday that many of its residents consider remarkable: it reelected its first black mayor with a biracial coalition and the largest victory margin in city history" (Russakoff 1983). The fact that whites' anti-black mobilization declined after only a few years and significantly more whites became willing to support black leadership was not only a positive sign for race relations in these cities—it was a positive change that many did not foresee.

A Broader Phenomenon: All Incumbent Black Mayors

The changes in white voter behavior noted above may be unique to the twenty-six cities in the data set or limited to the first few years of black leadership. To assess black incumbency more broadly, I collected data on the reelection bids that took place in the twentieth century of every black incumbent mayor in every city with a population over 50,000.[2] In each case, in addition to the outcome of the contest, I obtained information on the racial makeup of the city, the race of the opponent, the number of terms the incumbent had been in office, and the number of black mayors who had previously served in the city.

The findings from my analysis of this larger set of cases echo the results for the twenty-six cities. First, black incumbents won in the vast majority of the cases. Since 1965, black mayors have won 78 percent of their reelection bids (98 out of 126 cases). In fact, depending on the exact comparison, black incumbents do almost as well as or even better than white incumbents. Between 1970 and 1985, the only period for which I was able to obtain equivalent data for both black and white mayoral incumbents, black mayors were reelected 89 percent of the time (31 out of 35 cases), a slightly higher rate than white mayors, who were reelected 84 percent of the time (359 out of 429 cases). From these data, it would seem that black and white incumbents are treated almost equally by the American electorate.

Second, there was no sharp decline in black reelection rates over time, and thus little indication that the information provided by black incumbents was losing efficacy over time. Although the first African Americans to serve as mayors of their cities were particularly successful when they ran as incumbents for the first time (winning 83 percent of these reelection bids), they also did well in subsequent electoral bids, winning 74 percent of the time. Equally important, there does not appear to be a major distinction in success rates between the first black mayor of a city and others who follow. The overall reelection rate of cities' first black mayors (80 percent) by no means dwarfs the reelection rate of subsequent black mayors (73 percent).

But does the success of black incumbents have anything to do with white voters? After all, the majority of black mayors represent minority white cities. Given the fact that black voters tend to favor black candidates over white candidates, the success of black incumbents could merely be an artifact of black unity and voting strength and not the result of increasing white support. But this appears not to be the case: if we confine the analysis to minority black cities, where white voters presumably have a good chance of controlling the outcome of the contests, black incumbents still do well. Black mayoral incumbents in minority black cities won reelection over 80 percent of the time, only marginally below the overall white incumbent reelection rate. Moreover, black incumbents did not win these contests simply because white voters were forced to choose between two black candidates. Even in minority black cities in elections in which black incumbents faced a white challenger, black mayoral incumbents won reelection 73 percent of the time (19 of 26 cases). In fact, black incumbents actually did better against white candidates then they did against black candidates.

The Shifting Calculus of the White Vote

Across a wide range of cases and on a number of different measures, black mayoral leadership appears to lead to positive changes in white political behavior. These positive changes seem to favor the information model over both the backlash and the prejudice hypotheses, but they do not themselves demonstrate racial learning on the part of white voters. There are a number of possible reasons why black incumbents might be successful and why white voters might change their minds about black leadership. Most officeholders, whether they are white or black, get more support when they run as incumbents. To see if race and racial learning are behind the changes in the white vote observed in the data, more tests are required. In this section, I begin to examine the nature of the white vote more closely to see if the change in the vote can be linked to information. If the information model is accurate, we should see a distinct pattern emerge: in black challenger elections, the white vote should be largely based on racial fears; in black incumbent elections, fear should play a diminished role, and white voters should begin to base their votes on the track record of the incumbent and the specifics of the campaign.

I collected an array of data on the campaigns and candidates for each of the fifty-two elections in the original set of twenty-six cities. To assess the role of race and fear in each contest, I included two different kinds of measures. First, I used a measure of the black population size as a proxy for racial threat. The size of the black population is regularly employed as a measure of racial threat, and in a wide range of cases white political choices have been shown to be shaped by the local racial context (Giles and Hertz 1994; Key 1949). If fears about the consequences of black leadership are in fact driving the white vote in black challenger elections, we should find that white voters' preferences are closely tied to the size of the black community. The larger the black population and the more likely it is that blacks could actually gain control of the local political arena, the more we should see whites fearing black leadership and voting against black candidates.

Second, I included a measure of the racialization of each black candidate's campaign. If fear about racial change is behind white opposition, then what black candidates do or say regarding racial policy should also affect the white vote. The less black candidates talk about serving the black community and the more they run deracialized campaigns that promise a race-neutral administration, the less fear there should be in the minds of white voters and the more likely it should be that white voters will support black candidates. To measure the racialization of a given campaign, I coded the extent to which the black candidates' speeches, policy platforms, and mobilization efforts were targeted at blacks, whites, or both. This is admittedly a subjective measure, but in practice it was fairly easy to divide campaigns into three categories: campaigns that had any sort of explicit, pro-black focus; campaigns that addressed the black community implicitly through a generally pro-black policy agenda or by actively mobilizing black voters and speaking before black audiences; and campaigns that never mentioned black interests and were fairly race neutral. A comparison of the racialization measure employed in this study with a similar measure used in Lublin and Tate (1995) suggests that the coding is valid. If the information model is accurate, this measure should have a bigger effect on the white vote in black challenger elections than in black incumbent elections.

If whites cease to fear the consequences of a black takeover, conventional nonracial factors that are normally important determinants of electoral outcomes should begin to play a more significant role in black incumbent elections. To see if this is the case, I examine the extent to which three basic factors of the electoral context affect the white vote in black challenger and black incumbent elections: candidate quality, political endorsements, and campaign spending. In contests at almost every level of politics, each of these factors has proven to be critical to electoral outcomes. More-qualified candidates—with quality generally measured in terms of political experience—surpass the electoral fortunes of less-experienced candidates at both the congressional and local levels. Similarly, major endorsements have been shown to play a primary role in most local contests. In particular, both political party endorsements and city newspaper endorsements affect voting in local elections. Finally, campaign spending has been closely linked to the electoral fortunes of candidates from presidents all the way down to city council members. Candidates who are able to outspend their opponents by wide margins seem to be much more likely to win at the polls.

The Importance of Race in Black Challenger Elections

In Table 3, I begin to test these propositions by analyzing the aggregate white vote in black challenger elections. Although the number of cases is relatively small and is not necessarily representative of all American cities, the table does reveal a stark, clear pattern. As predicted by the information model, when black candidates challenged for the mayoralty for the first time, the aggregate white vote was tied almost exclusively to racial fears.

The first measure of racial fear indicates that the larger the black population in the cities in the sample—and hence the greater the perceived threat that blacks would gain some measure of control over the local political arena—the less willing whites were to support a black challenger. The size of the black population accounts for the bulk of the variation in aggregate white behavior; by itself, it accounts for 60 percent of the variation in white vote choice. Even considering the selection bias inherent in these cases, it is impressive how closely the white vote was tied to the size of a city's black population. In the

Table 3   Determinants of the White Vote in Black Challenger Elections

	White Support for the Black Candidate
RACIAL FEAR	
Percentage Black of City Population	−0.72 (0.13)***
Racialization of Black Candidate's Campaign	−0.58 (0.26)*
CONVENTIONAL POLITICS	
Candidate Quality	
Quality of White Opponent	0.01 (0.08)
White Incumbent Running	−0.09 (0.07)
Quality of Black Challenger	−0.05 (0.08)
Endorsements	
Democratic Party Endorsement	0.02 (0.05)
Local Newspaper Endorsement	0.01 (0.05)
Constant	0.64 (0.11)***
Adj. R^2	0.67
N	25

Note: OLS regression. Figures in parentheses are standard errors.
***$p < 0.01$
**$p < 0.05$
*$p < 0.10$

five cities with the highest proportion of African Americans, Baltimore, Birmingham, New Orleans, Memphis, and Newark, on average only 16.9 percent of whites supported the black challenger. In contrast, in the five cities where blacks represented the smallest proportion of the population and thus the smallest threat, a slim majority of white voters (on average 50.4 percent) supported the black candidate. Overall, the regression results indicate that a 10 percentage point increase in the proportion of a city's residents who were black led to a 7.2 percentage point drop in white support for the black mayoral candidate.

The importance of racial threat seems to suggest that these challenger elections were less about the candidates or the specifics of the election than they were about the size of the threat of a black takeover—a conclusion that is echoed over and over again in accounts of the elections. One of the most well-known accounts of Birmingham's election, for example, concluded that "whites worried not so much about Richard Arrington Jr. [the black challenger], but about blacks, the group they believed he represented. Had that day now come when 'the last shall be first, and the first shall be last?'" (J. Franklin 1989: 172). The transition was viewed very similarly in Atlanta, where Peter Eisinger found that "the change was understood not in terms of a turnover in the personnel of city hall but as a loss by one race to the other" (1980: 154). Wilbur Rich's account of Detroit reached the same conclusion: "Many white residents of Detroit responded to the 1973 election of Coleman Young with intense apprehensions and fear. . . . Many whites saw the race as the last stand before the takeover by the onrushing black majority" (1987: 208).

The role played by the black candidate's campaign, and in particular white voters' aversion to racially focused campaigns, also serves to confirm the critical importance of racial fears in these black challenger elections. What black candidates did or did not say about the interests of blacks apparently influenced the white vote in these contests. All else being equal, black challengers who ran essentially race-neutral campaigns garnered almost 60 percent more of the white vote than challengers who ran racially explicit campaigns. Even though all of the twenty-six black challengers tried in some way to assure white residents that they would not be ignored, white voters seemingly keyed in on small differences between campaigns. Thus, a candidate like Harold Washington probably lost substantial white support as a result of telling a black audience "It's our turn," even though most of his campaign was race neutral. And, at the other end of the spectrum, candidates like Thirman Milner, who emphatically told white voters that "there is no such thing as black legislation" and who often repeated his desire to be "mayor of all of Hartford," seem to have been rewarded with additional white votes. Candidate Charles Box recalled that "The key . . . was to take the fear of the unknown out of the equation" (quoted in Colburn and Adler 2003). Box was so concerned about racial fears that he centered his campaign in Rockford on having personal interactions with as many white voters as possible.

In addition to supporting the information model, these findings also contribute evidence toward the resolution of two ongoing debates in the literature on American racial politics. First, the clear negative relationship between white voting behavior and the size of the local black population in these mayoral elections reaffirms the important role that racial context plays in American race relations. Existing studies have reached very different conclusions about how the increasing presence of racial and ethnic minorities affects the white population. Although most studies have found that a larger black population is associated with greater racial antagonism, several recent works have concluded either that there is no relationship at all or that the relationship is positive. The results reported here support the position that a proportionately larger black population *does* represent a racial threat to white voters.

In addition, the relationship between the racial focus of a campaign and the white vote seems to suggest that deracialization can lead to increased white support. Again, there has been considerable debate on this point. Though many have maintained that black candidates can garner white support by deracializing their campaigns, others disagree. In one of the most extensive studies, Wright found that "black [mayoral challengers] in Memphis were unable to garner significant white crossover support regardless of their use of deracialized strategies" (1996: 151). Similarly, Starks contends that "There is no way in which a contemporary American campaign can utilize a deracialization electoral strategy and hope to eliminate race as a factor in that campaign" (1991: 217). But the documented results seem to indicate that whites can be quite sensitive to the kinds of campaigns black candidates run. When black candidates move from a racially explicit campaign to a less racially focused campaign, they are able to attract greater white support. This might lead some to recommend deracializing black campaigns as an effective strategy to increase white support and expand black representation. It is important to consider, however, whether any gains in white support are large enough to offset a possible erosion of black support and black turnout—to say nothing of the restraints on policy changes—that most likely accompany deracialized campaigns.

A Different Calculation in Black Incumbent Elections

But what happens the second time around? Is there, as the information model predicts, a real transformation in the nature of the white vote in black incumbent elections? A comparison of the aggregate vote in challenger and incumbent elections suggests that there is. Table 4 combines the results of the same set of black challenger and black incumbent elections and includes a series of interactions to directly determine if different factors matter more or less in the latter. In the table, each variable that is not interacted with black incumbent elections measures the effect of that variable in black challenger elections. Each interaction directly assesses how much more or less that variable matters in black incumbent elections. Thus, reading down the table, the significant interactions and the largely insignificant individual variables indicate that it is only after black incumbents have been given a chance to prove themselves that conventional factors begin to play an important role. As experience with black leadership grows and fear about its consequences declines, "politics" begins to play a primary role in voters' choices.

Table 4 The Transformation of the White Vote between Black Challenger and Black Incumbent Elections

	White Support for the Black Candidate
CONVENTIONAL POLITICS	
Candidate Quality	
Quality of White Opponent	−0.13 (0.07)*
Quality* Black Incumbent Election	−0.23 (0.11)**
Endorsements	
Democratic Party Endorsement	0.02 (0.05)
Party Endorsement* Black Incumbent Election	0.18 (0.08)**
Local Newspaper Endorsement	0.02 (0.04)
Newspaper Endorsement* Black Inc. Election	0.23 (0.12)*
RACIAL FEAR	
Percent Black of City Population	−0.07 (0.00)***
Percent Black* Black Incumbent Election	0.00 (0.00)
Racialization of Black Candidate's Campaign	−0.13 (0.06)**
Racialization* Black Incumbent Election	0.01 (0.09)
Black Incumbent Election	−0.30 (0.17)*
Constant	0.64 (0.11)***
Adj. R^2	0.72
N	48

Note: OLS regression. Figures in parentheses are standard errors.

***$p < 0.01$

**$p < 0.05$

*$p < 0.10$

More specifically, Table 4 reveals that conventional factors such as candidate quality and political endorsements matter much more in black incumbent elections than they do in challenger elections. As evidenced by the significant interaction between candidate quality and incumbent elections, the weight that white voters put on the quality of the white opponent grew sharply from the challenger to the incumbent elections. White voters may not have cared who the white candidate was when he or she faced a black challenger; at that point, any white would do. But in black incumbent elections, white voters gave white candidates with experience in citywide office almost 20 percent more votes than candidates with no experience in political office. As one white politician put it, "Race is not as much of a litmus test as it once was. The issue now is who is the best qualified man" (*Sun Reporter* 1993). The reduction in white fears also appears to have increased white voters' attention to newspaper endorsements. These endorsements were essentially meaningless in black challenger elections, but endorsement by the main local newspaper increased white support in the average incumbent election by another 20 percent. As well, party endorsements helped in the black incumbent elections, even though they did not in the challenger elections. The local Democratic Party's endorsement delivered an additional 16 percent of the white vote on average when blacks ran as incumbents.

A second important conclusion to draw from Table 4 is that race still mattered in these elections. The fact that interactions with both of the racial fear variables are insignificant indicates that the size of the black population and the racial focus of the black candidate's campaign remained important to white voters. This is not surprising; even a brief review of these elections reveals that many of them were highly racialized. Chicago, New York, and New Haven, in particular, represent cases where the general trend toward increased white support and diminished racial tension did not apply.

At the same time, there is evidence that race and racial fears were generally less powerful in the incumbent elections. Further analysis indicates that racial fear lost half of its explanatory power: whereas the size of the black population and the racial focus of the black candidate's campaign alone account for 67 percent of the variation in the vote in black challenger elections, these two variables account for only 36 percent of the variation when white residents voted in black incumbent elections. As one reporter put it in Chicago, "Something has changed. The paranoia and ugly racism that ripped the city apart [four years ago] are largely absent this time" (Bosc 1987). Another observer of several black incumbent elections in 1993 simply stated, "Race has faded in many places" (*Sun Reporter* 1993). This conclusion was echoed in a recent study of mayoral voting in Houston (Stein, Ulbig, and Post 2005). Using three different surveys of voters in the city, the study found that racial considerations faded over the course of Lee Brown's tenure in that city. As the authors note: "Racial voting appears to be more influential in minority candidates' first electoral bids. In successive elections, voters come to rely more on their evaluations of the minority incumbent's job performance than their racial-group affiliation" (Stein, Ulbig, and Post 2005: 177). Though the magnitude of the change should not be overstated, it seems that white residents became less likely to base their votes on the race of the candidate and their fear of a black takeover in the incumbent elections. Instead when black incumbents ran for reelection, white residents seemed to more deliberately assess the pluses and minuses of their candidacies. As Sharon Watson put it in her account of mayoral bids in eight cities, "In [reelection] campaigns, while race remains a special factor, it did not seem to overshadow the campaign, as was true of the first elections. Race as an issue appeared neutralized somewhat" (1984: 172).

The Black Incumbent's Record and the White Vote

The analysis to this point has ignored an important aspect of black incumbent elections. If the information model is accurate and white voters change their minds about black leadership largely because experience with black incumbents disproves many of their fears, then a black incumbent's record in office should be an important variable shaping the white vote. The model predicts that black incumbents whose policies take resources from the white community to serve the black community or who preside over cities with faltering economies should do less well than black incumbents who resist pro-black policies and govern under robust local economic conditions. To analyze the influence of black incumbents' records on the white vote, I assess a range of factors related both to overall conditions in each city and to the policies that each black incumbent enacted. Given that the main fears expressed by white residents before the election of a black mayor were a deteriorating economy, falling housing prices, and widespread crime, I included measures of each of these three factors in the model. Since residents might logically also gauge black leadership by local government policy, I assess the impact of local government spending patterns on the white vote by including a measure of how much a city shifted resources from developmental spending toward redistributional functions such as social services, housing, and education during the black mayor's first term. Spending is obviously one of the arenas where black mayors can affect a large number of white residents, and any emphasis on redistributive spending is likely to be perceived by white residents as a strong signal of a black mayor's underlying preferences for serving the black community.

This analysis is displayed in Table 5, which presents the results of a regression explaining the aggregate white vote in black incumbent elections in the same set of twenty-six cities. With a small number of cases and eleven independent variables, the model in Table 5 stretches the limits of what regression analysis can do and should therefore be read with some caution. Nevertheless, the results are suggestive.

The first conclusion is that there are signs of a link between the black incumbent's record and the white vote. The clearest evidence of this is that changes in the local housing market are significantly related to the white vote. If, contrary to white fears, housing prices do not collapse and homeowners do well under black leadership, white residents will tend to reward the black incumbent. This finding parallels emerging research on so-called performance models of mayoral approval (Stein, Ulbig, and Post 2005; Howell and Perry 2004; Howell and McLean 2001). These recent studies have shown that in a small number of cities for which there are survey data white approval of incumbent black mayors is related to white evaluations of local economic conditions and white perceptions of city services.

However, as Table 5 also reveals, for other aspects of the incumbent's record, the existence of any relationship to the white vote is less clear. None of the other factors assessing the incumbent's record significantly predicts the white vote. The most that can be said is that in all three cases the relationship between the incumbent's record and the white vote is in the expected direction.

Thus, another interpretation is that the relationship between a black incumbent's record and the white vote is not nearly as strong as some might have expected. In only the one case—housing prices—is the incumbent's record significantly related to the white vote, and even here the magnitude of the effect is not large. For every one point

Table 5 Determinants of the White Vote in Black Incumbent Elections

	White Support for the Black Candidate
RACIAL FEAR	
Percent Black of City Population	−0.27 (0.16)
Racialization of Black Candidate's Campaign	−1.03 (0.36)**
CONVENTIONAL POLITICS	
Candidate Quality	
Quality of White Opponent	−0.20 (0.08)**
Endorsements	
Democratic Party Endorsement	0.21 (0.08)**
Local Newspaper Endorsement	0.21 (0.12)*
BLACK INCUMBENT'S RECORD	
Local Conditions	
Change in Per Capita Income	0.40 (0.45)
Change in Median Housing Prices	0.21 (0.09)**
Change in Crime Rate	−0.03 (0.08)
Policy	
Change in Redistributive Spending	−0.11 (0.44)
Constant	0.01 (0.20)
Adj. R^2	0.71
N	25

Note: OLS regression. Figures in parentheses are standard errors.

***$p < 0.01$

**$p < 0.05$

*$p < 0.10$

increase in median housing prices, there is only a one-fifth of a point gain in white support for the black incumbent.

Why doesn't an incumbent's record matter more? Part of the answer may be related to the limitations of the empirical model. Too many variables and too few cases certainly cloud the analysis. The imprecise nature of the measures used in the analysis may also be a contributing factor. Whites, for example, may be more sensitive to housing prices and crime rates in their own neighborhoods than they are to overall changes at the city level. But a third and perhaps more critical answer here is the fact that almost all black incumbents exceed expectations. In the majority of the cities in the data set, per capita incomes grew compared to the national average, and in only two cases were gains in per capita income outpaced by more than 2 percent by gains made at the national level. Median housing prices rarely fell. And although crime rates did rise in the average city, in most cases they did not rise at a rate appreciably faster than in the nation as a whole. Likewise, local government policy under black incumbents did little to substantiate white fears. The average city did not shift *any* resources from developmental projects to such redistributive programs as welfare, health, and housing, and in only two cases was more than 4 percent of the city budget transferred to redistributive functions. Finally, few of the cities stood out in terms of affirmative action policies. All but one increased black hiring under the black mayor, but only one city increased the proportion of blacks in the public sector by more than 5 percent. The lack of any dramatic change under black incumbents is not surprising, as these results mirror accounts from a range of existing studies. But it is important, because it represents a stark contrast with the expectations and fears of many whites. In essence then, the lesson is the same in almost every city. By maintaining tolerable or even relatively robust economic conditions and by choosing not to shift substantial resources away from the white community, black mayors, in almost all cases, demonstrate that black leadership does not appreciably hurt the white community. The bottom line is that black incumbents can help themselves by introducing policies that benefit the city but in the end all they have to do is not attack the white community. That is often enough to convince some white residents that they are worth supporting.

Changes in the white vote, in the kinds of campaigns white opponents run, and in the success rates of black candidates in minority black locales all hint at a sea change in the views and perceptions of a large segment of the white community. Though it is impossible on the basis of the data presented here to assign this change definitively to the effects of white learning from black leadership, they certainly leave open the possibility that experience with black leaders is fundamentally altering the nature of biracial politics in this country.

CHAPTER 5

THE SUBURBS: THE POLITICS OF SPACE, RACE, AND ETHNICITY

IMMIGRATION AND THE SPATIAL MOSAIC OF THE SUBURBS

The suburbs of the contemporary metropolis reflect the dramatic changes wrought by globalization. In the popular imagination, if not always in reality, the suburban population of the twentieth century was made up of white families living on cul-de-sacs with green expanses of lawn. In the twenty-first century, the suburbs have been transformed. Many of them are now multiracial and multiethnic, and new suburban developments run the gamut from row houses and apartment clusters to McMansions to privatized, gated communities. The dramatic differences between one housing development and subdivision and the next gives a visual face to an important new development: the suburbs seem to be fragmenting into enclaves that work to separate suburban residents on the basis of class, race, and ethnicity. This trend may become a patchwork of spatial separation, but it is also possible that the movement of immigrants into the suburbs will break down historic patterns of segregation of rich from poor and white from almost everyone else. It is too soon to tell.

When assessing the ability of immigrants to exert political influence, it is essential to keep in mind the complexity of the recent immigrant streams. Many recent immigrants are focused on just getting by; thus it is their children and grandchildren who will enter the social and political mainstream. Selection 14, which is taken from *Picture Windows*, a book by Rosalyn Baxandall and Elizabeth Ewen, describes the social changes in the suburbs of Long Island, New York. There, recent immigration has exerted immense pressures on housing, schools, and social services. Many of the immigrants work in what the authors call an "underwater economy" of low-pay, informal jobs where they are employed as day laborers, maids, gardeners, babysitters, and the like. The consequences of the low-wage economy are becoming increasingly apparent in the suburbs where the immigrants live. Workers hang out at corners where contractors and other employers drive by to select them as day laborers. To find affordable housing, many of the immigrants crowd into substandard housing. Local health clinics and schools are overcrowded. In these and in other ways, the social consequences of ethnic division and inequality have come to the suburbs of Long Island, and increasingly to suburbs everywhere.

Selection 15, drawn from a book titled *Boomburbs*, by Robert E. Lang and Jennifer B. LeFurgy, traces the rise of the 54 suburbs with populations exceeding 100,000. These "boomburbs," many of them larger than the traditional large cities, are among the fastest-growing jurisdictions in the United States, and are among the few large cities that are still growing at a rapid rate. Nevertheless, they remain largely invisible in the public imagination because they lack the long sense of history of the older cities. They may have grown only recently, but most of them are complex and diverse. Defying the suburban stereotype, they have, in Lang and LeFurgy's words, "grown not because of white flight but because of immigration, influxes of retirees, and business expansion." They have attracted large numbers of Hispanics and Asian populations, and their black populations have been increasing. Boomburbs demonstrate that the old urban pattern, with racial minorities concentrated mostly in older central cities, is becoming a thing of the past.

In Selection 16, Eric Avila describes how the past pattern of "chocolate" cities and "vanilla" suburbs is giving way to a complex patchwork that continues to preserve racial, ethnic, and class inequalities. On one end of a spectrum is the high-tech manufacturing district, or "technopolis," which employs the highly skilled and highly paid workers at the top of the global economy. These workers tend to live in exclusive gated communities. At the other end of the spectrum are the low-wage workers who also give energy to the global economy, including people who work in sweatshops, do domestic labor, and work in temporary jobs. They live in older, often deteriorating suburbs. There is, finally, the middle class, who truly are caught in the spatial mosaic of the suburbs. Avila shows that the cultural interpretations of this complex landscape contrast sharply with the cultural legacy from the era of white flight.

Immigrants often lack citizenship status and do not vote; undocumented immigrants generally avoid engaging public officials and fear being sent back to their countries of origin. Nevertheless, local government officials routinely encounter these new groups and establish political relationships with them if only because immigrant-related issues, such as outdoor gatherings of day laborers or schooling immigrant children, are unavoidable. Who sets local policy in managing these kinds of issues? What interests get represented in dealing with groups that are not yet well enmeshed in local political systems?

In Selection 17, Paul G. Lewis and S. Karthick Ramakrishnan report that suburban governments in California are developing political connections with immigrant communities dominated by police bureaucracies, rather than elected officials. Their survey suggests that police chiefs and police departments generally are more deeply engaged in developing new policies and building political relations with immigrant communities than are mayors or council members. For example, police departments often provide language support, develop identity and registration procedures, and provide community representation through hiring personnel. In contrast, elected officials are often unaware of police efforts to accommodate immigrant groups. Even though the police are supposed to act as their agents in carrying out policy, elected officials frequently lack awareness of immigrant issues due to the lack of political incorporation of these groups. In contrast, the police are professionally motivated to gain the trust of immigrant communities and win their support in addressing law enforcement matters. Thus, public policies that affect immigrants are being forged through bureaucratic incorporation of these groups without a great deal of participation by elected policymakers.

The authors find that the police departments they investigated generally were even-handed and responsive to immigrants as they changed policing and addressed new immigrant issues. Nevertheless, relying on the discretion of civil servants to manage immigrant groups and create policies presents troublesome issues of political accountability. Should the police set policy directions on matters such as language services in public offices or the acceptability of identity documents? Do these not concern the whole community? Further, the professional interests of police departments in maintaining public order may well differ from those of immigrants or other residents in the community on many issues. As issues of immigration become more salient in the suburbs, the police role in setting policies toward immigrants seems likely to become more contested. Nevertheless, for good or ill, policing and law enforcement policies will continue to be an important element in immigration politics.

14

Rosalyn Baxandall and Elizabeth Ewen

NEW IMMIGRANTS IN SUBURBIA

New Immigrants

Beginning in the 1980s many older white residents began leaving Long Island suburbs for more rural places or warmer climes. At the same time, a mosaic of immigrants, mainly from Central America but also from South America, the subcontinent of India, Asia, and the Middle East, were moving to Long Island. Japanese, Iranians, Koreans, Cubans, Haitians, and Vietnamese, as well as Indians, Pakistanis, Guatemalans, and Salvadorans, were part of a national trend in immigration. No one knows exactly how many new immigrants live on Long Island. Even the Immigration and Naturalization Service cannot estimate the number. Some experts point to the growth of the Salvadoran population as an indication of the extent of the surge: "In 1979 before civil war broke out in El Salvador, there were as few as 5,000 Salvadorans living on the island. Today according to immigrant groups and outreach workers, the number is well over 100,000."[1]

Unlike their turn-of-the-century predecessors, these immigrants were not of one class. They were wealthy, educated, middle class, working class, uneducated, and poor. Traditionally families moved to suburbs to escape metropolitan exigencies and acquire a private house, with a car in the garage and a yard on a quiet, uncluttered street where children can roam freely. For poor immigrants this is not the case; they live and work in situations that rival the worst turn-of-the-century sweatshops and tenements, exposed by muckrakers like Jacob Riis and Lewis Hines. Few muckrakers today expose the suburban underbelly. Omar Enriquez, organizer for the Workplace Project, suggested, "The problem is much bigger on Long Island than most people will admit. We have a dirty secret here."[2]

Generally poor and unacculturated, the new immigrants challenge the suburban image while their labor helps to preserve and enhance it.[3] "With unemployment at 2.8 percent in Nassau and 3.7 percent in Suffolk, experts and local officials say many of these [low-paying] jobs would not get done without immigrant labor."[4] Nonetheless, some older residents—especially those who live near the immigrants—just don't want them in their backyards. As Vincent Bullock, seventy-five, of Farmingdale, Long Island, said, "[The] long and short of it [is], they're knocking down my property values and I'll be damned if I'm paying a dime to help them do it."[5]

Part of the problem is that many suburbanites and public officials see the issue as cultural rather than economic. Older residents, white and black, complain about men hanging out in groups on suburban street corners, talking and listening to loud music until late at night; yet none of them bother to ask why these new residents are out on the street.

One of the factors that had always differentiated suburbs from cities is the absence of street culture. Front porches and stoops rarely were found. Street life for new suburban immigrants, however, is a result of cultural traditions and overcrowding. As one longtime Freeport resident explains, "Suburbia does not like the idea of people congregating fifteen to twenty of them on suburban street corners, sitting on top of their cars blaring their big radios."[6]

Long Island villages need to both familiarize immigrants with the tacit customs of the suburbs and get longtime residents to accept the different mores of their new neighbors. The village of Glen Cove issued a short flier explaining what is and is not considered acceptable: public drinking is against the law, but outdoor gatherings are not illegal, unless they block the street.[7]

Another striking difference is that most newer immigrants bypass the city and go directly from the airport to the suburbs, a pattern that had begun in the late 1950s, when the majority of suburban immigrants were Puerto Ricans. Cubans joined them in the 1960s and 1970s; in the 1980s Dominicans, Haitians, Jamaicans, Salvadorans, and others arrived from the Caribbean. Jennifer Gordon, organizer of the Workplace Project in Hempstead, makes the point that, "Long Island has become a center for Central Americans in the New York Metropolitan area and is home to more of them than New York City or any other urban area."[8]

Advertisements promising cheap property, jobs in farms, greenhouses, nurseries, factories, and domestic service brought many rural Central Americans to the United States. Others, mainly from El Salvador and Guatemala, came because of political oppression and violent civil wars. Rural families tended to be attracted to Suffolk, while those from cities came to work in the non-unionized light industries of the South Shore of Nassau County, to towns such as Freeport, Rockville Center, Westbury, Glen Cove, and Hempstead.[9]

By the late 1980s pressures began to mount over issues related to the new immigrant presence in schools, housing, jobs, and suburban culture. Long Island, like other suburban areas, had little experience in dealing with newly arrived, diverse immigrant populations. Recession, budget cuts, a skyrocketing real estate market, and anti-immigrant sentiment all conspired against integration into the existing culture. Unlike large cities, suburbs have few local governmental agencies, social services, or homeless shelters to accommodate immigrants. Since many are not eligible to vote, politicians have no motivation to help these groups. Nonprofit advocacy organizations such as the Community Advocates in Nassau, the Central American Refugee Center, and the Workplace Project in Hempstead—an impressive center that assists immigrants with legal problems, holds classes in English and legal rights, and helps Hispanic residents in organizing labor co-ops—along with many churches have attempted, sometimes successfully, to fill the void. Like other pioneers to suburbia, immigrants rely on each other, their extended families, and informal networks.

Central American immigrants depend on an unconventional, illegal, and mostly informal economy—so hidden and secret that "Salvadorans call it by the Spanish phrase, *baja del agua* [underwater]. . . . In this economic underwater of Long Island there is nothing extraordinary about a suburban home doubling as a dental office or a restaurant, or a makeshift pharmacy in a bodega."[10] Most immigrants have to make use of this underwater economy. Sara Mahler, anthropologist, describes why: "You cannot survive on Long Island with the wages they are earning. In El Salvador, they hear they can make six dollars an hour and translate the worth to their home country. When they get here, they are shocked by the cost of living." In Hempstead, Westbury, and Brentwood,

> a licensed dentist charges about $55 dollars for tooth extraction, in the underwater, the bill comes to $25 dollars. A Main Street restaurant asks $1.25 for Salvadoran pupusas [made of thick tortillas and meat] but underwater cooks charge 75 cents. You can get your laundry done for two dollars and pharmaceuticals for about a dollar a pill.[11]

Although such networks offer the advantages of familiarity, language, and costs, they have disadvantages, too. Consumers have no legal recourse if service is shoddy or deleterious. Sometimes you get what you pay for, sometimes you don't.

The only work available to recent immigrants, who speak little English and sometimes are undocumented, is badly paid and erratic, with long hours and poor conditions. Immigrants often work as day workers doing landscaping or construction for local contractors. Some have more regular jobs in light manufacturing, building, cleaning, maintenance, and restaurants, or work as cashiers, stockroom clerks, gas station attendants, and domestics. Most of these jobs place immigrants at a disadvantage, because "They often take place outside the realm of the law. Employers are rarely registered with the appropriate authorities: many of them neither comply with labor laws nor pay taxes to the government and often, they fail to participate in mandatory insurance programs such as workers compensation or disability."[12]

Maria Luisa Paz (who used a pseudonym because she feared giving her own name) was undocumented and worked in a commercial laundry with 300 other Central American workers. Their work consisted of disinfecting, washing, pressing, and folding mounds of hospital linen. Her job was to fold the sheets that came off the presses. The damp sheets were scalding hot and seldom was she given anything to protect her hands. After a recent Occupational Health and Safety Organization (OSHA) inspection, the company was forced to hand out a few pairs of thin uninsulated gloves.

In the room where Paz worked the temperature was often 100 degrees. After a few weeks Paz's gloves had holes burned in every finger and her fingers were covered with large, watery blisters. Her shirt was splattered with blood from frequent heat-related nosebleeds, and her arms and legs were flecked with white chemical stains. She was not alone. Other workers had been injured as well: one man lost half a finger, another was severely burned on the chest by chemical water that had boiled over, and a woman fainted on the job from heat and fumes. When Paz complained, the owners responded, "We didn't do anything wrong; those health problems are your fault." She then was asked to produce work authorization and was fired when she couldn't. Paz then contacted OSHA about filing a discrimination complaint, but was discouraged because the OSHA investigator told her he couldn't do much for illegals like her.[13]

Suburbia would like simply to ignore these new faces, but often they become all too visible. One way they obtain work is by lining up along major thoroughfares in the morning so that work trucks can fetch them. This creates a problem for local residents, who resent this unsightly practice and gripe to the police, who then try to enforce local ordinances against loitering. In Glen Cove one policeman warned a group of men who had strayed into the street, "It's against the law to hang out in the street in groups, that's from the Mayor himself. We'll have to give you an appearance ticket or jail at worst, if we see you hanging around." When this message had been translated into Spanish, the full meaning sank in. Francisco Martinez, a Hempstead resident from El Salvador, "raised his hand and spoke, 'One question! We don't have the right to buy a coffee? If we go to buy a coffee, they are going to think we are hanging around.'"[14] After much ruckus Glen Cove resolved the visibility issue by creating an unobtrusive location for the shape-up (work truck pickup). There are at least five other similar shape-up stops scattered throughout Nassau and Suffolk counties.

In another Long Island town, Inwood, residents in 1994 attempted to remove workers from the corner where they were lined up waiting for employment. The residents complained that the workers were disrupting the neighborhood. Workers were videotaped, verbally harassed, and physically threatened by townspeople who eventually had the police blockade the street. With the help of the Workplace Project, the workers negotiated a settlement for a better place to wait. If towns see these gatherings as disruptive, organizers find them useful for making workers aware of their rights and helping them set new wage standards.[15]

Another hazard immigrant workers face is being cheated out of their wages by fly-by-night companies. Raoul Melendez (a pseudonym) waited on a street corner in the town of Franklin Square with sixty other Latino men at six in the morning. Melendez thought himself lucky to find a job with a landscape company that employed him at first for a few days, then for two weeks. He began to relax waiting for his first paycheck.

Unfortunately, his hand was badly cut by a lawn mower. His employer drove him to the hospital promising to return, but never did. Melendez was not paid for any of his work and was sorely in need of Workers' Compensation—but the company that hired him was not listed in the phone book and not registered with the Chamber of Commerce. Melendez was never paid.[16]

One of Raoul's friends at the Franklin Square street corner, Miguel Gueverra (also an assumed name) was not paid for nine days of work with another landscape company. He tried to confront the boss, who told him that the owner of the house didn't pay him and "when I don't get paid, you don't get paid." Gueverra, along with other workers and the Workplace Project, devised a strategy. They figured out where the landscape boss was working and went to the job site to confront him. Disturbed by the noise, the owner of the house came out and witnessed the confrontation. The home owner was horrified and the landscaper embarrassed by being caught. The boss agreed to pay the money because the home owner said to Gueverra, "If he doesn't pay you the rest like he promised, I won't be paying him what I promised either." The next week the debt was paid in full.[17]

In order to circumvent these irresponsible employment practices, the Workplace Project has set up a landscaping cooperative. The Cooperative Landscaping Innovation Project (CLIP) serves over fifty private clients and a church. Workers are responsible for both the administration of the business and the landscaping itself. Everyone votes on the issues and owns a part of everything. They make $12 an hour, far more than the going wage. As Jose Martinez, who fled the war in El Salvador, where he worked as an electrician, exclaimed, "The miracle is happening. After nine years as a day laborer, I have become my own boss."[18] Another sign of the Workplace Project's success is the passage of the Unpaid Wages Prohibition Act in New York State. This bill creates penalties for nonpayment or payment under the minimum wage. Enforcement remains spotty.[19]

Even when there are laws and redress agencies, enormous problems remain. The Hempstead office of the New York State Department of Labor

> seems designed to discourage immigrants from filing claims of non-payment of wages. A Spanish speaking interviewer is only available for three hours once every two weeks. Moreover because no one who answers the phone—if it is answered at all—speaks Spanish, it is impossible for Spanish-speaking workers to learn the hours of the Spanish-speaking interviewer.[20]

Also, many wage claims that are filed are not investigated for long periods of time, sometimes as long as eighteen months.

The New York State Division of Human Rights, charged with enforcing antidiscrimination laws, takes up to five years to investigate and decide discrimination cases. These practices, combined with requests for documentation concerning taxes, witnesses, and authorization of work "effectively turn a blind eye to the entire underground economy, the arena of the greatest labor abuses."[21]

Another often invisible occupation taken by immigrants is domestic work. In the hierarchy of domestic work, living with an employer is considered the lowest rung of the ladder. Women are isolated without transportation and often are compelled to work hours without defined limits. Hidden in the homes of upper-middle-class suburbs are immigrant women who work up to fifteen-hour shifts six days a week for wages amounting to $2 an hour. The popular Spanish term for this job, *encerrado*, "gets to the heart of the matter—locked up."[22]

Some domestics work by the day cleaning, doing laundry, and taking care of children. These female workers face problems similar to those of their male counterparts: working long hours for less than minimum wage, being subjected to the whims of employers, and having little guarantees of payment or benefits. Dina Aguirre worked for three weeks for a family in Garden City without getting paid. "I worked from seven in the morning until seven at night and sometimes until 11. I asked the woman to pay me and she said, 'I don't owe you anything, because you ruined my blouse.' She said, 'Give me your address and I will send you a bill for all that you owe me.'" Aguirre was finally paid, but only after suing in small claims court. Even when domestic workers go to court for back wages, often they remain unpaid. Yanira Juarez worked for an employer in Bellport, where she won her claim in court for more than $2,000 in back wages, but she was never actually paid. "I returned and returned again, with a friend who spoke English to tell her that I needed the money. She took my address and said, I will send it, I'm still waiting."[23] Other employers deny even having employed the worker, or falsely accuse them of stealing.[24]

The Workplace Project is organizing domestic workers by circulating an advice book about scornful bosses and their overworked maids, as well as forming Justice Committees of domestic workers who will appear at employers' homes to show their court orders and demand back wages. They plan to follow this up with a cooperative for domestic workers.

These low-paid, tenuous employment practices make decent housing for immigrants hard to find, especially in suburbia, where there is little inexpensive housing and
a market that favors single-family homes. Most communities have laws limiting the
number of unrelated people sharing a home. Town and village officials do not have
nearly enough inspectors to handle even a fraction of the hundreds of thousands of
illegal apartments believed to exist on Long Island.[25]

Often then, immigrants are forced to live in substandard, illegal makeshift housing
with five or six other families who share a single kitchen and bathroom. The situation
is even worse for undocumented immigrants, who have no legal recourse and sometimes are forced into renting beds by the day or night. Often "an extra bed in someone's
home is rented in shifts to day and night laborers who pay $300 dollars a month and call
them hot beds because they are rarely without a warm body."[26] Landlords frequently let
small rooms at inflated rents, from $250 to $500 a month; they can get as much as $5,000
a month leasing a house. In 1988 the Long Island Regional Planning Board estimated
that there were at least 90,000 illegal apartments, "which is obviously an underestima-
tion considering the massive new immigration and the difficulty in detection."[27]

Suburban neighborhoods by day present a tidy picture. By nightfall, when residents come home from work, the streets change to reveal telltale cracks in the suburban
facade. Cars on lawns, groups of people walking because they can't speak enough
English to get a driver's license, loud music, cookouts on the street, and general noise
are signs that homes meant to house a family have now become rental tenements. Only
catastrophe makes this situation fully apparent: a fire, a raid, or a fight.

In May 1999 in Huntington Station a fire engulfed a single-family house crowded
with thirty-three Salvadoran immigrants, killing three people and leaving sixteen injured
and thirty homeless.[28] Jose Santos Fuentes died of exposure in 1997, after falling into a
creek next to his bed under a Glen Cove overpass.[29] Another fire, in Freeport in 1996, revealed twenty-two people, most of them Central American immigrants, crammed into
makeshift cubicles of plywood and cardboard on every floor, from the basement up to the
third-floor attic. A raid by police and building inspectors in Hicksville turned up nearly
100 immigrants living in a hodgepodge of one- and two-story buildings. The building's
residents all worked, but they were living on the edge. Some, like the Delgado family, had
pooled their income to pay $2,700 a month to house fifteen people in an office suite that
had been converted into seven tiny bedrooms, two small kitchens, two bathrooms, and a
tattered former reception area that served as a living room. The Delgado family still lives
in this office suite, but now their bags are always packed in case of a raid.[30]

Even when inspections are made, there is no guarantee that living conditions will
improve. Huntington's public safety director, Bruce Richards, said that in 1994,

> "inspectors found men living in outdoor sheds on property, and more people living in two
> apartments carved illegally out of the garage. The sheds were removed and the owner,
> Estrella Martinez, paid $375 in fines." In 1997 Mr. Richards checked out a report of an over-
> flowing cesspool on the same property and discovered at least 15 people—all of them,
> apparently undocumented, living on the property: in a camper parked next to the garage;
> in four rooms in the cellar, two of which he likened to crawl space; and in an upstairs attic.[31]

The house was declared unfit for occupants and Ms. Martinez fined $1,100, but in
January 1998 inspectors returned to investigate another complaint and found people
again occupying illegal apartments and the cellar. She was given a summons and told

to report to court. This situation is not unusual. Landlords calculate the fines in their cost of doing business.

As Marge Rogatz, president of the nonprofit Community Advocates in Nassau County, explained, "We are turning our backs on the low income people working in our communities. We need them to run all kinds of enterprises, but we are perfectly willing to have them come to work from living in a place we don't want to know about."[32]

The black market in housing is a result of the unwillingness to build low income housing, or to change the zoning regulations that only allow single-family dwellings. The situation persists because of "the extraordinary collusion of landlords, tenants, real estate brokers and contractors tacitly abetted by judges and bureaucrats who are partly unwilling and partly unable to stop it."[33] Without new laws and protections, safety and health conditions cannot be assured.

The integration of this new population into the schools has also been difficult. Since 1990 Long Island has the highest level of students with limited English in New York State. Most of these limited-English districts are on the South Shore of Long Island. Some Long Island districts report that students speak thirty or more languages and dialectics.[34] Non-English-speaking students are expensive to educate; they need bilingual classes. Some school districts have tried to incorporate bilingual education into their curricula, at least for Hispanic students. The financial strain is greatest in poor districts that already are underfunded.

One solution is to place non-English-speaking students into special education classes, intended officially for the learning disabled. A 1994 special education report on teaching English as a second language noted that "the over representation of minorities and the foreign born in special education classes was not restricted to . . . Long Island. It reflects the failure of suburban school systems nationwide to adapt as their populations have changed." The report indicated that in many schools there is only "forty-five minutes of English instruction daily for students expected to master high school level mathematics, biology and history."[35]

One science teacher in Westbury, Long Island, taught twenty Haitian Creole-speaking students with no assistance. Eventually he became so frustrated that he slammed the door on a fourteen-year-old boy's finger, severing the tip. He landed in jail. The Haitian community then pressed school officials for Creole-speaking teachers and aides, but the Westbury school did not respond. Creole-speaking teachers were available, but the Haitian parents hadn't enough clout to ensure that their children's needs were met.[36]

Stringent residency requirements make it difficult for immigrant students to attend school. In many Long Island schools and other suburban districts in the country, one needs to prove residency by showing "lease contracts, mortgage statements and notarized letters from absentee landlords." Nine-year-old Daniel Amaya, whose family did not have these precious documents because they lived in a doubled-up dwelling, where such documents are difficult to attain, was barred from a Hempstead public school. Mrs. Amaya stated, "I have no idea who the owner is. I live with my two sisters." A meeting was arranged for immigrant women and children to explain the requirements. Unfortunately the Salvadoran group spoke no English and no official came to translate. Daniel Amaya captured the essence of this frustration when he said, "I don't understand anything they are saying, but they are really angry at all of us."[37]

In spite of these cultural skirmishes, the new immigrants have had an impact on Long Island. Street signs in a town such as Brentwood are in Spanish and English. In a delicatessen in Patchogue, a sign advertises a *cerveza light*. "The nearby mainstreet market sells baccaloo (dried cod fish) as well as t-bone steaks. Across the street at La Vida Christiana children receive religious instruction and adults learn English."[38] You can buy *platanos* (bananas used for cooking), Jamaican meat patties, curries of all varieties, and *Kim Chee* (Korean pickled cabbage). Video stores carry films in Indian dialects, Spanish, and Chinese.

> In Hicksville, a little India has developed encompassing a five block area offering food markets, restaurants, an Indian-owned hair salon and a duplex movie theatre showing only Indian films. The two biggest annual events [in Brentwood] . . . are the St. Patrick's Day Parade in March and the Adelante Day Parade, which celebrates Hispanic struggle, in June.[39]

There is such variety now that ethnic neighbors don't automatically bond. "Twenty years ago, if you saw a Hispanic person, you held him and said, 'I'm Spanish,'" Roberto Portal explained. "Now we are so many that if we see a Hispanic, we go across the street."[40]

Suburbs are now becoming—albeit not always willingly—multiclass, multiethnic, and multiracial. This assimilation continues to be knotty and remains in flux. Can older suburbs accommodate these new ethnic groups, or will outmoded decentralized government structures and prejudice keep them hidden *baja del agua*—underwater? Will these new populations revitalize the dream and energize suburbia to change once again?

15

Robert E. Lang and Jennifer B. LeFurgy

THE ETHNIC DIVERSITY OF BOOMBURBS

A primary LEGO showpiece, Miniland USA is a celebration of American achievements, a canvas to illustrate the diversification of its peoples and cultures, past and present.

—Legoland Website

The main attraction of Legoland, a theme park just outside of Carlsbad, California, is Miniland USA, which features miniatures of quintessentially American places built from 20 million Legos. Miniland has a replica of Washington, complete with federal museums, monuments, the White House, and the Capitol. It even has a miniature Georgetown and a working model of the Chesapeake & Ohio Canal. Other places in Miniland include the French Quarter of New Orleans, a New England fishing village, and Manhattan. The miniature of California is a hodgepodge of scenes, from an Orange County surfing town to Chinatown in San Francisco.

Adapted from Robert E. Lang and Jennifer B. LeFurgy, *Boomburbs: The Rise of America's Accidental Cities*, pp. 1–62. © 2007, the Brookings Institution. Used with permission.

What's missing from Miniland, however, is the built landscapes so typical of America—the housing subdivision, the retail strip mall, the office park—in short, suburbia. The irony is that Lego building blocks are perfectly suited to make such places, especially the commercial structures. The basic Lego is a small rectangular block. Think of the ease with which the Miniland model makers could depict big-box retail centers or the low-slung, banded-window suburban office building. Just snap a bunch of Legos together and, presto, instant "edge city."[1] It is not as if the Lego folks could have missed knowing about suburban malls and office buildings: Southern California is chock full of them. Such buildings even lie just outside the gates of Legoland, along Interstate 5 as it approaches San Diego. But apparently suburban sprawl does not count as an "American achievement."

Modern suburbia's absence from Miniland USA reflects a national ambivalence about what we have built in the past half century. We made the suburbs, and we increasingly live in the suburbs, but we still often disregard them as real places. Even though one could describe much of modern suburban commercial development as Lego-like, there was little chance that Miniland would include a replica of nearby Costa Mesa, California, which contains the nation's biggest suburban office complex and one of its largest malls.[2]

Boomburbs: The Booming Suburbs

While these booming suburbs may not capture the public imagination, they have consistently been the fastest-growing cities over the past several decades. This growth has not translated into immediate name recognition, except perhaps among demographers, who keep seeing the population growth of these cities exceed that of older cities.

The essence of a boomburb is that people know of them but find them unremarkable and unmemorable. As this book shows, all sorts of high-profile industries and activities occur in boomburbs, but few identify with the city. For example, over a dozen major league sports are centered in boomburbs, but only the Anaheim Mighty Ducks (a hockey team) carries the place name. The fact that the one professional baseball team that had a boomburb identity—the Anaheim Angels—has since become the Los Angeles Angels of Anaheim points to the problem. The city of Anaheim took the trouble to highlight this switch in its entry for Wikipedia.com, an online encyclopedia:

> On January 3, 2005, Angels Baseball, LP, the ownership group for the Anaheim Angels, announced that it would change the name of the club to the Los Angeles Angels of Anaheim. Team spokesmen pointed out that, from its inception, the Angels had been granted territorial rights by Major League Baseball to the counties of Los Angeles, Ventura, Riverside, and San Bernardino in addition to Orange County. New owner Arturo Moreno believed the new name would help him market the team to the entire Southern California region rather than just Orange County. The "of Anaheim" was included in the official name to comply with a provision of the team's lease at Angel Stadium, which requires that "Anaheim be included" in the team's name.

Thus Anaheim, a city with as many residents as Pittsburgh or Cincinnati, is reduced to an addendum on the Angels name—and only then because of a legal technicality.

Scratch most boomburb mayors and you may find that they have a Rodney Dangerfield complex: their cities get no respect. Michael L. Montandon, the mayor of North

Las Vegas (one of the nation's fastest-growing boomburbs), tells of an encounter in which the mayor of Salt Lake City dismissed the idea that the two places share common problems, despite the fact that North Las Vegas is both bigger and more ethnically diverse than Salt Lake City.[3]

North Las Vegas is not alone. Few big-city mayors seem to recognize boomburbs as peers, and visa versa. Mayor Keno Hawker of Mesa, Arizona (a boomburb that is now bigger than Atlanta or St. Louis), spent just one year in the U.S. Conference of Mayors before withdrawing his city. His problem (in addition to the stiff dues) was that the other mayors were simply not discussing issues that concerned him.[4] As of 2004 Mesa was the largest city in the nation that does not belong to the U.S. Conference of Mayors.

But boomburbs also have a hard time fitting into the National League of Cities, whose membership is dominated by smaller cities and suburbs. Although most boomburbs do belong to the National League of Cities, their size and growth rates make it difficult for them to share common perspectives and problems with the typical cities in the organization. As one boomburb mayor put it, "How do you relate to cities that are smaller than your city grows in just a year?"

We call boomburbs accidental cities.[5] But they are accidental not because they lack planning, for many are filled with master-planned communities; when one master-planned community runs into another, however, they may not add up to one well-planned city. Too new and different for the U.S. Conference of Mayors and too big and fast growing for the National League of Cities, boomburbs have a hard time fitting into the urban policy discussion. Washington's think tank crowd is simply stumped by them.

It seems that few boomburbs anticipated becoming big cities, or have yet to fully absorb this identity, and thus have accidentally arrived at this status. Part of the confusion may be that in the past the port, the factory, and the rail terminal fueled metropolitan growth. Today booms occur in places with multiple exchanges on new freeways, where subdivisions, shopping strips, and office parks spring up. This is the development zone that Bruce Katz refers to as "the exit-ramp economy."[6] Or as Jane Jacobs would say, boomburbs develop as "micro-destinations" (such as office parks) as opposed to "macro-destinations" (downtowns).[7]

Boomburbs are not traditional cities nor are they bedroom communities for these cities. They are instead a new type of city, a subset of and a new variation of American suburbanization.[8]

Boomburbs are defined as having more than 100,000 residents, as not the core city in their region, and as having maintained double-digit rates of population growth for each census since the beginning year (now 1970). Boomburbs are incorporated and are located in the nation's fifty largest metropolitan statistical areas as of the 2000 census, areas that range from New York City, with over 20 million residents, to Richmond, Virginia, with just under 1 million people.[9] As of the 2000 census, four boomburbs topped 300,000 in population, eight surpassed 200,000, and forty-two exceeded 100,000. The fifty-four boomburbs account for 52 percent of 1990s' growth in cities with 100,000 to 400,000 residents. (The fifty-four boomburbs are listed alphabetically in Table 1.)

Boomburbs now contain over a quarter of all residents of small to midsize cities. There may be just a few dozen boomburbs, but they now dominate growth in the category of places that fall just below the nation's biggest cities. Another way to grasp just how big boomburbs have become is by comparing their current populations with those of some better-known traditional cities. Mesa, Arizona, the most populous boomburb at

Table 1 Boomburbs, 2000 Census[a]

Anaheim, California	Gilbert, Arizona	Palmdale, California
Arlington, Texas	Glendale, Arizona	Pembroke Pines, Florida
Aurora, Colorado	Grand Prairie, Texas	Peoria, Arizona
Bellevue, Washington	Henderson, Nevada	Plano, Texas
Carrollton, Texas	Hialeah, Florida	Rancho Cucamonga, California
Chandler, Arizona	Irvine, California	Riverside, California
Chesapeake, Virginia	Irving, Texas	Salem, Oregon
Chula Vista, California	Lakewood, Colorado	San Bernardino, California
Clearwater, Florida	Lancaster, California	Santa Ana, California
Coral Springs, Florida	Mesa, Arizona	Santa Clarita, California
Corona City, California	Mesquite, Texas	Santa Rosa, California
Costa Mesa, California	Moreno Valley, California	Scottsdale, Arizona
Daly City, California	Naperville, Illinois	Simi Valley, California
Escondido, California	North Las Vegas, Nevada	Sunnyvale, California
Fontana, California	Oceanside, California	Tempe, Arizona
Fremont, California	Ontario, California	Thousand Oaks, California
Fullerton City, California	Orange, California	West Valley City, Arizona
Garland, Texas	Oxnard, California	Westminster, Colorado

[a] A boomburb is defined as an incorporated suburban city with at least 100,000 in population, as not the core city of their region, and as having double digit population growth in each census since 1970.

396,375 residents in 2000, is bigger than such traditional large cities as Minneapolis (population 382,618), Miami (population 362,470), and St. Louis (population 348,189). Arlington, Texas, the third biggest boomburb, with 332,969 people, falls just behind Pittsburgh (with 334,536) and just ahead of Cincinnati (with 331,285). Even such smaller boomburbs as Chandler, Arizona, and Henderson, Nevada (with 176,581 and 175,381 residents, respectively) now surpass older midsize cities such as Knoxville (with 173,890), Providence, Rhode Island (with 173,618), and Worcester, Massachusetts (with 172,648).

By the 2000 census, fifteen of the hundred largest cities in the United States were boomburbs. More significant, from 1990 to 2000, fourteen of the twenty-five fastest-growing cities among these hundred were boomburbs—including five of the top ten. Since the 2000 census, many of the largest boomburbs jumped ahead of their traditional (and much better-known) big-city peers (based on 2002 census estimates). Mesa (with an estimated population of 426,841) edged out Atlanta (estimated at 424,868). Both Arlington, Texas (estimated at 349,944), and Santa Ana, California (estimated at 343,413), passed St. Louis (which lost nearly 10,000 residents by 2002). Anaheim (with an estimated 2002 population of 332,642) is now immediately trailing St. Louis. Aurora, Colorado (286,028), has overtaken St. Paul (284,037). Finally, Peoria, Arizona (123,239), surged ahead of Peoria, Illinois (112,670), which has actually lost residents in recent years.[10]

To put the boomburb rise in perspective, consider that only about a quarter of the U.S. population lives in municipalities that exceed 100,000 people. The fraction of the population living in cities this size or above peaked in 1930. Boomburbs are among the few large cities that are actually booming. Much of the nation's metropolitan population gains have shifted to their edges.[11]

While some boomburbs are well on their way to becoming major cities, at least as defined by population size, it is not surprising that these places fall below the public radar. But it is interesting how little boomburbs register with urban experts, too. For instance, a recent encyclopedia of urban America that covers both cities and "major suburbs" fails to list even one boomburb exceeding 300,000 people; it does, however, have entries for comparably sized (and often even smaller) traditional cities.[12]

Websites and Wikipedia

The most comprehensive history available on boomburbs comes from city websites and wikipedia, an online encyclopedia.[13] All fifty-four boomburbs had a city website as of May 2006.[14] Histories appear on thirty of the sites and range from a few perfunctory sentences to lengthy and detailed entries. These histories provide an additional context for examining boomburb origins. They indicate what boomburbs think about their past. Website histories also offer an interesting extension of those found in the WPA Guides. Recall the WPA pre–World War II depiction of a sleepy Sunnyvale, California. The passage below is taken from Sunnyvale's web history and notes the impact of the war.

> Without a doubt, World War II is the single most important event that changed history in Sunnyvale, the San Francisco Bay Area and all of California. Some people date the beginning of the defense era in Sunnyvale with the arrival of Lockheed Missiles & Space Company in 1956. But defense industry roots were planted much earlier because Sunnyvale has a long history of actively recruiting industry by offering land and labor.[15]

The website and wikipedia histories share several common themes. As might be expected, rapid population growth is the biggest topic. In fact, more of the websites mention fast growth (thirty-six) than have full city histories. The forces that sparked this growth are also major themes. The most frequently cited causes for growth are highways, defense industries, water, and annexation. One even lists air conditioning as a factor.

Highways apparently loom large in the Denver area, with both Aurora and Westminster website histories referring to them. Aurora's website says that "the 1970s were prosperous for Aurora with the city benefiting from new highway construction." Westminster's notes that "with a population of 1,686 in 1950, Westminster was still a quiet rural town northwest of Denver. That all changed when the Colorado State Highway Department began construction of the Denver-Boulder Turnpike, a toll-road that operated between the City of Boulder and the Valley Highway (I-25)."[16]

Or consider this entry from wikipedia.org on the role that transportation played in promoting economic development in Olathe, Kansas: "After the construction of the transcontinental railroad, the trails to the west lost importance, and Olathe faded back into obscurity and remained a small, sleepy prairie town until the 1950s. With the construction of the Interstate Highway system and, more directly, I-35, Olathe was directly linked to nearby Kansas City and began an economic boom that accelerated in the 1980s and continues today."

The military turned the San Diego region from an American outpost near Mexico into a strategic metropolis on the Pacific, populating its boomburbs in the process. The Oceanside website has this to say:

> World War II saw Oceanside grow from a sleepy little town to a modern city. With the construction of the nation's largest Marine Corps Base, Camp Pendleton, on her border, the demand for housing and municipal services exceeded supply. The best illustration of the tremendous growth of the city is found in the census figures. The population of Oceanside jumped from the 1940 figure of 4,652 to 12,888 in 1950. In 1952 a special census showed the city's population exceeding 18,000 as the Marine Base grew with the Korean War and more service-connected families moved into the area.[17]

According to Chula Vista's website,

> World War II ushered in changes that would affect the city of Chula Vista forever. The principal reason was the relocation of Rohr Aircraft Corporation to Chula Vista in early 1941, just months before the attack on Pearl Harbor. Rohr employed 9,000 workers in the area at the height of its wartime production. With the demand for housing, the land never returned to being orchard groves again. The population of Chula Vista tripled from 5,000 residents in 1940 to more than 16,000 in 1950. After the war, many of the factory workers and thousands of servicemen stayed in the area resulting in the huge growth in population.[18]

The same kind of military-driven growth narratives appear in wikipedia.org. For example, consider the case of Clearwater, Florida:

> During World War II, Clearwater became a major training base for U.S. troops destined for Europe and the Pacific. Virtually every hotel in the area, including the historic Belleview Biltmore and Fort Harrison Hotel, became luxury barracks for new recruits. Vehicle traffic regularly stopped for companies of soldiers marching through downtown, and nighttime blackouts to confuse potential enemy bombers were common. The remote and isolated Dan's Island, now Sand Key, was used as a target for U.S. Army Air Corps fighter-bombers for strafing and bombing practice.

Of Fontana, California, wikipedia.org says, "Fontana was radically transformed during World War II by the construction of a steel mill belonging to the Henry J. Kaiser Company." A similar remark is made for the baby boomburb of Renton, Washington: "The town's population boomed during World War II when Boeing built a factory in Renton to produce the B-29 Superfortress. The factory has continued to operate since then, and still produces 737 aircraft. In 2001, 40% of all commercial aircraft were assembled in Renton. Boeing remains the largest employer in Renton."

As one would guess, water fed boomburb growth in the Southwest. This is especially true in the Central Valley of Arizona, where the Phoenix region, like the mythical bird, rose from the ashes of a lost Native American civilization—the Hohokam. The trick Phoenix used was rebuilding the ancient canal system left by the Hohokam. In Mesa, the Mormons got the water flowing early. Its website notes that "water entered the canals in April of 1878."[19] Two early twentieth-century major dam projects greatly enhanced the supply of water to Phoenix—Roosevelt Dam to the northeast and Hoover Dam (originally Boulder Dam) to the northwest. Both of these dams, and the lakes they formed, are often cited in metro Phoenix boomburb website histories. In fact, so many boomburbs around Phoenix mention water and canals one might think the place were Venice, Italy.

As their regions developed, boomburbs gobbled up unincorporated land wherever they could. Gilbert, Arizona, for example, aggressively expanded well beyond its original borders: "Gilbert began to take its current shape during the 1970s when the Town Council approved a strip annexation that encompassed 53 square miles of county land. Although the population was only 1,971 in 1970 the Council realized that Gilbert would eventually grow and develop much like the neighboring communities of Tempe, Mesa, and Chandler."[20] For Gilbert the plan apparently worked, because this boomburb is now the fastest-growing U.S. city above 100,000 residents so far in this decade.

The Boomburbs Keep Booming, 2000 to 2002

It is worth exploring how boomburbs are doing in the first years of the twenty-first century. Census estimates show that most boomburbs continue to boom.[21] In fact, boomburbs are the fastest-growing U.S. "cities" of over 100,000 people. The nine top growth cities over the period April 1, 2000, to July 1, 2002, were boomburbs.[22] Additionally, boomburbs made up six of the top ten fastest-growing cities from July 1, 2001, to July 1, 2002, including four of the top five of these cities.[23] The five fastest-growing boomburbs (and the five fastest-growing U.S. cities above 100,000 population from 2000 to 2002) are in the Phoenix and Las Vegas metropolitan areas. The next five quick growers are in Southern California—four in the Los Angeles region and one in the San Diego metropolitan area.

Gilbert, Arizona (the fastest-gaining boomburb), grew by nearly a quarter (23 percent) in just over two years.[24] At that pace, Gilbert could easily more than double its population in a decade. The next eight boomburbs following Gilbert all grew by more than 10 percent over the same period. Henderson, Nevada (south of Las Vegas), added 30,722 new residents from 2000 to 2002, leading all boomburbs in number of new people. Henderson was followed by Mesa, Arizona, with a gain of 30,466 people during the period. Almost a third (sixteen) of boomburbs gained over 10,000 residents each.

As a group, boomburbs jumped from 8,915,435 to 9,397,793 in population, or a gain of nearly a half million residents in just over two years. To put that in perspective, consider that that is about how many people lived in all boomburbs in 1950. Together, boomburbs now have a population larger than the Chicago metropolitan area (with 9,286,207 people as of July 1, 2002), the nation's third largest metropolitan area behind New York and Los Angeles.[25]

The "New Brooklyns" Slow Down

The term "new Brooklyns" applies to boomburbs that are now, or are rapidly becoming, immigrant-dominated communities, like the old Brooklyn (the full definition of what constitutes a new Brooklyn is presented later). This particular type of boomburb may also be losing steam. New Brooklyns such as Hialeah in Florida and Santa Ana and Anaheim in California have foreign-born populations that either match or exceed that of Brooklyn, N.Y. (which has a 38 percent foreign-born population). Other examples of new Brooklyns include Pembroke Pines, Florida, Irving, Texas, and Aurora, Colorado, all of which have a foreign-born population that greatly exceeds the national average of 11 percent.

New Brooklyns tend to be old, dense, and built-out suburbs, which dampens their population growth. As Rick Hampson observes, "Although the New Brooklyns were once new settlements on the suburban frontier, they're getting old. Their housing, accordingly, is more attractive to immigrants looking for bargains and is less attractive to longtime [mostly native-born] Americans, who can afford to move up."[26] Some new Brooklyns can continue to gain population (if not quite boom) provided that their foreign-born population maintains a high rate of natural increase. These places have also seen a turnover, as young immigrant families replace older empty-nest couples, which also adds to population growth. In time, the foreign-born population will age and assimilate, which should slow down the new Brooklyns even further.

The Future of Boomburbs

For now, most boomburbs seem to be humming right along. But many will experience relative decline in perhaps the not too distant future. One problem could be that the West (where most boomburbs are found) is running out of water. Almost all of the West's current water sources—from Denver to Southern California—have been overallocated.[27] Unless more water is diverted from agriculture or new supplies are tapped, the West will face a crisis that could significantly dampen the growth rates of its boomburbs.

Even assuming that the problem of water supply for new growth is resolved, the current group of boomburbs will ultimately experience much slower population gains. The fact is that no place can (or should) boom forever. Today's boomburbs are tomorrow's mature cities. But a whole new batch of boomburbs and baby boomburbs is already emerging. Look at the Central Valley of Arizona; as Tempe stalls and Mesa slows down, places such as Goodyear and Buckeye are just getting started. The future of boomburbs is discussed more fully in the final chapter of the book.

Finally, the economic drivers of urban growth are ever shifting. As noted, many boomburbs and baby boomburbs got a big lift initially from World War II and were sustained by cold war defense industries. Defense helped ratchet up boomburb growth just as suburbanization swept the metropolis. The general patterns that tilted U.S. growth to the suburbs in the post-World War II years as highlighted above—new highways, cheap mortgages—helped further develop boomburbs.

Recent boomburb expansion is due in part to a continued urban shift to the Sunbelt. Most boomburbs and baby boomburbs possess two qualities in particular that the urban economist Edward Glaeser argues drive growth: sun and sprawl.[28] Glaeser developed the idea that growth derives from a combination of sun, sprawl, and skills (or human capital). The Glaeser "three S" concept provides an alternative to Richard Florida's "three Ts," or talent, tolerance, and technology.[29] As a *New York Times Magazine* article on Glaeser's work notes:

> Glaeser likes to point out the close correlation between a city's average January temperature and its urban growth; he also notes that cars per capita in 1990 is among the best indicators of how well a city has fared over the past 15 years. The more cars, the better—a conclusion that seems perfectly logical to Glaeser. Car-based cities enable residents to buy

cheaper, bigger houses. And commuters in car-based cities tend to get to work faster than commuters in cities that rely on public transit.[30]

Boomburbs, as mostly warm, auto-friendly environments, fit this description. As a result, boomburbs and baby boomburbs should continue to grow until these drivers lose their steam and a new development model emerges.

Who Lives in the Boomburbs?

As much of the research based on the 2000 census reveals, the 1990s witnessed a radical departure from standard demographic trends. Hispanics passed African Americans as the nation's largest racial or ethnic group, while the Asian American population strengthened its presence by more than 50 percent.[31] The proportion of foreign-born persons reached 11.1 percent, the highest level since 1930. This surge of immigration is changing how communities plan and develop, especially since slightly more than half of all of immigrants who arrived in metropolitan areas in the 1990s chose to live outside central cities.

The country's median age is 35.3 years—the oldest it has ever been. Aging baby boomers are becoming empty nesters and fueling the development of "active adult" communities. Suburbs now contain more nonfamily households (largely young singles and elderly people living alone) than married couples with children.[32] In 2000 less than 25 percent of all households nationwide were nuclear families. This is a significant change from 1970, when the figure stood at around 40 percent. The nuclear family is a shrinking phenomenon, as acceptance of nontraditional approaches to marriage, divorce, childbearing, and cohabitation grows.

Overall, the share of racial and ethnic minorities living in the suburbs increased substantially in the 1990s—moving from less than one-fifth to more than one-quarter of all suburbanites. This trend is most evident in metropolitan areas that had a strong immigrant base. A study by the demographer William Frey finds that the growth of racial and ethnic groups fueled the 1990s population growth.[33] According to this study, in the largest 102 metropolitan areas, more than half of the Asian population and nearly half of the Hispanic population lived in the suburbs. Blacks showed the greatest increase in suburban living—in 1990 less than 33 percent of blacks lived in the suburbs studied; in 2000, almost 40 percent did.

During the past ten years suburban growth outpaced city growth irrespective of whether a city's population was falling, staying stable, or rising.[34] Minorities have driven most of this growth, and this is reflected in the boomburbs. Most but not all are ethnically and racially diverse. The majority of boomburbs have Hispanic populations above the national average, and Hispanics make up over half the population in six boomburbs and five baby boomburbs. Over three-quarters of boomburbs have Asian populations above the national average, and 85 percent of boomburbs had foreign-born populations above the national average of 11 percent.

Not only are boomburbs ethnically diverse, they also contain different strata of income. While most boomburbs are affluent, few are exclusive. Boomburb percentages, compared to the top fifty metropolitan areas, rank higher in categories such as race, foreign-born population, and median income. However, the percentages of families in poverty, postgraduate education, home ownership, and white non-Hispanic populations are lower. This chapter examines the demographics within boomburbs (using primarily census data); discusses their ethnic, educational, and economic diversities; and identifies two subcategories that emerge from the data: "new Brooklyns" and "cosmoburbs."

Race and Immigration

Some boomburbs defy the suburban stereotype put forth over the last four decades by cultural critics. They have grown not because of white flight but because of immigration, influxes of retirees, and business expansion. These suburbs have developed their own economies and diverse populations in boomburbs and baby boomburbs since 1980. Although baby boomburbs started off and remain more white, Hispanic immigration has grown as a greater share of their population over the last twenty years.

Boomburbs are surprisingly diverse in their Hispanic and Asian populations. For example, forty-five of the fifty-four boomburbs have Hispanic populations larger than the national percentage, which is about 12 percent. Five boomburbs are over 50 percent Hispanic. Hialeah, Florida, with 90 percent Hispanic population, tops the list; the other nine of the top ten are in California. Similarly, forty-two of the fifty-four boomburbs have a higher percentage of Asians than the U.S. percentage of 4 percent.

As of 2000, blacks were 12.3 percent of the U.S. population. The biggest gains were in Florida's baby boomburbs of Lauderhill, Miramar, and North Miami. Ten boomburbs lost black population during the 1990s (Irvine, Oceanside, Fremont, Thousand Oaks, Simi Valley, Oxnard, Sunnyvale, Daly City, Santa Ana, Hialeah), but the remaining forty-four boomburbs increased their black population. The black population of Gilbert, Arizona, rose from only forty-one persons in 1980 to well over 2,000 in the year 2000.

Boomburbs also contain a high percentage of foreign-born residents. Although only 11 percent of the U.S. population is foreign-born, a typical boomburb is 21 percent foreign-born. Forty-six of the fifty-four boomburbs have foreign-born populations higher than the national average. Further, there is a high correlation between share of Hispanic population and share of foreign-born population.[35]

New Brooklyns

Certain boomburbs with large foreign-born, working-class populations can be classified as "new Brooklyns." Much like Brooklyn New York, of a century ago, working immigrant families who speak English as their second language densely populate these cities. Although they have relatively large populations, as in the old Brooklyn, they play a secondary role in their region. Manhattan was home to the cosmopolitan tastemakers, while Brooklyn was Manhattan's bedroom community, where immigrants lived in tightly clustered neighborhoods and strived for middle-class existences.[36]

New Brooklyn boomburbs are characterized by a significant percentage of working-class, foreign-born citizens who speak another language besides English at home. They also contain populations claiming to have had no schooling at all, a higher than the national average of renters, and a relatively high population of families in poverty. Median household incomes are either slightly above or close to the national median. Baby boomburbs that meet similar criteria are Lynwood, California; South Gate, California; North Miami, Florida; and Rialto, California.

New Brooklyn suburbs are more ethnically diverse than their core cities, meaning they have a higher percentage of Hispanics and Asians than their core cities.

New Brooklyns tend to have larger than average family sizes. Most new Brooklyns rank above the national average family size of 3.1 members. Santa Ana has the highest (4.6), followed by Oxnard (3.9) and Ontario (3.6). The highest baby boomburbs are Lynwood (4.9), South Gate, California (4.2) and Chino, California (3.9). According to the 2000 census, three new Brooklyns—Santa Ana, Oxnard, and Hialeah—are among the top ten boomburbs with the highest incidence of crowded units. The incidence of overcrowding is now at record levels in California.[37]

16

Eric Avila

FEAR AND FANTASY IN SUBURBAN LOS ANGELES

In our present age of accelerated globalization, Los Angeles is undergoing yet another round of economic restructuring and demographic upheaval . . . another new Los Angeles has taken shape, and the cultural matrix of chocolate cities and vanilla suburbs is giving way to new social interactions that mirror the striking changes that have transformed the region since the postwar period. The city's capacity for rapid change and incessant innovation has perforated the physical and cultural boundaries that distinguished white space from black space, and although the noir city and its heterosocial interactions have made a certain comeback in recent decades, race continues to shape the cultural geography of the contemporary urban landscape in more powerful and less subtle ways. Once more, the cultural landscape of Southern California's everexpanding urban region holds clues to the countervailing forces of twenty-first-century urbanism.

Furthering the extremes between white wealth and nonwhite poverty, the demographic transformation of Los Angeles and its environs poses a powerful challenge to the regional hegemony of suburban whiteness. Since 1970, the vast influx of immigrant populations into Southern California has transformed the region from a bastion of middle-class whiteness into a Third World citadel. In 1970, 71 percent of Los Angeles County's population was non-Hispanic white or Anglo, and the remaining 29 percent of the population was divided among Latinos (15 percent), African Americans (11 percent), and Asian/Pacific Islanders (3 percent). By 1980, the non-Hispanic white population had dropped to 53 percent, and ten years later it had fallen further to 41 percent. Throughout the 1970s, large-scale immigration from Latin America and Asia, coupled with a moderate growth in the African American population, inflated the region's non-white population. Immigration to the region continued to expand throughout the following decade as the population of Asians and Latinos swelled. By 1990, Latinos comprised 36 percent of the city's population; African Americans and Asians constituted 11 percent respectively. Today's Los Angeles ranks among the most diverse urban regions in the world and the city once heralded as the "nation's white spot" now mirrors the polyglot diversity that defines the city and even its past.[1]

Fueling and fueled by demographic growth, economic restructuring in Southern California simultaneously enforces and enervates existing patterns of racial and ethnic inequality. Since the 1970s, the increasingly transnational currents of economic exchange have positioned the Los Angeles urban region to emerge as a "nodal point" within a new global economy. The manifestations of economic globalization in Southern California have furthered the sociospatial extremes of progress and poverty that have been manifest throughout every stage of capitalist urbanization. On the one hand, the region shelters a growing number of high-tech manufacturing districts, or "technopoles," which extend to the furthest corners of the urban region. In the southernmost portions of Orange County and the western fringes of the San Fernando Valley, where gated communities and high-end subdivisions guard the latest incarnation of suburban whiteness, high-tech manufacturers such as Hughes Aircraft Missile Systems Group, Micropolis, and Rocketdyne further the industrial and residential sprawl that began in earnest during the early 1940s. The region's high-tech economy, which has penetrated the entertainment industry to a certain extent, sustains the class standing of a highly skilled group of managers, business executives, scientists, engineers, designers, and celebrities who continue to reap the rewards of the region's economic prosperity.[2]

At the other end of the economic spectrum and concentrated within the region's multiple urban centers, a low-skill, low-wage, nonunionized workforce, comprising mostly women and undocumented Latino and Asian immigrants, has been taking shape alongside the growth of the manufacturing sector since the 1970s. In contrast to the high unemployment and economic decline that befell other major American cities through the phase of deindustrialization during the 1970s and 1980s, Los Angeles' manufacturing economy grew steadily throughout the 1970s and intensified during the following decade, when the infusion of Asian capital into the regional economy bolstered the production of manufactured goods such as apparel, furniture, jewelry, and machinery. Such growth, however, entails mixed consequences for Southern California's expanding immigrant populations, who are drawn by the prospects of job availability but face new depths of exploitation. The sweatshop has made a comeback within Southern California's industrial landscape in recent decades, providing an often overlooked reminder that the "new" Los Angeles runs on the sweat of immigrant labor.[3]

Between these extremes, the great white middle class, which dominated the image and reality of the postwar urban region, is making its departure. Throughout the Reagan era, the flight of major manufacturing firms from the region's industrial geography dislodged whites from their suburban neighborhoods, creating space for new concentrations of racialized poverty. This transformation was most visible in the communities of Southeast Los Angeles, which nurtured the suburban white identity explored in previous chapters: South Gate, Huntington Park, Maywood, Bell, Bell Gardens, Vernon, and Cudahy. The departure of industrial giants such as General Motors, Firestone Tires,

Weiser Lock, Bethlehem Steel, Dial, and Oscar Meyer from this area during the 1980s entailed a set of profound social consequences that undermined the cultural order of the postwar urban region. White workers and their families, who enjoyed full benefits and union representation, have taken flight, and, in their stead, recent arrivals from Mexico and Central America find work in the expanding low-wage, non-union sector and take shelter in cities crippled by shrinking tax bases and reduced services.[4]

While the brand of suburban whiteness that took shape within the cultural transition from the centralized, industrial city to the postwar urban region becomes a relic of the past, its legacy continues to shape California politics. The politics of white home ownership remains a powerful force in the state and its triumphs in recent decades have profound implications for the quality of race relations in the United States. In 1978, the passage of Proposition 13 marked a major victory for white homeowners and their brand of "identity politics" in California, much like the two-term presidency of Ronald Reagan. In the 1990s, California voters passed a series of measures that targeted immigrant groups and racial minorities. Looking back to the buoyant expressions of suburban whiteness that highlighted the cultural landscape of the postwar urban region, the current strategies to preserve white hegemony reflect a brazen attempt to maintain some semblance of the precarious social order that enjoyed a brief life span between the midcentury manifestation of the noir city and the current denouement of a Third World urbanism.

Film noir underscored the imperatives of suburban home ownership as a bulwark against the crisis of the public city; Proposition 13 surfaced in 1978 as a measure to secure that imperative for millions of California homeowners. The unbridled growth that swept across the region entailed a mixed set of consequences for suburban homeowners. On the one hand, the unceasing demand for homes generated higher property values, but, on the other hand, higher home prices brought higher property taxes, which basically doubled every few years. At the same time, the recession of the mid-'70s heralded a stagnation of real income and frustrated consumer efforts to live the suburban good life that California symbolized. Proposition 13, a measure that would lower property taxes by 60 percent, won by an overwhelming majority in California and inspired a similar set of homeowners' revolts in other states. In Los Angeles, Proposition 13 won by overwhelming majorities in white council districts, while it failed by a similar majority in the city's only black district.

Proposition 13 cannot be understood in isolation from the larger cultural context that dawned on Southern California during the postwar period. When Yvonne de Carlo warns Burt Lancaster in the climactic scene of the film Criss Cross, "You have to watch out for yourself; I can't help it if people don't know how to take care of themselves," she recites the creed that suburban homeowners adopted in their insular political outlook that disavowed any connection to other urban constituencies. Instead, the supporters of Proposition 13 campaigned with slogans such as "Vote for yourself! Vote for Proposition 13!" Proposition 13 upheld what Clarence Lo describes as a consumer model of citizenship, which is predicated upon the relentless pursuit of commodities that sustained popular idealizations of suburban domesticity. Such idealizations informed the dominant cultural narratives of Southern California's postwar urban region and guided the ascendance of tax-cutting conservatism that disavowed the interdependency of social groups and instead promoted self-interest as a primary goal of political struggle. Proposition 13 drastically reduced property taxes at the expense of public services such as schools, libraries, and police and fire protection, services that racial minorities have been increasingly forced to rely on. In this capacity, Proposition 13 continued the privatization of social life that began during the postwar period and widened the spatial and racial divide between chocolate cities and vanilla suburbs.[5]

Many proponents of Proposition 13 also endorsed the concurrent antibusing movement, in which white suburban parents sought to preserve the postwar racial order by resisting state efforts to send their children to schools in black and Latino neighborhoods. In suburban communities of both the San Fernando Valley and Orange County, where Proposition 13 won overwhelming support, local organizations such as the PTA marshaled opposition to busing programs, sponsoring constitutional amendments to limit busing, challenging busing in court, and seeking to elect public officials who opposed busing. The racist underpinnings of the antibusing campaign during the mid-'70s were not self-evident, but against the official effort to elide the racial geography of the postwar urban region through school desegregation, white suburban families defended their distance from the racialized city and, with it, the right to maintain school policies that sent white middle-class children to white schools in white neighborhoods.[6]

The political culture that sustained both Proposition 13 and the antibusing movement is essentially the same as that which bestowed two consecutive presidential terms on Ronald Reagan, who championed the rights of homeowners and consumers in their pursuit of privatized self-interest. Reagan's victory in the White House confirmed Southern California's prominence within the national political culture, not unlike the proliferation of homeowners' revolts throughout the nation following the success of Proposition 13 in 1978. The triumph of the New Right by the late 1970s was made possible by the support of various regional constituencies, but the course of political events in Southern California—beginning with the 1950 defeat of Helen Gahagan Douglas, bolstered by the simultaneous victory against public housing, and gaining further momentum with the 1964 cancellation of the Rumford Fair Housing Act—prefigured the subsequent victories of a new brand of Republican conservatism predicated upon the values enshrined in places like Disneyland. By the mid-1980s, at the height of the Reagan era, the brand of suburban whiteness that first took shape within Southern California's cultural landscape had entered the symbol iconography of the American Way and remained under the stewardship of a countersubversive coalition that targeted civil rights crusaders, feminists, antiwar demonstrators, and gay activists as culpable for the social ills and economic malaise wrought by economic restructuring, deindustrialization, and the dismantling of the welfare state.[7]

Reagan's legacy endured through the 1990s and found powerful expressions in the culture and politics of California. One year after the end of the Reagan-Bush-era and on the heels of the Rodney King uprising of 1992, the film *Falling Down* engendered controversy among national audiences for its neonoir portrayal of the white man's identity crisis in contemporary Los Angeles. "D-Fens," an unemployed engineer suffering a nervous breakdown, begins a killing spree as he walks from downtown Los Angeles to the beach. In the tradition of noir's white male antihero, D-Fens trudges through the racialized milieu of the city, attacking a Korean market, a fast-food outlet, a Chicano gang, and a neo-Nazi. The city that once resonated with compelling expressions of suburban whiteness is now alien territory for D-Fens, an inhospitable nonAnglo landscape that renders white male identity obsolete.

That filmmakers could market the fin de siècle crisis of white male identity as entertainment points to the very real challenge to whiteness posed by the demographic transformation of California and Los Angeles at the end of the twentieth century. In this context, California voters approved a series of measures that extended a note of nativist hostility to people of color. In 1994, Proposition 187 triumphed at the polls, denying public services to undocumented workers and their families. Although the measure's implementation has been indefinitely delayed by the courts, it targets California's immigrant population as a scapegoat for the economic woes that befell the state during the recession of the early 1990s. The specter of white identity politics surfaced twice again in the remainder of the decade. In 1996, as if the racial wrongs of the past had been righted, Proposition 209 brought a decisive end to affirmative action in both public service contracts and higher education, and in 1998, Proposition 227 terminated bilingual education programs in public schools to advocate "English only" as state law. The causes and consequences of these measures have been explored elsewhere; suffice it to say here that they signal last-ditch attempts to preserve what vestiges of suburban whiteness remain at the outset of the twenty-first century.[8]

Popular culture in the age of white flight thus maintains a powerful legacy, and although the future of that legacy is uncertain, the current phase of demographic upheaval in Southern California annihilates the racial identities imposed on the spaces of the postwar urban region. Watts, for example, no longer symbolizes the geographic core of black Los Angeles, as a massive in-migration of Latino immigrants dissolves the postwar boundary between white and black Los Angeles. South Gate and Huntington Park, where Southern California's Dust Bowl migrants reinvented themselves in the image of middle-class whiteness after World War II, are the current epicenter of *México de afuera*, as Mexican immigrants reestablish communal ties in the wake of deindustrialization and white flight. A large and expanding Koreatown lies just west of downtown Los Angeles, a new suburban Chinatown centered on Monterey Park has taken shape to the east, and a band of Cambodian and Vietnamese communities has grown to the south, extending from the older Japanese community of Gardena to Long Beach and into Orange County, where the city of Westminster is now known as Little Saigon.[9]

Perhaps even more striking, the San Fernando Valley now shelters a heterogeneous mix of Mexicans, Salvadorans, Guatemalans, Armenians, and African Americans. For a generation of white Americans in search of suburban domesticity, the Valley offered affordable housing and homogeneous neighborhoods, and its location on the northern side of the Santa Monica Mountains promised a comfortable distance from a Los Angeles mired in the mythology of film noir. The landscape of today's Valley, however, reveals a striking record of the demographic changes that have ensued over the past thirty years. On Van Nuys Boulevard, once the heart of white suburbia, Spanish has displaced English as the unofficial language of public signage. All around the Van Nuys business district, travel agents advertise discount tickets for international travel carriers such as Avianca and Aeroméxico. The native fare of El Salvador, Peru, India, Armenia, and a dozen other nations is served in the boulevard's myriad storefront diners. Most institutions that catered to the Valley's original white constituency are now gone: department stores have been replaced by *pupuserias* and *mueblerias*, the First Presbyterian Church closed after its English-speaking constituency plummeted, and the *San Fernando Daily News*, founded as the *Van Nuys Call* in 1911, left for tonier quarters in Woodland Hills. The "New Valley" harbors scant traces of the suburban good life that dominated the cultural imagery of postwar Los Angeles, and its public settings now echo the cultural dissonance of the polyglot noir city.

Amid the browning of the San Fernando Valley, homeowners there are mobilizing a campaign to authorize the secession of the Valley from the city of Los Angeles, in what would be the largest municipal divorce in national history. Valley VOTE (Voters Organized toward Empowerment), a grassroots organization established in 1998, has gathered sufficient signatures on petitions to push the secession drive to its most advanced stage ever. Whether or not the proponents of secession will have their way, the current move to secede from the city of Los Angeles inherits a tradition of municipal discord in Southern California and reflects a long-standing antipathy to the urban behemoth on the southern side of the Santa Monica Mountains.

The social, economic, political, and spatial transformations that engulf today's Los Angeles entail a set of cultural expressions that reflect both the extension and the extinction of popular culture in the age of the white flight. On the one hand, recent scholarship illuminates the cultural manifestations of contemporary urbanism by looking to Los Angeles as a window onto the "theming" of American culture and society. Through the disparate points of Southern California's urban expanse, scholars cite the most spectacular examples of the privatization of public life: From the self-contained citadel that has become downtown Los Angeles—including the cylindrical glass towers of John Portman's Bonaventure Hotel—to the gated communities of Orange County's "exopolis," to the ersatz urbanism of City Walk, Los Angeles and its environs support the many "variations on a theme park" that condition the experience of urban life at the outset of the twenty-first century. While generally eschewing the broader historical context that sanctions such cultural formations and often ignoring their immense popularity among white and nonwhite consumers alike, such observations generally deplore the corporate sponsors of contemporary public culture, emphasizing the manipulative and coercive strategies built into the design of contemporary public space.[10]

On the other hand, by looking "way, way below" the glass and neon facades of the contemporary metropolis, one can identify competing cultural expressions that emanate from the city's diverse neighborhoods. During the 1980s, amid the deindustrialization of South Central Los Angeles, black youth forged a cultural style that centered upon the distinctively West Coast sounds of hip-hop music. Gangsta Rap made its debut on the streets of Los Angeles through the innovative sounds of Ice-T, Eazy-E and NWA, Ice Cube, Snoop Doggy Dogg, and Dr. Dre, who drew upon African American cultural traditions such as descriptive storytelling and funk music, while utilizing samplers, drum machines, engineering boards, and other components of the latest in digital technology. Gangsta Rap of the late 1980s and early 1990s, as Robin Kelley and Tricia Rose point out, spoke to the realities of ghetto life for young black heterosexual men in postindustrial America, and proffered a genre of black popular culture that proved overwhelmingly popular not only in chocolate cities, but also, if not especially, in vanilla suburbs.[11]

Although the cultural palimpsest of contemporary urbanism supports the musical expressions of young black men, it also reflects the cultural stylings of the city's Mexican and Latino populations. A striking preference for big cities among Latinos brings a transformative energy to the texture of daily life in a "Latino metropolis" such as Los Angeles. As the old barrio of East Los Angeles gives way to the exponential growth of Spanish-speaking neighborhoods and subdivisions, the symbols and signs of *Mexicanidad* are visible throughout the urban region. Immigrant homeowners from Mexico and Central America are investing "sweat equity" in their homes, using paint and inexpensive landscaping materials to reverse the deterioration of urban neighborhoods

crippled by deindustrialization and white flight. Bohemian enclaves of Chicano communities in East Los Angeles and the San Gabriel Valley support the proliferation of
bilingual cafés and bookstores. Accustomed to the convivial spaces of *plazas* and
mercados in Latin American cities, Latino immigrants and their children make vital use
of playgrounds, parks, squares, libraries, and other endangered public spaces that their
more affluent counterparts in the city tend to ignore. Amid the current re-Mexicanization
of Los Angeles, with the addition of other Latino populations, we are witnessing an ethnic
transformation of the urban landscape on a scale unparalleled in history.[12]

So what's left of popular culture in the age of white flight? What remains of the cultural institutions explored in this book, and how have they fared in light of recent social
transformations? Hollywood continues to fixate upon Los Angeles in its dystopian
spectacles of urban decadence, and film noir and science fiction maintain their popularity at the box office. In the early 1970s, at the outset of an economic recession and in
the wake of the turbulent 1960s, Los Angeles occupied a starring role in a brief noir revival, climaxing with *Chinatown* by Roman Polanski, whose tragic and bizarre encounter with the Manson family in 1969 inspired his dark and morbid vision of Los
Angeles and its past. Disaster films such as *Earthquake* and *The Towering Inferno* also kept
the spotlight on Southern California, portraying Los Angeles as an epicenter of the
moral catastrophe that dawned in the era of Watergate. The following decade witnessed
Blade Runner, rendering its futuristic nightmare of a Los Angeles dominated by global
capital and teeming with Third World populations, while a spate of neonoir films of the
late 1980s and early 1990s, most notably *The Grifters, The Player, Reservoir Dogs, Pulp Fiction, Short Cuts,* and *L.A. Confidential,* keeps a tight focus on the darkness lurking behind
the sunny façade of the Los Angeles landscape.

More striking, however, is the recent arrival of new voices that add their own distinct inflection to the canons of film noir and science fiction. With a nod to Chester
Himes, Walter Mosley established his presence in American literature with the 1990 success of *Devil in a Blue Dress,* which portrays the investigations of Easy Rawlins, a black
private detective in 1940s Los Angeles who unravels the depths of white racism at the
core of Southern California's black city. In a similar vein, Octavia Butler brings a black
feminist perspective to her futuristic vision of Los Angeles in *Parable of the Sower,* which
renders a bleak portrait of a city overcome with violence and fear in the year 2027. Like
all durable genres of American popular culture, film noir and science fiction have incorporated new perspectives that extend and broaden their appeal over time; while Los
Angeles, ravaged by successive episodes of racial violence throughout the second half
of the twentieth century, remains a favorite site for collective fantasies of urban despair.

Meanwhile, Hollywood finds new ways to recycle its former glory as a means to
urban redevelopment. Responding to a cycle of decline throughout the 1980s and
1990s, Hollywood developers have enlisted the support of Los Angeles' Community
Redevelopment Agency to bring consumers and tourists back to Tinsel Town. Their
most recent *coup de main* has been the Hollywood and Highland Redevelopment Project,
built by the Canadian developer Trizec Hahn, the nation's largest owner of downtown
office space. At a price of 615 million dollars, the Hollywood and Highland complex
occupies one and a half city blocks of downtown Hollywood, containing a mazelike
425,000-square-foot retail mall, a two-thousand-seat multiplex cinema, and an auditorium designed as a permanent home for future Academy Awards ceremonies. With
architectural references to the glories of old Hollywood, including a partial reconstruction

of the extravagant movie set from D.W. Griffith's 1916 film, *Intolerance*, Hollywood is now reclaiming its former glamour as a means of reversing decades of urban decline.[13]

Disneyland is alive and well, though its constant renovation and ongoing expansion illustrate the extent to which today's audiences have outgrown the thematic imagery and cultural stereotypes that dominated the park's landscape in its postwar heyday. Racial difference no longer supplies a central theme of Disneyland. Aunt Jemima's Pancake House is now the River Belle Terrace and the grinning mammy has been retired from the kitchen. Audio Animatronic animals singing country music have replaced the Indians who once performed at Frontierland. And though Disneyland remains a cornerstone of "family entertainment," this did not preclude park officials from ignoring the vehement protests of the Christian Right and extending domestic-partner benefits to employees in 1995. Moreover, the recent successes of Disney films such as *Mulan* and *Pocahontas* indicate an openness to new stories and images that include the perspectives of racial minorities and women.[14] Would Walt Disney have approved of these changes? That question is impossible to answer, but the business acumen and sensitivity to the changing moral climate that Disney exhibited throughout his career would seem to imply his willingness to make such modifications in the midst of a rapidly changing world.

The Walt Disney Company's more sensitive portrait of racial and ethnic diversity, however, parallels the ongoing Disneyfication of public and private space. Today, Disneyland rests alongside Downtown Disney, a shopping and entertainment complex that presents Southern Californians with a neon-lit simulacrum of the noir city that Orange County residents shunned a generation earlier. While Disney executives repackage the noir city as their latest "attraction," American cities and suburbs today increasingly weave the themed experiences of Disneyland into the fabric of daily life. The brand of suburbanism that took shape in locales such as Orange County during the 1950s now extends its reach into the archetypal noir metropolis. In New York City, under the patronage of Mayor Rudolph Giuliani, the Walt Disney Company spearheaded an effort to revitalize Times Square, investing thirty-two million dollars in the renovation of the New Amsterdam Theater on Forty-second Street. Enticed by a slew of tax breaks and zoning incentives, Disney and other entertainment conglomerates—Nike, Warner Brothers, Virgin—are struggling against the presence of homeless vagrants and porn dealers to rescue Times Square from its previous noir incarnation.[15]

An even more portentous example of how Disney continues to blur urban fantasy and reality, Celebration, U.S.A., reflects the Disney Company's latest effort to establish its definition of community. Celebration, U.S.A., south of Orlando, Florida, extends across five thousand acres, complete with its own school, post office, downtown, pool, and parks. There is also a "town hall" designed by the noted architect Philip Johnson, though it serves no political function since the Disney Company retains the powers of planning and governance for Celebration's first twenty years. Not unlike the planners of Lakewood and countless other suburban housing developments, Disney and Osceola County arranged a mutually beneficial deal to keep low-income housing out of Celebration, U.S.A. Such an arrangement allows for larger profits on the sale of homes and higher property tax revenues, but, in the suburban tradition, minimizes racial diversity and severely limits civic experience.[16] If Celebration, U.S.A., maintains some remnants of suburban whiteness in Florida, Southern California harbors other reminders of Disney's cultural roots. Recently, the Ronald Reagan Presidential Library in Simi Valley, California, featured the exhibit "Walt Disney: The Man and His Magic."

The Dodgers retain their popularity among diverse Southern California baseball fans, and Dodger Stadium endures in the Chavez Ravine. Whatever ill will lingered between the Dodgers and local Chicanos over the Arechiga evictions, the arrival of a rookie pitcher from Etchohuaquila, Sonora, in 1981 sparked an intense passion for Dodger baseball among Chicanos and Mexican baseball fans alike. In his first year of pitching for the Dodgers, Fernando Valenzuela led his team to its fifth World Series victory, and with that, "Fernandomania" descended upon the Spanish-speaking world. Valenzuela's overwhelming popularity demonstrated the new cultural flavor of major-league baseball and illustrated how popular cultural institutions can reinforce distinct cultural identities, even as they appeal to broader audiences. The particular appeal of Dodgers baseball for the city's diverse constituencies continues, as Asian Americans also enjoy a special claim to the Dodgers in recent years. Representing the recent advances by Korean players in the major leagues, Chan Ho Park signed a ten-million-dollar contract with the Dodgers in 2001. Park follows in the footsteps of Hideo Nomo, who pitched for the Dodgers between 1995 and 2000, arousing the loyalties of Southern California's Japanese American community, which maintains an enduring enthusiasm for the game of baseball, dating as far back as the war years, when baseball games provided a momentary distraction from the indignities of internment. Today, as during the postwar period, the Dodgers continue to model interracial cooperation on the field before the city's diverse constituencies in the stands.[17]

Meanwhile, civic officials elsewhere look to Dodger Stadium as an example of how not to build a ballpark. On April 11, 2000, San Franciscans celebrated Opening Day for Pacific Bell Park (now known as SBC Park), a throwback to Boston's Fenway Park and its generation of urban ballparks. In contrast to the sprawling, 250-acre site of Dodger Stadium, SBC Park sits upon a mere 13 acres in the city's South of Market neighborhood, a newly gentrified area adjacent to downtown. Designed by Joe Spear of HOK Sport, the architect of Baltimore's Camden Yards and Cleveland's Jacobs Field, SBC Park offers a more modest—albeit more nostalgic—alternative to the monumentality of Dodger Stadium. Garbed in ivy, brick, and limestone, SBC Park rejects the solemn gray concrete that clothes Dodger Stadium, and its expansive view of the San Francisco Bay delivers a scenic connection to the surrounding region. Most unlike Dodger Stadium, however, SBC Park maintains a mere five thousand parking spaces, one fifth of which are usually empty during any given home game. The park's accessibility to public transportation and its close proximity to the city's many neighborhoods diminish the necessity for the automobile. While it might be unfair to compare SBC Park to a stadium built four decades ago, its success suggests that the designers of Ebbets Field, Fenway Park, and Wrigley Field just may have had it right all along.

Finally, although Southern Californians continue to exercise their preference for the private automobile, the freeway's benefit to urban life is more suspect than ever. Traffic congestion remains an enduring civic nightmare, and with recent population gains and a growing number of commuters willing to drive longer distances to work, today's freeways now more than ever fail to provide rapid access to the disparate points of the urban region. Freeway construction continues, though the master plan for freeways established by the Division of Highways in 1958 remains only half completed. Local residents are far more vocal in their opposition to highway construction, as the recent controversy surrounding the extension of the 710 Long Beach Freeway through South Pasadena illustrates. In the 2001 mayoral campaign, candidate Antonio Villaraigosa won the support of that community by announcing his opposition to the completion of the 710 project, denouncing that freeway as "a throwback to another era."

Growing frustration with the freeway and the automobile has intensified the search for alternative forms of public transportation. Today, the Metropolitan Transit Authority maintains its effort to build an extensive rail transit system throughout the urban region. The Blue Line from Los Angeles to Long Beach opened in 1990, and parts of the Green Line (from Norwalk to Hawthorne) and the Red Line (from downtown to the San Fernando Valley) have followed suit. Whether the vast majority of Southern Californian commuters will relinquish their automobiles in favor of rail transit remains uncertain, but hundreds of millions of dollars continue to pour into a transit system that may or may not alleviate traffic congestion on the region's freeways. Meanwhile, working-class communities of color continue to depend on the city's overcrowded and inadequate bus system. The Bus Riders' Union, a grass-roots organization dedicated to improving bus service, continues its fight against fare increases and route cancellations. During the age of the freeway, Los Angeles has sustained a kind of "transit apartheid" in which the experience of moving through urban space remains contingent upon class and color.[18]

The age of the freeway may be passing, but the street is making a comeback within the city's diverse communities. Los Angeles' emergence as the nation's preeminent Latino metropolis brings the street-oriented culture of Chicanos and Mexican immigrants to the very center of a new civic life. The city streets support the informal economy that relies upon the public display of goods and services. Day laborers congregate on sidewalks or parking lots, looking for a day's work in the vicinity of paint and hardware stores. *Vendedores* and *vendedoras* sell produce and flowers at freeway off-ramps and along median islands. Although such public interactions are commonplace within Latino neighborhoods, they are new to more affluent neighborhoods. Westside communities are taking their cue from their Eastside counterparts and learning to enjoy the pleasures of street life. Farmers' markets draw large crowds throughout the city's diverse neighborhoods, offering a weekly festival for adults and children. In the posh quarters of West Hollywood, planners have recently completed a massive redevelopment project to enhance street life along Santa Monica Boulevard. Sunset Strip and its more modest imitations throughout the Southern California metropolis continue to attract increasingly diverse crowds in search of the city's nightlife. Contrary to popular stereotypes about the freeway metropolis, the street is reclaiming its place at the center of a changing public life.

The cultural forms that nurtured a suburban white identity during the postwar period now include alternative perspectives and experiences. Since the postwar period, whiteness and white flight no longer have been the master narratives that shape the texture of American cultural life, at least in cities on the cutting edge of social transformations. Other narratives have been inserted into the built environment since the postwar period, and their vitality points to a new definition of urban life at the outset of the twenty-first century. Whether or not the recent appreciation of multiculturalism and diversity will empower marginal social groups, however, is an open question. If cultural expressions of suburban whiteness inaugurated a greater disparity between white suburban affluence and nonwhite urban poverty during the postwar period, can we expect the current incarnation of Los Angeles as a "world city" to bring about a more equitable reconfiguration of urban social relations? As whites have become a demographic minority in the Los Angeles urban region, new forms of urban popular culture model new configurations of race and space and encompass even more diverse cultural expressions. As the urban landscape mirrors the city's great diversity in more equitable ways, whiteness will lose its saliency as a defining principle of urban culture and identity. Once again, Los Angeles, a city often recognized as a cultural trendsetter, may be the first to model this development. Though the city once supported powerful expressions of suburban whiteness, it may be, in the not too distant future, that to imagine a white identity in a region teeming with nonwhite peoples will be to conjure a historical fiction from the city's past.

17

Paul G. Lewis and S. Karthick Ramakrishnan

POLICE PRACTICES IN IMMIGRANT-DESTINATION COMMUNITIES

In recent years, United States immigration policy and the presence of large numbers of undocumented immigrants in the country have been highly charged and salient elements of political debate, both at the national level and in the states and localities that play host to concentrations of foreign-born residents. In early 2006, immigrants and their supporters mounted large-scale protests in several American cities against proposed immigration legislation that they viewed as excessively punitive. Meanwhile, in some communities very visible influxes of recent immigrants were met with calls for local law enforcement crackdowns on outdoor gatherings of day laborers and on overcrowded or illegally subdivided rental housing units (Lambert 2005; Caldwell 2006). Pressure also mounted for local police to cooperate with federal authorities in enforcing U.S. immigration law (Jordan 2006).

These high-level policy questions on immigrants and immigration, however, take place at some distance from the everyday routines of interactions between local police officers and foreign-born residents in immigrant-destination cities. What is the nature of such interactions? To what degree have municipal police departments developed new procedures or policing styles in an effort to adapt to the presence of immigrants in the community and the new issues they present? Are police actions toward immigrants generally supportive or repressive? Finally, do police practices relating to immigrants emerge in response to the concerns of local elected officials, given the political salience of immigration issues? Or is there decision space for police bureaucracies to proactively develop their own approaches on immigrant-related issues, based on their own norms or professional ethos?

This article addresses these questions, based on quantitative and qualitative data collected as part of a wide-ranging study of municipal governments in immigrant-destination cities in California. One goal is simply to describe the emerging patterns of

From Paul G. Lewis and S. Karthick Ramakrishnan, "Police Practices in Immigrant-Destination Cities: Political Control or Bureaucratic Professionalism?" *Urban Affairs Review,* Vol. 42, No. 6, pp. 874–900, copyright © 2007 by SAGE Publications. Reprinted by permission of SAGE Publications.

police practices toward immigrants—an important task, given the lack of scholarly work on this topic. But we also seek to relate our empirical findings to larger theoretical questions about the nature of discretion in urban service delivery and the potential for what Michael Jones-Correa (2004) calls the "bureaucratic incorporation" of immigrants into local politics. That is, can local bureaucrats, in the absence of close guidance or support from the mayor and council, craft policies or administrative procedures that advance the interests of groups that are otherwise underrepresented in the public sphere?

Immigrants and the Challenge to Local Law Enforcement

The foreign-born population in the United States has grown substantially in recent decades, both in absolute numbers and as a proportion of the population, As recently as 1970, fewer than 5% of residents (or 9.6 million) were born outside the United States. By 2000, the immigrant population had grown to more than 31 million, or 11% of the national population. The impact of immigration on social and political relations is perhaps most apparent in California, where the proportion of foreign-born residents increased from 9% in 1970 to 26% in 2000, with the proportion considerably larger in many localities.

The growth of the foreign-born population poses a distinct set of challenges to local governance. Most immigrants lack much experience with the American political system, and many are not fluent English speakers. Furthermore, much of this immigration has occurred quite recently, presenting new issues for communities where these newcomers have settled. This is true even in states such as California, where there has been tremendous growth in the foreign-born population in small and medium-sized cities far from traditional destinations such as Los Angeles and San Francisco. Finally, immigration has also changed the racial and ethnic makeup of the United States, with the population now increasingly composed of Latinos and Asians.[1]

This article is part of a broader study in which we examine the extent to which city governments in California are receptive and responsive to immigrant concerns. Here we focus specifically on law enforcement and public safety. Among municipal services, policing is perhaps the most visible function, and it can touch the lives of immigrants and other residents in a very direct way. With their uniforms and patrol cars, police officers are probably the most obvious and frequently encountered representatives of municipal government. Indeed, Fairchild (1978, 443) views police as "gatekeepers" to local government and to the justice system.

The nature of recent demographic change in cities experiencing much immigration can make for a potentially very sensitive and challenging job for police. In their home countries, some immigrants dealt with law enforcement officials who were corrupt or who used force indiscriminately; others lived in fear of government authorities more generally. Thus fear or distrust of U.S. police might be expected even without the complication of language and other barriers. In addition, some immigrants are undocumented; their illegal status may make them inclined to avoid contact with authorities in general for fear of deportation. Such avoidance denies police a potentially important source of information about crime and public order in immigrant neighborhoods (Davis, Erez, and Avitable 2001; Menjivar and Bejarano 2004).

Finally, cultural practices among some immigrants—for example, dress, religious practices, or the presence of large households—are distinctive and may make them stand out from community norms or may arouse resentment among native-born residents. In some cities, immigrants' distinctiveness includes participation in underground economy activities such as day labor markets, where workers gather, typically outdoors, to seek "under the table" work from contractors or other passersby. Thus for reasons including limited English proficiency, undocumented status, and participation in informal economies, the growing immigrant presence in cities and suburbs poses a new and distinct set of challenges for law enforcement.

Accounting for Police Practices

Who really sets local police policy concerning immigrants? Drawing from relevant strands of the literature on urban politics, bureaucracy, and policing, two general hypotheses present themselves. One approach holds that bureaucracies take political cues and that police practices tend to follow the direction set by elected officials and local electoral outcomes. A second perspective holds that police departments increasingly are professional agencies that use discretion to engage in a search for practices that will help them to serve the local community in defending itself. Each perspective carries different implications for the likelihood that police departments develop policies and practices supportive of immigrants.

Political Control and Political Incorporation

Formally at least, police forces are the agents of local governing bodies, just as the U.S. military is the agent of the federal government. Local police chiefs must answer to the city council and mayor, either directly or through the city manager. Williams (1984, 19–23) argues that in the United States, municipal police departments have always been political institutions—initially controlled by partisan machines, but often subject to takeovers by state legislatures that sought to insulate the police from local party influence. At the national level, much of the literature suggests that political control of the bureaucracy is significant. Researchers have found, for example, that political shifts, such as changes in presidential administrations, have led to important changes in bureaucratic priorities and enforcement efforts (Wood and Waterman 1994; Moe 1985; but see Meier and O'Toole 2006).

Given this backdrop, and noting the emerging issues of day labor, crowded housing, and undocumented immigration in many immigrant-destination communities, one would anticipate that immigrant-police relations will take on a high degree of salience for local elected officials. Given the highly charged nature of immigration issues in recent years, the implication is that governing officials will take great interest in police procedures relating to immigrants and that police departments will follow these dictates.

Two classic studies of policing lend some support to this hypothesis. Skolnick (1994, original edition 1966) and Wilson (1970), each made the case, to varying degrees, that police practices tended to follow from the dominant political mores of the community in which they were located—whether those values were middle-class conformity, racism, the patronage politics of the machine, or veneration of expertise. "As an institution dependent on rewards from the civic community, police can hardly be expected to be much better or worse than the political context in which they operate" (Skolnick 1994, 239). Whether one can empirically detect a general linkage between elected officials' preferences and police practices across cities is less clear from these case studies of policing style. However, in a more recent aggregate study, Chaney and Saltzstein (1998, 762) found that the existence of a "cue" from elected officials—in this case, enactment by the city of a mandatory arrest law for incidents of domestic violence—helped predict police department actions regarding a "less-settled area," namely arrests in situations where domestic violence had been threatened but not perpetrated.

In a related vein, though not writing specifically about policing, several urban politics scholars have made the case that the incorporation of new groups into city electoral politics generally will precede any improvements in the way that local bureaucracies treat members of those groups (Browning, Marshall, and Tabb 1984; Saltzstein 1989; Meier et al. 2005). From this perspective, one would anticipate that improvements in the ways that police relate to immigrant communities would be a result of a growing electoral power among immigrants, either in becoming a major part of a victorious liberal electoral coalition or in electing coethnics to City Hall. According to political incorporation theory, then, police responsiveness would be predicated on two processes: the growing incorporation of immigrants into political institutions and the continued influence of elected institutions over the practices of police departments.

However, nearly all of the research on local political incorporation has focused on the influence and mobilization of African-Americans and Latinos. In the case of *immigrants* as a political minority, the political incorporation model may be of limited applicability in explaining bureaucratic responsiveness because in most municipalities the foreign born lack the votes necessary to influence local elections. Many immigrants are not eligible to vote because they lack citizenship, and even those who have completed the citizenship process are less likely to vote than native-born Americans, whether because of relatively lower levels of education and socioeconomic status, a lack of acquaintance with U.S. political practices, or the lack of mobilization by parties, interest groups, and political elites (Jones-Correa 1998; Ramakrishnan 2005; Wong 2006).

Nonetheless, immigrants are *constituents* of local government in the sense of being component parts of the community and are fully subject to the enforcement powers of local police. In the absence of increased political mobilization among immigrants or their supporters in local politics, then, the question becomes whether immigrants are primarily acted on—*objects* of local policing—or whether immigrants' concerns and needs are taken more seriously and somehow find a voice in policing policy. As it stands, the "political control" perspective suggests that local political controversies about immigrants, and the latter's relative powerlessness in elective politics, would lead toward relatively punitive law enforcement practices and a lack of support in such matters as language assistance. An exception might be if Hispanics or Asians hold one or more city elective offices, thus allowing coethnics in positions of power to shape the political agenda in ways perhaps more advantageous toward immigrants.[2]

Bureaucratic Professionalism and Bureaucratic Incorporation

Although scholars of political incorporation focus largely on the elected leadership of cities, a great deal of power potentially rests in relatively insulated local bureaucratic agencies that may be difficult for elected leaders to effectively control. Because agencies are often granted responsibility that greatly exceeds their resources, bureaucratic discretion results; lacking guidance, agencies must often set their own priorities (Bryner 1987). Principal-agent theorists have characterized circumstances under which bureaucrats are likely to be able to evade control by elected officials (see Waterman and Meier 1998 for a review and critique of this literature). In cities, civil service reform in particular, in combination with norms of bureaucratic expertise, can lead to "islands of functional power" since urban reformers sought and won insulation for bureaucracies from the vicissitudes of local politics (Lowi 1967; Brown 1988).

Police agencies have typically been thought to hold a large reservoir of discretion (Holmberg 2003; Mastrofski 2004). There are wide variations across cities in the style and stringency of law enforcement (Hahn 1971). Indeed, the "police power" is perhaps the most widely recognized of municipal prerogatives. Public choice scholars of urban service delivery have argued that the geographic decentralization of police authority is salutary, leading to more responsiveness to the particular needs and preferences of local residents (Ostrom, Parks, and Whitaker 1977). Others have pointed to the potential for inegalitarian and discriminatory outcomes because of police discretion, particularly in the absence of a formal rule-making process such as that prescribed for federal regulatory agencies by Congress (Bryner 1987, 10; Davis 1975). For example, Chaney and Saltzstein (1998) found that departments with a smaller share of female officers had lower arrest rates for domestic violence incidents. Unaccountable discretion is the dominant concern of now-dated research that viewed the police as a relatively out-of-control street-level bureaucracy (Lipsky 1980; Davis 1975). Stopping with these studies, one might anticipate a great deal of selective enforcement by police departments, probably carried out in a conservative or discriminatory way against immigrants.

More recent research, however, increasingly depicts policing in terms of a professionalist ethos. Although the police do not meet the classic Weberian definition of a profession, police officers nevertheless approximate professionals in that they are specialists who follow an ideal of service, which they handle with a wide degree of autonomy (Brown 1988, 41). This competence-oriented vision of policing initially emerged from the Progressive reforms of urban government, which stressed the application of technical knowledge and independent initiative by public employees not bound by a political hierarchy. However, the early concept of professionalism designated the realm of expertise of officers as fighting crime and imposing order on a chaotic society, rather than as serving the community. This conception served to distance police from the neighborhoods they patrolled (Brown 1988; Fyfe 2004).

Several authorities have described the emergence of a more empathetic, community service-oriented style of policing that, they argue, moves toward a vision of "good policing," or a more modern conception of police professionalism. An early work of this type was Muir (1977, 54), who saw the challenge facing the professional police officer as the ability to become "morally reconciled to using coercion and at the same time . . . [to reflect] empathetically upon the condition of mankind." Such policing refrains from "separating the world into Us and Them," basically treating people as equals (Muir 1977, 226).[3]

This ideal has been increasingly embraced by police departments as they move toward a "community policing" philosophy, and away from reactive crime fighting. Already by the mid-1980s, Skolnick and Bayley (1986) reported evidence of increasing innovation in urban police departments, innovation typically put into place by proactive chiefs who sought "to mobilize the entire community in its own defense" (p. 210), and who recognized that "when police alienate substantial segments of the community, they may lose not only electoral support for material resources but also information about the incidence of crime and identifications of criminals" (p. 20). For instance, Skolnick and Bayley described the progress of the Santa Ana, California, police from a former strategy of "kick ass and take names" (p. 13) to a department with a service orientation toward its increasingly heterogeneous population, thereby "subordinating its authority to community values" (pp. 37–38). Along these lines, the Santa Ana police chief viewed federal immigration "sweeps" of undocumented immigrants as threatening the trust of residents in government authority, and thus he refused to cooperate with federal authorities in such actions (pp. 33–35).

The new-style, strategically minded police chief actively searches for ideas of what is worthwhile for the organization to do, in furtherance of the agency's mission in the community. Such ideas need not come from political superiors—for example, they could be developed from bureaucrats' own experience or from community input (Moore 1994). Indeed, in this model of professionalism, "police serve, learn from, and are accountable to the community. Behind the new professionalism is a governing notion: that the police and the public are co-producers of crime prevention" (Skolnick and Bayley 1986, 213). The idea of coproduction (Whitaker 1980) highlights the importance of local agencies collaborating with their "clients" to improve patterns of service delivery and also to induce desired behaviors on the part of residents.[4]

The literature on professional policing, then, suggests that police are increasingly concerned more about keeping the peace rather than locking up criminals and will tend to develop rules and routines aimed at encouraging the support and cooperation of residents. However, much of this literature is based on field studies of single departments, and thus its powers of generalization may be suspect (Mastrofski 2004).

If political incorporation theory is the logical corollary of the political-control thesis, then *bureaucratic incorporation* may be the corollary of the bureaucratic professionalism thesis. Jones-Correa (2004), in a study of suburban school districts that have dealt with substantial immigration, developed the concept of bureaucratic incorporation of new groups into the political system. He argued that under certain circumstances, administrators—whether acting out of a sense of mission, professional norms, or personal ethos—may create de facto policies that advance the interests of groups that are otherwise marginalized in local public affairs and electoral politics.

Jones-Correa found that the large, generally affluent county-level school districts he examined in Virginia and Maryland pursued policies that redistributed resources and staff attention to language minorities and students in schools serving lower-income areas. These supportive bureaucratic actions occurred despite the general absence of any significant political power for immigrants in county or school district politics, and despite the contrary pressures of budget exigencies and anti-affirmative action court decisions. Jones-Correa argued that such patterns defy the predictions of political in-corporation theory. Electoral considerations were far less relevant than the egalitarian sense of mission of school superintendents, who viewed their districts' success in a com-munitarian fashion that emphasized the fate of the least fortunate.

It remains to be seen whether bureaucratic incorporation is applicable to other lo-cales and public services. Some may argue that the notion of bureaucratic incorpora-tion is likely to be found only among those agencies providing social services such as education and health. Furthermore, even if police departments engage in the bureau-cratic incorporation of immigrants, one may expect the dynamics underlying such in-corporation to be different, perhaps with the ideological commitments of agency chiefs playing a less prominent role and with a less direct impact on subsequent em-powerment of immigrants. Thus we turn our sights primarily to police practices re-garding immigrants in suburbs and smaller communities, where immigrants are present in increasing numbers but are often fairly recent and distinctive entrants to the community.

Evidence: Mail Surveys and Case Studies

Our quantitative evidence comes from mail surveys conducted in 2003 of police chiefs in California's immigrant-destination cities. We define immigrant-destination cities as municipalities where foreign-born residents comprised at least 15% of the population, as of the 2000 Census. In addition, we included five cities that were just below the 15% threshold but had a substantial presence of at least ten thousand foreign-born residents. Using these criteria, our study focus included 304 out of the 474 municipal governments existing in California as of the 2000 Census. Further investigation revealed that 82 of these cities contract out for police services, usually with the county sheriff's depart-ment. In the case of all but seven cities, we were able to identify the relevant com-manding officer through phone calls and web searches.[5] Although the 15% cutoff is somewhat arbitrary, one can assume that these 304 communities all have immigrant populations that are significant (relative to the size of the city) and visible. The cutoff also allows for considerable variation in the share of immigrant residents, with a mean of 29% and a maximum of 58%.

We used the Dillman (1978) mail-survey method to enhance response rates, and achieved a 62% response among police chiefs, with good response rates across a variety of city categories. To promote high response rates and in order that officials would feel comfortable answering, they were promised anonymity, and therefore we do not report the results in ways that would identify individual officials or cities.

In addition to the survey findings, we report on interviews conducted in three immigrant-destination cities—one in Orange County in Southern California and two in the San Francisco Bay Area. We chose cities that were similar in size and type—each was a large suburb of sixty to ninety thousand in population, relatively typical California municipalities in terms of size—but that varied in ethnic makeup, socioeconomic status, and the recentness of immigrants' entry. We spoke with leaders of civic, religious, ethnic, and immigrant organizations in these cities, as well as police chiefs and officers, elected officials, appointed commission members, and other observers.

Survey Evidence on Policing Practices

The surveys of police chiefs and elected officials enable us to help answer the question of whether police departments lag behind city councils and other city agencies in responding to the unique needs and circumstances of immigrant residents and neighborhoods, or whether they indeed take the lead on such matters. We can also examine whether councilmembers are knowledgeable about immigrant-related law enforcement policies and compare their responses to those of the local police chief. If elected officials lack knowledge, this suggests that they are not the primary movers in the formulation of policies that are of special concern to immigrant communities.

Translation and Language Issues

In police work, time is of the essence—either in responding to calls for assistance or in investigations soon after a crime has occurred. How do police departments deal with victims and witnesses who have difficulty understanding or speaking English? In the questionnaire, we presented police chiefs with the following hypothetical scenario:

> If an officer in your police department responds to a call, and a victim or witness is unable to speak English, how would the officer typically proceed? (Assume the responding officer is not fluent in the victim's language.) *Please check one response.* [emphasis in original]

As Table 2 indicates, 9% of the respondents refused to be pinned down to one answer, with some pointing out that the response would be dictated by the circumstances (i.e., whether an officer speaking that language was on duty, whether the incident was an emergency or a routine call, etc.). The vast majority, however, said that the police officer would typically ask the department to send an officer fluent in that language—an indication that departments have already recognized the need for language diversity and have recruited accordingly.

The priority given to language translation is further underscored by other survey responses indicating that 81% of departments count bilingualism in favor of job candidates during the recruitment process and 87% offer additional pay to bilingual officers. Although the survey did not include a question on the various languages supported, our case study interviews with police officials indicate that there is typically greater diversity in language support among police staff than among the staff in City Hall.

Table 2 Typical Response of Officer If Victim or Witness Is Unable to Speak English

Response	%
Ask the department to send an officer who speaks the person's language	69
Ask a civilian family member, neighbor, etc., to translate	14
Call on a translation service the department contracts with for this purpose	5
Call on a translator employed by the city or county	2
More than one of the above/it depends (volunteered)	9

Source: Authors' survey of police chiefs and commanders.

In cities with no language support among police officers, departments typically rely on civilian translators, with about one in seven chiefs indicating that they would rely on the family members or neighbors of victims and witnesses. Also, a small percentage of police chiefs indicated that they would call on a translator employed by the city or county, or a live translation service with which they contract.

By contrast, language support in other city departments remains quite limited. Our surveys of city elected officials broached the issue of language access differently, by asking how regularly the city provides interpreter services and translation of official documents. The results indicate that translated documents are regularly provided in only 6% of the cities, and interpreters are provided on a consistent basis in only 29% of cities.[6] We suspect the greater provision of language access and the hiring of a bilingual and multiethnic police force is due in large part to the critical importance of language assistance for an agency that seeks to gain the interaction and trust of diverse local residents in its efforts to combat crime and maintain order. As described below, these expectations were largely borne out by case study interviews.

Policies and Practices Regarding Undocumented Immigrants

One of the most controversial issues in recent years surrounding immigration concerns the question of whether foreign government identifications—particularly the *matricula consular* issued by the Mexican government for Mexicans abroad—may be used as a valid form of identification for a variety of official purposes in the United States. These identification cards have been issued since 1871 by the Mexican Consulate to Mexican citizens abroad. The card, which resembles a driver's license and typically expires after five years, includes the individual's picture, birth date, address in the United States, a phone number of the issuing consular office, and (on cards issued since March 2002) several visible and invisible security features.[7]

Proponents argue that the acceptance of the cards enables Mexican citizens the opportunity to open bank accounts, use libraries, and document their identification for minor police infractions. However, critics of illegal immigration argue that police officers should contact federal Immigration and Customs Enforcement (ICE) officials on the presentation of consular ID. Despite lobbying from the Mexican government, the matricula consular is not recognized as proof of identity at the federal level in the United States. In California, no statewide policy for the acceptance of matriculas consular existed at the time of our research, meaning that a policy (if any) would have to be set locally.

Our questionnaire asked both elected officials and police chiefs whether the local police generally accept consular or other Mexican ID cards as valid forms of identification. The results showed an interesting disparity in familiarity with local practices. Of the chiefs and commanding officers responding, 62% indicated that their departments generally accept these forms of identification, whereas 29% said they do not. The remaining 9% did not know, perhaps indicating that the issue had not yet presented itself in these communities. Lack of knowledge regarding the status of consular IDs was much greater among councilmembers and mayors. More than two-thirds of individual respondents (67%) did not know whether their city's police department accepted such forms of identification. It is possible that the collective knowledge of city councilmembers may help overcome the lack of knowledge of any particular elected official. However, even when we aggregate responses by city (by examining the modal response among elected officials in each city), we find no increase in the proportion of cities where elected officials have knowledge of the police department's acceptance of Mexican consular IDs.[8]

A somewhat related issue that has received some attention is whether local police make contact with federal immigration authorities (in ICE, now part of the Department of Homeland Security) after determining that a suspect is in the United States illegally. We asked police officials whether their department would typically contact federal immigration authorities "if an individual in police custody is unable to produce a valid ID and is suspected to be an undocumented immigrant." Only slightly more than one-quarter of respondents (27%) said their department would likely contact federal authorities, whereas 70% said this was unlikely and 3% did not know. This is generally in line with the position articulated by the International Association of Chiefs of Police (2004), which has expressed concerns that state and local involvement in immigration enforcement can have a "chilling effect . . . on legal and illegal aliens reporting criminal activity or assisting police in criminal investigations."

As in the case of consular IDs, the vast majority of city elected officials (74%) did not know whether their police departments would contact federal authorities if they had a suspected undocumented immigrant in custody. Once again, aggregating the modal responses by city council does not diminish the gap in knowledge regarding the police department's relationship with federal immigration authorities. Furthermore, lack of knowledge of police practices holds true regardless of whether the city's police department is supportive or restrictive in its approach toward undocumented immigrants (Table 3).

Thus far, we have seen that police departments in California have generally taken the lead in providing language support to immigrants when compared to the city council and other city agencies and that elected officials generally do not know the policies and practices of police departments regarding such matters as the acceptance of Mexican consular IDs and cooperation with federal authorities regarding deportation of undocumented immigrants. Together, these findings paint a picture of police departments that seem to be shaping policies and practices related to immigrants with little direction from, or knowledge among, elected officials in City Hall.

Questions remain, however, about whether such gaps between city councils and police departments vary according to the demographic and political characteristics of the city.[9] We estimated a multivariate logit model (results available on request) predicting whether police departments are more proactive than city councils in language provisions, controlling for such factors as city size, racial and immigrant composition, and

Table 3 Awareness of Local Police Policies Among Elected Officials (in percentages)

	Accept *Matricula Consular* (Know/Do Not Know)	Contact Federal Immigration Authorities (Know/Do Not Know)
Yes	40/60	28/72
No	25/75	26/74

Source: Authors' surveys or police chiefs and commanders and elected officials.

Note: Cells show proportion of councilmembers or mayors who say they know/do not know their police department's approach.

the racial and ideological composition of city council. We found that police departments are systematically "further ahead" of the council in cities with larger populations, but these gaps are not statistically significant when we use the Heckman selection procedure to take into account differences in response rates. The presence of one or more Latinos or Asians on the council was not associated with such differences; nor was the presence of district versus at-large elections or the proportion of Democrats in the electorate, further weakening the argument that police practices are a result of processes of political incorporation and political control.[10] Similarly, variables related to political incorporation are largely unhelpful in accounting for gaps in elected officials' knowledge regarding matriculas consular and cooperation with immigration officials, as are demographic factors such as the city's size or proportion of immigrants.

Case Study Evidence on Policing Practices

Although the survey evidence is valuable for its breadth of coverage of the many types of immigrant-destination cities across California, it does not lend itself easily to a detailed understanding of how these issues have played out in various communities. To do so, we provide vignettes of three cities where we investigated the relations between immigrants, police, and elected officials. All three communities are large suburbs with substantial local employment and with large immigrant populations. Two cities ("Bay Flats" and "Crossroads City") are in the San Francisco Bay Area, with the third ("SoCal Heights") being in Southern California. We use pseudonyms for these cities to protect the identities of interview respondents in our larger project.

Bay Flats is a traditional, White, working-class suburb where many Latino immigrants have recently entered, whereas Crossroads City is a middle-class, multiethnic community with no real ethnic majority and a substantial presence of high-tech businesses. Finally, SoCal Heights is a relatively affluent suburb with a fairly recent influx of immigrant residents, particularly Latino residents from a large neighboring city. We interviewed the police chief in each city, along with local elected and administrative officials, immigrant advocates, and representatives of nonprofits that work with immigrants. In each case, we find that the local police department made advances in working with immigrants largely on its own volition, without significant guidance from elected officials.

Bay Flats

Bay Flats has undergone a rapid shift in terms of its racial, ethnic, and immigrant composition. The proportion of non-Hispanic Whites living in the city fell from about 80% in 1960 to about 40% in 2000. Part of this decline can be attributed to a slow influx of African-Americans from Oakland and elsewhere. As of 2000, about 10% of the city's population was Black. However, the Asian-American (25%) and Latino (20%) communities were even larger. First-generation immigrants accounted for about one-quarter of the resident population. Moreover, noncitizens accounted for more than half of the foreign-born population, limiting the ability of immigrants to have an impact on electoral politics. Also, as some of our interviewees noted, even the immigrant *citizen* population in

Bay Flats is skewed toward young, recent arrivals, characteristics associated with low rates of political participation, whereas the White population is skewed toward long-term, elderly residents, who tend to have a high degree of participation in local affairs.

Bay Flats was well-known in the post-World War II period for racial exclusion, when it was tagged as one of the nation's most racist suburbs (Self 2003). Racial exclusion was felt primarily in housing, where residents entered into informal agreements to screen out Blacks, but our interviews with local officials and community leaders indicate that it was also felt in policing. As one councilmember told us, "the police would stop people if they were different, coming out of Oakland. They would sometimes pick them up and take them back over the border." Other respondents echoed similar sentiments, indicating that police misconduct was part of the more general problem of race relations in the city during the 1960s and 1970s. Little surprise, then, that it remained largely White despite the presence of a large Black population nearby in Oakland, a growing industrial base, and expanding real estate development.

Even when the racial and ethnic demographics began to change with the influx of immigrants, tensions between police and non-White residents remained a significant problem. However, most of our interviewees indicated that the situation had changed dramatically for the better in the past decade or so, attributable primarily to the "inclusive" and "proactive" leadership of the current police chief and his predecessor. For instance, one community leader noted that the department has hired several Latino and Asian-American officers, who in turn have been more involved in doing community outreach and working with families to prevent gang violence. The police chief indicated that, in addition to increasing racial and ethnic diversity in the police force, the department has also provided training to all its officers in issues such as handling domestic violence cases in different communities and learning about the needs of the Muslim community after the attacks of September 11, 2001. Finally, the department also makes it a point to attend various community events and neighborhood meetings, even if doing so involves significant overtime pay.

In many ways, the police department is more proactive in its outreach efforts to immigrants than other agencies and elected officials in this city. Many of the elected and appointed officials we spoke with said that they do not know much about the immigrant community. They also bemoaned the lack of civic involvement among immigrants; yet meetings between elected officials and immigrant business owners or advocates are rare, and very few city documents are translated. By contrast, the police department has succeeded in learning about various immigrant communities and has gained a modicum of trust in many neighborhoods. Finally, unlike other municipal agencies and governing bodies in Bay Flats that have minimal language assistance, the police department has full-time bilingual staff in Spanish, Chinese, and Tagalog to handle the language needs of immigrants with limited English proficiency.

At the same time, the relationship between the police department and various immigrant communities appears to be more oriented toward management than empowerment. Indeed, the department enforces certain policies that make life for some immigrant communities more difficult than it is, say, in large cities like Los Angeles or San Francisco. For one, it aggressively enforces some ordinances that are less likely to be tenable in areas of overcrowded housing (for example, a prohibition on fixing cars on the street even for a short period of time, or requiring that no storage items be visible from the street). The city's prohibition on loitering and solicitation means that day laborers often have to travel to Oakland to find work, and the police department is also vigilant in cracking down on informal businesses such as street vendors and unlicensed home enterprises.

Some may argue that these measures are based solely on concerns with public health, quality of life, and safety, and that immigrants themselves ultimately benefit from the enforcement of such laws. Yet if informal businesses and overcrowding are inevitable aspects of immigrant life in the urban areas (especially given the present state of wages, rents, and profit margins of immigrant-run businesses), then the enforcement of such ordinances places a greater burden on immigrants than the native-born. The city council has not addressed the issue of whether ordinances should be altered to suit the changing dynamics of the population and the local economy. Thus police involvement is more about enforcement and management than empowerment of immigrant communities. Yet, given Bay Flats's earlier history of contentious relationships between municipal institutions and minority communities, the police department has been more responsive than the city council to the needs of immigrant residents.

Crossroads City

Our second Bay Area case study is a multiethnic community. In 2000, nearly half of the inhabitants were immigrants, the vast majority of whom came from Asia (over 80%), with Filipinos, Vietnamese, Chinese, and Indians as the largest subgroups, in that order.[11] Moreover, about one-half of the city's immigrants had only recently arrived between 1990 and 2000. There is a significant Latino minority as well, and a small but long-standing Black population. According to the 2000 Census, about a quarter of the population reported not speaking English well, and about a quarter were noncitizens. However, given the variety of high-technology employment in the area, the city is relatively well off. The median household income in 2000 was over $80,000, although local neighborhoods are dominated by modest tract homes, small apartment buildings, and strip malls. Some portion of the high household income is explained by the presence of multigeneration and multifamily immigrant households. Asian populations are quite dispersed throughout the city, and neighborhoods are fairly mixed, although there is a more concentrated area of Latino settlement with a considerably lower income profile.

Current and former officials in the city noted that the local police department seemed well trained in cultural sensitivity and has achieved a high level of diversity. At the time of our visit, the chief was an African-American and the two captains ranking behind the chief were both Asian-Americans. About 15% of sworn officers were Hispanic, and about 28% were Asians, many of them recent hires. A Filipino community activist commended the police department for efforts to increase the force's representation of Asian and Pacific officers and to avoid racial profiling, saying that "the chief is a minority who is very sensitive to immigrant concerns." A Hispanic member of a city commission told us the department has proven to be "equal opportunity at busting crimes."

Interviewees brought up a number of examples of the importance of a diverse police force in resolving potential conflicts. An Asian-American former officeholder related an incident in which a Chinese-speaking motorist jumped on his car after a traffic incident and began waving a knife around. The police department dispatched a Chinese-speaking officer (among others) who was able to talk the man down. In other cities, the former official speculates, officers might have shot at the knife-wielding man and endangered bystanders because of the inability to communicate. A police officer noted that the department regularly sets up checkpoints for intoxicated drivers at various locations. On one occasion, the checkpoint was set up in an area with many Chinese restaurants. A resident called the mayor complaining that Asians were being targeted for DUI stops. The mayor asked the chief to investigate and was told that both the captain and sergeant leading the checkpoint that night were Chinese and several of the officers involved were Asian. This satisfied the city officials. "How would that have looked if we were a relatively White police department?" the officer wondered.

Beyond simple diversity of representation on the police force, sensitivity to different cultural backgrounds among immigrants is important when patrolling such an ethnically diverse community. The department has held occasional training courses on cultural customs and ethnic relations, though many issues are only discovered while on patrol. A White elected official brought up the example of the handcuffing of Vietnamese suspects. Given the conflicts of their home country, some Vietnamese American immigrants apparently feared execution if their hands were cuffed behind their backs. Police adapted to this concern and began cuffing suspects with hands in front. In another example, the police chief related that many Sikh men and boys in the community, as a cultural tradition, carry small ceremonial swords known as kirpans. The issue reached a head when school officials complained that some students were arriving at school with such swords. The chief investigated the issue and consulted with the district attorney's office and with police chiefs in nearby cities. Although "legally, we could take it and arrest them," a compromise was reached in which officers were instructed to allow Sikhs to carry the ceremonial swords, so long as they were not especially long or aggressively displayed. Ultimately, police and school officials and community members banded together to make a video explaining the tradition.

The police department collaborates with the local school district on outreach to youth of different cultures. Both the city council and school board have budgeted funds for this collaborative relationship, at the request of the bureaucrats involved. The department also reaches out by assigning one police officer to each of the city's many small shopping centers, requiring him or her to walk the shopping center "beat" at least forty minutes per day and to make regular contacts and inquiries with merchants. These include the many ethnic and immigrant merchants in Crossroads City, where shopping centers are dotted with signs in a variety of languages. The chief also attends many community events, typically in uniform. A neighborhood group leader noted that police were invited to, and typically attended, the group's community breakfasts, which often featured presentations from various ethnic or religious groups explaining their cultural traditions.

The department does not seek out undocumented immigrants or ask about the immigration status of persons who come in contact with the police. One officer related that police had gotten involved in one case where the teenage children in one undocumented family from Mexico were not enrolled in school; the father wanted them to work instead. A community affairs police officer and the school district at-risk specialist went to the family's home together, initially to reassure the father that they were not there to report him to immigration authorities. They then convinced him to register the children for school.

Overall, relationships between the police department and various immigrant communities in the city, if not always warm and close, appear respectful and not marred by gulfs of understanding and perception. Some of this is undoubtedly aided by the relative lack of grinding poverty, violent crime, or other conditions that often plague lower-income communities. Nevertheless, there are limits to what the police can do in "enforcing" tolerance. As the chief related, Sikhs at a community function once asked him why they were the targets of obscene gestures when walking past some people in Crossroads City. "I told them, 'because those people are stupid.' There's a lot of unwanted, unfocused attention, when there's different groups."

SoCal Heights

This medium-sized suburb in Southern California has more than doubled in population during the past twenty years and has also experienced significant transformations in its racial and ethnic composition. Between 1990 and 2000, the proportion of non-Hispanic Whites decreased from over 60% to 45%, whereas the proportion of Latinos increased from 21 % to 35% and the share of Asian-Americans rose from 10% to 15%. Immigration played a significant role in much of this diversification, with the foreign-born share of SoCal Heights's population growing from about 20% to about 33%.

As the city's population continues to grow, there is a gap between well-to-do areas in the north and more crowded areas near the southern edge of the city. Managing population growth is also a significant concern. The city government has tried to attract higher-income residents with luxury golf course subdivisions while contending with an influx of residents from the more modest neighboring cities.

Our interviews with social service providers and other community organizations indicated that the city was largely unprepared for the new challenges facing immigrant residents with low incomes and with limited English proficiency. Documents in City Hall are not generally translated into languages other than English, and interpreters are rarely provided in city government meetings, even though more than one in five residents lacks English proficiency. Advocates for immigrants also noted that the city's general level of affluence not only exacerbates the issue of overcrowded housing; it also makes it difficult to get elected officials and residents interested in the concerns of immigrants who live in less affluent areas. Social service providers thus perceived a growing socioeconomic divide in the city that was taking on a racial hue and saw little interest on the part of City Hall to address issues of concern to Latino immigrants, most notably affordable housing.

By contrast, the police department in SoCal Heights received high marks from everyone we interviewed. Respondents generally thought that the police department was fair in its dealings with immigrants and other residents. One Latino activist noted that "As kids we knew SoCal Heights cops were harder on Mexicans back in the 1960s. . . . [But] they realize that the community is changing so they try to develop relationships." He also noted that, unlike the city council, the police department does not care much about "whether someone is a voter or a nonvoter as much as what it takes to get the job done." A councilmember implicitly acknowledged the greater responsiveness of the police department to issues of language access. When asked about the provision of language access in City Hall, the councilmember noted that city officials sometimes call on bilingual police officers to assist with interpretation and translation.

In an interview, the police chief elaborated some of the ways in which the department has tried to reach out to immigrant residents. In addition to providing language assistance, the department posts a full-time officer in the high school and encourages officers to each "adopt" an apartment complex in the part of town where low-income residents live. As the chief noted, "One officer put on a summer-long swimming lesson after someone drowned in his complex. Some make newsletters. It's like a mini-community and they [tenants] feel like they have someone on their side."

In addition to making police officers a familiar face in immigrant areas, the department has also contracted with an outside firm to conduct city wide surveys of residents. In immigrant areas, the firm has translated the survey into different languages when necessary. These surveys have been used to modulate the outreach efforts of the police department based on the needs and concerns of various communities. As far as Latino immigrants were concerned, the chief noted, "We found out things that we thought would be important weren't important at all. For example, we thought gangs were important when after the survey, we learned that they were more worried about traffic."

Police, Immigrants, and Bureaucratic Incorporation

In recent decades, many American municipalities have undergone transformations, as immigrants have entered communities in large numbers and have begun to alter some of the norms and routines of these communities. Among the challenges presented for city governments by the entry of immigrants, law enforcement issues would seem to be among the most challenging and sensitive. Given the conservative reputation of the police and the history of strained relations between police and ethnic minorities, one might expect major conflicts to develop between police departments and immigrant populations. Our survey evidence makes it fairly clear, however, that police departments have developed policies that are generally supportive of immigrants. Furthermore, the case studies indicate that gaining trust and serving the community's unique needs were the spur for such policies.

These supportive policies are not being pushed on police departments by local elected officials. There is no evidence that mayors and councilmembers are setting policy or spurring innovations in these police departments, with respect to language assistance or matriculas consular. The survey and case study evidence both indicate that police departments and police chiefs are generally more likely than the mayor or councilmembers to be aware of the needs of immigrant communities. Police departments are also more likely than elected institutions and other municipal agencies to provide language support and to give priority to language skills and community representation when it comes to hiring new personnel. In line with this approach, police forces in immigrant-destination cities tend to be relatively diverse. According to the survey of police chiefs, about one-third of the total number of officers in our sample of cities are Latino or Asian—a much higher level of diversity than the elected officials of these towns, though less so than the population as a whole. We find little indication that this greater level of language support and diversity in hiring is because of pressure from elected officials.

Indeed, in some respects the elected officials do not even seem to know what their "agents" are doing. Elected officials are largely unaware of issues pertaining to immigrant residents and the practices of police departments on such matters as the acceptance of Mexican consular IDs and the decision of whether to contact federal immigration officials regarding undocumented immigrants. The lack of awareness of police practices holds true even in cities with high proportions of immigrants or with Latinos on the city council.

Rather than taking cues from the political leadership of the city, police chiefs are fashioning policies that aim to better police the city, using newer policing models of gaining trust and serving the community instead of older models emphasizing detached expertise in the imposition of order (Brown 1988). These findings are more congruent with the bureaucratic professionalism model—and, by extension, the "bureaucratic incorporation" of immigrants (Jones-Correa 2004)—than with theories of political control of the bureaucracy.

Moreover, even though the bureaucratic professionalism model, combined with our evidence, speaks to the wide degree of discretion enjoyed by municipal police, it departs from the implications of the classic "street-level bureaucracy" literature (Lipsky 1980; Davis 1975) that such discretion is exercised in a conservative or discriminatory fashion against minorities. Of course, our study is limited in that the survey evidence gathered from chiefs cannot determine whether patrol officers comply on a day-to-day basis with such departmental norms as providing language assistance, accepting Mexican ID cards, or not targeting undocumented immigrants—although studies like Skolnick and Bayley (1986) indicate that chiefs have substantial influence in setting the direction for the behavior of their subordinates. Still, our case-study evidence does indicate that these departments have sent a clear message that police officers need to seek the confidence and support of immigrant residents as they go about their patrol duties. This finding offers hopeful signs that these diverse cities can avoid crises of confidence in the police since such problems typically derive from concerns about the fairness with which police exercise discretion and express respect for the public, rather than from an inability of police to control crime (Mastrofski 2004, 109; Tyler and Huo 2002).

For purposes of analytical clarity, we have highlighted the dichotomy between political and bureaucratic control of service delivery and found that the police bureaucracies' professionalism and their routines appear more even handed than the political system, which is typically more responsive to group power. Nevertheless, over the long run, there may well be an iterative relationship between bureaucratic autonomy and political control. For example, it was political pressures in the Progressive reform era that led to the professionalization of and quest for expertise among police agencies; later, the social distance between police (who saw their "professional" duty as controlling misconduct) and the neighborhoods they served led to further political pressures that helped prompt the movement toward more community policing and new rules on the use of force. This iterative relationship may also help explain the puzzle of why police may show more foresight in their relations with immigrants in some areas than in others. For instance, police may accept Mexican IDs and may not be eager to jeopardize their relations with the community by actively seeking out illegal immigrants. However, as the Bay Flats case illustrates, where the city government has developed regulatory restrictions based on a certain conception of the community (such as a prohibition of street vending or outdoor storage), the police are still likely to enforce such ordinances, in spite of their disproportionate impact on immigrants.

We see potential to extend this line of inquiry in two ways. Further investigation might extend these research questions to a national sample of immigrant-receiving cities and broaden the array of immigrant-related law enforcement policies and practices examined. It would also be important to take into account cities with sizable Black immigrant populations and to tease out the relative importance of race, immigrant status, and ethnicity. In addition, scholars interested in issues of political control of the bureaucracy might wish to study a range of other local government functions to compare administrators' approaches in setting organizational practices and decision rules to elected officials' knowledge and understanding of those policies.

Finally, further research could determine whether the lack of political oversight of local police on immigrant-related matters has changed in the wake of the increased visibility of the immigration issue since our data collection took place in 2003. With the immigration issue being more salient in many communities today, there have been efforts by state and federal officials to induce or compel local governments and police to adopt more active roles in crackdowns on illegal immigrants. Initial evidence suggests that some police departments are resisting demands to play immigration cops and are limiting their cooperation with federal authorities (Johnson 2007, Thacher 2005). It remains to be seen, however, whether the concern of police departments to maintain the trust and confidence of immigrant residents will ultimately be trumped by efforts among some conservatives to reassert political control over police behavior.

CHAPTER 6

POLITICS, PRIVATIZATION, AND THE PUBLIC REALM

THE PRIVATIZATION OF URBAN SPACE

Many urban scholars have argued that fear is reshaping the geography and politics of urban America. In the twentieth century, affluent citizens escaped the problems of the city by moving to the suburbs. In the twenty-first century, people are finding new ways of separating themselves from the problems of urban life. Enclosed malls, gated communities, office parks, condominium towers, and tourist bubbles provide an escape from the public realm. What are the political consequences of this trend?

In Selection 18, Margaret Kohn maintains that a basic daily activity, shopping, has become politicized in a way that undermines individual civil liberties. According to Kohn, public areas are disappearing in cities and suburbs as a result of the proliferation of shopping malls. Unlike familiar Main Streets, these privately owned shopping enclaves usually exclude or severely restrict opportunities for face-to-face politics that take place in the public sphere, including handing out political leaflets, gathering signatures for candidates or ballot issues, holding protests, and other forms of political communication. Nevertheless, in many suburbs the malls are virtually the only available sites for these political activities.

Do mall owners have the right to exclude political activities or is there a legitimate state interest in making these spaces accessible for free speech? Kohn argues that in a series of "shopping mall" cases the U.S. Supreme Court has closed its eyes to the privatization of public space by insisting that the first amendment to the U.S. Constitution only limits what government agencies can do. Although some state courts have been more open to ensuring that private malls have public access responsibilities, there is no judicial consensus on this principle. Kohn contends that similar issues of exclusion arise in business improvement districts (BIDs), where business property owners essentially are entitled to control a private government in order to collect special revenues and to funnel the money into additional services for their own area. Although BIDs often exercise far-reaching governmental powers over public areas, they are largely beyond voter control. According to Kohn, they are also changing the nature of public space. BIDs mimic the suburban mall by transforming city streets into managed environments providing the same kind of security, order, and tidiness as suburban shopping malls.

In Selection 19, Jon C. Teaford argues that shopping malls are constantly evolving and that they are more complex than commonly supposed. The first generation of enclosed malls displayed a negative image as "soulless" "blank-faced hulks surrounded by vast parking lots." By the turn of the century, enclosed malls were losing customers and sales. Big-box megastores such as Wal-Mart began to draw shoppers away. Clusters of discount stores, so-called power centers, have also made inroads, as have lifestyle centers, which try to create a symbiotic relationship between upscale chain specialty shops, such as Banana Republic and Pottery Barn, and restaurant and entertainment venues. Another variant is the town center, which mixes an open-air ambiance of shopping and services with offices, housing, and even public facilities. The increasing variety of privatized spaces shows that developers are constantly adapting to changing preferences. These privatized spaces do not fit a singular stereotype, an impression one often suggested by the literature on suburban development. Despite their increasing public character, these venues remain only organized around consumption activities by their commercial overseers. Where will they evolve next?

The entire relationship of citizens to American cities has been challenged by the rise of international terrorism. In the aftermath of terrorist strikes here and abroad, scholars and citizens are debating whether terrorism is changing the use of public space in cities, especially prime targets, such as New York and Washington, D.C. Some believe these new security threats may fundamentally change urban life, forcing local governments and citizens to take radical defensive measures. This includes "hardening" tall buildings, dispersing economic activities, and undertaking an enlarged and intrusive police presence. Indeed, some have suggested urban terrorism challenges the viability of most densely settled communities.

In Selection 20, H. V. Savitch questions such a bleak scenario. He describes how even cities that have suffered the most attacks—such as New York, London, and Jerusalem—demonstrate great resilience to such disturbances. He believes these cities recovered with considerable speed due to their intrinsic value as centers of economic activity and social life, as well as because of their political capacity to address the consequences of terrorism. For example, traditional business activities sprang back to life in New York City within a short period after 9/11 and have flourished since. The author suggests the "natural dynamism" of large cities provides enormous capacity for recovery and revival, particularly when it is aided by national programs to further enhance it. He recommends coordination among all levels of government to enhance their security over a sustained period of time.

Savitch's positive assessment of the resilience of cities shows that their capacity to deal with terrorism has often been underestimated. Yet some of the long-term political consequences of terrorism remain uncertain. When cities suffer terrorist attacks, governments take new steps to minimize future violent events, as did the United States in the wake of 9/11. The Patriot Act signed into law in 2001 greatly increased the power of federal law enforcement agencies to fight terrorism and intrude into private communications. Local governments and police departments also increased their antiterrorist activities. How much will these new concerns over safety and security erode traditional civil liberties and undermine personal privacy in our cities? Collective action to defend the homeland poses new issues about the use of urban space.

18

Margaret Kohn

THE MAULING OF PUBLIC SPACE

Bridgewater Township is a community of 40,000 located in New Jersey. Like earlier cities that were traditionally situated at the intersection of transportation routes, it owes its location to the confluence of Routes 287 and 78, two superhighways. Although Bridgewater was originally a bedroom community serving professionals who worked in New York, it gradually developed its own local economy with offices, businesses, and services. What it lacked was a sense of place. Local residents dreamed of a town center, some ideal composite of a New England village green and a Tuscan piazza, a place where old people could gossip, young people could *farsi vedere* (make themselves seen), mothers could bring young children while getting a latté, a sandwich, or some postage stamps. After over a decade of discussion, in 1988 they inaugurated Bridgewater Commons—a mall.[1]

The Bridgewater Commons Mall was not originally the initiative of commercial real estate developers. After years of research and debate, local government planners and community groups decided that a carefully designed shopping mall was the form of development best suited to maintaining the small town's quality of life and avoiding the strip mall aesthetic. Individual retailers could not provide the capital necessary to implement a comprehensive plan that included environmentally sensitive landscaping and rational traffic management. More importantly, a traditional downtown could not guarantee the most highly prized amenities: safety, cleanliness, and order.

The Bridgewater Commons and hundreds of supermalls like it have long troubled architects and critics who bemoan the homogeneity, sterility, and banality of the suburbs.[2] Approaching the mall primarily as an aesthetic or even a sociological issue, however, overlooks the enormous political consequences of the privatization of public space. Public sidewalks and streets are practically the only remaining available sites for unscripted political activity. They are the places where insurgent political candidates gather signatures, striking workers publicize their cause, and church groups pass out leaflets. It is true that television, newspapers, and direct mail constantly deliver a barrage of information, including political leaflets. But unlike the face-to-face politics that takes place in the public sphere, these forms for communication do not allow the citizen to talk back, to ask a question, to tell a story, to question a premise. The politics of the public sphere requires no resources—except time and perseverance. Public spaces are the last domains where the opportunity to communicate is not something bought and sold.

And they are rapidly disappearing. Such places are not banned by authoritarian legislatures. The public is not dispersed by the police. Their disappearance is more benign but no less troubling. The technology of the automobile, the expansion of the

---

federal highway system, and the growth of residential suburbs has changed the way Americans live. Today the only place that many Americans encounter strangers is in the shopping mall. The most important public place is now private. And that is probably not an accident.

The privatization of public space poses a number of conceptual challenges for public policy makers. Does the ownership or use determine whether a particular place is truly private? How should the right to private property be weighed against the legitimate state interest in sustaining a public sphere? Does it violate the First Amendment right to free speech if a shopping mall prohibits orderly political speech? Are suburban malls meaningfully different from downtown developments?

The United States Supreme Court has tried to answer these questions in a series of decisions that have determined government policy defining the public sphere. The Supreme Court's doctrine in "the shopping mall cases" reflects a growing unwillingness to engage the broader political issues emerging from rapid social change. By insisting that the First Amendment only limits what government agencies can do, the Court has effectively closed its eyes to the privatization of public space.

The Shopping Mall Cases

The Supreme Court addressed the implications of private ownership of quasi-public spaces in a series of cases decided between 1946 and 1980. The Court first considered the issue in 1946 in *Marsh v. Alabama*, which dealt with a Jehovah's Witness who was arrested for distributing religious pamphlets in the business district of a company-owned town. The majority decided that the arrest violated the freedom of the press and freedom of religion guaranteed by the First Amendment and applied to the states under the Fourteenth Amendment. The opinion written by Justice Black emphasized that all citizens must have the same rights, regardless of whether they live in a traditional municipality or a company-owned town. He noted that a typical community of privately owned residences would not have had the power to pass a municipal ordinance forbidding the distribution of religious literature on street corners. Why then, should a corporation be allowed to do so?

The company, Gulf Shipbuilding Corporation, based its argument on the common law and constitutional right to private property. If an individual does not have to allow Jehovah's Witnesses into her home, why should the company have to allow them on its property? The court, however, rejected this logic. It cited a long list of precedents—cases involving bridges, roads, and ferries—to establish that the right to private property is not absolute. Especially when a private company performs public functions, it opens itself up to greater government scrutiny and regulation. Given that the town was freely accessible to outsiders, it implicitly invited in the general public, thereby voluntarily incurring quasi-public obligations. The concept of "invitee" went on to play an important role in desegregation cases. According to the Court, "The more an owner, for his advantage, opens up his property for use by the public in general, the more do his rights become circumscribed by the statutory and constitutional rights of those who use it."

The opinion concluded that property rights must be weighed against other state interests. Justice Black emphasized that a democracy had a compelling state interest in maintaining free and open channels of communication so that all of its residents could fulfill their duties as citizens: "To act as good citizens they must be informed. In order to enable them to be properly informed their information must be uncensored." A concurring opinion by Justice Frankfurter stated that fundamental civil liberties guaranteed by the Constitution must have precedence over property rights.

Based on the reasoning in *Marsh v. Alabama*, it would seem likely that the right to free speech would apply to other private arenas that are similarly open to a broad public. In a 1972 decision, *Lloyd Corp. v. Tanner*, the Court considered whether First Amendment guarantees extended to the shopping mall.[3] This time, however, the majority upheld the mall's policy forbidding the distribution of handbills on its premises. The owners could exclude expressive conduct, even when it did not disrupt the commercial functions of the mall. Writing for the majority, Justice Powell argued that a shopping mall was not the functional equivalent of a company town, because it was not a space where individuals performed multiple activities. It was simply devoted to shopping. Although it was true that the shopping mall implicitly invited the general public onto its premises, this did not transform it into a public space. According to Powell, political activists misunderstood the invitation if they turned the mall into a public forum; the invitation to the public was only to shop. Moreover, because the First Amendment only limited "state action" there was no constitutional basis to apply it to private entities.

In *Lloyd v. Tanner* the Court did not overrule *Marsh v. Alabama*; instead it emphasized how the two cases differed. The mall was no company town. Basically, the Court concluded that activists had other opportunities to engage in political activity. They could make use of the public roads and sidewalks on the perimeter of the shopping mall. The assumption was that citizens had other chances to be exposed to diverse ideas and viewpoints. Because they presumably spent at most part of their day at the shopping mall, they could become informed citizens elsewhere.

Although the Court tried to emphasize the differences of fact between the two cases, it actually modified its view of the relevant doctrine. In the *Lloyd* decision there was no idealistic discussion of the free exchange of ideas necessary to maintain an informed citizenry. Rather than considering the goal of the First Amendment—presumably to foster the free expression characteristic of a democracy—the Court focused narrowly on the supposed absence of state action. It decided that private property does not "lose its private character merely because the public is generally invited to use it for designated purposes."

It is puzzling that the justices in *Lloyd* did not really analyze the logic of *Marsh v. Alabama* on the critical issue of state action. In *Marsh*, Justice Black suggested that the enforcement of state criminal trespass laws constituted state action. If the state may make no law abridging freedom of speech, then it cannot pass a criminal trespass statute penalizing a citizen simply for engaging in nondisruptive expressive conduct in a place where he or she would be legitimately allowed to enter. This same logic was used in a much more famous case, *Shelley v. Kraemer*, which was decided by the same court in 1948. In that case, the Supreme Court struck down a restrictive covenant preventing residents from selling their homes to blacks. The contract was undeniably private, however, it could not be enforced without "the active intervention of the state courts, supported by the full panoply of state power." According to this decision, private actors could not use the police and the courts to enforce practices that violate constitutional rights. In *Lloyd v. Tanner* (1972) the Supreme Court decided to overlook these precedents, assuming a much narrower definition of what constitutes state action.

The last shopping mall case, *Pruneyard Shopping Center v. Robins* (1980) dealt with a group of high school students who attempted to gather signatures for a petition protesting a U.N. resolution condemning Zionism. The California State Supreme Court originally found in favor of the students, ruling that the state's criminal trespass law would constitute state action for the purposes of the First Amendment. The shopping mall owners appealed to the United States Supreme Court, claiming that their Fifth Amendment right not to be deprived of "private property, without due process of law" was violated by the California decision. They argued that the mall was no public forum. To require that the mall allow political solicitation was tantamount to "taking without just compensation." The owners also claimed that the right to exclude others is an essential component of the definition of private property.

The *Pruneyard* decision, which governs to this day, articulated a mediating position. The Supreme Court rejected the mall owner's claim to absolute dominion over its property. Drawing upon a long history of precedents regarding public regulation of private property, the court concluded that the due process clause only required that the laws "not be unreasonable, arbitrary, or capricious and that the means selected shall have a real and substantial relation to the objective sought." The right to exclude others would only be decisive if the mall owners could prove that allowing orderly political speech would substantially decrease the economic value of their property.[4]

The Court, however, also rejected the students' claims to protection under the free speech clause of the First Amendment. Because the facts of the case were substantially the same as those in *Lloyd v. Tanner*, the Court saw no reason to reconsider the issue. They still insisted that the mall was private and therefore beyond the reach of the Bill of Rights. But there was a second issue at stake. The students had challenged the shopping center's policy under both the U.S. and the California State Constitution. The language of the California free speech clause was more expansive. Article 1, § 2, of the California Constitution provides:

> Every person may freely speak, write and publish his or her sentiments on all subjects, being responsible for the abuse of this right. A law may not restrain or abridge liberty of speech or press.

The U.S. Supreme Court found that there was no reason why a state or federal statute could not guarantee access to the public areas of private malls. In other words, the Court did not find any constitutional prohibition against legislation protecting political speech in places where citizens were normally allowed to be. This finding was consistent with an earlier decision, *Hudgens v. NLRB* (1976), which held that striking workers had no First Amendment right to picket in a mall, but they could assert such a right under federal labor laws protecting the processes associated with collective bargaining.[5] Since the decision fourteen states have considered whether their own state constitutions protect expressive conduct in shopping malls. Only five—California, Oregon, New Jersey, Colorado, and Massachusetts—recognized broader protections for speech.[6]

Privatization and Public Policy

Over twenty years have passed since the Supreme Court's decision. Although the law has not changed in that period, society has. There is something quaint and anachronistic about reading the old shopping mall cases. They describe the world we take for granted as something new and marvelous and they could not even imagine the world in which we would soon live. Writing in 1972, Justice Powell described the Lloyd Center in Portland, Oregon, like this:

> The Center embodies a relatively new concept in shopping center design. The stores are all located within a single large, multilevel building complex sometimes referred to as the "Mall." Within this complex, in addition to the stores, there are parking facilities, malls, private sidewalks, stairways, escalators, gardens, an auditorium, and a skating rink. Some of the stores open directly on the outside public sidewalks, but most open on the interior privately owned malls. Some stores open on both. There are no public streets or public sidewalks within the building complex, which is enclosed and entirely covered except for the landscaped portions of some of the interior malls.[7]

This futuristic mall had 60 shops and 1000 parking spaces. Compared to today's supermalls, the Lloyd Center is a neighborhood corner store. By 1990 there were over 300 mega-supermalls with at least five department stores and three hundred shops. The West Edmonton Mall has over 800 shops, 11 department stores, 110 restaurants, 20 movie theaters, 13 night clubs, a chapel, a large hotel, and a lake.[8] In the United States there are twenty-three square feet of shopping mall space for every person.[9]

In 1972, the Court concluded that this new concept in shopping, "sometimes referred to as the 'Mall,'" in no way resembled a company town. It seemed obvious that a mall was simply devoted to a single activity, shopping, whereas a town was defined by the physical proximity of diverse spaces and activities, housing and services, leisure and work, consumption, education, and production. A mall is a place you visit; a town is a place you live. But this has been slowly changing.[10] Industry watchers report that the average visit to a "leisure time destination" (a mall with sophisticated design elements, restaurants, and movie theaters) lasted four hours as compared to just one hour at a conventional mall.[11]

The mall has become an entertainment mecca, a major employer, and a premier vacation destination. The Travel Industry Association of America (TIA) reported that shopping is the number one vacation activity in America. The Mall of America in Bloomington, Minnesota, attracts 42.5 million visitors annually.[12] Its hundreds of retail establishments are not the only attraction: it has a wedding chapel, the nation's largest indoor amusement park, a post office, a police station, and a school.

The mall is also a workplace. The West Edmonton Mall has over 15,000 employees. Although they do not manufacture automobiles or aircraft carriers, they do produce the spiral of fantasy, desire, and consumption that is the basis of the North American service economy.

The mall is becoming not only a genuine multi-use facility, but a completely self-contained homotopia of suburban life. In the morning the doors open to waiting seniors, the famous mall-walkers who appreciate the controlled climate, cleanliness, and safety. At night the security guards have to herd out the lingering teenagers, who are in no rush to go home to their monotonous housing developments.[13] The mall is clearly the nodal point of social life, but is it the equivalent of a downtown business district?

Not exactly. The shopping mall is so attractive because it combines the pleasures of public life with the safety and familiarity of the private realm. Ironically, the suburban megamall was intended to be an oasis of urbanity and civilization. Victor Gruen, the Viennese architect who designed the prototype of the modern mall, was motivated by a progressive vision. He wanted to recreate a vibrant, pedestrian-oriented; multi-use area that captured the excitement of urban space. An immigrant from Vienna, he was inspired by the glass-enclosed atriums of Europe, particularly the galleries of Milan and arcades of Paris. In 1956 he built Southdale in Edina, Minnesota, the first multi-level, enclosed; climate-controlled mall. He thought that the mall could serve as a community center and nodal point for civic identity in the suburbs.[14] He realized that many people long for the vitality, diversity, beauty, and stimulation of public space. Gruen astutely predicted that when public space is not available, people would flock to private simulacra. But the private provision of public places is a Faustian bargain. Once developers possess the power of property rights, they usually exercise them to create the highly orchestrated and controlled environments that eviscerate the diversity that animates public space.

Following in Gruen's footsteps, contemporary mall designers have used their formidable skills to simulate the old-fashioned downtown of our imaginations. Faux antiquarian signs suggest that shopping corridors are actually city streets and the central atrium is the town square.[15] Some malls, such as Faneuil Hall Marketplace in Boston, incorporate restored historical buildings in order to create the atmosphere of reassuring urbanity that many Americans identify with the past. Other malls play freely with period and place in order to incorporate images widely associated with a sophisticated and alluring public life. The Borgota, a mall in Scottsdale, Arizona, for example, was built to resemble a walled village in thirteenth-century Italy. Replete with an imitation church bell tower, bricks imported from Rome, and signs in Italian, it appeals to affluent consumers' fantasies about public space.[16] These design elements reflect the developers' claim that the mall is a "city within a city" (The Mall of America) or "an urban village" (Universal City Walk).[17]

When animal rights protesters went to court to gain access to the "public" areas of the Mall of America, they tried to make use of the mall's semiotic system for their own ends. They claimed that the mall presented itself as a multi-use downtown business district and therefore should be governed by the principles set out in *Marsh v. Alabama*. Faced with petitioners trying to engage in protest activity, the Mall of America, however, quickly retreated from the semiotics of "Main Street USA" and embraced a more conventional defense of private property.

In some cases, the claim that malls are contemporary community centers is based on more than imagineering.[18] Increasingly the mall is a civic center as well as a shopping destination. The local and county government in Knoxville, Tennessee, for example, has located essential government services in a shopping mall on the periphery of town, the Knoxville Center. In an effort to "take the services to the people," the city encourages Knoxville citizens to visit "City Hall at the Mall," where they can pay their property taxes, renew their drivers' licenses, mail letters, and apply for marriage licenses. There is also a police station and a community room.[19] The consequence of this convenience is that the shopping center effectively serves as a moat of private space that insulates public functionaries from protest activity. The leasing arrangement opens up a potentially Kafkaesque scenario in which the aggrieved citizens try vainly to gain access to the city hall only to be turned away at the gates of the mall by unaccountable private security forces. Lest this scenario seem fantastic, imagine a group of antiwar activists who want to deliver a petition to the city government, but they are turned away at the entrance to the mall because they are wearing T-shirts that say "Give Peace a Chance."

The "City Hall at the Mall" may be an extreme example, but it is emblematic of a trend toward multi-use malls. An April 1999 survey by the journal *Shopping Center World* found that half of the 150 new projects under construction are multi-use malls. Some of these are the New Urbanist-inspired developments that try to mimic the appeal of old-fashioned downtowns. . . . They link higher density housing with office and retail space, all unified by architectural cues evoking the turn of the century. Fifty of the new multi-use malls include office space, libraries, housing, or hotels.

One such project is the new Towers at Zona Rosa, a shopping mall situated ten minutes from downtown Kansas City. Although the plan relies on 30,000 foot department stores to anchor the retail plaza, it also includes loft-style apartments situated above boutiques and cafés. Underground parking, decorative street lamps, indigenous plants, and outdoor tables are among the lifestyle-enhancing amenities. As theme parks, megamalls, and gated communities merge, nostalgic recreations of the village green replace actual public space.[20]

Living at the mall might still seem unusual, but it is a culmination of a dynamic that has been accelerating throughout the 1990s—the emergence of what Joel Garreau has called Edge Cities. The growth of Edge Cities reflects a complete transformation of the spatial structure of postwar American life. The typical pattern of bedroom communities situated along the outskirts of urban cores is disappearing. He reports that Americans no longer sleep in the suburbs and work in the city. In dozens of cities including Houston, Boston, Tampa, and Denver, there is more office space outside the central business district than within it. This new office space is built in Edge Cities, suburbs that now incorporate millions of square feet of commercial development.[21]

There are undoubtedly positive sides of this development. As more companies relocate to the suburbs, the average American's commute time decreases. But as workplaces become more and more decentralized, the density needed to support public transportation such as commuter railroads also disappears. Your suburban office park may be closer to your home, but it is probably not served by the subway, which leads to greater automobile dependence, traffic congestion, pollution, and the blight of endless parking lots. It becomes increasingly commonplace to move from home to office to shopping mall in the automobile. The Edge City citizen need never traverse public space. It becomes possible to spend an entire day or lifetime without encountering street corners, bus stops, or park benches.

The new Edge City geography poses a challenge to the doctrine established by the Supreme Court. If private space takes on a public character in cases like the company town when it colonizes every aspect of life, then it is time to reconsider the character of the mall. But this is unlikely to happen. As recently as 1992, the Supreme Court held that labor organizers had no right to try to contact potential members by passing out leaflets in the parking lot of a Lechmere's store, this despite the fact that the only alternative space was a 46 foot wide grassy strip separating the lot from the highway.[22] In 1999 the Minnesota State Supreme Court heard a challenge from an animal rights group that was prevented from peacefully protesting in the common area of the 4.2 million square foot Mall of America. The protesters argued that the mall was a public space because it had been heavily subsidized by the state, which provided $186 million in public financing.[23] The Justices found that "neither the invitation to the public to shop and be entertained . . . nor the public financing used to develop the property are state action for the purposes of free speech" under the Minnesota Constitution.[24]

Politics and the Public Space

This string of defeats is a setback for political activists and proponents of an active public life. But it could have the unintended consequence of channeling debate over privatization into the political arena and out of the closed chambers of the court. If judicial intervention will not protect the public sphere, then political action still presents an alternative. Congress or state legislatures could pass statutes mandating that malls of a certain size must provide access to community groups. They could also establish guidelines to extend broader protections for political activity. One way to do this would be to pass legislation applying speech and petition guarantees to the functional equivalents of traditional public forums. As indicated in the *Pruneyard* decision, there is no constitutional provision that would invalidate these kinds of laws. Because labor unions are dependent on tactics such as the picket line, they would be powerful proponents of such a law and useful allies for other activist groups fighting to maintain access to public space. As the Seattle-inspired euphoria wanes, the struggle for such legislation could unify labor and other social movements.

Even in areas where such tactics were unsuccessful at the state level, it would still be possible to adopt similar strategies at the local level. The obvious place to start is to support downtown business districts and other public places that still encourage diversity and invite political activity. But this individualist solution, by itself, is naïve. Collective action is also necessary. When new large-scale mall developments are proposed, citizens have the most leverage to demand some form of continued public access. The support of local government agencies, town councils, and planning boards is crucial for a project on the scale of the modern mall. By building and upgrading roads, modifying zoning, and approving permits, localities still have bargaining power over some aspects of development. They could negotiate a policy guaranteeing free access to a community booth or public courtyard in the mall.[25] For example, in 1991 the Hahn Company, which owns thirty malls in California, signed an agreement with the American Civil Liberties Union that allows leafletting and petitioning in most of its malls. In New York, Democratic state legislators have introduced a bill mandating that privately owned complexes with at least 20 stores and 250,000 square feet of commercial space designate an area where citizens can congregate to engage in non-disruptive political activity.[26] In 1988 a similar bill was defeated in the state legislature.[27]

Why are these tactics seldom even employed let alone successful? Although malls like the one in Bridgewater manage to preserve natural oases such as "Mac's Brook," they fail to protect oases of publicness in a privatizing world. And this is not only the fault of greedy developers. Most people do not value the disruption and unease caused by other people's political speech. One of the appeals of the mall is precisely that it provides an environment carefully designed to exclude any source of discomfort. As Benjamin Barber put it, shopping malls and theme parks sell a sanitized substitute for public life "where people can experience the thrill of the different without taking any risks."[28] The soothing lighting, polished surfaces, pleasant temperature, and enticing displays are not the only allure; part of the fantasy involves entering a world where no homeless person, panhandler, or zealot can disturb the illusion of a harmonious world. We appreciate free speech in the abstract but often avoid it in reality.

In this mauling of public space, democratic theorists have confronted extremely sophisticated marketing experts, and the democratic theorists have been the losers. The political theorists who are most concerned with democracy have failed to offer a compelling rationale to challenge the privatization of public space. By concentrating on the value of speech rather than the importance of space, they turn the public sphere into an abstraction. We need to engage in more careful reflection on the reasons why we should protect free speech *and* public space.

In academic circles, theorists argue that deliberation between citizens is the most promising way to reach rational political decisions. Moreover, they stress that rational, public-spirited discussions are necessary to legitimate democratic procedures and make sure that politics does not degenerate into mere struggles over power. These theories of deliberative democracy are indebted to Jürgen Habermas's influential work on the ideal speech situation. The basic idea of the ideal speech situation is something like this: when we engage in conversation we assume that other participants are telling the truth, speaking sincerely, and oriented toward mutual understanding. When these conditions are realized, then a rational consensus can emerge.[29]

I believe that one reason for the popularity of deliberative democracy is that it is based on a certain optimism about the efficacy of ideas. Although our convictions may also be resistant to change, they are much more malleable than the built environment. Confronted with a landscape filled with strip malls, decaying supermalls, forbidding seas of concrete parking lots, and urban high-rises isolated in unkempt wastelands, it is tempting to focus on democratic theories rather than the more intractable problem of democratic practices.

At first it seems as if this emphasis on "deliberative democracy" is precisely what is needed to reinvigorate our commitment to the public sphere, whether it is comprised of street corners with soap boxes and speakers or their modern equivalents. Deliberative democracy reinforces traditional justifications of the speech clause of the First Amendment. But the concept of deliberation will not be useful if it emphasizes the rationality that emerges from the ideal speech situation. Let's face it. Nothing approaching the ideal speech situation ever happens in the mall. The ideal speech situation is basically an extremely idealized depiction of the norms of scholarly journals or conferences. We need free speech and public places not because they help us, as a society, reach a rational consensus but because they disrupt the consensus that we have already reached too easily. Reasonable arguments often just reinforce distance, whereas public space establishes proximity. This proximity has distinctive properties that democratic theorists often overlook. We can learn something from facing our fears and evasions that we cannot learn from debating principles. The panhandler and the homeless person—they do not convince us by their arguments. Rather, their *presence* conveys a powerful message. They reveal the rough edges of our shiny surfaces. The union pick-eter and right-to-lifer confront us with meaningful and enduring conflict. Provocative speech cannot be something that happens elsewhere—in academic journals, confer-ences, mass mailings, and highly scripted town meetings. It must sometimes be literally in your face for it to have any impact. For a robust democracy we need more than ra-tional deliberation. We need public places that remind us that politics matter.

In New Jersey, at least, malls will be part of this public. That is the implication of a decision reached by the New Jersey State Supreme Court on June 13, 2000. In a unani-mous vote, the Court held that Mill Creek, another New Jersey mall, could not restrict free speech by forbidding political groups from leafletting. Although the owners could place reasonable restrictions on expressive conduct to make sure that politics did not disrupt the commercial activities of the mall, they could not deny access to the only place left in New Jersey where there is an opportunity for face-to-face contact with large groups of people. By a circuitous route, the dream of Bridgewater comes true and the residents will get a commons.[30]

The Mall Goes Downtown:
Business Improvement Districts

. . . Business Improvement Districts (BIDs) have been at the forefront of the attempt to apply the logic of the shopping mall to downtown centers. There are over 1000 BIDs in the United States and more than forty in New York City alone.[31] BIDs are geographically contiguous areas that vote to assess property owners a special fee in order to provide additional services. These services include sanitation, security, and landscaping. Some BIDs employ uniformed personnel to provide tourists with directions and discourage criminal activity. Others install benches, enforce uniform exterior décor standards, and distribute maps featuring local businesses. They have been widely credited in the press for improving the quality of life in downtown commercial districts.

BIDs have been popular with both city officials and business owners. For govern-ment officials, they provide additional tax revenue to fund needed services in the most visible areas of the city. Business interests support BIDs because the structure allows them greater control over their own tax payments. Revenue collected through the BID is spent exclusively in the district and reflects the priorities of business owners. Because assessments are mandatory, setting up a BID overcomes the free-rider problem that plagues voluntary associations such as the Chamber of Commerce. At the same time, business interests maintain complete fiscal control, thereby avoiding the interference of government bureaucrats, local residents, and other citizens. With budgets in the tens of millions of dollars, these publicly regulated, private governments are reshaping the po-litical landscape of downtown.

The proliferation of Business Improvement Districts (a phenomenon that goes by many names including special assessment district or business improvement zone) is a response to competition from the suburban shopping mall. The BID is, in effect, a cen-tralized management structure that allows dispersed downtown retailers to imitate and incorporate successful elements of the mall. For a shopping mall it is fairly easy to pro-vide common spaces, maintain cleanliness, and orchestrate a high degree of visual and

234 The Mauling of Public Space

spatial coherence. Because the entire mall is owned by a single developer who leases space to individual stores, centralized control is guaranteed through property rights, rules, and detailed lease restrictions.[32] In most downtown business districts, streets and plazas are public; small businesses coexist alongside large chains in buildings that they may either rent or own. The BID, unlike the mall, has to rely on governmental powers such as eminent domain, taxation, fines, and zoning in order to mimic the effects of centralized control. The enabling legislation in Arkansas gives some idea of just how wide-ranging the power of business improvement districts can be. They are allowed:

> (1) To acquire, construct, install, operate, maintain, and contract regarding pedestrian or shopping malls, plazas, sidewalks or moving sidewalks, parks, parking lots, parking garages, offices, urban residential facilities including, without limitation, apartments, condominiums, hotels, motels, convention halls, rooms, and related facilities, and buildings and structures to contain any of these facilities, bus stop shelters, decorative lighting, benches or other seating furniture, sculptures, telephone booths, traffic signs, fire hydrants, kiosks, trash receptacles, marquees, awnings or canopies, walls and barriers, paintings or murals, alleys, shelters, display cases, fountains, childcare facilities, restrooms, information booths, aquariums or aviaries, tunnels and ramps, pedestrian and vehicular overpasses and underpasses; (2) To landscape and plant trees, bushes and shrubbery, grass, flowers, and each and every other kind of decorative planting; (3) To install and operate, or to lease, public music and news facilities; (4) To construct and operate childcare facilities; (5) To construct lakes, dams, and waterways of whatever size; (6) To employ and provide special police facilities and personnel for the protection and enjoyment of the property owners and the general public using the facilities of the district; (7) To prohibit or restrict vehicular traffic on the streets within the district as the governing body may deem necessary and to provide the means for access by emergency vehicles to or in these areas; (8) To remove, by agreement or by the power of eminent domain, any existing structures or signs of any description in the district not conforming to the plan of improvement; and (9) To do everything necessary or desirable to effectuate the plan of improvement for the district.[33]

In other words, BIDs can exercise far-reaching governmental powers against individual property owners in order to transform an existing neighborhood into a "managed environment" with quaint matching signs and manicured plazas. In some cases they can even eliminate seedy businesses that might scare off the target consumer demographic. All this is done with minimal input from neighborhood residents, citizen groups, or even commercial tenants.[34]

Business Improvement Districts have imitated the environment of the suburban shopping mall as well as its management structure. The shopping mall, like the theme park, tries to create an atmosphere "in which the emphasis on safety and tidiness is supposed to make visitors feel secure and happy so they'll spend money and come back."[35] To this end, BIDs devote, on average, twenty percent of their budget to sanitation and twenty-five percent to security.[36]

These downtown shopping districts try to achieve a mix of urban and suburban values. Their appeal is due to the energy, variety, visual stimulation, architectural distinctiveness, and cultural opportunities distinctive of urban centers.[37] At the same time they mimic the safety, cleanliness, order, and familiarity that has proven such an effective formula in suburban malls. This allows consumers to enjoy the traditionally urban pleasures of proximity to diverse strangers in a setting where any risk of threat, disruption, disorientation, or discomfort has been removed.[38] This is a formula that was perfected in "festival market-places" such as Faneuil Hall in Boston, Riverwalk in New Orleans, the Cannery in San Francisco, and South Street Seaport in New York. Each project transformed a historic district into a zone of leisure and consumption, filled with restaurants, chain boutiques, and kiosks specializing in local color. Wildly successful from a commercial point of view, these projects have been criticized for transforming distinctive, mixed-use districts into formulaic, sanitized tourist traps.[39] Festival market-places sell a simulacra of the city as tableau or spectacle, something to be enjoyed visually but not experienced kinesthetically: the city without its smells, sensations, or dangers. They cleverly integrate design cues that evoke nostalgia for an imagined urban past with the safety, cleanliness, and familiarity of the suburban mall.

Social and Political Consequences of Business Improvement Districts

Whereas most commentators have focused on an aesthetic critique of festival market-places and the Disneyfication of downtown, they overlook the political and social consequences of this transformation, particularly the impact of Business Improvement Districts on democratic governance. BIDs pose several challenges to a democratic polity. First, political influence in a Business Improvement District is usually directly proportional to the value of one's property, thereby violating the basic democratic principle of one-person, one-vote. Second, BIDs increase the impact of the already powerful business community on local government. Finally, BIDs, as private, nonprofit organizations, may be able to circumvent the constitutional provisions that require local governments to protect the civil liberties of their citizens.

In San Francisco, like most municipalities, the creation of a BID and its priorities depend on the support of the majority of property owners in the district. But all property owners do not have equal votes. Votes are apportioned in relation to the value of commercial property, therefore a very small cadre could effectively control the decisions of the BID. Although oligarchical control is acceptable, a monarchy is ruled out, at least in San Francisco, where the weighted vote of one individual cannot surpass forty percent.[40]

There have been several court cases challenging the anti-democratic decision-making structure of Business Improvement Districts. The most notable decision involves New York's Grand Central BID, which encompasses 71 million square feet of commercial space (nineteen percent of Manhattan's total office space) and has a budget of over $10 million. Robert Kessler, a shareholder in a co-op apartment building in the district, argued that the governance structure, which guaranteed thirty-one seats to property owners, seventeen seats to tenants, and four seats to government appointees, violated the constitutional principle of one-person, one-vote. In 1997 the United States District Court found in favor of the BID and the decision was upheld a year later by the Second Circuit Court of Appeals.

From a legal perspective, the issue was how to interpret the precedent established in *Avery v. Midland County*, the case in which the Supreme Court applied the doctrine of one-person, one-vote to local government. Although the Court clearly stated that cities and counties must guarantee personhood suffrage, it left open the question as to whether this doctrine applied to the myriad diverse and overlapping sub- and supra-local institutions. The Supreme Court noted that "a special-purpose unit of government assigned the performance of functions affecting definable groups of constituents more than other constituents" might be exempt from the principle of one-person, one-vote.[41] In subsequent litigation, the court recognized at least one such exception. It held that the governing board of a local watershed management district designed to provide irrigation could be elected exclusively by agricultural interests.[42] In *Kesslar*, United States Circuit Court Judge Kearse concluded that the Grand Central Business Improvement District (BID) was similar to the water management district: it existed for the purpose of promoting business. Due to its limited scope and disproprotionate impact on property owners, one-person, one-vote did not apply.[43]

Although it is certainly true that Business Improvement Districts exist in order to promote business interests, they still have a significant impact on local residents. The range of services provided by well-funded BIDs—security, sanitation, social services, and capital improvements—is similar to that of local government. Furthermore, the Grand Central BID's foray into social sevices illustrates some of the dangers that rise when a business lobby takes on quasi-governmental power. The controversy involved a program designed by the Grand Central Partnership (a Business Improvement District) to tackle the problem of homelessness by providing shelter and job training. There were two accusations levied against the program, which resulted in litigation.[44] Over forty participants in the job-training program claimed that the Partnership violated state and federal minimum wage laws. Under the auspices of "job training," homeless people were paid $1.16 per hour to serve as outreach workers.[45] The second accusation dealt with the nature of the work that fell under the category of "out-reach." Four former outreach workers claimed that they were told by supervisors to use all means necessary in order to remove homeless people from the district. They admitted to beating homeless people and destroying their belongings. These statements corroborated the stories of homeless people who claimed they had been beaten and threatened by Partnership employees.[46] After an investigation, the Department of Housing and Urban Development (HUD) requested that the BID return the unused portion of a $547,000 grant that had been awarded to subsidize its work with the homeless. Andrew Cuomo, assistant secretary of HUD, explained, "We are not in the business of subsidizing thuggery."[47]

The example of the HUD grant also illustrates another under-appreciated political consequence of the proliferation of BIDs. Although BIDs are widely lauded for raising additional tax revenue from businesses, they also are more effective at competing for scarce resources from city coffers. This is another lesson that BIDs have learned from shopping mall developers, who have been very successful at getting a variety of government subsidies in order to lure commercial development to a particular locality. In the suburbs, these subsidies usually include tax abatements and public funds for site development and roads. BIDs have made downtown more effective at lobbying for the enactment and enforcement of pro-business laws and gaining resources such as extra police protection or direct subsidies.[48] To take one example, the Wall Street BID offered to offset some of the costs (towards space and equipment) if New York City located a police substation in the district. Even though it was not an under-served area, the police department complied.[49] Decisions such as that one further exacerbate inequalities between neighborhoods in the distribution of essential services. Not only do Business

Improvement Districts benefit from their ability to pay for higher levels of service, they may also receive a greater proportion of city resources, as cost-sharing rather than need becomes a criterion for distributing scarce resources. Although it is true that a voluntary Chamber of Commerce, large corporation, or interest group will also be effective at influencing local government, the BID formalizes this influence by creating a strong institutional mechanism.

BIDs aspire to imitate the controlled environment and unified management of the shopping mall but public ownership of the streets and common spaces imposes a serious limitation on their ability to do so. Unlike mall owners, local police officers are limited in their ability to eject homeless people, preachers, street performers, and leafletters from common spaces downtown. But what happens if private security forces do so? Take, for example, the homeless people who were intimidated and forced to leave the Grand Central District. Had the police tried to evict them, they could have complained to the city review board in charge of police misconduct. The homeless victims also could have brought a complaint under a federal statute that provides redress to any citizen deprived of any right secured by the Constitution and laws. But because this statute only applies to rights violations undertaken by a person "acting under color of law,"[50] neither of these remedies is available to someone intimidated or threatened by a private security force.[51]

This raises the possibility that local governments may rely on private proxies to employ tactics that are forbidden to government actors. Although the Bill of Rights prevents the government from limiting individuals' right to free speech, movement, and assembly, it is unclear what would happen if a private government such as a BID tried to do so. Imagine a scenario in which a Business Improvement District adopted a code of conduct that banned skateboarding, lying on benches, loitering, and leafletting. A BID could claim that it was not a state actor, and therefore the Constitution did not apply. If this failed, the city could lease or give the streets, sidewalks, and plazas to the BID, which had already assumed the cost of policing and maintaining them. Armed with this designation as private property, the BID would be a step closer to its goal of transforming downtown into a specialty mall.

Conclusion

The malling of America is not limited to the suburbs. The shopping mall is an icon of fantasy, leisure, and consumption at the same time as it is a symbol of homogeneity, sterility, market stratification, and social control. If Rem Koolhaas is right and shopping provides the only public space that still exists, then the difference between the city street and the suburban mall may be diminishing. . . .[52]

The growing influence of Business Improvement Districts is problematic for two reasons. The governance structure of most BIDs violates norms of democratic accountability by giving a disproportionate voice to property owners over other community interests and possibly by circumventing statues and principles ensuring the protection of civil liberties. BIDs also exacerbate existing inequalities in the provision of government services in order to create marketable "Brand Zones" within the city. It is not surprising that the wealthy and powerful would prefer to govern themselves without interference from everyone else. What is surprising is that a democracy is willing to let them.

19

Jon C. Teaford

THE SPACES OF SUBURBAN RETAILING

The Varied World of Suburban Retailing

Perhaps no sector of American business is more suburban than retailing. With the decline of the great downtown department stores during the second half of the twentieth century, suburbia has emerged as the preeminent place to shop. It is the mother lode of modern consumerism, the destination for Americans seeking to satisfy their passion for spending. In America, shopping is a suburban pursuit.

During the last decades of the twentieth century the inescapable symbol of suburban shopping was the mall. Ridicule of the suburbs invariably included jabs at soulless malls, blank-faced hulks surrounded by vast parking lots where Americans accumulated consumer debt in the bland, climate-controlled environment of chain stores. The pinnacle of mall development was the gigantic Mall of America, which opened in Bloomington, Minnesota, south of Minneapolis in 1992. With 520 stores, this megamall was the largest enclosed shopping space in the United States, attracting over 42 million visitors each year; the Bloomington Convention and Visitors Bureau claimed it was "the nation's #1 visited attraction."[1] At the center of the mall was the seven-acre Camp Snoopy, the nation's largest indoor theme park, boasting two roller coasters.

Yet the opening of Mall of America did not mark the beginning of a new golden age for the suburban enclosed mall. Though the Mall of America attracted hordes of visitors its performance as a business investment was less than spectacular. In 1998 it earned $36 million for its owners, and the following year the operating income was up to $40 million. "That's a very shallow return for a project that cost $650 million to build," observed one leader in the shopping center industry. Ten years after its opening, two real estate experts estimated that the mall was worth at most $550 million, $100 million less than its cost of construction. "The Mall of America marked the culmination of the trend toward ever-larger enclosed malls," observed another expert in 2002. "I don't think we're going to see anything that big again."[2]

In the eyes of many knowledgeable observers, the Mall of America actually marked the beginning of the end of the nation's love affair with the enclosed suburban shopping center. By the turn of the twenty-first century, once-prosperous enclosed malls across America were losing customers and tenants. Americans were spending less time in malls; according to a New York real estate firm the average mall visit was down to only 40 minutes in 1999 as compared with an earlier average of 1.5 hours.[3] The International

Council of Shopping Centers estimated that the giant regional malls were the site of 40 percent of all retail sales in the early 1990s, but that by 2005 this was down to only 20 percent.[4] In 1999 one student of retailing predicted that 15 to 20 percent of the nation's 2,200 enclosed malls would soon close. In 2002 a leader in the retail real estate industry offered an even more dire prognostication when he claimed, "a thousand older shopping centers with a staggering 7 to 11 million square feet of commercial space will be taken off the market in the next 10 years." Confronted by the prospect of widespread mall closures, in 2000 the National Endowment for the Arts sponsored a conference on "redressing the mall," with participants sharing their views on how to reconfigure the giant suburban hulks that were expected to blight the American landscape. "A substantial percentage of shopping centers have become architecturally, economically, and socially obsolete," reported one participant. "Abandoned, boarded up, or still in their death throes, these malls no longer generate profits, no longer serve their communities, and worse, drain the financial base and social spirit from their neighborhoods."[5]

Indicative of the change in American retailing was the website deadmalls.com, which first appeared in October 2000. Dedicated to recording the gradual demise of the mall and the preservation of mall history, by 2006 deadmalls.com listed more than 220 dead or dying shopping centers across the nation with information and memories contributed by nostalgic mall aficionados. "I want to try and preserve what they were," confessed one of the website's creators who grew up during the heyday of the malls. "I'm a product of my generation."[6] Though many retailing experts felt the dead mall eulogies were premature, even the International Council of Shopping Centers had to admit that the mainstay of its organization was no longer on the cutting edge of American retailing. The organization reported that only one new enclosed mall opened in the entire nation in 2006. An executive of the corporation developing this lone shopping center expressed hope, however, that an era was not ending. "Let's remember that the best-producing centers are still the enclosed malls," he observed. "Hopefully, in time the pendulum will swing back into more equilibrium."[7]

Contributing to the decline of the enclosed mall was the slow death of the department store. America's great department stores had served as the mall anchors; they were expected to draw the customers who would not only buy their merchandise but that of the smaller specialty shops located between the big general merchandising emporiums. By the first decade of the twenty-first century many department stores had disappeared; others were consolidating, circling the wagons for a unified resistance to the assaults on their once impregnable status. "Major department stores are a train wreck now," commented one expert on consumer shopping patterns. "When you see major department store shopping is down, and they can only sell things when they're 40 percent off, that is not a formula of success. That is a disaster." The consequences were evident in Atlanta-area malls. In 2003 Lord & Taylor announced the closing of its Atlanta-area stores and Macy's and Rich's department stores merged, closing three Macy's mall sites and leaving one half-filled. More than 1.3 million square feet of empty department store space brought gloom to eight of the sixteen metropolitan-area malls, the vacant sites constituting nearly one-seventh of the total space in those shopping centers.[8]

Perhaps the chief enemies of the beleaguered department stores were the rapidly proliferating big-box stores that were becoming ubiquitous features of the suburban landscape. Among these were the huge discount retailers Wal-Mart and Target, which offered an even greater range of merchandise than the old department stores and at bargain prices. Others were mega–specialty stores known as *category killers* because their massive inventories and lower prices precluded the need for smaller competitors. Notable examples were the home improvement centers Home Depot and Lowes, and the office suppliers Office Depot and Staples. Wal-Mart, however, was the preeminent big-box retailer, having secured first place among world retailers with nearly four times the revenues in 2004 as the second largest American chain, Home Depot.[9] By 2004, 82 percent of American households shopped at Wal-Mart; it was the largest private employer in the United States with 1.2 million workers and the largest owner of corporate real estate with 911 million square feet of space, equal to about 215 Malls of America.[10]

Yet the giant discounter and other big-box retailers have not won accolades from all suburban Americans. Wal-Mart's enormous warehouselike superstores of 200,000 to 250,000 square feet, the size of five or six football fields, surrounded by acres of asphalt are too often deemed aesthetic eyesores that attract unwanted traffic, drive established retailers out of business, and underpay their nonunionized employees. To limit the behemoths, a number of communities have capped the size of retail establishments. Suburban Contra Costa County, northeast of San Francisco, effectively forbid construction of Wal-Mart superstores by limiting the size of such stores to 90,000 square feet.[11] In 2004, voters in Inglewood, California, outside of Los Angeles, defeated a referendum measure that would have permitted a 200,000-square-foot Wal-Mart superstore in that suburb.[12] That same year the founder of Sprawl-Busters, a group dedicated to curbing Wal-Mart, observed: "Ten years ago, fighting Wal-Mart was so unusual it was a national story— small town beats Goliath. Today, these battles are all over." Moreover, the Sprawl Busters website listed nearly 200 communities that had "beaten big-box stores" between 1998 and 2004.[13] Despite these supposed successes Wal-Mart, Target, Home Depot, and their ilk remain an ever-increasing feature of the suburban scene. Some localities may force modifications in size and design, but the big-box juggernaut has continued to sweep across suburbia, and suburban Americans continue to fill the Wal-Mart cash registers with their earnings.

Though Wal-Mart generally opts for freestanding stores, many of the big-box retailers locate in what are known as *power centers*. The International Council of Shopping Centers defines a power center as "a center dominated by several large anchors, including discount department stores, off-price stores, warehouse clubs, or 'category killers.'" with "only a minimum amount of small specialty tenants."[14] These meccas for bargain hunters are among the most formidable rivals to the enclosed mall. At a power center the shopper can find more for less, taking advantage of the prices and inventory offered by the hulking giants of twenty-first-century retailing.

Further undermining the enclosed mall is the *lifestyle center*. During the first decade of the twenty-first century, these open-air centers of upscale chain specialty stores with an ample supply of restaurants and entertainment venues became the latest rage in American retailing and a new feature of the nation's suburbs. The first of these lifestyle centers was Saddle Creek, which opened in 1987 in the Memphis suburb of Germantown. It, however, spawned few imitators until the first five years of the twenty-first century when the format attracted development dollars throughout the United States. By the close of 2005 there were 147 lifestyle centers nationwide, 17 having opened that year, and 50 more were planned or under construction.[15]

Basic to the lifestyle concept is the creation of a pleasurable ambience of well-designed and tastefully landscaped outdoor plazas and walkways. The centers are intended to be reminiscent of the small town main streets of yesterday, but with such upscale retailers as Ann Taylor, Banana Republic, and Pottery Barn never found in those small towns. In addition, they have plenty of parking, thus correcting a flaw that destroyed main street retailing. "The concept is a modernized version of the traditional marketplace," according to two leading retail developers writing in *Urban Land.* It is "a return to the character and ambience of a small town with enhanced offerings that include in-demand retailers, restaurants, entertainment, and services for a complete shopping 'experience.'"[16] A Massachusetts developer reiterated this when he explained that his lifestyle center was "designed to give the customer a sense of place that is more than just a place to shop. It creates something of a downtown feel."[17] Clay Terrace, a lifestyle center in suburban Carmel north of Indianapolis, attempts to recreate a small-town main street by producing façades that seem to date from periods of the past. "The idea was to create a small-town streetscape from an architectural series of prototypical buildings that represent different eras of architecture," remarked the center's designer. Moreover, the center includes a village green, "a place to sit on a bench and have lunch, or for the kids to stop and play."[18]

Not everyone is enamored with the lifestyle centers. The president of a corporation that owns some of the nation's largest malls has called the lifestyle centers nothing more than "malls in sheep's clothing"; another mall owner labeled them "glorified strip centers."[19] And the emphasis on pedestrian space does not mean that the lifestyle centers are actually recreating the main streets of the past. "The lifestyle centers that work best for us are where significant convenient parking is available to our customer," explained one chain store tenant.[20] Shoppers may enjoy strolling past charming storefronts and sidewalk cafes, but they do not want to stroll too far from their car.

A variant of the lifestyle center is the *town center*. Like their lifestyle cousins, town centers are open air with attractive public spaces and a main street ambience. They are mixed-use centers including not only retailing and entertainment, but also offices, housing, and often public facilities such as libraries. They are intended to be 24-hour venues, places where people live, work, and play that will recreate the liveliest urban streets. "A true mixed-use town center brings together everything people want in one attractive, exciting place, often generating two or three times the draw of a traditional shopping center," explained one town center developer. According to him, "many people are hungry for homes in a true town center that allows them to walk to stores, restaurants, entertainment, even work."[21] In 2004 Crocker Park opened in Westlake, Ohio, west of Cleveland; in true town center fashion its plans called for offices and apartments located over first-story retail space along the project's main street. Its developers were adamant in their declaration that it was something more than a lifestyle center. "Crocker Park is very different from a mixed-use point of view," claimed its builder. "We basically are building the city's desire for a mix of uses with pedestrian connectivity."[22] In Plano, Texas, Legacy Town Center is a development of stores, restaurants, apartments, and tastefully landscaped open spaces dropped down in a preexisting mega–office park housing the headquarters of such corporate giants as Frito-Lay, JCPenney, and EDS computers. City Center Englewood in the Denver suburb of Englewood combines offices, retailing, apartments, and a civic center complete with a public library, city offices, the local courts, and a cultural and performance center.[23]

Though lifestyle and town centers seem to have upstaged the older malls during the first years of the twenty-first century, many mall owners are not passively accepting obsolescence and a place on the deadmalls website. Instead, across the country older malls have adapted to the new fashion for open-air centers by adding outdoor lifestyle streets to their existing enclosed facilities. The owner of Long Island's Smith Haven Mall launched its makeover in January 2006 with plans to demolish the mall's vacant Stern's department store building and replace it with an open-air center featuring such lifestyle mainstays as the Cheesecake Factory, Barnes and Noble, and Dick's Sporting Goods.[24] Meanwhile, the Atlanta area's gigantic Cumberland Mall was adding "a 77,000 square-foot lifestyle, pedestrian-friendly streetscape," and in suburban Skokie, north of Chicago, the venerable Old Orchard Mall was proposing to level the spaces once occupied by Lord & Taylor and Saks Fifth Avenue and replace them with a lifestyle center of specialty stores along "a Main Street-style shopping promenade."[25] In Lynnwood, Washington, north of Seattle, Alderwood Mall added an open-air lifestyle component in 2004 complete with Borders Books, Eddie Bauer Home, and Pottery Barn.[26]

The lifestyle and town center options seemed especially popular in the Denver suburbs where older enclosed malls were being bulldozed and rebuilt as open-air venues. City Center Englewood arose on the site of the obsolete Cinderella City Mall, a new town center arose in Lakewood, replacing the former Villa Italia Mall, and in Centennial Southglenn Mall was giving way to The Streets at Southglenn with 950,000 square feet of retail space and 350 loft residences. "In addition to offering a wide variety of today's most desired retail shops and restaurants," the developer promised, "everything at The Streets at Southglenn will be designed to provide residents with urban convenience in an accessible, suburban setting."[27]

This adaptation and restructuring has resulted in the hybrid center, yet another retailing format that promises to be increasingly significant in the future. As its name implies, the hybrid center is a shopping area that combines the features of the enclosed mall, the lifestyle center, and possibly the power center. Thus some older malls are not only adding open-air lifestyle components but attracting such big-box stores as Target and Old Navy, more often found in power centers, to fill spaces vacated by department stores. The newly constructed District at Tustin Legacy in Orange County, California, combines such power center mainstays as Costco and Lowe's Home Improvement with entertainment venues in an open-air format reminiscent of lifestyle centers. "We have introduced into the power center an entertainment component and lifestyle elements to create a regional power-lifestyle-entertainment center," explained the developer.[28] As retailing adapts to the decline of the department store and changing consumer preferences, the mélange of power center, enclosed mall, and lifestyle center will probably become more common or possibly spawn some new and as yet unknown format.

In any case, suburban retailing is continually reinventing itself. It is not dependent on the fortunes of the traditional enclosed mall. Instead, suburbs throughout the nation are breeding grounds for the shopping options of tomorrow. The enclosed mall may no longer be on the cutting edge of retailing, but the suburbs remain the shopping frontier. In suburbia Americans spend their money and developers and retailers experiment and innovate in a continuing attempt to get them to spend more. Rather than a bland environment of look-alike shopping centers offering more of the same, suburbia is the testing ground where investors are creating the something different that will be the next magnet for consumer cash.

20

H. V. Savitch

CITIES IN A TIME OF TERROR

9/11 Dystopia

September 11 will best be remembered because it came to symbolize a new consciousness and brought about a new era. For all the rightful recognition that day brought, it also drew an extremely dismal picture of the urban future—or, as it is called here, 9/11 dystopia. The elements of 9/11 dystopia were manifested in different responses to the attack. One was an emotional response reflecting a deep pessimism that saw cities falling into stifling fear and dark repression. Another had more to do with a strategic response, and saw the path to national survival in movement away from cities and toward a "defensive dispersal" of people, housing, and industry. The last was burrowed in a belief that cities had gone astray because of their infatuation with "tall buildings." According to this creed, skyscrapers not only compromised the values of sound planning but made cities vulnerable to attack. Each of these responses is taken up.

The most emotional responses were drawn in the days immediately following 9/11 and denoted a new world of darkness. Often heard were predictions about growing repression by armed police, bounty hunters, and authoritarian rulers. Image makers produced a frightful picture. Brought into vogue again were films like Fritz Lang's *Metropolis*, an expressionist work made in 1920s Germany, and Ridley Scott's *Blade Runner*, an American cult classic released during the 1980s. While separated by more than half a century, both films show the city at its worst—lorded over by technology gone mad, ridden by social divisions, and headed for self-destruction.

At a scholarly level, Harold Lasswell's 1941 classic, "The Garrison State," was brought back to life to show the political temper of 9/11 dystopia. The article presaged an equally bleak urban future.[1] Lasswell wanted to "consider the possibility" that we would face a world where "specialists in violence" would become the most powerful group. He went on to write that "internal violence would be directed principally against unskilled manual workers and counter-elite elements, who have come under suspicion."[2] As he saw it, society was there to be ruled by those who could manipulate appealing symbols and dominate mass opinion through public relations. Lasswell's "garrison state" went far beyond Madison Avenue manipulation and took the coercive form of military control coupled with modern technology. Its cardinal rule was obedience, service, and work. In many ways, the idea of a "garrison state" was influenced by

From H. V. Savitch, *Cities in a Time of Terror: Space, Territory, and Local Resilience*, (Armonk, NY: M.E. Sharpe, 2008), pp. 148–154, 156–161, 162–167, 220–224. Copyright © 2008 by M.E. Sharpe, Inc. Reprinted with permission.

the rising fascism of the 1930s, but to some it seemed applicable to the days following 9/11 when the FBI launched large-scale searches and police swarmed downtown streets.

This was dystopia's emotional mindset, and it was filled by the speculation of newspaper columnists, popular writers, and academics. Little more than a month after 9/11, Mike Davis referred to "military and security firms rushing to exploit the nation's nervous breakdown." They would "grow rich," he wrote, "amidst the general famine." Davis predicted that "Americans will be expected to express gratitude as they are scanned, frisked, imaged, tapped and interrogated. . . . Security will become a full-fledged urban utility like water and power."[3] Davis was no less ominous about the economy as he declared that the coming days

> may likely be the worst recession since 1938 and will produce major mutations in the American city. There is little doubt, for instance, that bin Laden et al. have put a silver stake in the heart of the "downtown revival" in New York and elsewhere. The traditional city where buildings and land values soar toward the sky is not yet dead but the pulse is weakening.[4]

While Davis was at an extreme end of dystopia, others in the planning profession joined him. One professional voiced concern that "the war against terrorism threatens to become a war against the livability of American cities."[5] At about the same time, Columbia University planner Peter Marcuse flatly predicted of 9/11 that "the results are likely to be a further downgrading of the quality of life in cities, visible changes in urban form, the loss of public use of public space, restrictions on free movement within and to cities, particularly for members of darker skinned groups, and the decline of open popular participation in the governmental planning and decision-making process."[6] These were not isolated commentaries, and similar diagnoses were published along with Marcuse's article in the *International Journal of Urban and Regional Research*.[7]

In the midst of this, another group of writers took a different tack, arguing instead for a change in urban strategy. Their watchword was "defensive dispersal," and the idea was to find a path that would ensure safety. "Defensive dispersal" dates back to the 1950s, when interstate highways were lauded because they produced low-density suburbs that would elude a single devastating bomb. The Housing Act of 1954 had reinforced defensive dispersal by promoting low-density peripheral development. Other advocates of dispersal laid out a scheme to build "a dispersed pattern of small, efficient cities" with radiating expressways in order to thwart an enemy attack.[8] Once 9/11 hit, the idea of defensive dispersal was revised and linked to the digital age and a broader movement toward decentralization. As the theory went, compact cities had outlived their usefulness and were not as efficient as planners might have thought. Building density by vertically storing people and industry was outmoded, and modern industry would operate far more efficiently on an expanded horizontal scale. Even air pollution would be better controlled by dispersing population across wide-open spaces rather than confining people to compact cities. The digital age had rendered compact cities unnecessary by permitting people to communicate across vast distances.[9] Besides, since we were already a suburban nation, why not push this trend further and gain a defensive edge?

The theory of defensive dispersal was promoted by editorialists from the *Wall Street Journal*, who saw an advantage in sprawled cities, and by journalists at the *Detroit*

News, who noted that in the wake of September 11, the constituency for density had probably thinned out."[10] Other writers began to think aloud about the dangers of density and saw a trend in the making. In an article titled, "The De-Clustering of America," Joel Kotkin wrote, "the dispersion of talent and technology to various parts of the country and the world has altered the once fixed geographies of talent."[11] By this thinking, countering terror also coincided with low-density and unstructured patterns of settlement where anything could be done anywhere. As Kotkin saw it:

> This dispersion trend has been further accelerated by the fallout from September 11. Already, many major securities companies have moved operations out of Manhattan. . . . Many of them have signed long-term leases and aren't coming back. Financial and other business service firms are migrating to the Hudson Valley, New Jersey, and Connecticut.[12]

Finally, 9/11 dystopia was reinforced by a belief about the declining quality of urban life. This was a testimony about values that needed to be restored and it was based on an aversion to tall buildings. Far from being an effort to abandon the city, these writers wanted to reinstate a more traditional European-styled city, whose human scale would facilitate closer identity within a meaningful community. For these value-oriented theoreticians, tall buildings had not only robbed the city of its humanity, but brought suffocating congestion to its streets and overloaded its fragile infrastructure. Packing people into floor upon floor of skyscraper was intolerable, and it created an abysmal condition, which they labeled "urban hypertrophy."[13] Having discredited tall buildings because of their seeming threat to humanity, it was not a far step to point up the risks of inhabiting them and predicting their demise. Two urban writers mounted the campaign against tall buildings, writing shortly after 9/11 that "We are convinced that the age of skyscrapers is at an end. It must now be considered an experimental building typology that has failed. We predict that no new megatowers will be built, and existing ones are destined to be dismantled."[14]

To say the least, 9/11 dystopia was stark. It either saw little future for cities or argued for their complete reconception. It was predicated on some narrow possibilities. Either society had rotted from the inside and the attacks were to be expected, or cities had left themselves exposed to September 11 by misplaced development and they should be abandoned or revamped. Taken as a whole, the 9/11 disillusion was a reaction to recent decades of urban development and its remedies left little room for leeway.

The Resilient City

Understanding Resilience

At best, 9/11 dystopia missed the mark and at worst it ignored a city's capacity for resilience. Before exploring this proposition, we might ask how people who had observed and studied the city for so long could have been so mistaken. Any number of explanations is plausible. Among the more apparent reasons for the miscalculation was that lower Manhattan's devastation was so extensive that it distorted individual perspectives. A single stroke of so great a magnitude had so stunned the public, and created so dark a cloud, that it was to difficult to spot a silver lining much less see sunlight. Amid the gloom one could only portend additional gloom. Another explanation for the distortions of 9/11 dystopia is less generous. This rests on the ideology of its analysts—from both the political left and the political right. As this explanation goes, some commentators were so convinced about the righteousness of their belief that they saw its vindication in any act or circumstance. Their predictions were couched in a polemic that sought to justify its premises. A final explanation would deny that 9/11 dystopia was entirely wrong. It might go on to argue that most of the analyses and predictions were basically correct. Dystopia's defenders might cite the growth of surveillance and the shrinkage of urban space to convince an audience that their prognosis was correct. Those who held a dim view of the city might also point to the continuing flight to the suburbs. While this has some plausibility, the facts about what happened to New York (and other cities) after being attacked do not quite fit.

Any assessment of resilience works best when guided by the historic or empirical record, most particularly by other cities that underwent warfare, terror, or endemic violence.[15] While this is a complicated matter, the majority of findings point in a similar direction. The salient conclusion is that most cities have a remarkable capacity for resilience. Cities may well experience short-term negative effects from an attack, but under varying conditions and over varying periods of time they do recover. Moreover, recoveries are not accompanied by a period that gives to a rise a "garrison state" or repressive politics.[16] To the contrary, cities in free societies retain the fundamentals of local democracy, and while citizens may feel pangs of anxiety, their day-to-day habits are unchanged.[17]

To get a better idea of how resilience works, we can think of cities as large agglomerations of human settlement, social relations, and factors of production—held together and made dynamic by an extensive infrastructure. What makes cities dynamic is circular causation, where fortuitous circumstances trigger positive effects, which in turn feed those circumstances again to produce still more positive effects. Lying at the heart of this repetitive process is the magnitude of the city and its dynamic agglomeration. Generally speaking, the larger and more dynamic the city, the more difficult to set it in reverse. Any attack would have to be massive in order to permanently halt these self-generating processes. Even when subject to enormous shocks, cities seem to regenerate and spring back to life.

The most complete picture on the effects of violent shock to urban society can be found in studies of conventional warfare. Research on select cities examines their experience with intense periods of incessant bombing, firestorms, or even atomic warfare, and shows them to be remarkably resilient. In the United Kingdom and France, London and Paris experienced years of air bombing, close combat, or military occupation. In Germany, cities like Cologne, Hamburg, Berlin, and Dresden were subject to heavy aerial bombardment. In Japan, the devastation in Tokyo and especially Hiroshima and Nagasaki was much greater. Large sections of Japanese cities were destroyed and hundreds of thousands of people killed. Yet all of these cities in Europe and Asia recovered, and most went on to a period of unprecedented prosperity.[18]

A somewhat more complicated picture emerges from cities under terrorist attack. As we know, urban terror is a different type of warfare that emphasizes longer assaults on civilians, persistent attacks geared toward the decontrol of territory, and sustained efforts to paralyze normal life. Rather than extensive and abrupt shock, most terror consists of low-intensity warfare that is supposed to wear the enemy down through protracted friction.[19] It stands to reason that urban terror might affect cities in different ways than conventional military action. In these cases, the evidence points to varying degrees of recovery over varying periods of time. While the findings are qualified, they still are reasonably optimistic. Studies of American cities indicate that they are "highly unlikely to decline in the face of even a sustained terrorist campaign."[20] Other research on Italian cities demonstrates short-lived economic effects lasting for about a year after attack.[21] Another line of work on Israeli and Basque cities shows longer-term effects from terrorism, though in the absence of continued attacks these effects do wear off.[22]

We should understand that resilience is not an absolute or a matter of either being resilient or not. Cities are resilient to different extents, in different ways, and have different periods of recovery. Much depends on the size of the city, the strength of its economy, and its social coherence. These factors can then be coupled to the frequency and severity of attack to obtain a more nuanced picture of recovery. From all indications, the resilience of New York and London are different from that of Jerusalem.

How might we know whether resilience has been achieved? While it is normally difficult to precisely sort out the effects of one variable upon another, assessing resilience involves the simpler task of determining the extent to which a previous condition has been reinstated.[23] Simply put, the threshold for resilience can be satisfied by establishing whether a city has bounced back after sustaining an attack or wave of terror. For example, after a city experienced mega terror we would want to know whether the population has returned, or after a city incurred smart terror whether an infrastructure has been rebuilt. Measurable results should then tell us whether an area has recovered, the extent of that recovery, or whether any recovery took place. Resilience might also be achieved if an attack had not changed fundamental conditions or had no significant effect on normal life. This would mean a city had seen no adverse change and withstood an intended shock. A city meeting these criteria could be seen as resilient.

Different Cities/Different Resilience

As we know, New York's terrorism has been sporadic and marked by one enormous blow. With over 3.5 million jobs and a gross product of $400 billion, New York possesses one of the largest local economies in the world.[24] Almost 64 percent of the city's agglomeration is located in Manhattan, and most of that is concentrated in its midtown or downtown business districts.[25] High finance undergirds this great financial edifice, and its geographic concentration makes it vulnerable to attack. September 11 showed just how smart terror could pinpoint critical assets.

London's terrorism has been less murderous, though more frequent, and has occurred in cyclical patterns since the 1970s. Its economy is similar in size to New York's, with an employment base of close to 4 million jobs and a gross product of over $250 billion.[26] London's central business district is concentrated in The City and in the central boroughs of Westminster and Kensington, lying to the west. Much like New York's business cores, these areas are driven by high finance.[27] While the cycle of attacks in the 1990s targeted The City, the attack of 7/7 was somewhat more dispersed, occurring in Westminster and The City, but also just astride these boroughs.

By comparison with its two giant counterparts, Jerusalem's socioeconomic profile is quite modest and its pattern of continued terror differs. Jerusalem's 180,000 jobs and its gross product of $14 billion are a fraction of its giant counterparts.[28] Also, unlike the other two cities, Jerusalem is a not an economic capital but a political and religious one. Its central business district consists of moderately priced retail shops, restaurants, and a few important banks. Government buildings and cultural institutions are scattered throughout the city.

One asset that all three cities have in common is an important tourist industry, though this too greatly varies in size. London is one of the foremost tourist destinations of the world, and its tourism reached a zenith in 2005 with 14.9 million foreign visitors. New York's tourism is less than half that much, having reached its height in 2005 with 6.8 million international tourists. Tourism is one of Jerusalem's major industries, and its tourism reached a pinnacle in 2000 with 953,000 visitors. Unlike more stable industries, the elasticity of tourism relative to terror is a useful a barometer of local resilience.

Under the circumstances, we would expect the resilience of these cities to be markedly different from one another, and it is. Among the factors used to assess recovery in New York, London, and Jerusalem are employment, tourism, and office markets.

Resilience in New York, London, and Jerusalem

In the immediate period after 9/11, New York employment fell sharply and the city lost more than 100,000 jobs.[29] The drop was precipitous, linked directly to the collapse in lower Manhattan, and it occurred in the few months after September. The bulk of the lost employment occurred in the area around the World Trade Center, though it also spread to other parts of Manhattan and the rest of the city. For a time, the job situation was bleak, but by 2004 the city's employment began to move upward; by the end of 2005 the city's job base had reached 3.6 million.[30]

London's cyclical violence burst out again between 1990 and 1993, when financial institutions were targeted by the IRA. By comparison to New York, these attacks were pinpricks, though they engendered a huge psychological response, which eventually led to the "ring of steel." While it is not possible to attribute the subsequent drop in London's employment to these attacks, the falloff was significant. Once the cycle of terror had ceased, London was down by about 450,000 jobs from the previous period.[31] As in New York, the number crept up in subsequent years, and by the turn of the century employment reached a high that hovered around the 4 million mark.

For Jerusalem, the key period of terror occurred in the fall of 2000 through 2002. Here, too, the City Center was targeted, though neighborhoods within a short distance were also struck. Unlike London, the targets were people, rather than financial institutions. While businesses were severely affected and many closed, others waited out the storm. The Israeli government also stepped in to bolster the local economy.[32] Apparently, government programs made up for private business failures and through these years jobs remained at about 180,000. By 2003, terrorism subsided and employment rose to 183,000; it has since modestly continued on that trajectory.[33]

There are instances when employment falls after an attack and gradually rises as terrorism subsides. There is also variability in each city and instances where an attack had no discernible effect on employment. The first attack on New York's World Trade Center (1993) left no imprint. To the contrary, employment continued to rise through the 1990s. The second, much bigger attack (2001) left a deep imprint, but by 2004 the city showed signs of recovery. London fell into a trough just as the IRA struck in the early 1990s, but its employment dramatically accelerated through time. Jerusalem fared somewhat worse and also somewhat better. Its drop-off was not as steep, but its recovery was slower and more modest.

Might all this be coincidence and tied to other factors? No doubt exogenous factors played a role, though we can see the same fall and rise in other sectors of the local economy, particularly tourism. Foreign tourism is a useful gauge of resilience because of its sensitivity to large-scale, highly publicized violence. If a city were resilient, we would expect foreign visitors to return within a reasonable period of time. Indeed, in the immediate years after 9/11, New York's tourist traffic plummeted. A year after the attack, tourism had dropped by 25 percent compared to its pre-attack level, and by the second year it had fallen by more than 29 percent from its pre-attack level.[34] For a while it appeared the tourist industry would fade, but by 2004 it was back up and by 2005 the industry had fully recovered to its pre-disaster level of 6.8 million foreign visitors annually.

London's tourism was hardly touched by the attacks of 1990–93 and tourism actually increased. By 1995, London's tourism had grown to more than 13 million foreign visitors each year. Following some erratic years, London tourism continued to rise until the attacks of July 7, 2005.[35] The attacks of that summer changed everything, wreaking also a short-term effect on tourism. During the month after 7/7, tourism fell by 18 percent from the previous year and the decline persisted into August.[36] Not until September did tourism begin to revive, and it has now climbed to an all-time high. A possible explanation for the difference between the pre– and post–7/7 tourist reaction was the human toll of the latest attacks. London demonstrated again that mega terror aimed at people is more damaging to the tourist industry than smart terror aimed at things.

Jerusalem, where attacks have been especially aimed at people, [also] bears out this generalization. During the 1990s, low terror corresponded to high tourist visits and the number of foreign visitors surpassed 950,000 at the turn of the century. By the end of 2000, Jerusalem was in the throes of al Aqsa violence. Terrorism shot up and we can see tourism plummeting during this period. As casualties from terror continued to rise through the years 2001 and 2002, tourism continued to fall. By the end of 2003, terrorism had taken a sharp decline and tourism rose once again. The trend toward lower terrorism and higher tourism continues through 2004. With the decline of terrorism, Jerusalem began to bounce back, though it is still a distance from record levels.

Office markets also reflect a city's capacity for resilience. They indicate willingness to invest in a city, use clustered environments, and take a chance on tall buildings. Jerusalem has relatively little of this kind of investment and almost no tall buildings, and we put that case in abeyance. But New York and London are the world's corporate office capitals and exemplify the dynamics of urban agglomeration.

New York's rebound is instructive. After the loss and injury to lives, the most devastating effect of 9/11 was the loss of buildings and office space. The city's estimated property and attendant losses reach as high as $83 billion. The figure includes the loss of six buildings of the World Trade Center and the complete destruction of 13.4 million square feet of office space. Putting this in perspective, the destroyed space equaled the entire office stock in the city of Detroit.[37]

Under clouds of distrust for tall buildings, one might have expected the disaster that befell New York to have eliminated its market demand. Indeed, for a while the office market continued to soften, even in the wake of space shortages created by 9/11. In the two years after 9/11, office vacancies rose in Manhattan and elsewhere around the nation. By 2005, however, office markets had turned around. Mid-Manhattan vacancies shrunk to below 8 percent while lower Manhattan fell below 11 percent. Manhattan's office markets were not back to the halcyon days of the late 1990s, but they had considerably improved from the devastation of 9/11 and by 2005 they were the envy of much of the world.

The news was good on other fronts as well. Surveys showed that more than half the displaced tenants had returned to lower Manhattan and many other firms had chosen New York locations.[38] Most encouraging, the bulk of those who sought new locations chose tall buildings of twenty stories or higher.[39] Elsewhere in the country, tall buildings were doing quite well. From Boston to Dallas, developers continued to put up skyscrapers and fill them. Among the first to ride the tide was developer Donald Trump, who tried to build Chicago's tallest skyscraper. Trump has also set his sights for a tall hotel and tower in Toronto.

Office markets have been even stronger in London. Vacancy rates in the central boroughs have halved in just two recent years. By 2006, empty office space had fallen to under 5 percent. The largest development firms push hard to obtain construction permits for skyscrapers, albeit with great public controversy about their aesthetic desirability. The most fervid rush and the sharpest controversies transpire over who had already built or was about to build the tallest building. As of this writing, permission was granted to build London Bridge Tower, which will rise 1,000 feet (305 meters) above street level and will become Europe's tallest building. London also behaved in an untraditional manner when its plan explicitly endorsed tall buildings, cheered on by the effusive support of its socialist mayor.[40]

As Igal Charney points out, tall buildings have continued to appeal to cities.[41] Sometimes called "trophy" or "designer" buildings, they are now a source of prestige. Moscow and Seoul have already approved buildings that are twice the height of those planned for Chicago, Toronto, and London. Dubai has already granted permission to construct the world's tallest building. These new buildings exceed the height of the former Twin Towers.[42]

Finally, as if to defy the admonition against tall buildings (and possible attackers), skyscrapers are once again springing up at ground zero. The Freedom Tower is now under construction and so, too, is a 2 million square foot office tower not far away. As of this writing banks and financial houses are planning other skyscrapers in the area. While lower Manhattan's central business district had slipped after 9/11, it is now rising again as one of the nation's foremost financial centers.

Tall buildings have persisted against the wishes of dystopian value writers as well as the laws of economics. As commercial ventures, tall buildings are inefficient. Skyscrapers forever fight against their own weight because so much capacity is consumed supporting their upper height. Numerous airshafts, elevators, pillars, and other supports take up 30 percent of potentially rentable space. In the aftermath of 9/11, the idea of constructing still more vulnerable targets seemed inconceivable. One economist expressed his fear that "for at least a decade, the primary real estate issue regarding terrorist attacks will not be 60 versus 100 story buildings . . . but whether any unsubsidized buildings will be built by the private sector at all."[43] On this issue, modern economists have been outpredicted by architectural philosophers of another era. The "tall office building," wrote Louis Sullivan in 1896, "is one of the most stupendous, one of the most magnificent opportunities that the Lord of Nature in His beneficence has ever offered to the proud spirit of man."[44]

Resilience and Other Considerations

A fair assessment of these cities would conclude that they rebounded from disaster because of the strength of their social fabric, the dynamism of their economies, and the optimism of their citizenry. In his review of post–9/11 American cities, Peter Eisinger remarks, "If the texture and pace of city life are clouded somewhat by public anxiety about terror, the actual changes urban dwellers encounter in their daily lives in most places in the country and at most times are small and relatively unobtrusive."[45] With some qualification about *time of recovery*, much the same could be said for other cities around the world. For most other cities struck by terror, *time* is a key element in judging recovery because those cities lack the magnitude of New York or London.

Jerusalem presents the alternative view of a major, mid-sized city. In the midst of wave after wave of attack, the city looked as if it would never recover. This author was in Jerusalem observing the situation during one such wave and wrote in a later article:

> At least for the moment parts of downtown Jerusalem have begun to resemble older American urban cores that were shattered by de-industrialization. [Their] worn look creates a "broken windows" atmosphere that can only discourage business. . . . Once thriving retailers have now left and rental signs hang everywhere. Some rents have dropped by as much as 90 percent. Those properties that have been rented sell cheap, fast-turnover merchandise. Once upscale jewelry shops now offer inexpensive souvenirs for sale. Former clothing shops have been converted into storage facilities. Accessories and trinkets hang in store windows or lie on makeshift stands. The upper floors of some buildings have been turned into gambling rooms, exotic dancing studios and sex clubs. Downtown appears to be struck by the effects of a crime wave (bleak and downgraded) rather than war (complete devastation and rubble).[46]

The passages continue in this article, emphasizing that any pessimism about the city's future should be tempered by a number of caveats about drawing hasty conclusions. Among these was that "Jerusalemites are resilient, and even after a bloody attack they persevere."[47] Since then, the city has continued to recover. Foreign tourists have returned to its hotels, downtown streets are refilled, and restaurants have reopened. Tourism has not yet returned to its peak year of 2000, but it has come close and for a single recent year has now exceeded 850,000 foreign visitors. The city is also experiencing a real estate boom. Housing, retail, and office markets are robust and in many places prices have gone above pre-terrorism levels. While not all sectors have fully recovered, most have made substantial progress. Clearly, if Jerusalem's 700,000 residents show this capacity for resilience, we can say it is not the sole preserve of mega or global cities.

We should also acknowledge that while resilience entails recovery, it does not erase a disaster. Critical events, like terrorism, do leave a mark of one kind or another. Sometimes that mark can germinate into a movement that had been hardly discernible before terror struck; at other times it can accelerate recognized trends. Jerusalem's experience with attacks catalyzed an existing exodus of households from the center into the peripheries. The attack on New York catalyzed an existing movement of business from lower Manhattan to mid Manhattan. London's bout with terrorism took a society that was heavily ridden with surveillance and made it even more so. The final word on urban resilience may never be written, but Tom Wolfe's maxim that "you can't go home again" rings ever so true.[48] The challenge is to make that very different future a more secure one.

Sustaining a Better Future

The National Approach to Sustaining Resilience

Much of a city's resilience stems from its agglomerative nature and what might be called its natural dynamism. But this is hardly the end of the story, because a city's capacity for resilience is neither automatic nor is it unassisted. Rather, local resilience is helped and sustained by government. Government at all levels makes recovery possible and plays a critical role, whether that takes place by building infrastructure, educating the citizenry, stabilizing the social order, protecting society, or taking responsibility for a host of functions. For some, the laissez-faire state might have appeal, but it does not exist. Even private insurance is publicly regulated, publicly assisted, and often publicly subsidized. When great calamities strike, government is the foremost actor in rescue and reconstruction. Usually government at upper and mid levels takes the lead. At mid levels, states or provinces can play a role in staunching a crisis, but their geographic limitations and their resource constraints are insufficient to the task. Operating from the top down, national government is best able to cast the widest nets and most capable of coordinating local efforts. National government is also best able to enlist private enterprise or nonprofit organizations to work with authorities at all levels. Generally, the greater the breakdown the more it requires national attention.

This was certainly the case in the post–9/11 era, when free markets failed and most insurance companies refused coverage to high-risk clients. In the United States, the biggest and most vulnerable cities found themselves in a dire situation. Terrorism insurance was especially difficult to obtain in New York, Chicago, Los Angeles, and San Francisco. This put property developers in a quandary because lenders required insurance before a project could be financed. The absence of available underwriters went beyond new building construction and affected city debt ratings as well those of other public agencies. Since then, insurance premiums have risen dramatically, increasing the costs for both public and private sectors. On the public side, premiums for New York's transit system rose by 300 percent, and in the private sector, the owners of the Empire State Building paid 900 percent more for a lesser policy.[49]

Some insurance companies began to write "sunset clauses" into their policies that were designed to relieve them of future obligations. Other insurance companies have either refused to underwrite large-scale projects or charged enormous premiums to do so. Shortly after 9/11, more than $15.5 billion in real estate projects were suspended or canceled because developers could not obtain insurance.[50] In San Francisco, insurance for the Golden Gate Bridge doubled. In Baltimore, insurance companies refused to issue coverage for its International Airport and sporting events in Camden Yards. Under pressure from the state government of Maryland, the companies later relented.

America's federal government sought ways to fill the void and hastily strung together a broad safety net. The foremost means of doing this was the Terrorism Risk

Insurance Act of 2002, or TRIA. The act was extended in 2005 through the end of 2007, presumably allowing the insurance market to stabilize and resume normal pricing. Only commercial establishments are eligible and only foreign attacks are insured. In the event of an attack, TRIA covers 90 percent of losses, after deductible payments are met. Losses above $100 billion are not covered by the act. TRIA also limits liability by precluding payments for property damages due to a CBRN (chemical, biological, radiological, or nuclear) attack. Overall, the restrictions are intended to spread the risk between the federal government, private insurers, and the insured.

Elsewhere in the world, the part played by national government in providing terrorism insurance varies quite a bit. France, Spain, and Australia make coverage mandatory, and national government has a direct role in making sure that coverage is complete and equitable. France has established common insurance pools with higher premiums for developers who undertake new construction. The United Kingdom allows insurance to be optional. This has posed problems for British theatergoers and other mass audiences. As prospects of a mega attack increased over recent years, so too did insurance premiums, and public events have borne the brunt of the pain. Insurance rates increased by 200 percent or more for highly publicized events. In tangible terms, this meant that the cost for a concert at the National Theater jumped by 250,000 pounds; the cost of an event at the royal Opera House rose by 500,000 pounds. Given the circumstances, the public would have to forego some events or pay more for a ticket. Because many cities depend upon culture and entertainment to drive their economies, the increased prices for a time dampened the revenue capacity of these sectors. Troubled by this turn of events, Londoners referred to the change as the "Bin Laden effect."[51]

The most positive view of terrorism insurance would acknowledge that it establishes a net below which victims should not fall. More tenuously, the net can be broken by excessive damages (above $100 billion) or by attacks that are not covered. Terrorism insurance is a retroactive way of ensuring a degree of economic security. While post-disaster relief is important, proactive measures are just as important. These, however, are not quite as clear cut; they involve an amorphous array of actions and are conducted by governments and private actors at multiple levels.

Multi-Governance Approaches to Sustaining Resilience

Grand policies can be proclaimed from high political posts and ambitious goals can be announced by presidents, prime ministers, and cabinet members. When all is said and done, however, the action is accomplished at the local level. City politics is the politics of the trenches, where mayors and local officials take matters in hand, do the actual implementation, and face constituents. This is particularly true of the United States, where local police are responsible for public safety and exercise considerable autonomy over policy choices.

Referring to the American situation, Susan Clarke points out that the greater the national security threat, the more important the local role.[52] Clarke is correct, and it could be added that threats do not rest at a single level but in a skein of multiple governments at all levels. There is something about imminent crises that creates a need to pull together different levels of government, even when the immediate challenge is to clarify results in an incomprehensible tangle of relationships. Lyndon Johnson's War on Poverty invigorated intergovernmental relations just as George W. Bush's War on Terror has given intergovernmental relations a new twist Sloganeering aside, the agenda of each "war" has been considerably different. Johnson's war converted cities into centers of development and income redistribution, while Bush's war has brought to cities an agenda of security and watchfulness.

The attention paid to terrorism at a local level is far reaching. A recent poll of Americans showed that terrorism was at the very top of the agenda. Fully 79 percent of the American public believed terrorism was "very important" (compared to 66 percent for Europeans).[53] At the local level, nearly three-quarters of American municipalities have invested in some type of emergency preparedness (technology, security, disaster preparedness). Cities have conducted mock drills, closed off buildings, rerouted traffic, and added police and have begun to reorient their emergency medical services.[54] While homeland security no longer tops the list of local priorities, it does appear within the top thirty-eight issues that public officials consider most important to address.[55]

The jumble of intergovernmental cooperation is bound together by federal funding. The major distributor of this largesse is the U.S. Department of Homeland Security (DHS). Since 9/11, that department had dispensed over $18 billion in assistance to states and localities.[56] Because the Patriot Act requires a minimum distribution of assistance, all fifty states plus Washington, DC, and U.S. territories received some amount. Within the DHS money pot, the largest program pertaining to cities is the Urban Areas Security Initiative, or UASI, whose total funding in 2006 was approximately $711 million. UASI funding is based on a formula that assesses three basic risk factors—namely, *threat, vulnerability,* and *consequences.* In theory, this should gear funding toward cities facing the greatest probability of attack and potential damages. Realities are different, though, and UASI funding has now been distributed to over 50 localities; central cities ranging in size from New York's 8 million to Sacramento's 445,000 are included.

UASI funding for 2006 [shows] variation in amounts from a high of 124 million for America's largest city to the lesser amount of 7 million for smaller cities. The per capita amounts are revealing. Taking two high-risk examples, New York City and Washington, DC, were among the highest recipients in both absolute and per capita expenditures. Each city also received a handsome proportion of the total budget. New York City garnered 18 percent while Washington, DC, received 7 percent. Relative to the previous year, however, both of these high-risk cities were down by 40 percent. New York's mayor, Michael Bloomberg, and Washington's mayor, Anthony Williams, protested the cuts. As their reasoning went, each city had already incurred much higher expenses than other localities and each would continue to be an exceptionally sought-after target.[57] Homeland Security was not persuaded and instead awarded increases to smaller cities. Sacramento's allocation increased by 17 percent while Jacksonville's funding rose by 26 percent.[58]

For New York and Washington, DC, as well as other cities police protection and its costs are critical. In addition to heightened protection in densely packed built-up areas, the new War on Terror mandates that airports and other forms of interstate transportation be covered with additional local police. Yet legislation pertaining to homeland security often prevents federal support for police overtime or hiring new personnel.[59]

While the costs for protection flow to cities, not all the reimbursements follow. More often than not, states receive funding and pass it down to cities with instructions for the application of that funding. There are times when state priorities differ from those of their cities, widening the gap between response and need. Judgments about priorities are very subjective, and invariably political consideration will enter the mix, thereby shifting the emphasis from protecting targets to distributing rewards.

The conversion from a pinpointed policy measure to a more amorphous monetary benefit is hardly new to Washington.[60] Beneath the surface, a political pageant has been played out. In this pageant, allocations are spread to cities that can offer the rosiest presentation and summon the best rationales. What was once an initiative to concentrate funding in seven high-risk urban areas has been turned into pork-barrel legislation that distributes funding to a larger list of low-risk recipients. The allocations may very well be put to public use, but they are not well connected to the likelihood of attack. Policy analysts might say that a measure to ensure security has been turned into a distributive policy to reward friends and placate opponents.[61]

Inefficient spending may be the least of the obstacles confronting homeland security. The real problem lies in how to sustain the capacity for resilience over a lengthy period of time. At bottom, the objectives of homeland security are riddled by questions of how cooperation can be mustered across diverse metropolitan boundaries and how any momentum can be kept up. Individual metropolitan areas differ by size, number of jurisdictions, socioeconomic composition, political demands, and local culture. Ensuring security within any single area requires working with a great many parties—mayors, legislators, bureaucrats, and private contractors—where motivations differ, problems vary, and rewards are asymmetrical.[62] It is difficult enough to concert collective action among like-minded actors, but how to sustain a common objective amid this political cacophony is a challenge.

The challenge is magnified by the inherent inertia of public protection. Both *time* and *place* are critical but unknown elements. Given the perspective of time, we know that even the most frequently struck cities experience long periods of calm. Typically, assaults occur at the end of extended intervals and those periods can stretch into months or years. This is true even for one of the most incessantly struck cities—Jerusalem. That city experienced intermittent peace in the 1990s and has enjoyed another period of calm during the last three years. Taking New York as another example, more than seven years elapsed between the first and second attacks in lower Manhattan. Since 9/11, more than five years have gone by without an attack, and there is no telling when or if another such event will occur in New York. From the perspective of place, attacks could occur almost anywhere. Big, global cities have seemingly limitless targets. Is a transit system that stretches for miles most likely to be hit? Or is any one of the sixty-plus skyscrapers that fill Manhattan at greater risk? Or is a mass-attended concert most susceptible to attack?

It is by now commonplace in security circles to remind people that terrorists can choose both time and place, while defenders must always be on alert. Attackers require just one success, while protectors require a success rate of 100 percent. It is hardly surprising that over a period of time and at varying places, cities fall prey to what can be called asymmetrical reactions that swing between lethargy and hyperactivity. As used here, asymmetrical reactions are either not commensurate with the problem at hand or out of synchrony with the time trajectory of terrorism or not fully cognizant of realities.

The pattern is familiar to airline passengers during heightened periods of alert. It was particularly vivid for those who found themselves in the midst of an alert in August 2006 because of a threat to blow up aircraft flying out of London. The general scenario is something like this: During the first blush of training, security is ready and alert. In the absence of an emergency, alertness gradually fades. As readiness reaches a low point, an attack or threat catches personnel off guard. Having realized they were unprepared, security officials enter a period of hyperactivity or overvigilance. Picayune rules replace common sense, ordinary actions are viewed with unwarranted suspicion, and authority becomes overbearing. This behavior continues for a while, only to lapse again until the next real emergency.

Asymmetric reaction occurs in most cities around the world. Soon after terror struck Moscow, the militia closed roads, put public transport under intense surveillance, and began implementing strict rules concerning the possession of identification papers. Within a few months the alerts wore off and security forces fell into a state of indifference.

There are no easy answers to the problem of asymmetrical reaction. Any remedy must achieve a steadiness of response that is based on competence and practiced teamwork. The machinery of counterterrorism can be oiled by plans, drills, simulations, and "table-top" exercises. This might not be a substitute for the real thing, but it does enable first responders to be ready for the unexpected. Another remedy is to develop flexible responses that can be raised or lowered in measured steps. The key to achieving this lies in synchronized intergovernmental coordination. Governments can begin that process by clarifying and respecting mutual responsibilities. At the local level, officials should be able to comply with higher-level regulations, while avoiding the trap of goal displacement or becoming lost in mounds of rules. At national and state levels, authorities should exercise oversight while also delegating discretion to local actors, so they can exercise judgment and retain a sense of purpose. The balance between accountability and freedom of action is difficult to achieve, much less maintain over time. Terrorists depend upon surprise, and even modest reductions in uncertainty can mitigate the shock of attack.

Conclusions

The fears arising from 9/11 dystopia underestimated the city's capacity for resilience in the face of war or terrorism. That capacity not only varies by frequency and severity of attack, but also by the size of a city and the dynamics of its agglomeration. The ability of cities to bounce back from violent shock can be seen in the experiences of New York, London, and Jerusalem. In those cities, employment, investment in tall buildings, and tourism often suffered varying degrees of decline. However, over time, these sectors recovered and some went on to do exceedingly well. Tourism is particularly sensitive to outbreaks of large-scale violence, but this industry too sprang back to life once terrorism abated.

For all the natural resilience attributed to cities, government plays a critical role in their recovery. In Europe, national governments helped establish a better equilibrium between insurance carriers and consumers. In the United States, national policies were instrumental in restoring insurance coverage in high-risk cities. The U.S. federal government also provided a system of aid to localities in order to deal with threats from urban terror. This aid has a tendency to be spread and watered down because of political pressures. Terrorism is still an important concern in North America and Western

Europe, and still occupies an important place on the local government agenda. In many instances, local government is responsible for training and furnishing a cadre of first responders. While this has been a positive step, it is not without its problems. The challenges besetting government at all levels lie in bringing about collective action and sustaining long-term commitments. Governments also face problems in maintaining stable levels of performance. High performance is compromised by common patterns of asymmetrical reaction to terrorism, defined as a situation where behavior is not commensurate to an event. This is difficult to remedy, though a beginning can be made by synchronizing intergovernmental coordination and simulating critical events.

CHAPTER 7

THE POLITICS
OF METROPOLITAN REGIONS

THE DEBATE OVER REGIONAL GOVERNANCE

Population movement outward from the core has been a prominent feature of urban development in the United States for decades. The old urban form, which found a central city surrounded by spreading suburbs, is giving way to a metropolitan pattern characterized by many nodes of activity. While there are advantages to this arrangement, the disadvantages have attracted a great deal of concern. Urban sprawl is blamed for everything from traffic congestion and gridlock to air pollution, the loss of open space and farmland, polluted water, and even obesity. As the readings in this chapter reveal, a lively debate is being waged about how to solve these problems—and also over whether sprawl is the precipitating cause.

Since at least the 1920s, urban reformers have said that the answer to the worst problems of the metropolis is to implement comprehensive governmental reform. They argue that the political fragmentation of metropolitan areas into hundreds of jurisdictions makes it extremely difficult to address issues that exist at a regional as much as a local level. A few places, such as Miami–Dade County, Florida, and Minneapolis–St. Paul, Minnesota, have forged metropolitan-wide political institutions that help coordinate service delivery. Portland, Oregon, alone stands as a region with a growth boundary and some record of curbing sprawl. Cooperation is commonplace in urban areas as a means of coordinating such services as 911-dialing and county-wide parks and recreation and library services. But except for such arrangements, the governance of metropolitan areas is extremely fragmented.

The essays that follow provide a profile of a movement called the New Regionalism. In the past, most attempts to establish regional governance have failed. They are usually opposed by suburban local governments fighting threats to their powers and citizens wishing to keep the problems of the cities out of their backyards. In Selection 21, Myron Orfield describes how a measure of regional coordination was achieved in the Minneapolis–St. Paul region on the important issue of tax sharing. Orfield acknowledges that regional reform is difficult and controversial, but he claims it is possible because of the emergence of a new political center of gravity in urban politics. In the past, attempts to build regional political coalitions in Minneapolis–St. Paul were built on weak foundations—notably leaders dedicated to good government ideals. Their initial success in building regional coalitions was short-lived because they neglected to mobilize powerful interests sufficiently. By contrast, practitioners of the New Regionalism persuaded central-city interests to join with older suburbs who shared similar problems of decaying neighborhoods, sagging tax bases, and a retrenching local economy. The Twin Cities success in building some measure of regional tax sharing was enabled by this new political coalition—a coalition that potentially exists in other metropolitan areas around the country.

The case for challenging sprawl through more comprehensive forms of regional governmental intervention is made in Selection 22 by David Rusk. He believes that the core regional issue is growth management. His discussion shows that the way local government is organized is closely linked with the problems of social division and the quality of life in metropolitan areas. Rusk argues that sprawl has enveloped urban communities all over the United States, but that the problems it causes are worst in so-called "inelastic" cities where central cities have been unable to annex surrounding suburban communities for many decades. In these areas, social problems are concentrated in the inner cities while suburban governments capture a disproportionate share of regional wealth. By contrast, "elastic cities," mostly located in the Western and Southwestern rim of the United States, have been permitted to extend their governmental boundaries more easily. According to Rusk, this allowed them to mitigate some of the consequences of sprawl, resulting in less segregated and socially healthier cities and suburbs. Yet Rusk warns that even elastic cities are no longer able to keep up with the continued sprawl of people and jobs. He concludes that the answer is to create "big box" regional governments that can contain unplanned growth.

Are there alternatives to regionalism as the answer to sprawl? The two remaining selections offer contrasting responses. In Selection 23, Fred Siegel argues that sprawl " . . . is not some malignancy to be summarily excised, but, rather, part and parcel of prosperity." Siegel claims that fragmented government offers abundant advantages. It enables people who live in badly governed central cities to escape to other jurisdictions that provide an array of alternative places to live, shop, and conduct business. Most of all, he believes that fragmented government avoids the dead hand of a single, powerful regional government that will restrict choice. Although Siegel concedes that there may be cases of successful regional governments, as in Portland, Oregon, time will tell if such examples can be copied elsewhere. In the meantime, he prefers to address common regional issues through one-off measures like tax sharing and the prohibition of public policies that favor suburbs over cities.

Another approach to sprawl seeks to counter its worst effects by introducing small-scale planning and architectural design as a way of reviving a sense of community identity and reducing reliance on the automobile. In the 1990s a movement called the New Urbanism came together in reaction to the segmentation of urban space in the form of shopping centers, office parks, massive subdivisions, and traffic-choked streets and freeways. Advocates of the New Urbanism contend that people increasingly wish to escape the sameness of cookie-cutter housing developments and dull suburban spaces. The developers of New Urbanism projects respond to this impulse by designing enclaves that slow traffic and encourage walking and a sense of community by re-creating the look and feel of small-town neighborhoods. In Selection 24, Peter Calthorpe conveys the essence of this philosophy when he calls for a vision of a new Regional City. He argues that the old regionalism pulled everything apart—residential, retail, commercial, and civic activities became isolated from one another. The new regional form would be made up of small-scale development designed to human scale by bringing together the social, economic, and physical dimensions of the metropolis. He argues that urban regions should be viewed as complex ecologies that work best when the several components of the system are seen as a unit; "treating each element separately is endemic to many of the problems we now face."

Taken together, these selections add important voices in a continuing debate about how to manage the problems of urban regions in the twenty-first century. The debate will continue to be lively because the decentralization of metropolitan populations, whether called *sprawl* or some other name, will surely continue.

21

Myron Orfield

BUILDING CONSENSUS

Forty Years of Minnesota Metropolitan Politics

Skeptics tell me that regional equity reform will never happen in America's metropolitan regions because the suburbs are now in charge of American politics. It may be true that the suburbs are in charge of American politics. But the politics of metropolitan reform is not about cities versus suburbs or, for that matter, about Democrats versus Republicans.

The suburbs are not a monolith, economically, racially, or politically. Surrounding America's central cities, with their high social needs and low per capita tax wealth, are three types of suburbs. First are the older suburbs, which comprise about a quarter of the population of U.S. metropolitan regions. These communities are often declining socially faster than the central cities and often have even less per household property, income, or sales tax wealth. Second are the low tax-base developing suburbs, which make up about 10–15 percent of U.S. metropolitan regions. They are growing rapidly in population, especially among school-age children, but without an adequate tax base to support that growth and its accompanying overcrowded schools, highway congestion, and ground water pollution. Both the central city and these two types of suburbs have small tax bases, comparatively high tax rates, and comparatively low spending. Median household incomes are also comparatively low: $25,000–30,000 in central cities in 1990, $25,000–40,000 in older suburbs, and $35,000–50,000 in low tax-base developing suburbs. Families in these communities are thus extremely sensitive to property tax increases. A third type of suburb is the high tax-base developing community. These affluent communities, with the region's highest median incomes, never amount to more than 30 percent of a region's population. They have all the benefits of a regional economy— access to labor and product markets, regionally built freeways and often airports—but are able to externalize the costs of social and economic need on the older suburbs and the central city.

Suburbs and cities can also be surprisingly diverse in their electoral results. Not all suburbs are Republican—or all cities Democratic. In Philadelphia, Republicans

From Myron Orfield, "Conflict or Consensus? Forty Years of Minnesota Metropolitan Politics," *The Brookings Review*, Fall 1998, pp. 31–35. Copyright © 1998 The Brookings Institution. Reprinted with permission.

control almost all the suburbs and even the white working-class parts of the city. In Pittsburgh, Democrats control virtually all suburban seats except the highest property-wealth areas. In San Francisco, almost all suburbs are represented by Democrats, while in Los Angeles and Southern California, most of the white suburbs are represented by Republicans. In general, Democrats build their base in central cities, move to the older and low tax-base suburbs, and, if they are very effective, capture a few of the high tax-base suburbs. Republicans do just the opposite. In many states the balance of power rests on electoral contests in a few older suburbs or low tax-capacity developing suburbs.

Minnesota has been engaged in the politics of metropolitan regional reform for almost 40 years. Over the decades, three types of metropolitan coalitions have sought to move policy reforms through the state legislature. The first, a Republican-led bipartisan coalition, engaged in some bitter legislative fights; the second, a consensualist-led coalition, eschewed controversy; the third, a Democratic-driven bipartisan group, revived the real-world reform political style of their Republican predecessors. The following short history of metropolitanism in Minnesota suggests the complexity of coalition politics—and my own conviction that, while compromise and accommodation is the necessary essence of politics, regional reform, like all other real reform movements in U.S. history, necessarily involves some degree of controversy.

The Progressive Republican Vanguard

In the 1960s and 1970s, metropolitan reform efforts in Minnesota's legislature were led by "good government" Rockefeller Republicans and reform Democrats—in a sense the progressives that Richard Hofstader wrote of in his *Age of Reform*. Joined by leaders of local corporations, they took aim at waste in government and set out to plan and shape a more cohesive, cost-effective, efficient, and equitable region. Though they sought rough metropolitan-wide equity in Minnesota's Twin Cities, they were not typical practitioners of class warfare. They valued equity because they knew from hard-headed calculation the costs of inequity and of destructive competition for development among municipalities in a single metropolitan region.

In some ways progressive Republican regionalism was an elegant, direct, limited-government response to growing sprawl and interlocal disparity. Joining Minnesota's Governor LeVander were Oregon's Tom McCall, Michigan's Miliken and Romney, and the great Republican mayor of Indianapolis, Richard Lugar. Had the country heeded their far-sighted strategy, the 1980s and 1990s might have been much different for the central cities and older suburbs.

In Minnesota the progressive Republicans and reform Democrats created regional sewer, transit, and airport authorities for the Twin Cities, as well as a Metropolitan Council of the Twin Cities with weak supervisory powers over these authorities. (Making the Met Council an elected body was a top goal, but it failed in a tie vote in 1967.) They also created a metropolitan land use planning framework and enacted Minnesota's famous tax-base sharing, or fiscal disparities, law, which, since 1971, has shared 40 percent of the growth of our commercial and industrial property tax base among the 187 cities, 49 school districts, and 7 counties in our region of some 2.5 million people.

The battle to pass the fiscal disparities act was brutal. Though the legislation, introduced in 1969, had its origins in the ethereal world of good government progressivism, its political managers were shrewd vote counters who made sure that two-thirds of the Twin City region's lawmakers understood that the bill would both lower their constituents' taxes and improve their schools and public services. Some of the progressives' key allies were populists who did not hesitate to play the class card with blue-collar voters in the low property-value suburbs. Probably not coincidentally, the populists collected most of the votes. The progressives pragmatically swallowed their compunctions.

The fiscal disparities bill that passed in 1971 was supported by a coalition of Democratic central-city legislators and Republicans from less wealthy suburbs—essentially the two-thirds of the region that received new tax base from the act. A few more rural Republicans who had a strong personal relationship with the bill's Republican sponsor went along. The opposition was also bipartisan—Democrats and Republicans representing areas in the one-third of the region that would lose some of their tax base. Debate over the bill was ugly. Republican Charlie Weaver, Sr., the bill's sponsor, was accused of fomenting "communism" and "community socialism" and of being a "Karl Marx" out to take from "the progressive communities to give to the backward ones." One opponent warned that "the fiscal disparities law will destroy the state." "Why should those who wish to work be forced to share with those who won't or can't help themselves?" demanded a representative of the high property-wealth areas. Amid growing controversy, after two divisive failed sessions, the bill would pass the Minnesota Senate by a single vote.

Not until 1975—after court challenges that went all the way to the U.S. Supreme Court (which refused to hear the case)—did the fiscal disparities law finally go into effect. The last legal challenge to the law came in 1981, a decade after passage. High property-wealth southern Twin Cities suburbs were finally rebuffed in the Minnesota Tax Court. But representatives and state senators from high property-wealth Twin Cities suburbs have tried to repeal the statute in virtually every legislative session for the past 25 years.

A New Approach

The tough progressive reformers were followed by consensus-based regionalists whose preferred approach, it has often been joked, was to convene leaders from across metropolitan Twin Cities in the boardroom of a local bank to hum together the word "regionalism." Highly polished professional policy wonks, the new generation of leaders leaned more to touring the country extolling the virtues of regional reform, which many had no part in accomplishing, than to gritty work in city halls and the legislature to make it happen. To make matters worse, business support for regionalism began to erode. The rise of national and multinational companies created a cadre of rotating, frequently moving executives who, facing a more competitive business environment, eschewed controversy in favor of political action that would boost the bottom line.

By the 1980s, proponents of the regional perspective in Minnesota had dwindled to the chairman of the Citizens League, a local policy group financially supported by the region's big businesses; a half-dozen legislators; two or three executives of declining power; and the editorial board of the Minneapolis paper.

Meanwhile, some suburbs, particularly the high property-wealth developing ones that saw no gain but plenty of loss coming from metropolitan action, rebelled. Over the course of the 1980s, as the Twin Cities region rapidly became more like the rest of the nation—more racially and socially segregated—and as fundamental divisions hardened, those suburbs hired high-priced lobbyists and prepared for a fight to dismantle "regional socialism." Metropolitanism's opponents, tough and organized, began to control the regional debate.

During 1980–90, state lawmakers gradually dismantled the metropolitan authority that had been put in place in the 1960s and 1970s. They stripped the Met Council of its authority over major development projects: the downtown domed stadium, a new regional race track, and even the Mall of America—a local landmark that by its sheer size had a thunderous effect on the retail market in central Minneapolis and St. Paul and the southern suburbs. They severely weakened the land use planning statute by giving supercedence to local zoning. They also overturned the Met Council system of infrastructure pricing, abandoned a regional affordable housing system, and shelved well-conceived regional density guidelines. And they took a hard, well-financed run at the fiscal disparities system.

Sometimes the consensus-based regionalists would oppose the changes, but more often they seemed unable to stomach controversy. Their general response to the newly assertive high property-wealth suburbs was to seek accommodation. Meanwhile, developers in the high property-wealth suburbs and their lawyers obtained coveted seats on the Met Council itself.

The first generation of regionalists had fought bloody fights for land use planning, the consolidation of regional services, and tax equity. A decade later, the consensus-based regionalists were reduced to building regional citizenship through a proposal for a bus that looked like a trolley car to connect the state capital to downtown St. Paul. Times, and tactics, had clearly changed.

The proud legacy of the first-generation regionalists was in shambles. In 1967, the Twin Cities had created a regional transit system with a tax base that encompassed seven regional counties and 187 cities. By 1998, what had been one of the most financially broad-based transit systems in the nation was struggling with below-average funding per capita. The Met Council, now in thrall to developers, allocated virtually all federal resources to its large highway building program. Finally, the Citizens League and the consensus-based regionalists, perhaps to curry favor with the rebellious high property-wealth suburbs, used their influence both to defeat the development of a fixed-rail transit service and to fragment and privatize the transit system. By the early 1980s, the southwestern developing suburbs, the most prosperous parts of the region and those that benefited most from the development of a regional sewer and highway system, were allowed to "opt out" of funding the transit system that served the region's struggling core.

In 1991, the Met Council was on the verge of being abolished. A measure to eliminate the Council passed on the House floor, and the governor opined that the Council should either do something or disappear. The consensus-based regionalists, frustrated after a decade of difficulty, were not even grousing about legislative roadblocks. They had moved on to champion school choice and had joined the business community in an effort to cut comparatively high Minnesota business property taxes.

The Third Generation

Out of this state of affairs emerged a new type of regionalist, of which I count myself one. Most of us were new to politics in the 1990s, and we were spurred to action by worrisome conditions in the Twin Cities, where concentrated poverty was growing—at the fourth fastest rate in the nation.

To address the growing concentration of poverty in the central cities, we began to investigate reforms, particularly in fair housing, at a metropolitan level. We began to wonder, in particular, whether the sprawl at the edge of the Twin Cities area was under-mining the stability at the core and whether the older suburbs, adjacent to the city, were having equally serious problems. As we learned more about the region's problems, we came to appreciate the metropolitan structure that had been put in place 20 years before—a structure severely out of fashion and irrelevant in liberal circles. "What does land use planning in the suburbs have to do with us?" asked our central-city politicos. "We need more of a neighborhood-based strategy," they said. We were also received as fish out of water when we went to the Met Council and the Citizens League to discuss our regional concerns. "This is not what the Met Council is about," they said. "It is about land use planning and infrastructure, not about urban issues or poverty."

In addition to the concentration of poverty at the core, we grew interested in the subsidies and governmental actions supporting sprawl. We were inspired by the land use reforms in Oregon and the work of Governor Tom McCall, Henry Richmond, and 1,000 Friends of Oregon. We read the infrastructure work of Robert Burchell at Rutgers. We became aesthetically attached to New Urbanism and Peter Calthorpe, its proponent of metropolitan social equity and transit-oriented development.

Our third-wave regionalism gradually became broader based. We added environ-mentalism and the strength of the environmental movement to what had heretofore been a sterile discussion of planning and efficiency. We also brought issues of concen-trated poverty and regional fair housing into an equity discussion that had previously been limited to interlocal fiscal equity. The dormant strength of the civil rights move-ment and social gospel also readied itself for metropolitan action and activism. In only a few years, hundreds of churches joined the movement for regional reform.

We also mobilized the rapidly declining, blue-collar suburbs—angry places unat-tached to either political party—to advance regional reform. Blue-collar mayors, a few with decidedly hostile views toward social and racial changes in their communities, united with African-American political leaders, environmentalists, and bishops of the major regional churches to advance a regional agenda for fair housing, land use plan-ning, tax equity, and an accountable elected regional governance structure.

In fact, probably the most important element of the new regional coalition was the older, struggling, fully developed suburbs—the biggest prospective winners in regional reform. To them, tax-base sharing means lower property taxes and better services, par-ticularly better-funded schools. Regional housing policy means, over time, fewer units of affordable housing crowding their doorstep. As one older-suburban mayor put it, "If those guys in the new suburbs don't start to build affordable housing, we'll be swim-ming in this stuff."

Winning over these suburbs was not easy. We had to overcome long-term, powerful resentments and distrust, based on class and race and fueled by every national political campaign since Hubert Humphrey lost the White House in 1968. But after two years of constant cajoling and courting and steady reminders of the growing inequities among the suburbs, the middle-income, working-class, blue-collar suburbs joined the central cities and created a coalition of great political clout in the legislature.

In 1994 this coalition of central-city and suburban legislators passed the Metropolitan Reorganization Act, which placed all regional sewer, transit, and land use planning under the operational authority of the Metropolitan Council of the Twin Cities. In doing so, it transformed the Met Council from a $40 million-a-year planning agency to a $600-million-a-year regional government operating regional sewers and transit, with supervisory authority over the major decisions of another $300-million-a-year agency that runs the regional airport. That same year, in the Metropolitan Land Use Reform Act, our coalition insulated metro-area farmers from public assessments that would have forced them to subdivide farm land for development.

In both 1993 and 1994 the legislature passed sweeping fair housing bills (both vetoed); in 1995 a weakened version was finally signed. In 1995 the legislature passed a measure that would have added a significant part of the residential property tax base to the fiscal disparities pool. While the measure passed strongly, it too was vetoed. In 1996 a statewide land use planning framework was adopted, and a regional brownfields fund created. Throughout the process, we restored to the Council many of the powers and prerogatives that had been removed from it during the 1980s in the areas of land use planning and infrastructure pricing. In each area of reform—land use planning, tax equity, and regional structural reform—we were initially opposed by the consensus-based regionalists as "too controversial," only to have our ideas adopted by them a few years later as the political center of gravity began to change.

Worth Fighting For

Like all real reform, regional reform is a struggle. From the fight against municipal corruption and the fight against the trusts to the women's movement, the consumer movement, the environmental movement, and the civil rights movement, reform has involved difficult contests against entrenched interests who operated against the general welfare. Today, we are told that the Age of Reform is over. We are in an age of consensus politics, when calmer words— "collaboration," "boundary crossing," "win-win" strategies—carry more promise than "assertive" ones.

In every region of this nation, [roughly] 20–40 percent of the people live in central cities, 25–30 percent in older declining suburbs, and 10–15 percent in low tax-base developing suburbs. These communities, representing a clear majority of regional population, are being directly harmed by an inefficient, wasteful, unfair system. Studies indicate that the regions in the nation that have the least economic disparity have the strongest economic growth and those with most disparity are the weakest economically. The social polarization and wasteful sprawl that are common in our nation take opportunity from people and businesses, destroy cities and older suburbs, waste our economic bounty, and threaten our future.

Those who care about these problems must "assert" themselves to reverse these trends. We must engage in a politics that is free of personal attacks and sensationalism, that is conducted with a smile and good manners—like the progressives. At each road-block, we must seek a compromise that moves equity forward, before we entrench unproductively. We must achieve the broadest possible level of good feeling, gather for our cause as many allies as we can from all walks of life and from all points of the compass. We must educate and persuade. However, if there are those who stand in our path utterly—who will permit no forward movement—we must fight. We must fight for the future of individuals, for the future of communities, and for the future of our country.

In the end, the goal is regional reform, not regional consensus.

22

David Rusk

GROWTH MANAGEMENT
The Core Regional Issue

Urban sprawl is consuming land at almost three times the rate of population growth. On the threshold of the twenty-first century, the rate of outward expansion of low-density development is outstripping the ability of even the most annexation-minded central cities to keep pace. The leadership of almost all central cities (whether locked in like Cleveland or expansionist like Charlotte) faces a common challenge: defending their city's viability by controlling sprawl through regional growth management.

Regional growth management must also be a key target of the social justice movement in America. While barriers based purely on race are slowly coming down, barriers based on income are steadily rising in most metropolitan areas. Sprawling regional development patterns are closing off avenues of advancement for low-income minorities. Sprawl is leading to (1) greater dispersion of jobs, placing low-skilled jobs beyond the reach of many low-skilled potential workers; (2) growing fiscal disparities, which impair the quality of services in inner cities and older suburbs; and (3) greater concentrations of poverty, which have devastating impacts on the education of inner-city children.

Strong regional growth management practices, by themselves, will not be instant solutions for all these problems. Growth management is the essential framework within which access to low-skilled jobs can improve, fiscal equity can be achieved, and greater economic integration can be promoted. The political coalitions necessary to secure, through state legislatures, effective regional growth management will also be the source of support for other policies (such as regional tax-base sharing or fair-share affordable housing) that can achieve greater social equity.

Highways and Sprawl

Suburbanization has been a constant phenomenon in America, beginning with the first national census in 1790 that reported on the "suburbs" of Philadelphia.[1] America's urban experience has been a history of changes in transportation modes that constantly extended urban development outward from the core settlement. However, though suburbanization as we know it began in earnest with mass automobile ownership in the 1920s, it accelerated from the mid-1950s onward. Indeed, America's most influential urban planner may well have been President Dwight David Eisenhower.

In 1956 the Republican president convinced a Democratic Congress to launch the federal interstate highway system. In the midst of the cold war, the new law was styled the National Interstate and Defense Highway Act. In political myth, it was born out of young Major Eisenhower's experience in leading an army convoy coast to coast shortly after World War I—a journey of fifty-nine days!

From a vantage point four decades later, the interstate highway system has been militarily insignificant in our overcoming the Soviet Union. However, the interstate highway system has had a fateful impact on America's cities.

In order to build new interstate highways, federal highway appropriations were ratcheted up dramatically. In one decade, total federal highway outlays rose fivefold from $729 million (fiscal year 1956) to $4 billion (fiscal year 1966). By fiscal year 1996, the federal highway program had expended $652 billion (in 1996 dollars), compared to just $85 billion in federal mass transit aid (which was initiated in 1965).[2]

The great bulk of the 43,000-mile interstate system may be interurban—connecting different urban regions—but its primary impact has been *intra*urban—promoting low-density, sprawling development around core cities. With federal highway grants typically covering 90 percent of project cost, building sprawl-supporting highways was virtually cost-free for state governments. Other inducements to highway construction and sprawl were cheap gasoline (based on low federal and state taxes); easy, interest-deductible automobile loans; other federal infrastructure grants (such as $130 billion in wastewater treatment grants); and housing finance and tax systems that greatly favored homeowners over apartment dwellers.[3]

What picture emerges from calculating the growth of America's "urbanized areas" (as contrasted with the growth of county-defined metropolitan areas)? The 1950 census reported that 69 million people resided in 157 urbanized areas covering almost 13,000 square miles. By 1990 the population of these same 157 areas had grown to over 130 million people occupying almost 46,000 square miles. While urbanized population grew 88 percent, urbanized land expanded 255 percent (almost three times the rate of population growth). By 1990 the average resident of these 157 communities was consuming 90 percent more land area than just 40 years before.[4]

Central Cities as Quasi-Regional Governments

Many political commentators and scholars may decry the absence of metropolitan government in America. However, at midcentury there was still an implicit system of quasi-regional governance in place in the great majority of America's metropolitan areas: the dominance of the central city that spread a de facto unity over its region. Almost 60 percent of the nation's metropolitan population lived in 193 central cities. Most area children attended the city school system. Most area residents used city parks and libraries. Most area workers rode city buses, streetcars, and subways to blue- and white-collar jobs within the city or occasionally, to nearby factories just outside the city limits. Most of the region's voters cast their ballots for the same set of local offices. Although there were often fierce rivalries among ethnic and racial groups, city-based public institutions were unifying forces (except in the legally segregated South with its sets of parallel institutions).

Annexation and merger, of course, were the tools of municipal expansion, and they had been used by even the oldest American cities in their youth. In the nineteenth century, Boston grew from the compact, colonial port town that was besieged by General Washington's rebel forces from Dorchester Heights to a metropolis of 48 square miles. In the process Boston not only absorbed Dorchester Heights itself but the city of Roxbury (1867) and, leaping Boston Harbor in 1874, the city of Charlestown as well.[5]

In one afternoon in 1854, by act of the Pennsylvania General Assembly, the city of Philadelphia grew twentyfold in territory, filling all of Philadelphia County. In the process five of the nation's most populous cities disappeared: Spring Garden (ninth), Northern Liberties (eleventh), Kensington (twelfth), Southwark (twentieth), and Moyamensing (twenty-eighth).

In 1897 the New York General Assembly enacted the most ambitious restructuring of regional governance yet. The state legislature abolished the cities of New York and Brooklyn (the nation's first and seventh most populous cities), combined them with three largely rural counties (Queens, Richmond, and Bronx), and created the 315-square-mile New York City, the nation's first metropolitan government.

By the mid-twentieth century, of course, the territorial expansions of Boston, Philadelphia, and New York were history (and largely forgotten history, at that). In fact, throughout New England, New York, New Jersey, and Pennsylvania, the political boundaries of 6,236 cities, boroughs, villages, towns, and townships were set in concrete. On the threshold of accelerated urban sprawl, the Northeast had become a region of "inelastic" cities.[6]

Growing territorial inflexibility was also settling in over much of the Middle West, which through the Continental Congress's enactment of the Land Act of 1785 had inherited New England's pattern of township government. State laws might provide for municipal annexation, but cordons sanitaires of incorporated suburbs already surrounded many cities, such as Detroit and Cleveland. Throughout the Middle West, townships hastened to incorporate as independent municipalities as to avoid annexation. After 1950 Chicago would succeed only in annexing twenty square miles for the new O'Hare Airport.

Annexation versus Highways

At midcentury, central-city officials in regions other than the Northeast or Middle West could reasonably anticipate that annexation and mergers would continue to maintain their "elastic" city status as near-regional governments. They often had other tools available to shape development patterns. Many cities owned and operated regional water and sewage treatment systems; some exercised extraterritorial planning jurisdiction. With such powers, most southern and western cities expected to successfully maintain their "market share" of regional development.

By the 1990s, they had been proven wrong. The highway system decentralized America's metropolitan areas so rapidly and relentlessly that almost no city's annexation or merger efforts were able to keep pace.

Table 1 on pages 270–271 charts the territorial growth of the country's fifty most annexation-minded central cities from 1960 to 1990. Each added at least forty-six square miles to its municipal jurisdiction—an area equal to the city of Boston or the city of San Francisco. City-county consolidation was the mechanism for most of the largest expansions: Nashville-Davidson (1964), Jacksonville-Duval (1968), Indianapolis-Marion (1970), Lexington-Fayette (1973), and Columbus (Georgia)-Muskogee (1977). The champion of territorial imperialists was Anchorage, which by merging with Anchorage Borough in the mid-1960s ballooned from 13 square miles to 1,698 square miles.[7] Oklahoma City, Phoenix, and Houston annexed the most territory by conventional means. Collectively, the fifty cities more than tripled their municipal territory in three decades.

Running Hard but Falling Behind

Most of these fifty cities still lost market share of regional growth. . . . As a group, despite tripling their municipal territory, the percentage of the regions' urbanized populations that were city residents dropped from 65 percent in 1960 to 51 percent in 1990. The cities' share of metropolitan population declined more precipitously, from 60 percent in 1960 to 43 percent in 1990.

Over the three decades, only nine cities—Anchorage, Jacksonville, Nashville, Lexington, Columbus (Georgia), Colorado Springs, San Jose, Bakersfield, and Fresno—increased their market shares of both urbanized and metropolitan populations. However, the high-water mark for the consolidated jurisdictions' market shares typically occurred at the moment of the city-county mergers. During the 1980s, for example, Jacksonville, Nashville, Lexington, and Columbus experienced slower population growth than surrounding counties.

Even though these fifty most annexation-oriented cities are slowly losing ground in the face of accelerating urban sprawl, there is still strong justification for continued annexation. As suburban subdivisions are built around central cities, elastic cities are able to absorb some of that growth within their expanding municipal boundaries. By capturing shares of new, middle-class subdivisions, elastic cities maintain greater socioeconomic balance. Average incomes of residents in elastic cities are typically equal to or even higher than average incomes of suburban residents. Tapping broad, growing tax bases, elastic-city governments are better financed and more able to rely on local resources to address local problems. Although no community is free of racial inequities, minorities are more evenly spread out within the "big boxes" of elastic cities. Segregation by race and income class is reduced.

By contrast, "inelastic" central cities are frozen within fixed city limits and surrounded by growing, independent suburbs. By the 1990s, the downtown business districts of

Table 1 *Territorial Growth of the USA's 50 Most Elastic Cities, 1960–90*
Square miles unless otherwise specified

City[a]	Area			Percent Increase
	1960	**1990**	**Increase**	
Albuquerque	56	132	76	135
Anchorage-Anchorage	13	1,698	1,685	13,482
Austin	50	218	168	339
Bakersfield	16	92	76	474
Birmingham	75	149	74	99
Charlotte	65	174	110	169
Chattanooga	37	118	82	223
Colorado Springs	17	183	167	997
Columbus	89	191	102	114
Columbus-Muskogee	26	216	190	719
Corpus Christi	38	135	97	257
Dallas	280	342	63	22
Denver	71	153	82	116
Durham	22	69	47	215
Fort Worth	141	281	141	100
Fresno	29	99	71	247
Houston	328	540	212	65
Huntsville	51	164	114	224
Indianapolis-Marion	71	362	291	408
Jackson	47	109	63	134
Jacksonville-Duval	30	759	729	2,412
Kansas City	130	312	182	140
Knoxville	25	77	52	204
Las Vegas	25	83	59	237
Lexington-Fayette	13	285	272	2088

many inelastic cities may have revived as regional employment and entertainment centers, but most inelastic-city neighborhoods are increasingly catch basins for poor blacks and Hispanics. With the flight of middle-class families, inelastic cities' populations have dropped steadily (typically by one-quarter to one-half). The income gap between city residents and suburbanites steadily widens. Governments of inelastic cities are squeezed between rising service needs and eroding tax bases. Unable to tap areas of greater economic growth (their independent suburbs), inelastic-city governments rely increasingly on federal and state aid. Suburban areas around inelastic cities are typically fragmented into many "little boxes"—multiple smaller cities and towns and "mini" school systems. With, at best, a heritage of exclusionary practices or, at worst, continuing practice of such policies, the fragmented governmental structure of these little-box regions reinforces racial and economic segregation.

Table 1 (continued) *Territorial Growth of the USA's 50 Most Elastic Cities, 1960–90*
Square miles unless otherwise specified

City[a]	Area			Percent Increase
	1960	**1990**	**Increase**	
Little Rock	28	103	75	264
Memphis	128	256	128	100
Montgomery	32	135	103	325
Nashville-Davidson	29	473	444	1532
Oklahoma City	322	608	287	89
Omaha	51	101	50	97
Orlando	21	67	46	219
Phoenix	187	420	233	124
Portland	67	125	58	86
Raleigh	34	88	55	163
Reno	12	58	46	387
Sacramento	45	96	51	114
Salt Lake City	56	109	53	94
San Antonio	161	333	173	107
San Diego	192	324	132	68
San Jose	55	171	117	214
Shreveport	36	99	63	174
Tallahassee	15	63	48	316
Tucson	71	156	85	120
Tulsa	48	184	136	284
Wichita	52	115	63	122
Total	3,383	11,025	7,642	226

[a]Hyphenation indicates city-county consolidation.
Sources: Author's calculations based on census reports.

Big Boxes versus Little Boxes

A comparison of the very elastic cities with twenty-three "zero-elastic" cities illustrates these characterizations (Table 2). As a group, in four decades (1950–90), these twenty-three zero-elastic cities expanded their municipal areas by an average of only 3 percent—in sharp contrast to the very elastic cities' record of more than tripling their municipal areas in just three decades (1960–90).

By the 1990 census, the average income of zero-elastic city residents had fallen to 66 percent of suburban levels, while the average income of residents in very elastic cities was 91 percent of suburban levels. Zero-elastic cities averaged lower bond ratings (A) than highly elastic cities (AA).

In 1990, by a common demographic measure, African Americans were much more segregated within the metropolitan housing markets in zero-elastic core cities (an index

Table 2 Comparing Socioeconomic and Fiscal Health of 23 Zero-Elastic Cities and
        50 Very Elastic Cities and Their Respective Metropolitan Areas

Criteria	Zero-Elastic Cities/Metro Areas[a]	Highly Elastic Cities/Metro Areas
Income of city residents as a percentage of suburban income (1989)	66	91
City bond rating (1993)[b]	A	AA
Metropolitan Segregation Index[c]		
Housing (1990)	74	53
Schools (1990)	74	46
Poor households (1989)	42	31

[a]Zero-elastic cities are New York, Newark, Paterson, Boston, St. Louis, Providence, Detroit, Washington, D.C., Pittsburgh, Cleveland, Baltimore, Hartford, Minneapolis, Rochester, Syracuse, Jersey City, New Haven, Chicago, San Francisco, Philadelphia, Buffalo, Bridgeport, and Cincinnati.
[b]Bond ratings are those assigned by Moody's Investor Services in their 1991 Municipal Data Book.
[c]For segregation indexes, 100 = total segregation.
Sources: Author's calculations based on census reports.

of 74) than within metropolitan housing markets in highly elastic core cities (an index of 53).[8] For the 1989–1990 school year, the school segregation index matched segregated housing patterns in the zero-elastic regions (74 for both indexes), whereas schools were significantly less segregated (an index of 46) than neighborhoods (an index of 53) in the highly elastic regions. Finally, poor households living in zero-elastic regions were more likely to be segregated away from middle-class households (an index of 42) than those residing in highly elastic regions (an index of 31).[9]

Governance Structure Counts

A clear regional trend appears when the two groups of metropolitan areas are compared. Of the fifty very elastic cities, all but Indianapolis and Columbus (Ohio) are located in the South and West, while all twenty-three of the zero-elastic cities are in the Northeast and Middle West, except Baltimore, Washington, D.C., St. Louis, and San Francisco.[10]

However, the preceding discussion on racial and economic segregation is not just a disguised way of describing Rust Belt versus Sun Belt sectional differences. Within an urban region, how local governance is organized has an impact on issues of social mobility.

The clearest impact is on school segregation. In the decades after the U.S. Supreme Court declared segregated schools unconstitutional, school desegregation suits were brought in both southern and northern courts. Southern states (such as Florida, North Carolina, and Tennessee) tend to have big-box school districts that often are county-wide. Court-ordered school desegregation plans integrated schools not just within elastic central cities but across city boundaries into the central county's suburban areas.

In the North, however, little-box school districts mirror little-box city, village, and town governments. In its 1974 decision *Milliken v. Bradley*, the U.S. Supreme Court ruled that suburban school districts would not be required to participate with central-city districts in school desegregation plans unless it could be shown that state action had brought about such segregation. With white, middle-class anxiety about local schools intensifying the lure of new suburban homes, central-city school districts like Cleveland, Rochester, and Minneapolis were left to integrate systems that rapidly became heavily minority enrollment districts.

For example, with 115 independent suburban systems, metropolitan Detroit has the nation's most racially segregated public school systems. It is the unspoken mission of many little school boards to "keep our schools just the way they are for children just like ours"—whoever "our children" happen to be. That mission is more readily achieved with 115 separate school districts empowered to erect walls around themselves—a pattern repeated over and over again in little-box regions.

"Keeping our town just the way it is for people just like us"—whoever "us" happens to be—has also been the mantra of suburban town councils and planning commissions in little-box regions. Exclusionary zoning policies reign. By contrast, because planning commissions and city councils of big-box governments are accountable to more diverse constituencies, they are less likely to implement policies that divide residents as rigorously by income, with the attendant consequences for racial and ethnic segregation.

In the 1990s, southern metropolitan areas are less racially segregated than northern metropolitan areas, but not primarily because "black and white Southerners always lived closer together than Northerners did." That conventional wisdom doesn't stand up very well to historical analysis. In 1970 the average residential segregation index for eighteen major northern metropolitan areas (including San Francisco-Oakland and Los Angeles) was 85 compared to an average index of 79 for fourteen major southern metropolitan areas—hardly a major difference. By 1990 the northern average had edged down 7 points to 78, but the southern average had dropped 15 points to 64.[11] It is the dyanmics of housing markets within big-box central cities, reinforced by public school integration policies (and generally growing regional economies), that largely account for the greater pace of residential desegregation in the South.

Maintaining central-city elasticity is important both for the city's economic and fiscal health and for the region's social health. Wherever cities still have annexation powers, they should use them prudently. Whenever state legislatures or local voters can be persuaded to approve city-county consolidations, the effort should be made.[12]

However, even the most elastic central cities cannot hope to maintain their traditional role as quasi-regional governments that largely control regional development. Annexation strategies have been overwhelmed by the sprawl-inducing effect of the federal interestate highway system and the networks of state highways supporting it.

For example, Charlotte, North Carolina, has carried out successfully one of the most sustained annexation programs. From 1950 to 1996, Charlotte expanded from 30 square miles to 225 square miles. In the process Charlotte captured 83 percent of all population growth within Mecklenburg County, the boundary of its 1950 metropolitan area. However, in those same decades, Charlotte's actual metropolitan area expanded beyond Mecklenburg County to embrace seven counties and fifty municipalities covering 3,700 square miles in two states. Charlotte can no longer call the regional development tune. The Queen City must negotiate transportation and land-use issues with other local (and independent) governments.

If Charlotte could not annex new development fast enough to maintain regional hegemony, no elastic city can. Elastic cities of the South and West now face the same phenomenon of sprawling development beyond their grasp that in earlier decades victimized inelastic cities of the Northeast and Middle West.

The Regional Agenda

Don Hutchinson, president of the Greater Baltimore Committee, the area's regional business leadership organization, laid out the regional challenge most succinctly. "If regionalism isn't dealing with land-use, fiscal disparities, housing, and education," the former Baltimore County executive stated, "then regionalism isn't dealing with the issues that count."

In pursuit of that philosophy, in July 1997 the Greater Baltimore Committee issued a policy statement, *One Region, One Future*, that urged adoption of three major initiatives:

—Regional growth management policies that lead to redevelopment and reinvestment in older neighborhoods and reduce the infrastructure costs to the governments and taxpayers of the region.

—Policies that result in a system of tax-base sharing in the region. Any system should focus on the growth in the tax base and could draw upon a number of different models that have been adopted across the country.

—A policy for developing affordable housing throughout the metropolitan area. A key goal of this policy should be to avoid creating concentrations of people living in poverty.[13]

Baltimore's *One Region, One Future* is a policy statement that should serve as a model for business leadership in all metropolitan areas.

Land Use: The Key Issue

Land-use planning is the pivotal issue. Fiscal disparities, lack of affordable housing, and poor public schools all reflect uneven regional development patterns.

Fiscal disparities arise as new subdivisions, commercial areas, and office parks lead to devaluation and abandonment of older property. Wide fiscal disparities typically emerge most virulently in little-box regions where central cities and suburban jurisdictions alike have fixed jurisdictional boundaries. Elastic cities do not suffer from fiscal disparities. Indeed, elastic cities act as an internal revenue-sharing mechanism, taxing wealthier city neighborhoods to maintain adequate service levels in poorer city neighborhoods. (Highly elastic cities such as Charlotte, Lexington, and Albuquerque annex so much high-end new development that they are wealthier than their suburban neighbors.)

Growing economic segregation in most metropolitan housing markets is a reflection of postwar development patterns. Cities always have had richer and poorer neighborhoods. However, many older city neighborhoods contain a greater variety of housing types than typical postwar suburban subdivisions. As a result, many city neighborhoods contain households that range widely in income.

The greater economic homogeneity of suburban subdivisions partly reflects the fact that homebuilding has changed from a retail industry to a wholesale industry. Postwar homebuilders have learned to apply factory-like production techniques to building sites. Specialized crews (foundation layers, framers, plumbing and electrical installers, sheetrock hangers, roofers) move from site to site with factory-like precision. The result is that, within a given subdivision, a builder will erect large numbers of similar homes priced for a relatively narrow band of potential homebuyers.

Suburban planning and zoning policies often magnify the effect of such industry practices. By setting large minimum lot sizes, limiting the location of (or banning outright) townhouse complexes, apartments, and mobile home parks, local governments encourage economic segregation.

In too many urban regions, where a child lives largely determines the quality of the child's school experience. The problem is not primarily fiscal disparities among different local school districts—the target of many education reformers. The core issue is that a child's school performance is heavily influenced by the socioeconomic status of the child's family and classmates. For example, in communities across the country, 65 to 85 percent of the school-by-school variation in standardized test scores is explained by variations in the school-by-school percentage of low-income students.[14] The most effective education reform for improving poor children's school performance would actually be housing reform: mixed-income housing policies that integrate poor children into middle-class neighborhoods and middle-class neighborhood schools.

Target: New State Growth Management Laws

Growth management is rapidly emerging as the top regional issue of the next decade. There are two key targets: state legislatures, which control land-use rules, and federally required metropolitan planning organizations, which shape the allocation of federal transportation grants.

There are only twelve states that have enacted statewide growth management laws. They vary in effectiveness from strong (Oregon) to almost purely exhortatory (Georgia). In 1999, however, the Georgia legislature created a powerful Georgia Regional Transportation Agency to take charge of transportation and land-use decisions in sprawl-choked metropolitan Atlanta.

The two most recent state land-use reform laws have been adopted in Maryland (1977) and Tennessee (1998). Maryland governor Parris Glendening's Smart Growth Act strengthens a weak state planning law adopted in 1993. The Smart Growth Act ostensibly does not place new mandates on local planning, which is controlled almost entirely by county governments in Maryland. However, it restricts state highway, sewage treatment, and other infrastructure grants (and the federal grants they match) to established urban areas.

Tennessee's new state planning law popped forth virtually unnoticed by growth management advocates nationally. It had an unconventional origin—an obscure amendment to another Tennessee law that was adopted by voice vote in the waning minutes of the 1997 legislative session. To the Tennessee Municipal League's consternation, the stealth amendment suspended Tennessee's annexation laws for one year, wiping out existing cities' powers to veto the incorporation of new municipalities within five miles of their city limits. To ensure against annexation, proposals to incorporate mini-municipalities (dubbed "toy towns" by opponents) sprang up like weeds.

By the time the Tennessee Supreme Court declared that the amendment was unconstitutionally adopted by the legislature, residents of unincorporated areas had initiated proceedings to create forty-four toy towns (including one that was simply a condominium apartment building near Knoxville).

During the heated controversy, Tennessee's speaker of the house and the lieutenant governor (the presiding officer of the state senate who had created the stealth amendment) appointed a broad-based commission to review the state's annexation laws. Under the urging of the Tennessee Advisory Commission on Intergovernmental Relations, the commission expanded its mission to consider the broader need for regional land-use planning.

The result was enactment of the Annexation Reform Act of 1998—a title that reflects the law's origins but not its broad scope. Through a complex process, the new law requires counties to adopt comprehensive land-use plans. The plans must designate urban growth boundaries for existing municipalities (which will also be their twenty-year annexation reserve areas), rural preservation areas, and "planned growth areas" (which may allow some "new town" development).

Though undoubtedly not as rigorous a growth management directive as Oregon's law, the new Tennessee law has real teeth. Counties that fail to adopt a comprehensive land-use plan by July 2001 will no longer be eligible for a long list of state infrastructure funds, including participation in federal highway grants.

New Allies

Tennessee's new growth management law may have been born under unique circumstances, but there is growing public pressure for antisprawl legislation developing in many states, particularly in the Middle West, where no state has yet adopted a statewide growth management law. New recruits to the legislative struggle—business leaders, church coalitions, and inner-suburb mayors—are joining forces with environmentalists and farmland preservationists, growth management's more traditional advocates. Some key examples:

—A new association of business leadership groups in Pennsylvania, the Coalition of Mid-Sized Cities, has targeted enactment of a smart-growth, antisprawl law as its top priority.

—In Missouri a coalition of eighty churches—Protestant and Catholic, black and white, city and inner suburb—is lobbying for a new state growth management law for Greater St. Louis.

—In Ohio the recently established First Suburbs Consortium, initially formed by ten suburban mayors from communities around Cleveland, told the Governor's Task Force on Agricultural Preservation in 1997 that a strong state land-use law might be desirable to save farmland, but it was essential for the survival of older suburban communities.

"Since the late 1940's, policies have consistently encouraged the abandonment of boroughs and cities in Pennsylvania, and discouraged the redevelopment of existing neighborhoods and established commercial and industrial sites," explains Tom Wolf, president of Better York, owner of a multistate chain of builders' supply yards, and a leader of the Coalition of Mid-Sized Cities.[15] In addition to Better York, the coalition includes a dozen business groups such as the Lehigh Valley Partnership, Lancaster Alliance, and Erie Conference on Community Development.

"In the end, no one wins in a system that makes prosperity a temporary and fleeting phenomenon," Wolf continues. "No one wins in a system that has already condemned our cities and older boroughs to economic stagnation and decline. And no one wins in a system that ultimately threatens to do the same thing to our townships. The point is that public policies that encourage sprawl are neither smart nor right.

"We need to change the rules of the game," Wolf concludes. "Most of all we need to change the rules governing land-use planning.". . .

Land-Use Planning: The Portland Model

Across the continent, business and civic delegations, state and local politicians, and professional planners are flocking to Portland to see the practical results of nearly twenty-five years of operating under different rules of the game. In 1973 the Oregon legislature enacted the Statewide Land Use Law. It required that urban growth boundaries be drawn around cities throughout the state. Portland Metro, the nation's only directly elected regional government, is responsible for land-use and transportation planning in the 1.5-million-person metropolitan area. Anticipating a 50 percent growth of population over the next forty-five years, in November 1997 the Portland Metro Council voted 5–2 to add less than 8 square miles to Portland's existing 342-square-mile urban growth boundary. (The two dissenting votes felt the expansion was too little.)

Opposition to greater expansion was led by many local officials, like Mayor Gussie McRobert of suburban Gresham, as well as by many environmentally concerned citizens. Portland's urban growth boundary has succeeded in protecting farmland in Oregon's rich Willamette Valley. If the Metro Council sticks to its plans, over the next forty-five years, only about four square miles of current farmland will be urbanized— as much farmland as is subdivided in the state of Michigan every ten days.[16]

A big bonus is that shutting down suburban sprawl has turned new private investment back inward into existing neighborhoods and retail areas. Mayor McRobert's Gresham as well as Milwaukie, Oregon City, and other older suburbs are booming. Property values in Albina, Portland's poorest neighborhood, doubled in just five years. As Metro councilor Ed Washington, whose District 6 includes Albina, explained his vote for the small boundary expansion, "We are having redevelopment in my district for the first time in forty years; we don't want to lose it."

By the mid-1990s, Portland's economy had become superheated by a high-tech investment boom. With $13 billion in new, high-tech construction underway, workers flocked to the Portland area. From 1990 to 1996, the Portland area's population grew 16 percent, putting extreme pressure on the housing supply. Housing prices shot up 60 percent, and many area homebuilders and other allies launched a campaign against the region's tight land-use controls.[17]

In the midst of an affordable-housing crisis, the Metro Council adopted a wide-ranging package of regulatory actions and incentives to increase the production of affordable housing. A tough, mandatory inclusionary zoning ordinance (patterned on the successful program in Montgomery County, Maryland)[18] was deferred after several legal challenges before the state Land Conservation and Development Commission that regulates local growth management.

Citizen Accountability: The Portland Model

Portland Metro is the joint creation of both the Oregon legislature (1979) and local citizens (through three separate referenda, including adoption of a home rule charter for Portland Metro in 1992). Covering three counties and twenty-four municipalities, Portland Metro is responsible for regional solid waste disposal, regional air and water quality, the regional zoo, and the Oregon Convention Center. In the new home rule charter, the area's citizens affirmed that long-range planning is Metro's "primary" function. Metro's long-range planning function includes responsibility for both land-use and transportation planning.

Portland area citizens know where the crucial decisions affecting the future of their region are made: Metro. They know when and how such decisions will be made: in well-advertised public meetings after extensive public hearings. (In revising the Portland 2040 plan, Metro held 182 public hearings and presentations.) And citizens know who will make the decisions: the seven Metro councilors and Metro chief executive who are directly elected by the region's citizens. Land-use and transportation decisions are the issues that dominate political campaigns for Metro's elected offices. The result is that there is a much higher level of knowledgeable citizen engagement in regional planning issues in the Portland area than in any other regional community in the United States.

Transforming Metropolitan Planning Organizations

A Republican-controlled Congress dominated by self-anointed "conservatives" enacted in 1998 a $217 billion Transportation Efficiency Act (TEA-21). The country is poised for another massive round of federal transportation spending. Over the next six years, the federal government will spend almost one-third as much for highway and transit construction as was spent in the previous four decades. How this new generation of transportation investments will affect the growth and shape of America's urban areas will be determined largely by metropolitan planning organizations (MPOs).

For decades, deciding how federal transportation funds would be used was primarily the province of the Federal Highway Administration and state highway departments. That changed with the Intermodal Service Transportation Efficiency Act of 1991 (ISTEA). In the judgment of the National Association of Regional Councils, ISTEA "marked a radical and visionary transformation of the nation's transportation policy."[19]

Prior to ISTEA, local planning input was largely limited to prioritizing laundry lists of projects within narrow, federally prescribed program allocations. Under ISTEA, MPOs for all urbanized areas with at least 200,000 residents acquired broad discretion to allocate lump-sum federal funds among road, bridge, and transit projects.

About half of all MPOs are "regional councils," voluntary consortia of local governments with a variety of interests beyond transportation planning. Other MPOs are regional economic development organizations, transportation planning agencies, and arms of state highway departments.

In the years since ISTEA was enacted, most MPOs have not had as "radical" and "transforming" an impact as the National Association of Regional Councils originally anticipated. However, transportation planning certainly has acquired a much more local flavor. Had the MPO structure been eliminated (as several key congressional powers proposed), TEA-21 would have dealt a massive blow to the cause of regional planning; instead, TEA-21 will provide continued impetus to the evolution of regional land-use planning.

There has been a uniquely American asymmetry about the relationship between land-use planning and transportation planning. It is inconceivable that a land-use plan could largely ignore an area's network of roads and highways, yet transportation plans often have been developed as if they dealt only with transportation problems.

However, transportation decisions *are* land-development decisions. Who can doubt today that the primary impact of interstate beltways was not to route interstate traffic swiftly and conveniently around major cities (as originally justified) but was rather to generate major suburban commercial, industrial, and residential development? In urban areas the great majority of interstate highway users are local-origin cars and trucks.

Metropolitan planning organizations are federated bodies. Their boards are composed of individuals appointed by member governments and agencies. This raises two problems for organizations faced with increasingly tough, important decisions.

First, the primary loyalty of most board members is to their home jurisdictions. This is particularly true of local elected officials serving on MPO boards (who usually constitute all or a majority of board members). This makes it difficult to achieve an overall regional perspective. Second, federated boards can rarely survive judicial scrutiny when challenged under the "one person, one vote" standard.

Precedents for Elected Regional Organizations

Very limited precedents suggest that voluntary regional structures like MPOs will evolve into limited-purpose regional governments directly elected by the region's citizens. Portland Metro began as the Metropolitan Services District, with a seven-member federated board of local elected officials—one each from the city of Portland and Clackamas, Multnomah, and Washington counties and three representing other cities in each of the three counties. A parallel organization, the Columbia Region Association of Governments (CRAG), started as a federated board of representatives from four counties and fourteen cities and grew to represent five counties and thirty-one cities. As one observer noted, "The difficulty in building consensus around a [comprehensive regional land-use plan] reflected a fundamental tension in using the council of governments model to develop regional policies. . . . [CRAG board members] were often torn between the imperatives of regional issues and the need to protect their own community from unwanted costs, programs, or development initiatives."[20]

In 1977 the Oregon legislature abolished CRAG, assigned its regional planning responsibilities to the Metropolitan Services District, and authorized replacing the federated, appointed board with a directly elected twelve-member council and elected chief executive. In 1978 the Portland area electorate approved the changes. (The voters reduced council membership from twelve to seven and renamed the organization "Portland Metro" when the home rule charter was adopted in 1992.)

During the postwar years, another regional organization had evolved in the Seattle metropolitan area. Seattle Metro was a well-respected regional wastewater and transit authority governed by a federated board. By 1992, however, with the growth of region's population, the Metro Council had grown from its original sixteen members to forty-five.

Controversy increasingly revolved around the makeup and power of the federated Metro Council. After a dozen abortive efforts by the state legislature to reorganize Metro, the debate took a decisive turn in 1990 when a federal district judge ruled that the Metro Council's federated structure violated the constitutional one-person, one-vote guarantee. After further local controversy, legislative debate, and missed court deadlines, Metro Council members proposed merging Metro into King County government. Under the merger proposal approved by voters in November 1992, a single legislative body—the Metropolitan County Council—replaced the King County and Metro Councils, in effect expanding the King County Council from nine to thirteen members elected by district.

To give cities "a voice and a vote" in developing countywide comprehensive planning policies, three new bodies were mandated in a charter amendment to the King County charter: the Regional Transit Committee, Regional Water Quality Committee, and Regional Policy Committee. Each committee has twelve voting members: six Metro County Council members and six members divided between Seattle and suburban cities. The Metro County Council is the only body that is legally empowered to enact plans and policies. However, the County Council can override a regional committee recommendation only if at least eight of the thirteen council members agree. Otherwise, a regional committee's recommendations automatically become law.

A third nationally recognized regional body—the Twin Cities Metropolitan Council—is on the brink of passing from appointed to elected status. Since its legislative creation in 1967, the "Met Council" has been governed by a seventeen-member board appointed by Minnesota's governor. Although members are residents of sixteen districts into which its seven-county jurisdiction is divided, they and their full-time chairman are, in practice, accountable to the governor that appointed them, not to their neighbors. The Met Council functions like another state agency.

For three decades the Met Council carried out land-use planning functions and exercised loose oversight over three regional wastewater and transit agencies. The regional agencies, however, pursued increasingly independent directions. In 1994, seeking greater regional unity, the Minnesota legislature abolished the three agencies and placed their functions directly under the Met Council. The Metropolitan Reorganization Act transformed the Met Council from a planning body with loose supervisory control into an operational agency with a budget of more than $400 million and supervisory control over the $300 million Metropolitan Airports Commission. "After Hennepin County," noted state representative Myron Orfield, leader of the legislature's regional reform bloc, "the Met Council was Minnesota's second largest unit of government in terms of budget, and perhaps its most significant in terms of authority."[21]

A regional public agency with so much authority and spending so many tax dollars, Orfield and other colleagues argued, ought to be directly accountable to the citizens of the region. A bill to convert membership on the Met Council from gubernatorial appointment to direct election was defeated narrowly in the 1996 legislative session but passed in 1997, only to be vetoed by the governor. There are strong prospects that a similar bill will pass and become law in the near future.

Dealing with the Regional Issues That Count

The growing political support for state land-use planning laws and the increasing level of federal transportation grants are leading in the same direction: the evolution of stronger regional planning organizations. In some states existing regional planning organizations are likely to have their planning authority extended into housing policy, regional revenue sharing, and economic development policy. Some may also become vehicles for management of regionwide infrastructure programs formerly carried out by independent authorities.

I would like to offer some crystal ball gazing. Though there is little pragmatic evidence to date, I believe that as regional organizations become more operationally significant and the impact of their planning decisions becomes better understood, public demand may convert some of them into directly elected rather than appointed bodies.

Thus in coming decades, directly elected metropolitan governments are likely to evolve in a growing number of regions. They will not be unitary governments. (Anchorage is the country's only such example covering an entire metropolitan area.) They will not replace the mosaic of local governments as primary providers of local services. Their powers will appear limited but will be vitally important, since they will affect regional land-use and transportation planning, affordable housing, fiscal disparities, and major regional infrastructure investments—the "outside game." These evolving metropolitan governments will deal with the issues that count for the wealth and health of regions and the future of their central cities.

23

Fred Siegel

IS URBAN SPRAWL A PROBLEM?

Suburban sprawl, the spread of low-density housing over an ever-expanding landscape, has attracted a growing list of enemies. Environmentalists have long decried the effects of sprawl on the ecosystem; aesthetes have long derided what they saw as "the ugliness and banality of suburbia"; and liberals have intermittently insisted that suburban prosperity has been purchased at the price of inner-city decline and poverty. But only recently has sprawl become the next great issue in American public life. That's

---

From Fred Siegel, "Is Regional Government the Answer?" Reprinted with permission from *The Public Interest*, No. 137 (Fall 1999), pp. 85–98. © 1999 by National Affairs, Inc.

because suburbanites themselves are now calling for limits to seemingly inexorable and frenetic development.

Slow-growth movements are a response to both the cyclical swings of the economy and the secular trend of dispersal. Each of the great postwar booms have, at their cyclical peak, produced calls for restraint. These sentiments have gained a wider hearing as each new upturn of the economy has produced an ever widening wave of exurban growth. A record 96 months of peacetime economic expansion has produced the strongest slow-growth movement to date. In 1998, antisprawl environmentalists and "not-in-my-backyard" slow-growth suburbanites joined forces across the nation to pass ballot measures restricting exurban growth.

Undoubtedly, the loss of land and the environmental degradation produced by sprawl are serious problems that demand public attention. But sprawl also brings enormous benefits as well as considerable costs. It is, in part, an expression of the new high-tech economy whose campus-like office parks on the periphery of urban areas have driven the economic boom of the 1990s. And it's sprawl that has sustained the record rise in home ownership. Sprawl is not some malignancy to be summarily excised but, rather, part and parcel of prosperity. Dealing with its ill effects requires both an understanding of the new landscape of the American economy and a willingness to make subtle trade-offs. We must learn to curb its worst effects without reducing the wealth and freedom that permit sprawl to develop.

Rising incomes and employment, combined with declining interest rates, have allowed a record number of people, including minority and immigrant families, to purchase homes for the first time. Home ownership among blacks, which is increasingly suburban, has risen at more than three times the white rate; a record 45 percent of African Americans owned their own homes in 1998. Nationally, an unprecedented 67 percent of Americans are homeowners.

Sprawl is part of the price we're paying for something novel in human history—the creation of a mass upper middle class. Net household worth has been increasing at the unparalleled annual rate of 10 percent since 1994, so that while in 1970, only 3.2 percent of households had an annual income of $100,000 (in today's dollars), by 1996, 8.2 percent of American households could boast a six-figure annual income. The new prosperity is reflected in the size of new homes, many of whose owners no doubt decry the arrival of still more "McMansions" and new residents, clogging the roads and schools of the latest subdivisions. In the midst of the 1980's boom, homebuilders didn't have a category for mass-produced houses of more than 3,000 square feet: By 1996, one out of every seven new homes built was larger than 3,000 square feet.

Today's Tenement Trail

Sprawl also reflects upward mobility for the aspiring lower-middle class. Nearly a half-century ago, Samuel Lubell dedicated *The Future of American Politics* to the memory of his mother, "who pioneered on the urban frontier." Lubell described a process parallel to the settling of the West, in which families on "the Old Tenement Trail" were continually on the move in search of a better life. In the cities, they abandoned crowded tenements on New York's Lower East Side for better housing in the South Bronx, and from there, went to the "West Bronx, crossing that Great Social Divide—the Grand Concourse—beyond which rolled true middle-class country where janitors were called superintendents."

Today's "tenement trail" takes aspiring working- and lower-middle class Americans to quite different areas. Kendall, Florida, 20 miles southeast of Miami, is every environmentalist's nightmare image of sprawl, a giant grid carved out of the muck of swamp land that encroaches on the Everglades. Stripmalls and mega-stores abound for mile after mile, as do the area's signature giant auto lots. Yet Kendall also represents a late-twentieth-century version of the Old Tenement Trail. Kendall, notes the *New Republic's* Charles Lane, is "the Queens of the late twentieth century," a place where immigrants are buying into America. Carved out of the palmetto wilderness, its population exploded from roughly 20,000 in 1970 to 300,000 today. Agricultural in the 1960s, and a hip place for young whites in the 1970s, Kendall grew increasingly Hispanic in the 1980s, as Cubans, Nicaraguans, and others who arrived with very little worked their way up. Today, it's half Hispanic and a remarkable example of integration. In most of Kendall, notes University of Miami geographer Peter Muller, "You can't point to a white or Latino block because the populations are so intermixed."

Virginia Postrel, the editor of *Reason*, argues that the slow-growth movement is animated by left-wing planners' hostility to suburbia. Others mock slow-growthers as elitists, as in the following quip:

Q: What's the difference between an environmentalist and a developer?
A: The environmentalist already has his house in the mountains.

But, in the 1990s, slow-growth sentiment has been taking hold in middle- and working-class suburbs like Kendall, as development turns into overdevelopment and traffic congestion becomes a daily problem.

Regional Government

One oft-proposed answer to sprawl has been larger regional governments that will exercise a monopoly on land-use decisions. Underlying this solution is the theory—no doubt correct—that sprawl is produced when individuals and townships seek to maximize their own advantage without regard for the good of the whole community. Regionalism, however, is stronger in logic than in practice. For example, the people of Kendall, rather than embracing regionalism, are looking to slow down growth by *seceding* from their regional government. Upon examination, we begin to see some of the problems with regional government.

Kendall is part of Metro-Dade, the oldest major regional government, created in 1957. The largest of its 29 municipalities, Miami, the fourth poorest city in the United States, has 350,000 people; the total population of Metro-Dade is 2 million, 1.1 million of whom live in unincorporated areas. In Metro-Dade, antisprawl and antiregional government sentiments merge. Despite county-imposed growth boundaries, residents have complained bitterly of overdevelopment. The county commissioners—many of whom have been convicted of, or charged with, corruption—have been highly receptive to the developers who are among their largest campaign contributors. As one south Florida resident said of the developers, "It's a lot cheaper to be able to buy just one government." The south Florida secessionists want to return zoning to local control where developers' clout is less likely to overwhelm neighborhood interests.

When Jane Jacobs wrote, in *The Death and Life of Great American Cities*, that "the voters sensibly decline to federate into a system where bigness means local helplessness, ruthless oversimplified planning and administrative chaos," she could have been writing about south Florida. What's striking about Metro-Dade is that it has delivered neither efficiency nor equity nor effective planning while squelching local self-determination.

The fight over Metro-Dade echoes the conflicts of an earlier era. Historically, the fight over regional versus local government was an important, if intermittent, issue for many cities from 1910 to 1970. From about 1850 to 1910, according to urban historian Jon Teaford, suburbanites were eager to be absorbed by cities whose wealth enabled them to build the water, sewage, and road systems they couldn't construct on their own. "The central city," he explains, "provided superior service at a lower cost." But, in the 1920s, well before race became a central issue, suburbanites, who had increasingly sorted themselves out by ethnicity and class, began to use special-service districts and innovative financial methods to provide their own infrastructure and turned away from unification. Suburbanites also denounced consolidation as an invitation to big-city, and often Catholic, "boss rule" and as a threat to "self-government."

In the 1960s, as black politicians began to win influence over big-city governments, they also joined the anticonsolidation chorus. At the same time, county government, once a sleepy extension of rural rule, was modernized, and county executives essentially became the mayors of full-service governments administering what were, in effect, dispersed cities. But they were mayors with a difference. Their constituents often wanted a balance between commercial development, which constrained the rise of taxes, and the suburban ideal of family-friendly semirural living. When development seemed too intrusive, suburban voters in the 1980s, and again in the 1990s, have pushed a slow-growth agenda.

The New Regionalism

In the 1990s, regionalism has been revived as an effort to link the problem of sprawl with the problem of inner-city poverty. Assuming that "flight creates blight," regionalists propose to recapture the revenue of those who have fled the cities and force growth back into older areas by creating regional or metropolitan-area governments with control over land use and taxation.

The new regionalism owes a great deal to a group of circuit-riding reformers. Inspired by the arguments of scholars like Anthony Downs, one of the authors of the Kerner Commission report, and sociologist William Julius Wilson of Harvard, as well as the example of Portland, Oregon's metro-wide government, these itinerant preachers have traveled to hundreds of cities to spread the gospel of regional cooperation. The three most prominent new regionalists—columnist Neil Peirce, former Albuquerque mayor David Rusk, and Minnesota state representative Myron Orfield—have developed a series of distinct, but overlapping, arguments for why cities can't help themselves, and why regional solutions are necessary.

Peirce, in his book *Citistates*, plausibly insists that regions are the real units of competition in the global economy, so that there is a metro-wide imperative to revive the central city, lest the entire area be undermined. Less plausibly, Orfield in *Metropolitics* argues that what he calls "the favored quarter" of fast-growing suburbs on the periphery of the metro area have prospered at the expense of both the central city and the inner-ring suburbs. In order both to revive the central city and save the inner suburbs from decline, Orfield proposes that these two areas join forces, redistributing money from the "favored quarter" to the older areas. Rusk argues, in *Baltimore Unbound*, that older cities, unable to annex the fast growing suburbs, are doomed to further decline. He insists that only "flexible cities"—that is, cities capable of expanding geographically and capturing the wealth of the suburbs—can truly deal with inner-city black poverty. Regionalism, writes Rusk, is "the new civil rights movement."

There are differences among them. Orfield and, to a lesser degree, Rusk operate on a zero-sum model in which gain for the suburbs comes directly at the expense of the central city. Peirce is less radical, proposing regional cooperation as the means to a win-win situation for both city and the surrounding region. But they all share a desire to disperse poverty across the region and, more importantly, recentralize economic growth in the already built-up areas. The latter goal is consistent with both the environmental thrust of the antisprawl movement and the push for regional government. In a speech to a Kansas City civic organization, Rusk laid out the central assumption of the new regionalism. "The greater the fragmentation of governments," he asserted, "the greater the fragmentation of society by race and economic class." Fewer governments, argue the new regionalists, will yield a number of benefits, including better opportunities for regional cooperation, more money for cash-strapped central cities, less racial inequality, less sprawl, and greater economic growth. However, all of these propositions are questionable.

Better Policies, Not Fewer Governments

Consider Baltimore and Philadelphia, cities that the regionalists have studied thoroughly. According to the 1998 *Greater Baltimore State of the Region* report, Philadelphia has 877 units of local government (including school boards)—or 17.8 per 100,000 people. Baltimore has only six government units of any consequence in Baltimore City and the five surrounding counties—or 2.8 per 100,000 people. Greater Baltimore has fewer government units than any other major metro area in the United States. As a political analyst told me: "Get six people in a room, and you have the government of 2,200 square miles, because the county execs have very strong powers." We might expect considerable regional cooperation in Baltimore, but not in Philadelphia. Regionalism has made no headway in either city, however. The failure has little to do with the number of governments and a great deal to do with failed policy choices in both cities.

Rusk does not mention the many failings of Baltimore's city government. He refers to the current mayor, Kurt Schmoke, just once and only to say that Baltimore has had "excellent political leadership." In Rusk's view, Baltimore is "programmed to fail" because of factors entirely beyond its control, namely, the inability to annex its successful suburbs. In the ahistorical world of the regionalist (and here, Peirce is a partial exception), people are always pulled from the city by structural forces but never pushed from the city by bad policies.

Baltimore is not as well financed as the District of Columbia, which ruined itself despite a surfeit of money. But Baltimore, a favorite political son of both Annapolis and

Washington, has been blessed with abundant financial support. Over the past decade, Schmoke has increased spending on education and health by over a half-billion dollars. He has also added 200 police officers and spent $60 million more for police over the last four years. "His greatest skill," notes the *Baltimore Sun*, "has been his ability to attract more federal and state aid while subsidies diminished elsewhere." But, notwithstanding these expenditures, middle-class families continue to flee the city at the rate of 1,000 per month, helping to produce the sprawl environmentalists decry.

Little in Baltimore works well. The schools have been taken over by the state, while the Housing Authority is mired in perpetual scandal and corruption. Baltimore is one of the few cities where crime hasn't gone down. That's because Schmoke has insisted, contrary to the experiences of New York and other cities, that drug-related crime could not be reduced until drug use was controlled through treatment. The upshot is that New York, with eight times more people than Baltimore, has only twice as many murders. Baltimore also leads the country in sexually transmitted diseases. These diseases have flourished among the city's drug users partly owing to Schmoke's de facto decriminalization of drugs. According to the Centers for Disease Control and Prevention (CDC), Baltimore has a syphilis rate 18 times the national average, 3 or 4 times as high as areas where the STD epidemic is most concentrated.

Flexible Cities

Rusk attributes extraordinary qualities to flexible cities. He says that they are able to both reduce inequality, curb sprawl, and maintain vital downtowns. Rusk was the mayor of Albuquerque, a flexible city that annexed a vast area, even as its downtown essentially died. The reduced inequality he speaks of is largely a statistical artifact. If New York were to annex Scarsdale, East New York's average income would rise without having any effect on the lives of the people who live there. As for sprawl, flexible cities like Phoenix and Houston are hardly models.

A recent article for *Urban Affairs Review*, by Subhrajit Guhathakurta and Michele Wichert, showed that within the elastic city of Phoenix, inner-city residents poorer than their outer-ring neighbors are subsidizing the building of new developments on the fringes of the metropolis. While sprawl is correlated with downtown decline in Albuquerque, in Phoenix it's connected with what *Fortune* described as "the remarkable rebound of downtown Phoenix, which has become a chic after-dark destination as well as a residential hot spot." There seems to be no automatic connection between regionalism and downtown revival.

Orfield's *Metropolitics* provides another version of an over-determined structuralist argument. According to him, the favored quarter is sucking the inner-city dry, and, as a result, central-city blight will inevitably engulf the older first-ring suburbs as well. He is right to see strong pressures on the inner-ring suburbs, stemming from an aging housing stock and population as well as an influx of inner-city poor. But it is how the inner-ring suburbs respond to these pressures that will affect their fate.

When Coleman Young was mayor of Detroit, large sections of the city returned to prairie. But the inner-ring suburbs have done fairly well precisely by not imitating Detroit's practice of providing poor services at premium prices. "Much like the new edge suburbs," explains the *Detroit News*, "older suburbs that follow the proven formula of promoting good schools, public safety and well-kept housing attract new investment." Suburban Mayor Michael Guido sees his city's well developed infrastructure as an asset, which has already been bought and paid for. "Now," says Mayor Guido, "it's a matter of maintenance . . . and we offer a sense of history and a sense of community. That's really important to people, to have a sense of belonging to a whole community rather than a subdivision."

Suburb Power

City-suburban relations are not fixed; they are various depending on the policies both follow. Some suburbs compete with the central city for business. In south Florida, Coral Gables more than holds its own with Miami as a site for business headquarters. Southfield, just outside Detroit, and Clayton, just outside St. Louis, blossomed in the wake of the 1960s' urban riots and now compete with their downtowns. Aurora, with a population of more than 160,000 and to the east of Denver, sees itself as a competitor, and it sees regional efforts at growth management as a means by which the downtown Denver elite can ward off competition.

Suburban growth can also help the central city. In the Philadelphia area, economic growth and new work come largely from the Route 202 high-tech corridor in Chester County, west of the city. While the city has lost 57,000 jobs, even in the midst of national economic prosperity, the fast growing Route 202 companies have been an important source of downtown legal and accounting jobs. At the same time, the suburbs are creating jobs for residents that the central city cannot produce, so that 20 percent of city residents commute to the suburbs while 15 percent of people who live in the suburbs commute to Philadelphia.

The "new regionalists" assume that the prosperity of the edge cities is a function of inner-city decline. But, in many cities, it is more nearly the case that suburban booms are part of what's keeping the central-city economy alive. It is the edge cities that have taken up the time-honored urban task of creating new work.

According to *INC* magazine, the 500 fastest growing small companies are all located in suburbs and exurbs. This is because local governments there are very responsive to the needs of start-up companies. These high-tech hotbeds, dubbed "nerdistans" by Joel Kotkin, are composed of networks of companies that are sometimes partners, sometimes competitors. They provide a pool of seasoned talent for start-ups, where engineers and techies who prefer the orderly, outdoor life of suburbia to the crowds and disorder of the city can move from project to project. Henry Nicholas, CEO of Broadcom, a communications-chip and cable-modem maker, explained why he reluctantly moved to Irvine: "It's hard to relocate techies to L.A. It's the congestion, the expensive housing—and there's a certain stigma to it."

Imagine what the United States would be like if the Bay Area had followed the New York model. In 1898, New York created the first regional government when it consolidated all the areas of the New York harbor—Manhattan, Brooklyn, Queens, the Bronx, and Staten Island—into the then-largest city in the world. The consolidation has worked splendidly for Manhattan, which thrives as a capital of high-end financial and legal services. But over time, the Manhattan-centric economy based on high taxes, heavy social spending, and extensive economic regulation destroyed Brooklyn's once vital shipping and manufacturing economy.

In 1912, San Francisco, the Manhattan of Northern California, proposed to create a unified regional government by incorporating Oakland in the East Bay and San Jose in the South. The plan for a Greater San Francisco was modeled on Greater New York and called for the creation of self-governing boroughs within an enlarged city and county of San Francisco. East Bay opposition defeated the San Francisco expansion in the legislature, and later attempts at consolidation in 1917, 1923, and 1928 also failed. But had San Francisco with its traditions of high taxation and heavy regulation succeeded, Silicon Valley might never have become one of the engines of the American economy. Similarly, it's no accident that the Massachusetts Route 128 high-tech corridor is located outside of the boundaries of Boston, even as it enriches the central city.

The Portland Model

The complex and often ironic history of existing regional governments has been obscured by the bright light of hope emanating from Portland. It seems that in every generation one city is said to have perfected the magic elixir for revival. In the 1950s, it was Philadelphia; today, it's Portland. In recent years, hundreds of city officials have traveled to Portland to study its metropolitan government, comprehensive environmental planning, and the urban-growth boundary that has been credited with Portland's revival and success.

While there are important lessons to be learned from Portland, very little of its success to date can be directly attributed to the growth boundary, which was introduced too recently and with boundaries so capacious as not yet to have had much effect. Thirty-five percent of the land within the boundary was vacant when it was imposed in 1979. And, at the same time, fast growing Clark County, just north of Portland but not part of the urban-growth boundary, has provided an escape valve for potential housing pressures. The upshot, notes demographer Wendell Cox, is that even with the growth boundary, Portland still remains a relatively low-density area with fewer people per square mile than San Diego, San Jose, or Sacramento.

Portland has also been run with honesty and efficiency, unlike Metro-Dade. Blessed with great natural resources, Portland—sometimes dubbed "Silicon forest," because chipmakers are drawn to its vast quantities of cheap clean water—has conserved its man-made as well as natural resources. A city with more cast-iron buildings than any place outside of Manhattan, it has been a leader in historic preservation. Time and again, Portland's leadership has made the right choices. It was one of the first cities to reconnect its downtown with the riverfront. Portland never built a circumferential freeway. And, in the 1970s, under the leadership of Mayor Neil Goldschmidt, the city vetoed a number of proposed highway projects that would have threatened the downtown.

In 1978, Portland voters, in conjunction with the state government, created the first directly elected metropolitan government with the power to manage growth over three counties. Portland metro government has banned big-box retailers, like Walmart and Price Club, on the grounds that they demand too much space and encourage too much driving. This is certainly an interesting experiment well worth watching, but should other cities emulate Portland's land-management model? It's too soon to say.

Good government is always important. But aside from that, it's hard to draw any general lessons from the Portland experience. The growth boundaries may or may not work, and there's certainly no reason to think that playing with political boundaries will bring good government to Baltimore.

Living with Sprawl

What then is to be done? First, we can accept the consensus that has developed around preserving open space, despite some contradictory effects. The greenbelts around London, Portland, and Baltimore County pushed some development back toward the city and encouraged further sprawl as growth leapfrogged the open space. The push to preserve open space is only likely to grow stronger as continued growth generates both more congestion and more wealth, which can be used to buy up open land.

Secondly, we can create what Peter Salins, writing in *The Public Interest*[1] described as a "level playing field" between the central cities and the suburbs. This can be done by ending exurban growth subsidies for both transportation as well as new water and sewer lines. These measures might further encourage the revival of interest in old fashioned Main Street living, which is already attracting a new niche of home buyers. State and local governments can also repeal the land-use and zoning regulations that discourage mixed-use development of the sort that produces a clustering of housing around Main Street and unsubsidized low-cost housing in the apartments above the streets' shops.

Because of our strong traditions of local self-government, regionalism has been described as an unnatural act among consenting jurisdictions. But regional cooperation needn't mean the heavy hand of all-encompassing regional government. There are some modest, but promising, experiments already under way in regional revenue sharing whose effects should be carefully evaluated. Allegheny County, which includes Pittsburgh, has created a Regional Asset District that uses a 1 percent sales tax increase to support cultural institutions and reduce other taxes. The Twin Cities have put money derived from the increase in assessed value of commercial and industrial properties into a pot to aid fiscally weaker municipalities. Kansas and Missouri created a cultural district that levies a small increase in the sales tax across the region. The money is being used to rehabilitate the area's most treasured architectural landmark, Kansas City's Union Station.

Cities and suburbs do have some shared interests, as in the growing practice of reverse commuting which links inner-city residents looking to get off welfare with fast growing suburban areas hampered by a shortage of labor. Regionalism can curb sprawl and integrate and sustain central-city populations if it reforms the misguided policies and politics that have sent the black and white middle class streaming out of cities like Baltimore, Washington, and Philadelphia. Regional cooperation between the sprawling high-tech suburbs and the central cities could modernize cities that are in danger of being left further behind by the digital economy. In that vein, the District of Columbia's Mayor Anthony Williams seized on the importance of connecting his welfare population with the fast growing areas of Fairfax County in Northern Virginia. The aim of focused regional policies, argues former HUD Undersecretary Marc Weiss, should be economic, not political, integration.

Sprawl isn't some malignancy that can be surgically removed. It's been part and parcel of healthy growth, and curbing it involves difficult tradeoffs best worked out locally. Sprawl and the movement against sprawl are now a permanent part of the landscape. The future is summed up in a quip attributed to former Oregon Governor Tom McCall, who was instrumental in creating Portland's growth boundary. "Oregonians," he said, "are against two things, sprawl and density."

24

Peter Calthorpe and William Fulton

THE REGION IS THE NEIGHBORHOOD
Sprawl and the New Urbanism

At the heart of creating concrete visions for the Regional City is the notion that they can be "designed." We use the term "design" not in the typical sense of artistically configuring a physical form but to imply a process that synthesizes many disciplines. Regional design is an act that integrates multiple facets at once: the demands of the region's ecology, its economy, its history, its politics, its regulations, its culture, and its social structure. And its results are specific physical forms as well as abstract goals and policies—regional maps and neighborhood urban design standards as well as implementation strategies, governmental policies, and financing mechanisms.

Too often we plan and engineer rather than design. Engineering tends to optimize isolated elements without regard for the larger system, whereas planning tends to be ambiguous, leaving the critical details of place making to chance. If we merely plan and engineer, we forfeit the possibility of developing a "whole systems" approach or a "design" that recognizes the trade-offs between isolated efficiencies and integrated parts.

The engineering mentality often reduces complex, multifaceted problems to one measurable dimension. For example, traffic engineers optimize road size for auto capacity without considering the trade-off of neighborhood scale, walkability, or beauty. Civil engineers efficiently channelize our streams without considering recreational, ecological, or esthetic values. Commercial developers optimize the delivery of goods without balancing the social need of neighborhoods for local identity and meeting places. Again and again we sacrifice the synergy of the whole for the efficiency of the parts.

The idea that a region or even a neighborhood could or should be "designed" is central to creating the Regional City. We need to acknowledge that we can direct our growth and that such action can include complex trade-offs as well as unexpected synergies. The common impression is that our neighborhoods, towns, or regions evolve organically (and somewhat mysteriously). They are the product of invisible market forces or the summation of technical imperatives. There also is the illusion that these forces cannot and should not be tampered with. Planning failed in the past; therefore it will fail in the future.

The real illusion, of course, is that we cannot control the form of our communities. Historically, design played a large role in shaping our forms of settlement. The template that underlies much of our suburban growth was designed in the thirties by Frank Lloyd Wright with his Broadacre Cities plans and Clarence Stein's Greenbelt towns. These were then bastardized and codified by the HUD minimum property standards of the 1950s. The template for urban redevelopment was developed about the same time by Le Corbusier and a European group of architects called CIAM (Congres Internationaux d'Architecture Moderne). Their vision of superblocks and high-rise development became the basis of our urban renewal programs of the 1960s.

The problem is not that our suburbs and cities are lacking design but that they are designed according to failed principles with flawed implementation. They are designed in accord with modernist principles and implemented by specialists. The modernist principles of specialization, standardization, and mass production in emulating our industrial economy had a severe effect on the character of our neighborhoods and regions.

At the neighborhood scale, specialization meant that each land use— residential, retail, commercial, or civic—was isolated and developed by "experts" who optimized their particular zones without any responsibility for the whole. Regional specialization meant that each area within the region could play an independent role: suburbs for the middle class and new businesses, cities for the poor and declining industries, and countryside for nature and agriculture.

As a complement to specialization, standardization led to the homogenization of our communities, a blindness to history and the demise of unique ecological systems. A "one size fits all" mentality of efficiency overrode the special qualities of place and community.

Mass production (in housing, transportation, offices, and so forth) upends the delicate balance between local enterprise, regional systems, and global networks. The logic of mass production moves relentlessly toward ever-increasing scales, which in turn reinforces the specialization and standardization of everyday life.

Against this modern alliance of specialization, standardization, and mass production stands a set of principles rooted more in ecology than in mechanics. They are the principles of diversity, conservation, and human scale. Diversity at each scale calls for more complex, differentiated communities shaped from the unique qualities of place and history. Conservation implies care for existing resources whether natural, social, or institutional. And the principle of human scale brings the individual back into a picture increasingly fashioned around remote and mechanistic concerns.

These alternative principles apply equally to the social, economic, and physical dimensions of communities. For example, the social implications of human scale may mean more police officers walking a beat rather than hovering overhead in a helicopter; the economic implications of human scale may mean economic policies that support small local business rather than major industries and corporations; and the physical implications of human scale may be realized in the form and detail of buildings as they relate to the street. Unlike the standard governmental categories of economic development, housing, education, and health services, each of these design principles incorporates physical design, social programs, and economic strategies. These principles, then, are the ones that we believe should form the foundation of a new regional and neighborhood design ethic.

Human Scale

For several generations, the design of buildings, the planning of communities, and the growth of our institutions have exemplified the view that "bigger is better." Efficiency was correlated with large, centralized organizations and processes. Now the idea of de-centralized networks of smaller working groups and more personalized institutions is gaining currency in both government and business. Efficiency is correlated with nim-ble, small working groups, not large hierarchical institutions.

Certainly, the reality of our time is a complex mix of both of these trends. For ex-ample, we have ever-larger retail outlets at the same time that Main Streets are making a comeback. Some businesses are growing larger and more centralized while the "new economy" is bursting with small-scale start-ups and intimate working groups. Housing production is diversifying home types at the same time that it consolidates into larger financing packages. Both directions are evolving at the same time, and the shape of our communities will have to accommodate this complex reality.

Yet people are reacting to an imbalance between these two forces. The building blocks of our communities—schools, local shopping areas, housing subdivisions, apart-ment complexes, and office parks—have all grown into forms that defy human scale. And we are witnessing a reaction to this lack of scale in many ways. People uniformly long for an architecture that puts detail and identity back into what have too often be-come generic, if functional, buildings. They desire the character and scale of a walkable street, complete with shade trees and buildings that orient windows and entries their way. They idealize Main Street shopping areas and historic urban districts.

Human scale is a design principle that responds simultaneously to simple human desires and the emerging ethos of the new decentralized economies. The focus on hu-man scale represents a shift away from top-down social programs, from characterless housing projects, and from more and more remote institutions. In its most concrete ex-pression, human scale is the stoop of a townhouse or the front porch of a home rather than the stairwell of a high-rise or the garage door of a tract home. Human scale in eco-nomics means supporting individual entrepreneurs and local businesses. Human scale in community means a strong neighborhood focus and an environment that encourages everyday interaction.

Diversity

Diversity has multiple meanings and profound implications. It has the most challeng-ing implications for the social, environmental, and economic dimensions of community planning. Perhaps its most obvious outcome is the creation of communities that are di-verse in use and in population. As a planning axiom, it calls for a return to mixed-use neighborhoods that contain a broad range of uses as well as a broad range of housing types and people.

The four fundamental elements of community—civic places, commercial uses, hous-ing opportunities, and natural systems—define the physical elements of diversity at any scale. As a physical principle, diversity in neighborhoods ensures that destinations are close at hand and that the shared institutions of community are integrated. It also implies an architecture rich in character and streetscapes that vary with place and use.

As a social principle, diversity is controversial and perhaps the most challenging of all. It implies creating neighborhoods that provide for a large range in age group, household type, income, and race. As already stated, neighborhoods have always (to a greater or lesser degree) been defined by commonalties even if energized by differences. But today we have reached an extreme: age, income, family size, and race are all divided into discrete market segments and locations that are built independently. Complete housing integration may be a distant goal, but inclusive neighborhoods that broaden the economic range, expand the mix of age and household types, and open the door to racial integration are feasible and desirable.

Diversity is a principle with significant economic implications. Gone are the days when economic-revitalization efforts focused on a single industry or a major governmental program. A more ecological understanding of industry clusters has emerged. This sensibility validates the notion that a range of complementary but differing enterprises (large and small, local, regional, and global) are important to maintaining a robust economy, and that now more than ever, the quality of life and the urbanism of a place, as well as the more traditional economic factors, play a significant role in the emerging economy.

Finally, diversity is a fundamental principle that can help to guide the preservation of local and regional ecologies. Clearly, understanding the complex nature of the existing or stressed habitats and watershed systems mandates a different approach to open-space planning. Active recreation, agriculture, and habitat preservation are often at odds. A broad range of open-space types, from the most active to the most passive, must be integrated in neighborhood and regional designs. Diversity in use, diversity in population, diversity in enterprise, and diversity in natural systems are fundamental to the Regional City.

Conservation

Conservation implies many things in community design beyond husbanding resources and protecting natural systems; it implies preserving and restoring the cultural, historic, and architectural assets of a place as well. Conservation calls for designing communities and buildings that require fewer resources—less energy, less land, less waste, and fewer materials, but it also implies caring for what we have and developing an ethic of reuse and repair—in both our physical and our social realms.

The principle of conservation and its complements, restoration and preservation, should be applied to the built environment as well as to the natural environment—not only to our historic building stock and neighborhood institutions, but also to human resources and human history. Communities should strive to conserve their cultural identity, physical history, and unique natural systems. Restoration and conservation are more than environmental themes; they are an approach to the way that we think about community at the regional and local levels.

Conserving resources has many obvious implications in community planning. Foremost are the quantities of farmlands and natural systems displaced by sprawling development and the quantity of auto travel required to support it. Even within more compact, walkable communities, conservation of resources can lead to new design strategies. The preservation of waterways and on-site water-treatment systems can add identity and natural amenities at the same time that they conserve water quality. Energy-conservation strategies in buildings often lead to environments that are climate responsive and unique to place.

Conserving the historic buildings and institutions of a neighborhood can preserve the icons of community identity. Restoring and enhancing the vernacular architecture of a place can simultaneously reduce energy costs, reestablish local history, and create jobs. Although the preservation movement has made great strides with landmark buildings, it is correct now in extending its agenda beyond building facades to the social fabric of neighborhoods and to the ecology of the communities that are the lifeblood of historic districts.

Conserving human resources is another implication of this fundamental principle. In too many of our communities, poverty, lack of education, and declining job opportunities lead to a tragic waste of human potential. As we have begun to see, communities are not viable when concentrations of poverty turn them into a wasteland of despair and crime. In this context, "conservation" takes on a larger meaning—the restoration and rehabilitation of human potential wherever it is being squandered and overlooked. There should be no natural or cultural environments that are disposable or marginalized. Conservation and restoration are practical undertakings that can be economically strengthening and socially enriching.

Designing the Region Is Designing the Neighborhood

What happens to regions or neighborhoods if they are "designed" according to these principles? An interesting set of parallel design strategies emerges at both the regional and the neighborhood levels. First and foremost, the region and its elements—the city, suburbs, and their natural environment—should be conceived as a unit, just as the neighborhood and its elements—housing, shops, open space, civic institutions, and businesses—should be designed as a unit. Treating each element separately is endemic to many of the problems that we now face. Just as a neighborhood needs to be developed as a whole system, the region must be treated as an human ecosystem, not a mechanical assembly.

Seen as this integrated whole, the region can be designed in much the same way as we would design a neighborhood. That the whole, the region, would be similar to its most basic pieces, its neighborhoods, is an important analogy. Both need protected natural systems, vibrant centers, human-scale circulation systems, a common civic realm, and integrated diversity. Developing such an architecture for the region creates the context for healthy neighborhoods, districts, and city centers. Developing such an architecture for the neighborhood creates the context for regions that are sustainable, integrated, and coherent. The two scales have parallel features that reinforce one another.

Major open-space corridors within the region, such as rivers, ridge lands, wetlands, or forests, can be seen as a "village green" at a megascale—the commons of the region. These natural commons establish an ecological identity as the basis of a region's character. Similarly, the natural systems and shared open spaces at the neighborhood scale are fundamental to its identity and character. A neighborhood's natural systems, like the region's, are as much a part of its commons as its civic institutions or commercial center.

Just as a neighborhood needs a vital center to serve as the crossroads of a local community, the region needs a vital central city to serve as its cultural heart and as a link to the global economy. In the Edge City metropolis, both types of centers are failing. In the suburbs, what were village centers of human proportions are overcome by remote discount centers and relentless commercial strips. In the central cities, poverty and disinvestment errode historic neighborhood communities. Both fall prey to specialized enterprises oriented to mass distribution rather than the local community. Like the commons, healthy centers, both urban and suburban, are fundamental to local and regional coherence.

Regional and neighborhood design has other parallels. Pedestrian scale within the neighborhood—walkable streets and nearby destinations—has a partner in transit systems at the regional scale. Transit can organize the region in much the same way as a street network orders a neighborhood. Transit lines focus growth and redevelopment in the region just as main streets can focus a neighborhood. Crossing local and metropolitan scales, transit supports the life of the pedestrian within each neighborhood and district by providing access to regional destinations. In a complementary fashion, pedestrian-friendly neighborhoods support transit by providing easy access for riders, not cars. The two scales, if designed as parallel strategies, reinforce each other.

As we have pointed out, diversity is a fundamental design principle for both the neighborhood and the region. A diverse population and job base within a region supports a resilient economy and a rich culture in much the same way that diverse uses and housing in a neighborhood support a complex and active community. The suburban trend to segregate development by age and income translates at the regional level into an increasing spatial and economic polarization—the "secession of the successful," as Robert Reich articulated in *The Work of Nations*. Both trends can be countered by policies that support inclusionary housing and mixed-use environments.

These parallels across scales are not merely coincidence. The fundamental nature of a culture and economy expresses itself at many scales simultaneously. Sprawl and our lack of regional structure is a manifestation of an older and quite different paradigm. Since World War II, our economy and culture have accelerated their movement toward the industrial qualities of mass production, standardization, and specialization. The massive suburbanization that marks this period is the direct expression of these qualities. As a counterpoint, the principles and concurrences just outlined define a new paradigm of community and growth, one that leads from the Edge City to the Regional City.

CHAPTER 8

FEDERAL-CITY RELATIONS AND THE CAPACITY TO GOVERN

URBAN POLITICS IN A DECENTRALIZED FEDERAL SYSTEM

For more than two decades, federal policymakers have been shedding their responsibilities for urban programs and have been moving the responsibility for implementing important programs onto cities. Local public officials are searching for ways of managing their new roles while absorbing the shock waves caused by profound changes in their populations, economies, and political environments. How can localities best respond? In what direction is intergovernmental politics evolving after years of decentralization?

In Selection 25, Pietro Nivola points out that the hand of the federal government in local affairs remains a large and growing presence despite declining national financial assistance to localities. He argues that Congress is inclined to pass laws that force local governments to undertake new responsibilities without providing financial help in carrying out these mandates. Further, he argues that federal laws and judicial decisions are regulating matters that were left to local decision makers in the past. He describes how national prescriptions frequently deal with the minutiae of local affairs, such as requiring bright, standard-size yellow lines to separate drivers and passengers on school buses. He concedes that some national prohibitions and regulations are necessary when problems spill over local governmental boundaries, but asserts that many federal mandates go beyond that. According to Nivola, one-size-fits-all federal standards are becoming so ubiquitous that they undermine the ability of local officials to find sensible and effective solutions to their problems. Nivola reaches the conclusion that less national government would be better for all cities, but especially for central cities that disproportionately pay the legal bills and compliance costs that are generated by misplaced national regulations.

In the wake of Hurricane Katrina, which struck New Orleans in August 2005, and the attack on the World Trade Center in New York on September 11, 2001, a debate has broken out concerning the question of how local, state, and federal governments should prepare for, respond to, and recover from such disasters. In Selection 26, Stephen D. Stehr suggests that much is known about how to make cities and regions safer, but that political and economic calculations often make effective responses difficult. An inherent problem is that the mitigation of disasters is likely to be the responsibility of local governments, while the economic costs of recovery and reconstruction are borne by higher-level governments, especially the federal government. He asserts that local governments have few incentives to make preparedness for disasters or their mitigation high priorities because federal governmental programs and private insurance will provide assistance if and when the disaster occurs.

Stehr also believes that political pressures at all levels of government confound rational planning for disasters. The competition for local development encourages cities to give greater attention to economic growth, rather than to public safety and disaster recovery. Federal governmental attention to homeland security in an age of terrorism often diminishes interest of federal officials in planning for natural disasters even though they may be more likely to happen than terrorist events. Stehr concludes that the vulnerability of cities to disasters is essentially a political matter determined by the dominant narrative or interpretation of how such events should be managed.

Stehr's conclusion resonates in Selection 27. Since the devastation of New Orleans by Hurricane Katrina in August 2005, the beleaguered city still struggles to rebuild and recover. Peter F. Burns and Matthew O. Thomas describe how the impact of the disaster has not pulled the various political players at the state and local levels closer together in support of recovery efforts. This continues despite the suffering and losses to the city.

Burns and Thomas describe how the emergency brought opportunities for state and local political leaders as well as citizens to cooperate to change certain aspects of governance. This sometimes led to successful policy innovations, particularly in education. Nevertheless, lack of cooperation between the state and the city has generally prevailed in coping with the consequences of the disaster. Friction between state and local officials persists over most big issues, including the political control of recovery programs, funding, policy priorities, as well as on issues of political corruption. This has happened because the hurricane did not change enduring sources of state-local political rivalry. Burns and Thomas describe a long history of deep intergovernmental distrust and tension over money, control, and policy priorities. State and city electorates also tend to voice important differences about how New Orleans should be treated, with Louisiana residents less interested than city residents in restoring the historic city's economic role. The authors underscore how competing and overlapping control of many aspects of the recovery process by state and city governmental agencies makes political conflict inevitable. Indeed, at one time four different commissions representing city and state power brokers simultaneously claimed to lead the planning of the city's recovery.

State-local relations have not always obstructed emergency programs in other states in previous disasters. There may be some singular features in the New Orleans experience that increase distrust between city and state governments there. Yet this case demonstrates that city politics intersects with federal and state governments especially during a crisis. Cities are essentially creatures of states; city politics is often state politics, especially during a crisis. The various governments invariably tangle over questions about what should be done in times of crisis.

What is the proper relationship between the federal government and the cities? Do cities possess the capacity to respond to all problems that may face them? Making cities face the burdens once shouldered by the federal government does not help them to generate the resources necessary for responding to such events as Hurricane Katrina and the terrorist attacks; clearly, much of New Orleans's problem can be traced to the chronically dire straits of the city budget. Sometimes local governments demonstrate the capacity to respond; sometimes they clearly do not. There are problems that can overwhelm any local government, no matter how competently it may be run. This is an important problem in the American system of local government.

25

Pietro S. Nivola

FEDERAL PRESCRIPTIONS AND CITY PROBLEMS

It would be nice if America's local governments had a consistent history of good conduct. In reality much has gone wrong—at times so wrong any fair observer would have welcomed or at least understood an extensive federal usurpation of local powers. Think about the following episodes from various cities.

On the evening of May 31, 1921, a lynch mob in Tulsa, Oklahoma, descended on the municipal courthouse in search of a black man who had been charged with (and later acquitted of) raping a white woman.[1] After an altercation at the courthouse the mob invaded the city's black neighborhood, destroying thirty-five square blocks and murdering hundreds of residents. At one downtown location 123 blacks were found clubbed to death. How did city and state authorities respond as the bloodbath unfolded? The Tulsa police department deputized large numbers of the white vigilantes and, according to an account citing court records from the time, instructed them to "go out and kill." The state of Oklahoma appointed a Tulsa Race Riot Commission to launch an investigation— more than three-quarters of a century later.

In 1975 a strange thing happened: New York, the biggest city in the world's richest nation, neared bankruptcy. The sources of this fiscal crisis were complex, but at least one root cause was unmistakable: New York had spent beyond its means on redistributive social services.[2] This municipal welfare state could no longer be sustained by its vulnerable local tax base.

More recently the Atlanta metropolitan area has been experiencing a buildup of air pollution.[3] Along the eastern seaboard of the United States no metropolis belches more smog than Atlanta. It has one of the dirtiest coal-fired power plants in the country, and emission levels of nitrous oxides from motor vehicles have regularly exceeded the Environmental Protection Agency's (EPA) caps and projections. The local political establishment, however, has been slow to act. While Draconian steps such as ordering a four-day work week were rightly rejected, so were more modest proposals—like charging for parking spaces and converting to cleaner fuels. The idea of cleaner fuel, which implied a slight increase in energy prices, caused consternation in the Georgia legislature.

In 1989 a well-known journalist, staunchly committed to public education, described a problem his son experienced in a classroom of the public school system of the city in which they resided. "One of my children," the journalist wrote, "spent a year with an elementary school science teacher who had been shifted from teaching English. She was fully 'qualified' to teach, since she had her credentials, but she knew less about science than most of the children did."[4] One of the things this qualified science teacher did not know was how the moon revolved around the earth.

The Trouble with Localism

The derelictions of local government range from the barbaric to the regrettable, the irresponsible, and the merely ridiculous. What they imply, though, is that in the absence of enforced national standards some self-governed communities have proved capable of sinking below the most elementary regard for public competency, environmental safeguards, financial prudence, or even basic human rights.

The account about the public school teacher who did not understand the orbit of the moon was hardly unique. Reports of this sort or worse are sufficiently common to stir calls for national education standards. Nor was the Tulsa race riot of 1921 an isolated incident. In a wave of hysteria about rumored rapes of whites by blacks during the 1920s racial violence erupted in cities across the country.[5] The federal government may not have had at its disposal sufficient statutory powers to quell these atrocities or even to prosecute their perpetrators. Would that it had.

In the case of Atlanta's polluted atmosphere the argument for national "hammers" to compel an end to the local policy paralysis went beyond a need to protect the region's residents from possible health risks. Air pollution crosses boundaries. Concentrations of ozone can drift across hundreds of square miles. One place's foul air pollutes another region's water.[6] Why should people living in other jurisdictions have to inhale or swallow the poisons spewing from a neighboring urban area whose citizens year after year are not curtailing their wide-ranging effluents?

As Madison warned in *Federalist No. 10*, the inertia of local government has to do, at least in part, with the ability of entrenched interests to capture small polities: how can municipal school systems reinvent themselves when their administrations remain in the grip of obstructive teachers' unions? Will a one-company town, whose factory is the local economy's mainstay but also its worst polluter, put in a fix? Localism begets freeloading. When some jurisdictions become welfare magnets, others are tempted to lower their benefits below an acceptable minimum. A city or state whose contaminated air or water flows downstream to neighboring cities or states has little incentive to control the spillover for their sake. Indeed localities competing for business investment and taxable income might reciprocally "dumb down" standards.[7]

Clearly if interjurisdictional competition and externalities arbitrarily enrich certain communities at the expense of others or else draw too many into a "race to the bottom," or if local mismanagement is so endemic it corrupts the commonweal, or mischievous local factions egregiously violate the fundamental freedoms of citizens, the solution seems plain: "extend the sphere" of governance, as Madison recommended, shifting control from the "smaller" jurisdictions to "the Union."[8]

Mandating without Spending

In the past half-century most of this remedial enlargement of the national ambit has been purchased with federal dollars. As of 1990 nearly $120 billion in grants to state and local governments was being disbursed to patch alleged shortcomings of local policies in transportation, environmental protection, economic development, job training, education, public safety, and much more.[9] Because the purpose of this funding has not been to distribute unrestricted handouts but largely to make up for local deficiencies, receipt of the funds has been conditioned on compliance with a plethora of federal requirements. In theory those requirements could be ignored if the grantees simply turned down the money. In practice this became almost impossible. He who pays the piper calls the tune. New federal instructions are often affixed after the grant programs have been institutionalized. By then their constituencies are so well organized the programs have all but ceased to be voluntary. And typically the federal rules remain firmly in place even if congressional appropriations fall far short of authorizations. The local provision of special education for students with disabilities, for instance, is essentially governed by federal law, even though Congress has never even come close to appropriating its authorized share of this $43 billion-a-year mandate.

Federal grants feature these bait-and-switch dynamics because, despite considerable weaning during the past couple of decades, local governments remain dependent on whatever aid they can get. There are far fewer federal aid junkies today than twenty years ago (when more than three-quarters of the revenues in cities such as Detroit came from Washington), but federal aid remains a substantial source of state and local revenue, still exceeding in many places the proceeds from sales taxes or property taxes.

Going Off Budget

Paying the piper, however, is but one way of gaining influence. In recent decades the manner in which Washington exerts control changed. As the national government's deficits grew, and Congress's propensity to throw money at domestic programs bumped against budget caps, a tendency developed for the federal government to regulate local governments more stringently while aiding them less generously.[10] At the end of 1974 some forty federal mandates reflected this pattern. Twenty years later the number had grown by almost 160 percent (Figure 8.1).[11] Presidents Ronald Reagan and George Bush put up faint resistance to what the Advisory Commission on Intergovernmental Relations had come to call regulatory federalism, even in the realm of administrative rulemakings. Between 1981 and 1986 Reagan presided over the promulgation of some 140 agency rules that placed nearly six thousand new obligations on states and localities.[12]

To local entities, of course, many of these actions seemed unfair and irrational. To policymakers at the national level, however, there was method in the madness. Before a retrenchment commenced in the 1980s federal grant giving had gotten out of control. Between 1960 and 1980 expenditures increased one and a half times as fast as the growth of the economy. Funds were tossed hither and yon, sponsoring countless questionable "community development" needs—like the construction of a tennis complex in an affluent section of Little Rock, Arkansas, and the expansion of a municipal golf course in Alhambra, California.[13] Gradual curtailment of such waste after 1980 was a positive change regardless of whether a less profligate government might try to extend its influence by means of off-budget regulations.

Indeed, as the federal government applied the brakes to discretionary spending and eventually managed to bring a bloated budget into balance in the 1990s, inflation and interest rates fell, and the national economy surged. Federal austerity yielded by way of economic growth a large net gain for the nation and for the treasuries of most states and municipalities. With plenty of states and many cities now running

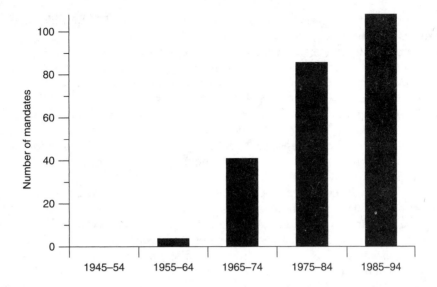

Figure 8.1 Federal Mandates on State and Local Governments, 1945–1994.

Source: National Conference of State Legislatures, as cited in Clyde Wayne Crews Jr., *Ten Thousand Commandments: A Policymaker's Snapshot of the Federal Regulatory State* (Washington: Competitive Enterprise Institute, September 1996), p. 17.

surpluses there was something to be said for devolving to them more chores and expenses.[14]

Passing responsibilities to local authorities can be fiscally prudent not only for the federal fisc but for society.[15] If local public works are mostly funded by Washington, their costs are harder to contain. States, cities, and counties do not print money; to spend they have to tax. Local resistance to taxation encourages cost consciousness.[16]

Stingy or Just Thriftier?

Local politicians wish Congress would simply shovel them cash and ask no questions. What the same politicians do not always acknowledge is that when Congress declines to write blank checks, and instead subjects state and local governments to uncompensated demands, some of the demands actually conform to local preferences.[17] A federal law that, say, asks states to administer particular licensing procedures for truck drivers using interstate highways is not an oppressive request if almost every state already has adopted, or willingly intends to adopt, essentially those same procedures. Hence, while the locals are often quick to say that, at a minimum, they should be paid back for the cost of meeting federal requirements, an indiscriminate policy of reimbursements would pose a moral hazard. States and municipalities that had been poised to take the desired actions anyhow would acquire an excuse to stop, sit back, and wait for federal payments.

Nor should taxpayers from afar be expected to indulge local governments that get themselves into trouble. In the early 1990s the governor of California, Pete Wilson, repeatedly complained that Washington was leaving his state too many of the burdens of servicing immigrants. In the next breath he insisted that his state had a rightful claim to hundreds of millions of dollars in federal disaster relief for property damage from earthquakes, floods, and mudslides, even in areas in which permissive California building regulations were substantially responsible for the losses.[18] The rotting rubbish at New York City's primary municipal dump discharges into the tri-state region not only one million gallons of polluted water each day but also large quantities of methane, a major contributor to global warming. People residing in Oregon or Oklahoma—or, for that matter, New Jersey and Connecticut—should not be taxed to detoxify the garbage New Yorkers generate. Efficiency and equity require that the polluters pay. Most federal environmental regulations operate on that logical principle.

Besides, though federal grants for mandatory pollution abatement have shrunk, other parts of the federal welfare state continued to support the nation's cities. Even during the Reagan years, the social safety net frayed less completely than many observers feared. Measured in constant dollars, federal welfare payments, Food Stamps, Medicaid, child nutrition, and supplemental feeding for women and children—all programs essential to cities—held up reasonably well between 1980 and 1990.[19]

Some would argue that the ability to deduct local property taxes and to exclude interest income earned by state and local debt instruments from the federal income tax represents a $70 billion concession to local control.[20] In 1988 the Supreme Court decided that Congress was free, if it wished, to tax the interest on municipal bonds.[21] Their tax-free status nonetheless has remained intact and continues to favor the beneficiaries with preferential rates of interest. The deductibility of local income and property taxes enables localities to raise more revenue than they otherwise could. Along with these constants at least one other remains in the equation: about half of the billions of dollars in revenues received annually from the sale of minerals, timber, and other commodities on public lands is shared with states and localities.

In sum in the United States as in any other country exactly what the central government "owes" subnational jurisdictions is a debatable matter. And certainly there are times when the Union, in Madisonian terms, has reason to take charge of local affairs—and can legitimately do so even without further indemnifying local governments.

The Yellow Line

But there also can be too much of a good thing.

Consider a small sample of the municipal functions now touched by national regulations. Federal law draws a line, commonly bright yellow, behind which passengers are forbidden to stand when they ride city buses. In many states, federal law may have a say in how firefighters should be deployed when fighting a fire. Federal law has influenced decisions about how long some unruly students in public schools can be suspended. Federal law has a bearing on how much a city pays for everything from snow removal services to contracts for sidewalk ramps. Federal law can affect whether the recruits for a police department are physically fit. Whether your child can walk to school or must commute by bus may depend on federal law. The degree to which a city's vacant industrial land parcels have to be cleared of toxic waste is dictated by federal law.

The salary your child's teacher is paid may be affected by federal law that reaches well beyond the national minimum wage. Federal law addresses what protective measures must be taken to secure municipal landfills, school buildings that contain asbestos, and housing units with lead paint. Federal law determines how a city has to purify its drinking water.

None of these examples are flights of fancy.

When charges for basic municipal services rise, personnel costs are typically the reason. In the wake of the Supreme Court's opinion in the 1985 case of *Garcia v. San Antonio Metropolitan Transit Authority* the entire local public sector became liable for retroactive pay to employees filing claims for overtime compensation.[22] Before that time, Congress had moved in 1974 to include state and local governments under the minimum wage and overtime pay provisions of the Fair Labor Standards Act, but two years later this exercise of the commerce clause power had been overturned.[23] *Garcia*, and the subsequent statutory reinstatement of FLSA coverage in the local public sector, can help explain the high cost of operating a fleet of city snowplows during a Sunday night snowstorm.

The Americans with Disabilities Act of 1990 (ADA) tells every municipality to install ramps so that streets and sidewalks can be wheelchair accessible. But when any federal funds help construct these special accommodations (or any other local public works projects) the Davis-Bacon Act, a vestige of the New Deal, requires that the municipal contracts go not to the lowest bidders but to those who pay the "prevailing" (that is, union negotiated) wage of laborers working comparable projects in the geographic vicinity.[24]

Antibias suits brought under the auspices of federal statutes are now so pervasive they shape the employment practices of every municipal agency. Sometimes this litigation appears to have discouraged police departments from testing rigorously for the physical qualifications of the men and women that apply for jobs. For example, after it interrupted such testing in 1986 because of legal challenges, the New York Police Department found itself with some hires who were unfit.[25]

The federally ordained special education program, frequently enforced in painstaking detail by judicial consent decrees, now takes so large a bite out of the budgets of urban school districts that many are unable to raise their regular classroom teachers' salaries, which lag behind those of wealthier suburban districts.

Beginning in the 1960s a number of federal court decisions greatly expanded the rights of students to appeal school suspensions.[26] Despite more modulated opinions by the Supreme Court in later years few teachers or principals can ignore the legal minefield they enter when they contemplate disciplinary actions, especially against students said to be suffering from learning disabilities.[27]

Whether children in a city attend neighborhood schools or are bused sometimes over great distances often hinges on whether and with what methods a federal court order is regulating the racial composition of the city's school system.

As for the instructions to firefighters and the federal pettifogging about where to stand on local public buses, the first fall under standard operating procedures formulated by the Occupational Safety and Health Administration (OSHA).[28] The second is a Department of Transportation (DOT) regulation, which reads as follows:

> Every bus which is designed and constructed so as to allow standees, shall be plainly marked with a line of contrasting color at least 2 inches wide or equipped with some

other means so as to indicate to any person that he/she is prohibited from occupying a space forward of a perpendicular plane drawn through the rear of the driver's seat and perpendicular to the longitudinal axis of the bus. Every bus shall have clearly posted at or near the front, a sign with letters at least one half inch high stating that it is a violation of the Federal Highway Administration's regulations for a bus to be operated with persons occupying the prohibited area.[29]

Crossing the Line

The immersion of the central government in most of these matters seems hard to understand. Why should a national cabinet department or regulatory bureaucracy concern itself with how "standees" ride city buses or with the deployment of firefighters? If local transit authorities or fire departments cannot be left to decide such minutiae, what, if anything, are local governments for? Surely few of the activities in question— putting out fires, riding buses, disciplining troublemakers in schools, hiring police officers, remunerating city workers or contractors—blow fallout across jurisdictions the way some forms of environmental pollution do. . . .

One Size Does Not Fit All

The point of federalizing standards is to set norms for society as a whole and hence ensure uniformity. However, uniform rules of little significance for some jurisdictions can be onerous for others. The reach of the amended Fair Labor Standards Act is illustrative. It extends to public employers the mandatory minimum wage and other provisions that the FLSA originally reserved only for private firms. Not only does this generic regulation of workplaces carry different implications for municipalities than markets, its effects vary from one location to the next. The law would not have for most suburban towns, with no unionized employees, comparatively small payrolls, and bountiful tax bases, the same costly consequences it has had for some major cities.

A federal lawsuit that contests traditional fitness tests can pose difficulties for a big city's police force like New York's, which has to cope with crimeridden slums. The same suit would be of little consequence for, say, Beverly Hills, a place so affluent and sheltered that, as the joke goes, the police department has an unlisted phone number.[30]

Green Mandates

The unequal impacts of federal environmental regulations are sometimes notorious.[31] In 1987 Congress concluded that every municipality in the United States would have to treat storm water much the same as discharge of polluted water from industrial plants. This requirement, appropriate for humid climates, was ill-suited to arid regions such as much of the Southwest. Never mind that Phoenix averages only seven inches of rainfall a year. This city nonetheless was required to spend large sums each year monitoring the runoff from extremely infrequent rain storms.

Between 1974 and 1994 American taxpayers poured $213 billion into upgrading their municipal water-treatment plants. Now the EPA predicts that $200 billion more will be needed through the year 2014 to bring local wastewater systems up to newly specified design criteria. To that estimate must be added another $132 billion for the replacement of aging plants. The projected total, therefore, rises to $332 billion—a figure that does not include the soaring increases in operating and maintenance expenses associated with more advanced technologies. If the recent past is prologue, local governments will be expected to come up with more than 90 percent of the funding for these capital improvements, plus 100 percent of annual operating expenses.

And for at least some cities the bill will be needlessly steep. Under the Clean Water Act cities have to install secondary wastewater treatment facilities that remove the remaining organic matter not treated in primary facilities. While secondary treatment is usually necessary for landlocked communities, according to a 1993 study by the National Academy of Sciences, the same precaution may not be essential for many seaport cities. Tides at coastal cities help flush organic residue from water bodies. Although the EPA has granted a number of waivers, arguably more oceanside cities ought to receive dispensations.[32]

So stringent are the federal criteria for cleaning up local land containing toxic wastes, and so unsparing have been the liability provisions, that developers and lending institutions have resisted investing in many abandoned industrial and commercial sites. A recent survey of more than two hundred cities by the U.S. Conference of Mayors reported no fewer than 81,000 acres of brownfields, including some undoubtedly entangled in Superfund suits. These sites continue to languish in the inner cities, costing them possibly as much as $2.4 billion in lost property tax revenue each year and foreclosing opportunities to create as many as 550,000 jobs. Meanwhile policymakers bewail the "sprawl" wrought by businesses that, steering clear of the legal liabilities, opt to locate on virgin acreage in the suburbs.

Under the rules of the Safe Drinking Water Act localities everywhere have been busy examining their water supplies for pesticides and other toxic residues that pose substantial risks only in particular areas. Before it was finally relieved from some of this duty in the mid-1990s Columbus, Ohio, found itself guarding against approximately forty pesticides. Many of them had long since been discontinued in the vicinity, including one product used chiefly on pineapple plantations in Hawaii.[33]

At times the nationalized regulations appear to have created new problems at the regional level. New York, for instance, ran afoul of a national prohibition on ocean dumping of sewage sludge. Banned since 1988 from disposing of any sludge at sea, the city resorted to dewatering and composting its waste. But this practice emits nitrogen-rich effluents that endanger marine life in nearby estuaries. In March 1998 the state of Connecticut filed suit against the city for contaminating Long Island Sound.[34]

Rights and Wrongs

If environmental standards often do not admit enough diversification, latitude, and cognizance of costs at the local level, the federal regulations that fall under the capacious category of civil rights permit even less. For the most part this is as it should be. "Rights tends to be viewed as absolutes," explains Robert A. Katzmann, "overriding considerations of cost effectiveness."[35] But no society can afford to extend "total justice" to an ever-increasing variety of petitioners.[36] What began in the 1960s as a long-awaited effort to secure equality of opportunity for African Americans has expanded into a vast apparatus of federally mandated protections and preferences for many additional groups. Whether every class of claimants has needed maximal compulsory remedies is a good question. So is whether each remedy should be determined from the top down.

Consider the rights of persons with disabilities. The ideal of accommodating the physically impaired is just and desirable, but should every municipality be told how to improve handicapped access in its public facilities? To modernize public buses and retrofit subways, as demanded by the Rehabilitation Act of 1973, New York concluded in 1980 that the requisite capital improvements and annual operating bills would amount to a budget-busting expense. Mayor Edward I. Koch figured, "It would be cheaper for us to provide every severely disabled person with taxi service than make 255 of our subway stations accessible."[37]

Mercifully, after pitched legal battles, the federal planners relented and lowered the costs. New York, with an old and extensive transit system, should never have been sidetracked from opting for alternatives to the federal retrofit policy. For this city it should have been obvious from the outset that investing in advanced paratransit or even subsidizing taxi rides would secure a greater net gain for the seriously disabled and for beleaguered local taxpayers.

In 1973 during the congressional debate on the Rehabilitation Act, the bill's authors seemed to have had no clue that in venues like New York the legislation's burdens might well exceed its blessings. One of the chief sponsors admitted afterward that neither he nor any of his colleagues "had any concept that it would involve such tremendous costs."[38] The deliberations were not altogether different sixteen years later when Congress took up the Americans with Disabilities Act of 1990, an even bolder piece of legislation mandating "fair and just access."[39] Local authorities pleaded for greater leeway or else for federal aid to cushion compliance costs, but Congress seemed untroubled. It wrote into the ADA a raft of requirements and almost no financial assistance.[40]

At congressional hearings on the ADA a representative of the Memphis Area Transit Authority guessed that the measure, if adopted, would force that city to eliminate hundreds of thousands of transit trips annually.[41] Dire warnings like this one about the fiscal havoc the bill portended proved mostly exaggerated. Nevertheless the law's seeming insouciance about local dissimilarities hit some communities hard. Faced with an ultimatum to construct some 65,000 wheelchair ramps by the mid-1990s the city of Phoenix reported that "it would be physically impossible to find enough skilled labor in the Valley to conduct such a massive construction program, even if the deadline were several years away."[42] Ordered to incorporate curb cuts and sidewalk ramps in its plans for downtown street repaving, officials in Philadelphia guessed that more than a third of its planned repavements would be unaffordable.[43] The Washington Metro in the nation's capital is America's most modern and beautifully designed subway system. Nonetheless it was directed to tear up parts of forty-five station platforms and install bumpy tiles along edges to accommodate the sight impaired. Interestingly the two leading organizations representing the blind—the American Council of the Blind and the National Federation of the Blind—disagreed about whether this multimillion dollar effort would protect sight impaired transit users or perhaps endanger them.

Zero Tolerance

How to handle municipal overtime pay, regulate the town water supply, or resurface city streets and sidewalks used to be judgments that local authorities dispatched. Now, more and more of these daily administrative duties are subject to federal guidance. Whatever the rationale for guiding so many quotidian decisions, however, the government's agenda would be less troublesome for many cities if its specifications sought to set only modest baselines. Alas the specifications are sometimes utopian.

Environmental Perfection

A number of U.S. environmental mandates certainly seem to qualify for that description. Their targets, timetables, and technologies seem specified without regard to whether the perils the rules are meant to diminish are great or small. Indeed policy in important instances proceeds as if risk should be banished at any price. This feverish pursuit of environmental purification, sometimes tolerating virtually no margin of health risk, is unreasonable for many municipalities and thousands of businesses.

When the EPA revised its goals for curbing effluents from municipal incinerators in 1995, for instance, it ordered the virtual elimination of emissions of mercury and lead as well as dioxin.[44] Most of these toxic substances had already dropped dramatically; overall lead emissions, for example, were down 98 percent between 1970 and 1995. The city of Tampa, which had finished building a state-of-the-art incinerator only ten years earlier, now had to refit that modern installation with another round of pollution control equipment costing scores of millions of dollars.[45]

How much the latest incineration standards would improve public health was uncertain. In a review of epidemiological research on the health of persons living near city incinerators in the United Kingdom one study discerned no consistent pattern of ill health.[46] The findings were interesting because the studies surveyed relied primarily on data from the 1970s and 1980s when pollution controls on incinerators were underdeveloped. After at least a decade of stringent regulation it was likely that the remaining health hazards from these facilities would be small—especially in the United States where a person's average exposure to poisons such as mercury is now less than half the average in Europe.[47]

In 1994 the Congressional Budget Office estimated that under the Comprehensive Environmental Response, Compensation and Liability Act the expense of cleaning up the nation's toxic waste dumps would run between $106 billion and a staggering $463 billion.[48] How could this environmental project cost more than twice the entire gross domestic product of Sweden? The excesses of Superfund bear some responsibility. Costs escalate when sites have to be decontaminated so pristinely that a child playing on them could safely eat their dirt for seventy days a year.[49] Thus the program had completed merely 52 of 1,320 designated sites as of 1993. City governments have incurred directly only a fraction of the multibillion dollar Superfund bill. But the persistence of old brownfields, at least partly shadowed by Superfund liabilities, continues to be for inner cities a financial sinkhole. . . .

Hypersensitivity

In bygone days almost anyone joining a big city police force, fire department, sanitation crew, or inner city school system understood that he or she would be entering an often unpleasant, indeed perilous, occupation. The clients of these tough "street-level bureaucracies" were not always polite company, and neither would be some of the supervisors and coworkers. Nasty or boorish encounters would occur; they went with the territory.

Expectations are rather different nowadays. U.S. legal theories have added new meanings to the pursuit of admissible and equitable employment conditions. "Hostile" work environments, unintentional discriminations ("disparate impacts"), even precautions misconstrued as insults or slights—all these imperfections and more are actionable.

Taxpayers, not philanthropists, pay the salaries of municipal employees. One would think that city officials accountable to voters might be permitted to set, say, basic health eligibility criteria and then unceremoniously ask prospective employees for their medical histories, especially if the jobs in question were physically demanding, stressful, or dangerous. Not so fast. To attain a bias-free environment for applicants with disabilities, such queries now have to be conducted with extreme delicacy, if indeed, they can be conducted at all. In one of many revealing vignettes in his 1997 book *The Excuse Factory*, Walter K. Olson relates what happened to a policeman in Boston who was disciplined after his superiors discovered that he had lied under oath about having received inpatient psychiatric care on five occasions. The policeman had to be reinstated, with back pay and damages.[50] What about the subway cleaner in New York who was refused a promotion to train operator because his corpulence prevented him from passing a basic stress test? He had standing to sue for alleged discrimination, did, and got the job.[51]

Sometimes the kinds of pains taken to ensure benign work environments are not without ironies. "A Los Angeles Police Department official," Olson recounts, "said the department was moving against a range of 'inappropriate' male doings even though 'very, very few' of them 'would rise to the level of true sex harassment.'"[52] But some years later misconduct of a different sort was disclosed in the LAPD: some members of the force had trafficked in narcotics and were accused of planting evidence, framing suspects, and shooting some unarmed ones.[53] What had been done to prevent *these* doings? Apparently too little according to newspaper accounts. Some of the officers implicated in the scandal seem to have been hired without adequately checking their backgrounds, which included histories of arrests and alcoholism.[54]

At all levels of government in the United States efforts to protect the civil rights of workers have moved beyond the original mission—to attain basic equality of opportunity for an oppressed minority in the labor force. State and local jurists often have been just as uncompromising as many federal ones in their efforts to sanitize employment procedures. (The Boston policeman took his grievance to a state court, though his could as easily have been a federal case.) The evolution of employment law at the federal level, however, has provided the legal foundation, and the main inspiration, for all concerned. . . .

Adversarial Legalism

Which brings up a third feature of the ubiquitous federal presence: it has helped stoke a firestorm of litigation. Between 1991 and 1995 the cost of routine liability claims in New York City increased 57 percent in constant dollars.[55] By 1992 these legal bills were totaling more than the city's entire budget for its parks and libraries.[56] The trend in some other cities was worse. During the same period Minneapolis experienced a 187 percent increase in liability expenditures.[57]

And that was only one portion of the jagged legal landscape. Alongside the mounting malpractice complaints, traffic accident claims, zoning appeals, slip-and-falls, and countless other petty municipal torts came new causes to sue city governments, now increasingly in the federal courts. Several Supreme Court opinions had widened the general exposure of cities to civil actions.[58] These and other stimulants made themselves felt.

The Long Arm of the Lawsuit

Litigation in the federal courts exploded after 1960. That year there was a total of only 2,483 civil filings under the categories of civil rights-related cases, for example, whereas the number of such cases reached 98,153 by 1995.[59] Of these lawsuits, the ones that targeted the local public sector left virtually no facet of municipal administration undisputed. Major cities found themselves awash in court orders determining everything from the racial balancing of schools to the placement of foster children and the schooling of learning-disabled students, to the provision of shelters for the homeless, the use of city jails, buses, and even public fire alarm boxes.

Fire alarm boxes? In 1996 a federal judge halted the New York City Fire Department's plan to replace 16,300 antiquated alarm boxes with public telephones wired to an emergency system. The rationale: hearing-impaired persons might be unable to use the phones; the new system violated a federal guarantee of "equal access" to public facilities.[60]

For years a federal court had told New York how to run its jails. Conditions in the jails needed reform. But under the terms of its decree, active since 1978, the court-appointed "special masters" became fastidious. No particular was spared—down to the ratio of cups of borax per gallon of water required to mop the bathrooms.[61]

In 1996, at the other end of the country, the Los Angeles Metropolitan Transit Authority (MTA) settled a federal suit in which the MTA was accused of discriminating against minorities because city buses on certain routes were very crowded. One of the plaintiffs characterized the conditions on the MTA's buses as "a brutal violation" of civil rights. The terms of the consent decree got into specifics: there could be no more than an average of fifteen people standing during bus rides for any twenty-minute peak period by the end of 1997; then no more than an average of eleven people by June 2000; then no more than eight by June 2002.[62]

While court orders like those in Los Angeles and New York had delved into details those in some other cities were detailed—and drastic. To relieve overcrowding in Philadelphia's prisons, for instance, a federal judge barred pretrial detention of any suspect not charged with a violent crime. The long-range purpose of this shock treatment was to ameliorate the city's jails, but in the meantime, according to the court's critics, the result was that the number of fugitive drug dealers soared.[63] By one count more than three-quarters of Philadelphia's drug dealers became fugitives within ninety days of their arrests.

To be sure, most legal threats to city authorities would fizzle well short of producing judicial injunctions, usually because the underlying grievances simply could not stand up even by the standards of the world's most accommodating civil justice system. That did not mean, however, that cities could ignore the threats. To limit liabilities millions of dollars have been spent each year paying lawyers, keeping legally bullet-proof records, purchasing insurance, commissioning consultants, administering sensitivity training to personnel, and so forth. . . .[64]

Litigious Workplaces

Employment cases, which already accounted for about a quarter of all civil suits against city governments by the mid-1980s, multiplied as well.[65] A growing number were brought by people expecting to be made whole by one or another of the federal civil rights statutes. Energized by various bold enactments, such as the Age Discrimination in Employment Acts of 1975 and 1986, the Americans with Disabilities Act of 1990, and the Civil Rights Act amendments of 1991, federal antibias suits fanned out to service a lengthening queue of clients. As in environmental advocacy cases plaintiffs acquired new incentives to sue. After 1991, for example, the burden of proof in cases of alleged racial or ethnic discrimination was tilted against defendants. The mere composition by race of an employer's payroll could be used as *prima facie* evidence of racism, leaving the truth to the accused, not the accusers, to establish. The accusers, moreover, could have the fees of their attorneys and expert witnesses recovered in multiples when prejudice was proved. And compensatory and punitive damages became available, with the odds of collecting large sums significantly improved by the use of jury trials.

Novel legal assaults on municipal employment practices also came from federal authorities acting directly. Closely scrutinized by the Equal Employment Opportunity Commission and the Department of Justice's Civil Rights Division have been the testing procedures for city job candidates. In city after city the physical fitness tests conducted by police and fire departments as well as other municipal agencies came under suspicion of victimizing some protected classes (women, for instance), while the pencil-and-paper examinations administered under typical civil service systems risked charges of excluding others (for example, blacks and Hispanics). Statistical discrimination was found even when respectable quotients of minorities ultimately made their way into hiring pools. Minority candidates were 30 percent of those who took a special civil service exam designed to increase minority representation in New York City's police department in the early 1980s. Nearly two thousand blacks and Hispanics reached the final pool. But that was not enough, according to a federal judge, who proceeded to set a standard for the department whereby half of all new hires had to be black or Hispanic until they reached at least 30 percent of the total force. . . .[66]

Suing the Schools

While the municipal workplace became increasingly litigious other sources of legal strife engulfed the delivery of city services, most notably the schools. For decades numerous cities had grappled with court-ordered desegregation plans, many of which had the unwanted consequence of aggravating racial imbalances by accelerating the exodus of white families from urban school systems.[67] These ordeals had finally run their course by the late 1990s, although not everywhere. As of 1995 several major city school districts, including those of Nashville, Buffalo, Indianapolis, and Memphis, were still operating under their original court orders or were still being supervised by a federal court though their original desegregation plans had been revised.[68] And as late as 1998 the DOJ was filing additional briefs requesting continued judicial supervision of the decades-old desegregation case in St. Louis.[69] But even as most of the forced busing experiments receded legal activists pressured school systems to secure other entitlements—such as a right to asbestos-free classrooms and the right of all children with disabilities to receive special educational services.

In 1975 Congress passed the Education of All Handicapped Children Act.[70] The aim of the law was to nationalize standards and procedures by which schools educated the handicapped. Teachers, administrators, and parents were to design jointly "individualized educational programs" for these children. The extensive tests and evaluations needed to prepare the programs could not be "racially or culturally discriminatory." Parents dissatisfied with a program were entitled to appeal up the line, ultimately to the federal courts. Schools would have to mainstream students "to the maximum extent appropriate" and provide for them "related services" such as physical therapy, psychological counseling, and recreational facilities. No school could change the placement of a special education student without parental approval. School districts would be required to identify all possible candidates for special education. This so-called child-find process involved discovering not only the eligible children, but also figuring out which ones were already enrolled but inadequately served.

Enforcing so elaborate a national code stirred legal conflicts as inevitable local infractions pertaining to one provision or another were revealed or perceived. "Every decision you make in special education you ask, 'Am I going to get sued for this?'"[71] That fear, voiced by the principal of an elementary school in Dade Country, Florida, could have been expressed by any number of other school officials around the country in the mid-1980s, at least in districts with sizable special education enrollments. One survey of state and local education boards published in 1987 indicated that more than a quarter of them had been sued.[72]

As the level of disputation rose the Supreme Court tried repeatedly to set boundaries. A decision in 1984 denied parents the ability to recoup attorneys' fees and one in 1989 went so far as to invoke Eleventh Amendment immunity of states from certain federal suits.[73] However, Congress promptly reversed these setbacks. Reauthorizations of the handicapped education act in 1986 and 1990 further enfranchised its citizen litigants, covered their legal expenses (now for administrative hearings as well as trials), and extended the whole program to preschool children.[74]

Predictably the law, presently titled the Individuals with Disabilities Education Act (IDEA), ratcheted the volume of litigation another notch (Figure 8.2). As in other spheres of adversarial excess (certain environmental programs, for instance) IDEA raised some bizarre expectations, not just legitimate requests, in the nation's courts of law. The superintendent of one California school district reportedly described confronting plaintiffs' lawyers who demanded such "related services" as karate lessons for a kindergarten child with an immune system disorder, horseback riding lessons as rehabilitation therapy for a child who had had seizures, and school trips to Disneyland for a child who was depressed.[75]

And predictably the distribution of the legal troubles has been uneven: besieged disproportionately have been the districts with large special-ed constituencies—the school systems of cities like New York, Baltimore, and Washington, D.C., that would have to cope for years with laborious consent decrees.[76]

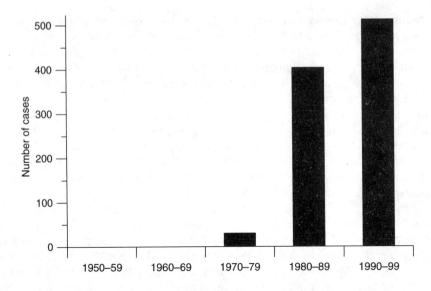

Figure 8.2 Special Education Litigation in Federal Courts, 1950–1999.[a]

Source: Perry A. Zirkel, "The 'Explosion' in Education Litigation: An Update," *West's Education Law Reporter,* no. 114 (1997), p. 348.

[a]Data for 1990–99 are a projection that is based on the actual number of cases through December of 1995.

Curing or Abetting the Mischiefs of Faction?

The Individuals with Disabilities Education Act is a monument to best intentions gone astray. Back in 1975, when Congress voted almost unanimously to plant this federal foothold in local public education, the lawmakers hardly anticipated what lay ahead. As its original title indicated the legislation was intended to assist the comparatively small number of children who were *handicapped*—that is, blind, deaf, paralyzed, or otherwise gravely impaired. In the ensuing quarter-century, however, definitions of disability widened to include categories of emotional, mental, or behavioral characteristics that had scarcely denoted a "handicap" in years past. Twenty-five years ago, for instance, there was no clinical classification for inattentive pupils. Now, diagnosed as suffering from "attention deficit disorder," they could be eligible for special services.[77] Twenty-five years ago underachieving students were simply called slow learners. Now, they, too, could qualify for special treatment; according to the U.S. Department of Education, "a severe discrepancy between achievement and intellectual ability" could signify that such students were learning disabled.[78] Partly in this fashion, IDEA eventually amassed about 6.1 million clients—and with them, colossal costs.[79]

The lawmakers of 1975 envisioned an expense that might rise to $8 billion nationwide, 40 percent of which would be defrayed by federal grants.[80] By the late 1990s the initiative's annual total was more than five times larger.[81] In the meantime, the federal contribution settled between 8 and 15 percent as congressional appropriators fled the oncoming budgetary behemoth.[82] State and local governments were left to confront it. New York City found itself allocating a quarter of its school budget to special-ed, an obligation so massive it crowded out more than $1 billion of other local priorities, from programs boosting gifted and talented kids to improved street lighting.[83]

Oversubscribed with students in special education, all of whom were entitled to customized "appropriate education" plans and some of whom required extraordinary facilities, many cities resorted to placing substantial percentages in private institutions. The premium for these schools, on top of the rest of the program's lopsided overhead, drove its average per pupil expenditures to twice the average for regular instruction, and in some cities (New York, for instance) to nearly three times the cost of instructing regular students.[84]

No affluent, civilized society can neglect the educational needs of disabled children. In 1975 the decision to assist them with what was supposed to be a large infusion of federal funds was decent and humane. But a responsible government also cannot, in effect, bring forth a blizzard of demands and then renege on its promise, shift the expense to communities that can least afford it, and run the risk of lowering the welfare of the remaining citizens in those communities. It is not too much to say that federal policy for special education has erred in just about all these ways. Its constraints on claims and eligibility are unclear; its appropriated funds have consistently fallen far below authorizations; and it has weighed most heavily on overtaxed cities with weak school systems. . . .

Summary

If each of these federal interventions decidedly improved the quality of urban life, the misgivings expressed in these pages could be shrugged off. But there is a point at which routinely subjecting municipal decisions to national supervision and regimentation risks doing more damage than good.

Federal regulation today reaches into so many details of municipal administration that picayune concerns are nationalized alongside weightier ones. Much of this spectacle is merely a nuisance. A federal court that interferes with the ability of a city to test, say, municipal clerk-typists for grammar, spelling, and punctuation (as the Fifth Circuit ruled a number of years ago) might trifle with the local community's own valued standards but probably does not put it in jeopardy.[85] At times, however, the stakes have been higher. The safety of community residents can be compromised, for example, by rulings that limit the testing of would-be firefighters and police recruits for endurance, strength, or agility (as some of the opinions handed down by the federal courts have done), or by rulings that turn loose hundreds of arrested suspects, including some charged with robbery, stalking, carjacking, drug dealing, and manslaughter (as a federal injunction against pretrial detention did for several years in Philadelphia).

Some federal mandates sock cities with unnecessarily large costs. Costs can soar, for example, amid the national campaigns for risk-free environments—such as perfectly bias-free workplaces, toxin-free tap water, asbestos-free schools, lead-free housing, hazard-free redevelopment sites, and more. The persistence of some 21,000 brownfields languishing in cities is a stark example of the debacle that a zero-risk mentality can create.[86]

Federal law has also enmeshed municipalities in new litigation, some of which manacles their managers, demoralizes their personnel, and ties their budgets in knots. Due in no small part to federal policy, the terms and conditions of municipal employment are cited as the realm most roiled by legal disputes or the threat of them.[87] City schools used to be relatively simple and trusted neighborhood institutions. Since the 1960s, however, they have been buffeted by federal regulatory and judicial directives, leaving many preoccupied with legal bills and compliance issues more than with the quality of instruction for most students.[88]

By the early 1990s New York City's costs of complying with the ten largest court orders and mandates, specifying protocols for various municipal functions, were said to corner 26 percent of the city's tax revenue.[89] Even if every dollar earmarked in this litigious fashion were a dollar well spent (a dubious proposition), local taxpayers could fairly ask whether less adversarial means would have allocated the desired resources better, or at least without as much costly friction. By the early 1990s the cumulative cost of settling New York's liability claims had reached bewildering proportions.[90]

Alongside these considerable vexations lies the fact that some federal regulations are relatively rigid templates, superimposed on cities and towns regardless of their diverse circumstances. In certain locations, therefore, the mandated expenditures are simply a waste of money. (Should Phoenix really be made to spend significant sums to monitor the runoff from practically nonexistent rain storms?) In other instances the costs of meeting a given standard, though not pointless, will vary wildly among localities. For example, all municipalities will have to bring their groundwater treatment up to the nationwide standards of the Safe Drinking Water Act. The charges for households could vary by several thousand percent between small and large cities.[91]

U.S. environmental strictures are hardly the only ones that beget interjurisdictional inequities. Many central cities in the United States continue to contain disproportionate percentages of the low-income residents of metropolitan areas. Hence these cities bear a disproportionate share of poverty-related public expenditures. National regulations can contribute to the imbalance when their costs are not adequately reimbursed and are a function of local poverty rates. The federal special education mandate, as we have seen, falls into this category, but so do quite a few others.[92]

At the end of 1996 the District of Columbia was home to 45 percent of the Washington region's poor.[93] A consequence, as in other cities that have to shoulder comparable concentrations of poverty, is that the expense of administering almost any city service is inherently higher in the District than in the surrounding suburbs.[94] Whatever the other reasons for the District's extraordinary administrative cost structure, the heavy lifting is scarcely alleviated by some thirty-nine federal court decrees, some of which have compelled steep increases in the costliest of municipal items—like overtime compensation for city workers.[95]

Race to the Bottom—or the Top?

It is generally assumed that Washington intervenes in local decisions primarily to prevent intergovernmental rifts and rivalries from degrading basic norms for public health, safety, or welfare. Federal authorities, the theory goes, chiefly step in to set suitable baselines—for Atlanta's air quality, or New York's fiscal practices, or the competence of school teachers in a bunch of cities. But in reality much federal preemption of local policies works the other way around. It subjects state and local governments to national directives even when those governments are emulating, indeed outdoing, one another to run standards up, not down.

In 1986 Congress moved to extend to preschoolers the universal right to special education for handicapped children. But forty-two states already had begun programs of this sort.[96] Similarly, by the time Congress proclaimed that no schoolchild should be exposed to asbestos risks most school districts already had programs to repair dangerous buildings. In 2001 a new administration in Washington proposed to coax the states to start rating the performance of all their local elementary and secondary schools. But less noticed during the national education reform debate was that seventeen states already assigned such ratings, four more were poised to initiate them in 2002, and at least two more planned to do so soon thereafter.[97] The concept of school accountability, in other words, was percolating and spreading at the local level well in advance of any coercive federal measures.

Proponents of central direction, however, frequently seem unimpressed. By their logic, if so many state and local initiatives have already blazed a trail, national standards only complete what the locals have started. The latter, it would appear, are as likely to have their independence shorn when they are proactive and progressive as when they are laggards.

Principled arguments are hard to advance for at least some of the specialized, coerced expenditures that have been pressed upon cities. But worthy or not, federally mandated programs, once established, are not easy to redesign. Program preservationists prevail.[98] The cementing of policies by vested interests was not what the framers of the Constitution had in mind when they sought to enlarge the orbit of national authority. What the founders intended was to check and counterbalance the power of calcified local elites. . . .

26

Stephen D. Stehr

THE POLITICAL ECONOMY OF DISASTER ASSISTANCE

The devastation wrought in the cities of the Gulf coast by Hurricanes Katrina and Rita has once again cast a spotlight on disaster policy and administration in the United States. Although presidential disaster declarations over the past decade have averaged approximately one per week, many go unnoticed except by those directly affected. But so-called "megadisasters," characterized by significant loss of life, widespread physical

---

Author's Note: Portions of the research reported here were supported by a grant from the National Science Foundation (CMS 0234100). The opinions presented in this article are the author's and do not necessarily reflect those of the National Science Foundation. The author would like to thank the anonymous reviewers who provided useful comments on an earlier draft.

and economic damage, and extensive media attention act as a catalyst for a reexamination of current policies and procedures. As the economic costs associated with disasters have grown (Cutter and Emrich 2005), these debates have increasingly focused on disaster relief and assistance programs and how urbanized regions might mitigate damages before they occur (Mileti 1999; Platt 1999). This is not an issue that is likely to go away anytime soon. Many of the nation's most populous urban areas are situated in coastal areas that are at high risk from naturally occurring events such as earthquakes or hurricanes. According to the Census Bureau, more than half of the nation's 297 million people live in coastal areas—most in major cities—and seven of the top 10 fastest-growing states are coastal. Cities nationwide are subject to an array of natural hazards such as riverine flooding, wildfires, ice storms, tornados, drought, and volcanic eruptions. In the post–September 11 environment, all cities are considered to be at some level of risk to terrorist attacks that have the potential of causing many of the same types of problems (e.g., large-scale evacuation of citizens; urban search and rescue; public health and environmental concerns; mass casualty management and victim identification; victim compensation; reconstruction of public infrastructure; business continuity) that are also associated with natural events.

Despite the increasing vulnerability of urban areas to catastrophic events, relatively little attention has been explicitly paid to issues that would inform both the literatures concerning urban studies and those that focus on the social science aspects of disaster.[1] This article represents a modest attempt to begin a dialogue between those who study more traditional topics in urban governance and those who study how communities prepare for, respond to, and recover from disasters. My primary focus is on two related questions: First, is it possible to reconcile the competing forces of economic development decisions and political calculations with hazard mitigation policies? Under the current structure, local officials have very few incentives to mitigate hazards secure in the knowledge that federal aid will be forthcoming following an event. Recovery from large-scale urban disasters also lays bare local political dynamics that may have been obscured prior to the event (Kantor 2002). But they also expose longer-term national political trends and priorities as they relate to disaster preparedness and response capabilities. A second question relates to the possibility of incorporating the idea of community resilience into discussions of sustainable development. As Savitch points out, our collective understanding of the life of cities goes through recognizable paradigmatic shifts (Savitch 2003). It remains to be seen if some of the forces discussed in this article have reached a critical mass and will launch a new paradigm focused on safe cities.

The history of disaster relief and assistance policy in the United States can be characterized as having brief periods of intense political activity typically following a major disaster or a series of disasters, followed by longer periods where interest in the subject wanes (May 1985). This has resulted in a fragmented set of policies that, over time, have significantly increased the financial exposure of the federal government (Platt 1999). There are four primary means through which postdisaster assistance is administered: (1) government programs (primarily implemented through the federal government); (2) charities and philanthropic organizations; (3) private insurance; and, (4) the court system chiefly through tort claims and bankruptcy filings.[2] Federal disaster assistance is provided through approximately 30 separate programs that offer aid to individuals and families, businesses, states and municipalities, special districts, and not-for-profit organizations (Jordan 2005). A wide range of financial strategies is utilized including direct grants to stricken communities and individuals, low interest disaster loans, federal public works programs to remove debris and rebuild public infrastructures, disaster unemployment benefits, mental health and legal services, environmental cleanup, and federal income tax deductions for uninsured casualty losses.

Federal aid is intended to be supplemental to funds dedicated by state and local governments. The Federal Disaster Assistance Act of 1988 (the Stafford Act)—the primary federal law governing disasters—specifies a 75/25 ratio of federal/nonfederal cost sharing of disaster assistance with state and local governments. However, recent presidents of both parties have raised the federal share or waived nonfederal contributions entirely (Platt 1999, p. 17). Although these waivers are no doubt motivated in part by compassion, presidents (and members of Congress) are also under intense political pressure to act quickly and generously, particularly in election years. Several recent studies have documented a connection between presidential elections, congressional politics, and level of disaster relief allocated to specific areas (Garrett and Sobel 2003; Reeves 2005).

Postdisaster response and recovery assistance has historically made up the vast majority of federal spending on disasters. According to a report issued by the Bipartisan Task Force on Funding Disaster Relief, approximately three-quarters of all federal spending on disasters between 1977 and 1994 was expended to pay for postdisaster recovery (U.S. Senate 1995). This same report charged that the federal government discourages state, local, and individual self-reliance by offering federal disaster assistance too readily. It seems reasonable to conclude that in some instances disaster assistance has become a form of political "pork barrel," particularly in cases where genuine need seems to be absent.[3]

The implementation of disaster assistance in New York City following the terrorist attacks of September 11 illustrates the basic structure of relief policies. According to a report completed by researchers at RAND, the total amount of direct disaster assistance delivered to victims, businesses, and government entities was $38.1 billion (Dixon and Stern 2004). Of this amount, slightly more than half ($19.6 billion, or 51%) was paid out by insurance companies. Through 2004, government programs accounted for $15.8 billion (42%) of total relief payments but this figure will grow as monies allocated but not yet expended are spent. Despite an unprecedented mobilization charitable distributions accounted for only 7% of total assistance.[4]

Soon after the attacks, President George W. Bush promised $20 billion in federal money to help the New York City area recover from 9/11. Although some may have interpreted this pledge to mean that New York City would receive a lump sum payment, in reality the aid package was structured to provide for both immediate needs as well as long-term assistance. The flow of federal aid to New York City and its inhabitants is being tracked by the New York City Independent Budget Office (IBO). By its accounting, approximately 30% ($6.3 billion) of the money was expended on emergency response activities. The majority of this money (approximately 70%) was provided to New York City to pay for debris removal and overtime costs for the police and fire departments and to establish an insurance pool to protect the city and its contract workers against lawsuits resulting from work at the World Trade Center site (IBO 2004). Only a small portion of the response funds (about 10%) were provided as direct aid to individuals or as low interest loans to property owners. About 20% ($4.4 billion) of

$20 billion appropriated by Congress was designed to spur economic recovery in Lower Manhattan and to help alleviate the budget crisis the city faced in the wake of the attack. Most of these funds were provided directly to New York City government (38% or $1.7 billion) or for business assistance grants (26% or $1.2 billion). The remaining $9.7 billion (most of which have not yet been spent) will go for long-term rebuilding projects primarily in the area of transportation improvements.

Although care should be taken in generalizing from this admittedly unprecedented case, several lessons emerge nonetheless. First, insurance companies provided about 50% of the total compensation provided. These monies went to individuals (mostly through life insurance policies) and affected businesses. As it turns out, there is empirical evidence to suggest that the 50% figure is a reasonable assumption in many natural disasters as well (Pielke 2005). Second, most of the assistance provided through federal programs was administered to New York City with a smaller portion going to businesses that were damaged, destroyed, or disrupted. In fact, aside from the approximately $7 billion that was expended through the VCF, a relatively small amount of direct assistance was provided to individuals. Finally, disaster recovery and reconstruction—even when the physical damage is relatively concentrated as it was in New York City—does not take place overnight. It is estimated that it will take approximately 10 years to fully expend the entire $20 billion authorized by Congress (IBO 2004).

Although disaster assistance is commonly thought to include only those activities that occur following an extreme event, a more comprehensive approach also includes pre-event mitigation and preparedness activities designed to eliminate or reduce event impacts. As Lindell and Prater (2003) point out, there are strong and important linkages between hazard mitigation and preparedness practices, and community recovery and reconstruction outcomes. An inherent problem in the structure of disaster assistance is the fact that the mitigation and preparedness are largely the responsibility of local governments while the economic costs of recovery and reconstruction are borne elsewhere. Subnational governments and individuals owning property in hazardous areas to a large extent control decisions that determine the ultimate effectiveness of mitigation and preparedness measures adopted at the local level; in most cases, these parties have few incentives to make these policies a high priority because federal programs will provide assistance should a disaster occur (May 1985; Stehr 1999). Adding to the problem is that well-intentioned government programs sometimes undermine each other. Rutherford Platt argues that a vast array of federal spending and economic development programs such as highway construction, housing, urban renewal, shoreline stabilization, water pollution abatement, and river control projects may undercut the goals of hazard mitigation by indirectly sponsoring development and redevelopment in areas of recurrent hazard (Platt 1999). It remains to be seen if a "paradigm shift" from a political-economic logic of urban development to one based in public security and protection will inform decisions regarding the rebuilding of New Orleans (Savitch 2003).

Going beyond the pressures associated with local economic development decisions and the problems it creates in creating workable response and assistance policies, disaster policy is also a by-product of other, seemingly unconnected policy decisions. For instance, decisions made in the arenas of national security policy, urban policy, and social policy have traceable impacts on current disaster policy. Following September 11, planning to detect and prevent terrorist attacks all but eliminated federal interest in preparedness and response activities and funding for natural disaster mitigation projects

(Holdeman 2005; Tierney 2005). Significantly, the Federal Emergency Management Agency (FEMA), the agency established to coordinate hazard mitigation, and disaster response and recovery policies, was stripped of its cabinet-level status when it was placed within the newly created Department of Homeland Security. Project Impact, a hazard mitigation program started during the Clinton administration to provide grants to cities, was eliminated in 2001 although it was costing only about $20 million per year. This devolution of responsibility can be seen as merely one part of a "new" urban policy whereby cities are expected to take on additional responsibilities for protecting their citizens (Eisinger 2004). This is also part of a larger trend. As William Barnes recently reported, federal funds as a percentage of municipal revenues reached a high in 1978 at about 17% and have declined steadily since then to less than 5% (Barnes 2005). Some observers have interpreted the events in New Orleans as resulting from decades of federal urban disinvestment, exurbanization, and "white flight," which have left the central cores of many cities "abandoned" (Graham 2005), or as "exposing the unacknowledged inequalities" that are the result of years of failed social policies (Frymer, Strolovitch, and Warren 2005).

Can We Create Resilient Cities?

For at least the past decade, community resilience has been a prominent topic among academic urban planners and natural disaster researchers. Dennis Mileti defines the concept this way: "Local resiliency with regard to disasters means that a locale is able to withstand an extreme natural event without suffering devastating losses, damage, diminished productivity, or quality of life and without a large amount of assistance from outside the community" (Mileti 1999, pp. 32–33). One aspect of community resilience focuses on hazard mitigation—that is, activities designed to reduce or eliminate long-term risk to people and property and break the cycle of damage, reconstruction, and repeated damage from disasters. These efforts include such actions as stricter building codes, engineering retrofits, land use planning, and property acquisition (Hardenbrook 2005; Godschalk et al. 1999; Burby 1998). How successful are these efforts likely to be? Certainly there will be localized success stories. However, as this article points out, there are strong political and economic forces at work that will make widespread urban hazard mitigation difficult to achieve. One promising avenue to pursue is the concept of "comprehensive emergency management." This idea is rooted in the notion that loss-reduction efforts should be oriented toward integrating mitigation, preparedness, response, and recovery activities suitable for a variety of localized hazards whether natural, technological, or human caused. But implementing this concept costs time and money and requires local political and administrative leadership. In the absence of national incentives to create resilient communities, the provision of public protection will continue to fall largely on urban governance structures.

In their recent book, *The Resilient City*, Vale and Campanella raise a number of important questions that could help inform a more robust dialogue between urbanists and those who study the social science aspects of disaster (Vale and Campanella 2005, pp. 12–13). For example, they pose the question: what does it mean for a "city" to "recover"? As regional hubs of economic, social, and cultural activities, cities recover to the extent that they return to some semblance of predisaster normalcy in human and economic relationships. But large-scale disasters also raise value-laden questions such as who will set the priorities for recovering communities? How will short-term recovery forces be balanced with long-range planning? Will predisaster inequities be replicated as part of the recovery process? Who will be displaced (and at what cost) as neighborhoods are rebuilt? What are the proper roles of local, state, and federal officials in an intergovernmental disaster assistance system? What dominant narratives will emerge to help us interpret what transpired and inform future hazard policies? By addressing these and many other important questions, a richer and more complete understanding of the vulnerability of cities to hazards could emerge that would serve to inform research from a variety of professional perspectives.

27

Peter F. Burns and Matthew O. Thomas

POLITICS, FEDERALISM, AND THE RECOVERY PROCESS IN NEW ORLEANS

A new New Orleans. That's what many thought, and even more hoped, would emerge after Hurricane Katrina attacked New Orleans. Local, state, and national figures thought that Katrina provided an opportunity for the city to start anew. In public, they advocated a new city, one that kept the New Orleans' charm, attractions, and culture but lost the area's negative aspects. In reality, much, but not all, of the new New Orleans resembled the old New Orleans. In particular, schisms between the public and private sector, whites and African Americans, and state and city government persisted in post-Katrina New Orleans. By contrast, a newer New Orleans appeared, particularly in the realm of governance.

Why, given such huge trauma, physical damage, and social disruptions, was there a reversion to some old patterns? Most stories on the friction between the state of Louisiana and the city of New Orleans attribute at least some of the tension to Mayor C. Ray Nagin's endorsement of two other gubernatorial candidates, one of whom was a Republican, instead of Kathleen Blanco, a fellow Democrat, in the 2003 gubernatorial primary and runoff. Certainly, personal animosity and political differences between the mayor and the governor complicated the relationship between Louisiana and New Orleans, but factors beyond personal politics also explain the endurance of state–local tensions.

Why did governance change while other policy areas remained stagnant? In this article, we examine how deeply rooted historical patterns of state–local conflict reasserted themselves even after the terrible destruction of Katrina and the redemptive promise of

From Peter F. Burns and Matthew O. Thomas, "A New New Orleans? Understanding the Role of History and the State-Local Relationship in the Recovery Process," *Journal of Urban Affairs*, Vol. 30, No. 3, 2008, pp. 259–271. Copyright © 2008 Urban Affairs Association. Reprinted by permission of Wiley-Blackwell.

a new beginning. We also explain how state government, some city leaders, and some New Orleanians took advantage of the opportunities presented by Hurricane Katrina to change certain aspects of governance in New Orleans.

To better understand how and why state government affects urban affairs, this article specifies those dimensions of the state–local relationship that influence how New Orleans rebuilds. It uses an historical analysis to identify the most important ways in which pre-catastrophe relations affect the recovery process. This article's broader implications illustrate the effect of state government on urban affairs and the influence of aspects of history on present conditions.

New Orleans: Then and Now

In July of 2005, the population of New Orleans stood at 452,170.[1] One month later, after the Katrina-breached levees flooded the city, the population all but disappeared. Essential city services, such as police and fire, barely operated, and all other governmental services halted. In essence, the city shut down.

Prior to Katrina, tourists flocked to New Orleans, feasting on its food, architecture, nightlife, and especially its music. The city's port, although diminished from its heyday, remained an important hub. A number of universities, including Tulane, Loyola, the University of New Orleans, Xavier, and Dillard, as well as the LSU Medical School, provided significant intellectual capital. These assets offered some promise for improvement after Katrina but New Orleans also needed to face the negative aspects of its past. Prior to Hurricane Katrina, the city struggled with issues of corruption; and city services, especially public schools, lagged far behind other jurisdictions. In the wake of Katrina, the city faced unfathomable challenges to recovery.

By July of 2006, a year after Katrina, the population of New Orleans had rebounded to 223,388, making the population about half of the pre-Katrina population. But other critical measures of capacity illustrate the challenges faced by the city. In that same month, only 22% of the child care centers, only 39% of the city's hospitals (9 of 23), and only 45% of the public transportation routes were open or operational. By August of 2006, only 41% of the city's public schools welcomed students.

Two years after Katrina, the population continued to increase, rising to almost 70% of the pre-Katrina population. Estimates in November 2007, indicate that blacks made up 58% of the city (*The Associated Press*, 2007). Prior to Hurricane Katrina, African Americans constituted slightly more than 66% of the city's population. Approximately 80% of New Orleans flooded as a result of the breached levees. The Uptown section of New Orleans, buffered by the city's natural levee, received the least amount of damage.

Whites in Uptown New Orleans lost some power and many elected positions, as the city's racial demographics changes over time, but they continued to exert considerable influence over public policy. They use campaign contributions, a good-government agency called the Bureau of Governmental Research (BGR), and access to the media, especially *The Times-Picayune*, to exercise power. One example of this influence occurred in 2004 when whites formed coalitions with some African Americans to stop the school board from firing Superintendent of Schools Anthony Amato. Of the five members who opposed Amato, three lost their seats and two did not seek reelection in the school board election of 2004.

The city's demographic shifts affected election results in post-Katrina New Orleans (Krupa, 2007b). In 2007, the New Orleans City Council became majority-white for the first time in 22 years. Throughout New Orleans, elected positions, including judges, city council members, and state legislators, which were held by blacks for years, have switched to white-officeholders in the post-Katrina period. At the time of the November 17, 2007, special election to fill a vacant, citywide council seat, black registered voters outnumbered white registered voters by more than 92,000, but turnout in majority-white districts was higher than turnout in majority-black districts (Krupa, 2007b).

Because of increases in the population, tax revenues, which plummeted in the immediate aftermath of the storm, continue to grow, reaching 94% of the pre-Katrina revenues. This positive sign is tempered by the city's continuing infrastructure dilemma. After two years, only 57% of hospitals, 62% of schools, and 38% of day care centers were in operation. When those within and outside New Orleans look at these figures and others like them, they characterize the rebuilding as slow.

Many displaced New Orleanians face the choice of returning to a city that cannot provide adequate healthcare, and those former residents with children must wrestle with the decreased capacity of the child care system and the limited number of public schools. Adding to those concerns, the city still struggles to adopt a comprehensive rebuilding plan, and the Road Home Program has a poor track record at issuing payments (see below). These two New Orleans, pre-and poststorm, are very different, but may in fact be influenced by similar trends. One of these historical patterns that continues to influence politics in the city is the character of state–local relations.

The Importance of State–City Relations

An investigation of the state–local dimension of the recovery is important because cities are creatures of the state (Burns & Gamm, 1997). Cities look increasingly toward state government for financial assistance in this era of devolution. Absent private leadership in cities, governors and state legislators have the potential to champion certain projects and policies in cities (Burns & Thomas, 2004). An analysis of the effect of state–local relations on rebuilding New Orleans also provides insight into other areas—race, culture, income, and class—that may affect how the city recovers from this disaster.

The Louisiana governor and legislature play important roles in the rebuilding of New Orleans. Because of devolution, the Louisiana governor maintains the authority to disperse federal recovery funds to New Orleans. The governor and state legislature propose and pass policies on how the city will not only govern itself but also execute police powers—including the education of New Orleans school children—in the aftermath of Katrina.

The focus on how state–city relations influence New Orleans' recovery does not indicate that this relationship is the only aspect of the recovery process. Clearly, other relationships, including those between races, public and private leaders, and community groups and government, also affect the manner in which New Orleans rebuilds after Hurricane Katrina. In addition to the aforementioned effects that state government exerts on city politics and policy, we also focus upon the role of state government because many critics argue that the study of urban affairs pays too little attention to extra-local actors, namely governors, state legislatures, and state bureaucracies (for example, see Burns, 2002; Burns & Thomas, 2004; Harding, 1995; Kantor, Savitch, & Haddock, 1997; Lauria, 1996; Sites, 1997).

Historical Tensions between Cities and States

Historically, states and large cities have had an antagonistic relationship (Berman, 2003). As Berman (2003) notes, "One of the most persistent themes in state–local relations has been the conflict between state legislatures and the largest cities in the states" (p. 53). Louisiana versus New Orleans, New York State versus New York City, Illinois versus Chicago, Michigan versus Detroit, Missouri versus Kansas City and St. Louis, Maryland versus Baltimore, among many other places, typify the conflict between state-level actors and big cities (for example, see Stonecash, 1989). But what are the sources of tensions between these levels of government?

Money

An overview of the history of state–city relations in the United States in general, and the interactions between the state of Louisiana and New Orleans in particular, suggests several potential explanations for prolonged conflict between these levels of government (Berman, 2003). Money, control, and differences between urban and rural areas constitute deeply rooted historical patterns that influence city–state relations (Berman, 2003). Historically, cities and state government fight over money. The battle over finances intensified in the 1980s when state government's involvement in urban and local affairs increased mainly because of three factors: A large federal deficit, President Ronald Reagan's view that the federal government failed to achieve victories in the war on poverty and other social problems, and the federal government's decision to devolve policy responsibilities to the states (Liner, 1989; Pagano, 1990; Stonecash, 1998). In this devolution period, cities wanted more money from the state government with fewer strings while states sought greater control and oversight over the dollars they allocated to urban governments.

Finances traditionally divide the state of Louisiana and the city of New Orleans. The rest of Louisiana argues that New Orleans receives a greater share of the state's resources than it contributes to Louisiana's coffers. Among other things, legislators from outside New Orleans opposed special state subsidies for the New Orleans Saints NFL team, the Superdome, a downtown arena in the city, an amusement park, and the state's only land-based casino.

In lobbying for mandatory crossing arms at all railroad crossings in the vicinity of schools, for example, a state senator from the northwestern corner of Louisiana argued, "There's a lot of people for giving millions and millions to the Superdome. But to save a child's life . . . we say it costs too much" (McGill, 2001). This kind of rhetoric has characterized state politics and relations between Louisiana and New Orleans for decades.

Editorials by *The Advocate*, a major newspaper in the state that is based in Baton Rouge, echoed what many outside New Orleans felt (and continue to feel) about state assistance to the city. After the state's bond commission approved millions for special projects in New Orleans in 1997, *The Advocate* concluded, "It's become an unfortunate and unpleasant fact of life: The New Orleans area grabs off the bulk of the state capital outlay money, and the rest of the state is left holding the bag" (*The Advocate*, 1997).

More than seven years later and in the midst of debates about state funding for a new football stadium in New Orleans, *The Advocate* (2004) argued, "We are delighted that the governor [Kathleen Blanco] explained the political reality to the New Orleans community: The rest of the state is not interested in paying $400 million-plus for a football stadium. And the existing state subsidy to the New Orleans Saints is widely resented" (*The Advocate*, 2004, p. 6).

A longstanding conflict exists over whether the state can trust New Orleanians to spend the aid it allocates to the city. Corruption and mismanagement afflict New Orleans' public bureaucracy, especially its school system. In 2003, for example, an audit revealed that the school system paid more than $31 million to former and even deceased workers (McGill, 2003). Less than a year later, a federal court indicted eleven people for this fraud and theft (Simpson, 2004). The federal government also charged two insurance brokers for receiving money in exchange for favorable treatment on school contracts (Simpson, 2004). In 2004, the federal government blocked the New Orleans' school board's attempt to fire Superintendent Anthony Amato, who by most accounts was succeeding in improving city schools. Most recently, Ellenese Brooks-Simms, the former president of the New Orleans School Board, pled guilty to federal bribery charges, further tainting the legacy of the school system (Maloney, 2007).

Control

Control over urban affairs traditionally divides state government and cities. State governments have attempted to control city politics and policy for several reasons. Some try to dictate urban politics for political and personal gains. In the mid 19th century, state legislators and political parties used patronage in the cities to gain electoral support in urban areas (Berman, 2003). State intervention into urban affairs has increased when governors and legislators either believed that cities could not handle the problems that confronted them or attempted to address corruption in city government. To say the least, urban actors, especially those in control, resent the assertiveness of state government.

In 2003, the state legislature and voters across Louisiana proposed and ratified a constitutional amendment to allow the state to take over failing schools. This amendment applied mainly to New Orleans. Proponents of the takeover amendment argued that the continual failure to improve the quality of education in some districts in general, and in New Orleans in particular, led them to support this policy reform. The president of the Louisiana Senate, a Republican who represented part of New Orleans, referred to the low quality of education in the city as tantamount to "intellectual slavery" (McGill, 2003).

In the vote on the amendment, three-fifths of the Louisiana electorate ratified the takeover amendment. New Orleans supported the takeover measure with 56% of the vote. The amendment received high support, 60–70%, among parishes in the New Orleans Metropolitan Statistical Area (MSA).

Part of the reason for the support for the amendment in New Orleans was the city's dismal view of the Orleans Parish School District. At the time, New Orleans' residents held negative views of the city's public schools. In a 2000 survey, half of the New

Orleans' residents who were surveyed characterized the city's elementary schools as poor whereas 61% held this view four years later (University of New Orleans Survey Research Center, 2000). Only 1% of respondents characterized these schools as excellent in 2004. In that year, New Orleans' residents regarded education as the city's second biggest problem behind crime. Despite these perceptions, 44% of the New Orleans electorate opposed the move to allow the state to assume direct control over schools that performed miserably.

The vote on the takeover amendment split along racial lines within the city of New Orleans. Voters in predominantly white districts overwhelmingly supported the amendment. Majority African-American districts strongly opposed state takeovers of failing schools.

In the pre-Katrina period, governors and state legislators were hesitant to provide exorbitant sums to the city because of New Orleans' reputation for corruption and patronage. They wanted a way to control the outcomes, and avoid sending good money after bad. In 2001, Louisiana Senator John Hainkel, who represented part of New Orleans, advocated the dissolution of the New Orleans Board of Education. He cited corruption, poor test scores, and overall mismanagement for his position; in response, a white member of the New Orleans school board regarded Hainkel's position as one dominated by a "plantation mentality," in which the senator assumed that the people of New Orleans could not govern themselves adequately (Gray, 2001).

New Orleans versus the Rest of the State

Cultural and racial divides between central cities and other areas throughout the state also heighten tensions between urban areas and state government (Gimpel & Schuknecht, 2002). Over time, a clear division existed between rural areas and cities. One source of this conflict involves which entities will control city politics. Another concerns stark differences in policy preferences. People outside of the cities, especially those in rural areas, were anti-immigrant, anti-Catholic, and anti-alcohol, among other things (Berman, 2003). By contrast, cities had high percentages of immigrants and Catholics and tolerant views on alcohol consumption. State legislatures translated these views into an anti-urban bias.

Stark differences between New Orleans and the rest of Louisiana, especially, but not exclusively, the northern part of the state, explain some of the tensions between the city and the state. Louisiana is a rural state; New Orleans is urban. Catholicism dominated New Orleans; Protestantism was the prominent religion in north Louisiana.

Over time, various governors, legislators, mayors, and other actors played out the animosity and even hatred that Louisianans in general, and those in the northern portion of the state in particular, felt toward New Orleans. Huey Long (governor from 1928–1932) and Earl Long (governor from 1939–1940; 1948–1952; 1956–1960 and lieutenant governor from 1937–1939) typified north Louisiana's disdain for all things New Orleans, namely its religion, racial composition, and culture.

Debates over control of the city and race continued to divide Louisiana governors and state legislatures against New Orleans after the Longs left office. Along with the Louisiana legislature, Governor Jimmie Davis (1944–1948; 1956–1960) opposed the *Brown v. Board of Education* decision and the integration of New Orleans public schools. In a special session of the legislature, the governor and state legislature passed a series of segregationist laws to circumvent the *Brown* decision (Garvey & Widmer, 2001). Governor Davis went so far as to take over the New Orleans schools to prevent desegregation. When that failed, he worked with the legislature to pass rigorous anti-integration laws (Crain, 1968; Parent, 2004, pp. 108–109).

Davis and the state legislature "abolished the Orleans Parish School Board, forbade all transfers, ordered the closing of any school under a desegregation order, and revoked the accreditation of integrated schools and the certification of any teachers at those schools" (Parent, 2004, p. 108). These actions to oppose racial integration illustrate the lengths state leaders went to in order to exert power over New Orleans. They also highlight the differences between the state and the city.

Edwin Edwards' (1972–1980; 1984–1988; 1992–1996) fourth and final gubernatorial election highlighted the enduring racial and religious tensions between the rest of Louisiana and New Orleans. David Duke, Edwards' opponent in the 1992 gubernatorial election and former Grand Wizard of the Knights of the Ku Klux Klan, received his strongest support from white Protestants and those in the rural parishes in north Louisiana (Robertson, 1991). In campaign speeches for the U.S. Senate in 1990, Duke "preached that the poor and minorities received too much assistance from the government and that the middle class did not get enough, instead being forced to pay for programs to assist the poor" (Renwick, Parent, & Wardlaw, 1999, p. 288).

New Orleans and Louisiana traditionally battle over the importance of the city to the rest of the state. Most actors in New Orleans claim that as New Orleans goes economically, so goes the rest of the state. Consequently, they argue that the state should provide financial resources to New Orleans because of the city's ability to generate revenue to state coffers.

Prior to his inauguration in 2002, Mayor-elect Ray Nagin told reporters, "Around the state, people understand that if New Orleans really gets going, it's good for the rest of the state" (Gyan, 2002). A year later, Nagin told the legislature, "We thank you for not hurting us yet" (*The Times-Picayune*, 2003). This statement clearly indicated that Nagin understood that legislators from around the state did not understand that what is good for New Orleans is good for the rest of the state.

In 2003, Governor Mike Foster's (1996–2004) former chief of staff, who served as president of the New Orleans Metropolitan Convention and Visitors Bureau at the time, argued, "The reality is that wherever you're from and whatever political bias you have, cultural orientation or background, if the city of New Orleans fails as an enterprise, so does the state. If New Orleans prospers, the state prospers" (Sayre, 2003).

Louisiana–New Orleans Relations in the Post-Katrina Era

How have these dimensions of the Louisiana–New Orleans historical-conflict played out in post-Katrina New Orleans? Which elements of the predisaster relationship affected the interactions between these levels of government and the manner in which New Orleans recovered after Katrina, and why? Which dimensions didn't have much of an impact at all, perhaps even when they were thought to possibly have such potential, and why?

An historical overview suggests that financial assistance, control over urban policies, programs, and bureaucracies, and cultural, socioeconomic, and racial differences
will be the greatest sources of conflict between New Orleans and Louisiana in the post-
Katrina period. We trace the interactions between Louisiana state government and New
Orleans city government in the aftermath of Hurricane Katrina in order to determine
which dimensions of the state–city relationship set the stage for what transpired after
Katrina. Specifically, we examine the extent to which financial aid and funding are cor-
related with enduring state and local tensions. Then, we address whether attempts by
Louisiana's state government to control governance and policy in post-Katrina New
Orleans continued the conflict between the state and the city. Finally, we examine how
residents from New Orleans and the rest of the state prioritize policy options in the post-
Katrina period in order to determine if significant differences continue to exist between
these parts of the state.

Money

Typically, urban politics involves struggles over scarce resources, including funding.
Ironically, in some instances of post-Katrina New Orleans, it appears that available
funding remains unspent. Nearly a year to the day after Hurricane Katrina hit New
Orleans, Mayor Nagin complained, "No real resources to help us stand up have gotten
down to our level. Zero" (Krupa, 2006, p. 1). The object of Nagin's criticisms was
Governor Blanco, who responded that the state allocated $225 million from the Federal
Emergency Management Agency (FEMA) to the city (Krupa, 2006). In response to the
governor, the mayor's assistant chief administrative officer noted that Blanco included
aid in her $225 million total that FEMA, and not the state, gave directly to city agencies
(Krupa, 2006).

As Blanco and Nagin fought over funding levels for the city, members of Blanco's
Administration insisted that Nagin need only request funds and he would receive them,
but the state seemed unwilling or unable to detail the process for these requests (*New
Orleans CityBusiness*, 2007). In a related example, FEMA recently indicated that New
Orleans was eligible for hundreds of millions of dollars in road and infrastructure repairs through Public Assistance grants, but that the city's Department of Public Works
had not yet produced a necessary list of storm-damaged streets. The city responded that
it was unaware of the grant program, and that it did not want to waste time catalogu-
ing damage when other pressing issues remained (Warner, 2007).

In his 2007 State of the City address Nagin touted the city's success, but he made it
clear that the state could be doing much more to help New Orleans. He blamed the
state for its repeated failures to issue Road Home monies in a timely manner, and criticized the federal government for not properly compensating the city (Krupa, 2007a).
The inability of the state and local governments to work together continued to affect
the recovery.

Control to Improve Governance

The city of New Orleans supported most attempts by the state to control or change governance in post-Katrina New Orleans. Local leaders and citizens tended to either support or not outwardly oppose efforts by the state to improve public institutions and

eliminate patronage, mismanagement, and corruption in the city. Hurricane Katrina provided an opportunity for the governor, the state legislature, and New Orleans citizens to attack the city's corruption and mismanagement. They took advantage of this opportunity by proposing, passing, and ratifying measures to make New Orleans government more efficient and leaner.

In the name of relief for New Orleans, the governor and the state legislature altered the structure of New Orleans public schools. According to Governor Blanco, Hurricane Katrina represented "a golden opportunity for rebirth" of New Orleans (Robelen, 2005, p. 1). The state seized the moment and reconfigured the Orleans Parish School system. This moment was met by some resistance but many others in the city either supported the transformation or held a neutral view.

In the first special session devoted to rebuilding New Orleans, the Louisiana legislature authorized the state to take over 107 of the 128 schools in the Orleans Parish School District (Ritea, 2006). At the beginning of the first full school year after Katrina, the School Recovery District (RSD), which is the entity created by the state in the takeover amendment in 2003, controlled nearly 90% of the schools in New Orleans (Gewertz, 2006). By August of 2007, the city had three school systems: the Recovery School District, which is operated directly by the state, charter schools, which were authorized by the state, and the old Orleans Parish School District (Simon, 2007). "The [RSD] system serves slightly more than a third of all city public school students, while close to 20,000 students attend the city's 40 charter schools and five traditional schools are still managed by the Orleans Parish School Board" (Simon, 2007, p. 1).

In the second special session, the governor and the state legislature proposed a constitutional amendment to eliminate the New Orleans levee board. More than 80% of voters in the state and 90% of voters in New Orleans ratified this amendment. Another constitutional amendment consolidated the number of assessors in New Orleans from seven to one. In the vote to ratify the assessors amendment in November of 2006, 78% of the voters throughout Louisiana supported this measure and 68% of the New Orleans electorate favored the consolidation. The state legislature also streamlined other offices in New Orleans, including the sheriffs and the clerks of court (Russell, 2006).

Control of Rebuilding

In the post-Katrina period, issues about how to rebuild, which entities should lead the recovery, and the allocation of federal relief funds deeply divided the state of Louisiana and the city of New Orleans. One of Nagin's initial attempts to provide a revenue stream for the city involved a plan to allow as many as seven new land-based casinos in New Orleans (Mowbray, 2005). Notwithstanding the monopoly state government previously granted to the downtown Harrah's Casino, Nagin's plan drew other criticism. Almost immediately, Blanco "urged caution" for the plan (The Times-Picayune, 2005). The idea would have required significant legislation, including the creation of a casino-zone in the city, as well as willing investment from the business community. Blanco's lack of support, as well as skepticism on the part of the state legislature, caused Nagin to eventually withdraw the plan (Wall Street Journal, 2005).

Louisiana and New Orleans created multiple commissions to deal with the city's recovery. Federal funding requires disbursement agencies, and a recovery commission is an appropriate mechanism to allocate these funds. Both Nagin and Blanco created separate recovery commissions to deal with the aftermath of Katrina. Not to be outdone, New Orleans' City Council created a third commission, and Lt. Governor Mitch Landrieu (the eventual run-off candidate in the 2006 mayoral race in New Orleans) instituted yet another. Of the four, Nagin's Bring New Orleans Back Commission and Blanco's Louisiana Recovery Authority (LRA) proved most consequential. The City Council and Landrieu commissions faded from the start, and while the Bring New Orleans Back Commission provoked significant debate about the character of the reconstruction of the city, its proposed blueprints were marred by the now infamous "green-dot" map, which covered formerly occupied neighborhoods with potential green space. The uproar from the plans of the Bring New Orleans Back Commission forced Nagin to distance himself from his own commission, and left the LRA as the only effective recovery commission in the state.

The creation and implementation of the state's Road Home Program illustrate the ongoing battle over control of programs. Governor Blanco designed this program to award housing funding for those affected by Hurricanes Katrina and Rita. She created the Road Home to disburse federal block grants when the federal government decided against creating a national-level bureaucracy. In a move that appeared politically motivated, the program was initially named Governor Blanco's Road Home Program. Blanco's public identification with the program served to promote a possible reelection campaign, and to lessen credit to Nagin, but, as time passed, Blanco decided to drop her name from the program as its performance dwindled.

Almost immediately, the Road Home Program faced a variety of difficulties. The LRA put together the proposal for the program without knowing the extent of federal funding for the program, leaving open questions about award sizes, and once the legislation to create the program was finalized, critics questioned the ethics of hiring the same consulting firm that helped draft the plan, to also administer the program (Maggi, 2006). The consulting firm, ICF International, started slowly, processing just a fraction of the applications received in the 2006 calendar year (Grace, 2006).

ICF continued to receive blame over the handling of Road Home claims. The firm, awarded a contract worth an estimated $756 million, infuriated the claimants with their plodding pace (Hammer, 2007). ICF blamed Parish offices for the lengthy closing process, and the mammoth tasks facing the LRA led Lt. Governor Landrieu to call for the establishment of a federal oversight committee, modeled after the Tennessee Valley Authority (Hammer, 2007). It turned out that parish government offices were not the only ones to blame for the delays. ICF, based in Virginia, failed to hire local appraisers to determine pre-Katrina home values, and when it recognized this flaw it turned to a subcontractor in California, which hired a subcontractor in Florida to procure a list of local appraisers in Louisiana, diluting the funding for the program while paying the subcontractors' fees (Gill, 2007).

Reacting to the failures of the LRA and the Road Home program, Nagin called for local control of the Road Home within the city limits. While highlighting the accomplishments of his administration in reviving city government, and the fact that his administration remained free of the historical corruption of the city, Nagin testified to a congressional subcommittee visiting New Orleans that he should be allowed to administer the funds to local awardees (Filosa, 2007). The state ignored Nagin's pleas, but the mayor's desire to control the funding for the rebuilding indicates a continuance of the tension-filled relationship between the state and New Orleans.

The state and the city never saw eye-to-eye on how to lead the recovery process. They disagreed about the creation of the recovery commissions, Nagin's casino plan, and the Road Home program. Recovery from such devastation is never easy, but other states affected by Katrina, such as Mississippi and Alabama, presented more streamlined processes. In previous disasters, states such as Florida proved able to unite to recover from past hurricanes, but New Orleans and Louisiana could not unify to pursue common goals.

Differences between New Orleans and the Rest of the State

Public opinion polls illustrate the continuing schisms between New Orleans and the rest of Louisiana. New Orleans residents and people throughout the state hold contrasting views of state government's spending priorities, the most important issues to the state, and the emphasis on rebuilding New Orleans (The Public Policy Research Lab, 2007).

In the spring of 2007, 46% of New Orleans residents regarded rebuilding as one of the state's three most important problems. By contrast, 30% of the people in the New Orleans metropolitan area excluding New Orleans, 29% of those in Baton Rouge, 20% of citizens in Southwest Louisiana, and just 13% of the residents in north Louisiana held this view (The Public Policy Research Lab, 2007).

In the spring of 2007, nearly 70% of New Orleanians agreed that Louisiana should continue to focus on rebuilding New Orleans, even if that effort meant paying less attention to the rest of the state (The Public Policy Research Lab, 2007). By contrast, 47% of residents in Baton Rouge, 36% of those in north Louisiana, 35% of citizens in the New Orleans metropolitan area excluding New Orleans, and 32% in Southwest Louisiana held this opinion. Overall, 51% of Louisiana residents believed that the state paid too much attention to rebuilding New Orleans and that it needed to think about other issues and other areas of Louisiana (The Public Policy Research Lab, 2007).

Enduring Tensions and Opportunities for Collaboration

Clearly, battles over finances and which entity allocates those resources constitute one of the most important ways that the pre-catastrophe relations influenced the recovery process. The state of Louisiana hesitated to provide funds directly to New Orleans in the pre-Katrina period and this tendency became amplified in the post-Katrina era. New Orleans and the state also battled over which entity would dictate how the city rebuilds. Residents in the city of New Orleans and those throughout the rest of the state continued to maintain contrasting views about the importance of New Orleans to the rest of the state. By contrast, the city of New Orleans collaborated with the rest of the state in approving the elimination of the levee board and the reduction in the number of assessors in Orleans Parish. Many even accepted major changes to the city's school system without much resistance.

Why did certain state–local tensions continue while others tended to subside? Distrust of public officials in New Orleans explains why friction persisted in some areas but waned in others. Hurricane Katrina did not alter the governor and state legislature's distrust of the city of New Orleans. Money drives the rebuilding of New Orleans and therefore, it sits at the center of the tensions between the city and state government. The state of Louisiana did not want the city to control hundreds of millions of federal recovery dollars. The city's continuing problems with corruption and mismanagement led the state to want to account for, oversee, and dictate the terms of the spending of federal funds.

Hurricane Katrina did not change how the city felt about not receiving aid. The city leaders complained about not getting the money in a timely fashion and the delay frustrated them. In the post-Katrina period, the pattern of state–local battles over money intensified.

The state's motivation for changing the number of assessors and eliminating the levee board also stemmed from a lack of trust in the ways that New Orleans managed its public policies. Hurricane Katrina gave an opportunity to the state and others to attack mismanagement. Many residents in New Orleans supported changes in the number of assessors and the elimination of the levee board because they too wanted an elimination of corruption and mismanagement in the public sector.

Hurricane Katrina resulted in key demographic changes in the city. Studies of the 2006 mayoral election indicate key shifts in the New Orleans electorate, with blacks losing 10% of their share of the electorate, while whites gained a 10% share. As noted above, these changes, including a higher percentage of white voters, as well as an upward shift in the income of voters, strongly influenced post-Katrina elections. The constitutional change to the levee boards illustrates this shift. In this instance, the business community also joined in the call for the levee board consolidation (*New Orleans CityBusiness*, 2006). The change in the racial composition of the electorate, and perhaps more importantly, the shift in class levels of the electorate, lead to the possibility that when the interests of the remaining electorate coincide with the interests of the state—in this example, the desire for increased accountability and a reduction in the possibility of corruption and malfeasance—the city and state can cooperate.

Several factors explain the favorable or neutral reactions to the state's control over so many schools in Orleans Parish. First, as a result of Hurricane Katrina, many residents of predominantly white districts, which strongly supported the takeover measure in 2003, remained in the city after the storm. By contrast, many residents of majority-African American, which opposed the takeover measure in 2003, had yet to return to the city by the start of the 2006 school year.

Next, the status of the school system was so awful that proponents of the reform saw the hurricane as an opportunity to improve the beleaguered district. Third, the RSD put the state in control of one-third of the schools, but other reforms increased local control. The creation of charter schools promised to increase local input in the functioning of New Orleans public schools, and many residents supported this change.

In areas other than education, elected officials and citizens in New Orleans wanted the city, not the state, to control the rebuilding of the city. Hurricane Katrina did not change how those who remained in New Orleans felt about local autonomy. Throughout time, localities have feared losing autonomy to higher levels of government, and certainly, the state's efforts to control the rebuilding enflamed New Orleanians' attitudes that the city was losing autonomy.

Hurricane Katrina did not change how the rest of the state felt toward New Orleans. In fact, it intensified the debate over the value of New Orleans to the rest of the state. State legislators from areas outside New Orleans will have to approve funding, policies, and other laws geared toward the recovery of the city. Decisions about how much to spend on New Orleans and whether to facilitate the rebuilding over issue-areas depends upon how these legislators regard the centrality of New Orleans to the state. Survey data indicate that people outside the New Orleans metropolitan area are much less enthusiastic about rebuilding the city than are those within this area. These opinions, which are often filtered through elected representatives, continue to heighten the tension between the city and the state. They influence the recovery because the state legislature will pursue spending and policy priorities that are not linked to the rebuilding of New Orleans. The tendency of those from north Louisiana and other parts of the state to want to focus on areas other than rebuilding New Orleans is a carryover from the pre-Katrina period.

The aftermath of Hurricane Katrina illustrates the significant role state government plays in urban affairs. The city's governance structure changed after Katrina and state government led this effort. The governor and legislature championed efforts to eliminate the levee board in New Orleans and to cut the number of city assessors to one. The sluggish speed of the recovery, especially in the area of housing rebuilding and payments, is attributable in part to the state's hesitancy to allocate federal funds to the city.

What we find, then, is that even in the face of utter chaos, where there appears to be a strong potential for a wholesale rearrangement of political relationships, historical patterns continue to affect these relationships. Continuing struggles over funding, the direction of the rebuilding, and the operation of key services illustrate the impact of these historical patterns. Critics fault urban scholarship for failing to acknowledge or investigate the role of the state–local relationship, and this research indicates this relationship can play a critical role in the governance of a city.

NOTES

Editor's Introductory Essay

1. Saskia Sassen, *The Global City: New York, London, Tokyo,* 2nd ed. (Princeton, NJ: Princeton University Press, 2001).
2. Richard Florida, *The Rise of the Creative Class* (New York: Basic Books, 2002).
3. Todd Swanstrom, "Semisovereign Cities: The Politics of Urban Development," *Polity* 21 (Fall 1988): 83–110.
4. John R. Logan, "The New Ethnic Enclaves in America's Suburbs," a report by the Lewis Mumford Center for Comparative Urban and Regional Research (Albany, NY: 2002), pp. 1–2.
5. William A. V. Clark and Sarah A. Blue, "Race, Class, and Segregation Patterns in U.S. Immigrant Gateway Cities," *Urban Affairs Review* 39, 6 (2004): 667–688.
6. Jim Hinch and Ronald Campbell, "Gated Enclaves One Future for Orange County," *Orange County Register,* May 15, 2002 (www.ocregister.com).
7. Ibid., quoting William Frey, a demographer in the Milken Institute of Los Angeles.
8. Dennis R. Judd, "Enclosure, Community, and Public Life," in Dan A. Chekki (ed.), *Research in Community Sociology: New Communities in a Changing World* (Greenwich, Connecticut: JAI Press, 1996), pp. 217–238.

Chapter 1

1 The Interests of the Limited City

1. Flathman, R. E. 1966. *The public interest* (New York: John Wiley).
2. Banfield, E. C. 1961. *Political influence* (Glencoe, Illinois: Free Press). Ch. 12.
3. Tiebout, C. M. 1956. A pure theory of local expenditures. *Journal of Political Economy* 64: 416–424.
4. Ibid., p. 419.
5. Ibid., p. 420.
6. Bruce Hamilton, "Property Taxes and the Tiebout Hypothesis: Some Empirical Evidence," and Michelle J. White, "Fiscal Zoning in Fragmented Metropolitan Areas," in Mills, E. S., and Oates, W. E. 1975. *Fiscal zoning and land use controls* (Lexington, Massachusetts: Lexington Books). Chs. 2 and 3.
7. See Weber, "Class, Status, and Power," in Gerth, H. H., and Mills, C. W., trans. 1946. *From Max Weber* (New York: Oxford University Press).
8. For a more complete discussion of roles, structures, and interests, see Greenstone, J. D., and Peterson, P. E. 1976. *Race and authority in urban politics.* Phoenix edition (Chicago: University of Chicago Press). Ch. 2.
9. Cf. Thompson, W. R. 1965. *A preface to urban economics* (Baltimore, Maryland: Johns Hopkins University Press).
10. I treat entrepreneurial skill as simply another form of labor, even though it is a form in short supply.
11. Elazar, D. J. 1976. *Cities of the prairie* (New York: Basic Books).
12. Weber, M. 1921. *The city* (New York: Collier Books).
13. United States Department of Commerce, Bureau of the Census. 1977. *Local government finances in selected metropolitan areas and large counties: 1975–76.* Government finances: GF 76, no. 6.

2 Urban Regimes

1. James G. March, "The Business Firm as a Political Coalition," *Journal of Politics* 24 (November 1962): 662–678.
2. Chester I. Barnard, *The Functions of the Executive* (Cambridge, Mass.: Harvard University Press, 1968).
3. Oliver E. Williamson, *The Economic Institutions of Capitalism* (New York: Free Press, 1985).
4. Ibid., 10.
5. See Norton E. Long, "The Local Community as an Ecology of Games," *American Journal of Sociology* 64 (November 1958): 251–261.
6. Cf. Graham T. Allison, *Essence of Decision* (Boston: Little, Brown, 1971).

7. See Philip Selznick, *Leadership in Administration* (New York: Harper & Row, 1957).

8. Cf. Bryan D. Jones and Lynn W. Bachelor, *The Sustaining Hand* (Lawrence: University of Kansas Press, 1986).

9. See especially Martin Shefter, "The Emergence of the Political Machine: An Alternative View," in *Theoretical Perspectives on Urban Politics,* by Willis D. Hawley and others (Englewood Cliffs, N.J.: Prentice-Hall, 1976).

10. Clarence N. Stone, Robert K. Whelan, and William J. Murin. *Urban Policy and Politics in a Bureaucratic Age,* 2d ed. (Englewood Cliffs, N.J.: Prentice-Hall, 1986, 104).

11. Stephen L. Elkin, *City and Regime in the American Republic* (Chicago: University of Chicago Press, 1987).

12. Ibid.

13. Cf. Jones and Bachelor, *The Sustaining Hand,* 214–215.

14. But see Elkin, *City and Regime;* Martin Shefter, *Political Crisis/Fiscal Crisis: The Collapse and Revival of New York City* (New York: Basic Books, 1985); and Todd Swanstrom, *The Crisis of Growth Politics* (Philadelphia: Temple University Press, 1985).

15. Robert H. Wiebe, *The Search for Order, 1877–1920* (New York: Hill and Wang, 1967), 10.

16. Russell Hardin, *Collective Action* (Baltimore: Johns Hopkins University Press, 1982); and Michael Taylor, *The Possibility of Cooperation* (Cambridge, Mass.: Cambridge University Press, 1987).

17. Mancur Olson, Jr., *The Logic of Collective Action* (Cambridge, Mass.: Harvard University Press, 1965).

18. Hardin, *Collective Action.*

19. Robert Axelrod, *The Evolution of Cooperation* (New York: Basic Books, 1984).

20. Hardin, *Collective Action;* and David D. Laitin, *Hegemony and Culture* (Chicago: University of Chicago Press, 1986).

21. Taylor, *Possibility of Cooperation.*

22. Charles Tilly, *Big Structures, Large Processes, Huge Comparisons* (New York: Russell Sage Foundation, 1984), 27.

23. Philip Abrams, *Historical Sociology* (Ithaca, N.Y.: Cornell University Press, 1982). For a similar understanding applied to urban politics, see John R. Logan and Harvey L. Molotch, *Urban Fortunes* (Berkeley and Los Angeles: University of California Press, 1987).

24. Cf. Anthony Giddens, *Central Problems in Social Theory* (Berkeley and Los Angeles: University of California Press, 1979).

25. Cf. James G. March and Johan P. Olsen, "The New Institutionalism," *American Political Science Review* 78 (September 1984): 734–749.

26. Abrams, *Historical Sociology,* 331.

27. Ibid.

28. Michael L. Porter, "Black Atlanta: An Interdisciplinary Study of Blacks on the East Side of Atlanta, 1890–1930" (Ph.D. diss., Emory University, 1974); Walter White, *A Man Called White* (New York: Arno Press and the New York Times, 1969); and Dana F. White, "The Black Sides of Atlanta," *Atlanta Historical Journal* 26 (Summer/Fall 1982): 199–225.

29. Kenneth T. Jackson, *The Ku Klux Klan in the City 1915–1930* (New York: Oxford University Press, 1967); and Herbert T. Jenkins, *Forty Years on the Force: 1932–1972* (Atlanta: Center for Research in Social Change, Emory University, 1973).

30. Charles H. Martin, *The Angelo Herndon Case and Southern Justice* (Baton Rouge: Louisiana State University Press, 1976); Kenneth Coleman, ed., *A History of Georgia* (Athens: University of Georgia Press, 1977), 294; and Writer's Program of the Works Progress Administration, *Atlanta: A City of the Modern South* (St. Clairshores, Mich.: Somerset Publishers, 1973), 69.

31. Lorraine N. Spritzer, *The Belle of Ashby Street: Helen Douglas Mankin and Georgia Politics* (Athens: University of Georgia Press, 1982).

32. John Bonner, *Introduction to the Theory of Social Choice* (Baltimore: Johns Hopkins University Press, 1986), 34.

33. Stein Rokkan, "Norway: Numerical Democracy and Corporate Pluralism," in *Political Oppositions in Western Democracies,* ed. Robert A. Dahl (New Haven, Conn.: Yale University Press, 1966), 105; see also [Steven Erie, *Rainbow's End: Irish-Americans and the Dilemmas of Urban Machine Politics, 1840–1985* (Berkeley: University of California Press, 1988)].

34. Matthew A. Crenson, *The Un-Politics of Air Pollution* (Baltimore: Johns Hopkins University Press, 1971); see also Edwin H. Rhyne, "Political Parties and Decision Making in Three Southern Counties," *American Political Science Review* 52 (December 1958): 1091–1107.

35. Clarence N. Stone, "Preemptive Power: Floyd Hunter's 'Community Power Structure' Reconsidered," *American Journal of Political Science* 32 (February 1988): 82–104.

36. Norman Frohlich and Joe A. Oppenheimer, *Modern Political Economy* (Englewood Cliffs, N.J.: Prentice-Hall, 1978), 19–31.

3 Rethinking the Politics of Downtown Development

1. http://www.greatergreenville.com/development/dt_fun.asp.
2. http://www.downtownstl.org/.
3. In some cities, downtown housing development benefits from an array of producer subsidies, so "market rate" is not an entirely accurate term. Most new downtown housing is not, however, "assisted" housing, with consumer subsidies and restrictions on residents incomes.
4. The extent of the downtown residential "boom" should not be exaggerated—Birch notes that, in the 45 cities she studies, the net gain in downtown population between 1970 and 2000 has totaled 35,000, while during the same period the suburban parts of these metro areas have gained 13 million residents. But these aggregate numbers obscure the significant downtown residential gains in some cities, where entire new residential districts have been established in downtown areas.
5. From the Greater Baltimore Committee statement of priorities, found on their website (www.gbc.org), accessed March 2006.
6. For example, the Allegheny Conference for Community Development, which had spearheaded the redevelopment of Pittsburgh's "Golden Triangle" through urban renewal programs, is now part of a larger regional alliance with no downtown program focus, while since 1994 a Pittsburgh Downtown Partnership has taken up the task of promoting the downtown.
7. BIDS are not only found in downtowns, but in outlying business areas as well. A 1999 survey found 404 BIDS in 43 states (although some states use other terms for them). Mitchell, 2001; Morçöl & Zimmerman, 2006.
8. Mitchell (2001) also finds many groups reporting involvement in "advocacy," but here advocacy is meant to describe activities working to link public and private sector actors engaged in downtown, rather than a broader involvement in political affairs.
9. Some of these observations are drawn from interviews with heads and board members of downtown organizations in Philadelphia, Seattle, Charlotte, and Detroit between 1999 and 2002 conducted by the author for an earlier research project. Several of those interviewed specifically talked about the decline of CEO board representation, and the strategies they employ to remain effective despite the diminished prominence of their board representation.
10. There is a professional organization, the International Downtown Association, to which most downtown organizations belong. See Gendron (2006) for more on this organization's significance.
11. Although, as Healey and Barrett (1990) note, this process is not unproblematic.
12. A few cities, such as New York or London, have such a concentration of very large real estate interests (developers, architects, financiers) that they do, indeed, export real estate services. In cities that are first-order tourism or second home/retirement magnets, real estate could also be seen as an export industry, as the end users of real estate products spend money earned somewhere else. In these cases, real estate is a more dominant economic sector, and prominent real estate capitalists may also have a more central role in political and civic life.
13. There are some interesting histories of the national real estate industry—see Weiss (1987); as well as local case studies that address the importance of real estate lobby groups in the policymaking process—see Gotham (2002)—but these do not really ask how and why individual property owners and developers organize to effect change in the central business district.

Chapter 2

4 Cities in the International Marketplace

i. Other parts of the world have also formed transnational associations, including the Association of South East Asian Nations (Brunei, Indonesia, Malaysia, Philippines, Singapore, Thailand, and Vietnam) and Mancusor (Argentina, Brazil, Paraguay, and Uruguay).
ii. Primate cities are giant entities, at least twice as large as the next largest city in the nation, and not infrequently they hold 20 percent or more of a nation's population. While primate cities are not always at the nexus of the global economy, they are central to a national economy and generate a substantial portion of its GDP.
iii. There are also cultural, social, and geographical reasons for this. Anglo-American traditions favor country and low-density living, while Continental traditions are more disposed to high-density or clustered environments. In America, the availability of greater space and racial enmity contributed to middle-class white flight.
iv. Instances of both democratic and antidemocratic movements can be traced in some ways to globalization. In 1999 the overthrow of the Indonesian government was made possible by Internet communication in that nation's archipelago.

Within the next year, populist, protest movements held large-scale demonstrations in Seattle and Washington, D.C. Populist demonstrations against Iran's repressive theocracy have also been held and gained resonance through telecommunications. On the other side, in the United States neo-Nazi and racist groups have been able to mobilize followers through the Internet. Also, marginal political parties in both America and Europe have capitalized on a reaction against global trade (in the U.S., Patrick Buchanan's Reform Party; in France, Jean-Marie Le Pen's National Front; in Italy Gianfranco Fini's neofascists).

v. Every action has its reaction, and globalism is no different. Vulnerability also has a more fortunate side that can be found in cross-national cooperation and synergy. This kind of complementary interdependence has brought about cooperation in regulating currencies, controlling AIDS and combating terrorism.

1. Knight and Gappert, *Cities in a Global Society*; Judd and Parkinson, *Leadership and Urban Regeneration*.
2. Population Action International, *Global Migration*.
3. Stoltz, "Europe's Back Doors."
4. A.T. Kearney, Inc., "Globalization Index."
5. Sassen, *Cities in World Economy*.
6. Savitch, *Post-industrial Cities*; Sassen, *Global City*.
7. Swanstrom, "Semisovereign Cities"; Hill, "Cleveland Economy."
8. Gappert, *Future of Winter Cities*.
9. Dangschat and Obenbrugge, "Hamburg."
10. Bernard and Rice, *Sunbelt Cities*; Ruble, Tulchin, and Garland, "Globalism and Local Realities."
11. Gotttman, *Megalopolis*.
12. U.S. Bureau of the Census, "Population of the 100 Largest Cities"; State of the Cities Census Data Systems.
13. Sternlieb and Hughes, *Post-industrial America*; Kantor with David, *Dependent City*; Kantor, *Dependent City Revisited*, chap. 6.
14. Mumford, *City in History*; Jacobs, *Death and Life of Great American Cities*; Garls, *Urban Villagers*.
15. Savitch, "Global Challenge."
16. Sassen, *Global City, Cities in a World Economy*; A.T. Kearney, Inc., "Globalization Index."
17. Held, "Democracy."
18. Knight and Gappert, *Cities in Global Society*; United Nations Centre for Human Settlements, *Indicators Newsletter*.
19. Smith, *Transnational Urbanism*.
20. Savitch and Ardashev, "Does Terror Have an Urban Future?"
21. Webber, "Order in Diversity."
22. Kresl, "North American Cities International"; Sassen, *Cities in World Economy*; Glickman, "Cities and International Division of Labor."
23. Prud'homme, "Les sept plus grandes villes du monde"; Savitch, "Cities in a Global Era."
24. European Foundation for the Improvement of Living and Working Conditions, *Living Conditions* (1986); Baugher and Lamison-White, *Poverty*.
25. O'Connor, *Fiscal Crisis of State*; Saunders, "Central Local Relations."
26. Judd and Fainstein, *Tourist City*.
27. Schumpeter, *Capitalism, Socialism and Democracy*.
28. Swyngedouw, "Mammon Quest"; Ascher, *Metapolis ou l'Avenir des Villes*.
29. Polanyi, *Great Transformation*.
30. Logan and Molotch, *Urban Fortunes*.
31. Rubin and Rubin, "Economic Development Incentives."
32. Mollenkopf, *Contested City*.
33. Williams and Adrian, *Four Cities*; Swanstrom, "Semisovereign Cities."
34. Muzzio and Bailey, "Economic Development"; Clavel, *Progressive City*.
35. Clark and Inglehart, "New Political Culture"; Clark, "Structural Realignments."
36. Miranda, Rosdil, and Yeh, "Growth Machines."
37. Peterson, *City Limits*.
38. Stone and Sanders, *Politics of Urban Development*; Stone, *Regime Politics*; Swanstrom, "Semisovereign Cities"; Logan and Molotch, *Urban Fortunes*.
39. Leo, "City Politics"; Clarke and Gaile, *Work of Cities*.

5 Globalization and Leadership in American Cities

1. Examples are the *Greater* Baltimore Committee, Charlotte *Regional* Partnership; *Greater* Cleveland Partnership, *Metro* Hartford Alliance, *Greater* Houston Partnership, Civic Council of *Greater* Kansas City, Council, *Greater* Milwaukee Committee, *Greater* Philadelphia Chamber of Commerce, *Greater* Phoenix Leadership.

7 Can Politicians Bargain with Business?

1. Urban Summit Conference, New York City, 12 November 1990.

Chapter 3

8 The Power of Place: The Creative Class

1. Adjusted for the costs of living differences, the average salary for an IT worker in Austin was

$65,310 compared to $47,173 in San Francisco in 2001 (based on salary data from the *Information Week* Salary Survey adjusted for cost-of-living).

2. Kevin Kelly, *New Rules for the New Economy*, 1998, pp. 94–95.

3. Some classic statements include: Robert Park, E. Burgess and R. McKenzie, *The City*. Chicago: University of Chicago Press, 1925; Jane Jacobs, *The Death and Life of Great American Cities*. New York: Random House, 1961; *The Economy of Cities*. New York: Random House, 1969; *Cities and the Wealth of Nations*. New York: Random House, 1984; Wilbur Thompson, *A Preface to Urban Economics*. Baltimore: The Johns Hopkins University Press, 1965; Edwin Ullman, "Regional Development and the Geography of Concentration." *Papers and Proceedings of the Regional Science Association*, 4, 1958, pp. 179–198.

4. See Michael Porter, "Clusters and the New Economics of Competition." *Harvard Business Review*, November–December 1998; "Location, Clusters, and Company Strategy," in Gordon Clark, Meric Gertler and Maryann Feldman (eds.), *Oxford Handbook of Economic Geography*. Oxford: Oxford University Press, 2000; "Location, Competition and Economic Development: Local Clusters in a Global Economy." *Economic Development Quarterly* 14(1), February 2000, pp. 15–34.

5. The literature on agglomeration economies is vast, for a recent review see Maryann Feldman, "Location and Innovation: The New Economic Geography of Innovation, Spillovers, and Agglomeration," in Clark, Gertler and Feldman (eds.), *The Oxford Handbook of Economic Geography*, pp. 373–394; Adam Jaffe, "Real Effects of Academic Research." *American Economic Review*, 79(5), 1989; David Audretsch and Maryann Feldman, "R&D Spillovers and the Geography of Innovation and Production." *American Economic Review*, 86(3), 1996; David Audretsch, "Agglomeration and the Location of Innovative Activity." *Oxford Review of Economic Policy*, 14(2), 1998, pp. 18–30.

6. Robert Putnam, *Bowling Alone: The Collapse and Revival of American Community*. New York: Simon and Schuster, 2000.

7. Joel Kotkin, "The New Geography of Wealth." *Reis.com, Techscapes*, December 2001; available on-line at www.reis.com/learning/insights_techscapes_art.cfm?art=1.

8. See Jacobs, *Cities and the Wealth of Nations*.

9. Robert Lucas, Jr., "On the Mechanics of Economic Development." *Journal of Monetary Economics*, 22, 1988, pp. 38–39.

10. See Edward Glaeser, "Are Cities Dying?" *Journal of Economic Perspectives*, 12, 1998, pp. 139–160. The human capital literature has grown large; other important contributions include: Glaeser, "The New Economics of Urban and Regional Growth," in Clark, Gertler and Feldman (eds.), *The Oxford Handbook of Economic Geography*, pp. 83–98; James E. Rauch, "Productivity Gains from Geographic Concentrations of Human Capital: Evidence from Cities." *Journal of Urban Economics*, 34, 1993, pp. 380–400; Curtis Simon, "Human Capital and Metropolitan Employment Growth." *Journal of Urban Economics*, 43, 1998, pp. 223–243; Curtis Simon and Clark Nardinelli, "The Talk of the Town: Human Capital, Information and the Growth of English Cities, 1861–1961." *Emplorations in Economic History*, 33(3), 1996, pp. 384–413. A comprehensive review is provided by Vijay K. Mathur, "Human Capital-Based Strategy for Regional Economic Development." *Economic Development Quarterly*, 13(3), 1999, pp. 203–216.

11. Spencer Glendon, "Urban Life Cycles." Cambridge: Harvard University, Department of Economics, unpublished working paper, November 1998.

12. Patricia Beeson, personal communication with author, winter 2000.

13. See Richard Lloyd and Terry Nichols Clark, "The City as an Entertainment Machine," in Kevin Fox Gotham (ed.), *Critical Perspectives on Urban Redevelopment. Research in Urban Sociology*, Vol. 6. Oxford: JAI Press/Elsevier, 2001, pp. 357–378.

14. Erica Coslor, "Work Hard, Play Hard: The Role of Nightlife in Creating Dynamic Cities." Pittsburgh: Heinz School of Public Policy and Management, Carnegie Mellon University, unpublished paper, December 2001.

15. Ray Oldenburg, *The Great Good Place: Cafes, Coffee Shops, Bars, Hair Salons and Other Hangouts at the Heart of a Community*. New York: Marlowe and Company, 1989.

16. Personal interview by author, spring 2001.

17. Bonnie Menes Kahn, *Cosmopolitan Culture: The Gilt Edged Dream of a Tolerant City*. New York: Simon and Schuster, 1987.

18. Personal interview by author, winter 2001.

19. I am indebted to Lenn Kano, a former Carnegie Mellon student for this term.

20. Simon Frith, *Performing Rites: On the Value of Popular Music.* Oxford: Oxford University Press, 1996, p. 273, italics in original.
21. Manuel Castells, *The Power of Identity: The Information Age: Economy, Society, and Culture,* Volume I. Oxford: Blackwell Publishers, 1997.
22. Richard Lloyd, "Digital Bohemia: New Media Enterprises in Chicago's Wicker Park. " Paper presented at the annual conference of the American Sociological Association, August 2001, p. 8.

9 Culture, Art, and Downtown Development

1. Major performing arts centers are defined as those with 1,000 seats or more. Major museums are those with annual attendance of 50,000 or more. Because this survey looks only at large cultural facilities, it understates the full extent of cultural building.
2. No doubt cultural institution capital campaigns have been aided by the unusually prosperous 1990s. States and cities had budget surpluses, and wealthy individuals could gain prestige and tax benefits by donating stock market gains to nonprofit arts institutions. Many of these projects, however, originated years before the economic boom.
3. Similar comments were made by cultural trustees of cultural organizations interviewed by the author as part of an ongoing study of Newark- and Philadephia-based organizations.
4. Comments of museum administrator made at the Art of the Deal conference, Rutgers University, New Brunswick, 27 March, 2001.
5. Arts administrators report that individual patrons have gained in importance in the late 1990s; individual giving has been fueled by the strong stock market (comments of museum administrator made at the Art of the Deal conference, 2001).
6. Whitt (1987) has questioned the methods by which the Business Committee for the Arts collects its data; as an advocacy group, it could well be inclined to inflate the importance of business contributions.
7. Comments of corporate foundation executive made at the Art of the Deal conference, 2001.
8. This strategy seems to be successful: Many museums point to big jumps in membership during blockbuster exhibits (Dobrzynski 1998).
9. The media play a role in cementing this convergence of interests. A study of newspaper arts coverage found that visual arts get short shrift in most newspapers, except when blockbuster exhibits come to town. Local media, then, become part of the system making highly visible and popular exhibits useful for arts institutions and local development officials (Janeway et al. 1999).
10. The National Endowment for the Arts studied the arts institutions of six cities and found that only in three did they generate as much or more local revenue than they cost the city in subsidies and services. Had these calculations included the costs of state and federal subsidies, the balance sheet would have even looked less favorable.

10 (Re)Branding the Big Easy

* Editor's note: Readers may wish to consult additional notes, references, and statistical appendices in the original text due to their elimination in this copy.

1. Tourism "practices" can include the socialization of locals to view their hometown as a tourist site, the aestheticization of space, and the development of promotional strategies to project a nostalgic view of local history and place. In the realm of law and public policy, tourism practices involve the development of legal and regulatory forms to facilitate the circulation of people to particular places, the growth of a hospitality industry, and the development of a transportation and cultural infrastructure to accommodate visitors. In this sense, tourism practices are multidimensional and can include forms of migration and mobility, flows of people and commodities, and different modes of consumption. In addition, tourism practices are about the production of cultural difference and the valorization of local authenticity to stimulate people to visit a place to consume its distinct characteristics including, for example, music, cuisine, culture, history, and identities. For overviews, see Gladstone (2005), Hoffman, Fainstein, and Judd (2003), Judd and Fainstein (1999), Desmond (1999), and Sheller and Urry (2004).
2. Figures on the growth in numbers of hotel rooms and conventions come from the New Orleans Metropolitan Convention and Visitor Bureau (NOMCVB), Ernest N. Morial Convention Center, New Orleans Aviation Board, Louisiana Office of Tourism, U.S. Travel Data Center, and Louisiana Hotel-Motel Association.
3. Local newspapers began to document the revenue problems of New Orleans as early as 1966. Media coverage continued throughout the decade. See *New Orleans States-Item* 1966, 1967, 1968, 1969; New Orleans Office of Policy Planning and Analysis 1976.
4. The changing ratio of tax revenue is reported in the City of New Orleans Operating Budget, 1964

and 1984. Calculations are by the Commission on the Future of the City (1985).

5. These fiscal constraints included (1) a reduction in the ability of local governments to collect income taxes, thereby increasing their reliance on revenue from sales taxes; (2) a statute that two-thirds of both houses of the state legislature had to approve any increase in an existing local tax, and (3) an expanded exemption on home owners' property taxes. The state legislature increased this homestead exemption from $50,000 of assessed valuation in 1974 to $75,000 in 1982 (Smith and Keller 1986, 150–154). On the local level, New Orleans's long tradition of elected assessors who owned their assessor databases and distribution of assessed property values meant that assessors appraised few homes over $75,000 (Smith and Keller 1986; Knopp 1990; Lauria 1984).

6. The specific subsidies of the GO Zone include tax-exempt bond financing, accelerated depreciation deductions of 50% for new development, an extension that allows carrying net operating losses for five years instead of two, allowances for demolition and clean-up expenses, plus other targeted tax breaks related to labor and restoration of commercial spaces.

Chapter 4

11 Racial Confrontation in Postwar Detroit

1. Joseph Coles, a prominent Democratic activist and an appointee to the Detroit Mayor's Interracial Committee (MIC), stated that 155 homeowners' associations existed in Detroit during the Cobo administration. Joseph Coles, Oral History, 15. Blacks in the Labor Movement Collection, ALUA. Coles slightly underestimated the number of associations. At least 171 organizations existed during the Cobo administration and at least 191 organizations thrived in Detroit from the end of World War II to 1965. This figure undoubtedly understates the number of such associations, for many were ephemeral and kept no records. The most important source is: "Improvement Associations of Detroit, List From Zoning Board of Appeals," July 12, 1955, DUL, Box 43, Folder A7–13, which includes names and addresses of 88 improvement associations. Through a detailed survey of letters and petitions on matters of housing and expressway construction sent to Mayor Albert Cobo, and especially through careful examination of letters in Cobo's separate files of correspondence from "civic associations," I was able to identify another

83 neighborhood groups not included in the 1955 list. See Mayor's Papers (1950) Boxes 2, 3, 5; (1951) Boxes 2, 3; (1953) Box 1, 3, 4; (1954) Box 2; (1955) Boxes 2, 4. The remaining associations were identified in a number of sources: a list of property owners' associations that joined the amicus curiae brief for the plaintiff in *Sipes v. McGhee* before the Michigan Supreme Court in Clement Vose. *Caucasians Only: The Supreme Court, the NAACP, and the Restrictive Covenant Cases* (Berkeley: University of California Press, 1959), 272, n. 41; Richard J. Peck, Community Services Department, Detroit Urban League, "Summary of Known Improvement Association Activities in Past Two Years 1955–1957," 6, in VF, Pre-1960, Folder: Community Organization 1950s; *Michigan Chronicle.* December 4, 1948, August 6, 1955, September 9, 1961; *Detroit News,* July 21, 1962; *Brightmoor Journal,* May 3, 1956, October 29, 1964, June 2, 1966, October 19, 1967, November 16, 1967; letters and brochures in SLAA; MIC, Incident Reports 1949, CCR, Part I, Series 1, Box 6, Folder 49–37; "A Study of Interracial Housing Incidents," January 20, 1949, ibid., Folder 49–3; CCR, Field Reports December 18, 1961, in RK, Box 2, Folder 4.

2. In 1955, housing activist Charles Abrams noted the importance of improvement associations in major cities and the dearth of studies of their activities. See Charles Abrams, *Forbidden Neighbors: A Study of Prejudice in Housing* (New York: Harper, 1955), 181–90. Abrams's call for research has remained largely unheeded, with the important exception of the brilliant discussion of Los Angeles' powerful grassroots homeowners' association movement in Mike Davis, *City of Quartz: Excavating the Future in Los Angeles* (London: Verso, 1990), 153–219.

3. Quotes from *Action!* the Newsletter of the Courville District Improvement Association, vol. 1 (February 15, 1948), attached to Mayor's Interracial Committee Minutes, April 4, 1948, CCR, Part I, Series I, Box 10; *The Civic Voice,* the newsletter of the Plymouth Manor Property Owners Association vol. 2, no. 9 (September 1962), in CCR, Part III, Box 25, Folder 25–128. For examples of ethnic diversity in Detroit, letters to Mayor Edward Jeffries, regarding the Algonquin Street and Oakwood defense housing projects, in Mayor's Papers (1945), Box 3, Folder: Housing Commission. See also Exhibit A, October 22, 1945, 1–2, attached to Memorandum to Charles S. Johnson et al. from Charles H. Houston, NAACP, Group II, Box B133, Folder: Michigan: *Swanson*

v. *Hayden: Neighborhood Informer*, Greater Detroit Neighbors Association—Unit No. 2 (December 1949), 2, UAW-CAP, Box 4, Folder 4–19. The editor of the *Informer*, it should be mentioned, was a James Sugrue, a first cousin once removed of the author. For derogatory references to Jews, see "Demonstrations Protesting Negro Occupancy of Homes, September 1, 1945–September 1, 1946: Memorandum J," 31, CCR, Part I, Series 1, Box 3; and "Activities of the East Outer Drive Improvement Association," February 8, 1947, ibid., Part III, Box 25, Folder 25–49. For a reference to "niggers, chinamen, and russians," see William K. Anderson to Herbert Schultz, October 17, 1958, SLAA. For housing incidents involving an Indian family, a Chinese family, and a Filipino family moving into white neighborhoods, see Chronological Index of Cases, 1951 (51–31) and (51–58), CCR, Part I, Series 1, Box 13; Detroit Police Department Special Investigation Bureau, Summary of Racial Activities, April 30, 1956–May 17, 1956, DUL, Box 38, Folder A2–26. On the ethnic heterogeneity of Detroit neighborhoods, see Olivier Zunz, *The Changing Face of Inequality: Urbanization, Industrial Development and immigrants in Detroit, 1880–1920* (Chicago, 1982), 340–51. In his examination of arrest records for whites arrested in anti-public housing riots in Chicago, Arnold Hirsch also found great diversity in ethnic affiliations. See Hirsch, *Making the Second Ghetto: Race and Housing in Chicago, 1940–1960* (New York: Cambridge University Press, 1983), 81–84.

4. See Dominic J. Capeci, Jr. and Martha Wilkerson, *Layered Violence: The Detroit Rioters of 1943* (Jackson: The University Press of Mississippi, 1991); on Briggs, see John M. Hartigan, Jr., "Cultural Constructions of Whiteness: Racial and Class Formations in Detroit" (Ph.D. diss., University of California, Santa Cruz, 1995); Arthur Kornhauser, *Detroit as the People See It; A Survey of Attitudes in an Industrial City* (Detroit: Wayne University Press, 1952), 104. On Southern whites and their organizational affiliations, see Cleo Y. Boyd, "Detroit's Southern Whites and the Store-Front Churches," Department of Research and Church Planning, Detroit Council of Churches, 1958, in DUL, Box 44, Folder A8–25; on their voting patterns, see Handwritten Vote Counts [1949], UAW-PAC, Box 63, Folder 63–2; "Degree of Voting in Detroit Primary," September 11, 1951, and "Indexes of Group Voting for Selected Councilmanic Candidates," September 11, 1951, ibid., Box 62, Folder 62–25. In 1956, Mrs. Cledah Sundwall, a Northwest Side resident and possibly a southern white migrant, called for the creation of a White Citizens Council in Detroit, calling it a "modern version of the old-time town meeting called to meet any crisis by expressing the will of the people. The primary aim of the council is to combat the NAACP and to preserve the upkeep of neighborhoods" (*Brightmoor Journal*, May 3, 1956). There is no evidence that the organization attracted any significant number of adherents in the city, perhaps because of the strength and ubiquity of improvement associations.

5. The South Lakewood Area Association had its humble origins in a protest against a proposal to expand off-street parking for stores on Jefferson Avenue: *East Side Shopper*, April 28, 1955. The SLAA papers offer evidence of the role of the homeowners' association in matters of zoning, traffic control, and parking. The South Lakewood area, on the Southeast Side of the city, was far enough removed from Detroit's black population that race seldom became an issue for the organization. The neighborhood association was concerned about what appeared to be a boarding house at 670 Lakewood, and noted "One colored" among the many boys who played in front of the house. ("Report—July 14, 1958," SLAA, Folder: 1957–1960). For a group concerned with city services, zoning enforcement, and streets and traffic, as well as racial transition, see Interoffice Correspondence, Subject: Meeting of the Burns Civic Association, April 1, 1963, CCR, Part III, Box 25, Folder 25–40. For concern about recreation, garbage pickup, and city services, see "Report on Puritan Park Civic Association Meeting," September 20, 1956, ibid., Folder 25–101. On the role of neighborhood associations in zoning enforcement, planning, and cleanups, see Detroit City Plan Commission, *Planner,* January 1945, 3–4, in the author's possession. Robert J. Mowitz and Deil S. Wright, *Profile of a Metropolis: A Case Book* (Detroit: Wayne State University Press, 1962), 426–29, describe the role of Northwest Side civic associations in battling the construction of the Lodge Freeway extension. For an excellent discussion of civic associations in Queens, New York (which, because of its distance from black populations, did not organize around racial issues in the 1950s), see Sylvie Murray, "Suburban Citizens: Domesticity and Community Politics in Queens, New York, 1945–1960" (Ph.D. diss., Yale University, 1944), esp. 78–131, 181–261.

For an example of the combination of civic uplift and racist rhetoric, see *Action!* vol. 1

(February 15, 1948). The Northwest Home Owners, Inc., met to discuss threats to the community including a city incinerator and "possible Negro residence in the neighborhood." Richard J. Peck, Community Services Department, Detroit Urban League, "Summary of Known Improvement Association Activities in Past Two Years 1955–1957," 6, VF, Pre-1960, Box 2, Folder: Community Organization 1950s. For a discussion of the role that improvement associations played in upholding restrictive covenants, see Herman H. Lond and Charles S. Johnson, *People vs. Property: Race Restrictive Covenants in Housing* (Nashville, Tenn.: Fisk University Press, 1947), 39–55; for examples of similar associations in Chicago, Baltimore, Washington, D.C., Los Angeles, Houston, Miami, and San Francisco, see Abrams, *Forbidden Neighbors,* 181–90.

6. U.S. Department of Commerce, Bureau of the Census, *U.S. Census of Population and Housing, 1940, Census Tracts Statistics for Detroit, Michigan and Adjacent Area* (Washington, D.C.: U.S. Government Printing Office, 1942), Table 4; U.S. Department of Commerce, Bureau of the Census, *U.S. Census of Population and Housing: 1960, Census Tracts, Detroit, Michigan Standard Metropolitan Statistical Area* (Washington, D.C.: U.S. Government Printing Office, 1962), Table H-1.

7. Kornhauser, *Detroit as the People See It,* 68–69, 75, 77–82. Kornhauser's team interviewed 593 adult men and women randomly selected from all sections of the city. For an elaborate discussion of the survey's methodology, see ibid., Appendix B, pp. 189–96.

8. Kenneth T. Jackson, *Crabgrass Frontier: The Suburbanization of the United States* (New York: Oxford University Press, 1985), 49–52, 117–18; on the desire of immigrants to own their own homes, see John Bodnar, Roger Simon, and Michael P. Weber, *Lives of Their Own: Blacks, Italians, and Poles in Pittsburgh, 1900–1960* (Urbana: University of Illinois Press, 1982), 153–83; a succinct synthesis of literature on homeownership and mobility can be found in Eric H. Monkkonen, *America Becomes Urban: The Development of U.S. Cities and Towns* (Berkeley: University of California Press, 1989), 182–205. On high rates of homeownership among ethnic Detroiters, see Zunz, *The Changing Face of Inequality,* 152–61.

9. The National Council of Churches conducted a census of church membership by county in the mid-1950s. It estimated that 65.9 percent of residents of Wayne County, Michigan, were Roman Catholics. Because so few African Americans were Catholic, the percentage of Wayne County whites who were Catholic was probably significantly higher. See National Council of Churches, Bureau of Research and Survey, "Churches and Church Membership in the United States: An Enumeration and Analysis by Counties, States, and Regions," series C, no. 17 (1957), Table 46; Paul Wrobel, "Becoming a Polish-American: A Personal Point of View," in *Immigrants and Migrants: The Detroit Ethnic Experience: Ethnic Studies Reader,* ed. David W. Hartman (Detroit: New University Thought Publishing Company, 1974), 187. "Survey of Racial and Religious Conflict Forces," Interviews with Father Constantine Djuik, Bishop Stephen Wozniak, Father Edward Hickey, in CRC, Box 70; Dominic J. Capeci, Jr., *Race Relations in Wartime Detroit: The Sojourner Truth Housing Controversy of 1942* (Philadelphia: Temple University Press, 1984), 77–78, 89–90; Memorandum Dictated by Major Jack Tierney, October 17, 1945, in NAACP, Group II, Box A505, Folder: Racial Tension, Detroit, Mich., 1944–46; Edward J. Hickey to Edward Connor, May 9, 1944, CHPC, Box 41. In April 1948, the pastors of Saint Louis the King Catholic Church and Saint Bartholomew's Catholic Church reportedly urged parishioners to attend City Council meetings to oppose the construction of houses for blacks on a Northeast Side site: See CCR, Part I, Series I, Box 4, Folder 48–80. Quote on Polish parishes from Mayor's Interracial Committee Minutes, February 19, 1947, 3, ibid., Box 10. On Saints Andrew and Benedict Parish, see Mayor's Interracial Committee Minutes, April 17, 1950, ibid., Part III, Box 25, Folder 25–114. John T. McGreevy, "American Catholics and the African-American Migration, 1919–1970" (Ph.D. diss., Stanford University, 1992) 56–58, 119–20, 159–160; also on the importance of Catholicism in Detroit, see Gerhard Lenski, *The Religious Factor: A Sociological Study of Religion's Impact on Politics, Economics, and Family Life* (Garden City, N.Y.: Doubleday, 1961).

10. See Report on Meeting, Temple Baptist Church, October 25, 1956, and States-Lawn Civic Association, February 14, 1957, DUL, Box 43, Folder A7–13; Metropolitan Tabernacle pamphlets, MDCC, Part I, Box 9, Folder: Civil Rights Activity Feedback and Box 10, Folder: Housing—Homeowner's Ordinance, Friendly; Jim Wallis, "By Accident of Birth: Growing Up White in Detroit," *Sojourners,* June–July 1983, 12–16.

11. Poster, "OPEN MEETING . . . for Owners and Tenants," n.d. [c. 1945], CRC, Box 66, Folder: Property Owners Association; *Action!,* vol. 1

(Feb. 15, 1948), 2; Guyton Home Owners' Association and Connor-East Home Owners Association, leaflets, in SLAA, Folder: 1957–1960; Peck, "Summary of Known Improvement Association Activity," *Southwest Detroiter,* May 11, 1950, copy in Mayor's Papers (1950), Box 5, Folder: Housing Commission.

12. Kornhauser, *Detroit as the People See It,* 62; "Integration Statement," anonymous letter, n.d., in MDCC, Part I, Box 9. For another example of economically vulnerable workers' insecurity about homeownership, see Bill Collett, "Open Letter to Henry Ford II," *Ford Facts,* September 15, 1951.

13. Kornhauser, *Detroit as the People See It,* 95; quotations from Kornhauser's analysis of survey response patterns.

14. The term "colored problem" was used most frequently by whites to describe black movement into their neighborhoods. See, for example, Property Owners Association flyer, 1945, in CRC, Box 66; *Action!,* vol. 1 (Feb. 15, 1948).

15. Kornhauser, *Detroit as the People See It,* 85, 185.

16. Ibid., 100. It should be recalled that there was already virtually complete residential segregation in Detroit when Kornhauser conducted his survey. In 1950, the index of dissimilarity between blacks and whites (a measure of segregation calculated on the percentage of whites who would have to move to achieve complete racial integration) was 88.8; the index of dissimilarity in 1940 had been 89.9. Respondents to the survey then supported even stricter racial segregation than already existed. Figures from Karl E. Taeuber and Alma F. Taeuber, *Negroes in Cities: Residential Segregation and Neighborhood Change* (Chicago: Aldine, 1965), 39.

17. Kornhauser, *Detroit as the People See It,* 87, 90, 91. For findings on the racial conservatism of Detroit Catholics that confirm Kornhauser's data, see Lenski, *The Religious Factor,* 65. On the importance of Catholic parish boundaries in preserving the racial homogeneity of a neighborhood and in shaping Catholic attitudes toward blacks, see McCreevy, "American Catholics and African-American Migration" and Gerald Gamm, "Neighborhood Roots: Institutions and Neighborhood Change in Boston 1870–1994," (Ph.D. diss., Harvard University, 1994).

18. Detroit Housing Commission and Work Projects Administration, *Real Property Survey of Detroit. Michigan,* vol. 3 (Detroit: Bureau of Government Research, 1939), maps and data for Area K. As Northwest Side resident Alan MacNichol complained: "I have watched the area within the Boulevard deteriorate into slums as the character of the neighborhood changed, restrictions were broken, and multiple flats came in," *Brightmoon Journal,* December 22, 1949.

19. Outer-Van Dyke Home Owners' Association, "Dear Neighbor," [1948], CCR, Part III, Box 25, Folder 25–94; Interview with Six Mile Road–Riopelle area neighbors in Incident Report, August 30, 1954, DUL, Box 43, Folder A7–13; William Price, "Factors Which Militate against the Stabilization of Neighborhoods," July 3, 1956, ibid., Box 38, Folder A2–17; woman quoted in Lenski, *The Religious Factor,* 66.

20. Longview Home Owners Association poster, n.d., MDCC, Part I, Box 10, Folder: Housing—Homeowners Ordinance—Friendly. Ellipsis in original.

21. For statistics on crime in Detroit, see Robert Conot, *American Odyssey* (New York: William Morrow, 1974), Statistical Appendix.

22. Alex Csanyi and family to Mayor Jeffries, February 20, 1945, Mayor's Papers (1945), Box 3, Folder: Housing Commission 1945. Ellipsis in original. *Home Gazette.* October 25, 1945: copy in CAH; Gloster Current, "The Detroit Elections: A Problem in Reconversion," *Crisis* 52 (November 1945): 319–21; "Program: General Meeting Courville District Improvement Association," April 2, 1948, CCR, Part III, Box 26, Folder 26–4; *Action!* vol. 1 (February 15, 1948); "Report on Formation of Area B Improvement Association," DUL, Box 38, Folder A2–22; Detroit Urban League Housing Committee, Quarterly Report, April–June 1966, ibid., Box 53, Folder A17–1. For other examples of fears of racial mixing, see John Bublevsky, Tom Gates, Lola Gibson, Victor Harbay, and Sally Stretch, "A Spatial Study of Racial Tension or 'The Walls Come Tumbling Down,'" CCR, Part III, Box 13, Folder 13–20; "Report on the Improvement Association Meeting at Vernor School," September 13, 1955, DUL, Box 43, Folder A7–13; Kornhauser, *Detroit as the People See It,* 28, 37, 101–2.

23. The original essays and a complete typescript are in "Compositions—6B Grade—Van Dyke School," CCR, Part I, Series 1, Box 3, Folder: Community Reports—Supplementing. Accompanying the essays cited were drawings and responses to another assignment, intended to foster racial harmony, on "Why Little Brown Ko-Ko Is My Friend," based on a short story about a black child. The name Mary Conk is a pseudonym.

24. All quotes and details regarding the Easby Wilson case are drawn from the following sources (unless otherwise noted): "Summary of Facts of Case Involving Mr. Easby Wilson," UAW

Press Release, July 25, 1955; and "Interview: Housing Discrimination" (Mrs. Easby Wilson and Harry Ross), all in UAW-FP, Box 14, Folder 14–8; *Pittsburgh Courier,* June 18, 1955; *Michigan Chronicle,* July 30, 1955; report on racial incident, in DUL, Box 43, Folder A7–13.

25. See, for example, George Schermer, "Re: Case 52–16, Petition—Courville Improvement Association Members," July 25, 1952, 1, CCR, Part I, Series 1, Box 9, Folder 52–16CP. When a white neighbor on the same section of Riopelle Street had offered his house for sale in the fall of 1953, a crowd of five hundred had gathered on the street to protest. See Incident Report, 18176 Riopelle, October 31, 1953, ibid., Folder 53–38; *Pittsburgh Courier,* October 31, 1953; Incident Report, November 7, 1954, DUL, Box 43, Folder A7–13.

26. U.S. Department of Commerce, Bureau of the Census, *U.S. Census of Population and Housing: 1960, Census Tracts, Detroit, Michigan Standard Metropolitan Statistical Area,* Final Report PHC(1)–40 (Washington: U.S. Government Printing Office, 1962) (hereafter cited as *1960 Census),* data for tract 606.

27. "A lot of firefighting": John G. Feild, oral history, December 28, 1967 (Katherine Shannon, interviewer), 11, Civil Rights Documentation Project, MSRC. The finding guide and interview transcript mistakenly spell Feild as Fields. John Feild, "A Study of Interracial Housing Incidents," January 20, 1949, 4, CCR, Part I, Series 1, Box 6, Folder 49–3, identified five "techniques employed" by improvement associations in the 1940s: warnings, street demonstrations, anonymous threats, picketing, and property damage. I have calculated the number of racial incidents through a comprehensive survey of records in CCR, DNAACP, DUL, and Detroit's African American newspapers, *Michigan Chronicle, Detroit Tribune,* and *Pittsburgh Courier* (Detroit edition). The number of reported incidents ranged from seven in 1953 to sixty-five in 1963. Unfortunately the Commission on Community Relations only kept complete data for a limited number of years.

28. An important discussion of territoriality is Gerald D. Suttles, *The Social Construction of Communities* (Chicago: University of Chicago Press, 1972). Suttles's discussion of defended neighborhoods is rich in its theoretical implications for studies of neighborhood change. But by building on the ecological model of Chicago School sociology, Suttles offers too deterministic a model of "invasion" and "succession," ignoring

the political and economic determinants of urban transformation. An important revision that has strongly influenced my own work is Gerald Gamm, "City Walls: Neighborhoods, Suburbs, and the American City" (paper presented to the American Political Science Association, New York, September 1994).

29. *Brightmoor Journal,* October 11, 1945; *Neighborhood informer,* December 1949, 1, 3, copy in UAW- CAP, Box 4, Folder 4–19; Handbill, "Emergency Meeting, March 11, 1950," CCR, Part III, Box 25, Folder 25–107; Ruritan Park Civic Association, "Dear Neighbor," ibid., Folder 25–101.

30. Detroit race relations official Richard Marks used the term "containment" (to describe white resistance to housing integration) in his testimony in the school desegregation case, *Milliken v. Bradley.* See Dimond, *Beyond Busing,* 43–44. For a development of the notion of "domestic containment" (though not applied to race), see Elaine Tyler May, "Cold War, Warm Hearth: Politics and the Family in Postwar America," in *The Rise and Fall of the New Deal Order, 1930–1980,* ed. Steve Fraser and Gary Gerstle (Princeton, N.J.: Princeton University Press, 1988), 153–81.

31. "Demonstrations, 1945–1946," 4.

32. National Association of Community Councils, "To Make a Long Story Short," CCR, Part III, Box 20, Folder 20–37.

33. *Action! The Newsletter of the Courville District Improvement Association,* vol. 1, February 15, 1948, 5–6, CCR, Part I, Series 1, Box 10.: *Michigan Chronicle,* March 6, 1948.

34. *Neighborhood Informer,* December 1949, March 1951, copies in UAW-CAP, Box 4, Folder 4–19; *Brightmoor Journal,* February 10, 1955, March 24, 1955; Richard J. Peck, "Summary of known Improvement Association Activities in Past Two Years, 1955–1957," 1–2, VF—Pre-1960, Box 2, Folder: Community Organization 1950s; "Report on Ruritan Park Civic Association Meeting," 3, September 20, 1956, DUL, Box 43, Folder A7–13; Richard J. Peck, "Report on Formation of Area E Improvement Association," 9, ibid., Box 38, Folder A2–22; "Activities Report, February 1–March 1, 1957, Current Status of Property, Cherrylawn Case," 4, ibid., Folder A2–23.

35. Detroit Police Department, Special Investigation Squad, Memo from Detective Sergeant Leo Mack and Detective Bert Berry to Commanding Officer, Special Investigation Squad, November 7, 1945, CCR, Part I, Series 1, Box 3, Folder: Incidents Housing 1945.

36. *Michigan Chronicle*, November 6, 1948.

37. Memo, n.d. [c. 1955], DUL, Box 43, Folder A7–13.

38. John Feild, "Special Report, Subject: Opposition to Negro Occupancy in Northeast Detroit," April 28, 1950, 3–4, CCR, Part I, Series 1, Box 7, Folder 50–18.

39. Commission on Community Relations, Field Division, Case Reports, January 21, 1963, CCR, Part I, Series 4, Box 4; see also Memo, Classification: Housing, September 27, 1954, DUL, Box 38, Folder A2–13.

40. *Southwest Detroiter*, May 11, 1950, copy in Mayor's Papers (1950), Box 5, Folder: Housing Commission (2); *Michigan Chronicle*, July 16, 1955; Commission on Community Relations, Minutes, June 17, 1957, CCR, Part I, Series 4, Box 2; Commission on Community Relations, Field Division Report, February 20, 1961, ibid., Box 3; McGreevy, "American Catholics and the African American Migration," 122.

41. See "Chronological Summary of Incidents in the Seven Mile-Fenelon Area," attached to John Feild, "A Study of Interracial Housing Incidents," January 20, 1949, CCR, Part I, Series 1, Box 6, Folder 49–3, ALUA.

42. Commission on Community Relations, Minutes, September 21, 1959, ibid., Part I, Series 4, Box 3. Nevada marked the boundary of Saint Rita's parish. See Saint Rita's Parish Boundary File, AAD.

43. *Michigan Chronicle*, December 4, 1948; "Demonstrations, 1945–1946": Memorandum J, 31. John Feild, "Special Report, Subject: Opposition to Negro Occupancy in Northeast Detroit," April 28, 1950, 3–4, CCR, Part I, Series 1, Box 7, Folder 50–18.

44. Thomas H. Kleene, "Report of Incident, Subject: Opposition to Negro Occupancy of Dwelling at 4227 Seventeenth Street (Continued)," ibid., Box 5, Folder 48–124H. On Courville, see Incident Report, November 7, 1954, DUL, Box 43, Folder A7–13. James Morris, the real estate broker who had originally called the police to the scene on Woodingham Street, was charged with driving with an expired license. The police, who did nothing to disperse the crowd, responded with remarkable efficiency to a neighbor's complaint that Morris's car was obstructing a driveway, the offense that gave occasion to ask Morris for his license. Another black realtist, John Humphrey, testified in the Detroit school desegregation case *Milliken v. Bradley* that he had suffered harassment by the police when he showed houses in predominantly white neighborhoods. See Dimond, *Beyond Busing*, 50–51. CCR Field CCR Field Division, Case Reports, September 18, 1961, in RK, Box 2, Folder 4; on Tuller and Cherrylawn, see CCR Field Division, Case Reports, August 11, 1961, October 23, 1961, ibid. See also *East Side Shopper* clipping, n.d. [September 1952], in CCR, Part I, Series 1, Box 9, Folder 52–30; *Michigan Chronicle*, December 4, 1948; "9423 Meyers," Case Reports for Period August 27–September 23, 1957, CCR, Part I, Series 4, Box 2.

45. John Feild and Joseph Coles, "Report of Incident, Subject: Protest to Negro Occupancy at 3414 and 3420 Harrison Street, August 23, 1948," in CCR, Part I, Series 1, Box 5, Folder 48–124; included in the file are Brock's card and the attached notice; see also "Buyer Beware," *Time* April 16, 1956, 24.

46. Richard J. Peck, "Summary of Known Improvement Association Activity in Past Two Years 1955–1957," 3, in VF—Pre-1960, Box 2, Folder: Community Organization 1950s; see also Report of Second Meeting of Ruritan Park Civic Association, Fitzgerald School, November 29, 1956, DUL, Box 43, Folder A7–13; Commission on Community Relations Minutes, February 18, 1957, CCR, Part I, Series 4, Box 2.

47. Successful purchases include Yorkshire and Evanston (1948), ibid., Series 1, Box 5, Folder 48–120; 7745 Chalfonte and Tracy and Chippewa in 1955, DUL, Box 38, File A2–15; 15550 Robson, *Detroit Free Press*, May 7, 1956; Richard J. Peck, "Summary of Known Improvement Association Activities in the Past Two Years, 1955–1957," pp. 1, 4, in VF—Pre-1960, Box 2, Folder: Community Organization 1950s. Attempts include "Report of Incident: Intimidation of Henry Lyons (Negro) by a White Group at 18680 Caldwell," September 22, 1947, CCR, Part I, Series 1, Box 4, Folder 47–59H; "Protest of Negro Occupancy at 18087 Shields," 1949, ibid., Box 6, Folder 49–33; Detroit Police Department Interoffice Memorandum, Subject: Racial Disturbance at 2966 Greyfriars, August 31, 1953, DSL, Box 20, Folder: Racial—Gang Activities and Complaints (2).

48. *1950 Census*, tract 603; *1960 Census*, tracts 603A, 603B.

49. Ibid., data for tracts 604, 605, 606.

50. *Michigan Chronicle*, September 10, 1955; Incident Report, DUL, Box 38, Folder A2–15. *1960 Census*, tract 261; tracts to the east, 170, 171, 172, 173.

51. *1950 Census* and *1960 Census,* tracts 9, 10, 35, 36, 37, 38, 39, 41.
52. *Detroit News.* October 4, 1961.
53. Hirsch, *Making the Second Ghetto.* 40–99.
54. Kenneth T. Jackson, *Crabgrass Frontier: The Suburbanization of the United States* (New York, 1985), esp. 190–218; Patricia Burgess Stach, "Deed Restrictions and Subdivision Development in Columbus Ohio, 1900–1970," *Journal of Urban History* 15 (November 1988): 42–68.
55. Albert Mayer and Thomas F. Hoult, *Race and Residence in Detroit* (Detroit: Urban Research Laboratory, Institute for Urban Studies, Wayne State University, 1962), 2.
56. A superb overview of patterns of racial segregation in Detroit is Donald R. Deskins, Jr., *Residential Mobility of Negroes in Detroit, 1837–1965* (Ann Arbor: Department of Geography, University of Michigan, 1972). For a perceptive discussion of similar patterns nationwide, see Douglas S. Massey and Nancy A. Denton, *American Apartheid: Segregation and the Making of the Underclass* (Cambridge: Harvard University Press, 1993).
57. Reverend Charles W. Butler, "Message to the Open Occupancy Conference," in *A City in Racial Crisis: The Case of Detroit Pre- and Post-the 1967 Riot.* ed. Leonard Gordon (n.p.: William C. Brown Publishers, 1971), 33. For an earlier statement of black suspicion of white homeowners, vandals, and the police, see *Michigan Chronicle,* September 24, 1955.

12 Minority Groups and Coalitional Politics

1. I use *non-White* and *minority* interchangeably throughout this article to refer to Blacks, Latinos, and Asians. I distinguish these three groups from Whites, who remain the majority racial population in this country. It should be noted that Latinos, unlike the other groups, are not classified as a distinct racial group by the census. In fact, they may identify as Black, White, or other under the census classification scheme. Most opt for White or other. Yet urban scholars typically define Latinos as a minority group by virtue of their numbers and cultural distinctiveness. This article follows that convention.
2. I use *Afro-Caribbean* to refer to Black immigrants from the Anglophone Caribbean region and to distinguish them from their counterparts from the French- and Spanish-speaking Caribbean. Anglophone Caribbean immigrants are the focus of this study. Although I use the term *Afro-Caribbean,* most of these Black newcomers refer to themselves as *Caribbean American* or *West Indian.* New York's Afro-Caribbean immigrants hail from throughout the Caribbean region, but the largest numbers come from Jamaica, Trinidad, and Guyana.
3. Scholars have puzzled over the absence of a strong minority coalition in New York. The city would seem to be fertile soil for this kind of alliance. The fact that one has yet to take root makes New York a "great anomaly" in the urban politics literature (Mollenkopf 2003).
4. Afro-Caribbean immigrants living in these overwhelmingly Black areas have carved out their own distinctive residential niches, often of marginally higher socioeconomic quality than surrounding African-American neighborhoods (Crowder and Tedrow 2001). Yet this modest economic advantage has not won them access to more integrated neighborhoods, a predicament they share with their middle-class African-American counterparts.
5. The obvious irony of this complaint is that African-Americans view attempts by a group of Black immigrants to achieve political influence as a threat to Black empowerment, rather than a step in that direction.
6. I borrow the term *racial agents* from a conversation with Jack Citrin.
7. The essentialist behavioral notions of racial identity that pervade everyday, commonsense thinking in this country follow the same perverse logic. That is, racial groups are deemed to "behave" or "act" in keeping with an identifiable mold. Blacks, say, are expected to be good dancers, or Asians good students. When group members deviate from the behavioral mold, they are labeled racially inauthentic. For a useful discussion of how this essentialist conflation of racial identity and behavior nonetheless allows for an antiessentialist critique of racial categories, see Jackson (2001).
8. Challenging the racial credentials or commitments of a fellow Black politician in electoral competition is a strategy that surfaces even among African-Americans themselves. The famously acrimonious 2002 race between Newark mayoral incumbent Sharpe James and young upstart Cory Booker is a recent example. Although both men are African-American, questions of racial solidarity and authenticity emerged nonetheless. The James camp took the tactic to bizarre extremes when they began circulating rumors that Booker was actually White and passing as Black to win the support of Newark's mostly

Black voters. Such strategies likely will become even more common as the Black population becomes more diverse in cities around the country.

9. For a thoughtful discussion on how White perceptions can engender conflict among subordinate minority groups, see Kim (1999, 2000).

10. Sampson's avoidance of the ethnic strategy may be due to his socialization in the United States. Born to Caribbean parents in New York, his ties to African-Americans run deep. His second-generation experiences and how they influence his political choices may be a precursor to the future of Black politics in New York. He is part of a new, expanding population of second-generation Caribbean New Yorkers. These children of Black immigrants likely will have a significant influence on the city's political future, as they become increasingly involved in the electoral process. It remains to be seen whether they will identify mostly as second-generation Caribbean ethnics or as African-Americans. But whatever the case, they may find coalition building with African-Americans easier than their parents have if they interact regularly with their counterparts in institutional settings.

11. African-American leaders at the time accused White party leaders of playing ethnic favorites by doling out the choicest patronage jobs to Afro-Caribbeans, who tended to be better educated than their native-born counterparts (Watkins-Owens 1996; Hellwig 1978; Holder 1980). But this was more job competition than political conflict, as the party structure was one of the few avenues of social mobility open to Black New Yorkers.

12. Social learning refers to the process by which potential coalition partners acquire knowledge and understanding of each other's interests (Stone 1989).

13. Taken together, these institutions comprise what Dawson (1994b) called the AfricanAmerican counterpublic.

13 Black Incumbents and a Declining Racial Divide

* Editor's note: Readers may wish to consult additional notes, references, and statistical appendices in the original text due to their elimination in this copy.

1. Including cases in which two black candidates run against each other would, obviously, reveal little about white acceptance of black leadership.

2. This data set was compiled using the National Roster of Black Elected Officials, local newspaper reports in each city, and a data set of mayoral names (Wolman, Strate, and Melchior 1996), and it includes the race of the mayor, the challenger, and the winner. As in the first data set, I focus on general or run-off elections rather than primaries, where factors such as multiple candidacies, lack of interest, and limited availability of empirical data complicate empirical analysis.

Chapter 5
14 New Immigrants in Suburbia

1. Charlie LeDuff and David Halbfinger, "Wages and Squalor for Immigrant Workers," *New York Times*, 5 May 1999.

2. *New York Times*, 24 July 1997.

3. Sara Mahler, "First Stop Suburbia," *NACLA* [North American Committee on Latin America] *Report on the Americas* 26, 1 (July 1992): 19.

4. LeDuff and Halbfinger, "Wages and Squalor."

5. Ibid.

6. Norman Appelton, interview by authors, January 1991.

7. Doreen Carvajal, "New York Suburbs Take on a Latin Accent," *New York Times*, 29 July 1993.

8. Jennifer Gordon, "We Make the Road by Walking: Immigrant Workers, the Workplace Project and the Struggle for Social Change," *Harvard Civil Rights Civil Liberties Law Review* (Summer 1995): 411.

9. Mahler, "First Stop Suburbia," 20–48.

10. Doreen Carvajal, "Making Ends Meet in a Nether World," *New York Times*, 13 December 1994.

11. Mahler, "First Stop Suburbia," 20–24.

12. Gordon, "We Make the Road by Walking," 412–13.

13. Ibid., 408, 418, 419.

14. Doreen Carvajal, "Out of Sight, Out of Mind, But Not Out of Work," *New York Times*, 8 July 1995.

15. Ibid.

16. Gordon, "We Make the Road by Walking," 408–9.

17. Ibid., 432.

18. Evelyn Nieves, "Day Laborer Stakes Out His Own Patch," *New York Times*, 10 May 1998.

19. *New York Times*, 24 July 1997; *New York Times* editorial, 31 August 1997; *New York Times*, 19 September 1997.

20. Gordon, "We Make the Road by Walking," 420–21.

21. Ibid., 418–21. See also Kenneth C. Crowe, "The Big Payback," *Newsday*, 7 January 1996.

22. Doreen Carvajal, "For Immigrant Maids, Not a Job But Servitude," *New York Times*, 25 February 1996.

23. Ibid.
24. *New York Times*, 24 July 1997.
25. LeDuff and Halbfinger, "Wages and Squalor."
26. Doreen Carvajal, "Making Ends Meet"; idem, "A Mayor Asks Help on Illegal Tenancies," *New York Times*, 11 October 1996.
27. Ibid., "A Mayor Asks Help"; LeDuff and Halbfinger, "Wages and Squalor."
28. Robert McFadden, "Fire in a Crowded Home of Immigrants Kills 3 and Injures 16 on L.I.," *New York Times*, 2 May 1999.
29. LeDuff and Halbfinger, "Wages and Squalor."
30. McFadden, "Fire in a Crowded Home."
31. Ibid.
32. Bruce Lambert, "Raid on Illegal Housing, Shows the Plight of Suburbs Working Poor," *New York Times*, 7 December 1996.
33. Frank Bruni, with Debra Sontag, "Behind a Suburban Facade in Queens, A Teeming Angry Urban Arithmetic," *New York Times*, 8 October 1996.
34. John Rather, "New Immigrants Transforming the Population," *New York Times*, 17 March 1996, Long Island edition.
35. Diana Jean Schemo, "Education as a Second Language," *New York Times*, 25 July 1994.
36. Doreen Carvajal, "Cultures Clash in Suburbs, Schools Struggle to Cope With Influx of Immigrant Students," *New York Times*, 8 January 1995.
37. Doreen Carvajal, "Immigrants Fight Residency Rules, Blocking Students in Long Island Schools," *New York Times*, 7 June 1995.
38. Sylvia Moreno, "Long Island Census Shows 3.9% Hispanic," *Newsday*, 27 April 1981.
39. Patrick Boyle, "Brentwood's a Melting Pot of Promise," *Newsday*, 1 December 1996; Lyn Dobrin, "The Spice Root in Hicksville." *Newsday*, 16 October 1995.
40. Ibid.

15 The Ethnic Diversity of Boomburbs

1. The term *edge city* was coined by Joel Garreau, *Edge City: Life on the New Frontier* (New York: Doubleday, 1991); also see Robert E. Lang, *Edgeless Cities: Exploring the Elusive Metropolis* (Brookings, 2003).
2. Observers began to note the trend in the late 1990s. See Haya El Nasser and Paul Overberg, "Suburban Communities Spurt to Big-City Status," *USA Today*, November 19, 1997, p. A4; David Brooks, *On Paradise Drive: How We Live Now (And Always Have) In the Future Tense* (New York: Simon and Schuster, 2004); David Brooks, "Patio Man and the Sprawl People," *Weekly Standard* 7, no. 46 (2002): 19–29.

3. Michael L. Montandon, personal conversation with Robert Lang, March 12, 2004. Interestingly, a referee for this book asserted that North Las Vegas is not comparable with Salt Lake City in part because it "does not confront an array of urban problems" and that Salt Lake City has a "more diverse population." The fact is that North Las Vegas has plenty of urban problems, including a high poverty rate. In addition, North Las Vegas's population is a quarter foreign-born and half minority. In other words, North Las Vegas is considerably *more* diverse than Salt Lake City (which is 70 percent non-Hispanic white) and even than Las Vegas itself. The misread of North Las Vegas by the referee shows that North Las Vegas's mayor was on to something. Apparently no one, not even urban experts who review books, think his city is diverse and has urban problems.
4. Keno Hawker, personal conversation with Robert Lang, March 10, 2004.
5. Jonathon Barnett first used the term *accidental cities*, but he was referring specifically to zoning. Jonathon Barnett, "Accidental Cities: The Deadly Grip of Outmoded Zoning," *Architectural Record* 180, no. 2 (1992): 94–101.
6. Bruce Katz, "Welcome to the 'Exit Ramp' Economy," *Boston Globe*, May 13, 2001, p. A19. Freeway exits as an economic development tool came up in several interviews with boomburb mayors.
7. Jane Jacobs, "The Greening of the City," *New York Times Magazine*, May 16, 2004.
8. The 2000 census marks the first time that a critical mass of suburban cities passed the 100,000-population threshold, and this study is the first-ever book-length treatment of those cities. But see Robert Fishman, *Bourgeois Utopias: The Rise and Fall of Suburbia* (New York: Basic Books, 1987); Garreau, *Edge City*; Carl Abbott, "'Beautiful Downtown Burbank': Changing Metropolitan Geography in the Modern West," *Journal of the West* (July 1995): 8–18; Carl Abbott, *The Metropolitan Frontier: Cities in the Modern American West* (University of Arizona Press, 1993); Carl Abbott, "Southwestern Cityscapes: Approaches to an American Urban Environment," in *Essays on Sunbelt Cities and Recent Urban America*, edited by Raymond A. Mohl and others (Texas A&M University Press, 1990).
9. This was done so that almost all boomburbs had full data for their starting point. Many boomburbs were unincorporated places before 1970, making it impossible to track their population changes before that date.
10. Lang and Simmons, in "Tale of the Two Peorias," note that Peoria, Arizona, passing Peoria,

Illinois, reflects the shift in population to the South and West.

11. Robert E. Lang and Dawn Dhavale, *Reluctant Cities: Exploring Big Unincorporated Census Designated Places*, Census Note 03:01 (Alexandria, Va.: Metropolitan Institute at Virginia Tech, 2003).

12. Neil Larry Shumsky, ed., *Encyclopedia of Urban America: The Cities and Suburbs* (Santa Barbara, Calif.: ABC-CLIO, 1997).

13. Wikipedia (www.wikipedia.org) is an open-source, web-based encyclopedia and as such it is subject to error. The information obtained from this site was crosschecked against other sources, including conversations with local officials.

14. Besides histories, many other interesting facts about boomburbs appear on their websites. For example, fourteen websites include detailed demographic profiles of the city.

15. See Sunnyvale.ca.gov/local/SVC%20CHRONOLOGY1.htm.

16. See www.auroragov.org/Visitors%20Guide/Pages/Our%20History.cfm; www.ci.westminster.co.us/city/history/default.htm.

17. See www.ci.oceanside.ca.us/community/history_print.asp.

18. See www.chulavistaca.gov/About/History.asp.

19. See www.mesalibrary.org/about_mesa/pdfs/Mesa History-0703.pdf.

20. See www.wikipedia.org.

21. The U.S. census produces yearly estimates for population change at the subcounty level, based on the distributive housing unit method. This method uses building permits, mobile home shipments, and estimates of housing unit loss to update housing unit change since the last estimate. The census developed a household population estimate by applying the occupancy rate and the average person per household from the latest census to an estimate of the housing units. The estimates obtained from this method are controlled for by comparing to the final county population estimate. "U.S. Bureau of the Census' Estimates and Projections Area Documentation Subcounty Total Population Estimates," 2003 (eire.census.gov/popest/topics/methodology/citymeth.php).

22. Ibid. The tenth-ranked city was Joliet, Illinois, which nearly qualified as a boomburb but failed to sustain double-digit growth for all five decades since 1950.

23. Quoted in Lori Weisberg, "Chula Vista No 7 in the Nation in Galloping Growth," *San Diego Union Tribune*, July 10, 2003, p. A1.

24. According to a *New York Times* story, Gilbert "issues building permits only to developers who build within an [homeowners] association." Quoted in Motoko Rich, "Homeowner Boards Blur Line of Who Rules the Roost," *New York Times*, July 27, 2003, p. 14.

25. Office of Management and Budget, *Metropolitan Statistical Area Definitions*, June 6, 2003.

26. Rick Hampson, "'New Brooklyns' Replace White Suburbs," *USA Today*, May 18, 2003, p. A1.

27. Shaun McKinnon, "Water: Growing Demand, Dwindling Supply," *Arizona Republic*, July 6, 2003, p. A1.

28. Edward L. Gleaser, "The New Economics of Urban and Regional Growth," in *The Oxford Handbook of Economic Geography*, edited by G. L. Clark, M. P. Feldman, and M. S. Gertler (Oxford University Press, 2000). Also see Richard Florida, "The Great Creative Class Debate: The Revenge of the Squelchers," *The Next American City 5* (2004): 18–24.

29. Richard Florida, *The Rise of the Creative Class: And How It's Transforming Work, Leisure, Community, and Everyday Life* (New York: Perseus, 2002).

30. Jon Gertner, "Home Economics," *New York Times Magazine*, March 5, 2006, pp. 20–31.

31. The 2000 census considered race and Hispanic origin to be distinct. This book uses the Office of Management and Budget definition of Asian, which is a person having origins in the Far East, Southeast Asia, or the Indian subcontinent. See also William H. Frey and Alan Berube, "City Families and Suburban Singles: An Emerging Household Story," in *Redefining Urban and Suburban America: Evidence from Census 2000*, edited by Bruce Katz and Robert E. Lang (Brookings, 2003).

32. Ibid.

33. William Frey, "Melting Pot Suburbs: A Study of Suburban Diversity," in *Redefining Urban and Suburban America: Evidence from Census 2000*, edited by Bruce Katz and Robert E. Lang (Brookings, 2003).

34. Robert E. Lang, *Edgeless Cities: Exploring the Elusive Metropolis* (Brookings, 2003).

35. Robert Suro and Audrey Singer, "Changing Patterns of Latino Growth in Metropolitan America," in *Redefining Urban and Suburban America: Evidence from Census 2000*, edited by Bruce Katz and Robert E. Lang (Brookings, 2003).

36. The Brooklyn of today is experiencing a renaissance and is becoming home to cultural institutions and young, urbane, middle-class refugees

from the Manhattan housing market. A *New York Times Magazine* article featured Brooklyn's emerging hipness and a bohemian culture that eclipses Manhattan's. James Traub, "The (Not Easy) Building of (Not Exactly) Lincoln Center for (Not) Manhattan," *New York Times Magazine*, April 25, 2004, p. 28.

37. Patrick A. Simmons, *Patterns and Trends in Overcrowded Housing: Early Results from Census 2000*, Census Note 09 (Washington: Fannie Mae Foundation, 2002).

16 Fear and Fantasy in Suburban Los Angeles

1. William A. V. Clark, "Residential Patterns: Avoidance, Assimilation and Succession," in *Ethnic Los Angeles*, ed. Roger Waldinger and Mehdi Bozorgmehr (New York: Russell Sage Foundation, 1996), 115.

2. Allen J. Scott, "High-Technology Industrial Development in the San Fernando Valley and Ventura County: Observations on Economic Growth and the Evolution of Urban Form," in *The City: Los Angeles and Urban Theory at the End of the Twentieth Century*, ed. Allen J. Scott and Edward W. Soja (Berkeley: University of California Press, 1996), 293.

3. Janet Abu-Lughod, *New York, Chicago, Los Angeles: America's Global Cities* (Minneapolis: University of Minnesota Press, 1999), 364–65.

4. Raymond A. Rocco, "Latino Los Angeles: Reframing Boundaries/Borders," in *The City: Los Angeles and Urban Theory at the End of the Twentieth Century*, ed. Allen J. Scott and Edward W. Soja (Berkeley: University of California Press, 1996), 374–75.

5. Clarence Y. H. Lo, *Small Property versus Big Government: Social Origins of the Property Tax Revolt* (Berkeley: University of California Press, 1990).

6. Ibid., 57–60; Abu-Lughod, *New York, Chicago, Los Angeles*, 379–82.

7. Michael Paul Rogin and John L. Shover, *Political Change in California: Critical Elections and Social Movements, 1890–1966* (Westport, Conn.: Greenwood Publishing Corporation, 1970), 173–78; George Lipsitz, *The Possessive Investment in Whiteness: How White People Profit from Identity Politics* (Philadelphia: Temple University Press, 1998), 136–38.

8. Abu-Lughod, *New York, Chicago, Los Angeles*, 383–85.

9. Edward W. Soja, "Los Angeles, 1965–1992: From Crisis-Generated Restructuring to Restructuring-Generated Crisis," in *The City: Los Angeles and Urban Theory at the End of the Twentieth Century*, ed. Allen J. Scott and Edward W. Soja (Berkeley: University of California Press, 1996), 443.

10. Michael Sorkin, ed., *Variations on a Theme Park: The New American City and the End of Public Space* (New York: Hill and Wang, 1992); Edward W. Soja, *Postmetropolis: Critical Studies of Cities and Regions* (Oxford: Blackwell Publishing, 2000), 233–63.

11. Robin D. G. Kelley, *Race Rebels: Culture, Politics and the Black Working Class* (New York: Free Press, 1996), 183–227. See also Tricia Rose, *Black Noise: Rap Music and Black Culture in Contemporary America* (Hanover, N.H.: University Press of New England, 1994).

12. Mike Davis, *Magical Urbanism: Latinos Reinvent the U.S. City* (London: Verso, 2000). See also Victor M. Valle and Rodolfo D. Torres, *Latino Metropolis* (Minneapolis: University of Minnesota Press, 2000); Gustavo Leclerc, Raul Villa, and Michael J. Dear, *Urban Latino Cultures* (Thousand Oaks, Calif.: Sage Publications, 1999); and Marta López-Garza and David R. Diaz, *Asian and Latino Immigrants in a Restructuring Economy: The Metamorphosis of Southern California* (Stanford, Calif.: Stanford University Press, 2001).

13. "Can Hollywood Get Its Glitz Back?" 12 November 2001, www.businessweek.com/magazine/content/01_46/b3757018.htm.

14. Jim Rawitsch, "Moving Right Along," *Los Angeles Times Magazine*, 13 July 1986, 1.

15. Samuel R. Delany, *Times Square Red, Times Square Blue* (New York: New York University Press, 1999); Ada Louise Huxtable, "Reinventing Times Square: 1990," in *Inventing Times Square: Commerce and Culture at the Crossroads of the World*, ed. William R. Taylor (Baltimore: Johns Hopkins University Press, 1991), 356–70.

16. Dana Cuff, *The Provisional City: Los Angeles Stories of Architecture and Urbanism* (Cambridge, Mass.: MIT Press, 2000), 334–35; Andrew Ross, *The Celebration Chronicles* (New York: Ballantine Books, 1999); Douglas Frantz and Catherine Collins, *Celebration, U.S.A.: Living in Disney's Brave New Town* (New York: Henry Holt, 2000).

17. Samuel O. Regalado, *Viva Baseball! Latin Major Leaguers and Their Special Hunger* (Urbana: University of Illinois Press, 1988), 122–28.

18. Roger Keil, *Los Angeles: Globalization, Urbanization, and Social Struggles* (New York: John Wiley and Sons, 1998) xxxi–xxxii; Kelley, *Race Rebels*, 232–33.

17 Police Practices in Immigrant-Destination Communities

1. We use the terms *Hispanic* and *Latino* interchangeably, as we do with *Black* or *African-American*. We use *White* to refer to non-Hispanic Whites, and *Asian* or *Asian-American* to refer to those who identify themselves as Asian or Pacific Islander.

2. The vast majority of immigrants in our California sample of cities are Hispanic or Asian.

3. Muir (1977) concluded from his fieldwork that the leadership of the police chief in setting a tone for the department was key to developing this professional model. As Moore (1994, 229) found, "It is the police executives who see most clearly the limitations of their current strategies, and it is they who are groping their way toward better ones."

4. Whitaker (1980) emphasized that especially in communities where the residents—and their circumstances and behaviors—are changing, agencies that rely on citizen requests for service need to be alert to, and even to encourage, requests for assistance with new types of problems. He also noted in passing (p. 242) that "in a strict sense, not even the formal status of 'citizen' is required for these sorts of participation." Thus under this approach noncitizens and even illegal immigrants would be dealt with as potential resources by police departments.

5. In the questionnaire sent to these contract cities, we specified on the cover which city we were asking about and instructed the police commanders to tailor their answers to the police practices and conditions prevailing in the community in question.

6. The difference in question wording—providing a hypothetical scenario to police chiefs, but a more general question on language access to elected officials—may account for some of the gap in language assistance. However, our case study interviewees indicated that language assistance is indeed more consistently provided by police departments than by other departments in City Hall.

7. More recently, Argentina, Colombia, and Guatemala have also issued secure consular identification cards. To our knowledge, no such card exists for immigrants from Asian countries.

8. Indeed, the likelihood of a "don't know" response is higher in cities from which we received multiple elected-official responses.

9. We focus here on predicting gaps in language support and knowledge of policies rather than predicting the actual policies themselves because it is difficult to distinguish the influence of possible council-initiated policy changes in cities where no gaps exist between the reports of police departments and city councils.

10. The race or ethnicity of the police chief and the racial and ethnic composition of the police force were also not significant predictors.

11. According to Census Bureau definitions, Filipinos are classified as Asians.

Chapter 6

18 The Mauling of Public Space

1. The story of Bridgewater is recounted in Joel Garreau's *Edge City: Life on the New Frontier* (New York: Doubleday, 1991), 42–45.

2. John Hannigan, "The Saturday Essay: Who Wants to Spend Their Life in a Theme Park?" *The Independent*, Nov. 28, 1998, T1.

3. In an earlier case, *Food Employees v. Logan Valley Plaza* 391 U.S. 308 (1968) the court ruled that a labor union could picket a supermarket located in a shopping mall, despite the objections of the mall manager. For a full discussion of the shopping mall cases, see Brady C. Williamson and James A. Friedman, "State Constitutions: The Shopping Mall Cases," *University of Wisconsin Law Review* (1998), 883–903; Curtis J. Berger, "Pruneyard Revisited: Political Activity on Private Lands," *N.Y.U. Law Review* 66 (1991), 663–691.

4. For a critical view of this argument, see Richard Epstein, "Takings, Exclusivity and Speech: The Legacy of *Pruneyard v. Robins*," *The University of Chicago Law Review* 64 (Winter 1997), 21–56.

5. *Hudgens v. NLRB* 424 U.S. 507 (1976) was an important decision because it overturned *Food Employees v. Logan Valley Plaza* 391 U.S. 308 (1968), the first shopping mall case. The decision held that striking workers did have a First Amendment right to protest unfair labor practices in front of their employer's store, even though it was located in a mall. In weighing the issues, the court concluded that the employees had no alternative place to protest, inasmuch as their message was directly linked to the commercial activity of a store located in the mall. In contrast, *Hudgens* stated that "property does not lose its private character merely because the public is generally invited to use it for designated purposes."

6. Mark Alexander, "Attenation, Shoppers: The First Amendment in the Modern Shopping Mall,"

Arizona Law Review 41 (Spring 1999), 1–47. Alexander notes that many of the nine states which have rejected petitioners' free speech claims rely on the Supreme Court doctrine of "state action" even though their own constitutional provisions provide a broader guarantee similar to the language in the California constitution.

7. *Lloyd Corp. v. Tanner* 407 U.S. 551 (1972).

8. Margaret Crawford, "The World in a Shopping Mall," in *Variations on a Theme Park: The New American City and End of Public Space*, ed. Michael Sorkin (New York: Hill and Wang, 1992), 3.

9. Eds. Chuihua Judy Chung, Jeffrey Inaba, Rem Koolhaas, and Sze Tsung Leong, *Harvard Design School Guide to Shopping* (Cologne: Taschen, 2001).

10. For a detailed account of the transformation of the shopping mall, see William Severini Kowinski, *The Malling of America: An Inside Look at the Great Consumer Paradise* (New York: Morrow,1985).

11. Jim Walker, "Visionary's Quest: Columbus-Based Developer Yaromir Steiner Determined to Build Better Shopping Center," *The Columbus Dispatch*, June 9, 2002, 1E.

12. Melissa Levy, "On the Road Again," *Minneapolis Star Tribune*, July 16, 2001, 1D.

13. Kowinski, *The Malling of America*, 26–52.

14. See Victor Gruen and Larry Smith, *Shopping Towns USA: The Planning of Shopping Centers* (New York: Reinhold, 1960). See also Witold Rybczynski, *City Life* (New York: Touchstone, 1995), 206–207.

15. Some of the Mall of America's promotional literature reads: "[The] Mall of America will be a city within a city, unlike other malls. . . . It will be divided into four distinctive city streets providing four unique shopping and visual environments." Brief of Amicus Curiae from the Minnesota Civil Liberties Union, presented in the case *State v. Wicklund.*

16. Kowinski, *The Malling of America*, 233.

17. "Universal City Walk: An Architect's Dream: A Conversation with Jon Jerde," Universal City Press Release, 1993. Cited in Adia Hozic, *Hollyworld: Space, Power and Fantasy in the American Economy* (Ithaca, NY: Cornell University Press, 2001), 6.

18. The term "imagineering" suggest "engineering and image" à la Disney. The term comes from Keally McBride, *Social Imagineering*, unpublished manuscript, 2002.

19. Jennifer Niles Coffin, "The United Mall of America: Free Speech, State Constitutions, and the Growing Fortess of Private Property," *University of Michigan Journal of Law Reform* 33 Summer 2000), 615–649.

20. Craig Kellog, "Shopping and Housing Mix in New Kanas City Mall," *Architectural Record* 187, no. 2 (1999), 56.

21. Garreau, *Edge City.*

22. *Lechmere, Inc. v. NLRB* 502 U.S. 526 (1992).

23. The mall is also protected by City of Bloomington police and the only police substation is located on mall property. For a more thorough discussion of this case see Coffin, "The United Mall of America."

24. Mike Kaszuba,"Megamall Not Public Space, Court Rules," *Minneapolis Star Tribune,* March 12, 1999, 1A.

25. Many other malls, including those operated by the Rouse Company (the developer of many visible projects such as Faneuil Hall in Boston), routinely provide a booth for community groups. See Witold Rybczynski, *City Life* (New York: Simon and Schuster, 1995), 209.

26. Anne Miller, "Mall Drops T–Shirt Charges," *The Times Union,* March 6, 2003, B1.

27. Anne Miller, "Mall, Main Street Intersect in Debate; As Anti-War Voices Seek a Public Outlet, Private Property Issue Arise, " *The Times Union*, March 7, 2003, A1.

28. Benjamin Barber, "Malled, Mauled and Overhaulded: Arresting Suburban Sprawl by Transforming the Mall into the Usable Civic Space," in *Public Space and Democracy*, ed. Marcel Hénaff and Tracy B. Strong (Minneapolis: University of Minnesota Press, 2001), 206.

29. See Jürgen Habermas, *Theory of Communicative Action, Vol. 1*, tr. Thomas McCarthy (Boston: Beacon, 1984); Jürgen Habermas, "What is Universal Pragmastics," *Communication and the Evolution of Society*, tr. Thomas McCarthy (Boston: Beacon, 1979). For an excellent secondary source, see Simone Chambers, *Reasonable Democracy: Jürgen Habermas and the Politics of Discourse* (Ithaca, NY: Cornell University Press, 1996).

30. Molly J. Liskow, "Leafletting Rules to Balance Mall's and Speakers' Rights," *New Jersey Lawyer*, August 28, 2000, B8. For the full text of the decision, see *Green Party of New Jersey v. Hartz Mountain Industries, Inc.*, New Jersey Supreme Court, A-59, June 13, 2000.

31. Richard Briffault, "A Government for Our Time? Business Improvement Districts and Urban Governance," *Columbia Law Review* 99 (March 1999), 365–477.

32. Kowinski, *The Malling of America*, 53–63.

33. See Arkansas Statue 14-184-115 (1995). Cited in Clayton P. Gillette and Paul B. Stephan III, "Constitutional Limits on Privatization," *American Journal of Comparative Law* 46 (1998).

34. Some BIDs, for example, those in New York, guarantee representation to non-property owners, but even there business people, especially landlords, dominate the membership of the governing boards. One study of eight BIDs in New York City found that 67% of members were business people; in the five remaining BIDs 75% of the board members were either business people or legal professionals. (Briffault, "A Government for Our Time?" 412.)

35. Stephen C. Fehr, "Property Owners Commit to Revive D.C.: In Heart of District a $38.5 Million Push for Safety, Cleanliness," *The Washington Post,* July 27, 1997, A20 (citing views of downtown business owners).

36. Briffault, "A Government for Our Time?" 396.

37. Paul Goldberger, "The Rise of the Private City," in *Breaking Away: The Future of Cities: Essays in Memory of Robert F. Wagner,* ed. Julia Vitullo-Martin (New York: Twentieth Century Fund Press, 1996), 136–137.

38. On festival marketplaces, see M. Christine Boyer, "Cities for Sale: Merchandising History at South Street Seaport," in ed. Michael Sorkin, *Variations on a Theme Park: The New American City and the End of Public Space* (New York: Hill and Wang, 1992), 181–204.

39. Bernard Frieden and Lynne Sagalyn, *Downtown, Inc.: How America Rebuilds Cities* (Cambridge, MA: MIT Press, 1990).

40. Tom Gallagher, "Trespasser on Main St.: (You!)," *The Nation,* December 18, 1995.

41. *Avery v. Midland County et al.* 390 U.S. 474 (1968).

42. The courts decided that local school board elections were not exempt from one-person, one-vote. In *Salyer Land Co. v. Tulare Lake Basin Water Storage District,* the Court determined that the water storage district, by virtue of its limited purpose and financing structure, could be governed by affected property owners exclusively.

43. "Voting Scheme for Board Okayed," *City Law,* November/December, 1998.

44. A similar lawsuit was brought by homeless plaintiffs against the Fashion District BID in Los Angeles. The suit was settled out of court. Although the BID denied wrongdoing, it also promised that its security contractor, Burns International Security, would not search, harass, or order homeless people to "move along." See Marla Dickerson, "Fashion District Group Agrees to Settle Homeless Lawsuit," *Los Angeles Times,* August 14, 2001.

45. "Homeless Workers: BIDs Failed to Pay Minimum Wage," *City Law,* March/April 1998. The article reported that U.S. District Court Judge Sonia Sotomayor ruled that the program participants were entitled to the minimum wage.

46. Heather Barr, "More Like Disneyland: State Action, 42 U.S.C. 1 1983, and Business Improvement Districts in New York," *Columbia Human Rights Law Review* (Winter 1997), 399–404. The accuracy of these later accusations is a matter of controversy. At least one of the four workers retracted the accusations and another claimed that he was pressured to retract. The BID did settle at least two lawsuits by homeless people injured by outreach workers.

47. Thomas Lueck, "Grand Central Partnership Is Subject of U.S. Inquiry," *New York Times,* May 26, 1995, A7.

48. Briffault, "A Government for Our Time?" 427–428. To cite one specific example, the Riverhead Business Improvement District successfully lobbied the town board to enact legislation requiring that any social service agency wanting to relocate in the district must get a special permit. See Mitchell Freedman, "Riverhead to Govern Downtown Tenants," *Newsday,* May 9, 2002, A30.

49. Briffault, "A Government for Our Time?" 462–463.

50. Barr, "More Like Disneyland," 404, 408–411. The statute quoted is 42 U.S.C. 1 1983.

51. Of course, a homeless person who was physically injured or whose property was destroyed could bring a criminal complaint or a civil suit for damages. The former is difficult, given how closely private security forces work with police (sometimes sharing a substation). The latter has been pursued successfully by homeless individuals. One plaintiff won a $27,500 judgment against the Grand Central Partnership. See David Stout, "For a Troubled Partnership: A History of Problems," *New York Times,* November 8, 1995, B6.

52. Eds. Chuihua Judy Chung, Jeffrey Inaba, Rem Koolhaas, and Sze Tsung Leong, *Harvard Design School Guide to Shopping* (Cologne: Taschen, 2001).

19 The Spaces of Suburban Retailing

1. "Mall of America," http://www.bloomingtonmn.org/mallofamerica.html (accessed 13 June, 2003).

2. Eric Wieffering, "10 Years Later, the Mall of America Still Stands Alone," *Minneapolis Star Tribune*, 4 August 2002, 1A.

3. Kevin Mattson, "Antidotes to Sprawl," in *Sprawl and Public Space Redressing the Mall*, ed. David J. Smiley (Washington, DC: National Endowment for the Arts, 2002), 40.

4. H. Lee Murphy, "Retail Revisions: Mall Seek Lifestyle Change," *Crain's Chicago Business*, 28 March 2005, 36.

5. Mattson, "Antidotes to Sprawl," 40–41; "Roundtable: Obstacles to Development" in *Sprawl and Public Space*, 91; David Smiley, "Addressing Redress" in *Sprawl and Public Space*, 14.

6. Teresa F. Lindeman, "Dead Mall Shopping" *Pittsburgh Post-Gazette*, 10 May 2002, C3; see also http://www.deadmalls.com.

7. Donna Mitchell, "Turtle Creek Sole U.S. Enclosed Mall to Open During '06," http://www.icsc.org/srch/sct/sct0206/feat_turtle_creek_mall.php (accessed 4 April 2006).

8. Renee Degross, "Room at the Malls," *Atlanta Journal-Constitution*, 6 August 2003, ID.

9. "State of the Industry," *Chain Store Age* 81 (August 2005): 6A.

10. Jennifer Evans-Cowley, *Meeting the Big-Box Challenge: Planning, Design, and Regulatory Strategies* (Chicago, IL: American Planning Association, 2006), I; Marlon G. Boarnet, Randall Crane, Daniel G. Chatman, and Michael Manville, "Emerging Planning Challenges in Retail: The Case of Wal-Mart," *Journal of the American Planning Association* 71 (autumn 2005): 433.

11. John Ritter, "California Tries to Slam Lid on Big-Boxed Wal-Mart," *USA Today*, 2 March 2004, 2B.

12. Boarnet, et al., "Emerging Planning Challenges," 434.

13. Ritter, "California Tries to Slam Lid," 2B.

14. "ICSC Shopping Center Definitions," http://www.icsc.org/srch/lib/SCDefinitions.pdf (accessed 30 July, 2006).

15. Kristina Kessler, "Refining Retail," *Urban Land* 64 (October 2005): 87.

16. David C. Scholl and Robert B. Williams, "A Choice of Lifestyles," *Urban Land* 64 (October 2005): 89.

17. Robert Preer, "Sharing the Wealth in Hingham," *Boston Globe*, 28 November 2004, Globe South Section, 1.

18. Paula Widholm, "Indiana's Clay Terrace; Small-Town Charm Meets Upscale Shopping," *Midwest Construction* 8 (1 May 2005): 39.

19. Jennifer Waters, "Lifestyle Centers Offer It All," *Albany* (New York) *Times Union*, 20 June 2004, E1.

20. Ed McKinley, "These Centers Made for Walkin," but Not Too Far Please," http://www.icsc.org/srch/sct/sct0206/feat_lifestyle_walk_park.php (accessed 4 April, 2006).

21. Charles Lockwood, "Raising the Bar," *Urban Land* 62 (February 2003): 77.

22. Sam Newberg, "Town Centers Open around the US," *New Urban News*, December 2004, http://www.newurbannews.com/TownCenters Dec04.html (accessed 11 October 2005).

23. Lockwood, "Raising the Bar," 74. See also Janet H. Cho, "Westlake Complex Growing Up to Be Success," *Cleveland Plain Dealer*, 15 November 2005, C1.

24. Lauren Weber, "Smith Haven Mall Makeover," *Newsday* (Nassau and Suffolk Edition), 3 November 2005, A54.

25. "Cumberland Mall—About Us," http://www.cumberlandmall.com/html/MallInfo.asp (accessed 3 January, 2006); Sandra Jones, "Giant Expansion for Old Orchard," *Crain's Chicago Business*, 6 June 2005, 1.

26. Monica Soto Ouchi, "Alderwood Alters Retail Image," *Seattle Times*, 3 November 2004, F1.

27. "Southglenn Shopping Center Is Reinvented," News Release, Alberta Development Partners, http://www.newsouthglenn.com/Documents/AlbertaSouthglennAnnouncement.pdf (accessed 8 January, 2006).

28. Katherine Field, "Power Surge," *Chain Store Age* 82 (March 2006): 123.

20 Cities in a Time of Terror

1. See Harold Lasswell, "The Garrison State," *American Journal of Urban Sociology* 46 (January 1941): 455–468.

2. Ibid., p. 455.

3. See Mike Davis, "The Flames of New York," *New Left Review* 12 (November–December 2001): 45.

4. Ibid., p. 44.

5. David Dixon, "Is Density Dangerous? The Architects' Obligations after the Towers Fell," in *Perspective on Preparedness*, Belfare Center for International Affairs and Taubman Center for State and Local Government, Harvard University (October 12, 2002): 1.

6. See Peter Marcuse, "Urban Form and Globalization after September 11: The View from New York," *International Journal of Urban and Regional Research* 23, 3 (September 2002): 596–606. For Marcuse's quote, see p. 596. Marcuse held much the same opinion in an earlier article. See Peter Marcuse, "Alternate Visions for New York City: By Whom, for Whom," *MetroPlanner* (January–February 2002), p. 3.

7. There appeared to be a uniformity of opinion in most of the published articles. See the *International Journal of Urban and Regional Research* 26 (September 2002): 589–590, and 27, 3 (2003): 649–698.

8. Michael Dudley, "Sprawl as Strategy: City Planners Face the Bomb," *Journal of Planning Education and Research* (Fall 2001): 52–63.

9. The idea actually began in the 1960s and was elaborated during the 1990s. See Melvin Weber, "Order in Diversity: Community without Propinquity," in *Cities and Space: The Future,* ed. Lowdon Wingo, Jr. (Baltimore, MD: Johns Hopkins University Press, 1963). For later and cruder versions, see Harry Richardson and Peter Gordon, "Market Planning: Oxymoron or Common Sense?" *Journal of the American Planning Association* 59 (Summer 1993): 59–77; and Peter Gordon and Harry Richardson, "Are compact Cities a Desirable Planning Goal?" *Journal of the American Planning Association* 63 (Winter 1997): 95–107.

10. Quoted in Keith Schneider, "Sprawl Not an Antidote to Terror," *Elm Street Writers Group* (Michigan Land Institute, December 2001).

11. See Joel Kotkin, "The Declustering of America," *Wall Street Journal*, August 12, 2002, p. A12. For extended discussion, see Joel Kotkin, *The New Geography: How the Digital Landscape Is Reshaping the American Landscape* (New York: Random House, 2000).

12. Ibid.

13. James Kunstler and Nikos Slingaros attribute the term "urban hypertrophy" to Leon Krier. See Leon Krier, *Leon Krier: Houses, Palaces, Cities* (New York: St. Martin's Press, 1984). See James Kunstler and Nikos Slingaros, "The End of Tall Buildings," *Planetizen* (September 17, 2001), available at www.panetizen.com/oped/item.php.

14. Ibid.

15. See Edward Glaeser and Jesse Shapiro, "Cities and Warfare: The Impact of Terrorism on Urban Form," *Journal of Urban Economics* 51 (March 2002): 205–224; and Ronald R. Davis and Weinstein E. David, "Bones, Bombs and Breakpoint: The Geography of Economic Activity," *American Economic Review* 92 (December 2002): 1269–1289. See also Steven Brackman, Harry Garretsen, and Mark Schramm, "The Strategic Bombing of German Cities during World War II and Its Impact on City Growth" *Journal of Economic Geography* 42, 2 (2004): 201–208.

16. For varying interpretations of the war on terror, including the garrison state, see Kathe Callahan, Melvin Dubnick, and Dorothy Olshfski, "War Narratives: Framing Our Understanding of the War on Terror," *Public Administration Review* 66, 4 (July–August 2006): 554–568.

17. See Peter Eisinger, "The American City in an Age of Terror: A Preliminary Assessment of the Effects of September 11," *Urban Affairs Review* 40, 1 (2004): 115–130.

18. Ibid. Brackman, Garretsen, and Schramm, *Strategy Bombing,* do point out that cities in West Germany (FRG) incurred a temporary impact but fully recovered, while those in East Germany (GDR) did not and the Allied bombing had a permanent impact. While the authors do not venture into why the FRG cities would show a different recovery than GDR cities, a plausible reason might be that FRG cities were located in more dynamic, aggressive, and productive national economies. Those economies acted differently on their respective cities.

19. In distinguishing between conventional warfare and terrorism, we can talk about the unbounded friction of urban terror. This friction is akin to the experience of the Middle Ages, where plunder and siege lasted for 20, 30, or 100 years. In these instances, constant invasions and centuries of pillage caused many cities to wither or disappear (see Pirenne, *Medieval Cities*). The Thirty Years' War resulted in a radical depopulation of German cities in which Marburg and Augsburg lost more than half their inhabitants, never to regain their predominant status (C.V. Wedgewood, *The Thirty Years War* [Garden City, NY: Doubleday, 1961]). Another way of understanding how the friction of terror might affect cities is to examine the relationship between crime and urban settlement. Like terrorism, crime creates chronic apprehension and paralyzes normal life. Much as guards, gates, and surveillance are used to thwart terror, so too are they employed to prevent criminal aggression.

20. James Harrigan and Philippe Martin, "Terrorism and the Resilience of Cities," *Economic Policy Review* (November 2002): 97–116.

21. Robert Greenbaum and Andy Hultquist, "The Impact of Terrorism on Italian Employment and Business Activity" (unpublished manuscript, 2006).

22. For the Israeli case, see Zvi Eckstein and Daniel Tsiddon, "Macroeconomic Consequences of Terror: Theory and the Case of Israel" (paper presented at the conference on "Public Policy," Carnegie-Rochester, November 21–22, 2003); and Daniel Felsenstein and Shlomie Hazam, "The Effect of Terror on Behavior in the

Jerusalem Housing Market" (unpublished manuscript, Institute of Urban and Regional Studies, Hebrew University of Jerusalem, 2005). For the Basque case, see Alberto Abadie and Javier Gardeazabai, "The Economic Costs of Conflict: A Case Control Study for the Basque Country," National Bureau of Economic Research (Cambridge, MA, September 2001).

23. Resilience can also be complex, and Vale and Campanella adumbrate its processes beginning with the onset of disaster to rebuilding. The purpose here is simpler and involves narrowing down a condition to see whether the disruption endures, for how long, and whether there has been a restoration. See Lawrence Vale and Thomas Campanella, eds., The Resilient City: How Modern Cities Recover from Disaster (New York: Oxford University Press, 2005).

24. For an account of New York's economy after 9/11, see Edward Hill and Iryna Lendell, "Did 9/11 Change Manhattan and the New York Region as Places to Conduct Business?" in Resilient City: The Economic Impact of 9/11, ed. Howard Chernick (New York: Russell Sage, 2005), pp. 23–61.

25. Ibid., p. 35.

26. Gross city product is calculated differently from one country to another, and this may account for the London's lower figure. See Corporation of London, London/New York: The Economies of Two Cities at the Millennium, Executive Summary (London: Corporation of London, June 2000), p. 16.

27. Ibid., sec: 2, "Driving Forces of Change in London and New York Economies."

28. Jerusalem Institute for Israel Studies, 1999–2000, The Jerusalem Yearbook, available at www.jiis .org.il/shnaton.

29. U.S. Department of Labor, Bureau of Labor Statistics, Current Employment Survey, 2006. See also Eisinger, "The American City in an Age of Terror," Urban Affairs Review 40, 1: 115–130; and Hill and Lendell, "Did 9/11 Change Manhattan and the New York Region as Places to Conduct Business?" in Chernick, ed., Resilient City.

30. See Chernick, ed., Resilient City, for the period up through 2004, and James Parrot, New York City's Labor Market Outlook with a Special Emphasis on Immigrant Workers, New York: Fiscal Policy Institute, December 2005.

31. The year taken for the previous period is 1989 and the year taken for the cessation of terror is 1994. As of this writing, data on London were not available to assess the employment effects due to the attacks of July 2005. See City of London Corporation, City Research Focus, available at http://www.cityoflondon.gov.uk/Corpo ration/business_city/research_statistics/Research+ periodicals.htm#focus, and Annual Business Inquiry.

32. See H. V. Savitch and Garb Yaacov, "Terror, Barriers and the Re-topography of Jerusalem," as well as Hank V. Savitch, "An Anatomy of Urban Terror."

33. Jerusalem Institute for Israel Studies, "Statistical Yearbook of Jerusalem 2001–2004."

34. The comparisons made are between the pre-attack year of 2000 and the post-attack years of 2002 and 2003. The tourist figures cited in this section deal with tourism from other nations, or "foreign tourists." New York statistics are obtainable on the New York City Official Tourism Website at http://www.nycvisit.com/content/index .cfm? pagePkey=57.

35. Visit London Corporate, London Monthly Trends, Monthly Visitor Index (London: Visit London, July–September 2005).

36. Ibid.

37. Franz Fuerst, "The Impact of 9/11 on the Manhattan Office Market," in Resilient City, ed. Howard Chernick (New York: Russell Sage, 2005) pp. 62–98.

38. Ibid. About 20 percent of firms chose to move out of the city.

39. Ibid., p. 81.

40. See Igal Charney, "Reflections on the Post-WTC Skyline: Manhattan and Elsewhere," International Journal of Urban and Regional Research 29 (March 2005): 172–179.

41. Ibid.

42. Ibid. The skyscraper in Dubai will rise to over 2,300 feet (705 meters). The antenna/spire of the World Trade Center was 1,731.9 feet (527.9 meters) and its roofline was 1,368 feet (417 meters).

43. Quoted in Edwin Mills, "Terrorism and U.S. Real Estate," Journal of Urban Economics 51 (2002): 198–204.

44. Quoted in "Special Report: The Skyscraper Boom," Economist, June 3,2006, pp. 65–67.

45. Eisinger, "The American City in an Age of Terror," p. 126.

46. Savitch, "An Anatomy of Urban Terror," p. 388.

47. Ibid., p. 389.

48. Thomas Wolfe, You Can't Go Home Again, 2d ed. (New York: Harper Perennial Classic, 1998).

49. Jonathan Schwabish and Joshua Chang, "New York City and Terrorism Insurance in a Post 9/11 World," Issue Brief (Partnership for New York City, September 2004).

50. National Underwriter Company, *Property and Casualty/Risks and Benefits* (National Underwriter Company, November 2002).

51. Editorial, *London Times,* December 14, 2002. p. 1.

52. Susan Clarke and Erica Chenoweth, "The Politics of Vulnerability: Constructing Local Performance Regimes for Homeland Security," *Review of Policy Research* 23, 1 (January 2006): 95–114.

53. German Marshal Fund, *Transatlantic Trends: Key Findings,* p. 7.

54. National League of Cities, "Cities Report Change in Financial Conditions," *State of American Cities Survey.* (Washington, DC: National League of Cities, 2001).

55. Ibid.

56. U.S. Senate, Undersecretary of Preparedness George Foresman, Department of Homeland Security, speaking "For the Record" to the Committee on Homeland Security (June 21, 2006), p. 3. This does not take account of other sources, and some have pegged the total amount at $28.9 billion. See Clarke and Chenoweth, "Politics of Vulnerability."

57. U.S. House Committee, Mayor Michael R. Bloomberg of New York City and Mayor Anthony Williams of Washington, DC, speaking on "DHS Terrorism Preparedness Grants: Risk-Based or Guess Work?" to the Committee on Homeland Security (June 21, 2006).

58. Department of Homeland Security, *FY 2006 Urban Area Security Initiative (UASI) by Urban Areas* sec. 2 (Washington, DC, 2006).

59. For a discussion of this see Peter Eisinger, "Imperfect Federalism: The Intergovernmental Partnership for Homeland Security," *Public Administration Review,* (July/August 2006): 537–545.

60. This is a political logic that decades ago marked efforts to create full employment and model cities. See, for example, Charles Haar, *Between the Idea and the Reality* (Boston: Little, Brown, 1975).

61. See Theodore Lowi, "American Business, Public Policy, and Case Studies and Political Theory," *World Politics* 16: (1964): 677–715; and Paul Peterson, *City Limits* (Chicago: University of Chicago Press, 1981).

62. See Clarke and Chenoweth, "Politics of Vulnerability."

Chapter 7

22 Growth Management: The Core Regional Issue

1. Unless otherwise noted, all data in this article are drawn from the author's calculations based on various decennial census reports; Department of Commerce, *Statistical Abstract of the United States,* various editions; and Department of Commerce, *Historical Statistics of the United States: Colonial Times to 1970 (1975).*

2. Executive Office of the President, *Budget of the United States Government, Historical Tables for Fiscal Year 1996,* table 8.7.

3. The outstanding value of all federally aided home mortgages (including Fannie Mae and Freddie Mac's portfolios) was $2.5 trillion in 1995. By contrast, the annual direct federal appropriation for rental housing assistance for low-income households was $26 billion. In 1996 the federal tax code provided $94 billion in tax incentives for homeowners compared to less than $9 billion in tax incentives for investors in rental properties.

4. Over the next three decades, the census recognized another 239 urbanized areas. By 1990, 396 urbanized areas contained 61,000 square miles of urbanized land—about 2 percent of our land mass.

5. By the centennial of the American Revolution, the site of the Battle of Bunker Hill (that is, Breed's Hill) and all other major landmarks of the siege of Boston lay well with Boston's city limits.

6. "Elastic cities" expand their boundaries through annexation or, more rarely, city-county consolidation to absorb many new suburban areas. "Inelastic cities" are trapped within fixed city limits by either bad state annexation laws or being surrounded by incorporated suburbs. For a full discussion of the consequences of city elasticity and inelasticity, see David Rusk, *Cities Without Suburbs,* 2d ed. (Johns Hopkins University Press, 1995).

7. As of 1990, less than one-tenth of the land within Anchorage's city limits was classified as "urbanized" by the Census Bureau.

8. The segregation indexes are "dissimilarity indexes" that describe the relative unevenness of the distribution of target populations. On a scale of 0–100, a score of 0 indicates an absolutely even distribution, or complete integration; a score of 100 indicates an absolutely uneven distribution, or complete segregation. The measurements are made on a census tract by census tract basis (that is, largely without regard to political boundaries). Dissimilarity indexes cited are drawn from a report by Roderick J. Harrison and Daniel H. Weinberg, *Racial and Ethnic Segregation in 1990* (Bureau of the Census, Department of Commerce, 1992).

9. With the assistance of the Urban Institute in Washington, D.C., I calculated dissimilarity indexes for

attendance zones of all public high schools in 320 metropolitan areas, based on computer tapes provided by the National Center for Education Statistics, for the 1989–1990 school year.

10. The term *South* refers to the seventeen states and the District of Columbia that maintained legally segregated school systems until the U.S. Supreme Court's epochal *Brown v. Board of Education* decision in 1954.

11. See David Rusk, *Inside Game/Outside Game: Winning Strategies for Saving Urban America* (Century Fund and Brookings, 1999), p. 73.

12. In the 1990s, voters have approved three new city-county consolidations: Athens–Clarke County and Augusta–Richmond County, both in Georgia, and Kansas City–Wyandotte County, Kansas.

13. Greater Baltimore Committee, *One Region, One Future* (1997).

14. See David Rusk, *Abell Report: To Improve Poor Children's Test Scores, Move Poor Families* (Baltimore: Abell Foundation, July 1998).

15. David Rusk, "Renewing Our Community: The Rusk Report on the Future of Greater York," *York Daily Record* (November 20, 1997), p. 2.

16. The Michigan Society of Planning Officials estimates that Michigan is subdividing farmland at the rate of ten acres an hour.

17. Housing prices escalated rapidly in other regions of the booming Pacific Northwest and Rocky Mountain states. Without any urban growth boundary in effect, Albuquerque, for instance, experienced a similar increase in housing prices and for much the same reason. In both Albuquerque and Portland, Intel was building $4 billion chip factories.

18. In 1973 the Montgomery County Council adopted the Moderately Priced Dwelling Unit (MPDU) ordinance. It requires that in any new housing development of fifty or more units builders must make at least 15 percent of the units affordable for households in the lowest third of the county's income range. To compensate builders for lost profits from developing 15 percent of their property at less than market potential, the MPDU ordinance provides up to a 22 percent density bonus. In the twenty-five years under the policy, home-builders have built over 10,000 affordable units in compliance with the MPDU policy. The county's Housing Opportunities Commission, which, by ordinance, has right of first purchase for one-third of the MPDU units, has purchased over 1,500 units as rental properties for very low-income tenants. While economic segregation has increased in most urban areas, Montgomery County's dissimilarity index for poor households has been stable at a low 27 rating—a direct consequence of the county's MPDU policy and other mixed-income housing initiatives.

19. National Association of Regional Councils, *Regional Reporter 3* (January 1992), p. 1.

20. Carl Abbott and Margery Post Abbott, "Historical Development of the Metropolitan Service District," prepared for the Metro Home Rule Charter Committee.

21. Myron Orfield, *Metropolitics* (Cambridge, Mass., and Washington, D.C.: Lincoln Institute of Land Policy and Brookings, 1997), p. 133.

23 Is Urban Sprawl a Problem?

1. "Cities, Suburbs, and the Urban Crisis," *The Public Interest,* No. 113 (Fall 1993).

Chapter 8

25 Federal Prescriptions and City Problems

1. For a full account of the Tulsa riot on which this paragraph is based, see Brent Staples, "Unearthing a Riot," *New York Times Magazine,* December 19, 1999, pp. 64–69.

2. See Paul E. Peterson, *City Limits* (University of Chicago Press, 1981), chaps. 10, 11.

3. See David Goldberg, "Heads Up, Atlanta: Cities Are Scrambling to Comply with the Clean Air Act's Strict New Rules," *Planning,* vol. 64 (July 1998), pp. 20–23.

4. James Fallows, *More Like Us* (Houghton Mifflin, 1989), p. 169.

5. Racial violence, sparked by alleged black rapes, exploded in Omaha, Kansas City, Knoxville, Rosewood, Fla., Longview, Tex., and Washington, D.C., among other towns, at about this period.

6. Nearly all the PCBs flowing into the Great Lakes originate from the air. An estimated quarter of the nitrogen in the Chesapeake Bay derives from polluted air drifting from at least four neighboring states. Mary Graham, *The Morning After Earth Day: Practical Environmental Politics* (Brookings, 1999), p. 80.

7. Susan Rose-Ackerman, "Does Federalism Matter? Choice in a Federal Public," *Journal of Political Economy,* vol. 49, no. 1 (1981), pp. 152–63. See also John H. Cumberland, "Interregional Pollution Spillovers and Consistency of Environmental Policy," in M. Siebert and others, eds., *Regional Environmental Policy: The Economic Issues* (New York University Press, 1979), pp. 255–81.

8. James Madison, "Federalist No. 10," in Pietro S. Nivola and David H. Rosenbloom, eds., *Classic Readings in American Politics*, 3rd ed. (St. Martin's, 1999), p. 34.

9. *Budget of the United States Government, Fiscal Year 1993*, 1, 5, pp. 164–65.

10. This was reflected in the nearly static level of aid to state and local governments between 1980 and 1995, excluding federal assistance for Medicaid, Annothy Conlan, *From New Federalism to Devolution: Twenty-Five Years of Intergovernmental Reform* (Brookings, 1998), pp. 204–06, 219.

11. Conlan, *From New Federalism to Devolution*, p. 204.

12. James Q. Wilson and John J. DiIulio Jr., *American Government: Institutions and Policies*, 7th ed. (Houghton Mifflin Company, 1998), p. 70.

13. Bernard J. Frieden and Marshall Kaplan, *The Politics of Neglect: Urban Aid from Model Cities to Revenue Sharing* (MIT Press, 1977).

14. As early as 1994, the states were enjoying surpluses that totaled more than 7 billion.

15. On how devolution has been a cost-controlling mechanism for social programs such as Medicaid, see James R. Tallon Jr. and Lawrence D. Brown, "Who Gets What? Devolution of Eligibility and Benefits in Medicaid," in Frank J. and John J. DiIulio Jr., *Medicaid and Devolution: A View from the States* (Brookings, 1998), p. 237.

16. See generally, on the efficiency gains from inter-jurisdictional competition within federal systems, Michael S. Greve, *Real Federalism* (Washington: American Enterprise Institute Press, 1999). For the leading analysis of its disadvantages see Paul E. Peterson, *The Price of Federalism* (Brookings, 1995).

17. Paul C. Light, *The True Size of Government* (Brookings, 1999), p. 32.

18. In 1995, for instance, California collected $1.2 billion in federal disaster relief, much of it to compensate questionable "victims." Dan Morgan, "Governors Bit Helping Hand in Mandates Fight," *Washington Post*, January 1995, pp. A1, A6.

19. Demetrios Caraley, "Washington Abandons the Cities," *Political Science Quarterly*, vol. 107, no. 1 (1992), p. 13.

20. For the subsidy argument, see James R. St. John, "Unfunded Mandates: Financing State and National Needs," *Brookings Review*, vol. 13 (Spring 1995), 12–15.

21. *South Carolina v. Baker*, 485 U.S. 505 (1988).

22. *Garcia v. San Antonio Metropolitan Transit Authority*, 469 U.S. 528 (1985). Nine months later Congress responded by amending the Fair Labor Standards Act (FLSA), extending it again to all public sector employees. Public Law 99-150, November 13, 1985.

23. *National League of Cities v. Usery*, 426 U.S. 833 (1976).

24. On the impact of Davis-Bacon, see U.S. Advisory Commission on Intergovernmental Relations, *The Role of Federal Mandates in Intergovernmental Relations* (January 1996), p. 13.

25. See Walter Olson, *The Excuse Factory: How Employment Law Is Paralyzing the American Workplace* (Free Press, 1997), p. 185.

26. For instance, *Tinker v. Des Moines Independent Community School District*, 393 U.S. 503 (1969); *Goss v. Lopez*, 419 U.S. 565 (1975). See Abigail Thernstrom, "Where Did All the Order Go? School Discipline and the Law," in Diane Ravitch, ed., *Brookings Papers on Education Policy, 1999* (Brookings, 1999), p. 213. In a North Carolina school district, for instance, a student who broke a teacher's arm was given a mere two-day suspension.

27. In *Bethel School District No. 403 v. Fraser*, 478 U.S. 675 (1986) and several ensuing decisions, the court sought to nudge the balance of authority back from students to school officials. However, lower courts have tended to restrict removals and even suspensions of special-ed students.

28. According to the so-called "2-in, 2-out" procedure, at least two employees have to remain outside the site of an "interior structural fire" when two go inside (Standard Number 1910.134 (g) (4) (i) through (iii)). OSHA, *Regulations (Standards— 29 (CFR): Standard Number 1910.134*. The rule may apply to many fire departments that have federally approved occupational safety and health (OSH) plans in effect. Section 18(b) of the Occupational Safety and Health Act of 1970 (Public Law 91-596) stipulated that states operating under their own OSH plans are required to provide OSH protection to public as well as private sector workers. And the standards of each state OSH plan have to be at least as stringent as those of the federal OSHA program, which covers all private sector workers. See U.S. Department of Labor, Office of Inspector General, *Evaluating the Status of Occupational Safety and Health Coverage of State and Local Workers in Federal OSHA States* (February 2000). Some two dozen states operate under federally approved OSH plans. Thus, California, as an example, follows the federal OSHA fire-fighting guideline verbatim. How much, if any,

flexibility localities might have in such states is not entirely clear. A note attached to paragraph (g) of the OSHA regulations, however, adds this proviso: "Nothing in this section is meant to preclude firefighters from performing emergency rescue activities before an entire team has assembled."

29. Motor Carrier Safety Administration, Federal Highway Administration, Regulation no. 393.90.

30. I owe the Beverly Hills joke to James Q. Wilson and John J. DiIulio Jr., *American Government: Institutions and Policies* (Boston: Houghton Mifflin Company, 1998), p. 68.

31. The ensuing discussion is drawn from Pietro S. Nivola and Jon A. Shields, *Managing Green Mandates: Local Rigors of U.S. Environmental Regulation* (AEI-Brookings Joint Center for Regulatory Studies, 2001).

32. San Francisco concluded that it was simpler in the long run to build an oceanside secondary treatment plant than to count on obtaining periodic waivers. This city's experience illustrates the kinds of local complications that arise, even under EPA policies intended to increase local flexibility. San Francisco had obtained a waiver in the early 1980s, but it was only good for five years. If, one day, the city would have to build a second treatment plant, a particular site was referred. Rather than risk that subsequent waiver applications might be turned down, and that by then the land at the site might not be available, the city broke ground for the new facility in the late 1980s and opened it in September 1993.

33. At one time, however, the product in question had been in use near Columbus as well. For a breezy account of this and other incidents, see Thomas DiLorenzo, "Federal Regulations: Environmentalism's Achilles' Heel," *USA Today Magazine*, vol. 123 (September 1994), p. 48.

34. Mike Allen, "Connecticut Joins Lawsuit over Pollution in Sound," *New York Times*, March 24, 1998, p. A24.

35. Robert A. Katzmann, *Institutional Disability: The Saga of Transportation Policy for the Disabled* (Brookings, 1986), p. 189.

36. The phrase is from Lawrence M. Friedman, *Total Justice* (Russell Sage Foundation, 1988).

37. Edward I. Koch, "The Mandate Millstone," *Public Interest*, no. 61 (Fall 1980), p. 45.

38. Representative Charles Vanik, quored in Timothy Clark, "Access for the Handicapped," *National Journal*, October 21, 1978, p. 1673. The Congressional Budget Office estimated that section 504 of the 1973 Rehabilitation Act would require $6.8 billion to equip buses with wheelchair lifts, install elevators in subway systems, and take other measures to expand access to public transit systems for the physically disabled. Congressional Budget Office, *Urban Transportation for Handicapped Persons: Alternative Federal Approaches* (Washington, 1979), p. xi.

39. For a definitive treatment of this initiative see Thomas F. Burke, "On the Rights Track: The Americans with Disabilities Act," in Pietro S. Nivola, ed., *Comparative Disadvantages: Social Regulations and the Global Economy* (Brookings, 1997).

40. Stephen L. Percy, "ADA, Disability Rights, and Evolving Regulatory Federalism," *Publius*, vol. 23 (Fall 1993), p. 87.

41. *Hearings on the Americans with Disabilities Act* before the Subcommittee on Surface Transportation of the House Committee on Public Works and Transportation, 101 Cong. 1 sess. (Government Printing Office, 1989), p. 2721.

42. James H. Matteson, "Americans with Disabilities Act Requirements: Community Sidewalks and Curbs," *City Council Report*, City of Phoenix, January 24, 1997, pp. 1–2.

43. Percy, "ADA," p. 104.

44. Pursuant to the Clean Air Act amendments of 1990, "Standards of Performance for New Stationary Sources and Emissions Guidelines for Existing Sources," *Federal Register*, vol. 60, no. 243 (December 19, 1995), pp. 65378–436.

45. City of Tampa, *Mayor's Strategic Initiatives* (January 1999), pp. 51–52.

46. Medical Research Council, *Health Effects of Waste Combustion Products* (Leicester, UK: Institute for Environment and Health, 1997).

47. U.S. Environmental Protection Agency, *Mercury Study Report to Congress: Volume II* (December 1997).

48. Katherine N. Probst and others, *Footing the Bill for Superfund Cleanup: Who Pays and How?* (Brookings and Resources for the Future, 1995), p. 1995.

49. Cleaning up urban waste sites, rivers, air sheds, and so on, by 90 percent may be practicable, but erasing the remaining 10 percent can be prohibitive. Stephen Breyer, *Breaking the Vicious Cycle: Toward Effective Risk Regulation* (Harvard University Press, 1993), pp. 11–12, 29.

50. Olson, *The Excuse Factory*, p. 17.

51. James Rutenberg, "Long Weight's Over," *New York Daily News*, March 5, 1998, p. 8.

52. Olson, *The Excuse Factory*, p. 253.

53. Rene Sanchez, "LAPD Reeling as Corruption Cases Multiply," *Washington Post,* February 12, 2000, pp. A1, A14.

54. James Sterngold, "Los Angeles Police Officials Admit Widespread Lapses," *New York Times,* February 17, 2000, p. A12.

55. Charles Epp, "Litigation against Local Governments: Expenditures on Legal Services, 1960–1995," paper presented at the annual meeting of the American Political Science Association, 1997, p. 5.

56. Allen R. Myerson, "Soaring Liability Payments Burdening New York," *New York Times,* June 29, 1992, p. B1.

57. Epp, "Litigation against Local Governments," p. 5.

58. See, for instance, *Monell v. New York City Department of Social Services,* 436 U.S. 658, 56 2d 611, 98 S Ct. 2018 (1978); *Owen v. City of Independence,* 445 U.S. 622, 633n., 13m 100 S Ct. 1398, 1406–1407 (1980); and *Maine v. Thiboutot,* 448, 100 S Ct. 2502 (1980).

59. Richard A. Posner, *The Federal Courts: Challenge and Reform* (Harvard University Press, 1996), pp. 57, 60–61.

60. Don Vannatta Jr., "U.S. Judge Says Removing Alarm Boxes Discriminates against the Deaf," *New York Times,* February 14, 1996, p. B3.

61. Greg B. Smith, "City Asks for End to Jail Regs," *New York Daily News,* May 30, 1996, p. 22.

62. "MTA Officials Admit Violating Federal Court Order to Reduce Overcrowding, Report Says," Associated Press State and Local Wire, September 9, 1998.

63. See Sarah B. Vanderbraak, "Why Criminals Would Rather Be in Philadelphia," *Policy Review,* no. 71 (Summer 1995), pp. 73–75.

64. See Charles R. Epp, "Litigation Stories: Official Perceptions of Lawsuits against Local Government," paper prepared for the 1998 annual meeting of the Law and Society Association, Aspen, Colorado, pp. 9–11.

65. Yong S. Lee, "Civil Liability of State and Local Governments," *Public Administration Review,* vol. 47 (March–April 1987), p. 160.

66. Koch, "Mandate Millstone," p. 53.

67. White student enrollment in Milwaukee stood at 58.9 percent in 1976. After the city's desegregation plan took effect, the percentage dropped to 45.3 percent by 1980. White students had been leaving city schools all along, but the annual rate of departures accelerated by almost 62 percent as the desegregation process unfolded. Paul E. Peterson, Barry G. Rabe, and Kenneth K. Wong, *When Federalism Works* (Brookings, 1986),

p. 185. Forced busing in Charlotte-Mecklenburg had been in effect for decades. As of the late 1990s, it had still to achieve racial balance. In fact, forty-two of the district's schools were not in balance as of 1998, compared with only seven in 1979. Busing in Denver began in 1974. Parents responded by moving away to suburban districts, sharply reducing the number of white students in city schools. In 1995 a federal judge finally ordered the busing to stop. "Stopping the School Bus," *Economist,* May 29, 1999, pp. 25–26. Boston's busing program also began in 1974. Today, only 15 percent of the city's public school students are white, compared with 60 percent in the early 1970s. Carey Goldberg, "Busing's Day Ends: Boston Drops Race in Pupil Placement," *New York Times,* July 15, 1999, p. A1.

68. National School Boards Association, *Survey of Public Education in the Nation's Urban Districts* (Alexandria, Va., 1995), pp. 130–32.

69. Clegg, "Lee," p. A19.

70. For an excellent chronicle of this program's evolution, see R. Shep Melnick, *Between the Lines: Interpreting Welfare Rights* (Brookings, 1994), chaps. 7 and 8.

71. Peterson and others, *When Federalism Works,* p. 127.

72. Roberta Weiner and Maggie Hume, *And Education for All: Public Policy and Handicapped Education* (Alexandria, Va.: Capital, 1987), cited in Paul I. Posner, *The Politics of Unfunded Mandates: Whither Federalism* (Georgetown University Press, 1998), p. 132.

73. *Smith v. Robinson,* 468 U.S. 992 (1984); and *Dellmuth v. Muth,* 491 U.S. 223, 230 (1989).

74. See *Congressional Quarterly Almanac* (Washington: Congressional Quarterly, Inc., 1990), p. 616.

75. Lisa Gubernick and Michelle Conlin, "The Special Education Scandal," *Forbes,* February 10, 1997, p. 66.

76. Urban school systems naturally have disproportionate numbers of pupils in special education because learning disabilities are closely correlated with poverty. Jay Gottlieb and others, "Special Education in Urban America," *Journal of Special Education,* vol. 27, no. 4 (1994), pp. 453–65.

77. See Wade F. Horn and Douglas Tynan, "Revamping Special Education," *Public Interest,* no. 144 (Summer 2001), p. 38.

78. Under the wide-ranging category of students said to suffer a "specific learning disability" (SLD) are those who may have trouble listening,

speaking, reading basic words, comprehending what they read, expressing themselves in writing, problem solving in mathematics, or doing mathematical calculations. According to the director of the University of Minnesota's National Center on Educational Outcomes, more than 80 percent of all schoolchildren in the United States could qualify as having SLD under one definition or another. Horn and Tynan, "Revamping Special Education," p. 38. See also Joseph P. Shapiro and others, "Separate and Unequal," *U.S. News & World Report,* December 13, 1993. Some diagnosed afflictions seem to have burst onto the scene in epidemic proportions. In the years 1994–99, for instance, the number of children considered autistic increased by 153.6 percent, David Brown, "Autism's New Face," *Washington Post,* March 26, 2000, p. A1.

79. The 6.1 million figure was for 1999–2000 and included children and youth ages three to twenty-one. In 1976–77 the number of children receiving special education services and accommodations had been 3.7 million. Horn and Tynan, "Revamping Special Education," p. 36. Jeffrey L. Katz, "Policy on Disabled is Scrutinized over Discipline Problems, Cost," *Congressional Quarterly Weekly Report,* May 11, 1996.

80. *Congressional Quarterly Almanac,* 1975, vol. 31 (Congressional Quarterly Inc., 1976), p. 651.

81. Tom Loveless and Diane Ravitch, "Broken Promises: What the Federal Government Can Do to Improve American Education," *Brookings Review,* vol. 18 (Spring 2000), p. 20.

82. U.S. Advisory Commission on Intergovernmental Relations, *The Role of Federal Mandates in Intergovernmental Relations* (January 1996). Loveless and Ravitch, "Broken Promises," give a more current 12 percent estimate. See also Jeffrey L. Katz, "Policy on Disabled Is Scrutinized," p. 1297.

83. Norm Fruchter and others, *Focus on Learning: A Report on Reorganizing General and Special Education in New York City,* New York University, Institute for Education and Social Policy, 1995; Sam Illon, "Special Education Absorbs School Resources," *New York Times,* April 7, 1994, p. A1; Scott Miner Brook, "The Cratering of New York," *U.S. News & World Report,* May 27, 1991, p. 31.

84. This distortion in New York was far worse than in the rest of the state. (Spending on special education grew much less rapidly elsewhere in New York State, and did not squeeze the resources available for regular students as badly.) Mark Lankgord and James Wyckoff, "The Allocation of Resources to Special Education and Regular Instruction," in Helen F. Ladd, ed., *Holding Schools Accountable: Performance-Based Reform in Education* (Brookings, 1996), p. 231. In the District of Columbia, as much as $49 million of the city's proposed $125 million special education budget in 1998 may have been claimed by the 17 percent of special education students that had to be sent to private schools. Beset by litigation, the District's program also anticipated paying between $6 million and $8 million in legal fees to plaintiffs' lawyers. Doug Struck and Valerie Strauss, "D.C. Special Ed System Still in Disarray, Report Says," *Washington Post,* July 20, 1998, p. B1.

85. Olson, *Excuse Factory,* p. 181.

86. U.S. Conference of Mayors, *Recycling America's Land: A National Report on Brownfields Redevelopment,* vol. 3 (February 2000), pp. 9–11.

87. Epp, "Litigation Stories," pp. 6–7.

88. Paul T. Hill, "Supplying Effective Public Schools in Big Cities," in Diane Ravitch, ed., *Brookings Papers on Education Policy, 1999* (Brookings, 1999), pp. 422–23.

89. Ross Sandler and David Shoenbrod, "Government by Decree—The High Cost of Letting Judges Make Policy," *City Journal,* vol. 4 (Summer 1994).

90. Allen R. Myerson, "Soaring Liability Payments Burdening New York," *New York Times,* June 29, 1992, sec. B, p. 1.

91. Congressional Budget Office, *Federalism and Environmental Protection: Case Studies for Drinking Water and Ground-Level Ozone* (GPO, November 1997), pp. 25–30.

92. Great variations in the intermediary roles of state governments translate into widely divergent federal impacts. The U.S. special education program does not pose the same financial complexities for the cities of Florida, say, as for the municipalities of New York. (Local districts in Florida are responsible for only 2 to 3 percent of special education spending.) Peterson, *When Federalism Works,* p. 156.

93. Brookings Center on Urban and Metropolitan Government, *A Region Divided: The State of Growth in Greater Washington, D.C.* (Brookings, 1999), p. 3.

94. For a general analysis of this unbalanced pattern in metropolitan areas, see Janet Rothenberg Pack, "Poverty and Urban Public Expenditures," *Urban Studies,* vol. 33, no. 11 (1998), pp. 1995–2020.

95. U.S. General Accounting Office, *District of Columbia Government: Overtime Costs Exceed*

Those of Neighboring Governments (September 1997), pp. 21, 32. The GAO found the District paying more in overtime as a percentage of municipal salaries than did any of the city's surrounding counties. For some poverty-related services (corrections, for instance) nearly 18 percent of the District's salary base went to overtime, compared with 0.2 percent in Maryland's Prince George's County.

96. Posner, *Unfunded Mandates*, p. 64.
97. "School Accountability: How Are States Holding Schools Responsible for Results?" *Education Week*, vol. 20 (January 11, 2001), p. 80.
98. See, more generally, the delightfully readable Jonathan Rauch, *Government's End: Why Washington Stopped Working* (New York: Public Affairs, 1999), especially chap. 6.

26 The Political Economy of Disaster Assistance

1. In the aftermath of the attacks of September 11, some urban scholars have turned their attention to issues related to homeland security (Gerber et al. 2005) and urban terrorism (Eisinger 2004; Kantor 2002).

2. This article will focus primarily on the governmental component of disaster assistance.
3. Reporters at the South Florida *Sun-Sentinel* examined 20 of the 313 disasters declared by the Federal Emergency Management Agency from 1999 to 2004. They concluded that 27% of the $1.2 billion paid out went to areas where official reports showed minor damage or none at all (Kestin 2005).
4. In exchange for establishing the September 11th Victim Compensation Fund (VCF) to provide compensation to families of those who were killed and to the seriously injured, Congress limited the role of the tort system in part to protect the airlines involved in the attacks and the owners of the World Trade Center.

27 Politics, Federalism, and the Recovery Process in New Orleans

1. All figures in this section are from The New Orleans Index (November 13, 2007), jointly prepared by The Brookings Institution and the Greater New Orleans Community Data Center (available at http://www.gnocdc.org/).

REFERENCES

Chapter 1
3 Rethinking the Politics of Downtown Development

Adams, C., Bartelt, D., Elesh, D., Goldstein, I., Kleniewski, N., & Yancey, W. (1991). *Philadelphia: Neighborhoods, division, and conflict in a postindustrial city.* Philadelphia: Temple University Press.

Alonso, W. (1960). A theory of urban land markets. *Regional Science Association Journal, 6,* 149–158.

Bergsman, S. (2004). The ground floor: Downtown is up in a revitalized L.A. *Barrons* March 8, pp. 40, 42.

Birch, E. (2005). *Who lives downtown.* Washington, DC: Brookings Institution. Available at www.brookings.edu.

Briffault, R. (1999). A government for our time? Business improvement districts and urban governance. *Columbia Law Review, 99* (2), 365–477.

Center City District (2006). *State of center city 2006.* Philadelphia: Center City District.

Cohen, L. (2007). Buying into downtown revival: The centrality of retail to postwar urban renewal in American cities. *Annals of the American Academy of Political and Social Science, 611*(1), 82–95.

Dahl, R. (1961). *Who governs.* New Haven: Yale University Press.

DeLeon, R. E. (1992). *Left coast city.* Lawrence: University Press of Kansas.

DiMassa, C. M. (2007). Downtown has gained people but lost jobs, report says. *Los Angeles Times,* 21 February, B1.

Dymski, G. (1999). *The bank merger wave.* Armonk, NY: M. E. Sharpe.

Fainstein, S. S. (1994). *The city builders.* Oxford: Blackwell Publishers.

Fainstein, S. S., & Judd, D. (1999). Cities as places to play. In D. Judd & S. Fainstein (Eds.), *The tourist city* (pp. 261–272). New Haven: Yale University Press.

Ferman, B. (1996). *Challenging the growth machine.* Lawrence: University Press of Kansas.

Fitzpatrick, D. (2000). The story of urban renewal. *Pittsburgh Post-Gazette,* May 21.

Fogelson, R. (2001). *Downtown: Its rise and fall.* New Haven, CT: Yale University Press.

Ford, L. (2003). *America's new downtowns: Revitalization or reinvention?* Baltimore: Johns Hopkins University Press.

Friedan, B. J., & Sagalyn, L. B. (1989). *Downtown, Inc.* Cambridge, MA: MIT Press.

Friedland, R., & Palmer, D. (1984). Park place and main street: Business and the urban power structure. *Annual Review of Sociology, 10,* 393–416.

Gendron, R. (2006). Forging collective capacity for urban redevelopment: "Power to," "power over," or both? *City and Community, 5*(1), 5–22.

Gleaser, E., & Kahn, M. (2001). *Job sprawl: Employment location in US metropolitan areas.* Brookings Institution, May. Available at www.brookings.edu.

Gotham, K. (2002). *Race real estate and uneven development: The Kansas City experience, 1900–2000.* Albany: State University of New York Press.

Hannigan, J. (1998). *Fantasy city: Pleasure and profit in the postmodern metropolis.* London and New York: Routledge, 1998.

Harrell, D. C. (2004). Old downtown hotel is on a new mission: Housing the homeless. *Seattle Post-Intelligencer,* 10 November.

Harrison, B., & Bluestone, B. (1982). *The deindustrialization of America.* New York: Basic Books.

Harvey, D. (1985). *The urbanization of capital.* Baltimore: Johns Hopkins University Press.

Healey, P., & Barrett, S. M. (1990). Structure and agency in land and property development processes: Some ideas for research. *Urban Studies, 27*(1), 89–104.

Hodos, J. (2002). Globalization, regionalism, and urban restructuring. *Urban Affairs Review, 37*(3), 358–379.

Holloway, S. R., & Wheeler, J. O. (1991). Corporate relocation and changes in metropolitan corporate dominance, 1980–1987. *Economic Geography, 67*(1), 54–74.

Isenberg, A. (2004). *Downtown America.* Chicago: University of Chicago Press.

Judd, D., Winter, W., Barnes, W. R., & Stem, E. (2003). Tourism and entertainment as local economic development: A national survey. In D. R. Judd (Ed.), *The infrastructure of play* (pp. 50–74). Armonk, NY: M. E. Sharpe.

Kanter, R. M. (2000). Business coalitions as a force for regionalism. In B. Katz (Ed.), *Reflections on regionalism* (pp. 154–181). Washington, DC: Brookings.

Lang, R. E. (2003). *Edgeless cities*. Washington: Brookings Institution Press.

Logan, J., & Molotch, H. (1987). *Urban fortunes*. Berkeley: University of California Press.

McGovern, S. J. (1998). *The politics of downtown development*. Lexington: The University Press of Kentucky.

McGraw, B. (2002). Hudson's name will fade, but family's legacy shines. *Detroit Free Press*, 26 June, B1.

Mitchell, J. (2001). Business improvement districts and the 'new' revitalization of downtown. *Economic Development Quarterly, 15*(2), 115–123.

Mollenkopf, J. H. (1983). *The contested city*. Princeton University Press.

Morçöl, G., & Zimmerman, U. (2006). Metropolitan governance and business improvement districts. *International Journal of Public Administration, 29*, 5–29.

Nolan, M. F. (1993). One inhabitant, able and discrete. *Boston Globe*, 12 September, 16.

Norman, J. (1989). Congenial Milwaukee: A segregated city. In G. Squires (Ed.), *Unequal partnerships: The political economy of urban redevelopment in postwar America* (pp. 178–201). New Brunswick, NJ: Rutgers University Press.

Perlman, E. (1998). Downtown: The live-in solution. *Governing, 11* (9), 28–32.

Salisbury, R. H. (1964). Urban politics: The new convergence of power. *Journal of Politics, 26*(4), 775–797.

Salter, S., & Scott, J. (1991). Problems at CAP top off a bad time for downtown. *Atlanta Journal Constitution*, 3 June, 1.

Saporta, M. (2000). Central Atlanta progress seeks new 'go-to' person. *Atlanta Journal Constitution*, 24 March, 3E.

Saporta, M. (2003). City looks to overcome scarcity of leadership for civic roles. *Atlanta Constitution*, 12 December, 3E.

Sbragia, A. (1989). The Pittsburgh model of economic development: Partnership, responsiveness, and indifference. In G. D. Squires (Ed.), *Unequal partnerships* (pp. 103–120). New Brunswick, NJ: Rutgers University Press.

Sharoff, R. (2001). In St. Louis, office buildings are becoming lofts. *New York Times*, 24 June.

Slobodzian, J. A. (2005). Center city renaissance. *Philadelphia Inquirer*, 27 December.

Stone, C. N. (1989). *Regime politics: Governing Atlanta, 1946–1988*. Lawrence: University Press of Kansas.

Strom, E. (2002). Converting pork into porcelain. *Urban Affairs Review, 38*(1), 3–21.

Strom, E. (2003). Cultural policy as development policy: Evidence from the United States. *International Journal of Cultural Policy, 9*(3).

Strom, E. (2005). The political strategies behind university-based development: The Philadelphia case. In D. Perry & W. Wievel (Eds.), *The university as developer: The university, the city, and real estate development*. Armonk, NY: M.E. Sharpe.

Swanstrom, T. (1985). *The crisis of growth politics*. Philadelphia: Temple University Press.

Turner, R. S. (2002). The politics of design and development in the postmodern downtown. *Journal of Urban Affairs, 24*(5), 533–548.

Wallack, T. (2005). Kaiser top employer on Bay area scene. *San Francisco Chronicle*, 22 February.

Weiss, M. (1987). *The rise of the community builders*. New York: Columbia University Press.

Wolfinger, R. (1974). *The politics of progress*. Englewood Cliffs, NJ: Prentice Hall.

Zukin, S. (1982). *Loft living*. Baltimore: Johns Hopkins University Press.

Chapter 2

7 Can Politicians Bargain with Business?

Almond, G. 1988. The return to the state. *American Political Science Review* 82:853–874.

Bachrach, P., and M. Baratz. 1962. The two faces of power. *American Political Science Review* 56:947–952.

Body-Gendrot, S. 1987. Grass roots mobilization in the Thirteenth Arrondissment: A cross national view. In *The politics of urban development* edited by C. Stone and H. Sanders, 125–143. Lawrence: University Press of Kansas.

Capek, S., and J. Gilderbloom. 1992 *Community versus commodity* Albany: State University of New York Press.

Caro, R. 1974. *The power broker*. New York: Vintage.

Christensen, T. 1979. *Neighborhood survival*. London: Prism Press.

Crenson, M. 1971. *The un-politics of air pollution*. Baltimore, MD: Johns Hopkins University Press.

Cummings, S., ed. 1988. *Business elites and urban development*. Albany: State University of New York Press.

Dahl, R. 1971. *Polyarchy*. New Haven, CT: Yale University Press.

Dahl, R., and C. E. Lindblom. 1965. *Politics, economics, and welfare*. New Haven, CT: Yale University Press.

Danielson, M. 1976. *The politics of exclusion*. New York: Columbia University Press.

Darden, J., R. C. Hill, J. Thomas, and R. Thomas. 1987. *Race and uneven development*. Philadelphia: Temple University Press.

Dreier, P. 1989. Economic growth and economic justice in Boston. In *Unequal partnerships*, edited by G. Squires, 35–58. New Brunswick, NJ: Rutgers University Press.

Dreier, P., and W. D. Keating. 1990. The limits of localism: Progressive housing policies in Boston, 1984–1989. *Urban Affairs Quarterly* 26:191–216.

Eisinger, P. 1987. *Rise of the entrepreneurial state*. Madison: University of Wisconsin Press.

Elkin, D. 1987. State and market in city politics: Or, the real Dallas. In *The politics of urban development*, edited by C. Stone and H. Sanders, 25–51. Lawrence: University Press of Kansas.

Etzkowitz, H., and R. Mack. 1976. Emperialism in the First World: The corporation and the suburb. Paper presented at the Pacific Sociological Association meetings, San Jose, CA, March.

Ewen, L. 1978. *Corporate power and the urban crisis in Detroit.* Princeton, NJ: Princeton University Press.

Fainstein, S. S., N. I. Fainstein, R. C. Hill, D. Judd, and M. P. Smith. 1986. *Restructuring the city.* 2nd ed. New York: Longman.

Fasenfest, D. 1986. Community politics and urban redevelopment. *Urban Affairs Quarterly* 22:101–123.

Feagin, J. 1988. *Free enterprise city.* New Brunswick, NJ: Rutgers University Press.

Foglesong, R. 1989. Do politics matter in the formulation of local economic development policy: The case of Orlando, Florida. Paper presented at the annual meeting of the American Political Science Association, Atlanta, GA, September.

Governor turns down UAL. 1991. *Courier-Journal,* 18 October, 1.

Hill, R. C. 1986. Crisis in the motor city: The politics of urban development in Detroit. In *Restructuring the city,* 2d ed., by S. S. Fainstein, N. I. Fainstein, R. C. Hill, D. Judd, and M. P. Smith. New York: Longman.

_____. Industrial restructuring, state intervention, and uneven development in the United States and Japan. Paper presented at conference: The tiger by the tail: Urban policy and economic restructuring in Comparative perspective. State University of New York, Albany, October.

Jobse, B., and B. Needham. 1987. The economic future of the Randstad, Holland. *Urban Studies* 25: 282–296.

Jones, B., and L. Bachelor. 1986. *The sustaining hand.* Lawrence: University Press of Kansas.

Kantor, P. 1993. The dual city as political choice. *Journal of Urban Affairs* 15 (3): 231–244.

Kantor, P. (with S. David). 1988. *The dependent city.* Boston, MA: Scott, Foresman/Little, Brown.

Levine, M., and J. Van Weesop. 1988. The changing nature of urban planning in the Netherlands. *Journal of the American Planning Association* 54:315–323.

Lindblom, C. 1977. *Politics and markets.* New Haven, CT: Yale University Press.

_____. 1982. The market as a prison. *Journal of Politics* 44:324–336.

Logan, J., and H. Molotch. 1987. *Urban fortunes.* Berkeley: University of California Press.

Logan, J., and T. Swanstrom, eds. 1990. *Beyond the city limits.* Philadelphia: Temple University Press.

Mamadouh, V. 1990. Squatting, housing, and urban policy in Amsterdam. Paper presented at the International Research Conference on Housing Debates and Urban Challenges, Paris, July.

Mollenkopf, J. 1983. *The contested city.* Princeton, NJ: Princeton Univ. Press.

Molotch, H., and S. Vicari. 1988. Three ways to build: The development process in the United States, Japan, and Italy. *Urban Affairs Quarterly* 24:188–214.

Muzzio, D., and R. Bailey. 1986. Economic development, housing, and zoning. *Journal of Urban Affairs* 8:1–18.

Nethercutt, M. 1987. *Detroit twenty years after: A statistical profile of the Detroit area since 1967.* Detroit, MI: Center for Urban Studies, Wayne State University.

Noyelle, T., and T. M. Stanback. 1984. *Economic transformation of American cities.* New York: Conservation for Human Resources Columbia University.

Parkinson, M., B. Foley, and D. Judd. 1989. *Regenerating the cities.* Boston, MA: Scott, Foresman.

Peterson, P. 1981. *City limits.* Chicago: University of Chicago Press.

Rich, W. 1991. Detroit: From Motor City to service hub. In *Big city politics in transition,* edited by H. V. Savitch and J. C. Thomas, 64–85. Newbury Park, CA: Sage Publications.

Rosentraub, M., and D. Swindell. 1990. "Just say no"? The economic and political realities of a small city's investment in minor league baseball. Paper presented at the 20th annual meeting of the Urban Affairs Association, Charlotte, NC, April.

Sassen, S. 1988. *The mobility of capital and labor.* Cambridge: Cambridge University Press.

Savitch, H. V. 1988. *Post-industrial cities: Politics and planning in New York, Paris, and London.* Princeton, NJ: Princeton University Press.

Savitch, H. V., and J. C. Thomas, eds. 1991. *Big city politics in transition.* Newbury Park, CA: Sage Publications.

Stone, C. 1989. *Regime politics.* Lawrence: University Press of Kansas.

Stone, C., and H. Sanders, eds. 1987. *The politics of urban development.* Lawrence: University Press of Kansas.

Swanstrom, T. 1986. *The crisis of growth politics* Philadelphia: Temple University Press.

UAL bidding goes on. 1991. *Courier-Journal,* 22 October, 1.

Van Weesop, J., and M. Wiegersma. 1991. Gentrification in the Netherlands. In *Urban housing for the better-off: Gentrification in Europe* edited by J. Van Weesop and S. Musterd, 98–111. Utrecht, Netherlands: Bureau Stedellijke Netwerken.

Vaughn, R. 1979. *State taxation and economic development.* Washington, DC: Council of State Planning Agencies.

Vogel, R. 1990. The local regime and economic development. *Economic Development Quarterly* 4:101–112.

Walsh, A. 1978. *The public's business.* Cambridge: MIT Press.

Chapter 3

9 Culture, Art, and Downtown Development

Alexander, V. D. 1996. *Museums and money.* Bloomington: Indiana Univ. Press.

American Association of Museums. 1999. *The official museum directory.* New Providence, NJ: National Register Publishing.

Bailey, J. T. 1989. *Marketing cities in the 1980s and beyond*. Rosemont, IL: American Economic Development Council.

Bourdieu, P. 1984. *Distinction*. Cambridge, MA: Harvard Univ. Press.

Bradsher, K. 1999. A horn of plenty for opera in Detroit. *New York Times*, 28 October, E1, 10.

Burrows, E. G., and M. Wallace. 1999. *Gotham: A history of New York City to 1898*. New York and Oxford, UK: Oxford Univ. Press.

Byrd, J., 1997. Culture at the core. *Seattle Post-Intelligencer*, 9 February, J1.

Clack, G. 1983. Footlight districts. In *The city as stage*, edited by K. W. Green. Washington, DC: Partners for Livable Places.

Clark, T. N. 2000. Old and new paradigms for urban research: Globalization and the Fiscal Austerity and Urban Innovation Project. *Urban Affairs Review* 36 (1): 3–45.

Conn, S. 1998. *Museums and American intellectual life, 1876–1926*. Chicago: Univ. of Chicago Press.

Courtney, M. 1984. Newark museum revives growth plans. *New York Times*, 8 April, B1, 4.

Cwi, D., and K. Lyall. 1977. *Economic impact of arts and cultural institutions: A model for assessment and a case study for Baltimore*. Washington, DC: National Endowment for the Arts.

Danielson, M. N. 1997. *Home team*. Princeton, NJ: Princeton Univ. Press.

Davies, P. 1998. Philadelphia could make big gains from Performing Arts Center visitors. *Philadelphia Daily News*, 17 April.

DiMaggio, P. J. 1982. Cultural entrepreneurship in nineteenth-century Boston: The creation of an organizational base for high culture in America. *Media, Culture and Society* 4:33–50.

_____. 1986. Can culture survive the marketplace? In *Nonprofit enterprise in the arts*, edited by P. J. DiMaggio, 65–92. New York and Oxford, UK: Oxford Univ. Press.

DiMaggio, P. J., and W. W. Powell, 1983. The iron cage revisited: Institutional isomorphism and collective rationality in organizational fields. *American Sociological Review* 48:147–60.

Dobrzynski, J. 1998. Blockbuster shows and prices to match. *New York Times*, 10 November, E1, 13.

Duncan, C. 1995. *Civilizing rituals: Inside art museums*. London, New York: Routledge.

Eisinger, P. 2000. The politics of bread and circuses. *Urban Affairs Review* 35 (3): 316–33.

Friedan, B. J., and L. B. Sagalyn. 1989. *Downtown Inc*. Cambridge, MA: MIT Press.

Gans, H. J. 1974. *Popular culture and high culture*. New York: Basic Books.

_____. 1999. *Popular culture and high culture*. Rev. ed. New York: Basic Books.

Hannigan, J. 1998. *Fantasy city*. London: Routledge.

Harvey, D. 1989. *The condition of postmodernity*. Oxford, UK: Basil Blackwell.

Holcomb, B. 1993. Revisioning place: De- and re-constructing the image of the industrial city. In *Selling places: The city as cultural capital, past and present*, edited by G. Kearns and C. Philo. Oxford, UK: Pergamon.

Horowitz, H. L. 1976. *Culture and the city*. Lexington: Univ. Press of Kentucky.

Janeway, M., D. S. Levy, A. Szanto, and A. Tyndall, 1999. *Reporting the arts: News coverage of arts and culture in America*. New York: Columbia Univ., National Arts Journalism Program.

Judd, D. 1999. Constructing the tourist bubble. In *The tourist city*, edited by D. Judd and S. Fainstein, 35–53. New Haven, CT: Yale Univ. Press.

Levine, L. W. 1988. *Highbrow/lowbrow: The emergence of cultural hierarchy in America*. Cambridge, MA: Harvard Univ. Press.

Logan, J. R., and H. L. Molotch, 1987. *Urban fortunes*. Berkeley: Univ. of California Press.

McDowell, E. 1997. Tourists respond to lure of culture. *New York Times*, 24 April, D1, 4.

Miles, M. 1998. A game of appearance: Public art and urban development—Complicity or sustainability? In *The entrepreneurial city*, edited by T. Hall and P. Hubbard, 203–24. Chichester, UK: Wiley.

Mollenkopf, J. M. 1983. *The contested city*. Princeton, NJ: Princeton Univ. Press.

Morey and Associates, Inc. 1999. Economic impact analysis of the Los Angeles County Museum of Art and the Van Gogh exhibition. Unpublished report.

National Association of State Arts Agencies. 2001. Retrieved 11 April 2001, from www.nasaa-arts.org.

National Endowment for the Arts. 1981. *Economic impact of arts and cultural institutions*. Washington, DC: National Endowment for the Arts.

Newark Museum. 1959. *The Newark Museum: A fifty-year survey*. Newark: Newark Museum.

Ostrower, F. 1998. The arts as cultural capital among elites: Bourdieu's theory reconsidered. *Poetics* 26:43–53.

Perryman, M. R. 2000. The arts, culture, and the Texas economy. Retrieved 15 April 2001, from www.perrymangroup.com.

Peterson, R. A. 1986. From impresario to arts administrator. In *Nonprofit enterprise in the arts*, edited by P. J. DiMaggio, 161–83. New York and Oxford, UK: Oxford Univ. Press.

_____. 1997. The rise and fall of highbrow snobbery as a status marker. *Poetics* 25:75–92.

Peterson, R. A., and R. M. Kern. 1996. Changing highbrow taste: From snob to omnivore. *American Sociological Review* 61:900–907.

The Port Authority of New York and New Jersey and the Cultural Assistance Center. 1993. *The arts as industry: Their economic importance to the New York–New Jersey metropolitan region*. New York: The Port Authority of New York and New Jersey.

Rosentraub, M. S. 1997. *Major league losers*. New York: Basic Books.

Rothstein, E. 1998. Arts centers are changing the face of culture. *San Diego Union-Tribune*, 6 December, E10.

Russell, J. S. 1999. Performing arts centers: Using art to revive cities. *Architectural Record*, May, 223–28.

Sanders, H. T. 1998. Convention center follies. *Public Interest* (summer): 58–72.

Stone, C. N. 1989. *Regime politics*. Lawrence: University Press of Kansas.

Strom, E. 1999. Let's put on a show: Performing arts and urban revitalization in Newark, New Jersey. *Journal of Urban Affairs* 21:423–36.

Toffler, A. 1964. *The culture consumers*. New York: Random House.

_____. 1973. *The culture consumers*. Rev. ed. New York: Random House.

Tomkins, C. 1970. *Merchants and masterpieces*. New York: E. P. Dutton.

Ward, S. V. 1998. *Selling places*. New York and London: Routledge.

Whitt, J. A. 1987. Mozart in the metropolis: The arts coalition and the urban growth machine. *Urban Affairs Quarterly* 23:15–36.

Whitt, J. A., and J. C. Lammers. 1991. The art of growth. *Urban Affairs Quarterly* 26 (3): 376–93.

Wyszomirski, M. J. 1995. The politics of arts policy: Subgovernment to issue network. In *America's commitment to culture: Government and the arts*, edited by K. Mulcahy and M. J. Wyszomirski. Boulder, CO: Westview.

Zolberg, V. 1983. Changing patterns of patronage in the arts. In *Performers and performances*, edited by J. B. Kamerman and R. Martorella, 251–68. New York: Praeger.

10 (Re)Branding the Big Easy

Brand Strategy, Inc. 2004. The brand science guide for destination research: The handbook to help convention and visitors bureaus manage tourism research for destinations. Brand Strategy, Inc. http://www.destinationmarketing.org (accessed September 6, 2006).

Chatterton, Paul, and Robert Hollands. 2003. *Urban nightscapes: Youth cultures, pleasure spaces, and corporate power*. London and New York: Routledge.

City of New Orleans. 2004. Mayor builds music industry. Mayor Nagin's Office of Communications, August 9.

Clark, Terry Nichols, ed. 2004. *The city as an entertainment machine*. New York: Elsevier Press.

Cohen, Lizabeth. 2003. *A consumer's republic: The politics of mass consumption in postwar America*. New York: Random House.

Coviello, Will. 2006. Roger Wilson's "Broadway South" initiative could rebuild downtown New Orleans as a theater district. *Gambit Weekly*, November 14.

Craig, Frank. 1977. Letter from the President of the Council for a Better Louisiana, to the Honorable Secretary of Commerce, Washington, DC, January 31. Records of the 1984 Louisiana Exposition, City Archives, New Orleans Public Library.

Desmond, Jane C. 1999. *Staging tourism: Bodies on display from Waikiki to Sea World*. Chicago: Univ. of Chicago Press.

Foster, Mary. 2006. Shootings tarnish New Orleans image. Associated Press report, July 30.

Gibson, Timothy A. 2006. City living, D.C. style: The political economic limits of urban branding campaigns. In *Urban communication: Production, text, context*, edited by Timothy A. Gibson and Mark Douglas Lowes. New York: Rowman and Littlefield.

_____. 2005. From pilgrimage to package tour: Travel and tourism in the Third World. New York: Routledge.

Goffman, Erving. 1957. *The presentation of self in everyday life*. Edinburgh: Univ. of Edinburgh Press.

Gottdiener, Mark, Claudia C. Collins, and David R. Dickens. 1999. *Las Vegas: The social production of an all-American city*. Malden, MA: Blackwell.

Greenberg, Miriam. 2000. Branding cities: A social history of the urban lifestyle magazine. *Urban Affairs Review* 36, no. 2 (November): 228–262.

_____. 2003. The limits of branding: The World Trade Center, fiscal crisis, and the marketing of recovery. *International Journal of Urban and Regional Research* 27, no. 2 (June): 386–416.

Harvey, David. 2001. Spaces of capital: Towards a critical geography. New York: Routlege.

Hoffman, Lily K. 2003. The marketing of diversity in the inner city: Tourism and regulation in Harlem. *International Journal of Urban and Regional Research* 27, no. 2 (June): 286–299.

Hoffman, Lily K., Susan S. Fainstein, and Dennis R. Judd, eds. 2003. *Cities and visitors: Regulating people, markets, and city space*. New York: Blackwell Publishing.

Hollands, Robert, and Paul Chatterton. 2003. Producing nightlife in the new urban entertainment economy: Corporatization, branding, and market segmentation. *International Journal of Urban and Regional Research* 27, no. 2 (June): 361–385.

Hotel Monteleone. 2006. Hotel Monteleone kicks off its literary luncheon series. News release, June 14.

International Association of Convention and Visitor Bureaus (IACVB). 2005. Developing a genuine destination brand. In *Nation's Cities Weekly*. May 9. http://www.iacvb.org/ (accessed September 25, 2006).

Judd, Dennis. 2003. Visitors and the spatial ecology of the city. In *Cities and visitors: Regulating people, markets, and city space*, edited by Lily K. Hoffman, Susan S. Fainstein, and Dennis R. Judd. New York: Blackwell Publishing.

Judd, Dennis, and Susan Fainstein, eds. 1999. *The tourist city*. New Haven: Yale Univ. Press.

Knopp, Lawrence. 1990. Exploiting the rent gap: The theoretical significance of using illegal appraisal schemes to encourage gentrification in New Orleans. *Urban Geography* 11(1): 48–64.

Lauria, Mickey. 1984. The implications of Marxian rent theory for community-controlled redevelopment strategies. *Journal of Planning Education and Research* 4: 16–24.

Lewis, Pierce F. 2005. *New Orleans: The making of an urban landscape.* 2nd ed. Univ. of Virginia Press.

Lin, Jan. 1998. Globalization and the revalorizing of ethnic places in immigration gateway cities. *Urban Affairs Review* 34:313–339.

Lloyd, Richard. 2005. *Neo-Bohemia: Art and commerce in the postindustrial city.* New York: Routledge.

McNulty, Jan. 2005. The Brennans family: A luscious legacy. www.frenchquarter.com/dining/brennans.php (accessed December 6, 2005).

Miroff, Nick. 2006. Taking a tip from Madison Avenue, towns buy into branding. *Washington Post* B1, July 17.

Moor, Elizabeth. 2003. Branded spaces: The scope of "new marketing." *Journal of Consumer Culture* 3(1): 39–60.

_____. 2000. $30 million for tourism OK'd: It's a good start; Visitors Bureau says. *Times-Picayune,* April 22.

Mowbray, Rebecca, Michelle Krupa, and Greg Thomas. 2006. Plan would reshape downtown to build Jazz Center. *Times-Picayune,* May 30.

New Orleans Jazz Orchestra. 2005. http://www.thenojo.com/mission.html (accessed December 12, 2005).

Novelli, Marina. 2005. *Niche tourism: Contemporary issues, trends and cases.* Oxford, England: Butterworth-Heinemann.

Scott, J. Allen. 2000. *The cultural economy of cities: Essays on the geography of image-producing industries.* London: Sage Publications.

Sheller, Mimi, and John Urry, eds. 2004. *Tourism mobilities: Places to play, places in play.* New York: Routledge.

Slater, Don. 2002. Capturing markets from the economists. In *Cultural economy: Cultural analysis and commercial life,* edited by Patrick D. Gay and Michael Pryke. London: Sage.

Sorkin, Michael, ed. 1992. *Variations on a theme park: The new American city and the end of public space.* New York: Hill and Wang.

Stafford, Leon. 2005. Las Vegas: Gambling. Orlando: Disney. New Orleans: Bourbon Street. Atlanta: Hmmm. . . *Atlanta Journal-Constitution,* May 10.

Urry, John. 2002. *Tourist gaze.* 2nd ed. London: Sage Publications.

World Tourism Organization (WTO).2006. Destination positioning, branding and image management. Addis Abada, March 27–29. http://www.world-tourism.org/destination/ethiopia/session_6.pdf (accessed January 19, 2007).

Yuen, Belinda. 2006. Reclaiming cultural heritage in Singapore. *Urban Affairs Review* 41, no. 6 (July): 830–54.

Chapter 4

12 Minority Groups and Coalitional Politics

Arian, A., A. Goldberg, J. Mollenkopf, and E. Rogowsky. 1990. *Changing New York City politics.* New York: Routledge.

Browning, R., D. Marshall, and D. Tabb, eds. 2003. *Racial politics in American cities.* 3rd ed. New York: Longman.

Carmichael, S., and C. Hamilton. 1967. *Black power: The politics of liberation in America.* New York: Random House.

Crowder K., and L. Tedrow. 2001. West Indians and the residential landscape of New York. In *Islands in the city: West Indian migration to New York,* edited by Nancy Foner. Berkeley: Univ. of California Press.

Dao, J. 1999. Immigrant diversity slows traditional political climb. *New York Times.* December 28.

Dawson, M. 1994a. *Behind the mule: Race and class in African-American politics.* Princeton, NJ: Princeton Univ. Press.

_____. 1994b. A Black counterpublic? Economic earthquakes, racial agenda(s), and Black politics. *Public Culture* 7:195–223.

Falcon, A. 1988. Black and Latino politics in New York City: Race and ethnicity in a changing urban context. In *Latinos and the political system,* edited by F. Chris Garcia. Notre Dame, IN: Note Dame Univ. Press.

Foner, N. 1985. Race and color: Jamaican immigrants in London and New York. *International Migration Review* 19:284–313.

Fuchs, L. 1990. *The American kaleidoscope: Race, ethnicity, and civic culture.* Hanover, NH: Wesleyan Univ. Press.

Green, C., and B. Wilson. 1989. *The struggle for Black empowerment in New York City: Beyond the politics of pigmentation.* New York: Praeger.

Greenhouse, S. 2000. Despite defeat on China bill, labor is on rise. *New York Times,* April 28.

Grimshaw, W. 1992. *Bitter fruit: Black politics and the Chicago machine,* Chicago: Univ. of Chicago Press.

Hellwig, D. 1978. Black meets Black: Afro-American reactions to West Indian immigrants in the 1920s. *South Atlantic Quarterly* 72:205–25.

Henry, C., and C. Munoz Jr. 1991. Ideological and interest linkages in California rainbow politics. In *Racial and ethnic politics in California,* edited by B. Jackson and M. Preston. Berkeley, CA: IGS Press.

Hicks, J. 2000a. Bitter primary contest hits ethnic nerve among Blacks. *New York Times,* August 31.

_____. 2000b. Term limits turn old allies into opponents; protege against mentor, backer against incumbent. *New York Times,* March 22.

Holder, C. 1980. The rise of the West Indian politician in New York City. *Afro-Americans in New York Life and History* 4:45–59.

Jackson, J. 2001. *Harlemworld: Doing race and class in contemporary Black America.* Chicago: Univ. of Chicago Press.

Jennings, J. 1997. *Race and politics: New challenges and responses for Black activism.* London: Verso.

Kasinitz, P. 1992. *Caribbean New York: Black immigrants and the politics of race.* Ithaca, NY: Cornell Univ. Press.

Katznelson, I. 1981. *City trenches: Urban politics and the patterning of class in the United States.* New York: Pantheon.

Key, V. O. 1949. *Southern politics in state and nation.* New York: Vintage.

Kim, C. 1999. The racial triangulation of Asian Americans. *Politics and Society* 27(1): 105–38.

———. 2000. *Bitter fruit: The politics of Black-Korean conflict in New York City.* New Haven, CT: Yale Univ. Press.

Kleppner, P. 1985. *Chicago divided: The making of a Black mayor.* Dekalb: Northern Illinois Press.

Lewis Mumford Center for Comparative Urban and Regional Research. 2002. *Separate and unequal: The neighborhood gap for Blacks and Hispanics in metropolitan America.* Albany, NY: Univ. at Albany Press.

Lewis Mumford Center for Comparative Urban and Regional Research. 2003. *Black diversity in metropolitan America.* Albany, NY: Univ. at Albany Press.

Macchiarola, F., and J. Diaz. 1993. Minority political empowerment in New York City: Beyond the Voting Rights Act. *Political Science Quarterly* 108(1): 37–57.

Marable, M. 1994. Building coalitions among communities of color. In *Blacks, Latinos, and Asians in urban America,* edited by J. Jennings. New York: Praeger.

Mink, G. 1986. *Old labor and new immigrants in American political development.* Ithaca. NY: Cornell Univ. Press.

Mollenkopf, J. 1992. *A phoenix in the ashes: The rise and fall of the Koch coalition in New York City.* Princeton, NJ: Princeton Univ. Press.

———. 1997. New York: The great anomaly. In *Racial politics in American cities,* 2nd ed., edited by R. Browning, D. Marshall, and D. Tabb. New York: Longman.

———. 1999. Urban political conflicts and alliances: New York and Los Angeles compared. In *The handbook of international migration: The American experience,* edited by C. Hirschman, P. Kasinitz, and J. DeWind. New York: Russell Sage Foundation.

———. 2003. New York: The great anomaly. In *Racial politics in American cities,* 3rd ed., edited R. P. Browning, D. R. Marshall, and D. H. Tabb, New York: Longman.

New York Carib News. 1996a. April 23.

New York Carib News. 1996b. October 1.

———. 1988. Black urban regime: Structural origins and constraints. *Comparative Urban and Community Research* 1:138–89.

Reid, I. 1939. *The Negro immigrant: His background characteristics and social adjustments, 1899–1937.* New York: AMS Press.

Rogers, R. 2000. Between race and ethnicity: Afro-Caribbean immigrants, African Americans, and the politics of incorporation, Ph.D. diss., Princeton University.

Skerry, P. 1993. *Mexican Americans: The ambivalent minority.* Cambridge, MA: Harvard Univ. Press.

Sleeper, J. 1993. The end of the rainbow. *New Republic,* November 20–25.

Sonenshein, R. 1993. *Politics in black and white: Race and power in Los Angeles.* Princeton, NJ: Princeton Univ. Press.

———. 2003a. Post-incorporation politics in Los Angeles. In *Racial politics in American cities,* 3rd ed., edited by R. P. Browning, D. R. Marshall, and D. H. Tabb. New York: Longman.

———. 2003b. The prospects for multiracial coalitions: Lessons from America's three largest cities. In *Racial politics in American cities,* 3rd ed., edited by R. P. Browning, D. R. Marshall, and D. H. Tabb. New York: Longman.

Stone, C. 1989. *Regime politics: Governing Atlanta, 1946–1988.* Lawrence: University Press of Kansas.

Stone, C., and C. Pierannunzi. 1997. Atlanta and the limited reach of electoral control. In *Racial politics in American cities,* 2nd ed., edited by R. Browning, D. Marshall, and D. Tabb. New York: Longman.

Tate, K. 1993. *From protest to politics: The new Black voters in American elections.* Cambridge, MA: Harvard Univ. Press.

Vickerman, M. 1999. *Crosscurrents: West Indian immigrants and race.* New York: Oxford Univ. Press.

Warren, C., and D. Moreno. 2003. Power without a program: Hispanic incorporation in Miami. In *Racial politics in American cities,* 3rd ed., edited by R. Browning, D. Marshall, and D. Tabb. New York: Longman.

Waters, M. 1996. Ethnic and racial groups in the USA: Conflict and cooperation. In *Ethnicity and power in the contemporary world,* edited by K. Rupesinghe and V. Tishkov. London: U.N. University.

Waters, M. 1999. *Black identities: West Indian immigrant dreams and American realities.* Cambridge, MA: Harvard Univ. Press.

Watkins-Owens, I. 1996. *Blood relations: Caribbean immigrants and the Harlem community, 1900–1930.* Bloomington: Indiana Univ. Press.

Wong, J. 2000. Institutional context and political mobilization among Mexican and Chinese immigrants. Paper presented at the Immigrant Political Participation in New York City Working Conference, New York, June.

13 Black Incumbents and a Declining Racial Divide

Bosc, Michael. 1987. "Chicago's Mayoral Primary: Racial Lines Are Drawn, But Tempers Are Cooler." *U.S. News & World Report,* February 23:20.

Bullock, Charles S., and Bruce A. Campbell. 1984. "Racist or Racial Voting in the 1981 Atlanta Municipal Elections." *Urban Affairs Quarterly* 20(2): 149–64.

Colburn, David R., and Jeffrey S. Adler, eds. 2003. *African American Mayors: Race, Politics, and the American City.* Urbana, IL: University of Illinois Press.

Eisinger, Peter K. 1980. *Politics and Displacement: Racial and Ethnic Transition in Three American Cities.* Institute for Research on Poverty Monograph Series. New York: Academic Press.

Franklin, Jimmie Lewis. 1989. *Back to Birmingham: Richard Arrington, Jr., and His Times.* Tuscaloosa: University of Alabama Press.

Giles, Michael W., and Kaenan Hertz. 1994. "Racial Threat and Partisan Identification." *American Political Science Review* 88(2): 317–26.

Howell, Susan E., and William P. McLean. 2001. "Performance and Race in Evaluating Minority Mayors." *Public Opinion Quarterly* 65(1) (Feb): 321–43.

Howell, Susan E., and Hugh L. Perry. 2004. "Black Mayors/White Mayors: Explaining Their Approval." *Public Opinion Quarterly* 68(1) (Feb): 32–56.

Karnig, Albert K., and Susan Welch. 1980. *Black Representation and Urban Policy.* Chicago: University of Chicago Press.

Key, V. O. 1949. *Southern Politics in State and Nation.* Knoxville, TN: University of Tennessee Press.

Lublin, David Ian, and Katherine Tate. 1995. "Racial Group Competition in Urban Elections." In *Classifying By Race,* edited by P. E. Peterson. Princeton, NJ: Princeton University Press.

Rich, Wilbur C. 1987. "Coleman Young and Detroit Politics: 1973–1986." In *The New Black Politics: The Search for Political Power,* edited by M. B. Preston, L. J. Henderson, and P. L. Puryear. New York: Longman.

Russakoff, Dale. 1983. "Birmingham Reelects Black: Once-Split City Unites at Polls." *Washington Post,* October 13: A1.

Sonenshein, Raphael J. 1993. *Politics in Black and White: Race and Power in Los Angeles.* Princeton, NJ: Princeton University Press.

Starks, Robert T. 1991. "A Commentary and Response to Exploring the Meaning and Implication of Deracialization in African-American Urban Politics." *Urban Affairs Quarterly* 27(2): 216–22.

Stein, Robert. M., Stacy G. Ulbig, and Stephanie S. Post. 2005. "Voting for Minority Candidates in Multi-Racial/Ethnic Communities." *Urban Affairs Review* 41(2) (Nov): 157–81.

Sun Reporter. 1993. "Black Mayors on the Rise." *Sun Reporter* 56(38): 1.

Vanderleeuw, James M. 1991. "The Influence of Racial Transition on Incumbency Advantage in Local Elections." *Urban Affairs Quarterly* 27(1): 36–50.

Watson, S. M. 1984. "The Second Time Around: A Profile of Black Mayoral Election Campaigns." *Phylon* 45: 165–75.

Wright, Sharon D. 1996. "The Deracialization Strategy and African American Mayoral Candidates in Memphis Mayoral Elections." In *Race, Politics, and Governance in the United States,* edited by H. L. Perry. Gainesville, FL: University of Florida Press.

Chapter 5

17 Police Practices in Immigrant-Destination Communities

Brown, M. K. 1988. *Working the street: Police discretion and the dilemmas of reform.* New York: Russell Sage Foundation.

Browning, R. P., D. R. Marshall, and D. H. Tabb. 1984. *Protest is not enough.* Berkeley: University of California Press.

Bryner, G. C. 1987. *Bureaucratic discretion.* New York: Pergamon Press.

Caldwell, C. 2006. A family or a crowd? *New York Times Magazine,* February 26, 9.

Chaney, C. K., and G. H. Saltzstein. 1998. Democratic control and bureaucratic responsiveness: The police and domestic violence. *American Journal of Political Science* 42 (3): 745–68.

Cooper, C. A., A. J. Nownes, and S. Roberts. 2005. Perceptions of power: Interest groups and local politics. *State and Local Government Review* 37(3): 206–16.

Davis, K. C. 1975. *Police discretion.* St. Paul, MN: West.

Davis, R. C., E. Erez, and N. Avitable. 2001. Access to justice for immigrants who are victimized. *Criminal Justice Policy Review* 12(3): 183–96.

Dillman, D. A. 1978. *Mail and telephone surveys: The total design method.* New York: John Wiley & Sons.

Fairchild, E. S. 1978. Organizational structure and control of discretion in police operations. *Policy Studies Journal* 7:442–49.

Fyfe, J. F. 2004. Good policing. In *The administration and management of criminal justice organizations,* 4th ed., edited by S. Stojkovic, J. Klofas, and D. Kalinich, 146–66. Long Grove, IL: Waveland Press.

Hahn, H. 1971. Local variations in urban law enforcement. In *Race, change, and urban society,* edited by P. Orleans and W. Ellis, 373–400. Beverly Hills, CA: Sage.

Holmberg, L. 2003. *Policing stereotypes.* Madison, WI: Galda & Wilch Verlag.

International Association of Chiefs of Police. 2004. Press release: Police chiefs announce immigration enforcement policy.

Johnson, G. 2007. Gov: Mass. police won't arrest illegals. Associated Press, January 11.

Jones-Correa, M. 1998. *Between two nations: The political predicament of Latinos in New York City.* Ithaca, NY: Cornell University Press.

———. 2004. Racial and ethnic diversity and the politics of education in suburbia. Paper presented at the annual meeting of the American Political Science Association, Chicago.

Jordan, M. 2006. The new immigration cops. *Wall Street Journal,* February 2.

Lambert, B. 2005. L.I. is ordered to give notice of house raids. *New York Times,* December 17, B3.

Lipsky, M. 1980. *Street-level bureaucracy.* New York: Russell Sage Foundation.

Lowi, T. J. 1967. Machine politics—Old and new. *Public Interest* 9 (Fall): 83–92.

Mastrofski, S. D. 2004. Controlling street-level police discretion. *Annals of the American Academy of Political and Social Science* 593:100–118.

Meier, K. J., E. Gonzalez Juenke, R. D. Wrinkle, and J. L. Polinard. 2005. Structural choices and representational biases: The post-election color of representation. *American Journal of Political Science* 49(4): 758–68.

Meier, K. J., and L. J. O'Toole, Jr. 2006. Political control versus bureaucratic values: Reframing the debate. *Public Administration Review* 66 (March–April): 177–92.

Menjivar, C., and C. Bejarano. 2004. Latino immigrants' perceptions of crime and police authorities in the United States. *Ethnic and Racial Studies* 27(1): 120–48.

Moe, T. M. 1985. Control and feedback in economic regulation: The case of the NLRB. *American Political Science Review* 79(4): 1094–1116.

Moore, M. H. 1994. Policing: Deregulating or redefining accountability? In *Deregulating the public service*, edited by J. J. Dilulio, Jr., 198–235. Washington: Brookings institution.

Muir, W. K. 1977. *Police: Streetcorner politicians.* Chicago: Univ. of Chicago Press.

Ostrom, E., R. Parks, and G. Whitaker. 1977. *Policing metropolitan America.* Washington, DC: Government Printing Office.

Ramakrishnan, S. K. 2005. *Democracy in immigrant America: Changing demographics and political participation.* Stanford, CA: Stanford University Press.

Saltzstein, G. H. 1989. Black mayors and police policies. *Journal of Politics* 51(3): 525–44.

Self, R. 2003. California's industrial garden: Oakland and the East Bay in the age of deindustrialization. In *Beyond the ruins: The meanings of deindustrialization,* edited by J. Cowie and J. Heathcott, 159–80. Ithaca, NY: Cornell University Press.

Skolnick, J. H. 1994. *Justice without trial: Law enforcement in democratic society.* 3rd ed. New York: Macmillan.

Skolnick, J. H., and D. H. Bayley. 1986. *The new blue line: Police innovation in six American cities.* New York: Free Press.

Thacher, D. 2005. The local role in homeland security. *Law & Society Review* 39(3): 635–76.

Tyler, T. R., and Y. J. Huo. 2002. *Trust in the law: Encouraging public cooperation with the police and courts.* New York: Russell Sage Foundation.

Waterman, R. W., and K. J. Meier. 1998. Principal-agent models: An expansion? *Journal of Public Administration Research and Theory* 8(2): 173–202.

Whitaker, G. P. 1980. Coproduction: Citizen participation in service delivery. *Public Administration Review* 40(3): 240–46.

Williams, G. H. 1984. *The law and politics of police discretion.* Westport, CT: Greenwood.

Wilson, J. Q. 1970. *Varieties of police behavior.* New York: Atheneum.

Wong, J. 2006. *Democracy's promise: Immigrants and American civic institutions.* Ann Arbor: University of Michigan Press.

Wood, B. D., and R. Waterman. 1994. *Bureaucratic dynamics.* Boulder, CO: Westview Press.

Chapter 8

26 The Political Economy of Disaster Assistance

Barnes, W. 2005. Beyond federal urban policy. *Urban Affairs Review* 40(5): 575–89.

Burby, R., ed. 1998. *Cooperating with nature: Confronting natural hazards with land-use planning for sustainable communities.* Washington, D.C.: Joseph Henry Press.

Cutter, S., and C. Emrich. 2005. Are natural disaster losses in the U.S. increasing? *EOS: Transactions, American Geophysical Union* 86(41): 381–96.

Dixon, L., and R. Stern. 2004. *Compensation for losses from the 9/11 attacks.* Santa Monica, CA: RAND.

Eisinger, P. 2004. The American city in the age of terror: A preliminary assessment of the effects of September 11. *Urban Affairs Review* 40(1): 115–29.

Frymer, P., D. Strolovitch, and D. Warren. 2005. Katrina's political roots and divisions: Race, class, and federalism in American politics. Understanding Katrina: Perspectives from the social sciences. Web site created by the Social Science Research Centre. University of Maryland, http://www.understandingkatrina.ssrc.org (accessed September 19, 2005).

Garrett, T., and R. Sobel. 2003. The Political Economy of FEMA Disaster Payments. *Economic Inquiry* 41(3): 496–509.

Gerber, B., D. Cohen, B. Cannon, D. Patterson, and K. Stewart. 2005. On the front line: American cities and the challenge of homeland security preparedness. *Urban Affairs Review* 41(2): 182–210.

Godschalk, D., T. Beatley, P. Berke, D. Brower, and E. Kaiser. 1999. *Natural hazard mitigation: Recasting disaster policy and planning.* Washington, D.C.: Island.

Graham, S. 2005. Cities under siege: Katrina and the politics of metropolitan America. Understanding Katrina: Perspectives from the social sciences. Web site created by the Social Science Research Center, University of Maryland, http://www.understandingkatrina.ssrc.org (accessed September 19, 2005).

Hardenbrook, B. 2005. The need for a policy framework to develop disaster resilient regions. *Journal of Homeland Security and Emergency Management* 2(3): Article 2.

Holdeman, E. 2005. Destroying FEMA. *Washington Post,* August 30, 2005.

Jordan, M. 2005. Federal disaster recovery programs: Brief summaries. CRS Report for Congress, Congressional Research Service. August 29, 2005.

Kantor, P. 2002. Terrorism and governability in New York City: Old problem, new dilemma. *Urban Affairs Review* 38(1): 120–27.

Kestin, S. 2005. FEMA battered by waste, fraud. South Florida *Sun-Sentinel*, September 18, A1.

Lindell, M. K. and C. Prater. 2003. Assessing community impacts of natural disasters. *Natural Hazards Review* 3(2): 176–85.

May, P. 1985. *Recovering from catastrophes: Federal disaster relief policy and politics.* Westport, CT: Greenwood.

Mileti, D. 1999. *Disasters by design: A reassessment of natural hazards in the United States.* Washington, D.C.: Joseph Henry.

New York City Independent Budget Office. 2004. Three years after: Where is the $20 billion in federal WTC aid? Inside the budget. August 11, 2004.

Pielke, R. 2005. Historical economic losses from hurricanes: Where does Katrina fit in? Center For Science and Technology Policy Research, University of Colorado, http://www.sciencepolicy.colorado.edu (accessed September 19, 2005).

Platt, R. 1999. *Disasters and democracy: The politics of extreme natural events.* Washington. D.C.: Island.

Reeves, A. 2005. Political disaster? Presidential disaster declarations and electoral politics. Department of Government, Harvard University (unpublished manuscript).

Savitch, H. 2003. Does 9–11 portend a new paradigm for cities? *Urban Affairs Review* 38(1): 120–27.

Stehr, S. 1999. Community recovery and reconstruction following disasters. In *The handbook of crisis and emergency management*, edited by A. Farazmand, 345–57. New York: Marcel Dekker.

Tierney, K. 2005. The red pill. Understanding Katrina: Perspectives from the social sciences. Social Science Research Center, University of Maryland, http://www.understandingkatrina.ssrc.org (accessed September 19, 2005).

U.S. Congress. Senate. Bipartisan Task Force on Funding Disaster Relief. Report of Senate task force on funding disaster relief. 104th Congress. Document No. 104–4.

Vale, L., and T. Campanella, eds. 2005. *The resilient city: How modern cities recover from disaster.* Oxford: Univ. Press.

27 Politics, Federalism, and the Recovery Process in New Orleans

Berman, D. (2003). *Local government and the states: Autonomy, politics, and policy.* New York: M.E. Sharpe.

Burns, P. F. (2002). The intergovernmental regime and public policy in Hartford, Connecticut. *Journal of Urban Affairs, 24,* 55–73.

Burns, N., & Gamm, G. (1997). Creatures of the state: State politics and local government, 1871–1921. *Urban Affairs Review, 33,* 59–96.

Burns, P. F., & Thomas, M. O. (2004). Governors and the development regime in New Orleans. *Urban Affairs Review, 39,* 791–812.

Crain, R. L. (1968). *The politics of school desegregation: Comparative case studies of community structure and policy-making.* Chicago, IL: Aldine Publishing

Filosa, G. (2007). Nagin wants to run Road Home in N.O.; Congressional panel gets earful on public housing. *The Times-Picayune*, February, 23, 1.

Garvey, J. B., & Widmer, M. (2001). *Beautiful crescent: A history of New Orleans.* 10th edition. New Orleans, LA: Garner Press.

Gewertz, K. (2006). Dual Orleans systems grow in storm's wake: Complex 'Overlapping circles' of governance, prevalence of charter schools mark landscape. *Education Week, 25*(1), 20–21.

Gill, J. (2007). Road Home goes through California, *The Times-Picayune,* February, 23, 7.

Gimpel, J. G., & Schuknecht, J. E. (2002). Political and Demographic Foundations for Sectionalism in State Politics: The Connecticut Case. *American Politics Research, 30,* 193–214.

Grace, S. (2006). Blanco struggles with balky Road Home. *The Times-Picayune,* November, 28, 5.

Gray, C. (2001). Hainkel: Stop electing school board: Bill lets mayor, university pick members. *The Times-Picayune,* 1.

Gyan, J. (2002). Healthy New Orleans good for La., mayor-elect says. *State-Times/Morning Advocate,* p. 7-B;S.

Hammer, D. (2007). LRA juggles money to pay parishes' costs: Despite precedent, feds won't pay the full tab. *The Times-Picayune,* 1.

Harding, A. (1995). Elite theory and growth machines. In D., Judge, G. Stoker, and H. Wolman (Eds.), *Theories of urban politics* (pp. 35–53). London: Sage.

Kantor, P., Savitch, H., & Haddock, S. V. (1997). The political economy of urban regimes: A comparative perspective. *Urban Affairs Review, 32*(3), 348–378.

Krupa, M. (2006). Nagin asks Blanco: Where's our money. *The Times-Picayune,* 1.

Krupa, M. (2007a). Nagin: City recovering despite failed promises; Bush, Blanco can make it up with cash he says. *The Times-Picayune,* 1.

Krupa, M. (2007b). Election results reflect racial shifts: White candidates win key black-held seats. *The Times-Picayune,* 1.

Lauria, M. (1996). *Reconstructing regime theory: Regulating urban politics in a global economy.* Thousand Oaks, CA: Sage.

Liner, E. B. (1989). Sorting out state-local relations. In E. B. Liner (Ed.), *A decade of devolution: Perspectives on state-local relations.* Washington, DC: The Urban Institute Press.

Maggi, L. (2006). Housing program contract draws criticism over ethics; company has conflict, GOP lawmakers say. *The Times-Picayune,* 4.

Maloney, S. (2007). U.S. Attorney: 23 convictions will deter N.O. school system corruption. *New Orleans City-Business.*

McGill, K. (2001). A $450 million stadium? Politically, it's too costly. *The Associated Press State & Local Wire.*

McGill, K. (2003). Senate oks BESE takeover measure. *The Associated Press State & Local Wire.*

Mowbray, R. (2005). Deck seems stacked against casino idea; Harrah's monopoly, river boat opposition create 'uphill battle'. *The Times-Picayune,* 8.

New Orleans CityBusiness. (2006). 37 business groups back levee consolidation for N.O. *New Orleans CityBusiness.*

New Orleans CityBusiness. (2007). Commentary: Powell should mediate funding dispute. *New Orleans CityBusiness.*

Pagano, M. (1990). State-local relations in the 1990s. *Annals of the American Academy of Political and Social Science, 509,* 94–105.

Parent, W. (2004). *Inside the carnival: Unmasking Louisiana politics.* Baton Rouge, LA: Louisiana State University Press.

Renwick, E. F., Parent, T. W., & Wardlaw, J. (1999). Louisiana: Still *sui generis* like Huey. In A. P. Lamis (Ed.), *Southern politics in the 1990s.* Baton Rouge, LA: Louisiana State University Press.

Ritea, S. (2006). Bell's about to ring. *The Times-Picayune,* 1.

Robelen, Erik. (2005). Louisiana eyes plan to let state control New Orleans schools. *Education Week, 25*(1), 26.

Robertson, A. W. (1991). All the Duke's men. *National Review, 43,* 43–45.

Russell, G. (2006). New assessor system to take effect in 2010: One-assessor amendment wins big statewide and in New Orleans. *The Times-Picayune,* 1.

Sayre, A. (2003). Former Foster aide says 'north versus south' must end. *The Associated Press State & Local Wire.*

Simon, D. (2007). New school era opens today: Recovery District has 13,400 students. *The Times-Picayune,* 1.

Simpson, D. (2004). Eleven indicted in federal probe of New Orleans school corruption. *Associated Press State & Local Wire.*

Sites, W. (1997). The limits of urban regime theory. *Urban Affairs Review, 32,* 536–557.

Stonecash, J. (1989). Political cleavage in gubernatorial and legislative elections: Party competition in New York, 1970–1982. *The Western Political Quarterly, 42,* 69–81.

Stonecash, J. (1998). The politics of state-local fiscal relations. In R. L. Hanson (Ed.), *Governing partners: States-local relations in the United States.* Boulder, CO: Westview Press.

The Advocate. (1997). Bulk of funding goes to Orleans. *The Advocate,* 10B.

The Advocate. (2004). Stadium issues still on the table. *The Advocate,* 6-B; S.

The Associated Press. (2007). Balance of power may be shifting in Katrina-shaped New Orleans. *The Associated Press.*

The Public Policy Research Lab. (2007). The spring 2007 Louisiana survey final report. Manship School of Mass Communication's Reilly Center for Media & Public Affairs and the E.J. Ourso College of Business. Baton Rouge, LA.

The Times-Picayune. (2003). Briefing book: News and views from the Louisiana Capitol. *The Times-Picayune,* 4.

The Times-Picayune. (2005). Gov. Blanco not sold on casino plan; Governor prefers tax credits for renewal. *The Times-Picayune,* 1.

University of New Orleans Survey Research Center. (2000). Quality of Life Survey: Orleans and Jefferson Parishes. Available at http://www.uno.edu/~poli/qual00.htm; University of New Orleans Survey Research Center. April, 2004. Quality of Life Survey: Orleans and Jefferson Parishes. Available at http://www.uno.edu/~poli/unopoll/previous.htm.

Wall Street Journal. (2005). New Orleans mayor drops casino plan. *Wall Street Journal,* D4.

Warner, C. (2007). FEMA, city sparring over street repairs; Agency still waiting on list of damage. *The Times-Picayune,* 1.